Praise for *Spiritual Light*

"A fascinating account of what is possible for humans as multi-dimensional beings. Since consciousness is a field of all possibilities, new worlds open up to us as we shift into different frequency domains of our own awareness."
—DEEPAK CHOPRA, renowned author and speaker.

"*Spiritual Light* is an encyclopedia of wisdom which should be understood by all humanity. It presents the essence of world religions and sacred lifeways and offers it in a unified text of universal teachings which is properly called "spiritual" rather than "religious." It is a guidebook to happiness, holiness and healing the material world by receiving the light of God, as transmitted to us by the Universal Spiritual Brother&Sisterhood."
—JOHN WHITE, author of *What Is Enlightenment?* and editor of *Psychic Exploration: A Challenge for Science* by astronaut Edgar Mitchell.

"*Spiritual Light* is an incredible read... I cannot recall another book in recent times which pays this much attention to the detail, and still manages to keep you wanting more. This is the book Spiritualism has been waiting for – comprehensive, concise and well written – The Spiritualist Bible for the twenty-first Century."
—MATTHEW HUTTON, Assistant Editor, *Psychic World*.

"Anyone who is familiar with the higher levels of mediumship will immediately recognize that this work is coming from the highest vibration. Breathtaking in its scope it answers all the questions in ways that are simple yet profound. As you read it you will find a resonance with all of the great spiritual teachers and yet a feeling of discovering further revelations. An amazing achievement."
—VICTOR AND WENDY ZAMMIT, co-authors of *A Lawyer Presents the Evidence for the Afterlife* and *The Friday Afterlife Report*.

"This inspired collection of spiritual teachings offers a depth of wisdom more necessary than ever in our current age of materialism."
—SUSAN FARROW, Editor, *Psychic News*.

"The seekers of *truths*, especially those dealing with the meaning of life and the survival of consciousness after death, who dare venture outside the boundaries of orthodox religion and mainstream science, can find many answers, but those answers often lead to more questions. Having read hundreds of books dealing with spiritual, metaphysical, and paranormal matters, I can, without hesitation, say that this book has many more meaningful answers than any other book I have read. Second place doesn't even come close."
—MICHAEL TYMN, author of *The Afterlife Revealed, The Articulate Dead*, etc.

"This book...is promoting ways for each of us to grow spiritually,... whether you practice any religion, or not, the only thing that matters is that you are able to discover the Truth. To discover the Truth, you will have to search for it, and this book is an excellent place to begin your search."
—PAUL HAUSER, reviewer for *The Journal for Spiritual and Consciousness Studies*.

"*Spiritual Light* is a collection of spiritual teachings from highly advanced souls who have been entrusted with the spiritual development of our planet for ages. Those teachings are in remarkable agreement with the spiritual knowledge entering into this world through near-death experiences (NDEs). The influence of these souls on bringing spiritual unity into this world cannot be overstated. I highly recommend *Spiritual Light*."
—KEVIN WILLIAMS, author of *Nothing Better than Death*, webmaster of *Near-Death Experiences and the Afterlife*.

Spiritual Light

UNIVERSAL TEACHINGS FROM THE HIGHEST SPIRIT REALMS

Spiritual Light

The Complete Official Edition

SPIRITUAL LIGHT
Universal Teachings from the Highest Spirit Realms

presented by

The Universal Spiritual Brother&Sisterhood

compiled and edited by

Michael Flagg and John Finnemore

USB Vision Press

SPIRITUAL LIGHT:
UNIVERSAL TEACHINGS FROM THE HIGHEST SPIRIT REALMS

First printed September 2014.

Copyright © 2014 by The Universal Spiritual Brother&Sisterhood, Inc.

All rights reserved. Except as permitted under copyright law and except as permitted in the next sentence, no part of this publication may be reproduced, stored in a retrieval system, or transmitted, in any form or by any means, electronic, mechanical, photocopying, recording, or otherwise, without the written permission of The Universal Spiritual Brother&Sisterhood (USB). Permission is hereby granted to reviewers, who may quote brief passages in their reviews, and to individuals who may make, during their lifetime, single photocopies of not more than 100 pages of this book provided such copies are for personal study or educational use only, are not sold, and the title of the book, its copyright, and the USB website are noted on the front page of the copies.

Publisher's Cataloging-in-Publication

Spiritual light : universal teachings from the highest spirit realms / presented by
   The Universal Spiritual Brother&Sisterhood ; compiled and edited by Michael
   Flagg and John Finnemore. – The complete official edition.
   pages cm
   Includes index.
   LCCN 2014945149
   ISBN 978-0-9912422-2-1 (pbk.)
   ISBN 978-0-9912422-1-4 (flexibound)

   1. Spirit writings. 2. Spiritual life.
   3. Spirituality. 4. Truth. I. Flagg, Michael,
   1903–1992. II. Finnemore, John, 1937–

   BF1290.S65 2014   133.901'3
                            QBI14-600106

Published by USB Vision Press, Cupertino, California,
publishing division of The Universal Spiritual Brother&Sisterhood, Inc.
www.TheUSB.org
Printed by Lightning Source, printing division of the Ingram Group.
www.lightningsource.com

This paperback book (1 lb 15 oz, 890 g) was simultaneously published in deluxe, compact, and durable form (1 lb 3 oz, 535 grams, ISBN 978-0-9912422-1-4). Translated into Spanish (paperback, ISBN 978-0-9912422-3-8).

Acknowledgments: The following have generously given permission for the use of quotations from copyrighted material: Brotherhood of Life, Inc. (502:7),the Estate of Estelle Roberts (many), The Leslie Flint Educational Trust, Ltd. (many), and The Society for Psychical Research (323:n17).

Dedicated:

To that great love, which has so inspired many on both sides of life to help bring higher and purer spiritual teachings to humanity.

To all those wondrous souls, who, over the ages, have devoted themselves to this mission, and who, more recently, dedicated themselves to delivering this book.

And to all those who seek and probe for the highest and strive to share it.

Liability Notice

To the best of our knowledge the information in this book is true and correct. The editors and the publisher offer no guarantees in this book, nor are they engaged in rendering legal, medical, or other professional advice or services, for which the expert assistance of competent professionals should be obtained. We repeatedly advise readers to not accept anything unthinkingly from anyone, ourselves included. The editors and publisher disclaim all liability in connection with the use of this book.

Contents

How to Use This Book   xv
Introduction   1
Preface   11
Greetings from an Illumined Soul   15
An Offer and a Call   17

THE BASIS

Chapter 1. The Universal Spiritual Brother&Sisterhood   21
Origins, values, outlook

Chapter 2. Teachings and Reason   39
Teachings of the new age, thought, reason

Chapter 3. Truth   49
The nature of truth, searching for truth, spreading truth

Chapter 4. The Laws That Govern   73
On laws, responsibility, service, justice, love, attraction, life

Chapter 5. Love   85
God, love, service, prayer

THE WORLDLY

Chapter 6. The Individual   107
Characteristics, knowledge and understanding, medical aspects

Chapter 7. Personal Responsibility and Behavior   123
Will, personal responsibility, integrity and standards, attitudes, behavior, right living, directing our efforts, personal progress

Chapter 8. Our World   191
This material world, humans, these times, good and bad, crime, leadership and example, freedom, challenges

Chapter 9. Everyday Life   251
Relationships, family, health, sleep, time and cycles, sound and color

Chapter 10. The Divining Arts   285
Prediction, astrology, palmistry, phrenology, psychometry, hypnosis

continued...

Contents

THE SPIRITUAL

Chapter 11. Phenomena 315
Types and methods of unorthodox healing, about healers, materialization and plasms, other phenomena, psychic experiences

Chapter 12. Survival and Communication 365
Survival, mediums, mediumship, spirit guides and friends, communication, home circles

Chapter 13. Spirit Life 421
The spirit world, our spirit makeup, spirit existence, living in the spirit world

Chapter 14. Spiritual Progress 467
Spirituality, challenges, responsibilities, forgiveness, enlightenment, the path, the USB view

Appendices 493

A. *Addresses by Illumined Souls* 495
B. *Error and Misteachings* 505
C. *Reincarnation* 533
D. *Operation of the USB* 537
E. *The USB Leaflet* 557
F. *Glossary* 565

Index 573

Acknowledgments

Most of all, we thank those Blessed Inspirers who guided the foundation of The Universal Spiritual Brother&Sisterhood (USB) on earth and then imparted their spiritual teachings for so many years.

Besides those highly illumined spirit teachers, it will doubtless be quite a long time before many people truly comprehend how indebted we are to all their helpers and to Michael Flagg, who worked so hard, painstakingly, and long to make these teachings available to humanity on earth.

This work would not have been possible without the assistance of a number of outstanding mediums, who made direct and clear communication possible between the so widely separated realms. In particular, two in England helped launch the enterprise and one American dedicated many years of her life to this mission.

We gratefully acknowledge the following people who generously helped with the preparation of this book: Janet Christensen, Patricia Eshagh, Gulshan Finnemore, Matthew Kwan, and Jarrell Siler helped with word processing the original manuscript. Janet Constantinou, Rudite Emir, Priya Finnemore, Riaz Finnemore, Ruth Flagg, Castillo Garrido, Robert Goodwin, William Gough, Roberta Grimes, Jeanne Gunner, Ann Harrison, Howard Losness, Tim Myers, Mary Lou Nelson, Karna Nisewaner, K. Linda Ortiz, Anjali Puri, Gabriele Rico, Balbir Singh, Deanna and Peter Sparks, and Manjula Waldron reviewed the manuscript and/or advised on its organization and content. Graphics were prepared by Riaz Finnemore. In particular I (John) thank Frederick Parrella for his important help on social and related issues, involving numerous reviews and extended discussions; Rosalind Finnemore and Guillermo Noffal for their many "catches" and so much other help; and my family for their loving support, especially that of my wife, Gulshan. Without her tolerance for my long hours of preoccupation and her assistance in so many ways, I would never have been able to accomplish this result.

Most especially, I also thank my own unseen helpers in spirit life, who, without question, have guided and inspired me during my process of compiling, editing, and promoting, and who I am sure have instilled in me so much enthusiasm for this project.

Acknowledgments

6   Bryan Clardy and Ann Harrison provided us with excellent guidance in the preparation of our documents for printing. Ann Harrison, Raman Mehra, Sumant Pendharkar, Anthony Raymond, John Sphar, and Michael Tymn gave valuable help on publishing and promotion.

7   All quotations in the main text of this book, other than those acknowledged on the copyright page, are taken either from Michael Flagg's writing in the USB *Letters* from 1958 to 1982, or from the recorded words of his spirit inspirers. All the uncredited poems in this book were composed by Michael Flagg.[1]

8   The Universal Spiritual Brother&Sisterhood thanks all financial contributors for their essential support, given freely and without our solicitation.

---

[1] Poems by Michael Flagg appear in the following topics: 301, 721, 727, 728, 1326, and 1426. They are copyrighted and were previously published in the USB *Letters*.

About the Contributors

1 **Spirit inspirers** who have given, discussed, and reviewed the material in this book and otherwise directed its development, include over a dozen Illumined Souls and Blessed Souls (see Glossary), many of whom are "of the highest [spiritual] attainment," and some of whom are today still revered by hundreds of millions of people on earth. Those Illumined and Blessed Souls were from time to time assisted by a number of other spirit inspirers. They asked us to not give any recognizable inspirer's name in this book, for reasons explained in the Introduction (paragraph 39).

2 **Michael Flagg** (1903–1992) was born in Shanghai, China into an English merchant family. He entered the U.S.A. in 1926 and worked as a freelance writer-researcher. He served in the U.S. Army from 1942 to 1946 and thereafter resided in California. He was the editor of an industrial safety magazine and he wrote speeches for government officials. Michael became interested in the spirit world in 1951–1952, and through top-class mediumship in England in 1956 he learned of his important mission (see Preface). Under spirit direction he founded the USB on earth in December 1956 and led it for the rest of his life. From 1956 to 1982 Michael received material for, prepared, and distributed 93 USB newsletters. From 1979 he began compiling them into topics for this book.

3 **John Finnemore** (1937–) was born in London, England, grew up in Hertfordshire, and became a civil engineer. He immigrated to Canada in 1962 and entered the U.S.A. in 1965 to attend graduate school at Stanford University. After a subsequent year teaching overseas he settled in California, performing research in water resources and environmental protection. Since 1979 he has been a professor of civil engineering, publishing research articles and coauthoring three editions of a classic textbook on fluid mechanics. John became interested in the spirit world and higher spiritual teachings as a teenager. He discovered the USB in 1959 and first met Michael Flagg in the mid-1960s. At Michael's request, John organized and edited the USB topics into book form after Michael's return to spirit life.

How to Use This Book

1   This book consists of mostly independent topics, arranged together on the basis of the subject matter. So if you have special interests in certain areas it will be perfectly all right to begin reading anywhere in the book. For example, for spiritual inspiration you might start straight into Chapter 14. There is only one proviso: I (John Finnemore, editor) strongly recommend reading the material before Chapter 1 first. This is because it "sets the scene" by explaining the background where the teachings came from, and why and how. That material also introduces certain terms that you may not otherwise properly understand.

2   Having said the above, however, I believe the shorter Chapters 1–5 do provide a helpful general background for the longer chapters that follow.

3   For your guidance, the table of contents is divided into three major areas. Each chapter in that table has subheadings that correspond to the chapter section headings, providing a quick guide to finding what interests you. Then, the list of topic titles at the start of each chapter is there to help you further. If you peruse these topic lists from time to time you will before long become quite familiar with the "lay of the land" as it were. The rather extensive Index provides you with an alternative and more detailed way to find items of interest.

4   In general terms, Chapters 1–6 contain many of the *basic truths and teachings* offered by the USB. Chapters 7–9 discuss *applications* of those teachings to our lives. Chapters 10–13 relate to *how* these teachings were received—to the psychic, the phenomena, and the spirit world. And Chapter 14 is about the USB's and hopefully your goals, the *purpose* of these teachings.

5   To facilitate citing them in references, topics are "numbered" by three or four characters, where the first one or two characters correspond to the chapter or appendix and the last two digits indicate their position in the sequence. Thus we might most conveniently read Topic 1006, say, as ten-oh-six, when referring to the sixth topic in chapter ten. Likewise A02 refers to the second topic in Appendix A. In many cross-references or citations, topic numbers are followed by a colon and then the number of the paragraph within that topic (the paragraphs are numbered in the left margin). So A02:3 refers to the third paragraph of Topic A02. If the colon is followed by an *n*, then the reference is to a footnote by footnote number. Thus 206:n2 refers to footnote 2 of Topic 206. To refer to the

How to Use This Book

items preceding Chapter 1 I suggest using "Ackno:," "Contrib:," "Howto:," "Intro:," "Pref:," "Greet:," and "Call:."

6   To help you find out more about subjects mentioned in passing, I have often inserted cross references or short notes in brackets [ ]. Sometimes I have inserted footnotes to provide more complete reference information, definitions of terms, clarifications, biographical information, and the like. Consider following up on such references and footnotes as entirely optional All such entries were *not* part of the original *Letters* or the manuscript for this volume and I have made clear all material that I alone prepared by keeping it separate.[1]

7   We have also given our definitions of terms used in the Glossary.

8   During my editing I found that inspiring passages and delightful little gems are sometimes tucked into unexpected places, so there is a lot to be gained from a complete reading when time permits. We hope that anyone who intends to teach from this book, or to lead a group to discuss or study these teachings, will strive to become familiar with them all.

9   If you appreciate these teachings as much as we hope you will, you will probably want to keep the book handy to reread and study it from time to time and to refer to it when helping others or whenever life presents you or a loved one with another of its many challenges.

---

[1] In summary, the material that Michael Flagg assembled and spirit leaders of the USB reviewed was all that in the Preface, Chapters 1–14 and Appendices B and D, except for the items that I prepared as noted below.

Appendix A gives the actual words of USB leaders (except for the footnotes and some clarifying inserts in [ ]), as taken from tape recordings and USB *Letters*. The Greetings from an Illumined Soul and An Offer and a Call are based on the words of those leaders, words that I drew largely from Appendix A. Michael wanted a Glossary (Appendix F), an Index, and the USB booklet to be included. He reviewed an early Glossary I prepared, requiring that it contain only USB definitions. The Index is based on a preliminary one Michael prepared. Because I believe the need for a USB booklet has been supplanted by the USB website, I have edited and considerably condensed the USB booklet into the form of a leaflet (Appendix E).

I (John Finnemore) prepared alone, without the help of spirit leaders to my knowledge, the following: all the footnotes, all the inserts in [ ], the endorsement page (from the indicated contributions), the title page, the dedication, the liability statement, the tables of contents, the Acknowledgments, About the Contributors, How to Use This Book, the Introduction, Appendices C and F, everything before the actual leaflet text in Appendix E, the "To order" page, and the back cover. I chose the chapter and section headings and I decided the organization and ordering of the topics. Also, from materials previously given (Appendix A) or approved (Intro:18) by the spirit leaders, I assembled the following new items: Greetings from an Illumined Soul, An Offer and a Call, and topic nos. 102, 109, 501, 508, 512, 517, 522, 608, 730, 739, 760, 1401, 1421, and D08.

Introduction

1   A group of beings of extraordinary spiritual elevation and wisdom, including many of the greatest spiritual teachers of all time, have striven to find the way to directly share with us on earth their knowledge and the spiritual principles they teach *today*. (By "spiritual" we mean having high and noble qualities of spirit.)

2   Overcoming tremendous difficulties and with the utmost patience, these great souls gave us their united teachings to record in this book so that all who wish to can learn their highest spiritual philosophy. The result reveals great beauty and wisdom—much needed in these times. It is a truly wonderful gift.

The Undertaking

3   Michael Flagg discovered his life's mission in the mid-1950s. It was to help great souls deliver high spiritual teachings and truths to us on earth. Living in San Francisco, Michael was contacted from the spirit world by leaders of The Universal Spiritual Brotherhood (USB), which has served humanity for many ages. These leaders are beings of extraordinary spiritual elevation and wisdom, who are surrounded by incredible love, auras, and bright light, so that they have often been described as "Beings of Light." We call them Illumined Souls. One such being describes them as "of the highest [spiritual] attainment," which suggests that they are the most like God (par. 4) of all humankind. These USB leaders include many of the greatest enlightened spiritual teachers of the past, many of whose teachings led to great world religions. Some of them, after their lives on earth, have become deified. But they do not promote a religion; they accept truth *wherever* it is found. They also include some of the most spiritual and wise spirit guides of the 19th and 20th centuries. As Michael describes in his Preface, these Illumined Souls regularly communicated with him for many years through exceptional mediums.

4   For readers who cannot wait to read what the Illumined Souls say about God, let me briefly mention that they recognize and worship only the one God. They refer to God as a God of Love and Wisdom, Law and Justice, and That Which Is All-Good; as the Creator, the Most High, and

Introduction

the Supreme Power. They say that God is unknowable, indescribable, eternal, and illimitable, noting that each of us has our *own* conception of God. They teach that every human being has a spark of God, linking us all with one another and with God. And it is clear that God's power and the workings of God's Laws are far more apparent to those in the spirit realms than they are to us on earth.

5   It is not necessary to believe in an afterlife or in the source of these teachings to benefit greatly from them. If your reason embraces them and your inner being senses them to be true, it is enough to realize that we are *all* God's creations and therefore all spiritual sisters and brothers. If your heart reaches out towards these teachings we hope you will desire to put into effect those that strike a responsive chord within you and that you will help spread them for the benefit of others, sharing all that has moved or enlightened you. While one should certainly seek truth wherever one can, my own lifetime's search has led me to determine that these USB teachings from Illumined Souls have provided a far better guide for living than any others I have found.

6   For perspective on the USB's various teachings, please note that its most important concerns are for the development of character and spirituality and for knowledge about spiritual truth including the spiritual laws that govern everything. Only *these* can unite humanity in love and service, and help make life on earth truly enjoyable and satisfying for all.

7   Illumined Souls teach us that the human race on earth is but a small part of a vast population of spirit people belonging to this planet. We all continually evolve in consciousness and spirituality as a result of our individual actions and learning. As spirit people become more advanced they inhabit more refined or higher spirit realms. Their most progressed leaders, out of love, desire to help their brothers and sisters facing earth's unique challenges. Their teachings in this book will help us take those challenges in stride, progress up the scale to higher spiritual consciousness, discover their loving assistance, avert massive disasters, enhance life on earth, avoid the misery and havoc we create, spread love, and embrace all our brothers and sisters on this journey with understanding, tolerance, and compassion. By doing these things and understanding these teachings all will be enriched, both givers and receivers, and we will better prepare ourselves for our return to the spirit world and a truly joyful life of progress there.

8   Of the vast population in the spirit world, a small fraction is not spiritually aware. And some of those are undesirables, either mischievous or

The Undertaking

malevolent. So teachings from less advanced or earth-bound sources are questionable. Moreover, teachings of the more spiritually advanced, even if well intentioned, often contain personal biases and errors. Teachings from the *highest* level of spiritual attainment, like these we present from the USB, are rare and of unusual quality.

9   From my many discussions with Michael while working with him on this project and from the recordings and transcripts of his sittings in 1956–1957 with mediums in England, I gathered he is a leading worker for the USB in the spirit world. I also learned that, because of the differences between earthly and spirit life and the remote, elevated level of his spirit inspirers, Michael's job as receiver of the teachings was to present them for today's ways of thinking on earth.

10   To facilitate this, in 1956 at the instigation of the Illumined Souls, Michael founded The Universal Spiritual Brotherhood (USB) on earth, a counterpart patterned and named after the organization in the spirit world; he registered it as a nonprofit organization. Open to all, it is devoted to teaching spiritual truth; it is not a religion, cult, or sect. During his life Michael dedicated himself to distributing its teachings. People who wished to could be part of the USB movement for free. Later, to be inclusive of all and to follow current gender-neutral practice, the USB on earth was renamed The Universal Spiritual Brother&Sisterhood.

11   Of course, some religious traditions believe it dangerous to contact spirit people. (Good people and "bad" people remain much the same when they pass on to spirit life.) Although the USB does teach about such dangers and how to protect against them, *anyone* can study, *without* risk, the teachings that noble and illumined spirit beings (Illumined Souls) have gifted to us.

12   It is our hope that readers who are stirred by these writings and the love that inspired them will feel the desire to join some or many of the activities suggested and so strengthen this movement to make the world a far better place for all.

13   A small fraction of humanity presently considers the pursuit and practice of *highest* spiritual philosophy to be of great importance. For such people this volume has been compiled; those seeking spiritually something more; those wanting to glimpse the love, beauty, and grandeur of the higher spirit realms; those interested in improving our world spiritually; those wishing to add a universal spiritual dimension to international friendship; and those hungry for advanced spiritual teachings from the

highest levels. Because these teachings are universal, they apply to everyone. All who value them will try to make them available to seekers.

The Writing

14 For 24 years after founding the USB, Michael compiled and published the USB teachings he received in quarterly worldwide *Letters*. Let me comment a little on his writing.

15 Michael's writing blended at least three different types of material: (1) direct and indirect quotes of USB spirit leaders, received through exceptional mediumship; (2) write-ups of topics that Michael had discussed directly with Illumined Souls through the same mediumship; and (3) write-ups of topics, poems, and songs received by Michael through inspiration. His own expression appeared in the second and third types.

16 His wording may not always have been the first choice of the Illumined Souls. Yet USB spirit leaders carefully reviewed and approved the *Letters* before their release. If their views differed, they tended to defer to Michael because of his familiarity with conditions on earth. Although Michael is a leading worker for the USB in the spirit realms, like everyone else on earth he was strongly affected by living here, enhancing different viewpoints.

17 I believe Michael's inability to complete this book of teachings during his life was part of a greater plan to allow him to see them from both points of view, on earth and from the spirit world, enabling him to consider refinements he might not have understood before his return to spirit life. In any case, we should accept only what strikes a responsive chord within us and we need not accept all to align ourselves with the USB. Readers and students can concentrate on those teachings that appeal to and are acceptable, to *them*.

18 After drafting each *Letter*, Michael checked it with spirit leaders of the USB, often on a word-for-word basis. He did this through deep-trance (direct voice) mediumship. After 1959 an American medium, who later became Michael's wife, provided most of the needed mediumship. She was an exceptional combination of a highly skilled medium and a very spiritual person. From 1958 to 1982 Michael distributed *Letters* numbered 1–93 free to people who requested them.

The Book

19 In 1979 I began to meet regularly with Michael in San Francisco to help him compile the teachings from the *Letters* into self-contained topics suitable for inclusion in a book he referred to as the "Golden Book."

The Book

First Michael combined and edited similar topics, making minor changes for additional clarity as a result of discussions with Illumined Souls. Next Michael's wife reviewed the topics with him. Then I reviewed the result and discussed any questions I had with Michael. If necessary, Michael asked spirit leaders about questions that arose. Once the topics had been largely compiled, but not yet assembled into any kind of appropriate sequence, Michael developed a health condition that prevented him from working. He asked me for a commitment to complete the project; I agreed. It was Michael's deep wish to see the teachings published in a single volume during his lifetime. He hoped to recover but it was not to be. In early 1992 Michael returned to spirit life and I inherited all the materials.

20   I have no academic training in philosophy or spirituality, although subjects relating to the spirit world and higher spiritual teachings have been my life's avocation. Instead, my training is in civil engineering (a particularly down-to-earth profession, requiring logic, accuracy, and responsibility), in which I performed research for 35 years and about which I taught and coauthored textbooks for over 20 years. I hope the professional skills I acquired there have benefited this effort.

21   I had many concerns about my responsibilities with this book. I had to make many decisions without the benefit of Michael's direct communication with USB spirit leaders. I searched for a medium like Michael used but without success. At least two different clairvoyants said I must do the editing by myself, that the manuscripts would not have come to me unless they were meant to, and that I could change the presentation to make it right for the times as long as the overall message was the same. I have tried to err on the side of caution since changes in presentation sometimes *imply* changes in the message. Michael briefly communicated with excellent evidence of his identity, providing great encouragement, but he seemed to be avoiding questions while I was editing. So as best as I could, I followed content and editing guidelines Michael left for me.

22   Later, in January 2011, I did have an exciting communication. While talking by phone with my sister, a medium, about mundane matters, she suddenly interrupted and said, "my voice is going squeaky, which means a spirit friend is drawing near." Immediately, a strong, deeper-pitched male voice spoke through her, saying "I want to speak to John." After I welcomed him he mentioned some of my spirit loved ones who were present, including some who had been dedicated to the USB while on earth. He said he had come to bring me the thanks of many, many spirit souls for my dedication to the book I was working on. I thanked him for

Introduction

his encouragement and said I felt guilty about how long it was taking because I wanted to be careful and thorough. He responded that many have been trying to help and influence me with my editing work and now they were laughing because on occasions they had to work with me on a certain point numerous times before I got it right. Although I had never been aware of their influence, I agreed I had sometimes come back to a topic three or four times before I was satisfied. He also said I was chosen for this work because they knew I "look into things" carefully. He then soon had to leave, but did mention that on earth he "walked in the snow" and had been an Inuit. After he had withdrawn I discussed events with my sister. Living in Spain did not know the details of my editing in California and as she pointed out she certainly had not known about my repeated corrections. So his mention of them was good evidence of spirit help.

23 Each numbered topic in this volume is complete in itself although the student of these teachings will soon find connections between them. I reorganized a few topics and arranged the resulting 511 topics into Chapters 1–14 and Appendices A, B, and D, ordering them on the basis of the subject matter and precedence.

24 I have carefully avoided blending any teachings or ideas of my own into Michael's material; and I have clearly indicated additional material I prepared. In a few cases where I felt it helpful I have created new topics by collecting together material extracted only from the USB *Letters*, an early USB booklet, and from other topics in this book.

25 I have been asked why I included teachings that are not new to humanity. I did this because Illumined Souls wished it. It shows which of the previously known teachings they approve of.

26 Since 1956–1982, when Michael received most of the USB teachings, the world has changed considerably. With the ending of the cold war and with liberal democracies outnumbering dictatorships for the first time, I found it appropriate to edit material relating to those earlier times and having little relevance now. In addition, traditional scientists have since made a number of discoveries, particularly in physics, that support or seem to support metaphysical and spirit teachings; they are often referred to as "New Physics." I have mentioned in my footnotes some interesting examples that relate to USB teachings.

27 About three weeks before he passed on Michael said "we *have* to add" a paragraph about reincarnation to the introduction or preface, explaining why the USB accepts it. I have not found a draft by Michael of such a

The Source

28   paragraph. So I am mentioning it here and I have addressed reincarnation further in Appendix C.

28   Michael wanted the word "Light" in the title, to indicate the enlightenment shared by our Illumined Inspirers. I adopted *Spiritual Light*, to try to capture this book's essence. And because our Inspirers said the USB colors are blue and gold I have used them on the cover.

29   Because the Illumined Souls initiated this project and they were the primary source of the material in this book (see below), I chose to not put Michael's and/or my name on the cover; our individual contributions are explained above. *Spiritual Light* contains the only complete official teachings of The Universal Spiritual Brother&Sisterhood (USB).

The Source

30   Since it was the illumined spirit leaders of the USB who made this book possible, let me speak briefly about them. But first, let us keep in mind that *all* high spiritual teachings given to humanity on earth have come through mediumship, albeit in different forms, some through the lives of great spiritual teachers who were also mediums and others through direct voice mediumship, clairvoyance, automatic writing, inspiration, and the like. And let us also not forget that all mediums are human.

31   It was the USB spirit leaders, not Michael, who selected the direct voice mediums through whom they would communicate, mediums truly exceptional in their combinations of skills and spirituality and who desired to serve at the highest levels. (Nowadays it is hard to find *any* true direct voice mediums.) Through more than 300 sittings with these mediums over a period of *thirty years*, our spirit communicators became well known to Michael and later known to me; USB records suggest there were *many* more than 300 sittings with spirit leaders during 1956–1986. Each sitting typically lasted about 45 minutes. Over 50 different spirit speakers came through, supportive of the USB and Michael's work with it. Some of the USB leaders and inspirers returned in many dozens of different sittings; the pre-eminent leader returned for over 140 sittings that I know of. A few of the foremost leaders spoke to Michael through two, three, and even four different mediums, thus confirming their identities and providing evidence of their independence through numerous so-called cross correspondences. Activities at these sittings included presentations of teachings by USB leaders and inspirers, many interactive discussions with Michael of philosophy and teachings, occasional

personal discussions, visits by well-known spiritual and philosophical figures of past times on earth, and reviews of proposed USB *Letters*.

32   Throughout all those sittings and years these USB spirit leaders always maintained their highest standards. The love they conveyed is undeniable. They always treated us and their students and readers with the greatest respect. They were humble, attaching little importance to themselves and their former lives on earth. They *repeatedly* emphasized that no one should accept their (or anyone's) teachings and philosophy unthinkingly and they strongly advocated the use of reason to assess all teachings. They did not claim any monopoly of light and clearly stated that they are not perfect. They never commanded or required us to do anything, nor did they threaten in any way. They never insisted that we take their advice; they only asked us to consider it. They answered hundreds (thousands?) of questions to the best of their abilities, stating clearly when they did not know the answers—such as how and when human spirits were created. Their messages throughout were consistent, sincere, and serious. Their teachings are of a high moral standard and contain no statements that are outrageous, flippant, or (to our knowledge) false. They stressed the need to present teachings simply, clearly, and accurately. Their teachings were not just dictated once, in their own words in final form; instead they were discussed, revised, and polished in cooperation with Michael through multiple reviews and revisions. They taught that no prediction is infallible, that each of us is our own personal savior, and that love is the greatest basis of spiritual life. And they emphasized that "in all things we do, there is no cause greater than Truth." Such teachings and many, many more, comprise this book.

33   I do not consider any of the illumined leaders' teachings or statements to be extravagant. Certainly they are not unsupported, because we have many records of Michael's discussions with USB leaders, including transcripts and tape recordings. Nevertheless, we must question whether those teachers are in fact many of the leading spiritual figures of history that they claim to be. We can best explore this and assess their motives by considering the teachings they have given us—this is what *they* advise. I cannot see how they are trying to "get" anything from us, other than a spirit of cooperation that benefits humanity. They are only offering humanity guidance, knowledge, and inspiration. Their teachings certainly include much enlightenment and many "nuggets."

34   If these spirit teachers were deceptive or evil, as some believe most spirit people to be, how could they achieve their insidious objectives with the behavior and teachings described two paragraphs above and in

the remainder of this book, particularly when they repeatedly advise us to not accept anything on their authority alone, "to partake only of what pleases us," and "to accept only what our reason and inner self unreservedly embraces"?

35 This volume of teachings has only the *highest* motivation, which is to teach the *purest* possible spiritual truth. The purpose of these teachings is "to uplift [and spiritualize] humanity, to awaken all people to the spiritual realities of life and to the [spark of] God within them," that will, in time, unite humanity.

36 My familiarity with the contents of these teachings and the circumstances of their delivery lead me to conclude that this book is the result of a rare historical event in which exceptionally illumined cooperating spirit teachers have delivered the essence of their wisdom to humanity on earth. As some topics explain, re-delivery of such teachings has been necessary from time to time because they have become distorted and disfigured over time, for various reasons, and because the presentation may need to be changed to best suit the times.

37 An important feature of the teachings in this book is that, rather than coming from one teacher, or from various individual teachers, they are the collective work of many great spiritual teachers (over a dozen to my knowledge) *in agreement*. These include many of the greatest that humanity has known, those even wiser and more enlightened now than when they lived on earth. They do not represent any particular religion. Their teachings include quite a few on contemporary and modern issues which earlier spiritual teachings do not address. So while these teachings are an updated presentation of spiritual truth, I believe they are far superior to most provided by single teachers. Based on my own extensive investigations, I conclude there is *no* higher credible authority and source of such teachings accessible to humanity on earth. These important features, combined with the highest motivation, make this book of spiritual teachings truly unique.

38 A number of reviewers have commented on similarities between some of the USB teachings and those in the major religions. We should *expect* similarities, because these teachings are given by many of their former teachers. But these teachings now come directly and purely, presented for our times, and from the entire leadership in accord rather than from an individual teacher.

39 These enlightened spirit teachers, many well-known for their spirituality and spiritual teachings, asked us to not identify them in this book;

Introduction

some of them have assumed humble names to cloak their identities. They did so because they wish to avoid wrong impressions and controversies where teachings have been incorrectly attributed to them, or because they have over time changed their understanding, or because people associate them with religions they did not establish. But the main reason they give is their desire for people to accept teachings that resonate well with *them*, rather than because of the "names" of those who presented the teachings. They stress that *what* they teach is more important than the identity of the teachers.

40   Although the stated source of these teachings is extraordinary and even incredible to some, it is their *content* that is the most important, particularly their uplifting and inspiring nature.

41   The delivery of this body of teachings was clearly a major project and a work of love for the individuals involved. The difficulties for such advanced souls to communicate with us directly and specifically are far greater than we can imagine. Many made major commitments to serve in various capacities. The recordings and transcripts of early conversations between spirit leaders and Michael contain repeated references to "this mission."

42   The amount of service on both sides of life involved in a project of this scope is extraordinary. This, and the absence of material benefit accruing to the people involved, is important to bear in mind when considering the motives for this work. During Michael's lifetime he was by far the USB's major financial contributor. May all of us who benefit from these teachings remember and appreciate the contributions of so many.

A Reminder

43   Michael specifically asked me to end these preliminary remarks with the constant reminder from our Illumined Inspirers, to not accept anything unthinkingly from anyone, themselves included.

                     John Finnemore
                     Cupertino, California, June 2014

Preface

by the founder of the USB on earth

1. This volume contains teachings and philosophy of The Universal Spiritual Brother&Sisterhood (USB)—teachings and philosophy for the new age we are in. As it is a claim that many organizations have made in the past, that many make today, and that many undoubtedly will make in the future, we present the basis for *our* claim.

2. Teachings are more important than the teacher, the USB holds. But the teacher is important, too; for if the teacher is endorsed by individuals that are known to be respected and esteemed, many are much more likely to at least *examine* those teachings. For this reason I go back more than two decades to communications received through two exceptional mediums known to thousands for the high quality of their mediumship.

3. I have nothing to promote for myself. I expect to rejoin loved ones on the other side of life before long, perhaps before this volume is completed, in which case others will finish compiling what the USB's quarterly worldwide *Letters* have shared with its followers for more than twenty years.

4. There is nothing I want *from* the world, much that I wish *for* it: awareness, or greater awareness, of The [Spiritual] Laws That Govern, and of the Love, Wisdom, Goodness, Law and Order, Justice, and Compassion that are expressed by that Being or Force or Power that we and many others call God.

5. This volume presents a multitude of truths shared by beings of extraordinary spiritual elevation; a few of those beings, under more than one name, have been revered by hundreds of millions of people over the centuries.

6. I neither expect nor desire anyone to accept these statements on my mere say-so. That is why I give chapter and verse, so to speak, of some private sittings with mediums in England in 1956 and 1957, when I was fortunate and blessed to receive an overwhelming flood of spirit testimony to the mission of the USB and to the almost incredible spiritual stature of its Illumined Inspirers.

7. The identities of those mediums, and of [some] other unnamed individuals in this preface, are on file at USB headquarters in California, and are available to individual inquirers.[1]

---

[1] The names of the mediums and others who assisted the USB (as well as the names of USB spirit leaders, Intro:39) were omitted upon the request of Illumined Souls.

Preface

8   All except the first two sittings with one medium were tape recorded. And what the distinguished guide of another said to me was taken down in longhand notes by the medium's daughter and then typed. The tapes and transcripts are also in the USB files.

9   It was through the two English mediums, whom I shall refer to as A and B, that most of the USB's aims, plans, and principles were given or approved. It was through the deep-trance mediumship of my beloved wife that most of the teachings and philosophy have come.

· · · · ·

10 At my sittings with A, a famous social reformer and head of state was among the first to pledge his support to The Brother&Sisterhood, a support he has since renewed on more than one occasion.

11 Others included an eminent spiritual leader and an illustrious philosopher, both of their own accord acknowledging changes in some of the views they once held.

12 On October 17, 1956, the spiritual leader vowed that he and others would be with "the great and glorious work" that was about to begin, and that they would be "behind every path, every step of the way." He declared:

13 There are *thousands* of souls on this [spirit] side who are *anxiously* awaiting their opportunity to make themselves known to your world, and to cooperate and work with you, and through you and others. It is an *immense* thing. This is an organization that is founded on *this* side, and *you* are going to be the instigator on *your* side. *You* are an instrument for this work, from this side, and we shall do *everything* in our power to bring it into being, through you and others with you...

14 It wasn't just by mere coincidence that you came to England. It wasn't mere coincidence that you came to London, that you came here, and that you went to B. *All* that was planned and arranged some years ago, in America, for you...

15 The organization would be a great and glorious thing, he said.

16 But we realize it's going to take time. But we know that you have the power to do it. You're the right man. After all, you've been prepared for this work for some years. In fact I would go as far as to say you've been prepared for it through *centuries* of time, by various lives and incarnations and development of the soul. And you're back in this earth world now, *waiting* to commence this great work.

Preface

17 On the following day—October 18, 1956—one of A's guides, speaking for many in attendance from the spirit side of life, said that the organization [the USB] would be

18 ... a continuation of a much older one that you formed centuries ago, which was lost to the world through people's ignorance.

19 Two days later, another member of A's spirit band [of co-workers] had this to say:

20 I am quite frankly *amazed* at the link that exists between you and certain souls here... I'm sure that with the links that you have with the wonderful entities and souls from our world, you are going to do *tremendous* work for humanity...

21 On December 12, 1957, the illustrious philosopher spoke to me. I can reproduce his words, but not his accent.

22 You have been *blessed!* Though you may not have much in the way of the goods of the world, you have inherited a great inheritance of spirit, and you have been given a great strength in a realization which will assist you always, and bring you out of the darkness in your world into great illumination of spirit... My friend, it is for me the greatest of pleasure to come to one who is prepared to serve God and to work for God's children. For me, that is a joy.

23 At the same sitting, a Blessed One had this, among other things, to say:

24 Of course many of our plans, my son, cannot obviously be brought into being perhaps even in your lifetime. For you have been chosen to plant the seed, and others will come and help you to nurture that seed; and though you will see the blossoming forth, remember, my son, you may not see *all* in your lifetime. But from this side of life, when your work and task is finished, you will be able to join us on this side, and work with us from this side to help humanity on earth.

25 It is a great and glorious task which you have undertaken, and I *know* that you cannot fail, for it is a task that has been given to you to do by [according to the plan of] The Most High. And we who come, who are but God's ministering ones, join in love and in harmony and in peace with you, that we might bring realization to those who will listen to our words...

Preface

The sittings with B perfectly complemented and corroborated the sittings with A. B's distinguished guide said much that was enormously encouraging and significant.

On October 3, 1956:

> I have met you before. I know you much better than you know me... I am happy to come to you. I would not let you go away without talking to you...

On October 8, 1956:

> You have been chosen to help humanity out of this darkened state... If we can strengthen and help you, that is our mission. That is why I myself come to talk to you; I do not come to all...

On October 18, 1956:

> You were in the 2,000 year cycle which is coming to fruition at the end of the 2,000 years. You were with us at that period. You walked with us by the Sea of Galilee. I knew you in Jerusalem. That was the last time I met you in the planetary life of dreams,[2] and it is now coming back into that cycle and you had to meet me...[3]

On October 23, 1956:

> Be of good cheer. With every step you go forward, I and the glorious Band go forward with you; every step you fall back, we fall back with you. Your joys are our joys; your sorrows, our sorrows.

On November 28, 1957:

> The torch which you hold in your hand is the replica of that of a great Crusader who lighted the torch of great understanding long, long ago. That torch is the very existence of humanity in the Armageddon of light and darkness which enshrouds your world today.

Michael Flagg
San Francisco, California, 1980

---

[2] The "planetary life of dreams" is the phrase this guide of great spiritual advancement used to describe life on earth.

[3] The need for truths to be restated in each new age is discussed in Topic 201:4–6.

Greetings from an Illumined Soul

> *Before Michael Flagg passed on to spirit life, he asked the preeminent USB spirit inspirer if he wished to write a foreword to this book, to which the inspirer replied that he would think about it. He never did dictate one, and we were unable to ask him again. Under the circumstances, as editor I have assembled the following greeting from this Blessed Inspirer's addresses to humanity (Appendix A).*

1. I greet you, and I look upon you, and I see my children, my sisters and brothers, each in your own fashion making your way unto the greater light of understanding, and each in your own way *living* your life in a fashion that you *alone* can live.

2. For each of you, in your *own* manner, serves your God. Each of you, in your *own* fashion, extends your hands and your heart to your fellow human beings. Each of you brings to your fellow traveller a bit of light as you *alone* can bring it, and as you *alone* can share it.

3. For each of you is personally making a way for not only yourself, but for those who travel with you. You are making the way a little lighter, and you are showing what *can* be done when one feels the glory of God within, and feels within that in order for that light to shine round and about, one must *share* some of that light with one's fellow travellers.

4. We come to develop the spirit, we come that we might inspire and give unto the earth world a great realization of the purpose of life, and what it can entail and what it can achieve when people approach all things from the spiritual aspect and desire only spiritual good for themselves and the world. For when people cast out all material condition, when they cast out fear, and put in its place that assurance within themselves that all is well because they are walking with the Great Spirit, then all these things shall come to pass, and each and every one shall be blessed.

5. Our [the USB] way of life is one that will teach you not to overlook the trials and tribulations that pass your way, but to accept them cheerfully and to renew your strength spiritually, and to realize and understand their purpose.

6. Our way of life will *give* you strength of character. Our way of life will plant the seed of service more deeply within your being. And our way of life will encourage you to extend your hands—*both of them*—in

Greetings from an Illumined Soul

brotherly and sisterly love across the seven seas to *all* the children of earth...

7   So I would say to you: Let not *one* day go by without a kindly thought, expressed in your *own* fashion, for a fellow traveller.

8   Our lives are judged not by results alone, but by *intent* as well.

9   A life well lived is a life devoted not only to self-realization, but to *service* to one's fellow human beings. And one cannot be of service to one's fellow human beings *without* being of service to one's God.

10 While we make our way, we *are* being served. And as we serve one the other, know that the blessedness that comes from such service shall bring to each of you that which is your soul's desire.

11 *The need is now, and the need is great*, for each of you in your *own* fashion to share your light with your fellow traveller; and to remember that as you do, so is added unto yourselves a still greater portion of what you are seeking...

12 We are sisters and brothers, and we shall continue to seek for what shall bring to the children of earth the peace that they are searching for. We shall continue to bring to those hungry souls [spiritual] food to satisfy their craving [516:7].

13 And there shall be a glow within each child of earth that shall shine brightly, that shall bring to those who walk in the shadows a light that shall better enable them to make their way along the path that leads to greater understanding.

14 Let your light so shine, that those who seek it shall absorb it! Let your heart so sing, that those who cross your path shall feel the joy that is yours!

15 There are those among you who have a *great* realization of our mission—to free the children of earth from the shackles that bind them, and to bring to them the truth of the brother-and-sisterhood of humankind in its fullest expression, encircling the globe, and at last bringing peace to the children of earth.

16 You, who are the custodians of this great truth, must be an example in your world, and each of you must give forth that light which will illumine the path of others. And know that spiritually *each* of you is given the banner of Truth! Walk upright! And *let your voice be heard!*

17 Realize that *each* of you is *indeed* linked... as brother and sister—[you] are indeed as brothers and sisters in spirit.

18 I leave my blessings with each of you. And I pray that the God of your heart's understanding shall grant unto each of you *everything* that is the soul's desire.

An Offer and a Call

1. A group of Illumined Souls from the spirit realms of the highest spiritual attainment, including the greatest souls this earth has known, offer their help to *all* humanity.
2. They see so much suffering on earth, in so many ways; they observe that from time to time human activities have placed life on earth itself in serious danger.
3. They offer to help us:
4. — Sweep away many undesirable attitudes and behaviors of earlier times;
5. — Break down barriers between people;
6. — See and know and recognize the power of God, and of God's love for us;
7. — Find a peace and joy in things of the spirit;
8. — Bring peace and harmony to our world.
9. They say that in order to bring these things about, humanity needs to *live in accord with God's perfect spiritual laws*, and so reflect God's love and universal spiritual values.

10. They offer to *advise* us how to bring this about.
11. They bring us assurance and the knowledge we need, in this book.
12. But it is up to *us* to do it.

13. These Illumined Souls call on all interested people to join them in their movement, The Universal Spiritual Brother&Sisterhood, to help organize and carry out this very important spiritual work for all humanity. They say (Appendix A):
14. — *We need helpers*, those who are humble in spirit, to join us in our commitment, to serve humanity, as instruments of God;
15. — We would like to instill more love of God into your hearts and minds;
16. — You need *not* accept every one of our teachings to join with us, and you need *not* give up other affiliations and/or beliefs you hold;
17. — We want us *together* to make this movement strong and powerful, for *good* in the world;
18. — Remember the truths of the great souls of the past; remember what they have sacrificed and done; try therefore to be like them.

"To comfort people in their hours of sorrow is very important. But what is even more important is to give them a way of life, and to help them live that way of life, to help them understand the Laws of God, and the purposes of their being."

— an Inspirer

The Basis

1

The Universal Spiritual Brother&Sisterhood

The USB

CHAPTER CONTENTS

1.1 Origins		**22**
101	The USB and The Great Brotherhood	22
102	The USB Movement	24
1.2 Values		**26**
103	Principles of the USB	26
104	Purposes of the USB	27
105	Universality	27
106	The Need for Humility	28
107	Worship Only God	28
108	Personal Freedom for All	29
109	Some Values within the USB Requirements	30
110	How the USB Is Different	30
1.3 Outlook		**32**
111	On Linking Up with the USB	32
112	How One Can Serve	33
113	A Message of Cheer	34
114	On Individual Interpretation	35
115	A Great Teacher—and the USB	36
116	A Word of Warning	36

1.1 ORIGINS

101 The Universal Spiritual Brother&Sisterhood and The Great Brotherhood

1   The Universal Spiritual Brother&Sisterhood (USB) is a part of The Great (White[1]) Brotherhood; [they both first came into being in the spirit world (1301) many ages ago].[2] Both are directed from the highest spirit realms by the same Illumined Souls,[3] and both organizations have supporters in the spirit world and on earth.

2   The Great Brotherhood (GB)—the word *great* represents its size—is an immense organization for good. A *spiritual* organization completely, it is composed of countless groups, each in its own fashion serving according to its understanding of what is good, and each in its own way sharing light. Some groups work in the spirit realms only; others work on both sides of life, either directly, or through their supporters on earth, or both.

3   In a sense, the GB can be likened to a huge earthly organization of service operating at various levels of authority and responsibility, from the highest national level to the humblest local level, all contributing their share to the overall process.

4   There are many supporters of the GB living on earth, and members who have been initiated into it psychically or in the spirit world. But there are *no* official representatives of the GB on earth, although many *claim* that distinction.[4]

5   Our organization, the USB *on earth* [Intro:10], does not represent the GB as a whole. However, it *does* represent, and *is* the earthly counterpart of, the USB in the spirit world, an organization that has long existed

---

[1] (All footnotes and inserts in [ ] in this book were added by the editor, they were not part of the original USB material.) With the word *White* representing the purity, spirituality, and holiness of the Illumined Souls who direct it (and having nothing to do with race, which is not an issue in the higher spirit realms), The Great (White) Brotherhood was and is also known as The White Brotherhood. It has recently also become known on earth as The Great Brotherhood of Light.

[2] Before these two organizations became known on earth, their original names were The Universal Spiritual Brotherhood and The Great White Brotherhood, in which everyone then clearly understood the word *Brotherhood* to equally include men, women, and children. (In the higher realms all people are, and always have been, considered equal. We further describe the founding of the USB on earth and an impact of gender issues in paragraph 10 of the Introduction.)

[3] Like a spirit-world council of leaders. See also Intro:3,37 and Topic 1225.

[4] This was written in 1966.

1.1 Origins

there, that is the *mainstream* of the GB, that is under the direction of the most spiritually exalted souls the earth has ever known, and that at the dawn of each new age has provided truth simply, clearly, and accurately, in a form suitable for that age.[5]

6 That the teachings and philosophy of various GB groups are sometimes far from identical is not surprising. In the filtering down or *indirect* transmission of teachings and philosophy, there are bound to be misunderstandings and misinterpretations of what comes from the highest source. We in the USB on earth are fortunate, for our teachings and philosophy have come *directly* from truly Illumined Souls, who form the "governing body" of the GB.

7 We can liken the teachings and philosophy of the USB to pure water from pure snow on the loftiest watershed; and those of many other GB groups to water making its way to the ocean through innumerable streams and rivers, and naturally losing some of its purity during the journey as it absorbs elements and other materials from the earth and the atmosphere.

8 However, despite any differences in teachings and philosophy, we welcome each and every organization devoted to uniting humankind and to removing the barriers that people have built in ignorance and blindness over the centuries.

9 Each organization works as it is inspired to do.

10 The USB—*our* organization—is not political in any manner, shape, or form. It is a movement to uplift humanity, to awaken all people to the spiritual realities of life and to the [spark of] God within each of them.

11 Its task is to truly *spiritualize* humanity, to make people aware of The Laws That Govern, of the truths that are eternal. When that is accomplished, all else will fall into its proper place. For when people become *truly* spiritual, it is bound to affect every aspect of their existence—their politics, their relationships with others, everything.

12 In this book, when we speak of The Brother&Sisterhood, we refer specifically and only to The Universal Spiritual Brother&Sisterhood (on earth);

---

[5] To summarize, paragraphs 1–2 indicate that supporters of the USB and of the GB live and work on both sides of life; paragraphs 4–5 indicate that both organizations have official representatives in the spirit world, whereas on earth the USB has had them since 1956 and the GB had none in 1966.

101 ☐

when we speak of the USB, we refer to The Universal Spiritual Brotherhood (in the spirit world) and/or to The Universal Spiritual Brother&Sisterhood (on earth).[6]

102 The USB Movement

1 A *host* of great souls in the spirit world are the inspirers and supporters of The Universal Spiritual Brother&Sisterhood (USB) on earth. The USB was formed in the 1950s[7] under their direction and guidance, much of which was given in their own voices, in their very own words [the procedure is further described in Pref:6–9].

2 The quotations in this topic are *their* words, recorded on tape in the 1950s at direct-voice sittings [1218].

3 Some of the greatest souls who lived on earth are the actual originators of the USB. As a Blessed Soul[8] says:

4 Many of the great prophets and teachers who once trod your earth are the instigators of this that we are endeavoring to do, and under their leadership are many souls bound in love to serve humankind, to follow out the directions of the great ones...

---

[6] When we changed our name to make it gender neutral (Intro:10) we chose the word Brother&Sisterhood because we believe it best explains that the USB is an organization of *brothers and sisters*; it represents our important understanding that *all* human beings, on both sides of life, are linked as spiritual brothers and sisters (601:2), and that we should live accordingly. (Please note that it is *not* Brotherhood&Sisterhood, which suggests two separate but joined organizations.) We kept the acronym USB unchanged, mainly because we felt that the many needed repetitions of the acronym would be unwieldy if we used four letters, but also because we found USBS to be undesirable. A spirit communicator in April 2007, who claimed to speak for the USB in the spirit realms and who otherwise seemed very credible, made a point to mention that our parent organization in the higher spirit realms (where there are no gender issues like ours) is still known as the "Brotherhood."

[7] Newspaper articles of the 1950s describe Michael's discovery of his/this important mission; more information about them is available from USB headquarters. The USB is not linked in any way with any other group or organization on earth. It is not a religion, cult, or sect. Headquartered in California, it does not solicit funds or charge any membership dues or fees; its work is sustained entirely by freely donated contributions that come from the heart. See 109:2 and D06:1,4 for more details.

[8] Blessed Souls are very enlightened spirit individuals, spiritually progressed and much revered, who may or may not be Illumined Souls. Blessed Souls referred to in this book are also leaders, inspirers, or supporters of the USB.

1.1 Origins

5   As this is an organization of spiritual truth for people on earth, patterned after the original that has long existed in the higher spirit realms, followers should always remember that *"in all things we do, there is no cause greater than Truth."* [304:1; in 301:2–3 we define Truth as that which is eternal.]

6   Open to all people everywhere, regardless of the color of their skin, the faith they were born in, the country they live in, or the views they believe in, this movement (the USB) will unify humankind within the lifetime of many of us. People

7   shall forget their differences in race, and in color, and in creed, and they shall [understand their connection] with God. And there shall be reborn upon earth a new heaven... where people might live in peace and love and tranquillity, and grow in stature and in strength spiritually.

8   The USB's goal is to unite all humanity in a peace and harmony based on love and service, knowledge of Survival [of death], communication with those in other expressions of existence, enlightenment from Illumined Souls, and on the power of spirit [helpers] to heal.

9   Each person who links up with The Brother&Sisterhood brings the day closer when the barriers that people have built in ignorance and foolishness will be demolished.

10 Each group that meets from time to time, in love and harmony for purely *spiritual* purposes, adds to the spiritual reservoir that will be used for great things in the years to come.

11 An Illumined Soul says:

12 There are *great* powers, greater than any that you or any soul upon earth know of—greater powers than any can *comprehend* upon earth! There are great forces that can be brought into being, whereby we can, through the right people, when the time comes, demonstrate the power of God that flows through us.

13 And then we shall demonstrate in such a way, that *none* can turn their face from us. [And people] shall say: "This is indeed the path of truth, for we have seen the signs! And these signs are unto us of a new life, and a new power, where love shall sway *all* people in the direction of truth and tranquillity and peace."...

14 But we need *thousands* of souls... souls afire with the desire to do the will of God.

15   We need souls with courage, souls that realize that "those who would serve must be prepared to sacrifice," souls that have been "waiting for direction as to what they shall do to propagate the work of the spirit."

16   Many such souls have already joined with us. Not only individuals, but groups, some of which have for years been blessed by spirit guides with inspiration and teaching of a high order.

17
> The foundation has been built ... and soon the lighthouse will be erected. Forth from it shall come a great light across your world..., and *many* shall see the illumination, and shall bless it. And they shall indeed grow in strength from it, and they shall be lifted up.

18   This movement, the USB, began in a humble way, but its power will grow with the years, and it will in time "sweep the world with love and tenderness."

19   But it will remain humble always, as must those who serve it. We have the inspiration and example of Illumined Souls who come with such a burning desire to bring enlightenment and knowledge and truth to the world. [See their humility in 107:4–5.]

1.2 VALUES

103 Principles of the USB

1. God is That Which Is All-Good—a God of Love and Wisdom, of Law and Justice.
2. All humankind are God's children, and this means we are *all* spiritual sisters and brothers without exception.
3. Our lives are eternal and we retain our individualities after the change called death.
4. Under certain conditions we can commune with those in other expressions of life.
5. We are each personally responsible for all we say, think, and do; and no belief in anyone, or allegiance to anyone, can absolve us from that responsibility.

1.2 Values

6. The law of cause and effect, like all other spiritual laws, knows no exception; and as we sow we reap, here or hereafter.
7. The doors to spiritual progress are never closed to anyone—and loving ones will help us if we but reach out our hearts and minds to God.
8. Aspiration and effort are inseparable, so one cannot *truly* aspire without making the effort.
9. We should serve selflessly, as best we can, to bring love and peace and harmony to humanity, to bring the day ever nearer when all shall live in a universal spiritual brother-and-sisterhood.

104 Purposes of the USB

1. To unfold to humanity a way of life, and a new understanding of God's will and purpose.
2. To bring a universal awareness of the spark of God within each of us, and a realization that love is the greatest basis of spiritual life.
3. To bring to humanity peace and tranquillity of spirit, and happiness of heart and soul.
4. To break down the barriers that stand between one nation and another, between one people and another, and between one individual and another.
5. To break down the barriers of creeds and dogmas.
6. To cast aside ignorance and replace it with truth.
7. To form one great spiritual brother-and-sisterhood throughout the world.

105 Universality

1 The USB recognizes that there were great teachers among all peoples, and in all ages. For that reason, it does not confine its acceptance to any one person or book or authority, but acknowledges truth *wherever* it is found.

2 Its teachings stress the importance of thinking and acting universally.

3 The USB considers all people to be equally important; at its meetings, there should be no activities or (if possible) things that tend to separate people spiritually [D03:7–8].

106 The Need For Humility

1. The spirit inspirers of the USB not only *counsel* understanding and humility, but *reveal* those qualities in all they say and do. They know that it is difficult for us who live in a material world to always act spiritually. They know that we may occasionally err, however we may try not to. Says an Illumined Soul:

2. > We do not expect perfection from *you*, because *we* are not perfect... We who worship at the feet of The Most High are most humble, because we are conscious of what *we* lack.

3. Says another:

4. > They who would serve God, they who would serve the mighty spirit forces, first need to learn humbleness of spirit. For it is mainly through the humble that we are able to bring forth great things...

5. > All the great saints, all the great teachers, all the great prophets, all the great seers through the ages, have always been most humble. These things you know. But there are those who *profess* to know these truths who are blinded through ignorance and self-seeking.

6. There is no room for selfishness in the USB. We have *spiritual* leadership. And even though there must be organization, there will be no leaders in a *material* sense.

7. > We who come [to you] from the spirit world are all, as you well know, one, in complete love and in complete harmony. And so it is that it must be so in your world among those who are called to serve. Though there may be in a sense leaders, or leadership, yet all must remember and realize at all times that *no one is more important than the other*.

107 Worship Only God

1. The USB discourages the worship of any thing or person, on either side of life.

2. We should love one another. We should respect one another. We should help one another. But when it comes to worship, *we should worship only God* [Chap. 5 Sec. 1].

1.2 Values

3   An Illumined Soul, known by various names and revered by hundreds of millions of people, expresses the following for all truly great souls:

4   We come in humbleness and in spiritual desire to work *with* you, and *through* you... We only ask that you accept us and treat us as sisters and brothers a little more enlightened.

5   We do not want adulation. We do not want those upon earth to bow to us, or to make of us saints, or to make of us gods. For we come in the true sense as true brothers and sisters, in love and in harmony and in peace.

6   They do *not* claim any special divinity other than the spark of the divine [601:2] that *every* child of God, on earth and in spirit life, possesses.

7   Furthermore, we must beware of those on either side of life who at any time expect worship and adulation, or who at any time *demand* acceptance of what they present. We should shun them resolutely, for they are false!

108 Personal Freedom for All

1   One need not accept every purpose and principle of the USB to join the USB movement. It is enough to realize that all human beings [on *both* sides of life] are God's children, and that this means we are all spiritual sisters and brothers.

2   Other realization will come in time.

3   We have no wish to make anyone give up beliefs that comfort them, even though those beliefs may not be held by Illumined Souls. People will discard incorrect beliefs themselves in due season, when they are ready, and when they themselves wish to.

4   Nor do we require anyone to give up other affiliations on joining the USB's mission. In fact, we do not ask our brothers and sisters to give up *anything*.

5   As an Illumined Soul has said:

6   We must give everyone above all things their personal freedom ... One of the most important facts, one of the most important tenets of our work, is that all ... shall be free to live and worship, and to die—as the world terms "die"—in their own way and fashion, in their own beliefs, or lack of beliefs.

7   Though we desire in many ways to break down the barriers of creeds, we are conscious of people's needs. And if one person finds joy or happiness and help in some direction of their religious convictions, we do not necessarily desire that they shall lose it. For we recognize *one* Divinity, *one* God.

8   When one considers the hundreds and thousands of different religious sects and bodies—yet all worshipping the same God—we realize that many people have been foolish...! But nevertheless, such is our love and compassion, that we would not have anyone change their thought if it is not their deep wish and desire to do so.

9   Those who love their fellow human beings insist on their right to be free—so long as they do not intrude on the freedom of *others*.

109 Some Values Within the USB Requirements[9]

1   Simplicity and humility should mark the work of the USB in all its aspects. It strives to avoid things, titles, dress, music, and activities which separate people spiritually, or which suggest specific groups, organizations, or belief systems [D03, D22, D32]. It does not have rituals, rites, or prescribed ceremonies [D16]. It disapproves of excessive praise [D14].

2   The USB does not solicit funds and contributions, nor does it charge membership fees [D06, D09]. It only accepts contributions and donations that are freely and voluntarily given, that come from people's hearts with love [D06:1,4, D20].

3   The USB expects its speakers to be prepared, disciplined, and clear; and it expects its mediums to be truthful and convincing [D23–D25].

110 How the USB Is Different

1   We sum up a few things that, in whole or in part, distinguish the USB from a great many other organizations that believe in human survival after death:

2   — it is inspired and guided by Illumined Souls;

3   — it stresses higher teachings and philosophy;

---

[9] Appendix D presents requirements and guidelines of the USB. Here, references in brackets identify topics that give more information on the subjects mentioned.

1.2 Values

4 — it emphasizes each person's direct connection with God and with all people through God;
5 — it emphasizes that we can best worship God by serving our fellow human beings, and by living in love and peace and harmony;
6 — it insists that no one should accept anything unthinkingly from anyone, including from the USB;
7 — the spiritual requirements it expects of its mediums and speakers;
8 — it is not linked in any way with any other group or organization on earth;
9 — it requires that its financial support must come freely, with love, from people's hearts;
10 — it is completely detached from commercialism of any sort; and
11 — its positive *no's* governing USB activities, which include:
12   *no* worship of any one or thing except God
13   *no* rituals or rites of any sort
14   *no* fees
15   *no* solicitation for funds
16   *no* "selling of blessings"
17   *no* titles that separate
18   *no* politics of any sort
19   *no* smugness
20   *no* excessive praise
21   *no* positions on certain controversial subjects; and
22   *no* unusual or outlandish attire while working for the USB.

23   Some groups and organizations exact a promise from members not to divulge the teachings they are given. We, on the contrary, *encourage* sisters and brothers to impart USB teachings and philosophy to anyone and everyone ready to receive them. We ask them to present teachings simply, clearly, without excessive decorations, and only as much as can be comfortably absorbed at any time.

24   Another thing that distinguishes the USB is that it is absolutely clear about not only what it *supports*, but what it *opposes*. This is not in order to attack others, but to make it impossible for corruption to creep into the USB as it has crept into and tarnished many movements in the past.

25   We also oppose the imparting of beliefs that are *known* to be wrong. And regardless of the motive, we oppose the *discouragement* of anyone from seeking or examining truths. We oppose these because all who learn and accept error, no matter why, must unlearn and discard it before they can advance much further spiritually.

26   But the *main* difference is this: The USB originated and was organized in the spirit world, not on earth. It will not be crushed by rules of organization that have extinguished the spirituality of many movements. What rules we have are *spiritual* requirements, approved by truly Illumined Souls, to be followed by anyone whenever *officially* representing the USB [Appendix D].

1.3 OUTLOOK

111 On Linking Up with the USB

1   The Brother&Sisterhood is an organization of spiritual truth open to all. As an Illumined Soul puts it: "It is our wish that not one soul shall be turned aside who desires to walk with us."

2   We bless all souls, whether or not they are supporters or members of the USB. We welcome *all* who wish to join with us.

3   The USB is a way of life, not a religion. It adheres to the principle that "in all things we do, there is no cause greater than Truth" [304:1]. It endorses all that is good, anywhere.

4   Is there anything in the USB's aims, principles, policies, teachings, and philosophy that could not well be adopted by *any* individual, group, or organization that has the welfare of humanity at heart?

5   In any event, one need *not* accept every purpose and principle of the USB to become a supporter or member, *nor* need one give up any beliefs or affiliations [108].

6   In what is still an early stage of our work, we especially desire those who would *serve*, instead of being served; who would *give*, rather than receive; who would *love*, rather than be loved; who seek light that they might *share* it, not just hoard it; who realize that nothing is achieved without effort; and who know that *one who would serve must be prepared to sacrifice*. In other words, we especially desire those who have not only been touched by the finger of spirit, but are conscious of its beauty.

7   We welcome even the humblest endeavor to spread truth and enlightenment. We know that every endeavor, small though it may seem, or be, is a stream that contributes to the strength of the river it joins, hastening the day when it will be irresistible—a spiritual river whose mighty waters

1.3 Outlook □ *112*

will sweep away the barriers that people have built in ignorance and foolishness through the centuries.

8   Who knows *which* drop of water causes the dam to finally break? And who can say that *this* drop, or *that* drop, was of greater effect? We know that *all* drops contribute to the breaking of the dam. And we know that *all* efforts count in breaking the dam of ignorance and foolishness that has kept one person apart from another, one nation or people apart from another, and one race apart from another. We need the efforts of all who share a glimpse of Truth to bring the day closer when the children of earth will live as they *will* one day live—in a human brother-and-sisterhood, as children of a living and loving God.

9   The strength or force of a river is much greater than the sum of the strengths of the streams of which it is composed: It is more than arithmetical. Likewise, those who join the USB movement, however humble their efforts, contribute more by being linked together than they could ever contribute separately.

10   Many who follow the USB are people who feel they can go no further on other roads, and who find in the USB the path on which they can go further.

11   The USB is linking up various individuals and groups throughout the world who desire to serve their fellow human beings. It is unifying the scattered potential. It is linking up spiritual pools of illumination, the united light of which will in time become powerful enough to dissipate the darkness in people's minds.

112 How One Can Serve

1   To those who ask how they can serve, we say this.

2   You can serve by spiritualizing your own life to an ever greater degree, remembering always that love is the greatest basis of all spiritual life, and therefore also the greatest basis of the USB's work.

3   You can plant the seed of spirituality in others—gently, unobtrusively —by the way you live, and by what you do.

4   You can discuss with others the USB's aims and principles, and how they can be put into effect in daily life.

5   You can send out healing thoughts and prayers for those in need.

6   You can meet with others who wish to be of service, who seek to open up the spirit within, and who in humility and love reach out to God.

112

7 If you wish to add your link to those on both sides of life who strive to bring peace and happiness to humanity, you can serve by joining the USB movement.

8 You can serve by meeting with others from time to time, for spiritual discussion and unfoldment or development [D28].

9 Even if you live far from USB supporters, you can *still* serve in many of the ways just mentioned.

10 Aware of your linkage with Illumined Souls in this great and noble mission, you can forge links with others on earth that encircle the globe —not merely from east to west, or north to south, but from one heart to another heart, one hand to another hand, one home to another home, thus adding the personal and caring touch.

11 As an Illumined Inspirer has told us:

12 Each child of light that bears the torch of Truth, and makes its way into the dark places, plays an important role in the scheme of things.

113 A Message of Cheer

1 The USB preaches no doctrine of fear or panic or calamity.

2 On the contrary, our message is one of hope, serenity, love, understanding, strength, and courage.

3 It is the tidings that the brother-and-sisterhood of all humanity *will* be a living reality within the lifetime of many on earth today.

4 It is the teaching that *each one of us*, by our *own* efforts, however humble, can bring that day nearer.

5 Illumined Souls have never promised that the path will be easy. The path *is* not, and *cannot* be, an easy one. But with each kind word or thought or deed of a sister or brother, we are one step closer to our goal. With each added link to the USB, we are another step closer.

6 And with each new pool of light linked with the rest, greater is the flow into the spiritual reservoir that is *being* used for great things, and that will be used for *greater* things—far greater than we can perhaps comprehend at the moment—when the time is right.

7 So we say to our brothers and sisters:

8 Lift up your hearts and rejoice!

1.3 Outlook

9. Ignore the lamentations of the prophets of doom. A new world is not built by the fearful. A new age is not ushered in by the despairing.

10. The brother-and-sisterhood of humanity will be accomplished by all those who share our ideals, strengthened by the unity of those who tread the USB path.

114 On Individual Interpretation

1. We have often been asked why the USB does not take a specific position on various issues of the day, as some organizations do.

2. There are several reasons.

3. First of all, as we make clear, this movement is *non-political*, and will never be political in any manner, shape, or form [D04]; whereas many of the issues of the day either are political, or have political undertones.

4. Secondly, we would not presume to speak for *all* our followers on any issue; nor do we desire to. In any case, we know that people with a common aim may strongly disagree on the *methods* of achieving it.

5. Thirdly, and *mainly*, we are primarily concerned with presenting the teachings and philosophy of Illumined Souls—the *true* teachings and philosophy of this new age—for people to live by according to their own highest perception of what they accept.

6. In describing God's Laws That Govern, or THE LAW, we emphasize that while THE LAW governs the entire universe, *our* understanding of it will vary according to the level of our consciousness [402]. As we say there: We should not expect others to interpret The Laws precisely as we ourselves do. Nor should we try to force our own interpretations on them.

7. We can say the same about the USB's teachings and philosophy. We present a broad canvas of truth, portrayed by beings of extraordinary spiritual stature; but we do not expect everyone to see it in exactly the same way, or from the very same angle, or to appreciate its various aspects in the very same degree.

8. For we champion for everyone else the identical freedom we cherish for ourselves: the freedom of each individual to think things out for themselves, to reach their own conclusions, and to take only such action as they themselves decide to take [108].

115 A Great Teacher—and the USB

1. We have been asked why we do not quote or mention by name in our writings, except indirectly, a certain Great Soul revered by many millions, although we once made it clear that he is a leader of the USB. There are several reasons.

2. First and foremost, *it is his wish.* For over the centuries, much that he taught long ago has been twisted and distorted by chroniclers and others, either in ignorance, or to suit their *own* ends or the aims of those who engaged or directed them. Some of the sayings and teachings attributed to him he did not say, and, being the soul he was, *never* could have said. It would serve no useful purpose, and in fact would make only for endless controversy and dispute, to now quote him specifically on such things.

3. As one can well understand, there is little joy over the way his teachings have been misinterpreted and mispresented, often deliberately, and over the stream of false prophets and teachers who have claimed, even as some do now, that *he* inspired or worked through them.

4. A second reason is his desire that people judge teachings and philosophy by their soundness or lack of soundness, by whether they appeal to or are repelled by people's reason, by whether they strike a responsive chord within them or leave them unimpressed—and not by whether they believe that he teaches them.[10]

5. For another thing, many people associate him with a particular religion only, although he did *not* found a religion, but taught a way of life for all people.

6. But while we do not quote or mention him by name, we can say this emphatically: nothing is dearer to his heart than the universal spiritual brother-and-sisterhood of humankind.

116 A Word of Warning

1. It is not uncommon for teachings and philosophy to become twisted and distorted over the years.

2. Sometimes the misrepresentation is accidental. At other times it is done wilfully and deliberately.

---

[10] It seems to me very likely that Michael remained "inconspicuous" in his life here for similar reasons. –Ed.

1.3 Outlook

3   In the latter case, misrepresentation may take the form of implying that what is being shared comes from a respected organization, or from a founder or inspirer of such an organization.

4   There have been several instances of such regrettable conduct. In one case, the ascribed spirit source of a book containing scores of misteachings was described as one of the Illumined Souls who brought the USB into being. But *he was not*; and we know that he himself would never make that claim. [We discuss many misteachings in Appendix B.]

5   We emphasize that all the *official* teachings and philosophy of The Universal Spiritual Brother&Sisterhood (USB) are contained in *just this volume*—and *nowhere else*.

6   They are compiled mainly from our quarterly worldwide *Letters*, Numbers 1 to 93, with minor corrections and changes made for greater clarity.

7   We do not object to others including any of our teachings with their own, [with our source material acknowledged, as is customary, not taken out of context, and not changing its "attitude" or "impression,"] for we hold that truths *should* be shared with those ready to receive them. But we *do* object to teachings of others *combined* with our own being *all* attributed to the USB, especially when the mixture contains views that we completely *oppose*. [It must be perfectly clear which parts are taken from the USB.]

2

Teachings and Reason

CHAPTER CONTENTS

2.1 Teachings for This Age   40
   201   This New Age—and New Age Teachings   40
   202   The Need to Clearly and Precisely Define Terms   40
   203   First Impressions   41

2.2 Thought   42
   204   Think Constructively—Think Positively—Visualize That Which Is Good   42
   205   The Need to Think Universally   42
   206   The Power of Thought   43
   207   The Effects of Thoughts   45

2.3 Reason   45
   208   Reason, REASON, REASON!   45
   209   A Priceless Possession   46
   210   Reason, Faith, and Knowledge   47

2.1 TEACHINGS FOR THIS AGE

201 This New Age—and New Age Teachings

1 The "new age," which some of us await, has already begun, and we are living in it! For *every* age, *every* era, is a new age to humanity when we discover more about the Laws that govern the universe—discover them to a degree that can transform our way of living, materially or spiritually.

2 The Universal Spiritual Brother&Sisterhood publishes the *teachings* of this new age, simply and clearly presenting what all can understand, that will, in time, unite humanity. The purpose of these teachings is "to uplift [and spiritualize] humanity, to awaken all people to the spiritual realities of life and to the God within them" [101:10–11].

3 Of course, Truth can never be completely expressed by any *one* person or group, for no one person or group of people can understand Truth in its entirety. [In Chapter 3 we define truth as that which is eternal.] It is such a huge and many-sided jewel that we cannot see all its facets. But we can see *some* of the facets of the jewel we call Truth—and appreciate their loveliness, and make them a part of our way of life, thus making our way of life more beautiful.

4 Truth itself never changes, and truths themselves never change. Unfortunately, however, people sooner or later so becloud truths with their own personal ideas and their own personal interpretations and misinterpretations, that the truths often become quite unrecognizable. The beclouding may be the unconscious result of such thoughts, or it may be the deliberate act of those in positions of power to help perpetuate their power.

5 The truly great spiritual teachers of the ages presented truths of shining simplicity and beauty, only to find those truths eventually obscured, if not completely buried, by dogmas and rituals and creeds, and by personal interpretations and misinterpretations, conscious and unconscious.

6 So in each new age, there is a need for truths to be *restated*, and in the way best suited for that particular age. What is most suitable for *one* era, may not be most suitable for another. But there is always a need for truths to be presented simply and clearly; humbly, and without fanfare; and without excessive decorations that rob them of much of their beauty.

202 The Need to Clearly and Precisely Define Terms

1 As time passes, it is not uncommon for a word or phrase to come to have a different meaning or meanings from what it originally possessed. In

2.1 Teachings for This Age

addition, the very same word or phrase may mean different things to different schools of thought. For both of these reasons, those who desire to share truth need to give clearly and precisely *their* definition of certain terms they use.

Spirit, soul, mind, truth, enlightenment, consciousness—these are just a few of the terms that are variously interpreted by various schools of thought; unless each school clearly defines the meaning or meanings of the terms it uses, the seeker becomes confused.

For example, if certain people call a table a chair, and a chair a table, it matters little if they mention both to others. But, if they refer to just *one* of the two, those they speak or write to may not understand unless an illustration is provided.

We repeatedly stress the responsibility of teachers to present teachings and philosophy simply, clearly, and accurately. Of course it makes for richness and variety of expression to use words in any of the several meanings they may possess. We may say, for instance, and quite correctly, that certain people are good souls, or that they show spirit, or that they are in their right minds. But when we use such terms as soul, spirit, and mind in an obviously limiting sense, our audience will not understand us unless they know *exactly* what we mean by those terms.

203 First Impressions

It is perfectly natural to have first impressions about anyone and anything; in fact it is almost impossible *not* to have them. And they are important. But to form hard and fast conclusions from them may be unsound. It is like taking phrases out of context: A phrase may mean one thing by itself, but quite another in the complete paragraph or article in which it appears. For this reason, it is wise, until we know people better, to form merely tentative opinions about them, not final ones.

The same applies to teachings and philosophy. Much that may seem profound or beautiful at first glance, proves to be less than that when viewed by the light of reason.

This volume provides many examples of injunctions and teachings that have been unthinkingly accepted and endorsed for years, and sometimes even centuries, by literally *millions* of people, but that lose their appeal to many who examine them thoroughly.

2.2 THOUGHT

204 Think Constructively—Think Positively—Visualize That Which Is Good

1 "Think, and know! Think, and be! Think, and express, according to your highest perception of Truth!"—A Blessed Soul.

2 Again and again the inspirers of this movement stress the power of thought. Again and again they remind us to *never underestimate the power of thought of even one person.*

3 Again and again they tell us to realize the tremendous power that lies in the united thought of hundreds and thousands of people, directed to one purpose.

4 Much good can be accomplished around the council tables; and Illumined Souls are doing all in their power to influence the minds of the leaders of peoples towards peace on earth and good will to all.

5 And at times when there are those who seem willing to provoke fear and alarm, our inspirers ask all who love their fellow human beings to do what so many are already doing individually:

6 — To direct thoughts of love and peace and brother-and-sisterhood to the leaders of peoples and of nations;

7 — What is at least equally important, to visualize them gathered around the council tables in trust and good will and selflessness. To visualize a world of peace and harmony and understanding.

8 If we set aside a few minutes each day for this purpose, and at a set time, many spirit co-workers will join us, to multiply the power for good.

9 "The time is *now*, and the need is *great!*"

10 Let us, by our thoughts, make this a better world for all.

11 Let us, by our thoughts, help to bring peace and harmony to humankind.

12 Let us, by our thoughts, bring to all people, including ourselves, a greater consciousness of how blessed we are in our kinship with the divine [601:2], and in the infinite potential that lies within each child of God.

205 The Need to Think Universally

1 Indeed there is nothing greater than truth. And one of the great truths is that we are God's children and it follows that *all* human beings are spiritual sisters and brothers. That is why we welcome one and all into

2.2 Thought

this movement, the USB, no matter what the color of their skin, the faith they were born in, the country they live in, or the views they believe in.

We encourage everyone to *think universally*—the great need of this time and age. It will bring the day closer that our inspirers are certain will come.

206 The Power of Thought

Thought is the realm of expression that precedes *all* that is. As an Illumined Soul says,

> On earth, thoughts are *not* things, but the magnificent power *behind* things—the power that *brings* things into expression! [1]

Thought is *vibration*—that is, *energy in motion*—either within our *own* mentality, or directed from one mentality to another. There is much that could be said about vibrations directed from one mind to another—the mental images sent winging on their way.[2]

Whether or not a thought reaches its destination in the precise form in which it is projected, or whether it reaches its destination at all, depends on several things: the *intensity* of the thought; the conscious or unconscious *receptivity* of the person to whom it is directed; the degree of *attunement* of the two mentalities; and whether the thought is *relayed*, in which case there is always the risk of distortion, however unintentional.

We should remember well that a thought once directed cannot be recalled. However, a second thought can be transmitted to nullify or at least partly offset the first, if the first has not already been received. If it *has* been received, another thought can be directed to make amends in some way for the first.

---

[1] In Chapters 11–13 we describe some of the far greater powers of thought (or "will") in *spirit* life.

[2] Many in the spirit world (1301:1) routinely and clearly receive thoughts if they are specific and directed to them (see Topic 1224:6 and Sec. 12.5 on communication with spirit people). For people on earth there are many factors (see 1232) that make it much harder to recognize receiving such thoughts, including our physical (earthly) bodies and our preoccupation with things physical, but I understand we do in fact receive many such thoughts as impressions, often weak or vague, that we usually do not otherwise recognize. –Ed.

6   Illumined Souls tell us that the speed of thought is much more rapid than the speed of light,[3] which travels at about 186,000 miles or 300,000 kilometers per second. It is something that should make us reflect, something that should make us realize how *important* it is to ponder well over sending out thoughts that are anything but kindly and constructive.

7   It is the incredible speed of thought, incidentally, that explains how we are time and again "miraculously" preserved. Our falls are often "cushioned," for instance, and seemingly unavoidable accidents and injuries are averted. In far less than the twinkling of an eye, a call for help can be heard and *answered*. Sometimes the call for help is our *own* thought, conscious or unconscious; usually it is the *conscious* thought of a spirit person who is with us at the time.

8   Few of us can fully appreciate how frequently spirit friends save us from death or disaster. Not many could survive on earth for any length of time without the help and ministrations, in most cases silent and unknown, of those spirit helpers who have our welfare at heart.

---

[3] This fact, published in a USB *Letter* of 1965, can be compared with some recent scientific findings. According to classical physics and Einstein's relativity, the speed of light is the upper limit of the speeds at which energy, matter, and information can travel. Scientists presently recognize that in certain circumstances processes travel faster than light (FTL) relative to an inertial frame of reference, but they say that such processes cannot convey any information. One example they cite is of a research team in 1982 at the University of Paris working with diverging twin subatomic particles (photons) having identical angles of polarization. They discovered that when they intentionally changed the polarization of one particle, the other particle 13 meters (14 yards) distant changed also. Although this suggests that the two particles somehow *communicated* at speeds far greater than the speed of light and possibly instantaneously (as previously predicted by quantum theory), scientists say this is not true communication because this process cannot be used to transmit classical information. Subsequent experiments have confirmed the same behavior at separations of many kilometers, indicating "communication" speeds many times the speed of light. The two particles are said to have been "entangled," and by virtue of the (theoretical) original big bang, this suggests that *everything* is connected.

207 The Effects of Thoughts

1. Thoughts of a noble nature reach their destination, and then return to bless us.

2. Unworthy thoughts also return to us, but with this difference: If they are repelled by the aura [1311] of the person they are directed to, they return to the sender with the additional energy they have gathered on the journey; as a result, the sender receives an even greater impact than the impact intended for another. That is The Law.

3. Unworthy emotions such as hate, bitterness, envy, and jealousy, corrode and consume the individual who harbors them. If long retained, they destroy any semblance of goodness in that individual, and often cause serious mental unbalance.

2.3 REASON

208 Reason, REASON, REASON!

1. Among the things our inspirers continually emphasize is the importance of exercising *reason*—the mental powers concerned with forming conclusions, judgements, or inferences.

2. Failure to exercise reason has caused multitudes to accept *as* truth much that has little or no basis in fact. And each misteaching accepted is a misteaching to *unlearn*; it becomes another barrier to progression, another obstacle to surmount.

3. The desire to learn is *good*; unaccompanied by reason, however, it invites disaster; for it is then more difficult to distinguish and separate what is true from what is false.

4. Says an Illumined Soul:

5. > There are many souls who *are* sincere, who *desire* to serve, who are *most* anxious to walk in understanding and in light, who are indeed *eager* to be taught. They pay heed to what is shared with them—but oftentimes unthinkingly, which is unwise. For unless they use subtle faculties of reason, they cannot differentiate between what *is*, what *can* be, and what is merely the figment of a vivid imagination—their own, or another's.

6   Spirit teachers may be well-meaning—many are—but that alone does not invest either wisdom or authority to what they say; and to follow anyone blindly is to court disaster.

7   If we use the gift of reason, we soon learn whether, and to what extent, those spirit people who come to us can be relied upon. We soon learn whether they merit our *faith*—by which we mean not automatic or unthinking acceptance of everything they say, but confidence and trust based on our *experience* with them.

8   We do this with people on earth, putting our faith in the doctor or teacher or friend who we have come to know can be trusted. We should do no less with spirit people.

9   "The light of reason shall be our beacon," a Blessed Soul declares. By that light, let us incorporate into our consciousness what we find to be true.

10   Of course nothing is part of our consciousness unless we *live* it, or live *by* it, in our daily lives. Otherwise it is just idle words that fall from our lips, and not a part of our real selves.

11   By the light of reason, let us examine *all* that is shared with us, no matter from which side of life it comes. For either deliberately or in ignorance, much false information is given from *both* sides of life.

12   Well worth pondering are phrases written about two centuries ago: "He who will not reason, is a bigot... he who dares not, is a slave."[4]

13   There are more slaves by choice than by conquest.

209 A Priceless Possession

1   One of the aims of this movement, the USB, is to make people think; and we wish that more and more people would think, and think again, and question when they do not understand, before incorporating anything into their universe.

2   "It is only the *questioning* mentality that grows," says an inspirer. For to question not idly, but with the desire to learn, is to open the door to knowledge and enlightenment—always provided of course that *reason* is exercised and that there is *no blind acceptance* of what is said by anyone, anywhere.

---

[4] By Sir William Drummond, 1770?–1828, English writer and philosopher.

2.3 Reason   □ 210

3   As another says: "The *seekers* of Truth are many; the *probers*, few." We particularly embrace the probers; for those who devote time and energy to thoroughly examining something are usually those who *share* what they accept with those they feel are ready to receive.

4   Time and again Illumined Souls have stressed the importance of *reason*, one of our priceless possessions. Time and again they have repeated the injunction: "Think, and accept. Think, and reject. Think, and suspend judgement. But *think!*"

210 Reason, Faith, and Knowledge

1   "Faith cannot bring reason," a Brother says, "but reason can bring faith."

2   If by faith he refers to a major meaning of the word—*a belief in God*—he is correct. For very few who are aware of the orderly movements of the planets, the regularity of the seasons, or spirit communion with loved ones on the other side of life, to mention just a few of hundreds of things that could be cited, can doubt the existence of The Supreme Power that we call God.

3   But an Illumined Soul points out:

4   Reason can bring not only faith, but *knowledge*. And knowledge, if applied *wisely*, is of far greater importance than faith in the development of the individual. It is the *knowledge* that reason brings that enables one to climb to ever higher levels of consciousness, and to an awareness of an expanded and ever-expanding horizon.

5   That is why we say: Reason *well*, before accepting *anything* from *anyone*.

3
Truth

CHAPTER CONTENTS

3.1 The Nature of Truth		**50**
301	What Truth Is	50
302	The Facets of Truth	51
303	Truth as Our Inspirers See It	51
304	No Greater Cause	51
305	Truths Can and Should Be Presented Simply	52
306	Truth and Beauty	52
307	No Individuals Possess, or Have Within Themselves, All Truth	53
308	Our Various Responses to Truth	54
3.2 Searching for Truth		**55**
309	Qualities Needed by the Earnest Seeker of Truth	55
310	Two Safeguards in the Search for Truth	57
311	The Lot of Many Seekers of Truth	57
312	The Error of Self-Satisfaction	58
313	On Hermetic Teachings	58
314	On "Esoteric" and Ancient Teachings	59
315	Of Psychical Research Societies	61
3.3 Spreading Truth		**62**
316	Truth and Illumined Souls	62
317	On Sharing Truth	62
318	The True Teachers of Truth	63
319	A Great Obligation	65
320	Let Us Not Plow the Ocean	65
321	On Teaching Simple Truths to Young Children	66
322	Can the Leopard Change Its Spots?	66
323	Scientists—and Truth	68
324	Misconceptions	71
325	The Duty to Expose and Destroy Error	71

3.1 THE NATURE OF TRUTH

301 What Truth Is

1 Truth slowly walks; the lie and half-truth fly.
But truth, in time, will pass the others by;
For truth is deathless, while the others die.[1]

2 What is truth?

3 Throughout the ages philosophers have pondered over this question, often without reaching any definite conclusion. The answer can be given in four words: *that which is eternal.* (We use the word *eternal* here in the sense of *that which has no end.*)

4 Fact and truth are both true, but while all truths are facts, not all facts are truths. For a fact is often a reality for the moment only, but a truth is a reality *always.* That you are reading these words is a fact; it is not a truth, however, for you may not be reading them a few minutes hence, and you certainly will not be reading them forever!

5 Similarly, it is a fact that the Titanic sank in 1912; but it is not a truth, for the sinking was a reality for the moment only.[2]

6 Like attracts like. We reap what we sow. The greater our gifts, the greater our responsibility to serve. Under the right conditions, we can commune with those in spirit life. *The real self* [605:2] is indestructible. There is variety not only of species, but *within* each species. There is no injustice in the long run.

7 These, and countless other Laws That Govern that together form THE LAW [401–402], are truths that collectively form Truth, for they are eternal, operating everywhere and on all levels of expression [Chap. 4].

8 And the most sublime truth of all is that The Supreme Being, that which we and many others call God, *created* THE LAW and *expresses* through THE LAW.

9 Can there be a greater quest than the search for Truth? Can any view of a jewel of such surpassing beauty be gained without endeavor?

---

[1] All uncredited poems in this book were composed by Michael Flagg, see paragraph 7 and footnote 1 of the Acknowledgments.

[2] When people say "it is true" (as in 866:1) I understand that they usually mean it is a (true) fact. –Ed.

3.1 The Nature of Truth

302 The Facets of Truth

1 *All* truths [as the USB defines them] are perfect, and *all* truths are necessary to the completeness and perfection of what we call Truth. Like a multi-faceted jewel, Truth has many perfect parts that make up the perfect whole.

2 Those facets never oppose or contradict, but supplement and complement one another. And no truth retards or restricts the operation of *other* truths.

3 But as a Blessed Soul has reminded us, we do not necessarily see the same facets as others do, nor do we see them from the same perspective.

303 Truth As Our Inspirers See It

1 Our inspirers stress that as we progress only our *perception* of Truth changes, but never Truth itself. The higher the spiritual peak we attain, the vaster is the expanse before our vision, the nobler the panorama unfolded to our gaze, and the truer (and less clouded) our perception of Truth.

2 Illumined Souls humbly point out that what they offer us is only truth *as they see it*. But, in all fairness to them, we should note that they come from the Celestial Realms, the spirit realms beyond the Spiritual, and are ready to move on into the still higher Kingdoms [1301]; as a result they have travelled much farther on the path of enlightenment, and are consequently free from the misconceptions that some still hold in the less advanced spirit realms.

304 No Greater Cause

1 If there is one thing that Illumined Souls have made abundantly clear, it is that *"in all things we do, there is no cause greater than Truth."* They also say:

2 There are those who will sacrifice Truth. There are those who will jeopardize it. There are those who will prostitute it for their own ends [Appendix B].

3 But Truth remains free, and Truth in itself makes one strong, makes one ever conscious of the things that are eternal and real and are of God. For Truth is Truth, and can never be altered by people!

304

4   "Truth is no beggar, hat in hand, seeking alms," observes an inspirer. "Truth is the *giver*, providing, to those who truly seek, the greatest riches of all."

305 Truths Can and Should Be Presented Simply

1   The truths taught by the great spiritual teachers of the ages were always clearly and simply stated, shining like nuggets of pure gold—except when for various reasons they had to be expressed in parables whose deeper meaning only the inner circle could grasp. For those teachers knew well of what they spoke; and so clear was it in their own minds that they could explain it simply enough for even a child to understand.

2   However, the beauty and simplicity of much of what those teachers could freely teach were lost on some who mistakenly felt that truths must be difficult to perceive, and must be dug out laboriously from a mountain of words. But today, we can avoid such struggles if we realize that golden nuggets are within our reach.

3   Truths can and should be expressed simply and clearly, as has always been the case with teachings and philosophy that have inspired people to noble ideals and high resolve. We should seek out what is simply said and easily understood, and we should shun presentations in which little or nothing is told obscurely and at length, even if made by someone with a "reputation."

4   What has harmed the cause of Truth throughout the ages, what has often completely buried the essential beauty of many movements, has been the additions that "disciples" have added for one reason or another —often surrounding an ounce [grams] of truth with a ton of fiction, so that what is shining and beautiful can become quite unrecognizable.

306 Truth and Beauty

1   Many are familiar with these lovely lines in Keats' *Ode on a Grecian Urn*:[3]

2   "Beauty is truth, truth beauty," — that is all
                 Ye know on earth, and all ye need to know.

---

[3] John Keats, 1795–1821, English poet.

3.1 The Nature of Truth

3 It is an inspiring thought, one that has stirred thousands of people, including some of us; but it cannot survive the light of reason. For while all truths are indeed beautiful, facets of the incredibly exquisite jewel that is Truth, *not* all that has beauty is necessarily truth as we define truth: *that which is eternal.*

4 A flaming sunset, a delicate flower, an ancient urn may all possess beauty. But do they endure forever? The sunset will last a few minutes, the flower a few hours or days, the urn a few centuries at most, as a rule.

5 In any case, we would do well, while still living on earth, to come to know much more than Keats' five words in quotes. Only then will we be able to make good use of our stay here, especially by learning any lessons we may need to learn of those that can only be learned on earth [1424].

307 No Individuals Possess, or Have Within Themselves, All Truth

1 There are some who hold that "there is an inmost centre in us all, where truth abides in fullness," and that to know anything, consciously, consists not so much in letting in "light supposed to be without" as in "opening out a way whence the imprisoned splendor may escape."

2 This belief is expressed in a famous poem, some lovely lines of which we have just quoted.[4] It is a beautiful thought, but it is just not true. Truth in its fullness is *yet* to be perceived or contained within anyone, anywhere.

3 If anyone on earth possessed, consciously or unconsciously, *all* truth, there would be little point in expressing in a physical body on earth—or, for that matter, even in bodies of vastly more rapid rates of vibration [1310] in the spirit world. There could be no progression, no possibility of expansion, no opportunity to elevate oneself further; and certainly that state of being is not remotely claimed or suggested by even the most exalted Illumined Souls who have enlightened the world throughout the ages. On the contrary, as an Illumined Inspirer has said:

4 > We who come to you, though we have progressed far beyond the conditions of earth, though our development through the spheres has been great, yet are we ever conscious of the greatness that can be...

---

[4] *Paracelsus*, Part I, 1835, by Robert Browning, 1812–1889, English poet.

307 ☐

5 For another thing, the truth [one possesses] that is either *within* one's consciousness, or within one's ability to perceive from *without*, cannot be beyond the scope of one's consciousness, for no vessel can hold more than its capacity. That capacity is one's mind or mentality, which can be enlarged, and which *does* enlarge as one evolves.

6 Apart from "God" or "The Most High," there is no one in whom "truth abides in fullness." There may be much of Truth that individuals, here or in the spirit world, *know* that they know. There may be also much of Truth that they know, but do *not* know that they know; and they can sometimes "open out a way" for *that* truth, *that* "imprisoned splendor," to "escape" to the surface.

7 But additional truth, truth that is not theirs, either within themselves or on the surface, must come from *without*, and of course it must come from one or more minds—*other* minds.

308 Our Various Responses to Truth

1 To those of us who know something about The Laws That Govern, it is distressing to see a loved one indifferent to lasting values, engrossed in a purely material existence, and unreceptive to the things that are eternal and of God.

2 We know that although we can point the way or try to plant seeds of truth into the consciousness of others, we cannot learn their lessons for them, or perceive truth for them. All individuals should go their respective ways, in their own fashion, and at their own pace, absorbing only what they can absorb, at the rate they can absorb it, in the manner they can absorb it, and only if and when they *desire* to absorb it.

3 We can find some comfort, however, in the knowledge that such is the Love and Goodness of The Indescribable Power that we and many call God, that there is *no* annihilation or everlasting punishment for anyone [1320:1–3]. One may misuse or abuse one's free will as is one's right, or stumble a thousand times, or advance one step and fall back two, or go astray, or even plunge into the deepest depths, but one is never beyond redemption; for indeed it is true that the doors to spiritual progress are *never* closed to anyone, anywhere [103:7].

4 And just as the intelligence in even the tiniest plant causes it to reach out for sustenance, usually the sunshine, so the soul, the spark of divinity within each being, eventually causes that being to reach out for Light. So although some individuals, by their way of life, may in a sense

choose to dwell in darkness, sooner or later—whether it be years or centuries or eons—their final choice will be for the Light that is Truth, however much they may reject or oppose it.

3.2 SEARCHING FOR TRUTH

309 Qualities Needed by the Earnest Seeker of Truth

1. The quest for Truth demands a wealth of virtues.

2. **Courage** is required. For only with courage can we sever our ties to organizations that others cling to because they are "respectable" or "genteel," despite their historical periods of tyranny and persecution—even unto death—of those who dared to think for themselves and to *say* what they thought.

3. It takes courage to endure the ridicule of others, too often those near and dear to us, who are uncomfortable with anyone whose thinking and beliefs differ from their own.

4. It takes courage to recognize and discard long-accepted misteachings, particularly those of teachers we have venerated.

5. It takes courage to be as free as the wind, to seek Truth anywhere and everywhere. Those who consider only what a particular organization offers, or who *blindly* accept all that it shares, show more regard for that organization than they do for Truth.

6. **Humility** is required. For only in humility can we be free of smugness, a great barrier to Truth.

7. The more the humble know, the more they realize how much there is yet to know. But the humble discover enchantment in any facet of Truth, just as some of us do in a single, exquisite rose. We need not see *all* the roses in the garden to rejoice in beauty.

8. **Simplicity** is required. When we are required to be as little children, it is only that little children are, in their simplicity, free from habits, prejudices, misconceptions, and self-satisfaction that tend to make one blind to Truth. (It does not mean unthinking acceptance of what is shared, but readiness to receive it, and, if it is weighed and found not wanting, to accept it.)

9. **Persistence** is required. Only then can we firmly and steadily continue in the quest despite opposition or objection from others, or difficulties and disillusionments along the way.

10 **Patience** is required. The *true* teachers of Truth have always been few. The rest are as the blind leading the blind: some because they sacrifice integrity upon the altar of material wealth or power; others because, well-meaning though they are, they possess but little knowledge.

11 So seekers must be prepared to wait, weeks or months or years, for teachings and philosophy that will be manna for their minds and hearts.

12 **An open mind** is required. It will prevent summary rejection of views that contradict our own. Opposing views are the very ones we should examine well, for they may make us aware of misconceptions and misteachings we had uncritically embraced.

13 Earnest seekers of Truth will acknowledge truth *wherever* it is found. They will not confine their acceptance to any *one* person or book or authority. And they will beware of any and all who say: "*Here*, and here *alone*, shall ye seek."

14 **Reason** is required. If we wish to sift any truth from the enormous volume of error that deluges us from all sides, we must *exercise* our mental powers concerned with forming conclusions, judgements, and inferences.

15 To accept without reason is to bring chaos into one's life.

16 If we do not think, we can easily become sponges absorbing many pseudo-sciences and pseudo-studies that come along, so that our universe becomes cluttered with enough error to completely bury or overwhelm whatever little truth we may have perceived. We then have much to eventually unlearn, and many shackling misconceptions to unchain ourselves from, before we can make our way much farther towards the mountaintop.

17 Millions of people seek Truth, but seek it in varying degrees. [See also 209:3.]

18 Some seek Truth only as long as it does not conflict with their established way of living, or customs, or beliefs.

19 Some seek Truth only as long as it does not require making sacrifices, or giving up anything held precious.

20 Some seek Truth regardless of all else, because of the burning realization that *the quest for Truth is the greatest quest of all.*

21 It is that burning realization, arousing a passion so compelling as to sweep aside all that stands in its way, that makes for success in the quest for Truth.

310 Two Safeguards in the Search for Truth

1. Ever swelling are the ranks of those who search for Truth, as more and more people, realizing that there must be *more* to existence than appears on the surface, seek answers to questions and solutions to problems.

2. But ever swelling, too, is the flood of printed material that is produced to capitalize on the quest. Unfortunately, most of this material does little to enlighten the readers and much to confuse them, so that it eventually discourages many from continuing the search [1424:28].

3. For as a rule, too many publications portray things vividly but inaccurately. They quote one another, or quote from books and "authorities" that usually offer at least as much error as truth and at least as much fancy as fact; and we emphasize, errors and fancies, repeated frequently enough, are often unthinkingly accepted by people. Such publications often present conflicting theories and conflicting philosophies, apparently in the hope that each reader will find *something* palatable; and unthinking individuals then are likely to accept a ton of fiction with an ounce [grams] of truth, not knowing which is which.

4. Among the safeguards the seeker has—safeguards that more people should exercise—are the following. To *suspend* opinion about any theory or statement that could not affect one's existence for the better. And to accept *only* what one's reason embraces and one's inner being senses is both true and vital to living according to The Laws That Govern.

311 The Lot of Many Seekers of Truth

1. Many seekers of Truth can expect opposition from family and friends. This is not surprising, for people often resent those who have the courage to break away from the beaten path of dogma, creed, and ritual that they themselves travel, or those who think not in terms of one sect or religion or people or nation but in terms of all humanity.

2. Those who would serve must be prepared to sacrifice. They must be prepared to be misunderstood—even by their family and friends. Says a Blessed Soul:

3. > Always remember that there are those who do not understand our way of life, and who are not willing or do not desire to secure for themselves that which is our lot...

4   There are always there those with critical eye and sharp tongue, *waiting* to point a finger—with malice in their hearts, criticizing the actions of others, misunderstanding the motives behind and beyond the actions of others, seeing only what they desire to see, and not seeking deep... for the fine qualities... within.

5   It is for *us* to be tolerant, and we *are*. It is for *us* to bless them, and we *do*. And it is for *us* to bid them walk their own pathway, which we *also* do.

312 The Error of Self-Satisfaction

1   The further a soul advances spiritually, the humbler is that soul. We can well follow the example of Illumined Souls, who become ever more humble the further they progress beyond the conditions of earth. And the greater their wisdom, the greater their knowledge, the greater their understanding of things on earth and beyond earth, the *more* do they urge us to accept—even of what *they* offer—only what our reason wholeheartedly embraces and our inner self unreservedly senses is true.

2   They never insist that we share their point of view, but ask only that we ponder over it. Nor will they debate matters, but only discuss them. For in discussion, the goal is truth; in debate, the triumph of personal views. And there is a vast difference between the two.

3   Self-satisfaction (smugness) has no place within the seeker of Truth, for it only closes the door to further truths.

313 On Hermetic Teachings

1   From time to time we are asked our opinion of the Hermetic Teachings; and some have said that much of what the USB shares greatly resemble those teachings.

2   The Hermetic Teachings are based on what was offered to sincere seekers of Truth thousands of years ago by *Hermes Trismegistus*—or "Hermes the thrice greatest"—who was described by ancient Egyptians and others as "the Great Great," "the Master of Masters," "the Scribe of the Gods," the father of occult wisdom, and "the Fount of Wisdom."

3.2 Searching for Truth

3   We know of no one wiser than Hermes Trismegistus [or Trismegistos], and of no purer or nobler teachings and philosophy than his. Unfortunately, some of his teachings and philosophy, like many others unwritten and handed down through the centuries, have been unwittingly misinterpreted in the process, so that several things that many students of Hermetic Teachings accept today are *not* what Hermes Trismegistus taught. Distortion and misinterpretation are inevitable when the spoken word is transferred from teacher to pupil, and from language to language, for untold generations. The exercise of reason becomes more necessary than ever in such circumstances.

4   However, one of the Illumined Inspirers of the USB is Hermes Trismegistus himself, and what we share has his full and complete approval. It is thus *natural* that there is a great resemblance with what many regard as his teachings. In fact, where there is divergence, be assured that we present his *actual* views.

5   Some students of "esoteric" teachings mistakenly believe, for instance, that Hermes Trismegistus was the founder of astrology; the belief brings glamour and "authority" to that study. But Hermes Trismegistus was *not* the founder of astrology; he taught a simple understanding of *astronomy*, which is a vastly different thing. In fact he was a *founder* of astronomy, the science of the material universe beyond the earth's atmosphere.

314 On "Esoteric" and Ancient Teachings

1   Those who have been part of our movement for any length of time know that we repeatedly emphasize the importance of exercising *reason* in considering anything from *any* source, ourselves included.

2   It is especially important in the study of the esoteric, whether the term is defined as: something understood by and meant for only the select few who have special knowledge or interest; something beyond ordinary understanding or knowledge; something belonging to a chosen few; or something intended to be revealed only to the initiates of a group.

3   We can well understand people exploring various avenues in their search for Truth, and we do not discourage it; for as we teach, it is only the *questioning* mentality that grows [209:2]. We can also understand the fascination exerted by the seemingly hidden or secret or obscure. And if we list a number of things to remember during the quest, it is only so that readers can, if they wish, remain on solid ground instead of being engulfed in the quicksands of error and delusion.

4   We emphasize that ignorance is the mother of misconceptions, with one false premise spawning a chain of many mistaken notions. So the thinking individual, who rejects even a single error, will thereby also reject others that stem from it.

5   It is wise not to accept teachings just because they come from the distant past. Even if correct as originally expressed, distortion and misinterpretation are inevitable when the spoken word is transferred from teacher to pupil, and from language to language, for untold generations. The pure and noble teachings of Hermes Trismegistus [313] and Jesus, to cite just two instances, have been encrusted with distortions, errors, and misinterpretations over the centuries.

6   As for the *written* word, the mere fact that something is ancient does not give it authority or accuracy [see also 764]. Documents, however old, are still either the opinions or findings of people, or what people who wrote them at the time wished others to believe—often for personal motives of their own, and sometimes in contradiction with their own knowledge. In any case, there is sufficient and enough confusion with what we have at hand, without adding to it from ancient archives—which at best are still *people's* word of their own beliefs and experiences, or their understanding or interpretation of the beliefs and experiences of others.

7   We have only to note how many conflicting opinions are written and spoken about many people and events *in our own times,* to realize that much that is presented today as fact consists merely of individual opinions and interpretations, correct or incorrect, some actually held, some expressed for ulterior purposes.

8   Certain schools of thought have produced volume after volume of "esoteric" writings purporting to relate, among other things, *how* and *why* and *when* humans came into being, *how* the world and planets and stars and everything else in the universe were created, and *what* "the Absolute" is. We find such teachings to be of little if any worth, and in many cases they spring from vivid imaginations and extreme susceptibility to impressions from others, on either side of life [see also 506, B08].

9   Founders of some of those schools of thought, and some prolific writers also, have spoken from the spirit world to acknowledge misteachings and errors they made when they lived on earth; but who of their present earthly followers would believe such admissions, especially from those who while on earth vigorously *denied* the reality and abundance of communication with spirit life?

315 Of Psychical Research Societies

1 We would advise seekers of truth about Survival [of death] and Communication [with spirit people] to be very cautious about studying the publications of psychical research [more recently termed parapsychology] societies before at least the mid-1960s. For their articles published on these two subjects were then at times more concerned with presenting *any* possible theory, however implausible and fantastic, to explain away evidence of the truths of Survival and Communication [323:2–4], than in impartially weighing the evidence itself, and, if it was convincing, accepting it.[5]

2 It is odd how some people will go to any lengths to discredit truths that should, in our opinion, be accepted with delight, especially when such abundant evidence was and is available [Chapter 12]. In most cases, it is probably because people would have to face the shaky foundations that are the basis of their lives, and would have to consider a completely *new* scale of values; and usually only the earnest seeker of Truth is prepared to do that.

3 If people will, without study, reject and discredit the findings of the giants among scientists, individuals of integrity and international renown —like William Crookes, a towering figure in physics and chemistry; and Alfred Russel Wallace, a naturalist second to none; and profound students such as Conan Doyle, to name just a few[6]—it is folly to try to convince them. Such people are not ready.

4 Eventually, in scores or hundreds or thousands of years, people who are now quite blind to such truths will see the light—for all individuals, *in time*, do reach some state of light, depending on the ability of each to absorb and express that light in accordance with The Laws That Govern.

5 Meanwhile, it is pointless to spend time and substance on the blind who do not wish to see, or the deaf who do not wish to hear. Too many are ready and waiting for the seed to scatter it on barren ground.

---

[5] While good research *was* done earlier, after the 1970s openness to Survival and Communication in parapsychology has greatly increased, although resistance does continue in a few areas and much more so among scientists in general. –Ed.

[6] Sir William Crookes, 1832–1919, English chemist and physicist, discoverer of thallium, inventor of physical instruments, winner of three medals for science, president of four leading scientific societies, founder and editor of scientific journals; Dr. Alfred Russel Wallace, 1823–1913, English naturalist, and co-discoverer with Darwin of the principles of evolution; Sir Arthur Conan Doyle, M.D., LL.D., 1859–1930, British physician and author, best known for his Sherlock Holmes detective stories.

3.3 SPREADING TRUTH

316 Truth and Illumined Souls

1 With the humility of truly Illumined Souls, our inspirers constantly remind us that they claim no monopoly of Truth. They claim no infallibility. All that they ask us to do is to ponder well over what they present, and to accept and make part of our life what we find, by the light of reason, to be good. They have said:

2 We present things as *we* find them to *be*, and as we pray that others shall one day *grow* to understand them.

3 Providing a feast and inviting us to the banquet table, they emphasize that ours is the freedom to accept or reject the invitation, and, if we accept, to partake only of what pleases us. As a Blessed Soul put it:

4 It is our joy to share. It is our joy to prepare food for the hungry soul, and to place before the seeker what we feel will provide a measure of enlightenment. But it is the prerogative of *all* to accept or reject what we place before them.

5 Our Illumined Inspirers do not expect or desire unthinking acceptance of either themselves or what they share. In fact they tell us to *question* all we are offered, including what comes from *them*. They tell us to sift *all* that we hear and read and see. They tell us to always exercise that most precious possession: *reason*.

6 This, of course, is what we *must* do. But as we do it, let us also remember the extraordinarily spiritually-advanced vantage points of our inspirers [303:2, 1225].

7 If we repeat this advice often, to be questioning, it is because Illumined Souls emphasized it whenever we have had the privilege and joy of communion with them.

317 On Sharing Truth

1 "Beauty was never meant to be unshared," our inspirers teach. And because its beauty is beyond compare, Truth must never be concealed from those who truly seek it.

2 People who hide any glimpse of what they possess of that priceless jewel from eyes that hunger for the sight of it, do not much serve others or Truth itself [B01:2]. *True* lovers of Truth, beauty, and good always

3.3 Spreading Truth

desire *others* to enjoy what brings rapture to *them*. And by another of the wonderful Laws That Govern, that rapture *remains* with them when they share it.

3   We pray that every true seeker of Truth will discover the teachings and philosophy of Illumined Souls.

4   *Their* prayer, as expressed by a Blessed Soul, is this:

5   May we *continue* to sow the seeds that we wish to sow among people who are interested [1429]. May the seeds find fertile soil. May they be nurtured. And may they grow and blossom and bloom, to inspire all who are moved by their beauty to forge *their* links with The Brother&Sisterhood.

6   Our purpose is to sow the seeds: *That* is our purpose. And great and momentous changes will come about, in time, within the lifetime of many on earth today, when more and more who live on earth join our ranks, and the seeds we sow take root in a multitude of mentalities, including some in positions of high responsibility.

7   There are those among our people who rejoice not only in receiving our teachings, but in *sharing* our teachings with others on the path. And while we bless all souls, it is *those* individuals, those *sharers* of Truth, whom we doubly bless!

318 The True Teachers of Truth

1   The *true* teachers of Truth have always been few, and lonely and uncrowded is the path they tread. For much that they proclaim is not always what the multitude wishes to hear, although it is what *needs* to be heard and, better still, *heeded*.

2   *True* teachers of Truth have no desire for pomp and luxury. They are unimpressed by worldly wealth and power, and will not sacrifice one iota of integrity to achieve them.

3   They will not twist and distort Truth, as they understand it, to seek or retain the approval of others.

4   They create no pedestal for themselves, nor do they accept and mount any that their followers may fashion for them.

5   *True* teachers of Truth point out that the path to the mountaintop is a difficult one, not attained at a single bound, but also that it is a joyous

path to those who have some knowledge of The Laws That Govern and of the Love and Wisdom and Goodness that are God.

6 They do not try to influence anyone by fear, nor do they threaten those who would leave the fold.

7 They know that not everyone is wise enough to learn from the experience of others, or to avoid pitfalls that earlier travellers on the road have marked. They recognize that each individual must be free to choose how to travel the road, both in what way and at what pace.

8 *True* teachers of Truth emphasize that the truth they present is as *they* understand it, and that they do *not* expect everyone to see it through *their* eyes.

9 *True* teachers of Truth are ever conscious of their responsibility to precisely define terms [202], and to make certain that their teachings are *correct, perfectly clear, and easy to understand*. Only then do they incur no debt if others intentionally or unintentionally misinterpret their teachings or hand on misinterpretations to others.

10 They are ever conscious, too, that Truth is always more important than those who present it, however distinguished they may be.

11 *True* teachers of Truth are aware that what is false may be of two kinds: in human form; and in the shape of teachings and philosophies that encourage the weak to reject reason or to abandon personal responsibility [e.g., Appendix B]. True teachers know that both lead to the depths, and not to the heights.

12 But while they expose what is false, as it is their duty to do, *they question no one's right to accept it.*

13 They realize that even predominantly decent human beings may not always be strong enough to resist snares and temptations of one sort or another.

14 They do not thrust their knowledge and wisdom upon others, nor desire others to give up comforting beliefs, however wrong [320].

15 *True* teachers of Truth emphasize that no one, themselves included, can walk the path for others, do the work of others for them, or absolve others from The Law of Cause and Effect or any other of The Laws That Govern.

16 They seek no adulation, no glory for their work. It is enough for them to serve. But there is reward from time to time in eyes that light up with understanding.

17 *True* teachers of Truth meet disappointments well, and do not let disappointments affect them for long. They are naturally disappointed

3.3 Spreading Truth

when people fall far short of their possibilities, and in consequence fail themselves much more than they fail their *teachers*.

18 True teachers know that they cannot please everyone, and that they may alienate some who cling to errors they expose.

19 They realize that some of the people they trust may abuse that trust; that some whose support they hope for may oppose them; and that they may be misunderstood, vilified, slandered, perhaps even hated. But they do not lose sight of the spark of divinity within every individual [601:2]. And they leave those who fall by the wayside with love and compassion —and with the prayer that light, or greater light, will one day enter their universe.

319 A Great Obligation

1 All who expound their understanding of Truth should realize the enormous *responsibility* that is theirs. They should also realize their moral *obligation*, especially to those they teach, to immediately speak out and *renounce* any of their teachings that they have come to discover are incorrect.[7]

320 Let Us Not Plow the Ocean

1 In their joy and enthusiasm over truths they have come to perceive, some servers of Truth become overanxious and overeager to convince others of what has brought them so much to be thankful for. This is a mistake.

2 The wise will drop a seed here, a seed there, and wait to see that the soil is fertile before trying to do more. As our inspirers emphasize: "It is *good* to plant the seed. It is *good* to water the soil. But it is *not* good to force growth."

3 Any attempt to in any way overwhelm others into understanding usually makes them draw tighter the shutters that obscure the light. In effect, it is to plow the ocean—the height of futility.

---

[7] The consequences of teaching errors are addressed in 917:7, 1131:3, 1209:7, and elsewhere.

321 On Teaching Simple Truths to Young Children

1 It is sad to see parents deprive their young of knowledge that it took some parents half a lifetime or more to acquire, often only after intense grief over the loss of loved ones. Of those parents who are aware of the reality of Survival and Communication, not only do too many not share these simple, beautiful truths with their children, but they actually permit their children to attend, and in fact even *send* them to, places of instruction where their receptive young minds are crammed with untruths [911].

2 People with some knowledge of spiritual Truth should attempt to give their children an insight of real and enduring values, of truths that give purpose and meaning to existence. They should impart what they know of a God of Love and Justice, and not perpetuate the misconception of a god of revenge and caprice. We would then have a generation better equipped and prepared to live as all people should live: in peace, in dignity, in brother-and-sisterhood, with love and respect and understanding for all beings, and with each of us aware of our responsibility to ourselves and to our fellow humans.

322 Can the Leopard Change Its Spots?

1 Among the things we stress over and over again is the use of reason.

2 How can anyone who knows the shameful record of organizations that have long repressed Truth, that have long denied Truth, that have persecuted the adherents of Truth—organizations that would wither away and die under the light of Truth—how can anyone who *knows* that record make apologies for those organizations, or seek Truth only *within* those organizations, or believe that those organizations can become bulwarks of Truth?

3 We should remember that organizations that exist mainly on the strength of dogmas and creeds and misteachings cannot be expected to promote only Truth. For Truth would sweep away those very same dogmas and creeds and misteachings that are the foundation on which those organizations were built.

4 If thinking people would examine, one by one, the principles or articles of those organizations—whether the principles or articles are 39 or 59 or 99 in number—and check how many of them they themselves still accept, it would surely be a revelation to them.

5 We should remember another thing. Tyrants, whether individuals, groups, or organizations, never relinquish power except when they are

3.3 Spreading Truth □ 322

6   compelled to—and then only with the idea of retaining what hold they still possess, and in time regaining all they have lost and more.

    Let us not be lulled into a false sense of security about any tyrant, no matter whether that tyrant is an individual, a group, or an organization.

7   Some, who are aware that a few individuals in certain organizations have come to accept the truths of Survival and Communication, rejoice in the prospect that the organizations themselves will do so too, sooner or later. We do *not* share their rejoicing.

8   Organizations that have lost ground on every front, that suffer dwindling membership, and that find their teachings and philosophy acceptable to ever fewer members, eventually may, *in self preservation*, embrace and demonstrate a truth they have long rejected: that communication with those who have passed on can take place under the right conditions [B04]. It is not a prospect we relish. For to what ends would those organizations use that truth? To liberate people, or to bind them more tightly? To open the door to additional truths, or to buttress age-old misteachings?

9   Would any of those organizations recognize, let alone accept, any former dignitaries who returned to *repudiate* the teachings of that organization? Or would it label them as impostors? Would it give *any* hearing to those who no longer endorsed its philosophy, principles, rites, and rituals? Or would it allow only those to come through who retained extraordinary fervor about certain convictions, right or wrong, and who could be trusted to excite or intensify that fervor in others?

10   Judging from history, would not such organizations ultimately proclaim that only the communications *they* approved, or that came through *them*, were genuine and good, and all others false or evil?

11   Also, The Law of Attraction does exist [411]. Could organizations that are insular in outlook and discourage inquiry, be guided or inspired by great souls who are universal in outlook and encourage others to think for themselves?

12   One thing more. We point out elsewhere [1319] that *thought forms* [resembling spirit people]—which, unlike other "visions," are created (usually quite unconsciously) by intensity of thought—can only project or echo the views of their creators, and no one else. There would most certainly be thought forms at any gathering powerfully united in beliefs and enthusiasms, especially one receptive to "miracles"; but if those thought forms spoke or behaved in any way, they would, by their very

nature, merely reflect, and thus perpetuate and reinforce, already-held convictions, however wrong. *Would that be desirable?*

323 Scientists—and Truth

1 With rare exceptions, wisdom is given *to* and *through* the humble and unlearned, those who come before Truth as a little child, with no walls of arrogance and prejudice and snobbishness and conceit and smugness surrounding them.

2 Whether it is individuals with little or no schooling, or gifted but humble and *spiritual* mediums, of whom, thank heaven!, there *are* a few—it is *they* who have served the truths of Survival and Communication far more than many of their formally educated contemporaries. For formally educated people, except for a handful possessing courage and integrity, rarely have supported these truths [before 1960].

3 None are more formally "educated"—as most people understand the word—than our scientists, state leaders, clergy, and professors. But how many of them, with a world of evidence available to them, are aware of the great truths of Survival and Communication, or, *if* aware of them, have the courage to openly support them?

4 The fact is that the majority of scientists have been most unscientific outside their own particular fields. As far as the truths of Survival and Communication, or spirit teachings and philosophy, or The [spiritual] Laws that Govern, are concerned, scientists on earth have contributed little knowledge. On the contrary, they have usually hampered the spread of Truth and enlightenment, often by condemning with little or no investigation, which of course is a far from scientific attitude.[8]

5 In any case, as [the previously mentioned famous naturalist] Alfred Russel Wallace pointed out long ago:[9]

6 ...[it does *not* require] immense scientific knowledge to decide on the reality of any uncommon or incredible facts... I assert,

---

[8] It seems quite apparent that such unscientific and unreasonable behavior, and ineffectual countervailing stands, taken by so many of society's leaders, have greatly contributed to a widespread belief (in spite of the abundant evidence to the contrary) that reality is only material, and that all things not material, like love, consciousness, and the spirit, are produced by things material, such as the brain. This belief, known in philosophy as *materialism*, occurs almost exclusively in secular cultures.

[9] Dr. Alfred Russel Wallace, 1823–1913, English naturalist, and co-discoverer with Darwin of the principles of evolution. He included this in his book, *On Miracles and Modern Spiritualism*, 1875.

3.3 Spreading Truth

without fear of contradiction, that *whenever the scientific men of any age* [before 1874] *have denied the facts of investigators on a priori grounds* [that is, before examination or analysis; emphasis ours], *they have always been wrong.* It is not necessary to do more than refer to the world-known names of Galileo, Harvey, and Jenner.[10] The great discoveries they made were, as we know, violently opposed by all their scientific contemporaries, to whom they appeared absurd and incredible... When Benjamin Franklin[11] brought the subject of lightning conductors before the Royal Society, he was laughed at as a dreamer, and his paper was not admitted to the *Philosophical Transactions.* When Young[12] presented his wonderful proofs of the undulatory theory of light, he was equally hooted at as absurd by the popular scientific writers of the day. The *Edinburgh Review* called upon the public to put Thomas Gray[13] into a straitjacket for maintaining the practicability of railroads. Sir Humphry Davy[14] laughed at the idea of London ever being lighted with gas. When Stephenson[15] proposed to use locomotives on the Liverpool and Manchester Railway, learned men gave evidence that it was impossible that they could go even twelve miles [19 kilometers] an hour. Another great scientific authority declared it to be equally impossible for ocean steamers ever to cross the Atlantic. The French Academy of Sciences ridiculed the great astronomer Arago,[16] when he wanted even to discuss the subject of the elec-

---

[10] Galileo Galilei, 1564–1642, Italian scientist who founded modern physics and telescopic astronomy; William Harvey, 1578–1657, English physician who discovered the circulation of the blood; and Edward Jenner, 1749–1823, English physician who discovered vaccination.

[11] Benjamin Franklin, 1706–1790, American printer, writer, scientist, and renowned public servant.

[12] Thomas Young, 1773–1829, British physicist who first demonstrated the interference of light, thus substantiating the wave theory of light.

[13] Thomas Gray, 1716–1771, English poet and professor, considered one of the most learned persons of his century.

[14] Sir Humphry Davy, 1778–1829, British chemist who invented the miner's safety lamp and isolated seven earth metals.

[15] George Stephenson, 1781–1848, English engineer who developed the first steam-powered locomotive.

[16] Dominique François Jean Arago, 1786–1853, prominent French physicist, astronomer, and public servant, who discovered the sun's surface atmosphere and played a leading role in establishing the wave theory of light.

323 □ CHAPTER 3 *Truth*

tric telegraph. Medical men ridiculed the stethoscope when it was first discovered...[17]

7   Wallace pointed out another thing well worth remembering. He noted that in experimental investigations it is standard procedure to accept the facts when they have been confirmed by three or four independent observers. Those facts are accepted at least provisionally and until disproved. But, he wrote, when investigating *psychic* or *spirit* phenomena

8   a totally different—a most unreasonable and a most unphilosophical course is pursued. Each fresh observation, confirming previous evidence, is treated as though it were now put forth for the *first* time; and fresh confirmation is asked of it. And when the fresh and independent confirmation comes, yet more confirmation is asked for, and so on without end...

9   We teach that people *can* learn from the experience of others [860]. Would it not be wise to do so?

10   If each individual, including each scientist, were to start from the beginning, blind to all the preceding experiments and observations and cumulative knowledge and wisdom, could there be much progress of any kind in any field?

---

[17] In the 130 or so years since Wallace wrote this, such closed-minded attitudes have largely continued in mainstream science, although exceptions have been increasing. Examples of more recent discoverers who were opposed and ridiculed are: Alfred Wegener (continental drift), Robert Goddard (rocket-powered space ships), Subramanyan Chandrasekhar (black holes), John Baird (television camera), Barbara McClintock (transposable genetic elements), Stanford Ovshinsky (amorphous semiconductors), George Zweig (quark theory), Fernando Nottebohm (brains *can* grow neurons), Gerd Binnig and Heinrich Rohrer (scanning tunneling microscope), Barry Marshall (*h. pylori* bacteria cause ulcers), Stanley Prusiner (prions), Robert Folk (nanobacteria), and Warren Warren (new magnetic resonance imaging theory). A respected member of the Society for Psychical Research wrote in its *Journal* of July 2003 (Vol. 67.3, No. 872, p. 224): "all the leading scientific journals... have long displayed open hostility to the concept of the paranormal. Professor... ignores the lessons of scientific history if he imagines that ideas which undermine current beliefs receive a warm welcome from the Establishment which upholds them. Nearly every major scientific advance of the past two centuries and more has been strongly resisted or simply ignored by the scientific establishment, from Harvey (blood circulation), Lister (antiseptics), Esdaile (hypnosis), and Young (light waves) to Edison's phonograph, Bell's telephone, Röntgen's X-rays and Tesla's alternating current, to say nothing of space travel and aeroplanes."

3.3 Spreading Truth   □ 325

11   Of course we all have the privilege to seek Truth in our own ways and in our own fashions, to cross what we consider to be the threshold of Truth, and to reach our own conclusions, right or wrong. But it is far from scientific for scientists to completely ignore the thorough and meticulous experiments and unanimous findings of scores of their predecessors, people of the highest caliber and repute, respected and acclaimed nationally and internationally for their distinction in various fields.

12   There is no question that in matters of really great importance, such as the truth and implications of Survival and spirit communication, and demonstrations [of mental or physical phenomena] whose value cannot be overemphasized, the average person is wiser than the average scientist, who by training tends to be limited by observations made with the physical senses.

13   It is sad but true that scientists and "educators" often complicate what is simple and obscure what is clear.

324 Misconceptions

1   Misconceptions are like pits in the road. If we cannot fill them, we can at least post a warning for others who will travel on that road, so that those who wish to span them can do so.[18]

325 The Duty to Expose and Destroy Error

1   Because one of the responsibilities of the true teacher of truths is to expose what is false, we point out errors and misteachings that grow like weeds in the garden—weeds that, if not uprooted, could flourish so thickly

---

[18] This book mentions dozens of misconceptions, including many that could affect one's subsequent life in the spirit world. Many are listed in the index, including some of their resulting effects.

In an early USB *Letter* Michael Flagg (founder) mentioned he once had harbored some misconceptions, which he later corrected after receiving enlightenment from USB Inspirers. Because he knew that earlier misconceptions, if not repudiated, can rise to confuse and confound others, in a 1956 newsletter he stated for the record that he stood foursquare by all the USB teachings, starting from its first *Letter*.

as to completely hide the exquisite blossoms of Truth that delight or enchant the lover of beauty.[19]

2   Fact and error about any particular cannot both exist in anyone's mind at the very same time. And when we expose misteaching, as it is our duty to do, it is never to condemn those who err. It is to enable others, who have the desire and the courage (if needed), to replace by the light of reason what is false with what is true.

3   Illumined Souls have said time and again: "We do not condemn any soul." And like its inspirers, the USB condemns no one. We wish to destroy error, not those who err. We condemn the sin, not the sinner.

4   In any case, it is not for us to judge others. In God's scheme of things, there is perfect justice [409], and its scales weigh every single grain.

5   If the USB wields a sword, and it *does* wield a sword, it is the sword of justice and of Truth—"not to harm or to kill, or in any sense do anything that would hurt" humanity, as an Illumined Inspirer has said, "but only to clear the path with others who have sincerity in their hearts and truth, and to make free the peoples from those who have so long held back truth."

---

[19] On a number of occasions Michael emphasized to me the importance of wiping out error. To enable the more serious investigator to exercise reason by studying and learning from the attitudes of USB inspirers to error and misteachings and from examples of what USB spirit leaders are convinced are errors and misteachings, and to help expose what we feel certain is false, we include topics on such subjects in Appendix B: "Error and Misteachings."

4

The Laws That Govern

CHAPTER CONTENTS

4.1 On Laws — 74
   401 Natural Laws and People's Laws — 74
   402 THE LAW—and the Laws — 74
   403 Translating "The Laws That Govern, or THE LAW" — 75

4.2 Responsibility — 76
   404 The Law of Personal Responsibility — 76

4.3 Service — 76
   405 The Law of Service — 76
   406 The Law of Reciprocation — 77

4.4 Justice — 77
   407 The Law of Cause and Effect — 77
   408 The Law of Compensation — 78
   409 The Law of Justice — 78

4.5 Love — 78
   410 The Law of Brotherly and Sisterly Love — 78

4.6 Attraction — 79
   411 The Law of Attraction — 79
   412 The Law of Affinity — 79

4.7 Life — 80
   413 The Law of Life — 80
   414 The Law of Vibration and the Law of Motion — 80
   415 The Law of Change — 82
   416 The Law of Variety — 83
   417 The Law of Multiplication — 84

4.1 ON LAWS

401 Natural Laws and People's Laws

1 Natural laws, the laws of Nature, the laws of God, like many other similar terms, refer to *laws that are not made by people.*

2 We in the USB prefer the term *The Laws That Govern*, or (collectively) THE LAW—The Law that enables all that *is*, to *exist*, and that enables humanity and all else to express. That Law includes all physical and spiritual laws, whether or not we are conscious of them.

3 Laws that are made by people often vary from place to place, from country to country, and from age to age. Laws made by people may change, and they may be good or bad. The Laws That Govern are unchangeable and eternal, and *they are always good.*

4 Observance of a law made by people brings light or darkness, depending on the law. Observance of The Laws That Govern brings only light.

5 A Blessed Soul has observed: "Where is there perfection in nature, except in the Laws[1] that govern nature?"

402 THE LAW—and the Laws

1 There are innumerable Laws That Govern, and that together make up THE LAW. They are Truth, being eternal and operating everywhere on all levels of existence.

2 THE LAW is universal in its application, but personal in its interpretation. In other words, while THE LAW governs the entire universe, our understanding of it will vary, according to the level of our consciousness. We should strive to live according to our highest perception of THE LAW; and the more we evolve, the greater will be our perception.[2]

3 We should not expect others to interpret the Laws precisely as we ourselves do. Nor should we try to force our own interpretations on them.

---

[1] We use a capital L to identify Laws of Nature, of God.

[2] We discuss in Topic 1425 how knowledge of THE LAW is very important to our spiritual progress.

4.1 On Laws

4 What we can do is to plant a seed here and there; and if the ground is fertile, the seed will eventually take root. Then we can nourish the plant with light and water, always taking care to provide no more than it can readily absorb. Too much sun would wither it; too much water could uproot it.

5 Whereas laws made by people, like creeds and dogmas made by people, cast only a shadow, the Laws that come from The Source of Light shed light.

6 The Laws That Govern are simple—as is all Truth and Beauty. And we should express the Laws simply if we wish to bring that light to others.

403 Translating "The Laws That Govern, or THE LAW"

1 In languages where as a rule words possess fewer meanings than English words do, a literal translation may not convey the precise intent of a phrase we often use: "The Laws That Govern, or THE LAW." So we present a few thoughts that may help translators in non-English speaking countries to provide satisfactory equivalents of their own.

2 *The law* of any country consists of *all* its laws made by people—laws designed to cover every facet of that country's concerns, including health, education, social welfare, industry, traffic, justice, and defense.

3 Similarly, the Laws that are the creation of that sublime Force or Power that we and many others call God together cover every facet of existence in the entire universe. The difference is that those Laws of God are *perfect in every way*. We call those Laws, Laws that apply to everything that is known or unknown to us, *The Laws That Govern*, or, collectively, THE LAW.

4 When, in following chapters, we speak of *living by* The Laws That Govern or THE LAW, however, we refer specifically to the *spiritual* Laws that apply to all people on both sides of life, and that govern or determine our rate of progression according to the degree we observe them. Those Laws of course include The Law of Personal Responsibility and The Law of Service.[3]

---

[3] Other Laws, mentioned in passing in this book but not defined, are The Law of Moderation (734:16) and The Law of Self-Preservation (a law of nature, not a *spiritual* law; 416:6, 812:1, 818:5).

4.2 RESPONSIBILITY

404 The Law of Personal Responsibility

1. Of the spiritual laws *we* know, the most important Law that affects the individual is: The Law of Personal Responsibility.

2. By that Law, individuals who *normally* can distinguish between right and wrong [839:3–4], are accountable for their thoughts, words, acts, and actions: No belief in anyone or anything, or allegiance to anyone or anything, or the voluntary taking of anything that we know or suspect may adversely affect our faculties or behavior, can absolve us from that responsibility [103:5].

3. It is a responsibility we can never escape, no matter what is our expression of existence, and no matter whose advice or teachings we follow.

4.3 SERVICE

405 The Law of Service

1. "The greater our blessings, the greater our gifts, the greater our awareness, the greater our opportunities, the greater is our responsibility to serve."

2. That is The Law of Service, the Law our inspirers stress so often, the Law that inspired the *formation* of the USB.

3. There is no one that cannot serve in some fashion or other. We can serve by bringing cheer to others in humble ways—a sympathetic look, a sunny smile, a friendly greeting, or a firm handclasp.

4. We can serve by spreading truth and enlightenment—by bringing light where there is darkness, beauty where there is unsightliness, knowledge where there is ignorance, courage where there is fear, and joy where there is gloom.

5. The avenues of service are limitless. We can fulfil the Law by pursuing the paths closest at hand, selflessly, with no thought of gain, and with joy in the serving.

6. Love and Service are inseparably linked.

7. How can we love without serving? What is selfless service but love in expression? How can we love God without loving and serving God's children?

8   Illumined Souls emphasize that individuals should be encouraged to serve in their own ways, in their own fashions, and to the extents they desire.

9   Our combined efforts, they say, are like

10 a tapestry that is woven with many threads. *All* the threads, even though they may not all be of gold, are important to the finished picture... We should not dislike the more somber hues and those that are more dulled, but remember that what is to become glorious to behold requires *many* threads and *many* colors.

11 *We* determine, each one of us, the thread and the color that *we* contribute to the tapestry.

406 The Law of Reciprocation

1   For kindness shown us when in need, we should, when the opportunity comes, gladly show the same kindness to another—to *any* one of God's children, not necessarily the one who helped us.

2   If we do that, we observe The Law of Reciprocation.

3   For that Law is not always the reciprocating or exchanging of things between *two* people or groups, as one might assume from its name. It is, at times, giving *someone else* what we have received from another.

4   It is not always possible to repay the very one who has helped us; but we can, in turn, help another less fortunate than ourselves—a thing to do at least equally good as repaying.

4.4 JUSTICE

407 The Law of Cause and Effect

1   As we sow, we reap. As we plant, so is the harvest. Each thing we say or think or do brings its inevitable result.

2   That is The Law of Cause and Effect which, like all other spiritual laws, is no respecter of persons and knows no exception.

3   The effect may not *immediately* follow the cause. In fact the effect is often deferred until after we pass on to spirit life. But the Law is unalterable, and the effect appears sooner or later.[4]

---

[4] There seems to be nothing to prevent many causes having a single, combined effect, or vice versa.

408 The Law of Compensation

1. Our actions, which bring their inevitable results to us, sometimes adversely affect others—*innocent* victims of our actions.

2. In that case, The Law of Compensation makes up for what others suffer through no fault of their own [1410].

3. If, for instance, a reckless driver runs over an infant, the driver is subject to The Law of Cause and Effect. The infant, by The Law of Compensation, is provided with care and affection in the spirit world. And its parents, if not unworthy, are permitted during sleep to visit their child, so that they are not strangers when reunited later, when they too shall live in the spirit world [1330:2–4].

409 The Law of Justice

1. The Law of Cause and Effect and The Law of Compensation together form The Law of Justice. Because of this Law there is *not*, and *cannot* be, *any* injustice *in the long run*. [See 325:4.]

4.5 LOVE

410 The Law of Brotherly and Sisterly Love

1. We cannot extend our hearts in love to fellow human beings without others eventually extending *their* hearts in love to us, and, in turn, sooner or later finding other hearts extended to *them*.

2. This is The Law of Brotherly and Sisterly Love.[5]

3. It is like links in a chain, one link forged to a second, the second to a third, the third to a fourth, and so on, and on, and on.

4. The Law of Brotherly and Sisterly Love is the Law that will unite humanity, as more and more people observe it, as more and more not only forge links to existing chains of love, but also serve as initial links in newer chains.

5. The Law of Brotherly and Sisterly Love is the Law that brings Illumined Souls to us in love and compassion and the burning desire to share *their* enlightenment, *their* peace and harmony, and brother-and-sisterhood.

---

[5] We discuss whether love is the *fulfilling* of a law in Topic 514.

6   For regardless of which globe or planet we live on, regardless of which expression of existence is ours, *we are all sisters and brothers, all children of the one God.*

7   The Law of Brotherly and Sisterly Love is related to The Law of Cause and Effect. And of course it is not unlike The Law of Reciprocation. Indeed the Laws are intertwined.

4.6 ATTRACTION

411 The Law of Attraction

1   The greater our spirituality, the nobler our character, ideals, aspiration, and efforts, the higher is the caliber of those spirit people who come to us for one reason or another, often as guides and teachers. Like attracts like.

2   That is The Law of Attraction.

3   And as we progress *spiritually*, we attract more advanced souls by the workings of this Law.

4   The Law of Attraction is a far more encompassing one than The Law of Affinity, which is so often misunderstood.

412 The Law of Affinity

1   The Law of Affinity is a closer, more delicate, more soul-satisfying Law than The Law of Attraction, of which it is part.

2   It is, in a sense, the finest distillation, the purest essence, of The Law of Attraction. For while we may attract or be attracted to many, *we have only one affinity—our twin soul*, whom few of us meet on earth [1321]. (We do not use the words *affinity* and *attraction* interchangeably, as most dictionaries do.)

3   People often say they have, or feel, an affinity with someone, when it is actually just an attraction to someone—a vastly different thing, as we define the terms here.

4   The Law of Affinity is definite: *one* has an affinity to *one*—and *only* one.

4.7 LIFE

413 The Law of Life

1. The Law of Life is the Law that enables the universe to be; and the magnificent power *behind* that Law is God! (Or The First Cause, or The One Great Source, or The Great Spirit, or whatever word or phrase is used in referring to The Supreme Being.)

2. It is a Law that may always remain a mystery to us. But we can know *some* of its blessings—just as we can know that the sun provides warmth without knowing exactly what the sun is or how it was formed.

3. It is The Law of Life that makes possible *all* manifestations of life, in all its aspects.

4. It is the Law that enables the individual to exist.

5. It is the Law that provides each of us with a spark of divinity.

6. It is the Law that gives us the priceless boon of free will.

7. It is the Law that provides intelligence to each and every cell of every living thing and every being.

8. It is the Law that enables each cell to produce and reproduce intelligently, according to a habit pattern.

9. It is the Law that in effect says to a blade of grass: "Your intelligence enables you to be a blade of grass. Reach out into the sunlight for what is vital for *you* to express yourself."

10. It is the Law that gives us freedom of expression, and freedom to *change* our thoughts and live accordingly.

11. It is the Law that makes what is called "spirit return" possible—the Law that allows us to feel the *touch* of a loved one, or hear the *voice* of a loved one, or even *see* a loved one who has moved on to spirit life.

12. It is the Law that enables Illumined Souls to bring light to individuals and groups that strive to attune themselves to the higher spirit realms.

414 The Law of Vibration and the Law of Motion

1. A few words about the Law of Vibration and the Law of Motion, concerning which volumes could be written.

2. The Law of Vibration, which is more comprehensive, includes the Law of Motion.

3. By The Law of Motion, all that *is*, either is *in* motion or has motion *within* itself. Or both.

4.7 Life   □ 414

4   Everything has motion. Nothing is motionless, no matter how still it appears to our eye or to instruments for detecting and measuring movement. Even the smallest grain of sand, and the tiniest speck of dust, are in ceaseless motion; for like all things visible to our physical eyes, they are composed of a great many atoms, each atom including protons and neutrons, and electrons moving around them.[6]

5   There is a specific *rate of motion*, and a specific *type of motion*—oscillating, revolving, or rotating, for instance—for the atoms of any particular element.

6   It is The Law of Vibration that gives every single thing and every creature an individual "pulse" or "beat" or "rate" that reflects its nature and quality.[7]

7   The *rate of vibration* is especially important, for it determines the *expression* of an object, and the *appearance* of that object to our physical senses.

8   In other words, it is the rate of vibration that makes a tree a *tree*, and visible to us *as* a tree; a rose, a rose; a dog, a dog; a cloud, a cloud; and so on.

9   Each species has its *own* range of rates of vibration, within which range it remains.

10   Trees, for instance, have their own specific range or band of vibrations. And it is the specific *rate* of vibration within that specific *range* of vibrations that determines whether a tree is an oak or an elm or a beech or any other variety of tree.

---

[6] Quantum mechanics holds that all physical particles are at the same time wavelike —the "wave-particle duality". This is the best understanding that modern science has of the inherent character of everything material. Thoughts are also waves of energy, as indicated by electroencephalography (EEG), so in essence *everything* is vibrating.

Apparently far more energy and matter exists than we can observe. For astronomers and cosmologists believe that the universe consists primarily of "dark matter" and "dark energy," both invisible. They infer dark matter from gravitational effects on visible matter and background radiation, and they infer dark energy from the accelerating expansion of the universe. In 2013 they estimated the total energy of the universe to be about 5% visible matter, 27% dark matter, and 68% dark energy.

[7] Traditional physics has long recognized that all physical bodies and their component parts emit electromagnetic radiations (wave patterns), which vary with body/part size and density. These radiations are caused by physical motions, some indirectly by piezoelectric effects.

11   The animal kingdom has *another* range of rates of vibration. And it is the specific *rate* of vibration within that specific *range* of vibrations that determines whether an animal is a lion or an elephant or a mouse or any other creature.

12   So too with all other species.

13   *We* are limited in *our* appearance by the specific range of rates of vibration of the *outermost* body we inhabit at any particular time: the physical [earthly] body, the astral body, the psychic body, the spiritual body, the celestial body, or *any* body of a still more rapid rate of vibration [1310].

14   *All* expression and appearance (manifestation) are governed by The Law of Vibration, which is one of the most important Laws that people can understand.

15   As to *what* is vibrating in *what*, we can say this: All that *exists* in nature vibrates *in* nature.

16   A physical body provides an excellent illustration of this truth.

17   Each atom in the body vibrates in the cell of which it is a part.

18   The cell vibrates in the organ (or other bodily component) to which it belongs.

19   The organ (or other bodily component) vibrates in the physical body.

20   The body vibrates in the atmosphere of our planet, earth, as does all else that is on earth.

21   The earth and its atmosphere vibrate in our solar system.

22   And so on, and on, and on, *up* to (but *not* including) The Original Source, or First Cause, or whatever is our term for what we cannot know and cannot limit.

23   We can see that there are vibrations *within* vibrations—less rapid rates within more rapid rates, and more rapid rates within less rapid ones.

24   Incidentally, to ponder over this truth—or any *other* truth for that matter—is to help us realize one thing: *All that exists* is the handiwork of a Power that we cannot more than dimly fathom, except through some of Its manifestations.

415 The Law of Change

1   Except for what is perfect as well as eternal—THE LAW, Truth, and the Creator of THE LAW and Truth—everything changes in one way or another, sooner or later, for better or for worse. That is The Law of Change.

2   We witness change all about us, in day and night, in the seasons of

4.7 Life □ 416

the year, in the plant and animal kingdoms, and, if we are perceptive, not only in others but in and within ourselves. Certainly we are not the same physically as we were ten years ago; and it would be tragic if we *were* the same, mentally and spiritually, and not farther along the path.

3   Change is natural. In fact The Law of Change, like all other Laws that constitute The Law of Life, is essential. While that overall Law "enables *all* demonstrations of life, in *all* its aspects, in *all* its expressions," the *varying* aspects and expressions of any one person or creature or thing are only possible *because* of The Law of Change.

4   We emphasize the ever vital need for change in our life, provided that the change is for the better [803].

416 The Law of Variety

1   The Law of Variety is the Law that allows all things and all species to express in different ways, with *unity of expression* but *variety of manifestation*.

2   We have only to look about us to realize that it is a good Law—as of course *all* God's Laws are—for there is beauty and enchantment in variety not only of *species*, but *within* a species.

3   All roses, for instance, express *as* a rose, for there is *unity* in their expression; but there is an innumerable variety of forms of that exquisite flower. The same with the lily. The same with the violet. The same with any and every other flower. Each species of flower shows unity of expression and variety of appearance. Together, they present a riot of color and a pageant of beauty to delight the heart and lift up the soul.

4   Consider the elm, a beautiful expression of nature. There are many varieties of elms, but they all belong to the same family. For in that family, as in every family, there is unity of expression and variety of appearance.

5   We find the same in the animal kingdom. The cat family, for instance, includes a wide variety of creatures, from the domesticated kitten to the lion, the so-called king of the jungle.

6   In the *human* species, we find the same law of variety. Tall ones, short ones; fat ones, thin ones; people of various colors—*all are humans*. And just as all other forms of life express themselves according to species, with variety of appearance and according to The Law of Self-Preservation, *so too do humans*.

7   The time will come when people everywhere will live as they all should

—in dignity, walking erect, aware that they are *sisters and brothers all, children of a living and loving God*. Then there will be not only unity of expression and variety of appearance among God's children, but a harmony and oneness of purpose that will mean many great things and much joy for humankind.

417 The Law of Multiplication

1 We have been asked whether there actually are individuals who, from just a handful of grain in a bowl, for instance, can in a few minutes produce enough of it to meet the moment's needs of scores or even hundreds of people.

2 There *are* such individuals, but there cannot be many of them. We know [in 1981] of only one person on earth who possesses that power or "gift"—an exceedingly rare form of mediumship demonstrating what is called *The Law of Multiplication*.

3 Various scriptures relate examples of that Law in operation. One is of a prophet who, during a time of drought and famine, promised a widow that the handful of meal and the little oil she possessed would sustain her and her household while there was a need; the promise was kept. Another is of the Being who, from a few fishes and a few loaves of bread, fed a vast multitude.

4 We learn in mathematics that no matter what the multiplier of *zero* may be, the result is *always* zero.

5 An increase is possible only when there is *something* to multiply. And in such "miracles" as we describe, there always *is* something to multiply.

6 The Law of Multiplication, which includes such taken-for-granted marvels of nature as a single watermelon seed becoming a watermelon containing hundreds of seeds with the very same potential, should make one thing plain:

7 *We* cannot create *anything*, not even a blade of grass, however much we may be privileged to multiply what The Source of All Good has created, or however much we may be able to mold or rearrange it.

8 It is enough to make us very humble and very grateful—*if we think!*

5
Love

CHAPTER CONTENTS

5.1 God		**86**
501	Excerpts and Quotations on God	86
502	God Is Not All—but All that Always Manifests In Order	87
503	PART of Us Is Part of God, but We Are NOT God	87
504	The Twenty-Third Psalm	88
505	"The Kingdom of Heaven" – "The Kingdom of God" Is Within	89
506	On Idle Conjecture and Pointless Speculation	90
507	Of Atheists and Agnostics	91
5.2 Love		**92**
508	The USB and Love	92
509	"Abou Ben Adhem"	92
510	On "Love Thy Neighbor As Thyself"	93
511	On Unselfish Love	94
512	Some Quotations on Love by Our Inspirers	94
513	Love with the Eyes Wide Open	95
514	Is Love the Fulfilling of a Law?	96
515	If We Cannot Love Them—	97
5.3 Service		**98**
516	Only in Selfless Service Can We Truly Serve God	98
517	Quotations on Service by Blessed Souls	98
518	On Helping Others	99
519	Let Not Thy Left Hand Know What Thy Right Hand Doeth	99
520	On the Responsibility to Serve	100
5.4 Prayer		**100**
521	A Little about Prayer	100
522	Some Excerpts on Prayer	102
523	A Prayer of a USB Inspirer	103
524	Two Prayers by Illumined Souls	103

5.1 GOD

501 Excerpts and Quotations on God

1   Let us rejoice in the knowledge of the Power that some describe as That Which Is All-Good, a God of Love and Wisdom, of Law and Justice.

2   A Blessed Inspirer, Alcoon, has said: "We preach a God of love,[1] of tolerance, of understanding, One who desires only that God's children shall find happiness, that they shall find the path of true progress in all spiritual things."

3   God is a word for our highest conception of The Supreme Power, or First Cause, or whatever other words and phrases people use in their attempts to describe The Indescribable, or All That Always Manifests in Order.[2] (Of course when we speak of "All That Always Manifests in Order," we refer not to manifestations themselves, but to The Supreme Power that brought them into being.)

4   What is God to each of us but our personal view or thought of That Which Creates and Expresses in and Controls the Universe? The opinion differs with each individual; the more spiritually evolved we are, the higher is our conception [1141:21].

5   There are literally millions of different conceptions of God [1111:3].

6   God is a God not of caprice, but of Law; God *expresses* through Law, let us never forget [1111:7].

7   In the sense of without *beginning* or end, the term *eternal* can be properly applied only to God.

8   "The scheme of things is perfect," says an Illumined Soul. "It is our *understanding* of it that lacks perfection."

---

[1] In a discussion in 1989, Michael said: "God's love is expressed in The Laws That Govern. The Laws that allow everyone to redeem themselves (103:7), for example, show God's love at work." –Ed.
[2] Native North American spirit guides have frequently used the term *Great Spirit* as a name for God.

5.1 God

502 God Is Not All—but All that Always Manifests in Order

1. Some schools of thought assert that *God is all*; that *all that is, is God*; and that *there is nothing that is NOT God*. Volumes have been written in support of that belief. The same schools also assert that *God is perfect*.

2. With the latter assertion, we agree completely; with the former, not at all. In fact we find the former and latter statements irreconcilable.

3. For one thing, if God *were* all, and all that is *were* God, then miserable human conditions, crimes of the worst kind, and undesirable human emotions—*all* these things would be God, or at least godly, a conclusion we could never accept, and that our reason totally rejects.

4. Certainly such conditions and crimes and emotions do not reflect or signify anything remotely resembling perfection!

5. For another thing, if God *were* all, then God would not be a creator. The earth and the heavens and the universe itself would all have sprung from themselves, and would have always existed—without a *cause* that conceived and created them. That too is something we cannot accept. For the universe reveals law and order—law and order of such degree, immensity, and beauty, that we can only bow our head in humility at the sublime wonder and majesty of The Master Mind whose handiwork we glimpse [507:3–6].

6. The following words of Allan Kardec[3] clearly, simply, and beautifully express that truth:

7. > The intelligence of God is revealed in God's works, as is that of a painter in his or her picture; but the works of God are no more God [alone] than the picture is the artist who conceived and painted it.

8. Anything that manifests in disorder *cannot* be of God. Disorder is created mostly by people, and results mainly from their misuse of freedom and free will and forces that can be used for either good or bad.

503 PART of Us Is Part of God, but We Are NOT God

1. Our inspirers emphasize that no affirmation, of itself, will raise us one rung higher on the ladder of consciousness; and that as one thinks, so does one *think* one is, but only too often is not.

---

[3] Allan Kardec, *nom-de-plume* of Léon-Dénizarth-Hippolyte Rivail, 1804–1869, the French author of early books on spirits and mediums, writing in 1857.

503   CHAPTER 5 *Love*

2   These truths are in strong contrast with the teachings of some "esoteric" groups, whose students learn to affirm (among other things): "I am God."

3   It is true, as we often state, that "within each one of us is a spark of God, our portion of divinity [601:2]. And as we evolve spiritually, the rest of what is *us* becomes more and more godlike." But for an individual to claim to *be* God, is to reveal not only great ignorance or imagination, or both, but a lack of the humility that marks those who are much, much farther along the road of progression. It is as if a pasture to which the wind has carried a drop of water from the ocean were to say: "I am the ocean."

4   For although an infinitesimal spark of the divine, a very, *very* small part of us *is* part of God, that does not invest us with all the powers or attributes usually associated with the Deity.

5   Certainly if a person *were* God there would be little point in existence on earth, and still less need to continually affirm it! In any case, a person could repeat that affirmation every minute of every day of every year without resembling "God" the slightest bit more. Only if we "live by The Laws That Govern to the extent that we understand them, consciously or unconsciously," can we hope to progress spiritually and become more godlike. Affirmations in themselves will not help us at all in that respect.

6   Instead of being unreasonable, let us enjoy immense comfort, assurance, strength, and elation in the knowledge that we possess a spark, however infinitesimal, of the divine. For it is *that* spark—the *part* of us that *is* part of God—that prevents any limit to expansion of our consciousness, so that there is no finality to what we can *become*.

504 *The Twenty-Third Psalm*

1   Few lines are spoken as often as the Twenty-Third Psalm. But only rarely is it said unhurriedly enough, and with emphasis on the words that should be stressed for its full meaning and beauty to be revealed.

2   Here is [one version of] the familiar psalm, with italics indicating the words that should be stressed, as an Illumined Soul sees it.[4]

3   The LORD is my shepherd; I shall not want.

4   *He* maketh me to lie down in green pastures: *he* leadeth me beside the still waters.

---

[4] Such emphasis can be added to other translations in the same way. Because this psalm was written before 500 B.C., the "Lord" mentioned could only be God.

5.1 God

⁵   *He* restoreth my soul: *he* leadeth me in the paths of righteousness for *his* name's sake.

⁶   Yea, though I walk through the valley of the shadow of death, I will fear *no* evil: for *thou* art with me; *thy* rod and *thy* staff, they comfort me.

⁷   *Thou* preparest a table before me in the presence of mine enemies: *thou* anointest my head with oil; my cup runneth over.

⁸   Surely goodness and mercy shall follow me *all* the days of my life: and I will dwell in the house of the LORD for ever.

505 "The Kingdom of Heaven"—"The Kingdom of God" Is Within

1. What is meant by "the kingdom"? It is a question that has been asked innumerable times throughout the centuries.

2. "The kingdom" means different things—it *must* mean different things—to different people.

3. Just as our conception of God changes as we reach a higher level of spiritual consciousness, and on so doing we perceive a grander idea of God "The Indescribable"—so too does our conception of "the kingdom" change as *we* change. As an Illumined Soul puts it:

4.   What we think of as "the kingdom" when we take our first step on the path that leads to the mountain top, is not "the kingdom" we will conceive when we have made our way for a while, or "the kingdom" we will envision when we complete our journey.

5.   And then we will find before us a still higher peak to climb. For there is indeed *no* limit to the expansion of one's consciousness. And as "the kingdom of heaven" or "the kingdom of God" is a state of consciousness, which is limitless, who can offer any *final* definition of the term?

6. Interpretation of "the kingdom" must obviously be a strictly personal matter for each individual, regardless of literature considered sacred and interpretations of that literature.

7. Our Illumined Inspirers consider "the kingdom" to be *a spiritual glow within*, a glow of which one may or may not be aware.

8. They emphasize that this is *their* interpretation, their *present* interpretation, one that they may not always continue to hold.

9   When individuals become conscious of that spiritual glow with every breath they take, then truly "all things...shall be added unto" them, though not necessarily on earth. However, all those things will not be of great importance to them by then, because they will have realized that they have already found the priceless treasure: "the kingdom."

10   The question arises: *Who* are those individuals who possess the spiritual glow within? Illumined Souls tell us they understand those individuals are the doubly blessed [516:7]—those who in unselfish service seek for the purpose of "feeding" the hungry souls of others.

11   We cannot conceive of any greater glow that could exist for people than the realization that in some mysterious and incredibly wonderful way they are in the presence of The Most High.

506 On Idle Conjecture and Pointless Speculation

1   The individual who thinks and reasons eventually realizes that there is a point beyond which it is futile to conjecture and pointless to speculate. For the more one delves, the more does one find a cause behind a cause, *endlessly*, so that one finally concludes that God or The First Cause, or The Supreme Power, or whatever other words and phrases are used in an attempt to describe The Indescribable, cannot be limited or circumscribed by definitions or by the limitations of one's own mentality.

2   It would be easier for an ant to fully understand a human, than for a human to fully understand God. But while we cannot perceive the fullness of The Supreme Power, we can recognize the *existence* of that Power by the abundant and unmistakable evidence of law and order throughout the universe, including the law and order behind our appearance in a physical [earthly] body [612:4–7].

3   Volumes have been written claiming to describe how and why humans came into being and precisely what humans are. But much if not all that is expressed on these matters is of little worth, Illumined Souls tell us. They themselves, comprehending vastly more than anyone on earth could ever consciously comprehend, do not pretend to have the answers to these questions. As a Blessed Soul puts it:

4   We know that *we are*; this we *know*. We know too *what* we are. But *why* we are, and *how* we are, this we do *not* know.

5.1 God

5   However, it is sufficient to realize that we exist, and that we can, if we wish, live by The Laws That Govern to the extent that we understand them, consciously or unconsciously.

6   We do know that within each one of us is a small spark of God, our portion of divinity. And as we evolve spiritually, the rest of what is *us* becomes more and more godlike.

507 Of Atheists and Agnostics

1   We champion the right of individuals to think as they please, regardless of how much their views might differ from our own.

2   But we are puzzled by the beliefs of the atheist, which *deny* the existence of an Intelligence or Being or Creator that hundreds of millions of people call God, and of the agnostic, which *question* that existence.

3   For if people, digging under desert sands, were to discover magnificent palaces, ornate fountains, marble columns, paved avenues, rich furnishings and attire, and a splendid drainage system, they would immediately and unquestioningly conclude that *some* being or beings of unusual intelligence and skill had produced them.

4   And if people, hacking their way through almost impenetrable jungle, came upon an immense glade with a well-trimmed lawn, a beautiful arbor, exquisite fruit-laden trees, and an imposing mansion, they would unhesitatingly accept that they were witnessing the result of the work of intelligences.

5   Or if, scaling a mountain peak far from the beaten path in a remote, seldom-travelled land, people discovered what obviously were the ruins of a temple, they would not for a moment question that it had been the handiwork of beings with intelligence.

6   But when it comes to anything *infinitely* more stupendous and marvellous, something of such magnitude, design, and imagination as the existence and orderly movement of the sun and planets in our solar system, operating so precisely that we can determine to the exact moment when eclipses will occur in the future, or the relative positions of the planets at any specified time, atheists and agnostics are *not* convinced that an *Intelligence* lies behind their creation and operation.

7   A theory that many atheists, and some agnostics, would rather accept is one propounded by people who cannot conceive of a mind greater than their own: the theory that the universe sprang from "a fortuitous concourse of atoms."

8   As to *how* those atoms came into being, the theory has little to say.

9   A related point is worth reflecting on here.

10   While humanity as a whole realizes the awesome power contained in the atom, few give thought to what to us is infinitely more remarkable: the Intelligence that created the atom and *confined* that power in it.[5]

5.2 LOVE

508 The USB and Love

1   A major purpose and goal of the USB is to bring about a far wider understanding of the importance of love in everyone's life.

2   This is expressed in our second stated purpose [104:2]:

3   To bring a universal awareness of the spark of God within each of us, and a realization that *love is the greatest basis of spiritual life*.[6]

509 "Abou Ben Adhem"

1   (There is much beauty and truth in Leigh Hunt's lovely lines.[7])

2   Abou Ben Adhem (may his tribe increase!)
Awoke one night from a deep dream of peace,
And saw, within the moonlight in his room,
Making it rich, and like a lily in bloom,
An Angel writing in a book of gold:
Exceeding peace had made Ben Adhem bold,
And to the Presence in the room he said,
"What writest thou?" The Vision raised its head,

---

[5] One gram of matter (about one 28th part of an ounce) contains enough energy to raise a weight of 91 million metric tons (90 million British/long tons, or 101 million US/short tons) to a height of 100 meters (328 feet). This weight is equivalent to 277 buildings the weight of the Empire State Building in New York City, 102 stories tall.

[6] It is not the *complete* basis, for as an Illumined Soul explained, knowledge, wisdom, and service are others.

[7] James Henry Leigh Hunt, 1784–1859, English journalist, essayist, and poet.

5.2 Love

And with a look made of all sweet accord
Answered, "The names of those who love the Lord."
"And is mine one?" said Abou. "Nay, not so,"
Replied the Angel. Abou spoke more low,
But cheerily still; and said, "I pray thee, then,
Write me as one who loves his fellow men."

3　The Angel wrote, and vanished. The next night
It came again with a great wakening light,
And showed the names whom love of God had blessed,
And, lo! Ben Adhem's name led all the rest!

510 On "Love Thy Neighbor As Thyself"

1　Few injunctions have been so misinterpreted and misunderstood as that of: "Love thy neighbor as thyself." The reason is that the word "love," as used in the injunction, has seldom been correctly defined.

2　The injunction was not intended to imply that we should love ourselves at all—certainly not in the sense of having an excessive regard for our own advantage or welfare, or in the sense of *overly* admiring what we might consider are our physical or mental attributes. (It is good to *recognize* and respect our own talents and abilities, not to make us feel superior, but to encourage us to use them. For we can respect ourselves and walk with our heads high if we do the best we can with our abilities, and if we try to be worthy of the spark of divinity each one of us possesses. Of course self-respect is far removed from self-love, which too often is destructive.)

3　Then, too, "love" was not intended to mean merely a warm personal attachment or deep affection for another, such as we usually have for family, close friends, and sweethearts.

4　Love in its noblest sense is far above affection for children and family. It is charity in thought, word, and deed. It is understanding and tenderness and compassion. It is service to others without thought of reward. At times, it is sacrifice.

5　From *this* viewpoint, we can perceive the significance of the injunction. It means being at least as charitable to another—our "neighbor"—as we are to ourselves. It means realizing that others, also being human, most certainly would have some of the faults and foibles and frailties of humans. It means having compassion for those who are stricken by misfortune. It means being gentle and understanding with others, not least when it is our duty to discipline them. It means lending a helping hand for a spell, if needed, to those who walk with us or cross our path. It means readiness to do with less, and on occasion even to do without for a time, that others might have.

6   It means, in short, showing by the way we live that we are *conscious* that we are sisters and brothers all, children of a living and loving God.

7   *Thus* understood, "Love thy neighbor as thyself" is among the greatest injunctions humanity has ever received.

511 On Unselfish Love

1   When the human heart holds love for those who walk in darkness, or for those who lie on beds of pain, or when there is love for right conduct—then one demonstrates one of the great principles of the universe, the principle of Love.

2   So says an Illumined Soul, speaking of course of *unselfish* love.

3   Love reveals itself in many ways. And to the one who shares it, love brings a sense of well-being, a sense of accomplishment, a sense of trust, a sense of beauty.

4   Those who love are radiant beings. Those who truly love, without thought of self-satisfaction, are *spiritual* beings.

512 Some Quotations on Love by Our Inspirers

1   All labors of love are made easy *because* of the love.

2   It is the power of love, not the love of power, that will bring peace— to an individual, to a nation, to humanity as a whole.

3   Human hands, inspired by the love of God, have wrought much beauty.

4   When one *loves*, with a love that enfolds the entire universe, then one indeed is like unto God.

5.2 Love   □ 513

513 Love With the Eyes Wide Open

1. Illusions obscure reality. And many of us have illusions, about people, about things.

2. Illusions are often created and perpetuated by the illusioned themselves. It is as though the illusioned blindfold themselves, so that reality cannot puncture the illusions. Disillusionment is inevitable, but not always swift, and, for people who exercise little reason, it may be deferred for years or even centuries, until long after they have passed on to spirit life. That is a sad waste of time.

3. We *invite* illusion if we let fancy invest fact with fiction. We should accept people for what they are. We should love people for what they are or can *be*—possessing, as we know each does, a spark of the divine. But we should not be blind to their faults and frailties.

4. It is an error to place *anyone* on a pedestal, to regard *anyone* as a paragon, to consider *anyone* a god. It is equally an error to expect too much from anyone at *any* time.

5. "People can share only as much as they possess," says an inspirer. "If we expect more than they can share, or are willing to share, the fault is ours—as is the unhappiness and disappointment that follow."

6. We should always exercise the faculty of reason. It is well, for example, to look up to those who are privileged to teach. It is natural to want to think highly of them. And it is tempting to sit at the feet of one who knows (or who we *think* knows) a great measure of Truth. But we should not *unthinkingly* accept anything and everything that is imparted, for it may contain error as well as truth.

7. Sometimes what is given, false and true alike, is designed to firmly entrench and embellish, in the mind and heart of those who listen, the personal image of the teacher, rather than the teachings and philosophy that are, or should be, above all personality. And what we should remember is not so much the person, but the *truths*, if any, that the person shares.

8. If we love with the eyes wide open, the personalities of those we love will be seen in their proper perspectives, and much heartache will be avoided.

9. If we love with the eyes wide open, and remember that teachings and philosophy transcend personality, we will not place people in a position where they might expect or demand homage from us, and acceptance without question of all they declare.

10. Too much that is shared today by various individuals and various schools of thought centers around a teacher instead of the teaching,

around a personality instead of a philosophy, around a person purporting to share truth, instead of around the truth itself.

11 Our inspirers frequently emphasize that "in all things we do, there is no cause greater than Truth." We are much more likely to remember this if we love with the eyes wide open [704:7].

12 An error of another kind is to expect others to live according to *our* standards; and to do so is to court regret. Even if we encourage others, as we should, to abide by noble conceptions of what is good and godly, we should not be surprised at occasional lapses. Which of us always lives up to *our* highest potentials?

13 We do not expect a sparrow to behave like an eagle. Why, then, expect a higher level of conduct from others than what is natural for them?

14 When we are disappointed with people, it is usually because we have looked for greater qualities in them than they possess. The fault is indeed ours.

15 We would stress this: Loving with the eyes wide open does not mean ignoring anyone who may have faults and frailties we dislike. Quite the reverse. Those aware of The Law of Service know their responsibility to try to inspire those on lower levels of consciousness—until or unless convinced it would be "plowing the ocean" [320]. For truly it is the ill, and not the well, who have greater need for a physician.

514 Is Love the Fulfilling of a Law?

1 A statement we hear expressed quite often is that love is the fulfilling of a law. Some are presumably quoting a line in scripture closely following "Thou shalt love thy neighbor as thyself" [510]. The latter, by the way, may be considered an injunction or a commandment, neither of which is a law. It certainly is *not* one of The Laws That Govern.[8]

2 "Love is the fulfilling of a law" has a nice ring about it; but like some other beautiful sayings we have examined, it should not be accepted merely because of its beauty, or because it is repeated over and over again by many people.

---

[8] Michael told me in 1989 that the (perfect) Laws That Govern are expressions of God's love, which is not the same as the everyday love of humans; and that the part of God (601:2) in each of us *draws* us to express love and respond to love. –Ed.

5.2 Love

3   For the questions arise: *What* law? What *kind* of love?

4   There are many expressions of that powerful emotion, not all of which are admirable or desirable. Most people think of love as a noble feeling or experience, which it could be, and should be, but sometimes is not.

5   For there is love, and there is love. There is conjugal love, and maternal and paternal love, and filial love, and fraternal and sororal love, and love of freedom, and love of country, for instance—all of which, *wisely* expressed, are forces for good.

6   But there also are loves that are *detrimental*. The love of a miser for gold and other possessions. The love of doting or neglectful parents who deprive children of experiences vital to their development and progress. The love for adulation, one of the baser desires. The love for power, to the extent of abandoning principles in order to obtain or preserve it.

7   Such loves, and others like them, *are* loves, but they are hardly noble loves.

8   It is good to love not only our neighbor, but *all* souls, as we define the verb [510:4]. But there is *no* law requiring us to do so.

515 *If We Cannot Love Them—*

1   On this subject an Illumined Soul said:

2   It is sometimes most difficult to express love towards *all* who cross our path. It is sometimes most difficult to show understanding and compassion for, and see the Godlight in, those who reveal selfishness, those who prostrate themselves before the shrine of material gain. And yet, they express love in *their* own fashion for what *they* feel is important to them.

3   It is *love* that inspires people—whether it is love of life, or love of self, or love of fellow human beings.

4   We can recognize that all people are brothers and sisters, without admiring all that they do. We can love people without loving what they represent. The Illumined Soul adds:

5   And if we cannot love them, let us pray to *understand* them. Let us pray for light, or greater light, to enter their universe.

5.3 SERVICE

516 Only in Selfless Service Can We Truly Serve God

1 There is much some seek besides purely material things.

2 Some seek the ecstasy of being in at-one-ment with "God"—*their* conception of God.

3 Some seek "the kingdom" [505] for the glory they believe will then be theirs.

4 Some seek "knowledge" for the sense of superiority it gives them.

5 Some seek to serve their fellow human beings [405].

6 The real glory comes to those who seek to serve others, humbly and selflessly, with no thought of glory, and with no thought of reward, material or spiritual, for what they would do. Says an Illumined Soul:

7 > Only in unselfish service to our fellow travellers can we truly serve God. Those who seek to feed the hungry [in their souls, 316:4], those who seek for the purpose of feeding others—*they* are the doubly blessed.

8 They are reaching, or have reached, "the kingdom," whether they know it or not.

517 Quotations on Service by Blessed Souls

1 Those who love and would serve God, love and serve God's children [737:10].

2 Let us walk the path of life with *each* day, or *a portion* of each day, set aside for service, extending a hand in sisterly or brotherly love, and rejoicing when eyes light up, or a voice rings with happiness, as a result of some effort on our part.

3 I do not know of any road to God but the path of love and service to our fellow travellers [1141:30].

4 Those who serve are indeed worthy to be called the children of God.

5 Every day that dawns is an opportunity for us to serve our brother and sister in our very own fashion. –High Mountain.

6 When there is *no* thought of self, to serve is to be blessed.

5.3 Service

7 Those who serve God know that the path is not easy. —Alcoon.

8 The hands that serve, and the lips that pray, can combine their service for the good of humanity [A11:4].

9 Each time we smile, each time we offer our hand, each time we express a positive and constructive thought—each time do we demonstrate the power that is within us. It is the power of the divine spark within us, the spark of That-Which-Is-All-Good that people call God.

518 On Helping Others

1 We should, of course, help those who cannot help themselves, or cannot help themselves sufficiently—the aged and infirm and ill and unemployed.

2 But the greatest service we can render others is to *help them to help themselves,* whenever that is possible. We can do this by providing skills to those who truly desire to learn, opportunity to those who truly seek to support themselves, and advancement to those who are truly anxious to work and work well.

519 Let Not Thy Left Hand Know What Thy Right Hand Doeth

1 They who truly share are those who give in silence, not trumpeting their gifts to obtain praise or plaudits. Whenever possible, they give quietly and in secret, for the pure joy of giving, and to avoid embarrassing those who receive.

2 Usually only what is given silently, unparaded, and unknown to others is of spiritual worth, for *that* giving comes from the heart.

3 The "martyr" who devotes much time and effort to another, but with a countenance that reveals to the world how much he or she is enduring, earns no high spiritual stature. The reward, a purely earthly one, is received in the commiseration of friends and acquaintances and the satisfying feelings derived from the "martyrdom."

4 The benefactor of a hospital or organization or charity who makes a contribution with a definite expectation of return—in the shape of plaudits in the press, or plaques to commemorate the benefactor's memory—

receives, in those plaudits or plaques, all the reward merited. Certainly few spiritual garlands, if any, are acquired.

5 The person who "serves truth" but lets the left hand know what the right hand does—so that everyone is aware of the "sacrifices" made—receives, in the impressions created upon others, a full measure of reward, a purely earthly one.

520 On the Responsibility to Serve

1 There are some who assert that the whole of our earthly life is worthwhile if we heal or bring light to just one person.

2 That may or may not be the case; in most instances it is *not*.

3 Much depends on our levels of development. We should not expect as much from infants as from schoolchildren, or as much from children as from mature adults. Certainly the more evolved adults are, the more that may rightfully be expected of them.

4 Abilities bring responsibilities, as The Law of Service, which we once again quote, makes clear: "The greater our blessings, the greater our gifts, the greater our awareness, the greater our opportunities, the greater is our responsibility to serve."

5 Whatever their fields, individuals who have the opportunity to serve many people but serve only one person, complete only a very small measure of their responsibility. Could that make their *whole* earthly lives worthwhile?

6 We should not expect perfection from anyone. Not even Illumined Souls are perfect, as they freely admit. But those who do not at least *try* to express themselves according to their highest abilities and capabilities fail in some respects; and those who consistently neglect opportunities to serve their fellow human beings, when physically and mentally able to do so, do not grow much in stature spiritually.

5.4 Prayer

521 A Little about Prayer

1 "Is one person's prayer, said in earnest, as effective as that of many people praying for the same thing?"

2 Questions to this effect are common.

5.4 Prayer

3   The answer is that it may or may not be so, depending on the *intensity* of the prayer. Certainly one person's prayer, if *intense* enough, is more powerful than that of many people who casually or with little fervor "pray" for the same thing. We place *pray* in quotes, because while major dictionaries give several definitions for "pray" or "prayer," the USB defines prayer as intense or concentrated thought expressed silently or aloud—and casual or listless expression does not meet that definition.

4   However, if the *intensity* of the prayer is the same, the prayer of a number of people *would* have greater force, and usually also greater effect, than the prayer of an individual. Many of the magnificent edifices, exquisite gardens, and other lovely things visible in the higher spirit realms are created by the united efforts of concentrated thought—or "prayer"—of several hundred or even several thousand souls.

5   Other things being equal, the intensity of prayer is much more important than the number of people who pray. Of course prayer is more effective when it has the benefit of both.

6   We can see, by the way, that the more individuals there are who pray for the hearts and minds of the leaders of peoples and of nations to be touched by light, and for peace and good will among all children of earth, the greater is the likelihood of these things coming to pass.

7   "Of course it is one thing to *pray* for peace," says an inspirer, "another thing to be *worthy* of peace, and yet another thing to take steps towards a *just* peace for all."

8   Two other important points about prayer are worth noting.

9   — We should know or learn how to pray most effectively. We should *concentrate* on a thought, even if just for a few moments, and at the same time *visualize and hold the visualization* of what we desire. (If, for instance, the prayer is for someone's relief from illness, we should visualize the person in complete and glowing health.) And then we should rejoice as if the prayer has been fulfilled, for the vibrations of rejoicing can be used by spirit friends towards the desired purpose.

10   — We should express the definite plea that the prayer be fulfilled *only* if it is for the highest good of the individual or individuals concerned and brings no harm to innocent souls. If a trial or tribulation provides a lesson that a person needs to learn, to defer the trial or tribulation would not be for his highest good; for while a needed lesson may sometimes be delayed by prayer, it must be

521 ☐

sooner or later learned, and delay merely postpones the opportunity to progress.

11   The application of The Law may be *deferred;* it cannot be *averted.*

12   The USB has *no* set prayers, and does not recommend any particular prayer. We know that words in themselves have little meaning or value or power unless they come from the heart, freely and fully. (In any case, we cannot advocate any specific prayer, and thus in any way, or in the slightest fashion, seem to suggest that something become a part of anything resembling a ritual, rite, or creed.)

13   We respect the prayers of others, regardless of whether *we* would or would not say them. And in a universal movement, such as ours *is*, it is only natural that prayers will be many and varied.[9]

14   One further thought.

15   There is often far greater wisdom in events than we can fathom at the time.

16   Most of us can look back with relief that some prayer or prayers were *not* answered in the way we had desired.

522 *Some Excerpts on Prayer*

1   Mental attitude, including expectation and a joyous anticipation of the result, is most important in prayer [1111:11].

2   We should not assume that we are praying to the very *same* God of everyone else's understanding [1111:2].

3   God *expresses* through Law. *When we pray, we set a Law in motion.* This invites others to help us if they can. But usually our own guides and spirit friends pass our prayers along or upward. It is as if our prayers climb a ladder until they reach their destination [1111:4,7,10].

4   When prayers are not answered, it could be that it is *necessary* for the requested outcome not to happen, or that the person the prayer is directed to has set up an impenetrable mental block or negation [1113:1–3].

---

[9] Regarding prayers at USB meetings, see also Topics 107 and D19.

5.4 Prayer

523 A Prayer of a USB Inspirer

1. (The following is shared merely to furnish an idea that, if rephrased and sincerely expressed, will help to bring about what we are all seeking. We emphasize that it is *not* a USB prayer, that the USB has *no* set prayers, and that it does not recommend any particular prayer.)

2. I forget self, remembering only love and service. In *Your* Holy Name, O Beloved Most High, I serve.

3. Flood me with greater love, greater wisdom, greater understanding, greater compassion, greater tenderness, that I may better reflect Your light and the light of Illumined Souls to all humanity.

4. In *Your* name, O Beloved Most High, I send the thought of love and peace and brother-and-sisterhood to the four corners of the globe, to the heart and mind of every soul.

5. Especially to the leaders of peoples and of nations I ask: "Forget self, remembering only love and service. Think not of benefit for yourselves or your peoples, but only of what will bring good to *all* humanity. Share what you have with those that have not. Gather around the council table in love, in trust, in good will one for another, to discuss and not debate the problems that may be.

6. "Above all, seek inspiration and guidance from That Which Is All-Good, by whatever name you may use for that magnificent supreme power that many call God.

7. "Take part in creating what is *being* created, what *shall* be established within the lifetime of many on earth today—a universal spiritual brother-and-sisterhood of *all* people, living in love and peace and harmony, each aware of their own spark of the divine, aware of the eternal Laws of God, aware that they are spiritual beings here and now, and not just at some remote future time and place—a brother-and-sisterhood of all human-kind, under the care of a living and loving God."

524 Two Prayers by Illumined Souls

1. I offer my prayer—not so much for the peace that *passeth* understanding, as for the peace that *bringeth* understanding within the hearts and minds of all the children of earth. May the leaders of nations gather together to resolve their differences around the council table, rather than on the field of battle. And may the weapons of war be transmuted into plowshares to

till the soil and bring abundance of supply for all people everywhere, so that there shall not be any child of earth without sustenance.

2 Let us live fully, to the greatest extent of our conceptions and perceptions of what is good and godly—one step at a time, one day at a time—with love in our hearts for all creatures, with compassion for those on lower levels of consciousness who are *less* fortunate and *less* enlightened. May the light that *we* shed reach them. May the thoughts that *we* share bring a greater understanding of humanity's purpose on earth. And may *all* of the children of earth be as blessed as *we* are.

The Worldly

6

The Individual

CHAPTER CONTENTS

6.1 Characteristics		**108**
601	Soul – Spirit – Mind – Mentality – Consciousness – Intellect – Intelligence	108
602	The Real Self	109
603	The Dwelling Place of the Soul	109
604	On Various Selves	110
605	Individuality and Personality	110
606	Our Individual Consciousness—a Comparison	111
607	A Little about Character	112
608	Excerpts on Spirituality	113
609	Conscience – Intuition – Instinct	114
6.2 Knowledge and Understanding		**115**
610	On Acquiring Knowledge	115
611	Know ABOUT Thyself	116
612	To Know Nothing—and to Know a Little	117
613	The Cosmic Pool, Cosmic Consciousness, Cosmic Sea, and Such	118
614	A Thought about Conscience	118
615	Wisdom and Humility	119
616	On False Humility	119
6.3 Medical Aspects		**120**
617	Some Reflections about Coma	120
618	On Certain Brain Surgery	121
619	Some Reflections about Clones and Cloning	121

6.1 Characteristics

601 Soul – Spirit – Mind – Mentality – Consciousness – Intellect – Intelligence

1. How does the USB define these terms, when used in an obviously limiting sense, and in reference to humans?

2. **Soul** is the spark of the divine in human beings, their portion of divinity. It is constant, unchangeable, and indestructible. It is this spark of God in each human being that makes us sisters and brothers all,[1] and that makes us eternal. Illumined Souls also tell us that humans are the *only* expressions on earth with a spark of the divine.

3. **Spirit**, in the sense we use it here,[2] is the animating factor in humans —as it is in all things. It changes with its vehicle of expression, according to the realm it expresses in.[3]

4. **Mind**, or **Universal Mind** (not *a* mind), is the source of supply. It is the overall term to encompass all that is known and unknown by humanity. It is power in essence, not power in action, nor direction of energy. It is an infinite reservoir of information that *has* been tapped, that is *being* tapped, and that will *continue* to be tapped.

5. **Mentality** is the *portion* of Universal Mind that an individual possesses. In other words, mentality is not Mind, it is *a* mind. (Thus it is correct to speak of one or more minds or mentalities impressing another, but not of *Mind* impressing an individual.) [604:7, 801:6, 1231]. An individual's mind or mentality is enlarged (without limit) as the person evolves.

6. **Consciousness** of an individual is the *sum total of what one is, what one has become*. Each of us is in a continuous state of *becoming*. The more evolved one is, the greater is our consciousness, and the higher the level of our consciousness [604, 606].

7. **Intellect** is a person's capability to understand.

8. **Intelligence** is the degree of intellect in an individual.

---

[1] Of note, according to research in population genetics using DNA indicators or "markers," is the finding that all human beings are also physically related by having common ancestry if we go back a sufficient number of generations; we all share the same single prehistoric ancestor. See also the ending of footnote 3 to Topic 206.

[2] For the animating factor, *spirit* is used with quite a different meaning from that used in *spirit people, spirit world, spirit phenomena, spirit communication*, etc. (202:4).

[3] The *vehicle of expression* refers to the outermost of the bodies it occupies (1310), and the *realm* of expression refers to the earth or the spirit realm that the outermost body inhabits (1301).

602 The Real Self

1. [Besides one's bodies[3],] each individual human is triune, a being composed of *soul, spirit,* and *mind*—that is, *a* mind or mentality.

2. These three components of an individual are indissolubly fused together, and cannot be separated from one another, regardless of one's realm of expression or one's vehicle of expression.[3] [We frequently refer to this triune as *"the real self."*]

3. Within this triune, the individual's *soul* (portion of divinity) is constant; the individual's *spirit* (animating factor) changes with its vehicle and realm of expression[4]; and the individual's *mind or mentality* can be enlarged without limit.

603 The Dwelling Place of the Soul

1. Where does the soul, the spark of divinity within each human being, reside? In the heart? The brain? The liver? The lungs? Precisely where?

2. It is a question often asked, but rarely answered correctly.

3. As we explain further elsewhere, our physical [earthly] body *envelops* our spirit [counterpart, etheric, subtle, beta] body or vehicle, which consists of many bodies of successively more rapid rates of vibration [1310]; that as we advance through the spirit realms we discard those bodies one by one; and that our soul, our infinitesimal but significant portion of divinity, is constant and unchangeable [601:2].

4. If we bear these points in mind, we can perceive where the soul *must* dwell: in the innermost and finest body of the spirit vehicle.

5. Incredibly pervasive substances—such as rhodamine and fluorescein, to name just two—when dispersed in water, will spread to a uniform concentration throughout it; and even if only *one* part of either substance is dropped into 1,000,000,000 parts of water, the substance can be detected (by means of a fluorometer) in *each* of those 1,000,000,000 parts!

6. In the same way, the soul suffuses and pervades *every* cell of our innermost and finest body: of its heart, brain, liver, lungs, and everything else.

---

[4] Changes its rate of vibration, for example.

604 On Various Selves

1. A common misteaching that some teachers still present is that each individual has a lower self, a middle self, and an upper or higher self.

2. There are *no* such compartments of one's self or consciousness.

3. However, *not* all portions of one's self or consciousness develop equally. And just as people do not all develop or progress at the very same rate, the various qualities of an individual do not all exist or progress in the same degree at the very same time [see 719:6–10].

4. A person's consciousness—the sum total of what one is—may be exceptionally developed as far as integrity is concerned, for instance, and yet be almost completely lacking in compassion and understanding and tolerance, as history bears distressing witness.

5. We are ever in the process of *becoming*, let us remember; and one's state of consciousness at any moment may contain, say, spirituality, wisdom, understanding, compassion, poise, and patience differing widely in the *degree* possessed. One may, for example, possess much spirituality and little knowledge, or much knowledge and little spirituality, or an abundance of facts and few if any truths.

6. In essence, a person's consciousness is their mind or mentality (of which they are seldom aware of more than a fraction). For it is only because we have a mind that we are conscious of *anything*. And, as we have pointed out, in the indissoluble triune of *soul, spirit,* and *mind,* as the USB defines these terms, the mind is the one ingredient that can be expanded without limit.

7. The more evolved a person's mentality—which includes one's emotions, desires, thoughts, and spirituality (if any)—the more expanded is that person's consciousness. But while that consciousness, the sum total of what that person is, will not be uniform in all respects, it is an *undivided* consciousness, not split into any "lower" and "middle" and "upper or higher" compartments.

605 Individuality and Personality

1. Some people confuse *individuality* with *personality*, words that are often not well defined by those who use them. We define them as follows.

2. One's *individuality* is *the real self* (or *the real "I"*), which few of us ever fully know. The individuality is a person's entire consciousness, the triune of soul, spirit, and mind that each of us is, and that is largely submerged and hidden, even from oneself.

6.1 Characteristics □ 606

3   One's *personality,* on the other hand, is what one *appears to be* to others, and it has many facets. We may present different personalities, or different facets of our personality, to different people, depending on our links and association with them—just as an actor, seen by various people in dissimilar roles, presents different portraits to them.

4   But while many people will have definite if varied impressions of our personality, it is not uncommon for even those we may have known all our life to have little inkling of our individuality.

5   Personality may change rapidly from moment to moment, depending on a number of things. Not so with individuality.

6   We can compare the individuality with the contents of a book; the personality, with the cover. The contents, if unaltered, will remain the same, whether issued in an elegant binding or in a paperback edition; the covers will vary.

7   We can liken the individuality to the actual dwelling within the outer walls of a house; the personality, to the facade. Rarely do we know what goes on behind the exterior even of residences we may pass a thousand times a year.

8   We can resemble individuality to *character;* personality to *reputation.* Of course the true measure of a person's worth is their character, and not their reputation, which may or may not bear *any* resemblance to their character.

9   In essence, the individuality is what *is;* the personality, what *appears to be.*

606 Our Individual Consciousness—a Comparison

1   As we have just said: One's *individuality* is *the real self,* which few of us ever fully know. The individuality is a person's entire consciousness, the triune of soul, spirit, and mind that each of us is, and that is largely submerged and hidden, even from oneself.

2   Much of what is submerged and hidden in our individual consciousness is not deeply buried, and can be instantly and accurately brought to the surface. The names of family and friends, our prized possessions, the multiplication tables of our childhood, and events that vividly impressed us at the time—all these and a thousand other things can be recalled in a flash, without effort.

3   Many other things can also be evoked, with varying degrees of ease or difficulty—sometimes only with outside assistance. Often, however,

much remains interred in our consciousness while we live on earth, and frequently even after we pass on to spirit life, unless and until we have reached the stage where it can be disclosed to us, or we ourselves can recall it, without severe shock.

4 We can liken our individual consciousness to a large, uncatalogued, personal library, crammed with volumes on a great many subjects—a library so crowded that the shelves are full to bursting, and the floor piled high with books. Some of the books may be constructive. Some may be destructive. Some may contain error as well as truth. Some may contain deliberate misteachings.

5 The volumes frequently used are within such easy reach that we can grasp them in an instant. Some take a little longer to get. Others are difficult even to *find*. Others are books we may have completely forgotten we possess—remembering them, if we ever do, only under rare and exceptional circumstances.

6 Still others are in an immense vault, to which we ourselves do not have the key. A wise custodian keeps certain things locked away from us; and The Wise Custodian locks away memories beyond the needs of our present existence, and until the time we can become aware of them without harm.

7 At some time or another, in some way or another, each volume we possess became a part of our library. Many of the volumes we ourselves selected, and our choice may not always have been of the best. Others we did not choose. But no matter how they were acquired, we ourselves are responsible if we continue to refer to any that are unworthy. Fortunately, we have the privilege of ignoring any undesirable volume, and of rereading or adding to those that are desirable and good—at times, only with the aid of others.

8 Let us remember this: Better a few gems of truth that we can read and reread with profit, that appeal to our reason, and that stimulate us to reflect and think—than a thousand flashy baubles that have no real worth.

607 *A Little about Character*

1 Nothing better reflects our individuality than our *character:* the sum total of traits that form our individual nature. The total is never final; it is ever changing, for better or for worse.

2 We can liken our character to a structure that we completely control. Whether the structure is sound and substantial, or a seedy, dilapidated

6.1 Characteristics

shell, is up to *us*. We can make sure that it is well kept up, or we can let it go to rack and ruin. We can maintain or enhance its value by making repairs and alterations when needed, or reduce its worth by letting one fault after another go uncorrected. We can expand it by making worthwhile changes and additions, or so neglect it that part or all of it must be closed. We can make it a glorious edifice, or a gloomy, forbidding wreck that brings a shudder to the passer-by.

3 But there is one important and vital difference. While a material structure may become so beyond repair and hazardous that it must be demolished, our character is never beyond improvement. No one is beyond redemption, for the doors to spiritual progress are never closed to anyone [103:7]—such is the Love and Goodness and Compassion of that Power that we and many others call God.

4 "Character is simply habit long ingrained," said Plutarch.[5]

5 "Sow a thought, reap an action; sow an action, reap a habit; sow a habit, reap a character," goes an old proverb. To which someone has added: "Sow a character, reap a destiny."

608 Excerpts on Spirituality

1 Spirituality is by far the most important of our noble qualities [1208:3].

2 It is part of our consciousness, and therefore part of our mentality [604:5–6].

3 The nobler our character and ideals and aspiration and efforts, the greater is our spirituality [411:1].

4 The higher our level of moral consciousness (with a compulsion to do right, not wrong), the more spiritual we are [609:1].

5 Spirituality is not necessarily related to mediumship, any more than it is to any other gift [1208:4].

6 Spirituality is evidenced less by words than by *deeds*. For those to have the eyes to see, spirituality, if any, and the *degree* of that spirituality, is evidenced by our way of life, by the way we express ourselves in all things, great and small [1403:2–5].

7 Our aura records the sum total of what we are, including our spirituality [1311:10].

---

[5] Plutarch, about 46–120 A.D., Greek philosopher and biographer.

8   Someone who is spiritual:
9   — lives simply [1401:1];
10   — will not knowingly do *anything* that remotely resembles craftiness [1403:2];
11   — does not seek anything that is not rightfully his or hers [711:16];
12   — shows consideration for others [1404:1];
13   — has the right mental outlook, or spiritual strength, and takes in stride what each day has to offer, the so-called good and the so-called bad alike [1408:12];
14   — corrects what can be corrected, and accepts all else graciously [744:13–16];
15   — is a channel for good [1407:4];
16   — expresses love, beauty, and the light of The Most High [1401:9];
17   — acts, speaks, and thinks in godly ways [1407:3];
18   — expresses his or her spirituality at every opportunity in daily life [1403:3];
19   — truly loves, without thought of self-satisfaction [511:4];
20   — is humble, sincere, and serves selflessly in the ways at hand [1407:3];
21   — serves others without any idea of personal gain or glory [1402:2];
22   — does not proclaim his or her spirituality for all to hear [1403:5];
23   — when more highly developed, is in mental attunement with great souls [1407:3].

24 We benefit spiritually from giving only if the motive is selfless, without any expectation of reward [1405:3].

25 We can grow in stature spiritually from the way we respond to challenges that problems present us [1408:13].

26 It is spiritual development, much more than psychic development, that makes contact with Illumined Souls possible [1407:2].

27 As we evolve spiritually, that greatest part of us that is *not* our divine spark becomes more and more godlike [503:3].

609 Conscience – Intuition – Instinct

1   **Conscience** is an inner knowledge or feeling of right and wrong, with a compulsion to do right. The higher the level of our *moral* consciousness, the more does conscience become a part of our very being, and the more spiritual we are—whether we know it or not.

2   Those on very low levels of moral consciousness have little conscience, and, without any qualm or idea that they may be doing wrong, will commit what society considers misdeeds. On the other hand, those on much higher levels of moral consciousness have a highly developed conscience, whether or not they are aware of it.

3   **Intuition** is a receptive quality—the immediate knowing or learning of something without the conscious use of reasoning. It is usually of great value to those who follow it, and it is generally surprisingly accurate, though not always so.

4   Intuition comes from a mind or minds, our own or others. It may come from an individual's personal storehouse of memory, however much submerged, or from the storehouse of memory of others. Nothing ever experienced, or heard, or read, or seen, is lost, though it may be so deeply buried in the storehouse of memory that it is only under special circumstances recalled.

5   **Intuition with conscience** is the immediate (and usually unconscious) moral appraisal of a situation, sometimes accompanied by the knowledge of what to do and *doing* it. Our intuition, if allied with conscience, will almost always guide us to the right path.

6   **Instinct** may be either the inborn tendency to behave in a way characteristic of a species, or a natural or acquired tendency, aptitude, or talent.

7   The distinction between intuition and instinct is sometimes rather thin. But as a general rule, intuition denotes *knowing;* while instinct denotes *doing*, without a *conscious* knowledge of why it is being done.

6.2 KNOWLEDGE AND UNDERSTANDING

610 On Acquiring Knowledge

1   We gain knowledge, *consciously*, in two ways.

2   One way is to discover, usually by reading, hearing, or observation, or by exercising reason, something that we did not consciously or unconsciously know.

3   The other way is to appreciate, often instantly, what others express clearly and precisely about what we have vaguely felt or known but never clearly thought through or voiced. We hear or read something, and in effect exclaim: *"That's it!"* It strikes a profoundly responsive chord within us, and we immediately make it a part of our universe.

611 Know ABOUT Thyself

1 Few injunctions are so commonly expressed as "Know Thyself"; for the famous inscription on the temple wall at Delphi[6] more than a score of centuries ago has been quoted by many a philosopher since. Yet few injunctions are so commonly misunderstood.

2 The injunction should not be taken literally, because to *really* know oneself would require knowledge of all one's past; and who among us is aware of our *entire* existence? Without that knowledge we could not fully realize why we are as we are, in tastes and talents and temperament, in desires, in philosophy, in intellect, in the degree of our ability to reason, in strengths and weaknesses, in character—or lack of character.

3 *But*—and this is a big but—we *can* know certain things *about* ourselves, things that apply to each and every human being: things that provide point and meaning to life, things that should make us rejoice and be grateful with every breath we take, things that should make us realize (or realize to a greater degree) the Love, Wisdom, Goodness, Law and Order, Justice, and Compassion of That which many call God.

4 While such things may not help us to know ourselves, they do help us to know *about* ourselves—which with few if any exceptions is vastly more important and desirable. Even when we pass on to spirit life, it is seldom that anyone becomes completely familiar at once with all aspects of his or her existence [1311:13]. In most cases it would not be good.

5 But to know *about* ourselves is always good.

6 Here are some things we can benefit from knowing about ourselves:

7 — We are eternal; *no* being is ever destroyed.

8 — We each possess a spark of the divine; there is, therefore, *no* limit to the expansion of our consciousness.

9 — We are the product of all that we have been, though we may little know all that has contributed to it.

10 — We are ever in the process of *becoming*, and *we* largely determine the stages in that process and the duration of those stages.

11 — We never lose our individuality, which, however, we have the privilege of changing.

12 — We are never so low that we cannot rise.

13 — Nothing that others do can halt our upward progress for long, if we live according to our highest conceptions of what is good and godly.

---

[6] An ancient Greek sanctuary renowned for its oracle of the Greek god Apollo.

6.2 Knowledge and Understanding □ 612

14 — We are our own saviors. We are our own prophets, and we reap the harvest of our own prophecy.

15 So we say to all: Know *about* thyself. And *live* by that knowledge.

612 To Know Nothing—and to Know a Little

1 There are some teachers and philosophers who say they know nothing—and then suggest the road a person should take!

2 There are others who also say they know nothing—and then proceed to demonstrate it.

3 To state that one knows nothing is foolish, for everyone knows *some* things; and there is much more that can be concluded by those who reason. To know a little is an altogether different matter; for even if what an individual *can* know is as a few thoughts compared with the vast expanse of Truth, those few thoughts are precious indeed and can be an inspiration to a noble or nobler way of life.

4 Certainly if we think and reason we should know enough to place our feet firmly on what to us is the spiritual path, for we will see the evidence of Law and Order, Love, Goodness, and Wisdom all around us.

5 We will recognize Law and Order in the countless manifestations of nature, such as the regularity with which day and night follow each other; the pattern of the seasons in temperate climes; the change from seed to fruit or flower; the way many plants bear leaves, blossom, bear fruit, and shed their leaves in an unfailing cycle during a great span of their existence; and the entire range of birth and growth and decay of all living things.

6 We will recognize Love and Goodness in the fact that the universe *and we* are enabled to *be*; that we are endowed with the priceless blessing of will; that we can, under the right conditions, commune with those who have passed on to spirit life; and that we never lose the freedom to change our thinking and revise our way of life accordingly.

7 We will recognize Wisdom in our departure from a physical body when it is no longer habitable.

8 We will recognize that things can exist whether or not we know of them, or whether or not we fully comprehend them. For just as the lowliest creature can recognize the warmth of the sun and put it to good use without having the faintest idea of just what the sun *is*—so can human beings recognize and rejoice in the knowledge of the Power that many call God, even though we cannot know just what that Power *is*.

9   The important thing is to realize that such a Power exists, to be conscious of some of its attributes, and to live according to our highest conceptions of it. Individuals who do so will know enough to walk the path that is right for *them*—and that is to know a great deal of what is *worth* knowing.

613 The Cosmic Pool, Cosmic Consciousness, Cosmic Sea, and Such

1   Some people talk or write or speak or think about a Cosmic Pool, or a Cosmic Consciousness, or a Cosmic Sea—as if it were actual waters that one can literally drink from, and, in drinking, imbibe knowledge or wisdom. Those terms are a few of the many symbolic expressions that confuse.

2   The "cosmic pool" or "cosmic sea" or "cosmic consciousness" is composed of *all* thought—of thoughts from everyone, everywhere, on both sides of life. Good thoughts and bad thoughts, positive thoughts and negative thoughts, constructive thoughts and destructive thoughts—*all* contribute to the pool. There are some important points to remember.

3   Anything we *receive* [mentally] comes from one or more minds, whether or not we recognize it. Each vision that we see, each impression that we get, is so presented. We receive it either directly or after it has been relayed through one or more minds.

4   Anything we are *aware of,* we are aware of because of a mind or minds—our own, or others on either side of life.

5   Not only do we, each one of us, receive from the "pool," but we *contribute* to it. If we contribute noble thoughts, we contribute, in a noble way, what *others* might receive. And each of us receives, in the degree that we are *capable* of receiving it, what we truly seek.

614 A Thought about Conscience

1   It is not so much that "conscience doth make cowards of us all," as the well-known quotation[7] goes, as that cowards resist or stifle their conscience.

---

[7] From Hamlet's soliloquy in Act III, scene i, written about 1601 by William Shakespeare, 1564–1616.

6.2 Knowledge and Understanding

2 By conscience, we of course mean "an inner knowledge or feeling of right and wrong, with a compulsion to do right" [609:1].

615 Wisdom and Humility

1 Wisdom is not the monopoly of individuals of any race or color or creed or gender or nation. Neither is stupidity or ignorance.

2 The wiser people are, the humbler they are; for the more they know, the more they realize the immensity of what is still a closed book to them.

3 And it is usually to the humble (and very often unlearned) that wisdom and understanding come.

616 On False Humility

1 People who repeatedly mention their humility do so to promote themselves in the eyes of those who do not realize one truth: To take *pride* in humility is to be far from humble. The truly humble do not glory in their "humbleness" or frequently point it out to others.

2 A booklet in which humility and other virtues are praised quotes the following: a teacher who "always prayed to God" to make him "the slave of his slaves"; a "saint" who said he had nothing to offer his students but humility; and a mentor who proclaimed that he was the wickedest of the wicked, that everyone else was better than he, and that those who saw it that way were his friends.

3 If those individuals believed their own words, was it not presumptuous of them to instruct others? If they did not believe them, were they not presenting a false appearance?

4 Too many in places of leadership display a facade of humility in an attempt to conceal their egotism—for it *takes* egotism to make statements such as we have quoted. Let us remember the words of a Great Soul:

5 > Humility does not wear a banner across the chest saying "I am humble. I am kind. I am gentle. I am good."

6 As he adds:

7 > People with virtues do not shout them from the housetops. To dwell on *any* self-claimed virtue is usually an effort to mask a diametrically opposite trait. Let our way of life speak for us— not our lips.

6.3 MEDICAL ASPECTS

617 Some Reflections about Coma

1 One thing that puzzles many is the fact that some individuals linger long in coma before either returning to normal consciousness or passing on to spirit life. To most of those who witness a loved one in a state of prolonged unconsciousness from which it is difficult or impossible to be aroused, their loved one's coma, when obviously a prelude to death, is beyond understanding.

2 But there *are* reasons, several good reasons, for such tenancy of a physical vehicle before passing on.

3 — The individual may be clinging with extraordinary tenacity to life on earth, although that tenacity may not be apparent to others.

4 — They may, by remaining for a time in coma, be paying off a karmic debt.

5 — They may be acquiring experience they need, the experience of *being cared for*. At the same time, those about the patient may be acquiring experience necessary for them, the experience of *caring for another*.

6 — The individual may, without realizing it, be *serving*—by providing physicians and scientists on both sides of life with the opportunity to learn more about coma, and thus be better able to help others in that condition.

7 In some cases of coma, the brain is damaged beyond repair. One thing to remember then is that even if the patient's brain is almost all "gone," their mind has not disappeared; it is merely more or less at rest as far as the physical body is concerned, because it no longer has a normal physical brain at its command.[8]

8 We can liken one's mind to a musician, and one's brain to an instrument the musician plays. If a vital part of that instrument is impaired, the musician can no longer use it satisfactorily, if at all; but *the individual* still exists, still retaining the same *skills*, though for a time unable to employ them exactly as preferred.

---

[8] Contrary to this, most investigators in the presently very popular area of brain research presume that consciousness is produced *by* the brain. But evidence of a mind outside the brain is suggested by many varied phenomena, including reports that stimuli such as light flashes or loud noises are registered by the body's energy field, as measured with an electromyograph (EMG), well before they are registered by the brain, as measured with an electroencephalogram (EEG).

618 On Certain Brain Surgery

1. Medical articles have discussed the idea of surgery to remove specific areas of the brain that some believe incline incorrigible wrongdoers to crime.

2. Those favoring it apparently do not realize that the earth is our proving ground, and that human beings should be free to choose between what is good and what is bad—subject of course, as we often emphasize, to swift and sure punishment for serious wrongdoing.

3. If, for example, part of a man's brain is removed, *use* of that part is ended. But while it would limit his opportunities to *express* as he might wish to, it [like being in a coma, 617] would not in itself change his character one iota, or his individuality—*the real self*—in any way at all.

4. It would be as though he was a musician seated at a piano with several octaves of the keyboard missing. He could evoke no sounds, pleasant or unpleasant, from that section nor could he demonstrate his skill, or lack of skill, in playing any composition that requires the use of almost all the piano keys. But while he would lack an instrument to *display* his ability, he would still *retain* that ability.

5. In sum, inclinations and propensities are neither altered nor eliminated merely if the means to express them are absent. Only when the means are *present* can it be shown whether, and to what degree, such tendencies still exist.

6. In our opinion, the removal of cell structure is *no* solution to the problem.

619 Some Reflections about Clones And Cloning

1. In recent years, there has been much discussion at various levels about *cloning*. An early stimulus was the publication of a book [around 1978] about a man who desired a son who would be his duplicate in all respects.

2. Cloning is a process of reproduction from just *one* parent, instead of two.

3. Originally, a clone was defined as a group of plants whose members are all directly descended from a single individual (plant). But more recently, the term has also come to include animals and human beings developed from a cell of only *one* parent.

4. The cloning of a human being—that is, one with genes precisely duplicating the parent—may not be impossible, but some of the speculations on the subject are extremely fanciful. In any case an exact reproduction

of the original in every respect is most unlikely. For as we explain [in 1009:3–4], while two individuals with identical genes are often indistinguishable *physically*, and usually inherit the very same *physical* strengths and weaknesses, their *mental* attributes may be vastly dissimilar, because *the real self* is not the same thing as the *vehicle* one inhabits.

5   Just as a fluid assumes the precise shape of the vessel it fills, but is *not* the vessel itself, so are we—*our real selves*—*not* the physical bodies we occupy.

6   An inspirer points out another important factor about cloning: Any cell placed in a womb for development will be affected by the woman carrying it, because while the cell structure is growing by repeated multiplication and division, it will be receiving sustenance from its "mother" —as of course it will throughout the entire period of gestation.

7   So, for example, while the genes of a father and his clone son will be identical, they will have received nourishment from different mothers, real and "custodial," while in the womb; and with nourishment playing a major role in the development of the embryo and fetus, any difference is bound to cause some variations in physical characteristics such as size, strength, stamina, and resistance or susceptibility to ailments.

8   But even identical twins, who of course received sustenance from the *same* mother during gestation, often are quite different in mentality; for as the USB emphasizes, we do not inherit *mental* qualities from our parents [1011:5–6].

9   All in all, therefore, the odds against a clone being identical with its human parent in *all* respects—that is, in both body *and* mind—are super-astronomical.

7

Personal Responsibility and Behavior

CHAPTER CONTENTS

7.1 Will — 126

   701 Our Unsurrenderable Possession—Our Will — 126
   702 Will and Inclination — 126
   703 Some Reflections on "Thy Will Be Done, Not Mine" — 127

7.2 Personal Responsibility — 128

   704 The Importance of Recognizing the Importance of Personal Responsibility — 128
   705 No One Can Absolve Another from Personal Responsibility — 129
   706 "Visitors" from Other Planets — 130
   707 We Are Not Responsible for Any Acts and Actions of Our Ancestors — 131
   708 Some Points to Note — 132
   709 On Being Provident — 132
   710 Laborers and Their Hire — 133

7.3 Integrity and Standards — 133

   711 Some Reflections on Integrity — 133
   712 Let Us Set Our Own Standards High — 135
   713 Unseemly Language — 136
   714 Some Reflections about Attire and Appearance. — 137
   715 Integrity—and Some Professions — 138
   716 On Promises — 141
   717 A Little about Resolutions — 141
   718 The Need to Return to Worthy Values — 142

continued...

7.4 Attitudes — 143

719	The Need for Tolerance	143
720	The Need to Be Flexible	145
721	On Recognizing Diversity	145
722	A Little about Motive	146
723	The Curse of Envy	146
724	A Note on Sorrow	147
725	Slavery to Empty Things	148
726	An Incident—and Some Questions	148
727	Some Reflections about Fear	149
728	Disappointments and Disillusionments—and the Secret	152
729	To Thine Own SOUL Be True...	153
730	Some Thoughts of Inspirers on Beauty	153
731	A Little about Pride	154
732	The Curse of Self-Pity	155
733	The Secret of Contentment	156

7.5 Behavior — 157

734	The Center Path—the Path of Moderation	157
735	Rage and the Individual	159
736	Slow to Decide, Then Quick to Act—a Worthwhile Philosophy in Most Cases	159
737	On Counting Our Blessings—and Being Grateful	160
738	Ingratitude and Ignorance	161
739	Quotations by Inspirers	161
740	The Importance of a Cheerful Countenance	162
741	On Regrets	163
742	On Denying a Condition	163
743	"Faith" and Material Commitments	164
744	On Certain Injunctions	164
745	Sports and Sporting Behavior	166

Chapter Contents

7.6 Right Living — 167

746	On Material Possessions	167
747	A Little about "Instant" Acquisitions	169
748	Some Reflections about Greed	170
749	Employers and Employees	171
750	Some Reflections about Tithing	171
751	Some Thoughts on Remembrance and Reflection	173
752	Patriotism	174
753	A Time to Speak, and a Time to Be Silent	175
754	On Resisting Evil	176
755	The Thought and the Deed	176
756	Another Note on Change	177
757	The Need for Effort	177
758	Perfect Peace?	178

7.7 Directing Our Efforts — 179

759	Let Us Do Our Part	179
760	Some Quotations by Inspirers	180
761	The Knowledge That Sustains	181
762	Wise Counsel	181
763	Remember the Similarities—Not the Differences	181
764	Of Ancient Scrolls and Such	182

7.8 Personal Progress — 183

765	Of Oneself, One Can Do Many Things	183
766	On Slates	184
767	A Sparrow Cannot Become an Eagle, But—	184
768	On Affirmations	185
769	Challenge and Opportunity	186
770	The Individual CAN Triumph	186
771	You CAN Teach An Old Dog New Tricks	187
772	Self-Determinism	188
773	Endeavor	188
774	Effort and Intent	188
775	There Is No Easy Path to the Mountain Top	189

7.1 WILL

701 Our Unsurrenderable Possession—Our Will

1. One of the greatest blessings the individual possesses is the God-given gift of *will*—the part of the consciousness that provides *the power of choice and deliberate action or intention* [1231:4]. It is a power that one cannot transfer to or share with anyone else.

2. Circumstances may compel one to act *contrary* to one's will. Obligations and responsibilities may chain one to what one finds distasteful. But like a tree that bends but does not break before a storm, one's will—one's *choice or desire or intention*—remains unchanged.

3. Some hold that individuals eventually reach the stage where they no longer possess will—the stage where they "surrender their will to God." But there is *no* force that can cause us to surrender our will, not even *that* force that we conceive as God. Of our own volition, which is the *exercise* of our will, we may "will" to be one with God (or our conception of God), but that is an entirely different process than surrender. And even if we *"become"* one with our conception, we remain so only as long as we will it, no longer.

4. There are untold thousands who dedicate themselves to pursuits or organizations, sometimes for many years, only to finally abandon them. *Both* actions result from the exercise of will.

5. Each individual's will is a precious birthright, untransferable, belonging to him or her alone. We may, for avarice or fear or any of a hundred other reasons, sell our votes or influence or decisions, or betray our principles and consciences. We may resignedly accept whatever happens to come our way, or we may "take arms against a sea of troubles." But in these cases, as indeed in all cases, it is because we so will it.

6. If individuals *could* surrender their will, they would be absolved from personal responsibility. We know, however, that personal responsibility is something no one can avoid or escape, something from which no one and no power can absolve us [404].

702 Will and Inclination

1. Many people do things against their *inclination*—which of us hasn't?—and then assert it was against their *will*, which was not the case at all. There is a vast difference between the terms, as an example will illustrate.

7.1 Will

2   Two men commit identical crimes. One goes voluntarily to the police, reports the offense, and turns in the weapon he used. The other, tracked down by police, exchanges shots with them; and only when he is out of ammunition, and they are closing in on him, raises his arms in surrender.

3   In *both* instances was there exercise of *will*—shown in the decision to surrender—but only in the *first* was it accompanied by the *inclination* to do so. The only inclination in the second case was for the lesser of two alternatives, capture rather than death.

4   Commonplace examples of the difference between will and inclination are legion. We get up in the morning and go to work, even if we are tired and would much rather remain in bed. We accompany a friend to a party, although we would prefer a quiet evening at home. We dress in a fashion that pleases someone we love, even if we ourselves may not particularly like it. In these cases, as in thousands of others that could be cited, our will and our inclination conflict. However, *we retain our will at all times*, even when we may be forcibly prevented from exercising it.

703 Some Reflections on "Thy Will Be Done, Not Mine"

1   Daily millions pray: "Thy will be done, not mine."[1]

2   (Some even go so far as to assert that it is one of only two prayers worth saying, the other being "Thank you.")

3   As we have pointed out, we cannot surrender our will. In any case, it is not another's *will* that should concern us—unless it must—but another's *wisdom*. Thus a noble prayer in any circumstance is the prayer for "the highest good of all concerned, with no harm to innocent ones;" certainly wisdom would desire that.

4   When people in a prayerful attitude cry out: "Thy will be done, not mine" they usually are in effect *resigning* themselves to whatever happens, and consciously or unconsciously attempting to relieve themselves of personal responsibility—something they cannot evade if they are normally capable of reasoning [839:3–4]. Advanced individuals make their *own* decisions, although they may quite properly seek inspiration and wisdom in reaching them.

5   However much we may consult others, *ours* is the responsibility to decide and to act accordingly.

6   In any case, far better than the prayer "Thy will be done, not mine" is the prayer: "May my will reflect Thy wisdom."

---

[1] Although many people interpret these words differently, this topic is addressed only to those who understand them in a literal fashion.

7.2 PERSONAL RESPONSIBILITY

704 The Importance of Recognizing the Importance of Personal Responsibility

1 As we say elsewhere [830:8], we who love our children *wisely*, discipline them when needed.

2 And we who love *wisely*, know that we must not deprive them—or anyone else, for that matter—of experience and the lessons that experience may teach them.

3 We who love *wisely*, know that the greatest good we can do for others is to help them to help themselves. We do not strengthen them or enable them to develop their character, or encourage them to unfold the divinity within them, if we strew their path with roses or perform their tasks for them. That would only postpone the inevitable, only delay and make more difficult the way they themselves must make if they are to reach spiritual heights.

4 In the words of an Illumined Soul:

5 It is well that we recognize that it is not possible for one individual to successfully bear the burden of another. But it *is* possible for one individual to inspire another to bear a burden with grace and dignity. It *is* possible to impress another with a desire to bear his or her burden well. And it *is* possible, by love and compassion and tenderness, and praise for nobly bearing what has been borne, to infuse another with the strength and determination to continue to bear it well.

6 It is essential that we recognize not only the *importance* of personal responsibility, but the importance of *fulfilling* that responsibility, and that we do nothing to deprive others of the opportunity of assuming and shouldering it—lest we ourselves assume a debt that must be paid, and without in any way helping others.

7 We should show love *and* wisdom in our relationship with others. For love *without* wisdom often brings calamity upon those expressing that love, as well as upon those receiving that love. Love *joined* with wisdom can bring only good.

7.2 Personal Responsibility

705 No One Can Absolve Another from Personal Responsibility

1. Before we can place our feet firmly on the path of unlimited spiritual progression, one realization is essential: the realization that we are our own saviors; that we are personally responsible for all we say, think, and do; and that no belief in anyone, or allegiance to anyone, can absolve us from our responsibilities [404].

2. To expect visitors from Venus or Jupiter or some other planet to "free" us, or to blindly follow any touted or self-proclaimed spirit or earthly savior, is to court disaster—to defer our spiritual evolution, perhaps for decades or centuries.

3. During our journey on earth, there are many souls who can, and do, inform and inspire us; who can, and do, encourage us spiritually; who can, and do, remind us of The Laws That Govern and of a God of Love, Wisdom, Law and Justice, and That Which Is All-Good. But none of these souls, however advanced, can assume *our* responsibilities, or shoulder *our* burdens.

4. Too long have people sought others on whom they could place their burdens and responsibilities. This is partly because some in high places —for one motive or another—have *encouraged* us to do so.

5. We might well remember these words of an inspirer:

6. > Be not deceived by those who would promise you a place in the sun. It is not the privilege of one individual to make a place in the sun for another.

7. And these words of another inspirer:

8. > Those who make pronouncements that cause others to follow them, that cause those who would believe to accept false promises; those who place themselves upon pedestals and by the spoken or written words about them, or by them, call the children of earth to follow *their* dictates; those who would lead others to believe that *their* way of life is the way of life promised them in the long ago—upon their heads and shoulders rests a great and grave responsibility for all that is spoken and written in their names.

9. > Many have placed themselves in that position. They have been heard, and they have been heeded. But time has revealed them as false prophets and teachers.

10. > Much *ill* is caused by false prophets and teachers.

11   Small would be their power, and few their followers, if each child of earth would realize that *no one* can absolve another from personal responsibility.

12   Look within your soul. Weigh *well* the tempting phrases that are proclaimed, phrases that could, in time, lure you into darkness.

13   Ponder well over all and anything others would have you absorb. Place it under the light of reason. Then accept what your soul *knows* is good. Cast all else aside!

14   We *cannot* express for others. We must express for ourselves. We must willingly shoulder our *own* personal responsibilities, if we would leave the lowlands and make our way to the mountaintop.

15 Let us always remember this: No one, not even the greatest spiritual leaders, can liberate or "save" us. They can show us the path. They can inform us. They can remind us of the Laws of God, a God that is all-love, all-wisdom, all-justice, all-good. But they cannot do *our* work for us. They cannot walk the path for us. They cannot embed their teachings and philosophy into our consciousness. *We* must do our work. *We* must walk the path *we* choose to tread. And what is embedded into our consciousness rests with *us*.

706 "Visitors" from Other Planets

1 Some "new age" periodicals from time to time report "accounts" of visitors from other planets who appear in the guise of men and women of earth, usually to bring warnings of impending doom and annihilation for the many, and salvation for the few.

2 We would not say that it is impossible for beings in other planets to communicate with us, but any such communication would have to be from a distance, and not face-to-face. For just as our physical [earthly] bodies could not withstand the vibrations of Venus or Jupiter, the bodies of beings from those planets could not withstand the vibrations of earth. Thus communication would necessarily be by *thought*. It would usually have to be *relayed*, for perfect attunement would indeed be rare; and relayed communication is subject to distortion, intentional or unintentional, by the minds of the relayers.

3 Many purported conversations with visitors from Venus or Jupiter are either nothing but vivid dreams, from which the dreamer awakens very gently and gradually without realizing he or she has been asleep, or they are "visions" created by his or her own mind or the minds of others.

7.2 Personal Responsibility

4   Another point that should be remembered is that one of the aims of the forces of evil—the forces of darkness—is to confuse humankind. Their desire is not to free humanity from the bondage of ignorance, not to teach humanity that we are our own saviors, not to encourage humanity to realize and accept the truth of personal responsibility—but to keep us in ignorance or greater ignorance, to have us "believe" rather than know, to have us retrogress rather than progress spiritually, and to delay the progress of the new age that has already dawned.

5   Some of the forces of evil, on both sides of life, *pose* as beings from other planets, the better to impress the unwary and unreasoning, those who do not know that each planet has its own spiritual leaders in the spirit side of life—leaders entrusted with the general stewardship of affairs of that particular planet, and that planet alone [1301:11].

6   There are other forces, not necessarily evil, who *also* pose as beings from other planets, in the hope of thereby receiving greater recognition and deference than they merit, and gaining greater acceptance of their teachings. As we constantly emphasize, mere passage to another expression of existence causes no changes whatever in character, and it often takes many, *many* years for some individuals to overcome weaknesses they displayed while on earth.

707 We Are Not Responsible for Any Acts and Actions of Our Ancestors

1   Some people believe that the sins of previous generations are visited on their descendants.

2   Such beliefs ignore the truth that *none* of us are responsible for anything our ancestors did or did not do. We *cannot* be.

3   Let us reflect a moment.

4   As the USB teaches, we *affect* all we meet, and are *affected* by all we meet, in one way or another, in one degree or another, and for one period of time or another [1410:3]. Some things that we do, or fail to do, may affect generations yet unborn; but no one using any reasoning at all could honestly hold those future generations accountable for our errors of omission or commission.

5   In the same way, then, *we* cannot honestly be held accountable for any errors of those who preceded *us*.

6   One's personal responsibility cannot be transferred to *anyone, anywhere, at any time*. And those who affirm otherwise show either ill will or lack of knowledge, or both.

CHAPTER 7 *Personal Responsibility and Behavior*

708 Some Points To Note

1 It is one thing to lose a home through no fault of one's own: It is quite another to put it to the torch and then look to the community to provide another!

2 Yet the latter happens, literally and metaphorically, in many places today.

3 Society benefits neither itself nor the individual when it rewards anyone who wilfully destroys property or evades his or her personal responsibility.

709 On Being Provident

1 In recent times some long-honored virtues have been discarded by much of humankind because of vast changes—not always for the better—in their thinking.

2 Providence is one of the virtues too often neglected today, and comparatively fewer and fewer are the ranks of the provident: those who try to provide for the future; who exercise foresight and wisdom in expenditures; who make what provision they can for a rainy day.

3 The mere fact that it has become a way of life for millions of people to live beyond their incomes does not commend it, and those with a high degree of integrity and responsibility will not go into long-term debt except for *necessities* of modern-day living. More luxuries of every sort, temptingly advertised, are now within the reach of more people than ever; but unless one can comfortably afford it, it is pointless to buy a country estate, a vacation hideaway, a second or third color television set, or whatever else is available, merely because it is available. The secure person with a sense of true values does not feel he must "keep up with the Joneses" or do what "everybody else" does.

4 The provident shun the extremes of extravagance and parsimony. They do not spend more than they consider necessary or wise, but neither are they excessively frugal. They try to guard against becoming a burden to others; and if they ever are, they can still hold their head high, knowing that they *were* prudent with their resources, and that circumstances beyond their control, and not they themselves, are to blame.

5 The provident are more likely to be content and at peace with themselves, as they are less likely to confuse desires with needs and waste their substance on unessentials. They consciously or unconsciously know that "to have *simple* wants is the secret of contentment."

710 Laborers and Their Hire

1   That "laborers are worthy of their hire" is true. What is equally true, but unfortunately often ignored, is that laborers should *earn* their hire, or at least do their utmost to earn it [749:4].

2   Too many take undue advantage of situations in every way they can, deliberately doing as little as possible, and often (as the saying goes) "getting away with murder."

3   But the "getting away with murder" is only apparent, and not real. For each thing we do or leave undone, like each thing we think and each thing we say, affects our spiritual appearance, which perfectly and exactly reveals *our real selves*, even though our physical appearance may not change [1311:11].

4   Those who cheat others, cheat themselves—a lesson they sooner or later learn, for unkind actions eventually recoil on those who commit them. It is The Law.

7.3 INTEGRITY AND STANDARDS

711 Some Reflections On Integrity

1   Poor indeed is the individual without integrity—uprightness, honesty, and soundness of character that nothing can impair.

2   For integrity is the root of a noble character: It is as essential to nobleness of spirit as oxygen is to water. Individuals may have the finest "education," the advantages of wealth and fame, a passport to every circle they desire to enter, and the means to gratify every whim; but without integrity they are spiritually poor, poorer than any homeless or penniless wanderer who exhibits that quality.

3   Integrity is a trait that may be possessed by *anyone*, regardless of his or her circumstances. It is a trait one should strive for, and be prepared to suffer if need be to *retain*. Like other qualities, it develops with use: The more it is exercised, the more firmly is it established, until it becomes second nature to its possessor, as normal and as unconscious as the act of breathing.

4   Integrity is usually put often to the test, to reveal whether it has indeed become an indestructible part of one's being, or a facade that crumbles before any severe temptation or onslaught. The earth is our proving ground, let us never forget.

5   People with integrity may not be always right, but they are never deliberately wrong. They do *not* sacrifice principle to expediency. They may often be silent, but not when silence is a crime. They do their utmost to fulfil pledges and agreements freely and voluntarily made. They prefer defeat with honor, to victory with dishonor. They repudiate the doctrine of too many of today's "leaders"—that winning is everything; for they realize that however old-fashioned it may seem to some, it is vastly more important to be just and honorable in all circumstances.

6   Customs and habits change. Some rivers *do* at times flow uphill. But the eternal values, of which integrity is one, never alter; they are unchangeable and imperishable.

7   Individuals with integrity may from time to time have to perform tasks that are not to their liking. In the capacity, say, of salesclerks, they may have to display items that little enchant them; but as long as they do not promote them on their *own* time their integrity is not compromised.

8   Throughout the ages, many who have had great opportunities to serve in one way or another have had talents that, spiritually used, would have brought immeasurable good to their fellow human beings. Too great a number of them, however, have used their talents for their own earthly ends, such as acquiring power, prestige, material riches, and the adulation of the unthinking.

9   Integrity is not as prevalent as it should be. To refuse to sacrifice principle for a so-called place in the sun is unusual. To prefer to be a foot soldier in the ranks of Truth rather than an officer in the legions of Error is rare. It is sad.

10   There are too many groups and societies whose leaders for various reasons, profit or petty prestige in particular, encourage expression of what is not truth.

11   This includes promoting the distribution of pamphlets and books that contain much that is known to be false. It also includes inviting individuals, perhaps distinguished in their own fields of endeavor, to speak on other, unfamiliar subjects, and who therefore perpetuate or expand error —thus adding to confusion and misunderstanding in people's minds instead of bringing light.

12   This too is sad. As is the debt such leaders of groups and societies incur.

13   Most people do not display integrity, or the same *degree* of integrity, in all their doings.

7.3 Integrity and Standards

14   Someone who would not take a penny too much from a friend, may unhesitatingly pocket the excess change that he or she realizes a cashier has provided by mistake. A person who would not dream of walking out of a store with merchandise not charged or paid for, may "forget" to declare taxable goods when going through customs. An individual who would not take even the most trifling office supplies for personal use, may think nothing of habitually taking an extra fifteen or twenty minutes for lunch.

15   Obviously, then, one may possess many and *various* levels of integrity.

16   Of course highly spiritual people neither seize nor seek anything that is not rightfully theirs, nor do they do unto others what they would not have others do unto them.

17   There is no *honest* compromise with wrong. They who sacrifice principle for expediency, or who repudiate agreements freely and voluntarily made, create debts that must eventually be paid.

18   It is a truth that millions of individuals have yet to learn. Sadder still for the world, it is a truth that scores of peoples and nations have still not learned.

19   The seeds of dishonor and deceit bear bitter fruit—and the sowers must eat of it. It is a Law.

712 Let Us Set Our Own Standards High

1   Just as respect for law and order as a whole is gradually worn away by both those who commit minor violations, and those who overlook them, so is character gradually eroded by the accumulation and disregard of little weaknesses, each in itself perhaps trifling, but each contributing to a marked decline in character.

2   It is sometimes tempting, for one's immediate advantage, to do little things that we know are wrong, things that other people do, and excuse our actions by saying, "*everyone* does it." It is a temptation we should strongly resist, however; for it is a hole in the dike that, if not plugged, eventually widens enough to allow the waters to pour through, to flood and destroy much of worth.

3   We would do well to remember that it is what *we* do that mainly matters to *us*—not what *others* do (although of course we are often affected by the actions of others). Unless this truth is part of our consciousness, we are bound to neglect many of certain opportunities for spiritual growth that earth alone offers [1424].

4   So regardless of what those around and about us do or do not do, let us set our own standards *high*—and do our best to *live* by those standards.

5   We can obtain inspiration and strength from the knowledge that nothing *others* can do can halt the upward journey of the individual who lives according to noble conceptions of what is good and godly.

713 Unseemly Language

1   Whether by design or ignorance, or from the desire for gain or notoriety, or from a combination of these causes, in many countries in recent times there has been a steady increase in unnecessary offensive language, particularly in the printed page, on the stage, and even on television. Such language, which offends some people and is distressing or abhorrent to others, and which usually has no justification, is used and encouraged by people who wish to bring others down to their own low level, or worse. In contrast to language of beauty, it does nothing to edify or uplift.

2   One thing is true in any field: We can choose the gutter or the stars; and the choice is our measure.

3   The language of noble souls, however unlearned, however small their vocabulary, and whatever their dialect if any, is simple, wholesome, and gracious, untainted by unseemly language.

4   The worth of a cause can often be judged by the caliber of those who promote or endorse it; and that caliber is suggested by the nature of the language they use. A noble cause deserves noble language. It is never served by offensive language, which usually reveals the spiritual deficiency of those who employ it, and the spiritual immaturity of those who enjoy it [803:11–12].

5   Some supporters of low language and behavior claim that it is art, because it reflects the speech or actions of a certain type of people. But the *main* value of art is not *merely* to reflect—it is to *encourage and uplift* others to more noble forms of understanding, appreciation, and *expression*.

6   The artist who studies classical paintings is inspired to strive towards perfection in his or her field. So is the musician who listens to music that has passed the test of time. So is the sculptor who gazes at an exquisite statue. So is the writer or speaker of lines that are simple, clear, and moving, each phrase a gem set in a jeweled crown. And so is the individual who is none of these things, but is stirred to exaltation by what is lovely.

714 Some Reflections about Attire and Appearance

1 One cannot help wonder at some attire apparently designed to adorn the female form. Much of it seems as if it could have been designed only by individuals who dislike women, and worn only by women who have nothing better to do than to fritter away time and energy in the belief that attractiveness lies in anything that is different, however odd or unappealing it is to most people. That in itself may not be objectionable; it is another matter, however, when apparel borders on excessive exposure. Says an Illumined Soul:

2   Modesty is a virtue many have long since set aside, but it is still becoming. Modesty is a virtue that should be instilled and encouraged in the young, so that it may in time form part and parcel of their nature.

3   Modesty is not prudery. There are times when the display of the human form is in *excellent* taste—and there are times when it is *far* from that.

4 The female form is too frequently presented in little more than a fig leaf, if as much as that. So adorned or unadorned, it stimulates the adolescent (who of course may be of any age), and usually that is harmless. But what is not harmless is that it often excites the frustrated to acts they might not otherwise commit, almost always not upon the persons who invite certain responses, but upon *innocent* ones.

5 Also deplorable is the slovenly attire and incomplete grooming of people outside their homes. Bad enough in the comparative privacy of their own home, it is inexcusable out of it. We owe it to others, and to ourselves, to present an outward exterior that is at least clean and half-way pleasing, instead of one that is unkempt and objectionable to those who must see it.

6 While we champion everyone's right to walk in their own path in their own way and in their own fashion, it is our considered opinion that each person, male and female alike, has a responsibility to present an appearance that is not unpleasant. Certainly that appearance should, whenever possible, be clean and well groomed and suitable for the occasion.

7 Temperance and taste are desirable qualities in anyone. Doubly so is modesty, which can well include them both.

715 Integrity—and Some Professions

When integrity is a characteristic of those who affect our lives out of all proportion to their number—we refer to physicians, lawyers, judges, and those in office—a nation benefits. When it is not, a nation suffers. And those who are less than affluent, particularly those who have great difficulty keeping body and soul together, suffer most.

It is well to know what is less than desirable in any profession; for as we teach, the first step in correcting a condition is to *recognize* it.

· · · · ·

There are thousands of men and women who excel in the practice of **medicine** who possess high ideals and a burning desire to serve their fellow human beings. But there also are those who are less dedicated or less than competent.

[Medical care is now far more complex than the simple doctor-patient relationship of earlier times; pharmaceutical companies, medical insurance companies, and hospital corporations establish the agenda for much of modern medicine. But physicians still have professional responsibilities.]

As it is with almost every other group, not all physicians possess the highest moral principles. Excesses and under-treatment both occur.

Other things being equal:

— We prefer physicians who have taken up the practice of medicine because of a profound desire to cure, alleviate, or arrest the ills of others, to those who have done so because it can be highly lucrative.

— We prefer physicians who are frank to admit when a condition baffles them, to those who inexcusably label as "psychological" any condition they do not understand or whose cause they cannot quickly determine.

— We prefer physicians who have experienced pain and suffering to those who have not. We do *not* subscribe to the proverb "no one is a good physician who has never been sick," but we do believe that physicians who have known illness and discomfort are likely to have greater understanding, patience, and compassion for those who are ill or who find it difficult to clearly and accurately describe what ails them.

Having said this, we would add that there are few fields providing such opportunities for arbitrariness as in medicine, and so many opportunities

7.3 Integrity and Standards □ 715

to "play God." Such powers and tendencies should be thoroughly discouraged.

. . . . .

11 Many *lawyers* serve their clients well and faithfully. Others, however, including some so-called leading lights in their profession, too often neglect the interests of their clients, sometimes even to the extent of going into court ill-prepared or completely *unprepared*.

12 Evidence of this can be found in the Chief Justice of the Supreme Court of the United States castigating a large percentage of lawyers on this score some years ago.

13 Some lawyers have been known to purposely delay trials and prolong litigation in order to line their pockets or serve themselves in other ways. They are much more concerned with winning in court than with seeing justice prevail.

14 Few fields provide such temptations as the practice of law. That Abraham Lincoln realized this is revealed by his words to law students in 1850: "Resolve to be honest at all events; and if in your judgement you cannot be an honest lawyer, resolve to be honest without being a lawyer."

15 It is questionable whether any nation or state is best served when lawyers predominate in the legislature, as is not infrequently the case.

16 Lawyers in general, like physicians in general, seem to be opposed to simple, clear, and concise wording and language that would make them appear less than Olympian. But more and more members in these professions now use language intelligible to the lay public, respect the average person, and do not find it beneath them to make things plain. It is a great step in the right direction.

. . . . .

17 No system of justice is better than its *judges*.

18 A judicial system is weak, and invites corruption, when judges are appointed not on the basis of integrity and knowledge of law, but as a reward for political favors rendered or expected.

19 Sometimes judges take over the legislative role that properly belongs to lawmakers. It is not a judge's function to make laws by interpreting the law, which of course should be clearly written [and revised as needed], but to hear and decide cases according to laws that are in harmony with the *constitution:* the fundamental laws and principles adopted by a people as the bedrock of government.

20 Judges should respect and be guided by all laws that do not violate the constitution, even those they may disapprove of. They should never forget that they represent the people and are their servant, not their master. They have *no* right to ignore the will of the people, once that will is clearly and properly established.

21 Judges should base their decisions on the laws themselves, taking circumstances into account, and treating precedents set by others in an advisory capacity only.

22 Those who absolve the guilty, or inflict a mere slap on the wrist for any major crime, on the one hand, or punish excessively and unfairly or set bail at unreasonable levels on the other, should be removed from the bench for irresponsibility.

23 A judge donning the robe of office should have one thing uppermost in his or her mind: *justice.*

· · · · ·

24 History reveals several major factors that contribute to the decay of comparatively democratic nations and civilizations.

25 One factor is the decline in the caliber of those appointed to positions of authority. Another factor is the cynical betrayal of campaign platforms and promises by elected **officeholders.**

26 In too many places, the "ins" take advantage of those who placed them there; are generous with *other* people's money, and not with their own; and are willing to feed the rest of the world while some of their own people starve.

27 The sad fact is that there are always many politicians, but few if any statesmen. Politicians are of course seekers or holders of office who are much more concerned with getting or retaining power or personal gain than with maintaining principles. Statesmen are those [men and women] with wisdom and skill in handling the affairs of government or in dealing with important public issues.

28 There is sometimes also a third factor: apathy on the part of a public long disillusioned by those in office. This apathy must be dispelled by mounting indignation against ills, if the selfish and corrupt are to be voted out of office and succeeded by men and women who have the welfare of the people at heart.

716 On Promises

1   How many heartaches are caused by broken promises. How much trouble and confusion spring from promises that people make with no intention of keeping. The trail of broken promises is full of distress and tragedy and shattered dreams.

2   Those who fail to exert every effort to keep promises freely made do not do so with impunity in the long run. They may think they can "get away with it," and they may appear to succeed. But we emphasize: To break one's word or repudiate an agreement freely and deliberately made, except for very good reason or highly mitigating circumstances, is to incur *a debt that must be paid.* It is a lesson that many individuals and many nations have not yet learned, but will eventually learn.

3   People who seldom keep their word, or keep it only if it suits them, are of little stature spiritually. One is not much of a human being if one's word is not one's bond.

4   *A promise made should be a promise kept*, except if it becomes plain that it would bring harm to innocent ones.

5   Even in trivial matters, it is far better to say "No" or "We'll see" than to say "Yes" merely to quiet someone or to end a situation—unless we intend to *honor* that "Yes."

717 A Little about Resolutions

1   At the approach of a new year, millions of people make resolutions for change of one kind or another; but after a few hours or days or weeks, they usually break their resolutions, returning to ways that they were used to, that had become simple and comfortable, and that required no effort of will whatever.

2   Most people who make resolutions plan to begin keeping them at some *future* date—and what better date for a milestone than New Year's Day?

3   But the very act of setting a future day on which to begin to change a habit or pattern, or to start a new one, usually shows that the desire is not deeply rooted. And the delay only affords time for a habit or pattern to become still more firmly established, and thus more difficult to discard, or, if not established, still more difficult to *form.*

4   Procrastination is the thief not only of time, but of effort.

5   When the desire to do something is intense enough, we do not defer the attempt to do it. As the USB principle puts it [103:8], and we empha-

size two words here: "Aspiration and effort are inseparable, so one cannot *truly* aspire without making the *effort*."

6 There is no need to wait for New Year's Day or any other notable day to commence anything of worth. *Any* day can be the beginning of a new life for us, a day in which we can make a fresh start. Of course it is wise not to set too difficult a goal. As an inspirer says:

7 If we plan for but *one* day at a time, and live for that *one* day with our resolve firm and clear in our mind, it will be much simpler to abide by our resolve, for it is much easier to extend ourselves for one day than for one year.

8 The next day, heartened by success the day before, we can renew our resolve, again for just *one* day. And so on, day by day, until the pattern is so strongly established that it becomes a part of us.

9 A mountain presents a formidable climb if we think of the thousands of steps that lie ahead. But if we take the *first* step, then another, and yet another—thinking only of the one step we are *about* to take rather than the entire journey—we shall, with much less difficulty than expected, make our way to the top.

718 The Need to Return to Worthy Values

1 It is not only in the field of sports [745] that a return to a *worthy* set of values is desirable—in fact *essential*—to prevent further moral decay, and to encourage cultivation of moral virtues.

2 All too often, the virtues of responsibility, integrity, dependability, thrift, prudence, perseverance, consideration for others, pride in craftsmanship, and self-respect and dignity seem to have gone by the board.

3 It is sad to see people wanting something for nothing; confusing desires with needs; or deliberately doing as little as possible to get as much as possible; in fact, wanting to have everything their *own* way—but with *others* providing for them! Such life styles abandon all sense of responsibility, expecting society to take care of all needs while making no real attempt to give anything in return. Pleasure and excitement, which inevitably cloy, are preferred to visions and ideals of love and service to others. And a pay-as-you-take philosophy, except when it is obviously impractical or unwise, is often rejected in favor of a take-now-pay-later philosophy.

7.4 Attitudes

4   These character deficiencies are encouraged by many leaders and would-be leaders who, for the sake of votes, promise all things to all people. What is worse, the upward price spiral resulting from such behavior penalizes those who exercise thrift, who try to avoid being a burden on others, who endeavor to do their share, and who are prepared to make sacrifices for what they consider worthy. Especially penalized are those with limited incomes and pensions who find their struggles and thrift over the years nullified and devoured by the ensuing inflation.

5   Not enough leaders of nations make provision during the fat years to take care of the lean. How can nations pay off their debts in bad times if they do not do so in good times? Leaders need to take into account the fact that any live-only-for-today philosophy reaps its inevitable effect for nations as well as for individuals.

6   We can emphasize helping others wisely [518]. We can emphasize right relationships.

7   But most importantly, we can stress the Law of Personal Responsibility [404], a Law that applies to every individual everywhere—for like all other *spiritual* Laws, it is a Law from which no one is exempt.

7.4 ATTITUDES

719 *The Need for Tolerance*

1   In these trying times, when people are tugged in scores of different directions by scores of different philosophies, and with so many individuals and organizations impatient with the views of others and claiming to possess the *only* solutions for the problems of the day, there is ever greater need for *tolerance*, which is a vital part of the philosophy of the USB.

2   By tolerance, we do not mean the mere enduring of the opinions of others. We do not mean any superior, condescending, patronizing attitude towards others.

3   By tolerance, we mean a respect for the opinions of others, however much we may differ with them, or even oppose them; a respect for others,

and for their views and understanding, and even misunderstanding, as they exercise *their* privilege of personal interpretation.

4 The tolerant and wise person is one who is willing to listen to others, blesses them, understands that all souls are striving to reach what *to them* are the heights of expression, and recognizes that their motives may be sincere, however wrong they are to *his or her* way of thinking.

5 Such a wise person is tolerant even of the intolerant, even of those who would destroy others—while at the same time realizing that society has a right to protect itself from those who would destroy others, and, if need be, to deprive them of the power to harm others.

6 Such a wise person knows that people do not all develop or progress at the same rate. He or she knows that the various facets of every human being do not develop in the same degree at the very same time.

7 An Illumined Soul puts this beautifully in a parable.

8 Time and the sun ripen the grapes in the vineyard. Time to absorb the rays of the sun, the rain from the heavens, and the food from the soil.

9 We walk in the vineyard and find a vine here, heavily laden, awaiting the harvest. And in *that* vine, *one* cluster riper than the others. And in *that* cluster, *one* grape riper than its fellows. And in *that* grape, *one* portion riper than the rest.

10 For while *all* reach out to the sun, not all absorb the *same* measure of the sun's rays. And not one absorbs the sun's rays in the *same* degree throughout its *entire* being.

11 Intolerance of opposing views results in the severing of many acquaintanceships and friendships, sometimes over the most trifling things.

12 Certainly friends should at least *respect* one another's views and beliefs, however much they may disagree with them. If friends do not respect one another, and agree to disagree without bitterness or strife or dissension, especially when their opposing opinions in no way affect their own rights or safety, could there be much hope for peace and understanding and brother-and-sisterhood throughout the world?

720 The Need to Be Flexible

1 As we emphasize, much that happens to each of us may not be the result of our *own* acts and actions [1410]. So we should not expect plans, however painstakingly and meticulously prepared, to be never affected or sometimes even nullified by unforeseen events beyond our control. Therefore, the wise individual is *flexible*, with plans that can be modified if necessary.

2 The storm that fells a thick and mighty oak may not even bruise the slender reed flexible enough to bend before its fury.

3 The individual who lacks flexibility, who cannot or will not adapt to circumstances beyond his or her control—who cannot or will not "correct what *can* be corrected," and "accept *all* else gracefully, graciously, gratefully, and courageously" [744:16]—often is a loser not just materially but, what is vastly more tragic, spiritually.

4 Nothing on earth is perfect. Few relationships on earth are ideal. These are good reasons for us to strive to be flexible, to "love with the eyes wide open" [513], and to take a broad, overall view of people, plans, and circumstances.

5 To fail to do so is to invite disappointment and disillusionment.

721 On Recognizing Diversity

1
Be these your fiercest passions from your youth:
A love for Justice and a love for Truth.
The first reveals that everyone is equal;
The second shows a more important sequel:
That we, though equal, are of different breeds,
And so have different moods and different needs.
Thus what to one is fine is often crude
To others with another strain imbued;
And what one finds too obvious for rebuttal
Another finds most delicate and subtle.
Have, then, more than one gesture and one word,
And don't reduce the highest to the herd.[2]

---

[2] This poem by Michael Flagg was published in the *New York Times* on 16 February 1932—over 20 years before he discovered the USB and established it on earth. Subsequently he included the poem in a USB *Letter*.

722 A Little about Motive

1. Motive weighs heavily on the scales of Justice, the USB teaches. But what is at least equally important as motive is the understanding, tolerance, and compassion that should accompany it.

2. Without those qualities, actions inspired by even the sincerest motives can be most destructive. Much of history's long chronicle of bloodshed, including the slaughter of entire populations, lies at the door of those who were genuinely sincere in their beliefs and who truly believed that their motives were noble. It is plain, then, that *motive and sincerity are not enough.* Like other forces and qualities that can be used for good or bad, they benefit humanity only when they are attended by a profound regard for the life and rights of others.

723 The Curse of Envy

1. One of the saddest traits a person can possess is *envy*—the jealousy and resentment, usually with ill will, at seeing another's advantages, superiority, or success.

2. The pettiness of character revealed by envy is generally noted with regard to material things—mainly money and the things money can buy.

3. Less common, but far more harmful, is the envy of another's ability or spirituality. This type of envy often takes cruel forms, especially towards subordinates. It may express itself in seizing every opportunity to find fault with them, even if none exists; in placing unduly heavy or additional responsibilities on them, with the hope that they will not be satisfactorily fulfilled, and with vexation if they are; in attempts to disparage or humiliate them; and in extreme cases, in dispensing with their services even though it means "cutting off one's nose to spite one's face."

4. The same type of envy, but expressed in different ways, may be observed in some leaders (usually of small organizations) who, behind a facade of humility, have such a consuming desire for adulation bordering on worship that they will go to great lengths to achieve it.

5. These include undermining anyone who is popular, or becoming popular; stopping at nothing to break up incipient friendships that they fear may in some way threaten *their* position on the pedestal they themselves have created and mounted; belittling anyone in their organization who surpasses them in knowledge or wisdom; and attempting to curb anyone else's skill in any sphere in which they themselves express but do not excel.

7.4 Attitudes

6 How wide a gulf are these illustrations from the USB's words:

7 We rejoice when others serve as well, or better. We rejoice when others hold the torch as high, or higher [D13:4].

8 In some cases, envy springs from a sense of insecurity and inferiority, and the refusal to recognize that "a sparrow cannot become an eagle" [767]. But whatever the reason, envy is a trait that impoverishes the possessor. As an Illumined Soul says:

9 To be envious is to be a pauper spiritually, for envy and spirituality cannot dwell together. Spiritual individuals may wish for themselves the same state and circumstances as others, but they will not begrudge others their advantages or wish them ill on that account.

10 No spiritual laurels go to the envious, whatever good they may do, for envy weighs heavily enough on the scales to outweigh any good.

11 The sooner people who harbor envy realize the destructive effects upon *themselves*, the sooner they can rise above it, provided the desire to do so is there.

724 A Note on Sorrow

1 Sorrow can serve us well, if it opens the windows of our being to greater light and understanding. Often it is sorrow, and sorrow alone, that makes us *aware* of ourselves and the many blessings we possess, or that provides us with a glimpse of the Love and Wisdom and Goodness that are God.

2 Robert Hamilton[3] summed up the thought beautifully in eight lines:

3
> I walked a mile with Pleasure;
> She chatted all the way;
> But left me none the wiser
> For all she had to say.

4
> I walked a mile with Sorrow,
> And ne'er a word said she;
> But, oh! the things I learnt from her,
> When Sorrow walked with me.

---

[3] Robert Browning Hamilton, 1880-1974, American lawyer and occasional poet, wrote this poem, *Along the Road*, in 1913.

725 Slavery to Empty Things

1 Among the saddest forms of slavery is the voluntary slavery of the mind to what is trivial and pointless and time wasting.

2 Examples are the custom of immediately and blindly following every whim of "fashion"—a "fashion" often introduced by "authorities" with "reputation" but little sense of the beautiful. Or frequenting a restaurant only if it is "in," regardless of whether or not the food is good and the atmosphere pleasant. Or striving to visit places which *this* set or *that* set patronizes at the moment.

3 Behind almost every instance of such voluntary slavery lies snobbery, and an inner sense of insecurity, immaturity, and incompleteness. The mature, especially the spiritually mature, do not waste their time and substance on such trivialities and weaknesses. Nor, of course, do they condemn those who do; instead, they feel compassion for those whose life is bounded by inconsequential things, who find much worth and set great store by what is empty.

4 Those *born* in slavery have an excuse for being a slave; those who voluntarily accept it, none.

726 An Incident—and Some Questions

1 A collector of priceless books, in a fit of rage against the person from whom he had acquired them, consigned the precious volumes to the flames.

2 *Whose* was the loss? Was it a mature or a childish mentality that inspired the act of destruction? Was the collector worthy to possess the precious volumes in the first place? *Which* had he esteemed more—the volumes themselves, or the personality of the previous owner?

3 To worship the personality of an individual is to blind oneself to the value or lack of value of what the individual presents [513]. We should respect the bearer of a message, we should respect a teacher, but the message and the teachings should stand on their own merits, not on who expresses them.

4 Gems of truth are more important than those who present them. But those who present them are important, too; and each person who recognizes the jewels for what they are, and shares them in turn with others, also plays a valuable role in the scheme of things.

727 Some Reflections about Fear

1. A certain chain letter does not ask the recipient to send money to anyone. But after describing windfalls that it states were received by some people on the chain letter list, it relates dire consequences, in some instances sudden death, to those who it asserts did not, in turn, make and distribute copies of the letter within a few days.

2. We disapprove of such communications, especially when a threat, however veiled, is included; and we emphasize that it is not to anyone's good, *spiritually*, to be associated in any way with any such threat to another human being.

3. Fear itself often invites disaster. There are many recorded instances of individuals who, doomed to death by a council of fellow tribesmen, retired to their hut to perish from fright. Any "old wives' tale" handed down from generation to generation, with each generation enlarging and embellishing the tale, in time acquires power, effective power, over those who accept it.

4. There are many superstitions that some people cling to for fear of what might happen if they ignored them. Some say that little is lost by observing superstitions, or by bowing to a threat as the one in the chain letter discussed; but they are wrong. Strength of character and mind is lost. One purpose of our existence on earth is to improve our character and expand our mind, let us never forget; and the more superstitious we are, the more we fail in those respects.

5. We would add this. Not all fear is harmful; fear is sometimes actually helpful. It is true that in many cases fear robs one of reason, or creates panic, or paralyzes one into yielding without a struggle. In other instances, however, fear inspires us to prudence, or lends us wings, or gives us incredible strength, at the very moment when prudence, speed, or strength is needed.

6. Fear has two hands, two weapons to employ:
One to preserve, the other to destroy.

7. Fear—and we use the word in its main meaning of a distressing emotion aroused by real or imagined impending danger of disaster, pain, disapproval, or other undesired things—may indeed be unhealthy or healthy, depending on what inspires it.

8. It is a *healthy* emotion if it serves to protect or preserve. Those who fear poverty will tend to be provident instead of wasteful. Those who fear automobile accidents will tend to drive defensively, making ample allowance for possible errors and incompetence of other drivers. Those

who fear robbery will usually bolt the door against intruders. Those who fear heat exhaustion will usually not overdo a stay in the sun. Those nations that fear attack by others that have oppressed or gobbled up their neighbors will arm themselves and be prepared for any eventuality—if they are determined to preserve their freedom at all costs.

9 Despite what some psychologists and psychiatrists discourse about a so-called "death instinct" or "death wish" that they claim people unconsciously possess, deep within almost every individual is an intense if often unrecognized instinct or desire for *self preservation*—and a healthy fear is its most powerful ally. Few are born with any consciousness of fear; and as a rule fear is not innate but acquired or developed, usually as a result of experiences, warnings, or threats. A healthy fear may be acquired without personal suffering if one is old enough or wise enough to learn from the experiences of others, but more often than not it is learned from personal experience.

10 The toddler who reaches out and pushes or strikes a bigger child and is pushed or struck in return, quickly learns to fear hitting others indiscriminately. A newly born kitten may frolic happily and safely with a puppy in the same household, but it soon learns that dogs in general are not its friends, and only an acquired healthy fear of them will keep it out of their reach. The electrician who experiences an electric shock will usually disconnect the power supply in future.

11 People sooner or later learn that almost anything can be used constructively or destructively. The elements that provide light and heat and nourishment can destroy as well as sustain, and are to be feared unless understood and controlled. Those who fear the ravages of swollen streams and rivers will build levees and dams. Those who fear earthquakes will erect structures that are strong enough to resist earth movements, especially in villages and towns and cities situated on a fault. Those who fear the holocaust of fire will usually create a fire prevention program and a skilled and mobile fire fighting force.

12 A healthy fear is plainly the first step to security.

13 *Unhealthy* fear, on the other hand, is often the first step to slavery, mental or physical. And worse than slavery itself is its effect on the character of those who make no effort to resist it.

14 There are millions of souls who no longer accept most of the principles of an organization they belong to, but who for one reason or another fear to leave it. The organization is recognized, it has long existed, it may at one time have served a good purpose for many (and may still do so for some), and it is "genteel" and "respectable"; and it takes courage

7.4 Attitudes

to break away from it and, incidentally, reduce its power to perpetuate error.

15 One of the most common fears is the fear of disapproval—the fear of what people will say. It is a crippling emotion that prevents too many from living according to their highest standards, and that overwhelms many into hypocrisy. What is puzzling is that anyone who is aware of Survival [of death of the earthly or physical body] and other truths should fear the disapproval of others; but many do. Of course they should not flaunt or impose their views, if unwelcome, upon others, or needlessly offend the sensibilities of others; that would be uncivil and unkind. To refuse to sacrifice ideals on the altar of public opinion is, however, an entirely different matter.

16 An inspirer has said:

17 On earth, knowledge can reduce fear, or end fear. And yet—some knowledge will give rise to *greater* fear. The knowledge that enabled human beings to split the atom unleashed power that can be and is being used for good, but it can also wreak immense devastation and loss of life—something devoutly to be feared and avoided. And as scientists understand more and more about chain reactions, they become more and more fearful of the effects of any misuse of chemicals that are available to humanity.

18 So knowledge can *dispel* fear on one hand, and create *greater* fear on the other.

19 No one is immune from fear. There are some who say: "I have no fear. I fear nothing!" But if, for instance, they were unarmed and face to face with a ferocious beast in the jungle, they would experience fear as they realized they were no match for that expression of life.

20 Fear is present in the spirit world also—to those who have not rid themselves of errors in thinking. Some fear that they may not be invited to sit "at the right hand of the throne of God." Some fear that they will meet those they have wronged; some *will*. Some who dwell in darkness and gloom because of the earthly lives they led, fear that they may never walk in light. Some who have not learned of Survival fear that they are in the wrong body, especially if they find themselves free from pain or illness that was theirs before they passed on to spirit life. Only knowledge can free them from such fears.

21 Some other observations about fear:

22 — We fear the unknown far more than we fear the known.

23   — Most things that we fear do not come to pass.

24   — To fear something or someone is in a sense to be in bondage to that thing or person.

25   — It is better to *fear* to do wrong, than to *do* wrong; it is still better to do *right*.

728 Disappointments and Disillusionments—and the Secret

1   Life not infrequently brings disappointment and disillusionment—in things, in people, in events.

2   Those we trust, may fail us. Those whose support we expect, may oppose us. What we have taken years to build, may topple in an instant. Whichever way we turn, a wall may face us. Strive though we do, we may make no progress. We may be misunderstood, hated, vilified, or slandered.

3   If disappointment and disillusionment flood us from time to time, let us not reproach ourselves. Living in this world, how can we escape such emotions?

4   Even great souls, who remain human despite the spiritual heights they have attained, at times know disillusionment and disappointment in some of us from whom they hope so much. And if they, with their far vaster wisdom and enlightenment, and their greater perspective of life, can be touched by such feelings, much *more* so can we.

5   We can do what *they* do at such moments. We can send out love, where there is hate. We can pray for light, where there is darkness. We can be tolerant, even of the intolerant. Most important of all, we can reject all feelings of revenge and bitterness and every other unspiritual emotion.

6   It may be difficult to resist the impulse to meet hate with hate, bitterness with bitterness, unkindness with unkindness; but it *can* be done.

7   *Resist* the impulse, and with every stand
         The impulse is the easier to command.

8   As we have said elsewhere: It may be hard to be patient with those who are consumed with envy and jealousy, or who lie and vilify and slander. But if we are patient with the blind and the lame, and others who are physically afflicted, surely we should be patient with those who are spiritually afflicted—for spiritual ills are far greater than physical ills, and have far greater consequences.

7.4 Attitudes

729 To Thine Own SOUL Be True...

1. Among the loveliest lines in the English language are these from the Bard[4]:

2. > To thine own self be true;
> And it must follow, as the night the day,
> Thou canst not then be false to any man.

3. With the change of three letters in one word, we could unreservedly embrace this thought.

4. An individual's self—*the real self*—at any precise moment is composed of all that one *is* at that moment; and not everyone's self is at *all* times altogether admirable.

5. Deceit and unscrupulousness are only two of many unwholesome qualities that not only poison the self, but could become *part* of the self. Individuals, then, whose selves include such qualities, would be true to *themselves* in expressing those qualities, but at the same time unquestionably false to others.

6. However, if we replace *self* with *soul*—with soul as the USB defines it: "the spark of divine in human beings, their portion of divinity" [601:2] —we can see the lines in a new and more beautiful and magnificent light:

7. > To thine own *soul* be true;
> And it must follow, as the night the day,
> Thou canst not then be false to any man.

730 Some Thoughts of Inspirers on Beauty

1. Love and beauty go hand in hand. Beauty is an expression of love. Love is an inspiration for beauty.

2. On springtime: At this time of the year especially, when nature has reawakened and is in bloom, expressing that certain beauty that only nature can portray, let us remember that all of us, endowed as each of us *is* with a spark of divinity, can also portray beauty in *our* very own way, in *our* very own fashion.

3. A thought of beauty is a jewel rare, a jewel to be treasured, and a jewel to be *displayed*. Only when a jewel *is* displayed can its rays be observed.

---

[4] William Shakespeare, 1564–1616, English playwright and poet; in *Hamlet*, circa 1601, Act I, Scene iii, as spoken by Polonius.

CHAPTER 7 **Personal Responsibility and Behavior**

731 A Little about Pride

1. Is pride a sin? Or is pride a virtue?

2. The answer to both questions is "Yes," depending on the *kind* of pride. For there is pride, and there is pride, and they bear little resemblance to each other.

3. If by pride we mean excessive self-esteem; or exaggerated satisfaction in what one thinks are one's own accomplishments; or conceit over real or imagined superiority of abilities and talents; or glory in prestige and power and position and possessions—then indeed pride is a *sin*. Then it is the pride that "goeth before destruction."

4. But if by pride we mean a proper sense of one's own dignity and worth and self-respect; or a delight in the accomplishments of *others;* or a reluctance to act below one's capabilities and standards; or a refusal to take part in anything one considers base and unworthy—then indeed is pride a *virtue*.

5. One pride is material, the other spiritual. The difference between them is vast, for one is destructive, the other constructive. As an Illumined Soul puts it:

6. Pride is a double-edged sword. It can uplift, and it can destroy.

7. Pride can bring hope; it can bring despair. It can raise one to the mountain top; it can grind one into the dust. It all depends on the *nature* of the pride.

8. Honest pride in work well done is wholesome, and an incentive for continued excellence.

9. Those who serve for the joy of serving, and not in the hope of reward or recognition, may justly exhibit pride in what they do, if they recognize the part others play in what is done. In other words, if they are humble and realize that *one accomplishes nothing of worth by oneself* (with *worth* defined as something of great use or good to a large number of people.) For there are truly many, usually unseen and unknown, who join their efforts with ours. There are truly many, usually serving silently in the vineyard, who encourage us to develop one facet or another of our being, and who inspire us to greater heights.

10. To demand recognition for oneself is a sign of immaturity. To accord recognition to others, is a sign of maturity.

11. The pride in what an individual does alone (as he or she thinks) is poles apart from the pride in what one does along with others. To have pride, for instance, in what one might mistakenly think are one's own

7.4 Attitudes

accomplishments for the USB, would not be good. However, to have pride in being a part of the USB movement, joined with others on both sides of life who have done, and are doing, so much to bring love, peace, and understanding to humankind, is something altogether different. *This* pride can be a source of strength. *This* pride can be a source of happiness. For there *is* strength and happiness in the knowledge that, however small one's own efforts may appear, one is a link in a spiritual chain forged between heaven and earth, a link in the movement that will bring about a comparative heaven on earth within the lifetime of many now living here.

732 The Curse of Self-Pity

1. Some people are so deeply immersed in self-pity that they consciously or unconsciously resent anyone who is happy. Most of them enjoy being miserable, and for that reason usually prefer the company of others in the same mold, especially those they can outdo in lamentation, and outvie in aches and pains, real or imagined.

2. Self-pity often creates the delusion that *few* can have borne so much. *Few* can have experienced such an excruciating toothache, or miserable cold, or distressing illness, or known such sorrow or loss or disillusionment. *Few* can have suffered such adversities. *Few* can have been so abused by "fate."

3. Those steeped in self-pity often have a tremendous appetite for commiseration, but little relish for attempts to cheer them or to persuade them to look at the bright side of things, particularly the advantages they may possess. They prefer to dwell on their "misfortunes," and to "count their ills (actual or fancied) and not their blessings."

4. What a contrast they present to the many who uncomplainingly and courageously accept burdens and illnesses that cannot be corrected, and who seldom let slip any sign of the pain or discomfort they suffer, even when they know or suspect that it heralds a major bend in the road [1316]. Admirably bearing ills that are well nigh unendurable, they are more articulate about the suffering of *others* than of their own; and they try, in their own way and fashion, to ease the burdens others bear.

5. Such individuals are among the real heroes on earth. *They* are among those who merit and will receive spiritual jewels of great beauty when they pass on—though they may not be aware that life continues, and that no act or action goes unweighed.

733 The Secret of Contentment

1. It is too common to confuse *desires* with *needs*. Or to think that the more people amass of the things of the world, the greater will be their happiness; some *do* find happiness in them. But the individual who strives full time to acquire far more material possessions than he or she will ever need, frequently becomes a slave to them, instead of their master. For such a person, more possessions lead to more desire, and rare satisfaction; and often the things cherished become as dust and ashes in one's mouth.

2. How much better to realize the truth an Illumined Inspirer of the USB so well expresses: "To have *simple* wants is the secret of contentment." By contentment we of course mean the peaceful kind of happiness one can possess even though not every wish is gratified.

3. A place to live in, however humble; loving companionship; a few friends; enough for simple needs; time to read and discuss and reflect; counting our blessings from time to time, lest we take them for granted; and gratitude for the gift of life, particularly for the spark of God within us—what *more* does one need for contentment!

4. To desire always *more* of the things of earth, is pointless; it only lessens the joy in what we do have. To ever travel in search of what can be found only within, is fruitless; yet too many do so.

5. Only the *tranquil* water can perfectly reflect the sky. Only the *open* vessel can be filled with wine. Only the *quiet* mind, shutting out the blare and distractions of much of today's "living," can clearly hear the still small voice within.

6. We ourselves must conclude what is essential or unessential for us. As a Blessed Soul puts it:

7. > Just as individuals must decide what the moderate path is for *them,* so must they distinguish between their needs and desires —between what is vital to them, and what is *added* to what is vital to them.

8. Of course contentment should not mean inactivity. It should not mean indifference to the welfare of others. It should not mean disregard for what is right and just. It should not mean refusal to take a stand. It should not mean unwillingness to assume a proper share of the responsibilities of society. And it should not mean lack of endeavor in making desires a reality—provided the desires are noble ones.

7.5 BEHAVIOR

734 *The Center Path—the Path of Moderation*

1. The Brother&Sisterhood preaches no doctrine of fear, no doctrine of calamity, no doctrine of panic.

2. On the other hand, we do not close our eyes to the evils that exist. We do not imagine that we can correct or remove them merely by ignoring them. We know that *the first step to curing a condition is to recognize it for what it is.*

3. We walk the center path, straying neither to the right nor to the left. *Always* the center path—the path of moderation, moderation in all things.

4. We know that there are evils in the world. We know that there is ignorance, which is the great sin. But we also know that the world in general is a good and beautiful place to *live in*, a splendid place to *express in*, a wonderful place to *evolve in*, if we make the most of all that comes our way, good and bad alike.

5. We know that we are the product of all that we have been; that our level of consciousness is one that we have made and earned for ourselves; and that all that comes our way gives us a magnificent opportunity to raise that level. We can indeed change our level of consciousness—if the desire within us is great enough, if our prayer is sincere enough, and if we make the effort in the things that are at hand.

6. We do *not* preach continence, or asceticism, or abstinence, or fasting. *We preach the moderate path.* The physical body *does* have its needs, and these needs should be met if it is to be as fit a vessel as possible for the spark of divinity it houses while we inhabit it.

7. No one becomes saintlier by neglecting our physical needs. No one becomes saintlier by abstaining from what is natural and normal. No one becomes saintlier by living in a cave or monastery or ivory tower. No one becomes saintlier by self-mortification or rigorous denial of the normal pleasures of life. No one becomes saintlier by fasting, regardless of the volumes written and said in its favor. Gautama Siddhartha himself, he whom millions call the Buddha, fasted until he became a mere skeleton, so weak that he could not take more than a few steps without falling—to realize then that fasting brings *no* superior insight or knowledge. He came to recognize and to teach the wisdom of "the middle path of moderation."

8. Of course no one becomes saintlier by overindulgence, either. *The extremes are equally unsound.* But the path of moderation, while it will

not in itself make anyone saintlier, will tend to keep the body in good health, and the mind clear and strong, so that one is better equipped to do, say, and think what is good and godly.

9   There are other important points to bear in mind. An Illumined Soul points out:

10   When we speak of the path of moderation, we recognize that all individuals must decide for *themselves* just what is moderate for *them*. What is moderate for *one* might not be moderate for another.

11   We recognize, too, that the path of moderation changes as the *individual* changes. What was a moderate path for a *youngster*, would not be a moderate path after becoming an *adult*. And what would be one's moderate path in *one* walk of life, would not necessarily be one's moderate path in *another* walk of life.

12   We do not expect the moderate path an individual treads to remain the same path indefinitely.

13   The *seeker* of Truth and the *bearer* of Truth should be particularly careful to walk the moderate pathway. Too many seekers, in their eagerness, are like a sponge or a piece of blotting paper, lapping up everything from all available sources. Much that comes from those sources is quite contradictory. Much is quite inaccurate. As a result, many seekers become highly confused, and some of them abandon the quest.

14   It is better for seekers of Truth to absorb knowledge a little at a time, and only after weighing it and finding it not wanting. When *one* little bit of knowledge has been thoroughly assimilated, then and only then is it time to digest *another* morsel.

15   The bearer of Truth should be careful not to share too much at any one time. For in this regard each of us can be likened to a pipe; and a pipe can carry only so much as its diameter permits. If, in trying to share too much truth with others, we choke the mouth of the pipe, little if anything will pass into it.

16   Some of those who are now on earth to help bring light to humanity are among those who must learn the importance of moderation in all things. They know that there is much to do, and little time to do it; and in their desire to waste not even a moment, they sometimes overtax their physical [earthly] bodies. The penalty is a period of fallowness, or a period of enforced rest. For The Law of Moderation—and it *is* a Law—cannot be broken with impunity by anyone, regardless of motive.

7.5 Behavior

735 Rage and the Individual

1. Rage, which is unrestrained or violent anger, is a costly emotion, regardless of the pleasure some derive at the time from ranting and raving. Rage has no place—it *cannot* have a place—within a highly spiritual being, and it should for many reasons strictly be avoided. Rage robs one of judgement, often when judgement is needed most. It is difficult enough for an angry person to reason; for one in a rage, it is well nigh impossible. So it is wise to make no decision of importance during anger or rage, but to "sleep on it."

2. The *thoughts* of anyone in a rage cannot be uplifting. As for the *actions* of anyone in a rage, they often seem to reflect, and sometimes in fact *do* reflect, a completely alien personality. This is not surprising; for during rage an individual is much more easily impressed or possessed by undesirable beings, in or out of the physical, who would injure or destroy. In some cases that is why people have little recollection of acts and actions committed during rage.

3. Rage borders on insanity, which it sometimes becomes. Whatever its effects on anyone else, it is always harmful to those who express or harbor it; and when it cannot be vented upon others, it sometimes drives its possessors to self-destruction.

736 Slow to Decide, Then Quick to Act—a Worthwhile Philosophy In Most Cases

1. One cause for concern in the world today is the *reluctance* of many individuals and nations to act when action is needed. Instead of grasping the nettle firmly, they lose valuable time hesitating, hoping against hope that by some miracle the nettle will disappear.

2. Another cause for concern is the *eagerness* of other individuals and nations to rush into action, with little or no thought of the likely consequences to themselves or others.

3. Both extremes are equally unsound. When committed by those in positions of power, the results may be catastrophic.

4. Except when instant decisions are imperative, *the wise are slow to decide, then quick to act*. Once they reach a conclusion after due and thorough reflection, they act with as little delay as possible.

737 On Counting Our Blessings—and Being Grateful

1. There are millions of people who set aside one day a year for "thanksgiving." Usually it is the only day in the 365 or 366 in which some of us give *any* thought to our blessings, if we do so then; for to many people it is just another occasion for feasting, drinking, and boisterousness.

2. Partly due to acquiring too many things too easily, and partly due to insufficient knowledge of history, such people have come to consider the bounty of nature and the comforts of their environment as things *deserved*, rather than as things which one should be thankful one can *earn*.

3. More of us would count our blessings and give thanks for them, even as we strive for a more abundant life, if we had to *work* for the things we desire, and if we learned something of the appalling conditions of the multitude, women especially, little more than a hundred years ago.

4. "Gratitude is the least of virtues, ingratitude the worst of vices," goes the old saying. Gratitude should be as natural and easy as breathing, but it is rare. And too many of us unwisely dwell only on what we lack or think we lack, and not on what we have: It is not an ingredient for happiness or contentment.

5. Not all days can be as perfect as one might desire; nor would it be well and good if they were. But every day, every hour, every moment, can be one of thanks for the many blessings that are ours, particularly *the blessing of life as a human being*. That priceless gift provides avenues of expression and opportunities to change our lot if we are willing and anxious to do so and to take what steps we can in that direction.

6. Says an Illumined Soul:

7. > As we act, so do we help our dreams to become realities. The mere dream is not enough. But when we aspire and also make the *effort*, it is amazing how often a helping hand, visible or invisible, is extended.

8. We have a right to express in dignity as a human being. We have a right to opportunities to sustain ourselves and our family. But we have *no* right to expect luxuries at the expense of others. We have *no* right to expect others to present us with what we can, with effort, ourselves obtain.

9. As for giving thanks, it is surprising how many "successful" people attribute their success to themselves alone, little aware of the individuals, usually unseen and unknown to them, who augmented their endeavors.

7.5 Behavior

Some *do* express thanks for what they have acquired, but neglect the opportunity it provides to help deserving ones who cannot sustain themselves by their own efforts.

10 *Those who love and would serve God, love and serve God's children.* They can best show their gratitude to God not by endless recitals of God's worth, but by befriending those in need, offering a hand when others find the road too long or the load too heavy—always with the purpose of helping them to help themselves.

11 Truly grateful people are usually spiritual people, ever ready to serve others and to share what they have, however little, with those less fortunate than themselves. Consciously or unconsciously, they know that every day is a day of opportunity to serve someone, somewhere, in some way.

12 They do not waste time pining for what is not, but gratefully remember what *is*.

13 They meet misfortunes well, correcting what they can correct, and accepting the rest courageously.

14 They are on the path to a spiritual mountaintop, whether they know it or not, and whether they know of its existence or not.

738 Ingratitude and Ignorance

1 There are those who find little complimentary to say about the land they live in, even when it provides them with glorious opportunities not found elsewhere, or certainly not in such profusion.

2 To such souls everything foreign is much more desirable no matter how inferior it may actually be.

3 Such thinking reminds us of Gilbert's

4
> …idiot who praises with enthusiastic tone
> All centuries but this, and every country but his own.[5]

739 Quotations by USB Inspirers

1 Oysters provide a lesson worth remembering. Pearls are formed not from irritation, but from efforts to control it. The more successful the efforts, the lovelier the pearl.

2 People build shelters. Against what? —the minds of people!

---

[5] *The Mikado*, 1885, by Sir William Schwenck Gilbert, 1836–1911, English dramatist and librettist.

740 The Importance of a Cheerful Countenance

1. We point out more than once that we affect all we meet, and are affected by all we meet, in one way or another, in one degree or another, and for one period of time or another. And as one's countenance can be remarkably expressive, it can leave a distinct impression on almost all who see it.

2. Apart from those who revel in self-pity, who among us does not find life brighter on meeting someone with a cheerful countenance? Who among us does not find a sunny smile contagious? Who among us does not find good reason to be with those who radiate sunshine even on the gloomiest day?

3. One's features can be transformed by a cheerful countenance, which affects not only those who behold it, but the one who possesses it; and, if genuine, the more habitual the cheerful countenance, the more pronounced and prolonged is its effect on the owner.

4. Just as the cheerful countenance usually elicits a striking response from others, so does the sour one, although the latter provokes quite a different reaction. In some fields, especially those concerned with the displaying or serving of food, the chemical changes wrought within those who view a sour exterior can result in discomfort, and occasionally actual harm, to those who eat at that time—a fact that has not received enough attention by those who cater to the public.

5. An inspirer says to us:

6. > It is much easier to smile than to frown. It takes *little* energy to be happy. We have only to look about us to be inspired by the glory God has provided, partly obscured though that glory may be as the result of human foolishness and ignorance.

7. > Those who understand something about The Laws That Govern, and *live* according to that understanding, cannot help being happier. For when people have a realization of what *is*, and what awaits them, how can they help but rejoice. How can they help but sing songs of joy. How can they help but wish for their sisters and brothers the *same* knowledge, the *same* understanding, and the *same* exaltation.

741 On Regrets

1   Regrets are usually quite useless. They are only useful if they keep us from repeating the mistakes that caused them.

2   We can never undo what is past. As the *Rubáiyát* of Omar Khayyám[6] so eloquently puts it:

3
> The moving finger writes; and, having writ,
> Moves on: nor all your piety nor wit
> Shall lure it back to cancel half a line,
> Nor all your tears wash out a word of it.

4   But while we cannot erase the past, we can learn from it: *To the apt pupil, experience is a good teacher.* And as we stress, the wise learn not only from their own experience, but from the experience of others [860]. We can profit from it if we *wish* to, and if we *know* or are *shown* how to do so.

742 On Denying a Condition

1   We should not make the mistake so many commit of *denying* a condition —whether it is a cold, or a serious disease, or anything else unpleasant. We need not accept a disagreeable condition that can be cured or avoided, but we should *recognize* it, and, by the very act of recognition, refrain from sowing the seeds of illusion, which is the enemy of Truth, and which seldom benefits anyone.

2   It is like a puddle in the street, or a pit in the road. If we recognize them for what they are, we can perhaps avoid them; and if we cannot avoid them, we can at least try to find a way of *bridging* them—something we are not likely to attempt if we deny their existence.

3   It is one thing to *recognize* a condition; it is another to *accept* it.

---

[6] *Rubáiyát,* by Omar Khayyám, c1022–c1122, Persian poet, philosopher, mathematician, and scientist; from the fourth version (1879) of rendering in English verses by Edward FitzGerald (born Edward Purcell), 1809–1883, English poet.

743 "Faith" and Material Commitments

1. Some schools of thought advise their members to have "faith"—enough faith to make definite material commitments and assume that the means will be provided.

2. At first glance, this might seem to be a noble and beautiful thought. But it is not, and we cannot endorse such advice.

3. To make financial commitments when one cannot foresee how they will be met, is foolhardy at best. At worst, it is cruelly unfair to those who would suffer if commitments to *them* were not fulfilled.

4. To build, mentally, is good. To visualize the finished work, and then take every possible concrete step to transform the picture into actuality, is also good. But it is not good to expect what is vital to appear out of the blue and turn dreams into reality. It is a matter not of faith, but of common sense and fairness to others.

5. People with integrity will make no commitments or promises until and unless they know that they can keep them, barring unforeseen events beyond their control.

6. A community or nation would do well to insist that this same principle be embraced by those it elects to office. As a first step, it could require that no measure or proposal be considered that does not spell out precisely *how* or from what source any needed funds would be obtained.

744 On Certain Injunctions

1. Many of the words attributed to great teachers of the past are words they could not possibly have spoken, enlightened as they were, but words ascribed to them by others for one purpose or another—often to allay unrest and dissatisfaction of the multitude with conditions of the times.

2. Among such *ascribed* teachings are the injunctions to resist not evil but to turn the other cheek and to forgive "until seventy times seven" the sins committed against us.

3. In our opinion, in this day and age one would be less than wise to live by these injunctions. And if we imagine we gain in spirituality by meekly submitting to attack or repeated wrongs, we need wise counsel. So do the aggressors, regardless of whether their victims enjoy being abused or passively suffer it. *Neither* side grows in stature in such circumstances; in fact *both* lose ground spiritually.

7.5 Behavior □ 744

4   We have emphasized that while we can *overlook* wrongs [or cease to hold them against another], it is not in our power, or anyone else's, to forgive anyone (in the meaning of cancelling a debt) [1415, 1416].

5   As for not resisting evil, the record shows that evil waxes fatter and more powerful the longer it is unopposed. And if there is *one* lesson history teaches, the USB affirms, it is the folly of appeasement.

6   To those who accept the turn-the-other-cheek injunction in either its literal or metaphorical sense, we put the following questions.

7   — If a man broke *one* of your arms, would you invite him to break the *other?*

8   — If a woman swindled you of half your possessions, would you offer her the rest?

9   — If a man harmed *one* of your children, would you invite him to harm the *rest?*

10   — If someone violently attacked your spouse, would you stand by quietly?

11   We consistently maintain the importance of *reason*, which should be exercised about *all* things, including the actual or ascribed injunctions of *anyone*.

12   A few who discuss "turning the other cheek," mention the *fight or flight* philosophy, and recommend *flight*.

13   Circumstances alter cases, of course, and discretion is indeed often the better part of valor, with flight frequently the wise course to adopt. In many instances, however, flight is cowardly, and it is then a sign of spiritual weakness rather than spiritual strength. To cowardly endure what is wrong or run away from it is not a sign of spirituality; nor is it meeting problems that, well met, enable one to grow in stature spiritually.

14   In any event, the range of choices is better expressed by *fight, flight, or surrender;* and surrender is unfortunately recommended by too many of the "friends" as well as the enemies of freedom [853].

15   Rather than either the "fight or flight" or "fight, flight, or surrender" philosophies, we much prefer the wisdom of an Illumined Soul's counsel, which we quote more than once:

16   Correct what *can* be corrected. Accept *all* else gracefully, graciously, gratefully, and courageously.

17   *There* is a design for living!

745 Sports and Sporting Behavior

1. Competitive sports have been praised for many decades as a valuable means of promoting good sporting behavior—fairness, courtesy, good temper, and the ability to lose gracefully—qualities desirable in anyone. The important thing, we at one time heard over and over again, is not victory itself, but the *way* the game is played.

2. Those who truly hold that view must lament the unsporting behavior displayed more and more frequently by promoters, players, and spectators alike. In too many instances it is plain that all that matters is victory, by fair means or foul.

3. Too many players are loud, insulting, and quarrelsome towards opposing players and umpires. Many fans are intensely partisan, booing every decision against the team they happen to be favoring. In a number of cases scores of people have been killed or injured as the result of rioting following a so-called "game" or sporting event.

4. Commercialism and widespread betting on sports are undoubtedly at least partly to blame. Lack of courtesy and good manners is another cause. But the roots of the problem go far deeper.

5. The fact is that a thoroughly deplorable state of affairs exists in many lands, where vice and corruption have a stranglehold on several sports that have become "big business." With one thought uppermost in their mind—money—the criminals who reign in those fields have no compunction about using bribery, blackmail, and corruption, to control promoters and players in their toils. Those criminals often will stop at nothing, not even murder, to attain their ends.

6. Several fields of "sport" are notably lacking in moral leadership—leadership of powerful individuals of unimpeachable repute who could clean house if they were so minded and united in purpose. Only when this moral leadership is successfully displayed, and players completely respect their sponsors, will sports in general ever become a fit field in which to earn a living.

7. Even tennis, once a model of fairness and courtesy and good behavior, is now sometimes the scene of unpardonable and even ugly conduct.

8. The situation cries for correction.

9. What each of us can meanwhile do, at least in our own groups, and especially with the young, is to emphasize a new set of values, or a return to the old set of values in which sporting behavior is a worthy end in itself, far more worthy than victory over another could possibly be.

10. We should stress that the way a game is played *does* matter; that the greatest victory we can accomplish is not mastery over others, but mastery

7.6 Right Living

11   of *self;* and that our great aim should not be the plaudits of the throng, but nobility of character.

11   We should emphasize, too, something that is still too seldom realized and accepted—that as we sow, so do we reap, sooner or later, here or hereafter, with not one thought or word or act failing to bring its inevitable effect. That is The Law.

12   It is not only in professional sports, but in amateur sports too, that more and more emphasis is placed on winning. It is a deplorable trend that should be reversed; but the reversal is not encouraged by "educators" who also stress the unedifying winning-is-everything doctrine.

13   Worth remembering is a quatrain by Grantland Rice,[7] a noted sports writer of the earlier 1900s:

14

> For when the One Great Scorer comes
> To mark against your name,
> He writes—not that you won or lost—
> But how you played the Game.

7.6 RIGHT LIVING

746 On Material Possessions

1   It is the custom in some circles to pooh-pooh money and other material possessions of value.

2   To consider them an end in themselves, or the be-all-and-end-all of existence, is of course foolish and ignorant and little sign of spirituality. But to place *no* value on them, and go about cup in hand seeking alms, *also* is little sign of spirituality—even if the alms-seeking is accompanied by singing or affirmations or chants of one kind or another.

3   "One's worth or importance is not in what one *has*, but in what one *is*," says a Brother. He is right.

4   But there is another side to the coin, a side that should not be overlooked. An Illumined Soul points out:

---

[7] Grantland Rice, 1880–1954, American sportswriter, columnist, author, poet, and film producer, who believed that good sporting behavior was capable of lifting individuals, societies, and even nations to remarkable heights of moral and social action. This quatrain is excerpted from his 1908 poem, *Alumnus Football*.

5   What one *has* sometimes helps to pave the way to what one *is*. More important still, it can help to pave the way to what one can be.

6   Without a violin, a material possession, violinists could not maintain or improve their mastery of that instrument, or evoke strains to soothe or stir the heart and mind. Violinists *need* a violin if they are to *be* what they *can* be in their field.

7   Without the printed page, a material thing—and thank heavens, we say, for the printed page—the minds of many truly great souls would be closed to us. We could expand our consciousness somewhat by personally observing our fellow human beings and the growing things in nature, but not to the degree we can from volumes of history and philosophy, whether or not we completely agree with their contents.

8   Without such things as textbooks, and test tubes, and chemicals, and blackboards, and paper and pencils—all material things—many *more* people would languish in ignorance, lacking the basic tools to greater skills and greater knowledge.

9   Without food, a material thing, many more millions of people would be starving. And it is *not* easy for the hungry to think of spiritual things, or in fact of much of anything but something to eat. Spirituality does not particularly thrive in poverty, asceticism, or austerity: It is at least as easy to be spiritual in a comfortable home as in a cave or hovel.

10   We could give many other examples.

11   The fact is that material possessions of importance, including money, can be of *immense* value for *good*.

12   Those who express contempt for material possessions, but depend on others to supply them with what they need or want, including sustenance and shelter, and sometimes even luxuries, are less than mature spiritually.

13   As for those "spiritual advisers" who dwell on a plateau remote from worldly matters and feel they are *above* exerting themselves to provide for *their* material needs, we can say this: They who do not at least try to avoid being a responsibility or burden to others, fail one of earth's major tests, and share no lofty rung of the spiritual ladder.

14   The Illumined Soul reminds us:

15   *Moderation* is a virtue [734]. While it is folly to place too much value on material possessions, it is no less folly to ignore those that are *vital* to your way of life, and of importance in your being what you *are* and in what you *become*.

7.6 Right Living

747 A Little about "Instant" Acquisitions

1. In countries highly advanced technologically, speed plays an ever greater role in the environment. Buildings go up overnight. Continents are spanned in a few hours. Ultramodern equipment cooks food in a few seconds, or in a few minutes at most. Not only is there "instant tea" and "instant coffee," but a wealth of other drinks and foods that are prepared and packaged for almost immediate use when desired.

2. All these things, and many, many others, have had their effect on average people in these countries. Speed becomes a way of life for us except, as a rule, in our daily work. We hurry from home to work, from work to home; and our leisure hours are crammed as we race from one activity to another, except, usually, the activity of *thinking*.

3. With more time for ourselves than our grandfathers ever would have conceived possible, we have less time *for* ourselves.

4. We are so carried away by the pace to which we have become slave instead of master, that we even seek instant knowledge—which in a computerized age is often available.

5. We begin to expect more or less *instant* fulfillment of our desires; so much so, in fact, that we become easy marks for almost anyone and everyone who promises means for rapid achievement of them. We are offered techniques for acquiring power of one sort or another that will in practically no time bring us anything we wish, and that will open new and incredible horizons for us. We are offered formulas for praying that will obtain fantastic results—wealth, success in any field we choose, and all other material things we may crave. We are offered crash courses in health and beauty, and in becoming irresistible to others. We are told that we can, by reciting certain words and phrases, evoke invisibles who will do our bidding. We are offered power to easily erase all past errors. We are offered methods that will, in a flash, bend others to our will. And so on, and so on. *All* the tools and weapons we need, and at only a nominal cost and all designed for practically instant success, with little or no real effort of our *own*.

6. The tragedy is that with all the time this age provides for us, most of us use so little time for contemplation, for quietude, for becoming acquainted with our inner selves, for obtaining a realization of the purposes of existence and the importance of learning any needed lessons of those that can be learned on earth only [1424].

7. With so many material resources at our command, too many of us become blinder than ever to the eternal riches of the spirit and the spiritual

resources that, with effort, are available to us from within ourselves and from others.

8   With all our getting, most of us fail to get wisdom—for no computer will ever be able to furnish what only *a* mind or *minds* can provide. And without wisdom we will rarely discover the secret of contentment, or the value of opening up and developing ourselves spiritually.

9   Many of us will sadly discover one day, sooner or later, here or hereafter, how we have neglected the vast opportunities on earth to advance spiritually. We will learn that lasting values cannot be instantly acquired, however much this may sometimes appear to be the case.

748 Some Reflections about Greed

1   Devoting too much time to acquiring more and more material possessions, some of which may never be used, and all of which must eventually be relinquished, is tragic. Far better instead to use the precious time for seeking wisdom and other treasures of the spirit, which can be owned forever, and which no one else can take away.

2   Greed is revealed in an excessive and extreme desire for something, often for more than one's proper share, or in the desire to have *others* supply what one could provide for oneself.

3   People's material needs vary with geography, with climate, with life styles, and with natural resources. But there are certain fundamental things that everyone should have the *opportunity* to possess: a roof over one's head, enough food and clothing for oneself and one's family, a sound basic education, and the right to work and to live in dignity as a human being.

4   To have enough for one's needs but to still envy those who live in luxury, shows greed, thus compounding one undesirable trait with another.

5   Of course people have every right to obtain as many possessions as they fancy, if they acquire them honestly, and if it does not deprive others from acquiring any.

6   Greed, whether for material possessions or power, is the major cause of inhumanity to others. The world would be a vastly better and happier place if greed was rarer, and if more people realized that "to have *simple* wants is the secret of contentment."

7   Also insufficiently common is living according to one's needs rather than one's desires, with neither greed nor envy in one's heart.

7.6 Right Living 750

8 (Our comments do not of course apply to the emotionally unstable, those unfortunates who starve although their larders are full, or who are so fearful of the future that they amass and hoard much that is never used for either themselves or others.)

749 Employers and Employees

1 In the constant (but what should be unnecessary) tug-of-war between employers and employees, several things are too often overlooked as the pendulum swings from one extreme to the other. The most important is the principle of *personal responsibility*, from which no one, anywhere, at any time, under any circumstances, if *normally* capable of reasoning, is exempt.

2 An Illumined Soul has said:

3 > That responsibility is not only to oneself, but to others. And for relationships between employers and employees to be harmonious and of mutual benefit, each side must fulfil its own obligations, not the least of which is to recognize and respect the role and rights of the other. Both should be fair and considerate.

4 Employers should remember that employees *are* worthy of their hire; employees, to do their best to *be* worthy of it [710]. Employers should pay employees a full day's pay for a full day's work; employees should do a full day's work for a full day's pay. The only exceptions to "a full day's pay for a full day's work" should be when wages are reduced by mutual agreement in special circumstances.

5 In summary, employers and employees should respect one another, be concerned for each other's welfare, and recognize that *both* in their own ways are workers entitled to the fruits of their labor.

750 Some Reflections about Tithing

1 In the mid-1900s we witnessed a great increase in the number of organizations that assert that *tithing*—the giving of a tenth part of one's income or possessions—is a prime and vital part of a person's existence. That in itself may be of little moment. But when it is claimed or implied, as is usually the case, that tithing is required or demanded by *God*, or that

those who advocate and collect tithes *represent* God, then it is a matter for concern.

2   A few facts about tithing are worth reviewing.

3   — While the custom of tithing was supported by the lawgiver Moses, it was not a forced tribute. Only in the priestly code did it become a fixed and expected due.

4   — Tithing is a custom purely created by humans, one established mainly for the benefit of organizations that *presume* to speak for God, and, in their presumption, imagine they are entitled to respect and tribute.

5   — Tithing has almost always been a measure designed to secure a greater hold on the people; and too many comply with the custom only from fear of otherwise incurring displeasure, human or divine. (We shall not dwell on the long and shameful record of oppression, corruption, and cruelty on the part of some organizations in connection with tithing.)

6   — Tithing demands unremitting adherence from those wishing to have "a clear conscience" or wishing to remain in the good graces of organizations that *expect* tithes from them.

7   — Tithing often places the heaviest burden on those who can least afford it, but who in fear or ignorance (or sometimes love) place their *fancied* responsibility to tithe before their very real responsibilities to themselves and their families.

8   — Tithing, often of so-called "first fruits," is frequently made with the expectation of material or spiritual *return;* and in some cases organizations provide the former. But no one can buy a place in the sun spiritually, either for oneself or others, and vain are all gifts of any sort made with the purpose of securing spiritual blessings.

9   It is good when those who are blessed with riches share those riches with the less fortunate. Of course that sharing need not be limited to a tenth part of one's income or possessions, or to any single individual or organization. And when sharing is selfless and *wise,* it benefits those who give and those who receive.

10   The flames of expectation of reward for tithing are kindled and fanned by organizations and individuals who not only suggest or claim that they represent *God,* but proclaim that *God* will repay, many times over,

7.6 Right Living

contributions given to *them* [see D10]. Asking people to "test" or "try" God, they list names or initials of individuals who receive windfalls or other benefits attributed as returns from God for contributions to those "representing" God.

11   Upsetting though this is, still worse is another practice: persuading people to deed over all their possessions, including home and money, under ironclad legal provisions that cannot be successfully contested. Some organizations and individuals even induce others to hand over all their earnings except for a bare pittance. Gullible victims, impressed by what they regard as the power and authority of those they contribute to, often mistakenly believe that they are ensuring spiritual security!

12   Misteachings absorbed in infancy and childhood cause millions of souls to think they can buy "salvation." Only by exercising *reason*, only by realizing that *no one* can escape personal responsibility, only by knowing that *we are our own saviors*—only *then* can people be completely blind and deaf to flattery and persuasion suggesting that they can "pay now" and go to "heaven" later.

13   — As a rule, tithings enable individuals and organizations to go far afield, sometimes even to distant lands, to introduce the same custom to others who are induced to think they can make a "down payment" on the future.

14   — Considering the vast increase in the number and rates of taxes today, and the greater number of necessities of present-day existence compared with the past, tithing now exacts a larger proportion than ever of one's real earnings or income.

15   — If a legal *business* operation promised such handsome dividends for tithing, would it not be accused of fraud?

751 Some Thoughts on Remembrance and Reflection

1   Remembrance of momentous events in a nation's history has a fitting and proper place in the lives of its people, one reason being a truth the USB teaches—that one *can* learn from history and the experiences of others. Too often, however, days originally set aside for remembering and reflecting upon those events, and sometimes also for expressing gratitude for them, have for many people become occasions merely for excessive feasting and drinking and even boisterousness, with no thought to the significance of the events themselves.

751 ◻

2 But there is, or should be, a time for remembrance. There is, or should be, a time for reflection. Certainly it would be well to devote a few minutes of every twenty-four hours to these things. As an Illumined Soul says:

3 *Every* day is a day for reflection, not only to thank for that which is—for all of us have at least one thing to be thankful for—but more important still, to take stock of ourselves and judge whether we have lived up to our highest ideals. To honestly look back on the occurrences and experiences of the day, particularly our responses to them, will help us to resist repeating any unworthy thought or word or deed.

4 *Every* day is a day to remember or reflect about something, or someone. And when we do so, let us hold fast to all that is noble, all that gives us courage and strength to do right, as we see right; to take stands that we know are correct—to take those stands, and to take them well; and to voice, as best we can, what we feel will bring greater light to those who seek it, and what will inspire them with greater understanding of their fellow human beings—their views, their convictions, their stands—not necessarily to agree with them, but to give them the same courtesy we would wish for ourselves.

752 Patriotism

1 Patriotism is devoted love, support, and defense of one's country.[8] It is the very least to be expected from those who are fortunate to live in lands where by and large they have opportunities to make their own way in their own way in their own fashion, where unfailing help is extended to those in need, and where they possess a degree of liberty that is only a

---

[8] In a global world, patriotism today also means loyalty to the wellbeing of all humanity. While nationalism may be on the rise, there is also a new international spirit, a sense of common humanity and common destiny among all peoples. An example of this is the response to global warming and the awareness that all human beings, no matter where they live, must work together to solve this crisis. This new sense of commonality has also been fostered by the rise of instant communications over the Internet and 24-hour news channels, and the emergence of truly global corporations that transcend all national boundaries. All of this now makes a person not only a citizen of a state or nation, but also of the world.

7.6 Right Living

dream to most of humanity: the right to vote by secret ballot,[9] the right to travel about freely, the right to an occupation of one's choice, and the right to freedom of expression within proper bounds.

2 Individuals who take such blessings for granted seldom appreciate them, and rarely feel a sense of obligation to the country or province or city that provides them. They would do well to remember that in many parts of the globe a chair is a luxury, hot water a rarity, food a scarcity, and freedom conspicuous by its absence. If they remembered these things, many more would strive to be upright citizens, with love for their country and a willingness, even an eagerness, to support and defend it.

3 Of course we should not be *jingoistic:* boasting about patriotism and favoring an aggressive, threatening, and warlike foreign policy. But we should be patriotic. We should have pride in a land that offers us much. We should resolve to be worthy of it in every possible way. We should be ready and anxious to protect it from enemies within and without. And not for just one day in a year, or one year in a century, but during every day of every year.

4 Patriotism is the last refuge of a scoundrel, some cynically say, and it may be true in some cases. But patriotism certainly is the first sentiment of a heart full of gratitude for abundant opportunities for a fuller, freer, and nobler life.

753 A Time to Speak, and a Time to Be Silent

1 There is a time to speak, and a time to be silent. When it is time to speak, then silence is a crime.

2 When someone is falsely accused, who is known to be innocent, to be silent is unworthy of a human being; and the more powerful that silent person, the greater is his or her unworthiness.

3 Those who do not raise their voice when they know another is unjustly vilified, those whose lips are sealed when they know the condemned are innocent, and those who do not lift a finger when they know the assailed are upright—one should pity them. For *them*, conscience has been stilled by fear, courage has bowed its head, honor no longer is as dear, and justice no longer their proud banner.

4 It will be a sad day for humanity when there is no wide outburst of indignation over the most severe injustice to any person or any people.

---

[9] Voting is an essential indication of a real patriotic spirit.

754 On Resisting Evil

1. In the life of almost every individual, as in the life of every people or nation, there are times when one must either stoutly resist injustice and other evils, or meekly submit to them.

2. At such times, if resistance is possible, it is good to take a stand and take it well. Especially when situations can be remedied with no harm to innocent ones, there is little virtue in accepting wrongs. For then accepting wrongs is a sign not of strength, but of weakness; not of courage or spirituality, but of timidity or remissness.

3. There is something else to remember: Constant submission or retreat or appeasement is a grave error, whether committed by a nation or an individual. The less *we* resist bullies or tyrants, the more do we whet their appetites for abusing or intimidating not only us, but *others*.

4. As has been truly said: "All that is necessary for the triumph of evil is that good men do nothing."[10]

5. But while we should vigorously *oppose* what is evil or unjust, we can oppose it without hatred or malice in our hearts for those who err. We can be resolute in resisting wrongdoers, and even in isolating them when necessary to prevent them from doing further harm, and *still* pray that light will enter their universe.

755 The Thought and the Deed

1. Some quotations, scriptural and other, imply that the *thought* of an unworthy deed is as unworthy as the deed itself—an implication some uncritically accept. We in the USB do not agree.

2. The person who resists and subdues an impulse to do wrong is certainly not as much to blame as one who actually commits it. The person who dismisses or stifles the thought of revenge is certainly less to be reproached than one who carries it out. The person who desires but does not seize the possessions of another, is certainly less blameworthy than one who yields to that desire.

---

[10] This quote, and its large number of variants, has *not* been found in the writings of the English political philosopher Edmund Burke (1729–1797), as so many people claim.

7.6 Right Living

3   Those who resist temptation to do wrong are on a higher level of consciousness than those who succumb to it. They may not be as evolved as those who would not wilfully injure others, but their feet are on the right path.

4   Similarly, those who just think or speak of helping others but make no effort in that direction, are less evolved than those who actually *do* good, and still less evolved than those who selflessly serve with no thought of reward because it has become part of their nature to do so.

756 Another Note On Change

1   A popular plea of uncertain origin is: "God grant me the serenity to accept things I cannot change, courage to change things I can, and wisdom to know the difference."

2   Widely quoted, the plea appears on many things, including greeting cards, plaques, embroidered hangings, and decorative cushions.

3   With "correct" replacing "change" in both places, we could endorse the sentiments expressed. For as we observe, change may mean deterioration; and it is surely better to have *no* change than a change for the worse. But, "correct," whose major meaning as a verb is "to set or make right; remove the faults from," denotes *improvement*, which of course is always desirable.

4   So *we* would ask for "the serenity to accept things I cannot correct, courage to correct things I can, and wisdom to know the difference."

5   Or as an Illumined Soul has so beautifully and more fully expressed a similar thought:

6   Correct what *can* be corrected. Accept *all* else gracefully, graciously, gratefully, and courageously.

757 The Need For Effort

1   We should bear in mind that to wait for ideal conditions is usually to do nothing, for little on this plane of existence, lovely though it can be, is ideal. However, we *can*—by what we say, think, and do—make the world more receptive to truth and enlightenment.

2   And if we have love in our hearts, and the desire to serve God as best we know how, the door to service will be opened to us.

757 ☐

3   We should remember, too, that while spirit friends may open the door for us, *we* ourselves must make the effort to walk through the open doorway. No one else can do that for us. We emphasize the USB principle that aspiration and effort are inseparable: Without effort, there is no real aspiration.

758 Perfect Peace?

1   Throughout the ages, people have sought perfect peace, even as they do now.

2   Some seek it in ivory towers—places or situations far removed from worldly or practical affairs. Some in remote, almost inaccessible regions so far from the beaten path that few if any travellers come their way. Some in a degree of wealth that allows them to satisfy every material desire. Some in a close family unit thinking only of itself, and oblivious to everyone else. Some in positions of power where their commands are unhesitatingly obeyed. Some in the ability to avenge any real or fancied wrongs. Some in unquestioningly observing the rules and regulations of those who furnish them with food and shelter. And some in still other ways.

3   Who can tell what would provide perfect peace for another? We know of *no one*, anywhere, who can be certain what would bring that state to anyone but himself or herself.

4   Some may find it, or *think* they may find it, by travelling a certain path; others, by travelling a different path. And there are a thousand paths that can be taken. The way will vary not only with the individual, but *for* the individual. For just as our conception of God changes as we evolve, so, too, does our conception of perfect peace. As we advance spiritually, as our horizons expand spiritually, there will be changes within ourselves; so that what we once thought would bring us, or what once *may* have brought us, complete tranquillity, no longer will do so.

5   The way to perfection is endless: There will always be new paths to take, new heights to climb.

6   In any case, can those who love their fellow human beings be at perfect peace knowing of the turmoil in the world, the hundreds of millions less fortunate, and the homeless and hungry in almost every part of the globe?

7   However, and this is important, we can achieve a *measure* of peace if we realize that to have *simple* wants is the secret of contentment.

7.7 Directing Our Efforts

8   And if we put our hand to the tasks before us; if we selflessly serve where and when we can, taking care not to deprive others of opportunities to serve themselves; if we bring some cheer to those we meet on our journey; if we share whatever bounty comes our way; if we project thoughts of love and good will to all humanity; if we are as a lighthouse to vessels on a stormy sea; and, above all, if we increasingly realize the Love and Wisdom and Goodness and Justice and Compassion that are God—*then* we can possess a great *measure* of peace.

7.7 DIRECTING OUR EFFORTS

759 Let Us Do Our Part

1   There is *much* that each one of us can do towards making this world a better place.

2   We can try to rid ourselves of such weakness as envy and jealous and bitterness and pettiness, so that we can work lovingly with one another, with no thought of self, and with the welfare of humanity uppermost in our minds.

3   We can sit in the stillness for a few minutes each day, if possible at a set time, and *ask* to be used in some way to help bring peace and understanding and brother-and-sisterhood to a weary world. We all possess far greater powers than we know—certainly far greater than we exercise —and these powers can be put to *good* use if we so desire and will it and place them at the disposal of enlightened souls, who can often use those powers in ways undreamed by us, and who are making every effort to divert humanity from the folly of another cataclysm of its own making. We must remember that we have free will, and no one else, not even great souls, can use our powers unless we place them at their disposal.

4   We can *direct* our minds to thoughts of love and peace, and away from all that is destructive.

5   We can *visualize* the leaders of peoples and of nations gathered around the council tables in an atmosphere of harmony. We can direct to them the thoughts that they wish to successfully resolve their differences, not on the battlefield but in the council room; that they realize that *no* people or nation is more important than any other; that they display reasonableness and good will in their deliberations; and that they recognize their

responsibility to help bring the day closer when *every* individual on earth can express in dignity as a child of God.

6   Thoughts are far more powerful than is generally realized [Sec. 2.2]. And the *combined* thoughts and visualization of thousands of individuals, focused on such an objective, could be a mighty force for good, and perhaps could be the very force needed to tip the scales in the direction of lasting peace and good will on earth.

7   We can share a word or two of truth with others, going no further unless we note a genuine desire for additional knowledge. Today, more than ever before, people are *hungering* for light, and we can serve by providing it, in most cases slowly and gradually: Too much light may blind those unaccustomed to it, just as brilliant sunshine may blind those who suddenly emerge from a deep, dark cavern.

8   Precept [1002:3] is good. Example is better. Precept *and* example are better still.

9   The best example *we* can provide is the way we live.

760 *Some Quotations by Inspirers*

1   Our thoughts are seeds sown in the garden of life. We should carefully analyze them, and then express only what is good. Then indeed will beauty fill our garden.

2   We deny no one the privilege of his or her own opinions, but we do suggest some measure of *judgement* in forming them.

3   We cannot overcome for others what they must overcome for themselves.

4   This is a time for people to consider and reconsider their purpose in life.

761 The Knowledge That Sustains

1   To those of us who have even the faintest glimpse of the Goodness that is God, the Love that is God, the Wisdom that is God, the Law and Justice that are God—how can *anything* daunt or dishearten us for long? How can *anything* discourage us from spreading enlightenment? How can *anything* still the rejoicing in our being?

2   We can well understand the words of Illumined Souls who urge us:

3   Let your thoughts and your doings be of such calmness, such serenity, such assurance in The Most High, that there will radiate from your being a glow that, even though unseen, will touch and brighten the lives of all who cross your path.

4   Bring light where there is darkness, strength where there is weakness, knowledge where there is ignorance, courage where there is fear, and love where there is hatred. *Go forth and do good.*

762 Wise Counsel

1   It is quite understandable—the feeling of many whose overriding desire and concern is the spread of Truth: so *much* to do, so *little* time to do it.

2   But if we will not let the earth lie fallow now and then, if we burn the midnight oil when the body cries for rest, eventually we will pay the piper, and in the long run we usually achieve less than we would have otherwise accomplished.

3   Well worth heeding is an inspirer's counsel: "Do not *undo* in any way by *overdoing* in any way."

763 Remember the Similarities—Not the Differences

1   One thing we should all strive to do is to emphasize the similarities between peoples, not the differences.

2   Certain differences there will always be, not only between nations, but between peoples within a nation, between families within a people, and between individuals within a family. But these differences are trifling, compared with all that we hold in common. And variety there will always be, whether in flowers, or scenery, or people; which is good, for variety adds a richness that sameness never can.

763 □   Chapter 7 *Personal Responsibility and Behavior*

3   The thing we should look for is the soul—the spark of God—within each person. The thing we should do, unobtrusively, is to try to fan that spark into a flame.

4   We should try to see the goodness in *all* people. At times that goodness may be submerged almost beyond recognition. At times we may find people repellent at first glance. But underneath that repellence, under "the rubble and the ruin," is a spark of the divine, that spark that is within each one of us, and that makes us sisters and brothers all.

5   It is at best pointless, and at worst harmful, to accentuate the "differences" between peoples—as some do, for instance, in emphasizing the differences between the various [indigenous] peoples of Britain, or between the Americans and the English.

6   Any attempt to show one person or one people as superior to another can do little good, and sometimes much harm.

7   The thing to remember is that we are *all* God's children, no matter what the color of our skin, the faith we were born in, the country we live in, or the views we believe in.

8   Being all children of the One God, this can mean nothing to us unless it means the brother-and-sisterhood of all humankind.

764 *Of Ancient Scrolls and Such*

1   The discovery or rediscovery of ancient scrolls possesses a powerful fascination for many, who set great store by them. We wonder why.

2   As we have said before [314:6], the mere fact that something is ancient does not give it authority or accuracy. History provides ample evidence of that. And documents, however old, are still either the opinions or findings of people, or what the people who wrote them at the time wished *others* to believe—often for personal motives of their own, and sometimes contrary to their own *knowledge*. (We see the same thing today, in some people in high places who *know* the truths of Survival [of death] and Communication [with spirit people], but deny them; and in the vastly conflicting expressions of opinion, real or assumed, about people and events in our own times.)

3   Another thing to remember is that many "researchers" and "scientists" of one sort or another seek ancient scrolls purely with the desire to substantiate their *own* opinions and theories. In any case, all that researchers and scientists or anyone else will find in any ancient scroll is *someone's*

7.8 Personal Progress

opinions or interpretations of *some* thing or things, to which they usually will then add *their* opinion or interpretation.

4   There is sufficient and enough confusion with what we have at hand, without adding to it from ancient archives—which at best are accounts by people of their own beliefs and experiences, or of their understanding or interpretation of the beliefs and experiences of *others*.

5   In The Laws That Govern, we have enough to chart our course, enough to live the good life if we wish to.

6   Yesterday is gone, and our tomorrow will soon be our today. If we but realized this, and prepared accordingly—for we are ever in a state of preparation, of *becoming*—how much more wisely would we devote our time, than in seeking to discover declarations (honest or otherwise) written many centuries ago, or in pondering over someone else's present-day interpretations of those ancient declarations.

7   We know that there are those in the spirit world who also set great store by ancient scrolls. Some of them devote much time impressing their channels about lost or forgotten parchments of ages past, and welcome expeditions to try to recover those documents.

8   Far better, in our opinion, for such spirit friends to teach truths that, *lived by*, would help their friends on earth to make greater progress spiritually.

7.8 PERSONAL PROGRESS

765 Of Oneself, One Can Do Many Things

1   The Brother&Sisterhood teaches that one accomplishes nothing of worth by oneself [731:9]—with "worth" used in the sense of great usefulness or importance to many.

2   But this does not mean that there is little we as individuals can do to brighten the life of others, or that we should feel or say, as many mistakenly do: "Of myself I can do nothing."

3   For *of ourselves* we can show affection and understanding and compassion for our fellow human beings. We can lighten for a while the burden that another finds too heavy to bear. We can by our countenance or greeting or smile or handclasp bring a touch of warmth and cheer and

comfort to those we meet. We can share truth with those we feel are ready to receive. We can be honest and open in our dealings. We can bravely accept things that cannot be corrected. We can be faithful to principles we hold dear. We can be true to our highest ideals. We can, by our way of life, be examples and an inspiration to others.

4   Of ourselves, then, as individuals we can do *many* things. Of course we should be humble, remembering what was brought to us over the years. But that does not mean we should belittle or underestimate what we can do, for ourselves and for others, as we journey along the path.

766 On Slates

1   It is impossible for anyone to begin with a new slate [record] on which to write only what he or she is convinced is true and good.

2   The best thing, then, is to *erase* from our slates what we discover is unworthy or untrue, as we discover it, and to refrain from filling the spaces with pointless facts or theories that cannot help us to live according to The Laws That Govern, or THE LAW.

767 A Sparrow Cannot Become an Eagle, But—

1   There are a number of reasons for the widespread discontent in the world today. One is the common confusion of *desires* with *needs*, as we have pointed out, and seeking to acquire more and more of material things, not heeding the truth that to have *simple* wants is the secret of contentment.

2   Another reason is trying to be what one's present physical [earthly] body is not suited for. It is good to strive to be anything one considers worthy and desirable, *provided* that no insurmountable physical or material barriers bar the way. As an Illumined Soul says:

3   The wise distinguish between the limitations that they can and cannot overcome, live serenely within those limitations that they cannot overcome or overcome at the moment, and make the best of their lot. They do not aspire to be what they know they cannot be in this stage of their existence.

4   Those whose hands are gnarled from toil cannot lure from a violin the exquisite tones a master violinist can entice. Those who are extremely slight and frail of body cannot become Samsons.

5   But those whose hands are gnarled from toil can labor in the vineyard or in the garden. They can become the best tillers of the soil that *they* can be, and take just pride in contributing to the richness and beauty of vine and flower. And those who are extremely slight and frail of body can teach and encourage *others* to become Samsons, if they have the desire and the makings.

6   It is important to realize that there is worth in every *honest* work, however humble, and that any and all can have dignity and morality and integrity, whatever their circumstances, whatever their occupations, whatever their physical and material handicaps. They can walk with their heads high and take their places in the community so long as they do *their* work to the best of their ability.

7   A sparrow cannot become an eagle. But it can maintain worth and dignity as a sparrow. It can become the best sparrow *it* knows how to be.

768 *On Affirmations*

1   Much is said and written concerning the value of affirmations recited regularly and frequently.

2   In themselves, affirmations do *not* bring to people who affirm them what they affirm they are. They may gain some strength from being positive, from affirming this or that. They may even *think* that they are what they affirm they are. But *are* they?

3   Affirmations may or may not lack value. But in itself, *no* recited affirmation will raise us one rung higher on the ladder of consciousness, just as *no* thought in itself will make us what we think we are.

4   Only by living according to The Laws That Govern, by *applying, for good,* the knowledge we possess and by *doing* rather than merely affirming or thinking, do we enlarge our consciousness or tend to *become* what we desire to be.

5   A fundamental principle of the USB is that aspiration and effort are inseparable, and that one cannot *truly* aspire without making the effort [103:8].

769 Challenge and Opportunity

1 It is not things in themselves, but the *way* we respond to them, that is so important to us [1408:1].

2 Everything that comes our way, so-called good and so-called bad alike, is a challenge to us—and an opportunity to use it as a spiritual stepping-stone.

3 If we remember this, we will not be dispirited for long by anything we meet. We may bend, but we will not break. We will know that we can meet it well, with courage, and with the realization that it is only in the test that we can prove ourselves. We will look at the stars, not at the mud beneath our feet.

770 The Individual CAN Triumph

1 As we sow, so do we reap. The Law applies not only to individuals, but to nations and peoples as well.

2 The chaos and confusion in the world today—like other times of unrest and turbulence—are no accident, but the inevitable results of seeds sowed by human beings. Only when there are changes in the *thinking* of humanity, only when humanity as a whole becomes aware of the true and eternal values—*spiritual* values—will there be an end to the sowing of seeds of discord and destruction.

3 Changes in the thinking of humanity are taking place, because of the efforts of spiritual men and women (and their spirit inspirers) throughout the world. And the time *will* come, within the lifetime of many on earth today, when love will replace hate, knowledge will replace ignorance, understanding will replace fear, and human beings will at last be united in love and peace and brother-and-sisterhood.

4 Until that time, nations will continue to rise and fall, and wars will occur. Says a Blessed Soul:

5 > But the *individual* can rise above both. For if one lives according to THE LAW, one will rise above nations, and one will rise above wars. One will not flounder in a sea of indecisiveness, regardless of what peoples and nations do; for one's soul will be strong and untroubled, with a confidence and serenity nothing can shake.

6 > One will live a day at a time, and take one step at a time, sure and certain that by living according to noble conceptions of what

7.8 Personal Progress

is good and godly, nothing that *others* can do can halt one's upward journey for long.

7   Joy and strength come with the realization of this truth.

8   As Illumined Souls have emphasized more than once, *the world is our testing ground.* As far as *we* are concerned it is what *we* do that counts, and when we recognize this, we realize it is a blessing to us beyond price, that no one can deprive us of.

771 You CAN Teach An Old Dog New Tricks

1   We remark more than once that sayings repeated over a long period of time are, even if incorrect, usually unquestioningly accepted by the multitude.

2   A popular saying that many uncritically echo is that "you can't teach an old dog new tricks." But that really is not true. What *is* true is that it is most difficult to teach a dog to *unlearn* old tricks, for the habits and patterns of years are not easily broken. (That, by the way, is one of many reasons why we emphasize how *vital* it is to pass on to the spirit world with as few misconceptions as possible [particularly about spirit life and Truth; 324].)

3   It takes both *willingness* and *courage* to discard old ways, old relationships, and old misteachings that one comes to realize are wrong. As we have pointed out, there are millions of people who no longer accept, and in fact privately reject, the tenets of organizations of which they have long been members, but who nevertheless remain in them (and thus *strengthen* them) because they are "genteel" and "respectable." That of course is their privilege; we do not criticize them, but merely point out a fact.

4   It is to the credit of the human race that throughout the ages there have always been individuals who, sometimes quite late in life, having perceived a facet of Truth, had the courage not only to endorse it, but to repudiate what they had come to recognize is false. To such individuals the world owes much, for they are among the wayshowers; they also blaze the trail others may tread. And though they seek no reward, such individuals, on leaving the physical world, discover that their courage in striking off the shackles of error that had bound them has earned them spiritual heights they would not otherwise have attained.

772 Self-Determinism

1 We have pointed out time and again that as far as any individual is concerned, it is what *we* do that counts; for it is what *we* do that is of the utmost importance to us in the endless process of *becoming*.

2 For many, it is glorious and exhilarating to realize that *we* are the architect of our *own* future.

773 Endeavor

1 Heights are not reached by those who dare not climb. Barriers are not breached by those who will not pound them. Obstacles are not skirted or surmounted by those who do not try.

2 Two other points should also be remembered.

3 One is that the first step towards achievement is to concentrate on the *goal*, rather than on the impediments along the way, while *recognizing* that the impediments must be faced, and removed or skirted or surmounted.

4 The other is that those who strive, selflessly, to reach the heights or break down barriers or overcome obstacles, advance spiritually, regardless of the material outcome.

774 Effort and Intent

1 An Illumined Inspirer has said:

2 Not one day is wasted, when a portion of that day is devoted to directing thoughts of love, and thoughts of upliftment and enlightenment, to those who are in need.

3 Not one day is wasted, when a portion of that day is devoted to an attempt to reach a higher level of consciousness.

4 Not one day is wasted, when a portion of that day is devoted to attunement of a spiritual nature for the purpose of receiving what may be shared with others.

5 And a Blessed Soul has said:

6 *Every* effort is recognized. *Every* tender thought directed to a soul in need, *every* kindly expression of brotherly and sisterly love—be it the spoken word, the silent prayer, the sincere hand-

7.8 Personal Progress

clasp, the friendly smile—every thought and expression are *recognized*, whether they are received, or whether they are repelled.

7   This recognition is manifested in the form of spiritual development, whether one is *aware* of that development or not; for by the very effort to help another, one reaches a higher state of consciousness. And so I would say to you: Let not *one* day go by without a kindly thought, expressed in your own fashion, for a fellow traveller.

8   Our lives are judged not by results alone, but by *intent* as well.

9   A life well lived is a life devoted not only to self-realization, but to *service* to one's fellow human beings.

10   And one cannot be of service to one's fellow human beings without being of service to one's God.

775 There is No Easy Path to the Mountain Top

1   The USB emphasizes time and again that *we* are our *own* saviors, that *we* are our *own* prophets and reap the harvest of our *own* prophecy—which consists of all that we say, think, and do.

2   We repeat these truths as we note the ever growing number of individuals and organizations that make glittering but empty promises of one sort or another to induce others to join them. We would say this:

3   — *False* are any "prophets" who assert they can "save" another or place another on a higher level of consciousness. And less than wise is anyone who believes them.

4   — *They err* who preach that humans will eventually have everlasting life on earth, with their physical bodies "transmuted" to a more rapid rate of vibration. Any body of a more rapid rate of vibration than the physical would be a *spirit* [counterpart, etheric] body, which, unless living *in* a physical body, would reside in the *spirit* world [1310].

5   — *False* are any "teachers" who offer to make a place in the sun, spiritually, for another. And misguided is anyone who thinks they can.

6   — *False* are any "masters" who claim that they can erase all or part of another's karma, or assume it themselves. And unaware of The Laws That Govern is anyone who accepts that claim.

7   For there is *no* easy path to the mountain top, and *no one* can walk that path for us [1423]—not even the USB's Illumined Inspirers, who are of almost incredible spiritual stature.

8   However, if we *live by* the USB's teachings and philosophy, we shall *be* on that path. And to be on that path will add to our strength and integrity of character. It will plant or nourish the seed of selfless service within our being. It will encourage us to extend our hands—*both* of them—in sisterly and brotherly love to all the children of earth. It will aid us to understand the purposes of life on earth, and to cheerfully accept any trials and tribulations that cannot be corrected. It will bring us closer to The Most High.

9   The path is not strewn with roses; it *cannot* be. But it can be a joyous path, however difficult, if we realize that it is the right path, and that *nothing* can halt our upward journey if we persevere in making our way on it, step by step, slowly but surely [Sec. 14.6].

10   And in the first exquisite, breathtaking view from the mountain top, the long, steep climb will be forgotten.

8
Our World

CHAPTER CONTENTS

8.1 This Material World — 194
- 801 The World IS Real—the Things of the World ARE Real — 194
- 802 Scientists Will Never Create Life — 195
- 803 The Ever Vital Need for Change in Our Lives — 196
- 804 Some Reflections on the Landings on the Moon — 197
- 805 No New Thing under the Sun — 198
- 806 Machines with Intelligence and Emotions? — 199
- 807 Think and Thank God — 200

8.2 Humans — 202
- 808 Some Thoughts about Species—and Humans — 202
- 809 Nature and Humans — 203
- 810 The Animal Kingdom and Humans — 204
- 811 The Survival Instinct — 205
- 813 A Little about Color and Prejudice — 205
- 814 NOT Every Person Has a Price — 206
- 815 In Praise of "Average" People — 207
- 816 Sunspots—the Human Mind—and Other Things — 208
- 817 "As One Thinks..."? — 209
- 818 On Human Nature — 210
- 819 On Inhumanity — 211
- 820 The Physical Body—and the "Sport" of Prizefighting — 212
- 821 Population—and "Overpopulation" — 213

continued...

8.3 These Times — **215**

822	"These Are the Times That Try Men's Souls"	215
823	The Curse of Complacency	215
824	The Hour and the Need	216
825	A Prayer for These Times	217
826	The Dangers of Some Modern Music	217

8.4 Good and Bad — **218**

827	NOT All That Happens Is for Good	218
828	Of Good and Evil	219
829	Good and Evil are NOT Opposites Sides of the Same Coin	220
830	An Often-Asked Question	220
831	The Doors to Spiritual Progress Are Never Closed	221
832	On Non-Interference	222
833	The Dangers of Some of Today's Entertainment	222
834	The Swing of the Pendulum	223
835	The Best of Both	224
836	The Decline in Standards	224
837	On What Is Holy	228

8.5 Crime — **229**

838	The Need for Respect for Law and Order	229
839	The Age of Responsibility	229
840	Punishment—and Deterrents to Crime	230
841	On Capital Punishment	231
842	Poverty and Crime	232

8.6 Leadership and Example — **234**

843	The Good Shepherd	234
844	Of Some "Debunkers"	234
845	The Tyranny of the Few	235
846	The Abuse of Power	235
847	Some Lessons to be Learned	236
848	The Big Lie	237

Chapter Contents

8.7 Freedom — 237

849	Freedom for All—a Major Principle of the USB	237
850	The Freedom of Personal Interpretation	238
851	The Rights of the Individual	238
852	The Right to Privacy	239
853	Some Notes on Freedom	240
854	A Right and Responsibility of Nations	241
855	The Right to Dissent	241

8.8 Challenges — 241

856	The Battle Goes On	241
857	Some Reflections about War and Freedom	242
858	Some Questions	243
859	Two Tragedies	243
860	We CAN Learn from the Experience of Others	243
861	Some Reflections on Democracy	245
862	A One-World Government?	245
863	Eternal Vigilance	247
864	Utter Folly	248
865	On Tragic Happenings in Many Places	248
866	On "News" Disseminators	250

8.1 THIS MATERIAL WORLD

801 The World IS Real—the Things of the World ARE Real

1   Some schools of thought assert that the earth and things of the earth are nothing but illusions, with "mind"—and their definitions of "mind" vary—as the sole reality.

2   According to them, a tree, a street, coin and currency, stone and brick and mortar and wood and steel, are, like everything else except "mind," merely illusion. Among those who assert this, however, are people responsible for the *building* of edifices of stone and brick and wood and steel—all "illusions"—to assemble in; and they have no hesitation in accepting, and in fact welcoming, currency, coin, and checks—also "illusions"!

3   They travel by bus and car and boat and train and plane, although according to their teachings or misteachings those means of transportation do not actually exist, to go from one place to another—although those places, too, by their own philosophy, are not realities.

4   Electricity and coal and gas are, by their own admission, mere figments of the imagination; nevertheless, they use these things to light and warm the houses they inhabit, houses that are of course not actualities according to *their* teaching.

5   The schools they send their children to are of course also illusions, to their way of thinking, or perhaps we should say assertion. So are the paper and ink of the pamphlets that they print by the thousand in which to declare that nothing exists except *mind*.

6   Certainly without a mind (that is, a mentality) we could not be conscious of any thing [physical object]. We would not be aware of things, however much those *with* a mind were conscious of them. It is *because* of a mind that we are aware of things.

7   The world *is* real. Matter *is* real. The things of the world *are* real. This is so despite those who proclaim otherwise in books (which they say are illusions) that are sold for money (which they claim is imaginary) to people in physical [earthly] bodies (which they assert are unreal).

8   It is puzzling how some people will refuse to admit that the beds they sleep on, the physical bodies they inhabit, the food they eat, the clothes they buy, and a thousand other objects they see or use daily, are not illusions but in fact very real indeed. An Illumined Soul has said:

8.1 This Material World

9   To those who live in physical bodies, the earth is anything but an illusion. It is an actuality. It is substantial. It is real. It is just as real, just as solid and firm, as any other plane of expression is to those who live in it.

10   The "illusionists" set forth a volume of contradictions. That in itself may not be too tragic. What *is* tragic are the prolonged illnesses and premature deaths suffered by children who, under the parental control of those accepting such a philosophy, are denied measures that might cure or at least alleviate their conditions.

802 Scientists Will Never Create Life

1   From the vast laboratories of science have come from time to time reports of discoveries by biochemists that are described as placing humanity "on the verge of creating life."

2   Scientists may continue to unlock many of the secrets of nature. They may continue to arrange *different* combinations of substances, or different combinations of the *components* of various substances. They may even be able to form what *to them* are new expressions. But they will *never* be able to create life; for the life force or spirit [601:3] that animates all things and creatures and people, and that comes from a Source that cannot be fully comprehended, is beyond our power to duplicate.

3   Like any other people, scientists can apply some of The Laws That Govern, whether or not they are aware of those Laws—just as any one of us, by merely flipping a switch, can turn the electric light on or off, whether or not we know anything about electricity. We have, for instance, long discovered, or rediscovered, the laws that make radio and television a commonplace. *But we did not create those laws*—laws that were always in existence, as far as human conception of time is concerned; we merely *utilized* them.

4   In fact, we cannot create *anything*, however much we may be privileged to mold or rearrange what God has created; and the life force will never be manufactured in a test tube—or anywhere else! Says a Blessed Soul:

5   With human beings at the stage where they are rapidly making one momentous discovery after another, it is natural for them to think that they may one day uncover all the secrets of the universe. But while experiments to "create" life have taken place, are taking

place, and will continue to take place, life as we know it cannot be duplicated by humans. Certainly no individual or group of individuals, on earth or in the spirit world, has ever been successful in doing so.[1]

803 The Ever Vital Need for Change in Our Lives

1 As we have stated [415], except for what is perfect as well as eternal—THE LAW, Truth, and the Creator of THE LAW and Truth—*everything changes.*

2 We witness continuous change all about us and *within ourselves.*

3 Change is natural. In fact The Law of Change is essential, because it makes possible the *varying* aspects and expressions of any one person or creature or thing.

4 How we respond to that Law is up to each individual, in the final analysis, regardless of whether or how we may be influenced by others. We can use whatever comes our way to become wiser, more understanding, more compassionate, more loving; or we can become embittered, blind, harsh, cruel, and immersed in self-pity. We can use every opportunity, so-called good and so-called bad alike, as a millstone that drags us down into the dust, or as a stepping stone to higher ground. The choice is ours.

5 Change is vital in our lives, because without change we cannot progress. Of course change in itself does not necessarily mean a change for the better; and it would be folly to change merely for the sake of change, if it meant turning our footsteps toward the valley of darkness instead of towards the mountaintop.

6 It is by *change* that we grow. We add this, or remove that, to alter what is ours. In growing in stature spiritually, we set aside what no longer serves a noble purpose, however much it may at one time have been a part of our being and conducive to our growth, and replace it with other ideas, other ideals, and other visions. (The one thing that we never need discard are truths [302:1]).

7 It is good to recognize change when it faces us; and no matter how we view it, to welcome any opportunities it brings to alter our thought patterns for the better, and to turn our way of life to a more spiritual one.

---

[1] Cloning and similar techniques do not create life; by manipulating living cell components (DNA) they only initiate reproduction artificially (619).

8.1 This Material World

8 There are some who lament that life holds little in the way of change for them, but this is usually because they fail to recognize opportunities when they arrive. Even the most apparently humdrum existence presents some opportunities for change—even if it is just the chance to bear one's lot more cheerfully, to learn to be content with simple wants, to express a genuine and warmer welcome to those who cross our threshold, and to be, by example, a living encouragement to others of the way ills and afflictions can be borne.

9 If we did not change, or try to change for the better, from day to day, from week to week, from month to month, and from year to year, it would be high time to take stock of ourselves. We might then *recognize* the ever vital need and importance of change in our lives.

10 That change in itself is not necessarily good is demonstrated in a score of fields, including music, writing, poetry, sculpture, and painting, in all of which there have been many changes that in our opinion have often not been for the better [836].

11 It is unfortunately sad but true that too many people in various spheres of activity seemingly cannot or will not discipline themselves to the extent of setting high standards for themselves. Instead, they compromise or ignore standards altogether, if by so doing they can gain materially. (Of course they cannot gain *spiritually* by it.)

12 But regardless of general standards and trends, as Illumined Souls often remind us, *the individual can rise above all things.* If we set our *own* standards high, and if, whenever possible, we not only give of our best, but incorporate nothing into our universe that is below our standards—then debasements by others will not affect our own integrity and character and consciousness.

804 Some Reflections on the Landings on the Moon

1 Few would deny that the [1969–1972] moon landings were a remarkable and magnificent achievement far exceeding the expectations of most people. They were a complete triumph, and striking examples of what can be accomplished, technologically, when humanity harnesses knowledge and channels it towards a specific goal.

2 The fact that human beings, superbly prepared and superbly protected in every way, tarried for a few hours on the earth's lunar body, does not mean, however, that they could ever inhabit the moon without the same or similar protective equipment (for their physical bodies) that the astro-

nauts had, or that the protective equipment would, over a long period, prevent discomfort or harm to their bodies.

3 But even if human beings eventually could live on the moon for days or weeks or months or years, what value could it provide for humanity, other than the acquisition of lunar minerals and forms? In any event, undeveloped areas on earth exceed the moon's entire surface, which is less than one-thirteenth as large as the surface of the earth.

4 Whether the time and effort and money expended on the successful landings on the earth's satellite could not have been put to vastly better use is a matter of opinion.

5 The individuals who actually walked on a little of the moon's surface cannot have helped but experience a sense of awesomeness in the knowledge that they were the first beings in physical bodies, protected though those bodies were, to do so. But we cannot see where humanity in general has gained one iota *spiritually* from the moon landings. Of itself, it certainly has brought no one closer to solving the riddle of the universe, or to an understanding either of The Laws That Govern or the purposes of human existence on earth.

6 We have only to look about us; we have only to see and hear what is going on in the world today, to realize that physical and technical accomplishments, however immense and marvelous, do not necessarily bring any spirituality to human beings.

805 No New Thing under the Sun

1 As it has done for ages, the pendulum continues to swing from one extreme to the other, for human beings have yet to learn the wisdom of *moderation* and the value of *the moderate path.*

2 Whether it is dress or styles or education or ways of living or anything else, the pendulum swings from one apex to the other. What was once the custom or fashion, will be the custom or fashion again; many will consider it new, but those well versed in history will know it is not appearing for the first time.

3 Some will think: "What about our supersonic planes, our methods of transportation, our weapons of destruction, our virtually instantaneous communication systems?" They are not novel (Illumined Souls tell us), but duplicates or variations of some human inventions throughout the ages, and certainly not superior to those of long-lost civilizations such as Lemuria and Atlantis.

8.1 This Material World

4   Certainly in what is of unparalleled importance—the realm of *mind*—humanity today far from surpasses the ancients, particularly those of only twenty to twenty-five centuries ago, about whom we know comparatively much. And to leaf through the pages of the past is to discover that anything *we* think, has *already* been thought, and that anything *we* express, has *already* been expressed, very often much more ably. For every age has contained individuals of remarkable mental stature, king and slave, rich and poor, learned and unlearned.

5   As for present-day languages and "slanguages" that may be novel to us, much is definitely not new, as any truly comprehensive dictionary will show; and who would assert that the rest has never been phrased before? We know this: We have still to find a single *idea* that has not previously been put into words. As an Illumined Soul says:

6   > We do not know of *any* thought that is original. *Every* thought has been expressed at some time, by someone, somewhere. It may be garbed in what may seem to be a new fashion, so to speak; but whatever the garment it wears, the thought itself is not new. Indeed there is *nothing* new under the sun.

7   It is yet another thing to make us humble—if we think.

806 Machines with Intelligence and Emotions?

1   Many theories would be amusing if they were not so likely to impress the credulous or unthinking because of the academic stature of some of those who express them.

2   We noted [in the late 1970s] the declaration by two professors, one holding a position at two leading universities, that machines would be produced by the year 2000 with intelligence that will equal or surpass that of humans. They predicted that computers and robots would have emotions such as anger, affection, aggressiveness, and even jealousy.

3   Some years earlier, a computer expert had expressed the belief that it will be possible to design a computer that *thinks*.

4   Computers, a boon to society in countless ways, can more or less instantly provide information that has been *fed* into them. They can furnish the answers to complex mathematical problems in an incredible fraction of the time it would take an individual, or in some cases hundreds of individuals working together, to do so. They have revolutionized paper work. They can collate a mass of medical information and

806

    provide a diagnosis in a few moments instead of many hours. Their great use in scores of other areas is also a matter of record.

5   But what these professors and some other individuals surprisingly seem to overlook is that whether it is solving mathematical problems, or sorting and selecting information, or providing medical diagnoses, or doing any of a hundred other tasks it can perform so quickly and well, a computer, given sufficient energy, can only provide what in effect has been *programmed* into it. Let us not be overawed by academic qualifications.

6   *No* machine can think, nor will it ever be *able* to think. For to think is to form or conceive in the mind; and human beings with all their accomplishments cannot *create* mind, despite their lively and vivid imaginations, which are activities of their minds.

7   Humans can devise and build computers and robots to make life easier for themselves. They can rearrange combinations of elements and compounds. *But they have yet to create even a blade of grass.* They certainly will never create *mind,* and without a mind or mentality there can be nothing to think with or, of course, to express *emotion* with, for emotions are a part of one's mentality.

807 Think and Thank God

1   We can understand the despondency that from time to time may assail individuals who love and serve those they meet in life, as they read or hear or witness shocking evidence of some people's inhumanity to others.

2   Is the world making any progress? they ask.

3   The answer is "Yes." Definitely "Yes," though the progress may be obscured by the unending barrage of sensational headlines that too often blazon only what is low or bad.

4   One sign of betterment, despite the general decline in standards [836], is the search by literally millions of individuals around the globe for *something* that will give point and meaning to existence.

5   Too many, unfortunately, either do not find it or are drawn into movements created or led by those who are less than noble. The *true* teachers of Truth are few, as we point out elsewhere [318:1].

6   We who are linked in this Brother&Sisterhood in a vital mission that will, *in time,* change the thinking of humanity generally; we who are blessed to receive such a full measure of *truths, and nothing but truths* from truly Illumined Souls; we who are privileged to share those truths

8.1 This Material World

with those who are ready to receive them—let us never doubt the eventual success or the great endeavor of which we are all a part.

7 We do not walk with the prophets of doom. We do not share the gloom of one or two who have written to us. We do not share their pessimism. We do not share their feeling that all is lost.

8 We cannot in any case share their belief that the world is worse than it has ever been, for that is just not so.

9 *Think and thank God*, says an ancient proverb.

10 If we think, we *will* thank God, for we will remember the many blessings we posses but too often forget.

11 We will realize that the world *has* advanced, and advanced in many ways, in even just the last hundred years or so.

12 We no longer hang someone for stealing a lamb. We no longer work men and women twelve and fourteen hours a day, six days a week. We no longer ignore the needy. We no longer possess only the barest necessities of life. We no longer burn mediums at the stake.

13 Much remains to be done, it is true. But that should not blind us to what has been accomplished.

14 And what remains to be done will not be achieved by those who wring their hands and lament and sit idly by and do nothing to build a better world [757]. It will not be achieved by being disappointed if others do not see the flame from the torch the USB holds high.

15 It will be achieved by the persevering—who know that the path is not, and cannot be, easy.

16 It will be achieved by the patient—who know that they build slowly who build for the centuries.

17 It will be achieved by the selfless—who know that one who would serve must be prepared to sacrifice.

18 It will be achieved by the stout of heart—who know that God is a God of Love and Wisdom, of Law and Justice, and is That Which Is All-Good.

19 It will be achieved by the understanding—who know that there is much work for all, and that there is a role for each and every one who wishes to serve.

20 Every servant in the vineyard has a part to play, a purpose in the scheme of things; and each of us, from our individual vantage points, can perform what only we can do [759, 112, D27].

8.2 HUMANS

808 Some Thoughts about Species—and Humans

1 There are some who assert that humans are spiritual beings, evolved from the lower forms of life.

2 Others assert that it is specifically from the protozoan, a one-celled animal belonging to the lowest division of the animal kingdom, that all other forms of expression, including human beings, are evolved.

3 Let us reflect a little.

4 More than one million different species in the animal kingdom have already been described, with some 10,000 added species being identified each year, according to the *Encyclopedia Britannica*. Estimates by various authorities of the *total* number of all species living on earth, including those uncatalogued and undiscovered, commonly range from 5 to 15 million, but extend to 200 million.

5 Evidence exists *against* the evolution of one species into another. The *Britannica*, for instance, points out that a certain class of mollusks, *Monoplacophora*, thought to have been extinct for 350 million years, was found a few decades ago living in the ocean deeps. And entomologists say that there has been no change in the common cockroach during the past 300 million years. Other similar examples can be cited.[2]

6 Species that show no change over such incomprehensible periods of time certainly justify the presumption that they do not change at all.

7 Misconceptions about species may arise from unfamiliarity with two important truths that we have discussed [in Sec. 4.7, etc].

8 One is that *The Law of Variety* [like all spiritual laws, 402:1] operates everywhere and in all levels of expression, providing variety not only *within* species but *of* species [416].

9 The other is that each species has its own range of rates of vibration, within which range it is confined, with the specific rates of vibration *within* that range determining the expression of specific varieties of that species [414:9–11]

10 The two assertions initially mentioned imply *either* that there is *no* Creator, *or* that *whatever* created the one-celled protozoan was limited in its creation to just *that*. One could as logically limit a writer to one word, a speaker to one syllable, a musician to one note, and a painter to one stroke of the brush! [see 502:7].

---

[2] Fossils indicate that the horsehoe crab (genus *Limulus*) has existed unchanged for about 450 million years. (Vegetable life did not exist on land much before this.)

8.2 Humans

11 We have stated that Illumined Souls tell us they do *not* know *how* and *why* humans came into being [506:4].

12 They add that humans are the *only* expressions on earth with a spark of the divine [601:2]. It is a spark that did *not* originate from or within any of "the lower forms of life," but from the very Creator, which we and many others call God.

809 Nature and Humans

1 Some of today's prophets of doom cry that humans are irretrievably despoiling or destroying the natural world as it would exist without our presence and civilization. They are unaware that nature always strikes a balance, in one way or another. [This does not mean that humans need not strive to protect nature and their environment to the extent possible.]

2 For while human beings, through greed or ignorance, may harm *themselves* by their actions towards nature, they cannot inflict any lasting harm on nature, for The Law so operates that nature in some mysterious and unfathomable way [in time] offsets detrimental acts by humans.

3 If "disasters" destroy or damage a certain form of life in one area, nature increases that form in other areas, and/or increases other forms of life in the same area.

4 Two things should be noted.

5 One is that *nothing* in nature is wasted.

6 The second is that we humans do *not* have dominion over nature, however much some scriptures may proclaim that we have, or however much we may like to *think* we have, or however much we may misuse or abuse what nature makes so lavishly available to us.

7 There are beings and intelligences that guide nature in its operation; humans are not among them, although we have become increasingly able to alter some of the expressions of nature to provide for our needs.

8 Nature includes three kingdoms: *animal, vegetable* (or *plant*), and *mineral.* We provide a fourth: the *human.*[3] On earth, each kingdom contributes to others (and sometimes also to itself) in a multitude of ways.

---

[3] Since this was written in 1977 the kingdoms have been undergoing redefinition. Six kingdoms of living things becoming standard now are: Animalia, Plantae, Fungi, Protista (protozoans and algae), Eubacteria, and Archaea (ancient, bacteria-like but quite different, adapted to extreme habitats).

9   Humans benefit immeasurably from nature's other kingdoms, without which we could not survive on earth, let alone flourish as we do. We should appreciate nature's generosity and abundance, and not squander them, especially those resources that took millions of years to form. Above all, we should be ever grateful to that power, which many call God, which provides us with the riches of nature and with such unlimited opportunities to express for good.

810 The Animal Kingdom and Humans

1   One common misteaching, shared by some "teachers" on both sides of life, is that if humanity learned to live in peace and harmony, all creatures on earth would do the same. The lion would lie down with the lamb; all creatures would live side by side with no species attacking or consuming another.

2   This misconception reveals a misunderstanding of Nature: the natural world as it would [and did] exist without human beings and our civilization.

3   Of the estimated million or more of different species of insects, most species subsist on others. They are also a major source of food for many other creatures: birds, fish, reptiles, and mammals.

4   If one fact stands out clearly with respect to the animal kingdom, it is this: *life consumes life.* The overwhelming majority of that kingdom are flesh-eating creatures. (Some forms of animal life consume even their own kind.)

5   Many may consider this cruel, and conclude that Nature is indeed "red in tooth and claw"; but it is Nature expressing itself in its own way, usefully, and, as we have just emphasized [in 809], to strike a balance, as Nature always does.

6   Nature's laws and methods are millions or hundreds of millions of years old, humans have discovered. Can the *thinker* believe that those laws and methods would change if humans no longer lifted their hands against fellow humans?

7   Would animals stop eating each other for food?

8   The answer to these and similar questions is a clear and resounding "No."

8.2 Humans

811 What Sets Humans Apart

1   Throughout the last twenty centuries, many have accepted Cicero's[4] assertion that it is in *reason and speech*, more than anything else, that humans are "removed from the nature of wild beasts."

2   The statement may not be entirely true, however. For animals do communicate by vocal sounds and gestures [some have learned and used limited sign language to express themselves].

3   However, there *are* two important things that human beings possess that distinguish them from animals, and reason *is* one of them. The other is man's *soul*, the spark of divinity within each human being [601:2].

812 The Survival Instinct

1   Because of The Law of Self-Preservation, we share with animals, as we do with all other growing things in nature, *the instinct to survive*.

2   But despite that inherent instinct, there are people and animals, notably family pets, that will risk their lives to save others. There are many instances of dogs taking that risk to save family members from death by fire or flood or other dangers. There are also many instances of people who have faced death to rescue pets they cherished.

3   Some heroic deeds of family pets are undoubtedly inspired by spirit people. For animals are, as a rule, much more psychic than humans; and many pets, knowing and recognizing the family's close spirit friends, would be inclined to obey their instructions to aid someone in peril.

813 A Little about Color and Prejudice

1   "Why do people differ in color?" It is another often-asked question.

2   People of various "races" differ in color because of The Law of Variety [416]. Even within each race itself, because of that Law, men and women are of various shades and hues.

3   As we have pointed out, there is beauty and enchantment in variety—not only of *species*, but *within* a species. That truth applies to everything: to jade and diamonds, roses and violets, oak and maple, ants and butterflies, cats and dogs and horses, and every other species, including *humans*.

---

[4] Marcus Tullius Cicero, 106–43 B.C., Roman statesman, orator, and philosopher.

4   There is variety in every expression of life, but only in *humans* do we find prejudice because of differences in color!

5   Humanity as a whole has yet to learn that the outer garment is no sign of the caliber of the being within. It is human *ignorance* of The Law of Variety and others of The Laws That Govern, and misconceptions of superiority, that are responsible for many of our ills today.

6   The greatest whirlwinds have been reaped by those who sowed the winds of discrimination or of self-assumed superiority. It has been these hideous things that have caused so much *inhumanity to others*, and that have kept this globe from being the comparative heaven on earth it could be, and that it one day will be.

7   Human beings will only make rapid progress in that direction when it is generally realized, despite all misteachings to the contrary, that *there is not, and there has never been, any superior race or people*, and that the slant of the eye or the color of the skin is no indication of one's level of consciousness.

8   Too many have been too blind too long. Fortunately, "the doors to spiritual progress are never closed to anyone," nor to any people or nation.

9   Individuals, peoples, and nations should take stock of conditions today, and unite in erasing evils that exist. As a Blessed Soul says:

10 This is a time to search one's soul and conscience, to search one's consciousness, to show understanding, and to extend oneself to others. It is not too late to *love* one's brothers and sisters, to *walk* with them, to *talk* with them, to help them gain a *broader* view, and to help them make their pathways brighter. *It is not too late.*

814 NOT *Every Person Has a Price!*

1   There have always been *cynics*—those who believe that all human actions are motivated by only selfishness, and who cannot understand selfless acts or disinterested points of view. And according to cynics, "every person has a price."

2   Too many people either echo this idea, or some equivalent of it, to endorse the belief that anyone would do anything for money, power, fame, or other material gain.

3   But the saying has no truth.

8.2 Humans

4   For in every age, in every land, in every clime, there have been individuals, often in the hundreds or thousands, who could *not* be bought: who with dignity endured abominable indignities; who suffered torture, and in many cases even death, rather than abandon or pretend to abandon principles or ideals they deeply cherished.

5   The world owes them much, as indeed it does to such courageous individuals of *this* day and age.

6   Many people unquestionably *can* be bought. Fortunately for humanity, however, the sweeping generalization that every person has a price is *not true;* and those who proclaim it reveal a flaw in their *own* character, not a flaw in the character of *all* people.

7   It is wise to ignore cynicisms, for they tend to condone or encourage actions that are less than noble.

8   We should note that the word *Cynic*, initial letter capitalized, has a far loftier meaning than the uncapitalized word.

9   A Cynic was one of a sect of Greek philosophers twenty-four centuries ago who taught that virtue—in the sense of righteousness and moral excellence—is the only good; that the essence of virtue is self-control; and that surrender to the desire for more material possessions than necessary is beneath human dignity.

815 *In Praise of "Average" People*

1   The world is made up, in the main, of "average" people. They may not be the same in one era as in another, or the same in one area as in another; but they all have many things in common.

2   "Average" men and women have little lust for power or dominion over others. They have little desire to control the lives of their neighbors, or the lives of peoples in faraway places. They have few dreams of grandeur. All they ask is to be able to take care of the needs of themselves and their families, to have some common comforts, and to live and let live.

3   "Average" people are immensely more important than they themselves realize. For it is *they* who are the most vital cog in the economy. It is *they* who keep the wheels of industry rolling. It is *they* who till the soil and harvest the crops. It is *they* who perform hundreds of other tasks. It is *they* who bear the heaviest burden of taxes. It is *they* who pay for many of the privileges enjoyed by what is often called "the upper classes."

815

It is *they* who receive little credit when things go right, but much criticism when things go wrong. It is *they* who are in the front line of battle, risking their lives for what they believe or are led to believe is a noble cause. It is *they* who rise to extraordinary heights of heroism and sacrifice in times of peril. In a word, it is *they* who are there when the *need* to be there arises.

4   Like others, "average" men and women may be swayed and deceived by interests that control the channels of news and opinion. But they have a common sense that too many of their self-assumed superiors lack; and given the facts, "average" people will usually reach the right conclusions as to what procedures would be successful in a given situation.

5   "Average" people have faith in democracy; indeed they are the *backbone* of democracy.

6   We would say this to those in high positions: "Do not underestimate 'average' people, or their power when aroused. Do not forget that wherever liberty survives, it is because *they* have stoutly and courageously responded to its call."

7   Too many in positions of power regard "average" people as a commodity, rather than as people who deserve and should *enjoy* commodities. It is tragic, shameless, and inexcusable.

8   "Average" people are courted when there is a shortage of labor for roads to be built, farms to be plowed, coal to be mined, machines to be run, and other work to be done. Then they are welcomed. They are invited to immigrate. They are encouraged to have big families; in some instances they are even paid a bonus for each child.

9   But at the first signs of a recession or depression—events caused by humans that "average" people had no part in but of which they are the *victims*—the picture changes. The welcome mat is withdrawn, and "intellectuals" start speaking about "overpopulation" and suggest restricting the size of the family.

10   *We* do not disparage "average" people. *We sing their praise.*

816 Sunspots—the Human Mind—and Other Things

1   Some assert that sunspots—the dark spots sometimes seen on the surface of the sun—are the result of disharmonious mental and magnetic forces generated by humanity. This is a misconception.

8.2 Humans

2. Human minds are indeed powerful, the USB emphasizes, but they are far from powerful enough to affect a star never closer than 91 million miles [146 million kilometers] from the earth, and more than a million times as large.

3. It is the laws *of* Nature—and not human minds—that control the expressions *in* nature.

4. If the sun were affected by the minds of those who live on earth, it would also be affected by the minds in vehicles of expression in the *other* planets of our solar system [1301:11]. In any event, we would not know the cause of any changes we observed.

5. The sun and its orbit have been in existence a long, long time; and human minds cannot change the sun's appearance one jot, or alter its orbit one iota. Human minds cannot even affect the orbit of the earth itself [1124:6].

6. Our solar system—like any other solar system—is indeed a complex one, but it is in order.

7. The universe is in order.

8. All expression *of* and *in* nature is in order.

9. The human race, as an expression in nature, is in order. Any chaos on earth between people at any time is created by people; it is not an expression *of* nature or *in* nature, but the result of individuals misusing the free will that each of us possesses.

10. Conditions in any other orb of our solar system are largely of academic interest only. For people have more than enough to keep them occupied in the problems of life here on earth—problems that *they* have created, and that they certainly have not resolved with notable success so far.

817 "As One Thinks..." ?

1. Sayings repeated again and again over a long period of time are generally accepted without question by the unthinking—even though the sayings may contain little truth. They are also endorsed by some who usually weigh all things well before accepting or rejecting them.

2. A common adage, repeated in various forms throughout the ages and accepted as true by millions, is: "As one thinks, so is one."

3. The chronicles of history, which in large measure are a record of inhumanity to others, contain many pages written in the blood of men, women, and children slaughtered by those who *thought* they were fulfill-

ing God's wish in torturing or killing all who did not share their personal beliefs. We who are aware that God is a God of Love know that they were *not* fulfilling anyone's wish except their own or that of their evil-minded spirit inspirers, however much they *thought* they were doing as God directed.

4   We can say the following with certainty: "As one thinks, so does one *think* one is. But is one? Only too often, the answer is 'No.'"

818 On Human Nature

1   Many are prone to attribute weaknesses in character, particularly if they recognize that they themselves possess them, to *"human nature"*: the psychological and social qualities that in almost all cases distinguish humans from other living things.

2   But making light of those defects by mislabelling them does not alter them in any way or justify them at all.

3   Cheating, stealing, unkindness, neglect of responsibilities, greed, avarice, envy, jealousy, and a host of other undesirable expressions are *not* human nature, but the nature of *some humans*, which is an altogether different thing.

4   There *are* characteristics that can rightly be ascribed to human nature, and we possess them in a degree that varies with our level of consciousness.

5   It is human nature *to preserve oneself*. In fact The Law of Self-Preservation applies not just to humans; but humans often rise to exceptional heroism by risking life and limb to preserve others. So do some animals at times.

6   It is human nature *to laugh or weep* when emotionally affected. Indeed, humans are the only [known] expression of life to display emotion by laughter or tears. (Contrary to some misconceptions, the distinctive howling of the laughing hyena and the loud braying of the laughing jackass do *not* indicate merriment or amusement.)

7   It is human nature *to be kind and affectionate*. However depraved and unregenerate an individual may seem to be, there is usually at least *one* person or creature that he or she loves or is kind to.

8   It is human nature *to have a conscience*—"an inner knowledge or feeling of right and wrong, with a compulsion to do right [609:1]." No other living thing possesses a conscience.

8.2 Humans

9 We should recognize that human nature is always *good*, though the nature of *some humans*—remember the difference—gives little if any cause for rejoicing.

819 On Inhumanity

1 We point out that human beings must be free to choose between what is good and what is bad, with society of course having the responsibility to curb those who would curtail or abuse the rights and freedoms of others [849:2].

2 We also point out that many find affluence a much more difficult test to meet than poverty, and that too many use power for selfish ends instead of for the common good of all [846].

3 We reflect on these things as we think of tragic conditions around the globe from time to time, particularly those involving food and natural resources. Says a Blessed Soul:

4 The lavish contributions nature makes, and makes for *all*, can be used either for good or for bad, for constructive *or* destructive ends. They should be used for noble purposes. But when greed and avarice and lust for power enter the picture, some of those who *control* nature's contributions employ them as weapons to blackmail or crush anyone who resists their demands.

5 The Blessed Soul reminds us:

6 Human beings have not profited much from history. They have not learned their lessons well, if they have learned them at all.

7 Lack of concern and consideration for others is a failing not only of some leaders of nations, but also of some leaders of organizations that exert great influence and power on conditions affecting the community or nation.

8 There are those who would rather plow food into the ground than accept a little less for their efforts. Anyone who wilfully destroys food while there is hunger or starvation anywhere, has a lesson to learn and a spiritual debt to pay.

9 It is not surprising that Illumined Souls find nothing to approve or condone in the needless slaughter or waste of sustenance. As one of them exclaims:

10   How can humanity continue to expect to be provided for, if people deliberately do away with a resource instead of seeing that it benefits someone, somewhere.

820 The Physical Body—and the "Sport" of Prizefighting

1   The physical [earthly] body that envelopes us, that serves as our vehicle of expression for a time, should be cherished as a chalice, a vessel—a holy vessel—while we inhabit it and express through it. For whatever its appearance, it *is* a holy vessel, containing, as it does, while we occupy it, the spark of the *divine* that each of us is blessed with.

2   Because of the spark of divinity it houses while we inhabit it, it is our responsibility to care for our vehicle of expression, and to preserve it well. We cannot neglect that responsibility with impunity.

3   To deliberately subject the physical body to battering and injury is to violate a spiritual law. Those who risk such battering and injury for gain, and those who promote it for gain, alike are guilty.

4   So too are those who get pleasure from such violence. The penalty is certain and sure. For the pandering to brutal, cruel, violent instincts *lowers* one's level of consciousness; and the more one enjoys an exhibition of violence, the more does one spiritually retrogress.

5   To call prizefighting [professional boxing] a "sport" is a mockery of the term, because the speediest way to win, and the primary objective, is to knock one's opponent senseless, thereby inflicting brain damage;[5] and because the prizefighting ring is an arena for entertaining many people who enjoy seeing human beings injure one another.

6   We are not, on the whole, far along the path of progression, when hundreds of millions still delight in such spectacles.

---

[5] The American Medical Association reports brain deterioration in 75% of boxers who have had 20 or more professional fights. Wearing helmets would not reduce this. Over 350 amateur and professional boxers have been killed in the ring since 1945. Neurological associations and the medical associations of at least four nations (including the United States and Britain) have called for a ban on boxing.

Concerns about concussions sustained in American professional football rose to the level of investigations in the U.S. House of Representatives in 2009 because of publicity that retired players were experiencing a far-above-normal incidence of memory-related diseases due to brain trauma.

8.2 Humans

821 Population—and "Overpopulation"

1 Many are puzzled by the tremendous increase in the number of people on earth in the last few hundred years, especially in the light of teachings of some schools of thought. The increase has indeed been phenomenal, particularly during the 20th century. The following estimates of world population at 50-year intervals are compiled from U.S. Government sources.

2
1650	-	500,000,000	
1700	-	630,000,000	[+ 26%][6]
1750	-	795,000,000	[+ 26%]
1800	-	1,002,000,000	[+ 26%]
1850	-	1,265,000,000	[+ 26%]
1900	-	1,656,000,000	[+ 31%]
1950	-	2,516,000,000	[+ 52%]
2000	-	6,085,000,000	[+142%]

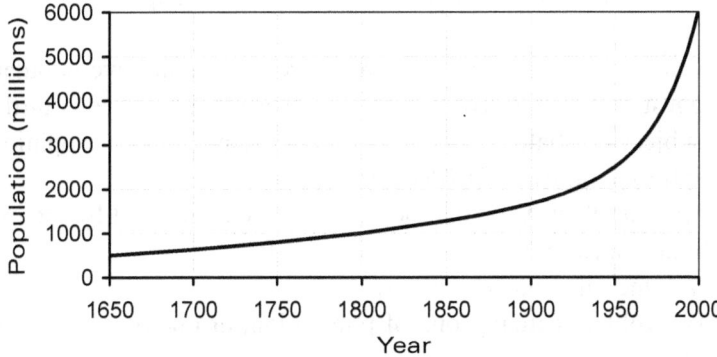

3 There are several reasons for the immense growth in the world population; but to catch any glimpse of the picture, we must first realize that even the thousands of millions of souls on earth today are only a very small percentage of the souls that exist—for there are many, *many* times as many souls in the spirit world as there are on earth.

4 As the USB teaches, there are some lessons that can be learned on earth *only* [1424]. But until comparatively recent times there was *no* opportunity for such vast numbers of individuals to come to earth.

---

[6] For each 50-year period we have calculated the average percentage growth rate, and we see that this has *also* been increasing. According to these figures, in the 18th century the world population increased by 59%, by 65% in the 19th century, and by a tremendous 267% in the 20th century. In the year 2000 it was increasing at a rate near three million per week. The graph was added by the editor.

821

5   All who come to earth come according to Law, and only according to Law; and there must be *opportunity* to come, *according* to Law, before anyone can live in the physical.

6   The opportunity is now greater than ever, because of medical and scientific advances. The earthly life span is far longer than it used to be. Deaths from plague and pestilence are few, compared with other times. The infant mortality rate is much lower than formerly. People as a whole are far healthier than in the past. And the fertility span of most women is longer than ever before.

7   All this of course encourages and promotes a greater number of births than was possible in other ages; so that despite wars that have claimed millions of lives, the world population soars.

8   To those who know a little about Truth, this is not a calamity, but a blessing—a *double* blessing. For it not only gives more souls the opportunity to learn the lessons that can be learned on earth only, but provides individuals and nations with greater opportunity to help one another.

9   Some who do not realize all this are concerned about "overpopulation," and suggest measures to correct it. One measure advocated is birth control, a subject we shall not touch on except to say that in our opinion it is a matter for the *individual* to decide.

10 We can say this: Any "overpopulation" seen is beheld by the eyes of those living on earth, not of those in spirit life.

11 We ask the following questions.

12 Is the problem actually one of population, or one of production and distribution?

13 Is not Nature truly bountiful—in fact *so* bountiful that in some places cultivation of crops is discouraged, with people paid to *not* grow them?

14 Is it not inhumanity that prevents proper distribution of Nature's ample supply?

15 Can human conscience be clear while there is abundance in one place and starvation in another?

16 Does one whose larder is well stocked, but who withholds a crust that would sustain a hungry sister or brother, know the meaning of compassion?

17 In the final analysis, is it not *human beings*—by creating and seeking for self and self alone—that are the greatest problem to overcome?

18 One more thought.

8.3 These Times

19 With more and more machines doing the work of humans, the "problem" may become ever more acute unless automation is used to benefit all humanity. In that case, automation would prove to be one of the greatest boons the earth has ever known, a boon contributing to a golden age.

8.3 THESE TIMES

822 *"These Are the Times That Try Men's Souls"*

1 In late 1776, Thomas Paine—a spirit member of the USB—wrote while on earth:

2 These are the times that try men's souls. The summer soldier and the sunshine patriot will, in this crisis, shrink from the service of their country; but he that stands it NOW, deserves the love and thanks of man and woman.

3 The greater the crisis, the greater the need, the greater and more glorious are the opportunities to be of service; to prove our spiritual worth; to be an example and inspiration to others, by the way we live; to display tolerance; to have love and understanding for *all* people, even those whom we must in all conscience oppose; and above all, to direct thoughts of love and peace and brother-and-sisterhood to the leaders of peoples and of nations, and to *visualize* a world of peace and harmony and understanding.

4 We know that there are thousands who are not "summer soldiers" and "sunshine patriots." We know that the greater the crisis, the greater the need, the more time they will set aside for directing, with tranquillity and power, the thoughts that will counteract and nullify the disordered thinking of others.

5 Paine, incidentally, like most people of vision and universality, was maligned and crucified by many; but he was far from the reprobate some made him out to be.

6 He said: "My country is the world, and my religion is to do good."

823 *The Curse of Complacency*

1 These are indeed difficult times, times to try our souls [822]. But such times have been faced by many people, many generations, in many eras;

823

1. for every age has its own trying experiences, and every generation its own obstacles—some that it *creates*, others that it *inherits*.

2. Trying times are aggravated when administrations do not serve the people well. Some other points should be remembered.

3. A community or nation invites destruction if it does not repudiate and hold to account an administration that fails to preserve law and order; if it does not *swiftly* apprehend and discipline those openly committed to its destruction or to changing it by violence and terror; and if it allows a *second* opportunity to those who take the law into their own hands, or who use freedom of expression to *deny* that freedom to others.

4. Without determination, strength, courage, and a firm hand by those who head any administration, in the face of disruption and destruction law and order will gradually give way to anarchy and chaos.

5. And if a community or nation invites destruction by its failure to meet challenges to law and order, how long can it expect to remain *free*?

6. Liberty and license are *not* the same, and all the sophistry in the world will not make them so.

7. It is one thing to allow an individual to denounce a government official. It is quite another thing, and a criminal thing, to call for his or her murder. Equally criminal are those apologists who term such incitement mere "rhetoric," or who by word or action disparage law and order in nations dedicated to freedom, justice, and progress.

824 The Hour and the Need

1. Every time of change, of changes such as we are now witnessing on earth, is a time to try our souls [822]. Today is no exception. As an Illumined Soul exclaims: "The time is *now* and the need is *great!*"

2. Perhaps more than ever before, the present *is* a time of trial, a time of testing, for almost everyone: individuals in their personal lives, and leaders of peoples and of nations. Whether we have responsibility for only ourselves and those about us, or for the fate of millions, the qualities required are the same: courage, patience, fortitude, principle, love, wisdom, and readiness to sacrifice for what is precious to us.

3. Those who abandon the helm in the midst of a storm are not worthy to command. Those who withdraw from a just cause in the hour of peril are not worthy to march in the vanguard. Those who surrender principle when defeat or stalemate seemingly stares them in the face, are not worthy of victory.

825 A Prayer for These Times

1 Just as an individual may be noble and heroic to an undreamed-of degree in the hour of trial, so too may a people or a nation.

2 Times of peril may produce great individuals—those who lead their people out of the depths and towards the hilltops.

3 The times cry for such leaders.

4 Meanwhile let us pray that those who gather around the council tables will think not only of themselves and their peoples, but of *all* who live on earth; and that they will hear and heed the voices reminding them that we are all sisters and brothers, children of a living and loving God.

826 The Dangers of Some Modern Music

1 Just as color affects people whether or not they are aware of it [930], so too does *sound*, which of course includes music.

2 Some of the music that modern youth enjoy [since the 1960s] has a rhythm and sound that stimulates the senses, and that brings young people a feeling of release from the tensions and pressures of what they see as an adult world.

3 In all eras, the young have been criticized for what pleases *them* but did not appeal to their elders. Their elders have not always been justified in their reactions. But modern elders cannot rightly be blamed if, to them, some music of the young suggests the primitive beat of the tom-tom, which raises the senses to a very high pitch, and if some young people's dancing resembles primitive rites, mimics sex acts, and over-emphasizes animal passions.

4 A great deal of this music and dancing is harmless, let there be no mistake about that. But when the volume of the music is excessive, or it consists, for example, of certain sustained or repetitive sounds, or if it contains many off-notes (between two adjacent halftones in the chromatic scale); or when the dancing includes unnatural contortions—it is then a different matter.

5 For excessively loud music is actually injurious[7]—it is something for parents to think about. The sounds and off-notes mentioned are offen-

---

[7] Because decibels (db), the unit of measurement of sound, are on a logarithmic scale, each additional 3 db indicates a *doubling* of sound intensity. Thus some "rock music" at 120 db is not just 1½ times the intensity of 80 db (the commonly considered dividing line between "loud" and "very loud"), it is *10,000 times as intense*, causing serious loss of hearing.

sive to sensitive people, and may also be harmful. And many unnatural contortions are harmful to the spine, which was not designed for them.

6 Parents would be wise to make sure that their children, from their earliest years—in fact from their very infancy—hear a variety of good music, harmonious music, music that soothes the soul, music that stirs it to heights of great and noble feeling, or that is pleasant just to listen to.

7 Of course it should not be forced on anyone. But in a home where the atmosphere is one of love and harmony and consideration and beauty, good music will have a natural setting, and will in almost all cases so lodge itself into the consciousness that nothing inferior will be able to displace it.

8.4 GOOD AND BAD

827 NOT All That Happens Is for Good

1 It is surprising how some people assert that *all* that happens is for good. Consoling as the thought may be, it is just not true.

2 We say this with no wish to have individuals give up a belief that comforts them—that is never our aim—but to stimulate them to *think*. And as always, we remind them not to blindly accept as fact or truth anything expressed by others [including ourselves], but only to ponder over it and reach their own conclusions.

3 To accept that all that happens is for good is in effect to deny that evils exist, and, by that denial, to do little if anything about ending them.

4 If all that happens *were* for good, then tyranny and oppression and murder and robbery and terrorism and other abominations should be welcomed! But who except those horribly ill in mind could welcome them?

5 This is not to say that sorrow and suffering do not often serve a valuable purpose, or that certain experiences and opportunities available just on earth are not essential for lessons that can be learned here only [1424]. But it *is* to say that some sorrow and suffering, and some experiences, spiritually profit no one.

6 Says an inspirer:

7 > The flat statement so many make, "all that happens is for good," provokes two questions. W*hat* good? And for *whom?*—questions that could well be asked about almost anything.

8.4 Good and Bad

8   Of scores of instances that we could mention, we cite one, and assume that it does not happen for karmic reasons. (Elsewhere we emphasize that *not* all that happens to us is the result of our own acts and actions [1410].)

9   A shopkeeper, a spiritual man, is robbed and slain by an intruder. *What* good is accomplished? And for *whom*? The victim? His widow and children? The murderer? The last only creates or adds to karmic debts that sooner or later must be paid.

10   And certainly The Laws That Govern do *not* require innocent ones to suffer tragedy and hardships, which result mainly from inhumanity to others.

11   It is important to realize that *not* all that happens is for good, because such awareness usually is the first step, a necessary step, to correcting or helping to correct what can be corrected.

828   Of Good and Evil

1   Some schools of thought assert that there is no such thing as evil, and that what others describe as evil is merely the absence of good.

2   But evil is *not* merely the absence of good; it is the presence of that which is *bad*.

3   The average person goes his or her way, without either harming or doing very much for others, trying to take care of personal material needs, but showing little awareness or interest in developing spiritually. "Good" may be absent from the average person's actions, but that absence is far removed from the actual commission of what is bad—murder, rape, pillage, arson, robbery, slander, and a thousand other things.

4   The fact is that there *are* forces of darkness, there *is* evil; and all the hairsplitting, euphemism, and twisting and manipulating of words and terms cannot alter that fact.

5   Of course there are *degrees* of evil—many degrees, as we all should know. There is a vast gulf between the man who steals a loaf of bread to feed his starving children, and the scoundrel who robs a widow of her mite. There is a vast gulf between someone who tells a lie to protect the innocent, and someone else who deliberately lies to injure them. There is a vast gulf between one person who violates a human law to save helpless individuals, and another who violates it for self enrichment at their expense. There is a vast gulf between someone who kills another in self-defense, and someone else who orders the slaughter of thousands of defenseless people.

829 Good and Evil are NOT Opposite Sides of the Same Coin

1 As we have pointed out, many things, repeated often enough, are assumed by the unanalytical to be correct. An example of this is a quotation that has received wide currency in certain circles: "Good and evil are opposite sides of the same coin." *That is just not so.*

2 To use a corrected metaphor along the same lines: Good and evil are *separate* coins—one of worth, the other worthless.

3 To accept the quotation at face value is to believe that evil must exist wherever there is good—a belief we completely *reject*. For in the higher spirit realms there certainly is no evil whatever; it is *impossible* for it to exist there. The quotation also implies that the greater the amount of *good*, the greater must be the *evil* that exists—something we *equally* reject. If the quotation contained any truth, any attempt to progress would be *pointless*, for *any* increase in good would be offset by an increase in *evil*.

4 There are *many* good people on earth without one iota of evil existing in their nature, whatever their flaws or frailties. And they—and others too, of course—*can* grow in goodness without any corresponding growth of evil within their own being or elsewhere.

5 The same comment applies to other pairs of opposites such as love and hate, light and darkness, and peace and turmoil. They are *not* opposite sides of the *same* coin, but *separate* coins entirely.

830 An Often-Asked Question

1 One question many ask is why God "allows" tragedy to occur. Many cannot reconcile the idea of a loving God with the pain and suffering they see about them, or that they themselves endure. Many others reproach God for "permitting" this or that to happen.

2 Missing is the realization that is it *not* God but *humans* who are responsible for the evil and suffering that exist, and that it is people's *ignorance* of The Laws that Govern, and people's *inhumanity* to one another, which are responsible for our ills [819].

3 Missing is the realization that the greatest blessings a loving God has given us are *freedom and free will,* and that freedom and free will by their very nature include the privilege of *selecting* the path we would tread [701].

4 *Choice* is implicit in *freedom*, which means the power to choose or decide without constraint from any source.

8.4 Good and Bad

5 Would our children be free if they did nothing except at our command? If they did not get up, or stand, or sit, or open their mouth, or speak, or eat, or take a step, or run, or walk, or smile, or laugh, or do any of a thousand things, without *our* word? We would think they were robots, and robots they would be. And we would be robots too—and there would be *no* purpose in existence—if we had no choice of words or actions.

6 *We* show understanding of *our* children by the latitude—which should be within reason—that we give them. Could a God of Love and Wisdom show *less* understanding of *God's* children?

7 *We* give our children freedom to speak and think and act—all of course within proper limits, if we have a sense of parental responsibility. Could a God of Love and Wisdom give us *less* freedom?

8 Of course there is a great difference between *liberty* and *license*. And as we who love our own children wisely, discipline them when needed, so does a loving God discipline *us* when needed. The discipline we receive takes place automatically, by The Law of Cause and Effect, even though it is sometimes deferred until after we pass on to spirit life.

9 We may not understand *why* it is deferred, for there is often greater wisdom in events than we can perceive at the moment. But knowing, as we do, that God is a God of Love and Wisdom, of Law and Justice, and is That Which Is All-Good, we know that in the long run the scales are always balanced. We know that *in the long run* there is not, and cannot be, any injustice—for The Law of Cause and Effect governs what we ourselves are responsible for, and The Law of Compensation makes up for what we suffer through no fault of our own [Sec. 4.4].

831 The Doors to Spiritual Progress Are Never Closed

1 As the USB principle puts it: The doors to spiritual progress are never closed to anyone [103:7]. Nor are they ever closed to humankind as a whole.

2 The world *continues* to have problems. It has *always* had problems—problems created by *human beings*. But as we have said more than once, we do not despair [807].

3 We have only to compare present conditions with those of a century ago, or even less, to realize that the world *has* advanced, and in *many* respects, though not so much spiritually as materially, and not as rapidly as we would wish.

4 [It is the goal of the USB to hasten the world's *spiritual* development (770:2–3).]

832 On Non-Interference

1. We have the shining example of Illumined Souls who, though they come to inspire and inform, and gladly give us advice and counsel if desired, make *no* attempt whatever to interfere with our free will. Nor would they if they could. As one of them has said:

2. > We who come to you realize that you are *individuals*, that you are separate entities, though yet belonging to the One Cause. But we have *no* right to take from you what is your inheritance. Individuals must be free to choose between what is good and what is bad.

833 The Dangers of Some of Today's Entertainment

1. What is harmful is not the use, but the misuse, of any force, we emphasize. And *any* force, *any* instrument, can be used either for good or for bad. The choice is ours.

2. These thoughts apply to modern entertainment media.

3. We are convinced that certain types of television programs and movies, [and more recently video games, all of which are becoming more and more available over the Internet,] are considerably and increasingly to blame not only for the rise in crime in recent decades in many countries where such entertainment has become part of the way of life, but also for a general deterioration of standards and morality.

4. Apologists for television have long asserted that the frequent appearance of ruthless and often pointless crime and violence in many of today's programs does not affect the attitudes and behavior of viewers. This is a strange claim to make regarding an industry in which advertisers pay thousands of millions of dollars a year to *influence* people to desire or more greatly desire products advertised. To suggest that a steady diet of advertisements *is* effective, but that a steady diet of horror and violence is *not*, is hard to believe.

5. The fact is that television *does* influence people.

6. Crime and violence [and glorifying the life styles of gangsters] in entertainment media *do* tend to foster, and especially in the young to *create*, undesirable values and standards that have no place in a decent society—for they are values and standards in which crime and violence are the solution to many problems. Let us bear this in mind:

7. The difference [especially for young people without soundly-established values] between the *effects* of watching actual crime and violence

8.4 Good and Bad

in one's own personal environment and the effects of watching them on the screen is very questionable.

8   Another point to remember: For too many people, the steps are short between repudiation and indifference and acceptance of anything offensive. As Alexander Pope[8] expressed it:

9
> Vice is a monster of so frightful mien,
> As, to be hated, needs but to be seen;
> But seen too oft, familiar with her face,
> We first endure, then pity, then embrace.

10   There still *are* some television advertisers who will not sponsor anything that lacks sound social values, regardless of so-called "ratings" of what the "public" supposedly prefers. They know (as also do other advertisers, of course) that people, particularly those of tender years, *are* affected by what they see and hear; and so they only sponsor programs in which such noble qualities as courage, integrity, compassion, understanding, kindness, love, and reason are favorably portrayed. Crime and violence, if part of the plot, are not depicted in unnecessary detail, or just for their own sake.

11   But the ranks of enlightened sponsors are not legion. And so it falls on *parents* to decide what their children may or may not see on television. Like all other responsibilities, it is one that, if unmet, creates a debt that must sooner or later be paid.

834 The Swing of the Pendulum

1   Throughout history there have been many who complained and took issue against what they considered bad or unjust. With few exceptions, they had integrity and courage: They had a firm conviction and certainty that their cause was right, and they were ready to suffer for it.

2   In more recent times, however, we have seen individuals and groups with complaints increasingly go to extremes. And *extremes breed extremes.* Permissiveness is followed by repression, which in turn is followed by permissiveness (and lawlessness). For the pendulum swings

---

[8] Alexander Pope, 1688–1744, English poet. From *An Essay on Man*, Epistle II, 1733.

both ways [805:1–2]; and the greater the swing in one direction, the greater the swing in the other.

Says a Blessed Soul:

> When we speak of the swing of the pendulum, let us be conscious that the pendulum is *always* in a state of movement. It never remains in one position, but is constantly making its way in one direction or the other.
>
> Humanity has reached a point, symbolically speaking, where there is need for the pendulum to reverse its direction. People of good will and wisdom will strive to see that it does so in an orderly fashion, and not to the opposite extreme. And they will endeavor to confine its path in future, and to a moderate pace, so that it can no longer swing too far in *either* direction.
>
> For the *moderate* path is the best path—the only path to steady and lasting progress.

835 The Best of Both

One lesson history teaches is how impermanent as a rule are changes produced by violence, terror, oppression, and tyranny, which contain within themselves the seeds of their own eventual destruction. Enduring changes are usually introduced gradually and peacefully, with the approval of the majority, and with the aim of raising lower levels and standards rather than demolishing higher ones. It is senseless to destroy what is good and useful just for the sake of change. It is folly to destroy the good with the bad.

Progress results from blending the best of the old with the best of the new.

836 The Decline in Standards

While the world has advanced, *materially*, in many ways in the past hundred years or so, it has not done so in all other respects. In some ways, in fact, it has *retrogressed*, and the observer who thinks about this cannot be unaware of the decline in too many countries of standards in literature, arts, education, morality, and related areas [see 718]. [These standards are vital because a major measure of the greatness of a civilization or a nation is its greatness in these areas.]

8.4 Good and Bad

2. Instead of endeavoring to improve their work by striving towards perfection in their fields, and thus reaching higher levels of consciousness and performance, too many practitioners today have become content with mediocrity—or worse. It is a sad commentary on the low standards that have crept into the arts, for instance, that much that is popular is quite undistinguished, to put it kindly.

3. If unchecked, the cult of mediocrity inevitably leads to ever lower standards, and an ever greater failure on the part of individuals to discipline themselves and struggle to reach the heights.

4. We can agree that there *is*, and *should* be, variety in the arts, as elsewhere, and still recognize that much that passes for some forms of art is puerile and juvenile if not altogether offensive.

5. ***Education*** presents a classic example of the disarray that can result from a continuous bombardment of "new approaches" of one sort or another.

6. When the school system in any area is lax in discipline, or is devoted more to entertaining children or keeping them quiet than to instructing them in at least the "three Rs," or advances pupils automatically to a higher grade even if they have made no progress at all, it is no wonder that a great number of students, often a majority of them, "graduate" virtually illiterate.

7. Unable to read well, or to comprehend much of what they read; unable to correctly compose or parse a simple sentence; unable to spell the simplest common words; and unskilled in elementary multiplication tables —their education is a farce. What is worse, they are tragically unequipped to meet many demands of normal adult life, and the range of occupations open to them is limited indeed.

8. When schools teach little if any history—of peoples and nations and ideas—the failure is compounded, for we cannot *learn* from history if we don't *know* history. It is often because of people's lack of awareness of past events that they endure situations and conditions that lead to poverty, war, or the erosion of sound moral values.

9. History, by the way, discloses, among other things, that much that is described today as "the new morality" not only existed in other eras in other lands, but contributed to the weakening of family life and the collapse of society and civilizations.

10. Ineffective school systems need to revert to *basic education*, to the *fundamentals* that, once acquired, provide individuals with many and varied paths to greater knowledge.

11 Schools should not have to provide "frills" or instruction in subjects that the home normally could provide equally well or better.

12 As for the seemingly endless controversy whether prayer should or should not be part of the school program, we say two things:

13 — We favor the separation of church and state.

14 — Parents who attach importance to prayer, as we do, certainly could devote a few moments daily to family prayer.

15 Some of today's **music** is actually *injurious*, we have noted [826].

16 And too many current songs lack two desirable elements: a tuneful melody and a literate lyric, suitably "wedded."

17 The **news media** much too often feature the low or violent or criminal, and report too little of what is decent and wholesome [833].

18 Television reporters and camera crews sometimes encourage violence or destruction, to make "news."

19 Newspapers too often contain incorrect grammar and punctuation. Not all newsreaders on television know the correct pronunciation of some frequently-used words.

20 As for **writing** or **literature**, we repeat our previous comment [713:5] that the main value of art is to *encourage and uplift* others to loftier forms of appreciation and *expression*. If writers wish to express at low levels, that is their right. But we should not encourage them by purchasing their wares, and thus stimulate others to follow in their footsteps.

21 It is in **poetry** that we witness one of the saddest declines in standards and in *appreciation* of standards.

22 Poetry is not the mere splitting up into separate lines of what is often merely pedestrian prose. By definition, poetry is rhythmic composition that excites pleasure by beautiful, imaginative, or elevated thought. It should be *clear*. It should have an *intensity and beauty* far beyond prose, except for that rare and sublime prose that is characterized by great beauty of language or thought. It should be *compressed*, saying much in a few words; it should be *taut*, like the strings of a violin, from which no lovely music can be drawn if the strings are slack. It should have a fervor and finality that is almost impossible in prose. It should at least in some degree amuse, inform, delight, enchant, or inspire.

8.4 Good and Bad   □ 836

23 As for *sculpture* and *painting*, these are not wonderful just because they are *unidentifiable*.

24 As for, *morality*, it is sad to note that integrity is too often lacking in those who could be shining examples to others, notably the young. Not only nations, but individuals, professional athletes in particular, one-sidedly break their written word if it suits them, repudiating agreements freely and deliberately made.

25 Standards of morality should be high in any role we play, or we cheat others—and in the long run ourselves. As employers, for instance, we should give a full-day's *pay* for a full-day's work; as employees, we should do a full-day's *work* for a full-day's pay [749:4].

26 Right conduct should *always* be the basis for our acts and actions.

27 In many countries, the public display of indecent and even immoral material (pornography) continues in movies, popular publications, advertising, and related media. It is offensive to many, and of special concern where the susceptible young are likely to become accustomed or attracted to it [833:9–10].

28 We have emphasized that individuals must be free to choose between what is good and what is bad. Further, we have pointed out that society *also* has that right; and in fact it is a *duty* for society to prevent *public* demonstration or display of what it considers offensive or immoral.

. . . . .

29 What can *we* do to combat, and if possible *reverse*, the continuing decline in standards?

30 Much.

31 We can set our *own* standards high, as the USB constantly exhorts, regardless of what others do.

32 We can strive to maintain, and if possible improve, the quality of our *own* work, whatever the field we are in. We can strive for a high level of skill in whatever *we* do, and not be guilty of slipshod or faulty work even if we know it would pass muster.

33 We can express our displeasure with anything unsatisfactory that is completed for us or that is placed before us, and if possible reject it. To passively accept poor work in any field only encourages poorer work in that field.

34 We can, as individuals, or as a group of individuals, demand *quality* in the things we buy.

35   We can refuse to patronize what is low or indecent.

36   We can make our voices heard.

37   If enough of us do this, we shall stem the drift to ever lower standards, and, better still, perhaps lead the way back to standards of comparative excellence.

38   Eternal vigilance is not the price of liberty alone: It is the price of high standards in *any* sphere. And those who are in a position to oppose, combat, or reject a debasement of standards, but fail to do so, do not merit any thanks.

39   For progress in general comes from raising what is low, not from reducing what is high. And a nation's levels of education, music, news media, language (spoken and written), writing, literature, poetry, painting, sculpture, and morality, are *key* indicators of its level of consciousness.

837 On What Is Holy

1   Where there is love and harmony among those who gather together in the desire to selflessly serve others, there indeed is a holy place, however small or humble it may be.

2   Where there is love and peace and friendliness among the people who *live* in it, there indeed is holy ground.

3   Of itself alone, *no* place or land is holy, or holier than any other. It is those who *live* in it, or who have *lived* in it, that make it holy or unholy.

4   Some places and lands considered holy have been the scene of so much bitterness and strife, so much destruction, and of so many perishing by the sword—all in the name of what was "holy" to the *slayers*—that one wonders why that adjective is still used in describing them.

5   The vibrations left on a scene by powerful individuals or events—whether for good or bad—may literally take ages to dissipate, unless meanwhile cleansed or nullified by equally powerful vibrations of an opposing nature.

6   Water, as we point out, is a great cleanser of vibrations [913:5]. More than one portion of the earth's surface has been cleansed of bad vibrations (impressed upon it by people and events) only by a powerful and prolonged deluge of one sort or another.

8.5 CRIME

838 The Need for Respect for Law and Order

1   A prime cause of some distressing conditions in the world today is disrespect for law and order. Each nation that breaks its pledges, each official who flouts the laws he or she has sworn to uphold, each individual who evades or violates laws prepared for the common good by the people or their duly-elected representatives—*each* contributes to the ills that afflict humanity.

2   We cannot expect human laws to match the perfection of The Laws That Govern. Nor should we expect human laws to please everyone. Not even The Laws That Govern do that! But as long as there are avenues for demonstrating, in law-abiding fashion, against what we consider unjust or unwise, we should *observe* human laws that do not infringe on any personal privacy that poses no nuisance or danger to others.

3   Law and order are necessary on earth—as they are elsewhere too, for that matter. We cannot hope to live in peace, we cannot hope to have order in our existence on earth, if each individual and each nation obeyed only those laws that please them, and disregarded all others.

4   People have the choice of law or anarchy. They have the choice of the great measure of freedom that law provides, or the virtual loss, from anarchy, of *all* freedom.

5   Respect for law is not fostered by laws that are ill-prepared or ill-advised or allowed to be broken with impunity by anyone. Only truly-needed laws should be enacted, and they should be strictly enforced. The desirable aim is a minimum of laws, a maximum of compliance.

6   Nor is respect for law fostered if laws do not equally affect *all*.

7   No human law is *just* that does not apply to everyone, mitigating circumstances excepted. By no stretch of the imagination can wealth, position, or power be considered a mitigating circumstance.

8   Laws should be as just and wise as people can enact, and revised whenever they can be improved in the light of added knowledge.

839 The Age of Responsibility

1   *When* does an individual's responsibility begin?

2   It is a question often asked, by those who are understandably dismayed by the fact that in many places the law *prohibits* newspapers from pub-

lishing the names of those under eighteen who commit crimes, even when the offenses are particularly violent and offensive.

3   An individual's responsibility begins when one is *normally* capable of distinguishing between right and wrong. There is no specific age that applies to everyone; children today mature earlier than their forebears. We should not, for instance, blame an infant who plays with matches and sets the house on fire; the blame lies on those who keep matches within its reach. But average teenagers who commit arson certainly know the act is wrong; and they should not, merely because they are under a certain age, escape appropriate punishment, which could well include the unwelcome publicity that might deter others from the same transgression.

4   The USB teaches that no one who is *normally* capable of reasoning is exempt from personal responsibility. We emphasize the word "normally" because one is *not* absolved from responsibility for acts committed under the influence, say, of drugs or alcohol freely and voluntarily taken.

5   Rarely do we help people by shielding them from the consequences of their behavior. On the contrary, that usually encourages them to further errors and excesses, as events in the past few decades have dramatically and sometimes tragically demonstrated.

6   Wrongdoing will be discouraged only when fitting punishment is swift and certain, with the names published of *all* (normally capable of reasoning) who commit major crimes, especially crimes of violence.

840 Punishment—and Deterrents to Crime

1   The USB stresses that sooner or later the scales are always balanced, and that in the long run there is not, and cannot be, any injustice—for the Law of Cause and Effect governs what we ourselves are responsible for, and the Law of Compensation makes up for what we suffer through no fault of our own.

2   Of course this does not mean that we should overlook crime. Society *should* attempt to correct conditions that lead to crime [and try to prevent them from arising], and it should discipline, punish, and protect itself from wrongdoers, especially those who wilfully and deliberately harm others. Penalties, however, tend to lose effect in *deterring* wrongdoing unless they are justly and promptly applied.

3   Certainly on earth, where [human] justice is not automatic, *justice delayed is often justice denied.*

8.5 Crime

4   The greatest deterrent to crime is not severity of punishment—although the punishment *should* fit the crime—but *the certainty and swiftness of it*. By swiftness we mean neither undue haste nor undue delay, but a fair, lawful and orderly process while a crime is still fresh and vivid in the public's mind, and without unnecessary postponements before penalties are enforced.

5   Those convicted of severer offenses such as crimes of violence or threats of violence, looting or destruction of property, or inciting to lawlessness and riot, should be required to begin serving their sentences without delay. Certainly they should not be released from custody during any appeal to higher courts—to give them a golden opportunity to commit *further* offences or to fan the flames of lawlessness that others or they themselves had kindled.

6   Another important deterrent to crime would be to *enforce* laws and ordinances against anyone and everyone guilty of excessively provoking others.

841   On Capital Punishment

1   There are several things to weigh well with respect to the death penalty.

2   One is that execution prematurely returns to the spirit world many who are so unremorseful, so corrupt, so inflamed with the bitter passions of hate and revenge, that they are completely deaf and blind to all spirit efforts to enlighten them. In fact they are consumed by the desire to incite the weak and debased on earth to the same or similar violence that brought *them* to the bar of justice, and in many cases they succeed in inducing or *controlling* individuals on earth to do just that.

3   In discussing sleepwalking [921:6–11], we relate circumstances that impel some spirit individuals, in bitterness, to gain possession of the physical body of someone who is asleep, with the aim of destroying it, and we emphasize that people under the influence of alcohol or narcotics are especially susceptible to such possession. And in explaining the reenactment of battle scenes hundreds of years old, we say that in most cases it is because those slain in battle are still so possessed by bitterness and the desire for victory that they are not conscious of anything else... and they continue to enact and reenact the last earthly experience they recall. Time means nothing to them, and they remain as yet unteachable... [1136:5].

4   That same bitterness more often than not *adds* to the unrepentance of those executed for crimes.

5   When criminals remain in the physical, however, as a rule they take less time to realize the error of their ways. For then in many cases the acute bitterness usually bred by what some call "the supreme penalty" is not present to cement their destructive feelings.

6   Advanced ones in the spirit world have a great deal to cope with in attempting to aid the billions of less-than-highly-evolved occupants of the lower realms and the large number from earth who daily return to spirit life. That burden should not be increased by dispatching defiant individuals to their side of life.

7   For these and other reasons, The Brother&Sisterhood's Illumined Inspirers are opposed to the death penalty.

8   This does *not* mean that society should refrain from punishing and protecting itself from wrongdoers, or in some cases *isolating* evildoers from their fellows.

9   Nor does it mean, as some strangely assert, that punishment is no deterrent. Would anyone say that penalties for infractions of traffic rules do *not* deter many people from committing or repeating them? Or that the likelihood of imprisonment, if caught, does not restrain at least *some* individuals from theft or vandalism or other crimes?

10   But appropriate punishment *can* be applied without the death penalty.

842 Poverty and Crime

1   From time to time we hear that the main cause of crime is poverty. But poverty is not the main cause of crime, it is one of the causes, although it often presents *temptation* to do wrong.

2   Many of the most illustrious men and women in history came from families that were extremely poor in material things, but they nevertheless stirred the heart and mind of generation after generation by their lofty thought, their noble aims, their unfailing integrity, and their unconquerable spirit in the face of seemingly hopeless circumstances.

3   "As the twig is bent, the tree's inclined," goes the proverb. It is in the home and family where *inclination* to wrongdoing, or *repugnance* to wrongdoing, is best developed or nurtured. Crime results largely from unwholesome attitudes that are not sufficiently discouraged in a child's formative years, or that are actually encouraged by the example parents

8.5 Crime □ 842

set. The fact that many of the materially wealthy also commit various forms of crime—including shoplifting, swindling, extortion, promoting drugs, and murder—demonstrates that it is not poverty but *lack of character* that is the great source of crime.

4 Boredom, as we note elsewhere [907:26], is another factor, and quite a few individuals resort to crime for the "thrills" they get from it. Idle hands are ripe for mischief or worse.

5 But the main fault, the main burden, as we say elsewhere, lies with parents who abdicate their responsibilities as parents [907:3–7]. And among the parents who are most remiss are those who out of mistaken kindness desire to spare children the struggles that they themselves overcame, not realizing that any *honorable* endeavor to cope with difficulties develops or strengthens character. This does not mean that parents should create hardships for their children, but that they should not deprive them of opportunities for growth that lie in overcoming, or doing one's best to overcome, obstacles.

6 If the young receive the care and affection that is their due, and at the same time have to *earn* things above and beyond their normal needs; if they learn the value of a dollar or pound or whatever is their national currency; if they learn to distinguish between right and wrong, most of them will then be well equipped for life. They will not expect to get something for nothing, or by dishonorable means. They will not enter or linger in a drug culture for either the peace or excitement they believe it may offer. They will not find an irresistible lure in anything forbidden. They will not evade their responsibilities. They will not find pleasure in straying from the path for real or fancied grievances against their elders. They will not resort to crime.

7 As we also say, it is in the home and family that sound values and morals and philosophy can be most thoroughly instilled into children [905:3], so that undesirable pressures by others can be successfully resisted. Of course some children will turn wayward even if the home and family environment are all that they should be: In that case, of course, the parents are spiritually blameless and incur no debt.

8 It is a tribute to the human race that despite years or even a lifetime of material poverty, untold millions of individuals make no attempt to harm other people in any way.

8.6 Leadership and Example

843 The Good Shepherd

1 The good shepherd does not *knowingly* allow wolves into the fold.

2 The good shepherd does not throw *any* sheep to the wolves, knowing it would but whet their appetite for more.

3 The good shepherd *realizes* a responsibility to the flock and a duty to protect them in every way possible.

844 Of Some "Debunkers"

1 Some writers have made a habit of "debunking" popular heroes of the past.

2 However, a nation *needs* heroes. We do not mean military conquerors, of course, at least not those who wage wars of aggression, but heroes who by their words and example arouse others to goodness and courage and love of liberty and zeal for what is right.

3 A nation needs *tradition:* traditions based on virtues such as honesty, integrity, compassion, principle, self-reliance, and concern for others. Many of the wrongs around the globe are caused or aggravated by the absence of wholesome traditions.

4 A nation needs a sense of purpose and continuity. It suffers when schools minimize history, or when teachers distort it. To accentuate the harmless and often endearing foibles of good and great men and women, and disregard their magnificent qualities and achievements, is like emphasizing insignificant flaws in an exquisite painting and ignoring its overall beauty.

5 A nation without heroes is rarely heroic. A nation without pride in its history is rarely inspired. A nation without ideals is rarely noble.

6 Individuals should be judged, in part at least, in the context of the times they lived in. For example, when slavery was common, there were still people who treated their slaves with kindness and consideration. When savagery and brutality were common, there were still conquerors who were magnanimous and compassionate in victory.

8.6 Leadership and Example

845 The Tyranny of the Few

1 In recent decades some determined and vocal minorities have taken part in various types of demonstrations in numerous countries. Many participants are undoubtedly inspired by the purest motives. But where there are ample avenues to demonstrate, in law-abiding fashion, against what one considers wrong, there is little excuse for inconveniencing or endangering others.

2 Just as the many should not tyrannize the few, neither should the few tyrannize the many.

3 Cruel and inhuman as have been the tyrannies of the many throughout history, they have been matched, and in fact exceeded, by the tyrannies of the few.

4 Some demonstrators who protest against what democratic nations do, remain [along with some democratic nations themselves] silent about the actions of totalitarian nations that deny freedom to individuals, and their right to protest.

5 The few have always included some who thought that they alone were uniquely equipped to decide what is best for humanity in general, and for fellow citizens in particular.

6 But truly great thinkers and leaders have always shown respect for democracy and the common sense of the average citizen. They have been patient with views differing from their own, and open to alternative solutions to problems. And they have been tolerant, respectful of others, knowledgeable of history and the lessons of history, flexible, practical, forthright, broad-minded, wise, and understanding. But most notably they bear the hallmark of truly great souls—*humility;* and it is usually to the humble that wisdom and understanding come [615:2–3].

7 A nation or administration governed by leaders with the qualities we have described would have little difficulty responding to "the tyranny of the few."

846 The Abuse of Power

1 There are individuals whom circumstances place in positions of power, and who, lacking any real wisdom or humility beneath their outward facade, strut their hour upon the stage as if dominating the universe. It is even worse when they allow themselves to be overcome by power or pride, and then *glory* in power. The saying "Power corrupts; absolute power corrupts absolutely" is unfortunately demonstrated more often as not.

2   "The path of glory leads but to the grave," said Gray.[9] To those in any level or position who misuse or abuse their power, who sacrifice integrity for self-aggrandizement and domination, the grave, if that indeed *were* the end, might be a welcome alternative to what actually awaits them. For as we know, the grave provides *no* escape for debts incurred, and all debts, large or small, must be paid to the last uttermost measure.

3   Inspirers of the USB repeatedly stress that the earth is our proving ground, and that all that comes our way here, so-called fortune and so-called misfortune alike, provides tests that determine the degree if any of our spiritual mettle. Strange as it may seem to some, people often find affluence a much more difficult test to successfully meet than poverty; and as history reveals, countless individuals and many peoples and nations display a more heroic mold and show greater unselfishness and concern for others in times of crises such as war and devastation, than in times of peace and material prosperity.

4   Those who know that life on earth is little more than a flash in eternity, those who consciously or unconsciously realize that *the greatest wealth is nobility of character*, will *not* use power for selfish ends, but as a trust to be exercised for the common good of all.

847 *Some Lessons to be Learned*

1   As the USB teaches, there are *some* lessons that can be learned only on earth [1424]. This truth applies not only to the individual, but also to organizations, peoples, and nations.

2   One lesson is that those who use the sword, except in self-preservation, eventually *perish* by the sword, metaphorically or literally.

3   Another is that those who put profits before people, and politics before principle, sow the wind, and eventually reap the whirlwind.

---

[9] Thomas Gray, 1716–1771, English poet and professor, considered one of the most learned persons of his century.

848 The Big Lie

1 The responsibilities of today's leaders of nations are grave indeed. One responsibility is to avoid the technique of the big lie, which has caused grievous suffering in the world. However monstrous and outrageously wicked, the big lie, if proclaimed ceaselessly over and over and over again, is accepted by many who do not *reason*, who do not *reflect*, and who do not *realize* that the mere incessant repetition of a lie does not convert the lie to fact.

2 The individual, with eyes and ears assailed by a barrage of claims and counter-claims, would do well to remember the words of an Illumined Inspirer of the USB:

3 > Think, and accept. Think, and reject. Think, and suspend judgement. But *think!*

8.7 FREEDOM

849 Freedom for All—a Major Principle of the USB

1 If there is one thing The Brother&Sisterhood stands for, it is the freedom of the individual [108].

2 Human beings *should* have that freedom, that liberty. *But liberty is not license.* Freedom—the freedom that is our right—does not give us the privilege to abuse with impunity the rights of others. And society has the responsibility to take measures to curb any individual or group of individuals who would curtail or abuse the rights and freedom of others.

3 Those measures should of course be applied with tolerance, with love, with understanding, and with the desire to enlighten.

4 We should also remember that each right, each freedom, should be exercised with a due regard for the welfare of others. As Oliver Wendell Holmes, an Associate Justice of the United States Supreme Court, put it so well in 1919:

5 > The most stringent protection of free speech would not protect a man in falsely shouting "fire" in a theater and causing a panic.

850 The Freedom of Personal Interpretation

1   Few of us are stirred in the very same degree by the very same sunset. Few of us see the very same beauty in the very same rose. Few of us are touched to the very same extent by the very same truth.

2   All that we see, all that we hear, all that we read, all that we sense, affects us differently, according to our different levels of consciousness.

3   And even on the very *same* level of consciousness there may be differences in personal interpretation.

4   So we should not expect everyone or anyone to respond to anything exactly as we ourselves respond to it—whether it is the melody we hear, or the flower we see, or the truths Illumined Souls present.

5   We should know that for all God's children, wherever they may live, freedom would not be complete without the freedom of personal interpretation.

851 The Rights of the Individual

1   In these times of turmoil and upheaval, when many of our ways of life, good as well as bad, are under fire, and when a multitude of problems clamors for solution, it may help us to see things in better perspective if we reflect upon one question: What does an individual have a *right* to?

2   Volumes could of course be written on this subject, and have been, for the rights of the individual are many; but they can be encompassed in one basic right. As a Blessed Soul puts it:

3   The individual, *every* individual, has the right to an *opportunity* to express in dignity as a human being.

4   Each of us has the right, unless we forfeit it by our actions, to be treated with respect and consideration, no matter whether we are rich or poor in the things of the world, and regardless of our race or color or faith or national origin.

5   If some are in need, we should help them. Indeed, it is our moral duty to do so. We can best do this by providing aid in developing *skills* to those who truly desire to learn, *opportunity* to those who truly seek to support themselves, and *advancement* to those who are truly anxious to work and work well. We should do what we can to encourage initiative, legitimate initiative, in individuals, especially if they have never had the

8.7 Freedom

opportunity to express it. And we should try to help them develop a sense of worth in themselves and in anything they can do that is of value.

6 But their right to an opportunity to express in dignity as human beings does not give them the right to impose *their* views upon the majority. It does not give them the right to demand more than they merit. It does not give them the right to rob and steal and destroy if their "demands" are not met. It does not give them the right to burn down their dwellings and then insist on other dwellings because they have no roof over their heads. It does not give them the right to decide *which* democratically-established laws they will obey, and which they will ignore. It does not give them the right to disrupt the life of the community if any of their desires are unfulfilled. And it does not give them the right to imperil the safety of their country.

7 For the rights an individual possesses do *not* include the right to infringe on the rights of *others*.

8 We emphasize that many of the problems of the free world are created, or at least compounded, by those within and without who would destroy the democratic way of life. We emphasize that those who use the sword, except in self-preservation, eventually perish by the sword, literally or metaphorically. And we emphasize that the pendulum swings in *both* directions [834].

852 The Right to Privacy

1 We point out elsewhere a vital element of freedom: the right not only to do, but the right *not* to do [903:7].

2 There is another right, a most important right, and one that is too often violated by too many governments: the right to privacy.

3 Not, in our opinion, particularly well defined in dictionaries, *privacy* was simply and illuminatingly described several decades ago by Associate Justice Louis Brandeis of the United States Supreme Court as "the right to be let alone—the most comprehensive of rights and the right most valued by civilized men."

4 We have a right to go our own way, in our own fashion, so long as we do not harm or imperil others by our acts and actions. Without that right, can freedom truly exist?

853 Some Notes on Freedom

1. Freedom and free will are our heritage, and no one has the right to take from us that which is our inheritance. It is only unevolved individuals, on either side of life, who would do so if they could.

. . . . .

2. There are those on earth who spread confusion, either deliberately or in ignorance. Wittingly or unwittingly, they foster fear and alarm and panic.

3. Slogans are sometimes part of their armory of disruption. Subtly they suggest that slavery is preferable to death. A far cry from the ringing declaration of another year: "Give me liberty, or give me death!"

4. Freedom is our priceless heritage. But things are worth only what we are prepared to pay for them. Whether it is Truth or Freedom or anything else, its value to us is only what we are ready and willing to sacrifice for it. If we are not prepared to defend Freedom, we do not deserve it.

5. To have liberty, people must love it enough to die for it if need be. To the lasting glory of the human race, there always are such souls. It is they who make tyrants tremble. For tyrants know that while one lover of freedom breathes, freedom lives.

6. Of course true lovers of freedom want liberty not only for themselves but for *others*—just as those who strive for brother-and-sisterhood know that it must include *all* human beings, no matter who they are, no matter what the level of their consciousness.

7. Weigh well the words of those on earth who would have us surrender our birthright without a struggle.

. . . . .

8. To *have* freedom, we must yield a part of it. It is a small price to pay for that blessing.

9. We cannot have a police force to protect us, or law courts to enforce justice, or traffic control to make for smooth and safe flow of vehicles and pedestrians, without giving up any individual "right" to harm others, to damage and steal property, and to drive or walk exactly when and where and how we wish.

10. In any democratic society, there must be rules for the general welfare. The rules may sometimes restrict the complete freedom of *individuals*, but that is indeed a trifling price to pay for the many freedoms they would otherwise lack.

854 A Right and Responsibility of Nations

1 As we have stated, individuals should be free to choose between what is good and what is bad, with society responsible for curbing those who would curtail or abuse the rights and freedom of others. In the same way, a *nation* should have the same freedom, with a society of nations being responsible for curbing any nation or group of nations that would infringe on the rights and freedom of others.

855 The Right to Dissent

1 In the freer nations, the right to dissent is taken for granted. What unfortunately is often not equally recognized by some dissenters, is the right of others to dissent from *them*.

2 Dissenters do not have the right to harass and embarrass those who disagree with them.

3 We cannot too often emphasize that *liberty is not license*. The tragedy resulting from those who confuse liberty with license, or from dissenters who themselves brook no dissent, is that the repressive measures they invite often affect not just them, but entire populations.

8.8 CHALLENGES

856 The Battle Goes On

1 The forces of darkness, the forces of evil, are unrelenting, tenacious, implacable, insatiable, ruthless, devious, and *patient*. They will resort to any lie, any deception, any terror, any killing, in their drive to dominate the world by enslaving or destroying all who oppose them. But their greatest weapon is their *patience*. They do not weary of the battle—as many who resist them do—and they retreat, if they must, only to regroup and rearm before returning to the attack. And all the while, to camouflage their purposes from the unthinking, they debase terms that have long represented the highest ideals of noble men and women everywhere.

2 They unfortunately receive breathing spells, sometimes when on the very brink of disaster, from those who become impatient during any prolonged struggle, who will not seize the initiative, who will not acknowledge the *nature* of the forces they face, and who will not learn the *lessons* that history so abundantly provides.

3   The forces of darkness are helped by the selfish who desire aid for themselves, but lend no hand to another; who desire any commitment to protect *them* honored, but condemn the honoring of that commitment to *others*.

4   Anyone should be able to realize that while it takes only *one* to make war, it takes at least *two* to make peace. It takes *wisdom* to maintain eternal vigilance, which is indeed the price of liberty. It takes *courage* to resist aggression, and to continue to resist it despite a ceaseless flood of hostile propaganda from without and within.

5   The forces of darkness place no value on human life, and are prepared to sacrifice millions of people to achieve their aim.

6   The forces of light, on the other hand, wish to *preserve* life—life with freedom. As an Illumined Soul says:

7   *Our* way is to keep people in their mortal frames as comfortable as possible until the time they can with dignity leave the physical —*not* shedding the blood of sisters and brothers—and only after a full and useful life that may inspire others. We are not enthusiastic about war as a solution to problems. We are not enthusiastic about the battling of human beings among themselves. But we know that an *unjust* peace is not a good peace, and is sometimes *more* calamitous than no peace at all.

8   Until humankind in general realizes certain fundamental truths—until people are profoundly concerned not only with their *own* lot, but with the lot of *others*—the struggle between the forces of light and darkness will continue.

857 Some Reflections about War and Freedom

1   In almost every case, war is an unmixed evil, except for the noble and heroic impulses it stirs among many who act magnificently in times of travail.

2   The countless tragedies that occur; the inevitable toll of death and injury; the long chronicle of hardships and sufferings; the many physical and mental illnesses created; the wanton destruction of much that is beautiful; the ravages that can never be repaired; the mischief that takes

8.8 Challenges

years or even centuries to undo—all these are only *some* of the evils war brings.

3   But there are *worse* things than war. One is to surrender liberty without a struggle.

4   To any people, the enemy of freedom may be within their borders, or an aggressor from without. In either case, freedom means little to them if they will not do all they can to achieve or retain it.

5   However, even when war is necessary to preserve freedom, even when it is waged in self-preservation, it can still be conducted without hatred, without vindictiveness, without thought of annihilating another in the moment of victory. It can still be waged with understanding of the opponent's view, however repugnant. It can still be accompanied by the longing for an honorable peace, the resolve to bind up the wounds of war as soon as hostilities end, and the desire to extend the hand of friendship and brother-and-sisterhood to the former foe.

6   Revenge breeds revenge. Hatred breeds hatred. Only love and understanding can, *in time*, dissolve emotions that are not in the makeup of spiritual people.

858 Some Questions

1   If a man is hemmed in by others, each with a knife against his throat, and he somehow manages to disarm them and put them to flight, is *he* the assailant?

2   Has he no right to defend himself *until* his throat is slashed?

859 Two Tragedies

1   It is always a tragedy when a small nation or country is invaded.

2   It is a greater tragedy when other nations or countries do not come to its defense.

860 We CAN Learn from the Experience of Others

1   We learn from experience, many say. But the fact is that we learn from experience only if we *choose* to profit from it, and if we *know* or are helped and *shown* how to profit from it.

860 ☐   Chapter 8 *Our World*

2   Mere experience, of itself, is usually of little avail. Many wrongdoers, for instance, do not learn that crime does not pay. Instead, they conclude that their *methods* of committing crime were faulty; and often they plan, while still in confinement, not on mending their ways, but on amending their methods.

3   The wise learn not only from their own experience, but from the experience of others.

4   One need never have been a thief or a murderer to be aware that stealing and murder are wrong. One need never have been consumed by avarice or envy or meanness to be aware that those emotions are unworthy.

5   The world as a whole would make negligible progress if individuals had to undergo every experience, desirable and undesirable, for themselves.

6   What is tragic is that the world has learned so little from its experience over the centuries. And if events reoccur, as they often do, it is only because of lack of wisdom on the part of the leaders of peoples and nations. History repeats itself; but it need *not* repeat itself if people would profit from the example of others.

7   And if there is one lesson history teaches—a lesson that humanity should by now have learned well—it is the folly of appeasement. The more aggressors are fed, the stronger they become. Aggressors who at first would be comparatively easy to cope with, become more and more difficult to resist the more they are appeased. The path of appeasement leads either to failure and surrender, or to a climax more terrible the longer it is delayed.

8   Some other points to remember:

9   — Stupidity and timidity in high places can be as disastrous to a nation as treason. Major examples of that stupidity are the refusal to learn from history, the refusal to recognize the folly of appeasement, and the refusal or inability to see the lack of wisdom of leaving to the enemies of freedom the immense advantages of initiative and the choice of time, place, and plans.

10   — It is indeed tyrannous for a giant to use its strength to bully others; but it is the height of folly and stupidity not to use that strength when needed in a just cause. It is the abuse of any power that is bad, not the wise use of it.

8.8 Challenges

11 — The world would be better off if leaders of nations devoted less thought to achieving a notable place in history, and more thought to learning *from* history; if they displayed the trust they should have in the people—whom they represent, and to whom they are responsible to depict conditions as they truly are; and then, if supported by the people or their duly-elected representatives, they had the courage and resolve to do right, as they see the right, come what may.

861 Some Reflections on Democracy

1 Despite its imperfections, which spring from the imperfections of many individuals, by far the best kind of government yet devised is democracy—a form of government in which the supreme power is vested in the people and exercised by them or by those they elect under a free electoral system.

2 Democracies are frequently threatened from all sides, in these times more than ever. However, their gravest peril often lies *within*, usually when a party in office, fearing loss of power, is unwise enough to form a coalition with those whose express purpose is to overthrow free systems of government and seize control.

3 Never has such a coalition benefited an entire nation in the long run. For just as impure water pollutes or tends to pollute all it enters, so do enemies of freedom contaminate in some degree *any* democratic group in which they gain a foothold or are allowed to link with in any way.

4 We have stressed that there is no *honest* compromise with wrong; and that it is society's responsibility—which of course includes the responsibility of government—to take measures to curb any individual or group that would curtail or abuse the rights and freedom of others.

5 Leaders who lack *wisdom*—knowledge of what is true or right coupled with just judgement as to action—can bring disaster to a nation, as history so abundantly illustrates.

862 A One-World Government?

1 We have been asked why we, who strive for a universal spiritual brother-and-sisterhood, do not support a one-world government.

2 For a very good reason.

3   In the *present* state of nations and peoples, a one-world government could lead only to disaster for humanity. Until nations in general, and the leaders of nations in particular, are immensely more spiritual than they are now; until they are so advanced morally that they would never sacrifice principle for expediency; until they wholeheartedly seek justice for *all*, rather than personal or national aggrandizement; until they unswervingly hold that the state exists to serve the people, and not the other way around; until they are unreservedly dedicated to the freedom of individuals everywhere so long as they do not corrupt others or infringe on the rights of others—*until then,* one-world government could be an unmitigated calamity.

4   Democracies[10] inspire many who live under tyranny with the hope or dream of someday, somehow, making their way to lands where freedom exists. That hope or dream could be extinguished if a one-world government fell into the hands of a dictator or an oligarchy.

5   For many decades of the 20th century, immensely powerful rival groups were striving for world domination. They were led by "elitists" and "intellectuals" of one ism or another who did not share our concern or regard for the average person; who in their ignorance and arrogance thought that they, and they alone, knew what was best for the thousands of millions of people on earth; and who proved by their aims and actions, that they would not hesitate to use absolute power to introduce a serfdom and reign of terror worse than the world has ever known. Individuals would be manipulated like puppets, to be used or "relocated" or even destroyed at the whim of "leaders"—as indeed happened in some parts of the globe.

. . . . .

6   Even a world parliament—a *true* world parliament—which idealists have long envisioned, is as yet nothing but a dream. So it will remain unless an impregnable foundation based on highly moral and spiritual values is established.

7   The two principal world-wide organizations of nations of the 20th century have a mixed record of success. Many members have not aban-

---

[10] When this was written in 1976 democracies were few compared with the many dictatorships. Although the number of democracies on earth today has increased considerably in recent decades, many of them (flawed democracies, hybrid regimes, and "illiberal" democracies) are not considered by authorities on freedom to be liberal democracies. Liberal democracies have outnumbered dictatorships since about 1990.

8.8 Challenges

doned selfishness. Slavery still exists in parts of the world. Totalitarian regimes still flourish.

8 Only an organization of nations with clear and definite principles of peace and humanity and justice for all, principles that must be accepted by those wishing to join; only an organization that would automatically expel *any* member, weak or powerful, who violated those principles; only an organization resolved and prepared to resist aggression by *anyone*—only *such* an organization could create a true moral climate in the world and real hope for those in bondage.

9 Worth repeating and emphasizing in this connection, are some points we have stressed elsewhere:

10 — If there is one thing the USB stands for, it is the freedom of the individual. One of the most important tenets of our work is that all... should be free to live and worship... in their own way and fashion [108:6].

11 — To have liberty, people must love it enough to die for it if need be. To the lasting glory of the human race, there always are such souls. It is *they* who make tyrants tremble. For tyrants know that while one lover of freedom breathes, freedom lives [853:5].

12 — There is no *honest* compromise with wrong. It is society's responsibility—which of course includes the responsibility of government—to curb any individual or group of individuals who would curtail or abuse the rights and freedom of others [849:2].

863 Eternal Vigilance

1 There are individuals, including the leaders of some nations, who possess a genius for maliciously twisting and distorting words that have long expressed the noblest conceptions of honorable and enlightened men and women. More and more have *democracy, civil liberties, freedom,* and *peace*, for example, become banners used to camouflage the purposes of some who would *destroy* those very ideals.

2 So it has now become more necessary than ever to judge not only the *words* that are expressed, but the *record* and *motives* of those who express them.

3 Indeed is eternal vigilance the price of liberty!

864 Utter Folly

1. In the continuing struggle between light and darkness, the latter is from time to time strengthened, often when on the verge of collapse, by the inexcusable actions of some of the very ones it would destroy.

2. Some individuals and some nations have yet to learn the folly of providing sturdier boots to those who kick them, or stouter cudgels to those who strike them.

3. When a foe is aided at the *expense* of an ally, the folly is compounded. So are the inevitable consequences.

865 On Tragic Happenings in Many Places

1. We should show both love and wisdom in our relationship with others. To show love without wisdom is to invite calamity. To show neither is to court disaster, as the chronicles of history abundantly record.

2. The inhumanity and cruelty that have been committed in recent years by peoples in various parts of the globe are, in some instances, the direct result of the lack of love and wisdom on the part of those who held stewardship over those peoples—the love and wisdom that would have revealed and expressed the recognition that *all human beings are sisters and brothers, children of a living and loving God, and equal in God's sight;* that would have educated people in the responsibilities of government *to* the governed; and that would have extended equal opportunities to *all* to live in dignity, and to open and expand their consciousness.

3. Individuals should be given full opportunity to express as human beings —*not* in the extremes of overlords or tyrants on one hand, or beasts of burden on the other, but in the role that is their rightful heritage: people who walk erect, with heads held high, free to go where they will, and do what they will, so long as their actions injure no one. There must be greater realization and greater emphasis on the worth and dignity of individuals, *all* individuals, no matter where they live, no matter what their circumstances.

4. Just as we have a grave responsibility to our children—the responsibility to show them the *right* path, as we believe that path to be, and to plant the seeds of right living into their consciousness, or to nourish the seeds already there—so do nations have a grave responsibility to the peoples under their jurisdiction or control.

5. Failure to educate children results in many mistaking liberty for license. Failure to educate peoples produces the very same effect. In such cases,

8.8 Challenges

the fault lies more with the teacher or should-be teacher, rather than with the taught or untaught.

6   Liberty is not something to be exercised without wisdom; for like all other powers, it can be used for good or ill. It cannot be forever denied, for it is the inalienable right of every soul; it must be given, or it will be claimed by force. But it should be given *gradually*, whether to children or to peoples, with guidance and encouragement in the proper use of it.

7   Some of the distressing and heartrending excesses in many places lie squarely at the door of those who had the responsibility and opportunity to be of love and service to their fellow human beings by preparing them for freedom, and preparing them well, but *neglected* that opportunity and responsibility—because of the philosophy of *profits before people*, or the desire to continue dominion over others, or both.

8   So before we condemn those who, in the first flush of freedom, revert to the law of the jungle and to inhumane actions none should condone, let us *remember* that they were often little removed from a rudimentary pattern—and that they were in many instances deliberately *kept* at that level, or forced even lower, by others who knew it is easier to exploit the uneducated than to exploit the educated. Let us remember, too, the atrocities, numbering in the millions, perpetrated in the last hundred years by so-called "civilized" nations, nations with centuries of experience in governing and being governed.

9   Inhumanity at *any* time is to be deplored, but it is far more deplorable in the case of those who by education and experience should know better.

10   The quest for freedom is stirring human minds as never before, as the light from the beacons of Truth reaches into almost every darkened corner of the earth. Some people and some leaders, blinded by the unaccustomed light, will act in ways we may not approve; but as they become more used to the light, and interpret it correctly and are transformed by it, they will live in greater harmony with their fellow human beings. We are saddened by many events, but not discouraged, for we realize that many of them were the inevitable effects of many causes.

11   Freedom is the right of *all* human beings, *all* peoples. But they must evolve in that respect (as in all others): from freedom for self, to freedom for one's own tribe, to freedom for one's own people or nation, to freedom for *all people everywhere*. Those of us who are a little farther along the path are remiss if we do not try, by love and wisdom, to make that evolution less painful.

12   Against tyranny and oppression and injustice *anywhere*, let us as individuals raise our voices for those who cannot speak.

866 On "News" Disseminators

1. It is sad but true that even in some nations with freedom of the press impartiality is a far-from-general attribute of newspapers, magazines, radio, and television.

2. With the small number of individuals and groups of individuals controlling many channels of information, the power to say *what* news is reported, or *when* news is reported, or *where* news is reported, or *how much* news is reported, or *whether* news is reported, is becoming concentrated in ever fewer hands.

3. As a result, news that the general public should be aware of is sometimes never publicized, or it appears only in channels of very limited circulation. Not reporting newsworthy items is a practice much more common than generally imagined.

4. In addition, news may also be slanted by presenting half-truths, which frequently are far more damaging than falsehoods. It may be slanted by quoting statements out of context, to wilfully mislead others. And it may be slanted in several other ways of "editing," including the omission of vital facts that would portray a contrary but correct picture.

5. [Governments themselves can distort the news by presenting one-sided views. In an age of spin doctors, photo opportunities, and twenty-second sound bites it is very difficult for individuals to find the whole truth.]

6. So nowadays the individual should weigh well not only the news reported, and the alleged source of it, but, what is more important still, the *degree* of impartiality and integrity of those responsible for disseminating that news.

7. With rare exceptions, the day of the truly independent newspaper or radio or television channel is over. But we can take heart from the few that still exist, and also from fearless individuals who, on their own time and often at their own expense, publish articles and reports enlightening others about the forces dedicated to misleading them.

8. They are among the true heroes of the age.

9

Everyday Life

CHAPTER CONTENTS

9.1 Relationships		**253**
901	Some Reflections on "The Golden Rule"	253
902	On Personal Relationships	253
903	On Freedom in Relationships	254
904	On Personal Love or Affection	254
9.2 Family		**255**
905	The Importance of the Home and Family	255
906	Working Parents	257
907	Today's Youth—and the Responsibility of Parents	258
908	On Seeing Loved Ones Suffer	261
909	Of Some Psychotherapists and Psychiatrists	265
910	A Little about the Care of Infants	265
911	No Child Is Too Young to Learn Simple Truths	264
9.3 Health		**265**
912	Correct Breathing—and Some Valuable Breathing Exercises	265
913	Some Reflections about Water	267
914	A Question about Water	268
915	A Cruel Misteaching about Cancer	268
916	Not All Illness Springs from the Mind	269
917	Other Misteachings Relating to Health	269

continued...

Contents □   CHAPTER 9 *Everyday Life*

9.4 Sleep		**270**
918	Why We Need Sleep	270
919	Our Sensitivity in the Sleep State	271
920	Effects of Activity During the Sleep State	272
921	A Little about Sleepwalking	272
922	Talking in One's Sleep	274
923	A Little about Dreams	274
924	Dreams—and Droes	275
925	Some Misconceptions about Sleep and Dreams	275
9.5 Time and Cycles		**277**
926	Some Reflections about Time	277
927	Enjoying the NOW	278
928	A Little about Cycles and Human Beings	279
9.6 Sound and Color		**280**
929	A Little about Sound, Color, and Odor	280
930	More about Color—and Colors	281
931	A Little about Color and Music	283

9.1 RELATIONSHIPS

901 Some Reflections on "The Golden Rule"

1. There are many versions of what has long been called the golden rule, which millions of good men and women have used over the centuries as their design for living. Among those versions are the following:

2. Do unto others as you would have them do unto you.
3. Do not do unto others what you would not have them do unto you.
4. Whatsoever ye would that men should do unto you, do ye even so unto them.
5. Do as you would be done by.

6. Of the four versions quoted—which, like several others, are more or less the same in meaning—we prefer the second, because it is comparatively selfless: It does not in any way suggest doing something with the hope or expectation of receiving or gaining anything.

7. Whatever the merits of the different versions, which have inspired many people to live better lives than they would have done otherwise, they do not strike a particularly responsive chord within us.

8. For the USB does not recommend doing *to* or *unto* others, but doing *for* others, and doing so not from any idea of return, but for the sheer joy of serving. As always, of course, we stress that the doing should be *wise*: Then it will not deprive others of the opportunity to grow in stature spiritually by learning any needed lessons that can be learned on earth only, or by doing what they can for themselves. As we have pointed out more than once, the best way we can help others is *to help them to help themselves*, if possible—an accomplishment that should make all concerned happy.

902 On Personal Relationships

1. For any close relationship between two people to endure, the wiser must be prepared to understand more and overlook more, to be more patient and tolerant of weaknesses, and to be more aware that we should not expect people of different levels of consciousness to have the very same standards.

2. However, that does not mean that the wiser should be willing to become a doormat for the other, or to be continually imposed upon, or to

suffer anything and everything just to preserve the relationship. That would do little good to either; in fact it would be detrimental to both. For both would miss a golden opportunity to grow in stature spiritually—the first by refusing to be constantly taken advantage of, the second by being just and considerate of others.

903 On Freedom in Relationships

1. In any comprehensive dictionary, *freedom* has many definitions. We use the word here in its emphasis on the opportunity to exercise one's rights, powers, desires, or the like—always provided, we would add, that it does not violate the rights of others.

2. Freedom is something that should be fostered and treasured in any relationship between two people.

3. In some relationships there is a conscious or unconscious desire within one person (and sometimes both) to limit the freedom of the other: to wish the other to be always by one's side; to censor the other's friendships; to stifle the other's venture and expression in fields one has little interest in; and to demand attendance at groups and gatherings that the other finds less than exhilarating, and the expenditure of time that the other feels could be put to better use.

4. Such cases usually indicate either of two things: a feeling of insecurity in the relationship, or a wish to possess the other. And possession is the foe of freedom.

5. Any worthwhile relationship between two people should expand the orbit of *both*; certainly it should not contract the orbit of *either*.

6. While their main pathway should preferably be the same, a few differing—and perhaps even *opposing*—interests may enliven and lend spice to a relationship by introducing new subjects, encouraging thinking on fresh lines, and stimulating an exchange of ideas.

7. They would also reflect a vital element of freedom: the right not only to *do* but the right *not* to do.

904 On Personal Love or Affection

1. To be of the greatest value, personal love should from time to time be not only demonstrated but also declared. The same applies to affection, which is a milder form of personal love.

2   Actions speak louder than words, it is true. But actions *and* words speak louder still, and their combined effect is greater than that of actions alone.

3   Few fail to respond to demonstrations of personal love or affection, or to words and the tone of the words expressed. Actions and words are *both* important in keeping the stream of personal love or affection clear and sparkling.

9.2 FAMILY

905 The Importance of the Home and Family

1   While the role of head of the family—more often than not played by the father, but sometimes by the mother—has varied throughout the ages and from civilization to civilization, one thing has remained virtually unchanged: the importance of the home and family in the life of the individual, the people, and the nation. (We use *family* in its most common meaning of parents and their children, whether living together or not, and we use *home* in its meaning of the dwelling of a family.)

2   The well-being of the family should be the first concern of governments that have the welfare of the people at heart. For it is *in* the family, not outside of it, that sound values and morals and philosophy are most thoroughly and successfully instilled. It is *in* the family, not outside of it, that children, if inspired by both word and example, most naturally develop or expand the virtues of gentleness, kindness, courtesy, compassion, integrity, understanding, and personal responsibility. It is *in* the home where, if love and laughter reign, much treasure is gathered for the storehouse of memory. It is *in* the home where any needed discipline, if applied wisely and with love, provides the surest and most lasting results.

3   It is in a home and family enjoying fine parental guidance that children can best be taught the folly of learning only from personal experience.

4   It is not necessary to be confined in a "drunk tank" to realize the tragedy of overindulgence in alcohol. It is not necessary to use drugs to realize that many addicts resort to crime to obtain money to relieve the craving they have become a slave to, and that drugs often rob individuals of reason, or give them a false and dangerous feeling of indestructibility.

5   Many of the young, immature and insecure, are greatly influenced by the attitude and behavior of others of their own age; for despite their clamor for "independence," the young, as a whole, are conformists conforming with one another. Only when they possess wholesome attitudes developed or nourished in the home can they usually withstand undesirable pressures from their peers outside the family.

6   Others things being equal, children thrive best in a family where loving parents play different but complementary roles, with only one parent going to work, at least while the children are young. But one-parent families have become very common, for various reasons; and in one-parent families, or when both parents work outside the home, a guiding parental hand may often be late or lacking when most needed.

7   Some assert that parents should never show disagreement in front of their children. We disagree. Minor disagreements, even if accompanied by flashes of temper and sharpness, do little injury if the atmosphere is usually one of harmony and affection. In fact occasional differences between parents may help prepare children to cope with life, by making them aware at an early age of things it is important to learn: to give and take; to live and let live; to realize that differences are a normal part of everyday existence, and, if not carried to extremes, harmless.

. . . . .

8   In lands where freedom of expression is banned, and *the state*—by which we mean *the governing body*—exercises dominion over everyone, parents have little say in raising their children. It is unfortunate for at least two reasons.

9   One is that we come to earth and into a particular family according to Law, although we seldom fathom the precise reason for it while here. In many instances, it is to provide specific opportunities and experiences for certain people: the child, or one or both parents, or all of them. Of course with the freedom that is our birthright, we have the privilege, unless robbed of it by the state, of altering our circumstances and relationships, for better or worse.

10   The second reason is that the state should exist to serve the people, *not* the other way around. Certainly any government *of* the people, *by* the people, and *for* the people is, or should be, the *servant* of the people, not their master.

11   Full freedom of expression is the right of individuals as long as they do not infringe on, or incite others to infringe on, the rights of their

9.2 Family

12   Proper stewardship during the formative years of those entrusted to their care at birth is the *greatest* responsibility of parents. Governmental authorities should not interfere with that stewardship unless children are inhumanely treated or flagrantly neglected.

13   Of course the state should, if needed, aid parents who make every attempt to properly provide for their children. Only in exceptional circumstances, however, should the state be a family's *complete* source of supply: That could weaken or destroy parental initiative, and deprive parents of much from which they might learn or profit.

14   One thing we should always remember: the more we look to the state to provide us with things that we could provide for ourselves with effort, the more do we lose control over our lives. The more power the state possesses, the greater the danger of dictatorship.

15   A government is best that has those at the helm steering us to the port of *our* choice, not theirs.

16   Much of history, much of humanity's fight for freedom, is a record of the struggle between the family and the state. We should resist any unjustified intrusion into the home and family.

906 Working Parents

1   Many consider it a deplorable state of affairs for both parents of young children to have jobs that take them away from home much of the day.

2   We ourselves would not express any blanket condemnation of two parents working. Too often both *have* to work, so that the family is not deprived of necessities. At the same time, a young child who returns home from school to find no parent [or substitute parent] awaiting it is deprived of the warmth, love, and discipline it needs at that time—and for the loss of which nothing else can compensate. It is then very easy for children to drift into undesirable activities with undesirable companions.

3   Parents should distinguish between needs and desires in their consumer habits; they should weigh well the effects of excessive consumerism on the time they spend with their children, especially during the formative years.

907 Today's Youth—and the Responsibility of Parents

1. We are most sympathetic to young adults, every generation of which has problems to face.

2. It has become the fashion to condemn today's youth on many counts: lack of ideals; lack of enthusiasm; lack of purpose; reluctance to earn what is desired; distressing behavior; twisted conceptions of life; and many other failings.

3. The same condemnation, the same blanket disapproval of youth, has been expressed throughout history, at various times in various ages. But it is only a *minority* of youth who deserve it, although it is often an offensive and noisy minority.

4. Who is to blame? Primarily those parents—too many of them—who neglect their parental responsibilities.

5. When parents for any reason abandon the helm, the ship of youth is rudderless, at the mercy of changing tides and rapid currents on the waters of life. The surprising thing is not that so many of today's youth lack admirable qualities, but that so many *possess* them despite the inadequate guidance they have received.

6. Whenever parents display a lamentable lack of courtesy, sincerity, integrity, self discipline, and consideration for others; live by the philosophy that the end justifies the means; deem it clever to obtain advantages in questionable ways; do as little as possible to get as much as possible; put great store on material things, but little on spiritual values [not necessarily religious]; or preach one thing and practice another—who can blame young people for being disenchanted with their elders, for being discouraged and disillusioned by the hypocrisy they witness, and for seeking distractions that they hope will make them forget what is around and about them. It is not surprising that some of these young adults revolt against their elders as a way of protesting against their behavior.

7. No matter how they "love" their children, it is certainly not wisdom that parents reveal when they fail to set a good example, and neglect to provide incentives, direction, and (to the degree they are aware of them) an inkling of the real and eternal values.

8. Those nearing adulthood have a right to express in their own way, a right to be *different*, a right to *experiment*—always of course so long as they do not harm themselves or others. They also have a right to expect stability on the part of their parents, an anchor to which they can secure themselves when the sea of life is stormy, as it often is for those approaching full manhood or womanhood.

9.2 Family

9. To add to their confusion and frustration, most of today's youth, as in ages past, do not possess the vital knowledge that might spare them the insecurity and instability and loneliness they feel. Their parents, through ignorance or neglect, have not acquainted them with The Laws That Govern; the fact that there is *no* death to *the real self;* the knowledge that there *is* purpose to life on earth; the realization that we are never alone; and the truth that endless spiritual progression can be the lot for any and all of us.

10. In an age of reason, or of greater reason, those of today's youth who *think* about such things cannot embrace pointless rituals, dogmas, and creeds; and having no values to cling to, unaware of the vast ocean of Truth before them, and uninformed of truths that bring point and meaning to existence, some flounder in bewilderment.

11. Too many parents fail in their moral and spiritual responsibilities *as* parents.

12. It is sad to witness, in all levels of society, the tragic effects of the failure of such parents: failure to sufficiently instill an early sense of personal responsibility in their children; failure to provide necessary discipline (and the feeling of security that comes from *justness* in discipline); failure to sufficiently inspire and stimulate desirable qualities and attitudes (e.g., knowing the difference between liberty and license, speaking and acting only within proper limits); and failure to sufficiently guide the tremendous energy of the young into constructive channels. When parents are remiss in these ways, they neglect their responsibility and incur a debt that, like all other debts, must be paid in full sooner or later. For as we stress, no responsibility [parental or societal] can be evaded with impunity. It must eventually be met, and met well, if one is to make much progress spiritually.

13. [In addition to parental lack of responsibility, the complexities of post-modern culture are factors in the formation of today's youth. These include the media and technology, especially the Internet, cable television, movies, cell phones, iPods, etc.]

14. Today's youth are tomorrow's leaders.

15. On *them* will fall the burdens and responsibilities of a civilization that has made enormous strides in unlocking the secrets of nature, but has not made as much progress in utilizing those discoveries for the good of humanity—a civilization that has made great advances materially (at least in some countries), but has barely advanced spiritually.

16   On *them* will rest many obligations, together with vast opportunities for service, vast opportunities for the exercise of love and wisdom in relationships within countries and between countries, and with their own people and other peoples.

17   There is great need for them to be educated and prepared for what will be expected of them. And it is in the home that they can best learn what they should learn. For it is in the child's early years that it is easiest for lasting impressions to be created, excellent habits to be formed, and admirable qualities to be inspired or nurtured.

18   The vast majority of young adults do have a decent and wholesome respect for the rights of others; they seek only for opportunities to express themselves in dignity; and they are willing and prepared to work, and work hard, to achieve their goals.

19   The unhappy state of a minority of today's youth is largely the result of the age we have lived in, and live in, for the mentalities of the young usually reflect the influence, or lack of influence, of those to whom they have looked, or look, for inspiration—grandparents who survived truly trying times, in particular the World War II period, when many lived only for the moment, with no thought for tomorrow, and parents who grew up in the ensuing strongly materialistic period. Those live-for-the-moment and materialistic philosophies continue to grow in many families, so that there are many parents who do not properly prepare their children for adult responsibilities.

20   The twin enemies of youth are boredom, and lack of discipline and direction from parents and others, [especially in the media (833),] who exert enormous influence on young people.

21   Such spiritual emptiness is true of rich and poor youth alike.

22   In poor families and neighborhoods, many of today's youth have too little to do, and too few opportunities for healthy play or the wholesome and satisfying expression of their energies.

23   They have too little, too seldom—and usually too late.

24   In rich families and neighborhoods, material wealth is too often not only of little value, but of positive harm. Children who receive all that money can buy, the moment they desire it, are deprived of the delight of hope and anticipation, of waiting for something and thus *appreciating* it when it comes, or of earning it in some way.

25   They receive too much, too soon—and usually too easily.

26   In many of these instances, in attempts to escape boredom the inevitable result is a perpetual search for thrills—exhilaration of one sort or

9.2 Family

another, in one form or another, sometimes destructive, but usually a waste of time. The thrills sooner or later pall; and when they pall, ever newer and more thrilling experiences are sought and snatched.

27 It is a significant commentary on today's society that vandalism, violence, addiction to narcotics, and other crimes are acts not of the underprivileged alone, but of the overprivileged also.

28 The great tragedy is that too many children in all levels now seek one new and exciting experience after another, experiences that are often not good for them or worse, when they should be receiving preparation for the adults they will soon be, the responsibilities they will soon have, and the duty they owe to both themselves and society.

29 Certainly there is a lamentable lack of structural meaning in the lives of many of today's youth. This is indicated by the high rate of teenage suicides and juvenile crime.

30 Many parents *do* teach moral and spiritual values to their young. Many parents, by their philosophy and example, *do* set an inspiring pattern for their children. But too many do not, or not sufficiently.

31 Society needs to reflect on these important issues.

32 It is indeed time for some changes. It is time for *all* parents to assume their full responsibilities; time to insist on a return to fundamentals in education, with less emphasis on frills and on what should be taught at home, and more emphasis on the basic subjects that will equip one to be more than just barely literate; time to teach history and the lessons of history; and time to expound sound values, the worth of character and integrity, the virtue of tolerance, the importance of personal responsibility, and above all, what too few are aware of, something about The Laws That Govern, or THE LAW.

33 Today's youth have no easy future awaiting them. They will face two tremendous tasks: correcting the disarray they did not create; and giving *their* children a sounder upbringing than they themselves received. Let us do all in our power to prepare them for the years that lie ahead.

908 On Seeing Loved Ones Suffer

1 It is distressing, even for those who know the truth of Survival [of death of the earthly or physical body], to see a loved one suffer, especially one reaching the end of life on earth [Sec. 12.1].

908

2 An Illumined Soul says:

3 Many have a most difficult time when they enter the valley of the shadow of death. While some of their violent contortions and struggles may be merely automatic reflexes, others may spring from *consciousness* of unbearable pain, at moments when those who hover between the two worlds are more in the realm of earth than the spirit realms. Often it is agony not only for the departing one, but for those who witness the agony they are powerless to relieve.

4 She draws an illuminating and comforting analogy between death and childbirth.

5 We can liken the release of the spirit [etheric, counterpart] body from its physical dwelling [earthly body] to the birth of a child in a physical body. In a great number of cases of imminent or approaching childbirth there are days, sometimes *many* days, when the mother-to-be is in such acute discomfort that only *immediate* skilled care can prevent the loss of mother or child, or both. But just as excruciating labor pains are, as a rule, quickly forgotten by a mother once she holds her newborn babe in her arms—so, in most instances, is a long and painful illness quickly forgotten by those who pass on, once they embrace and are reunited with spirit loved ones.[1]

6 There are those who wonder why some suffer pain during certain experiences, while others suffer no pain at all. In fact there are cases, as you know, of women being unaware, until the very moment of giving birth, that they were with child. But as the USB teaches, The Law of Variety operates *everywhere*, and on *all* levels of expression.

7 Some who see loved ones lying on beds of pain are puzzled and disappointed, and sometimes even bitter, because they have been led to believe that prayer and the power of spirit can overcome *all* things. But that is *not* so. With all our love, with all our desire to aid those in need, we do not *always* succeed.

---

[1] The USB's wonderful, highly spiritual, American medium often gave healing to people approaching death. She once told me that "death is the greatest experience that life has to offer." I would add "...for those who have treated others at least decently and do not have serious misconceptions (see Index) about the afterlife." –Ed.

9.2 Family

909 Of Some Psychotherapists and Psychiatrists

1 As a rule, those on earth engaged in any noble endeavor are able to do immeasurably greater good if they know of Survival [of physical death] and Communication [with spirit people] and other truths. Certainly a vastly larger number of people would obtain greater relief from mental and bodily ills if more members of the medical profession directly or indirectly consulted skilled spirit colleagues—colleagues, known or unknown to them, who have a rich store of knowledge in medicine and allied fields.

2 Psychotherapy and psychiatry by no means resemble an exact practice or science. Practitioners in these fields as a rule are not equipped to delve into those areas where only spiritual wisdom and insight should be the norm of healing and spiritual transformation. They must recognize the limits of their abilities to cure and heal patients. By their unawareness of the truths we mention, in many instances they not only hinder a patient's progress by misdiagnosing his or her ills, but aggravate or compound them by inadequate or incorrect treatment.

3 Fortunately for the world, there *are* some therapists—may their number increase!—who are in tune, consciously or unconsciously, with spirit colleagues highly advanced in their common field; who recognize the power of love when joined with wisdom; and who know that hate never builds but often destroys those who harbor it.

4 It is sad to realize that there are individuals on earth in prominent positions in various professions who during their lifetimes expound error after error to thousands or tens of thousands and sometimes even millions of people.

910 A Little about the Care of Infants

1 Whatever experts on the bringing up of infants may say or have said to the contrary, it is an elementary fact that during the earliest period of its life it is *vital* for a child to have an abundance of affection. It needs to be cuddled and embraced. It needs to be loved, and by someone that it knows and with whom it feels a sense of closeness, most important to an infant.

2 An infant needs a focal point of love—either its own mother or a substitute mother—with that focal point available to it day and night during the time it is so completely helpless.

3   No nursery school can furnish that.

4   Where possible, parents would be wise to fulfil their role in the family unit. To neglect it and leave the care of their children to others, is not only to miss many wonderful experiences, but to fail in their responsibility to inspire, and as much as possible *properly* mold, those entrusted to their care at birth.

5   Good parents can do much more than any group or organization can do to provide love to a child, to gradually teach it the things it should learn, and to encourage it along or towards the right path.

6   Some decades ago, it was the fashion of "modern" educators of the day to recommend a most Spartan regime for infants: *Ignore* them if they cry. *Don't* pick them up or lavish love on them.

7   But it is *cruel* to refuse an infant the attention and reassurance and love that only a familiar touch and voice can provide, not least when it awakens from a deep sleep and is cold or hungry or wet or frightened or uncomfortable.

8   Among some peoples an infant is carried on the mother's back or elsewhere on her person as she goes about her daily chores: It thus remains enveloped in her aura [1311], from which it deprives a great sense of security, a continuation of what it possessed in her womb.

9   Anyone who advocates a child being physically remote from its mother before the child itself desires it, knows little about children, in our opinion. Bringing up a child *wisely* includes giving it the choice of leaving its mother for increasing lengths of time; it does *not* mean thrusting it out.

10   Psychological tests have shown how *important* it is for a mother to hold her baby immediately after it is born, rather than a day (or more) later. It is still more important for the *infant*, we would add.

911 No Child Is Too Young to Learn Simple Truths

1   Some fathers and mothers of young children offer the lame excuse that their children are "not old enough" to be taught truths [321]. Apparently they are always old enough to be taught *untruths!*—even though, in most cases, untruths impose a greater strain upon the mind, and, in all cases, must sooner or later be unlearned.

2   To the impressionable, untruths are often far more dangerous than material weapons.

9.3 Health □ *912*

3   But people who would not dream of giving matches to an infant to play with, or a loaded revolver to a child to carry, sometimes think nothing of acquainting the easily impressed and immature with teachings that they know or suspect are false or far from noble.

4   For such dereliction, or shortsightedness, or indifference, or laziness, or lack of courage on the part of parents to be "different," there are consequences.

5   For one thing, it is a neglect of parental responsibility towards those entrusted to their care at birth. This neglect is serious enough in itself, and creates a debt that must be paid. But to *know* and *still* permit misteaching is much more serious than to permit it in ignorance, and a far greater debt is incurred.

6   For another thing, it injects into the mind of children, during their formative years, misteachings that frequently remain with them the rest of their days on earth—and often long after.

7   The problem is not simple. Most parents recognize that children are usually uncomfortable if they feel they are "different" from other children—if, for example, their playmates go to Sunday school and they themselves do not. For the unfortunately still small minority of parents in any area who know a little about spiritual Truth, a good solution, whenever possible, is to band together to open their own Sunday school, where their children can meet one another and together receive instruction from someone well versed and skilled in working with young minds.

8   As a rule, it is better for a child to learn with *other* children (than to learn with adults). But if that is not practical, the child's *parents* should instruct it. In any case, and whoever the teachers may be, parents cannot evade *responsibility* for what their children are taught.

9.3 HEALTH

912 Correct Breathing—and Some Valuable Breathing Exercises

1   Almost everyone knows that breathing through the nostrils is the best way to breathe, and that breathing through the mouth invites or aggravates disease and ill health.

2   Breathing of course means taking air or oxygen into the lungs and then expelling it: inhaling and exhaling. To inhale through the nostrils is

especially important, for the cilia (hair-like outgrowths) in the nostrils help to strain the air of impurities—which, incidentally, are usually expelled when the air is exhaled.

3   There are three common forms of breathing, sometimes described as *low breathing, mid breathing,* and *high breathing.*

4   **Low breathing** (or abdominal breathing) is by far the best: The lungs get fuller play in this method than in the others, as more air is inhaled. It is the way animals breathe, as may be noticed with dogs and cats at rest, and as infants naturally do at birth and until they acquire incorrect habits.

5   It is important to get enough air, *clean* air, into the lungs, because of the vital life force contained in oxygen [913:3].

6   **Mid breathing** fills the middle part of the lungs and a portion of the upper part.

7   **High breathing**, the worst form, requires the most energy but does the least good: As only the upper part of the chest and lungs is used, only a very small amount of air enters the lungs.

8   There have always been groups that recognized the value of specific breathing exercises for specific purposes.

9   Elsewhere [1138:4–6] we describe a simple breathing exercise to help stimulate receptivity of the psychic centers.

10 Breathing exercises long used to promote better health include what some call *the complete breath* and *the cleansing breath.*

11 **The complete breath** exercises every part of the lungs and the muscles used in breathing.

12 Sit or stand erect; or lie flat, face up, with no pillow under the head. (A pillow or cushion or bolster under the knees will make the last position more comfortable.) Then:

   1. Inhale slowly and steadily, first filling the lower part of the lungs, then the middle part, and finally the upper part, in one continuous movement. Inhale to any count that is *comfortable*, silently counting six, eight, ten, twelve, or any other *even* number.
   2. Retain the breath for half the count.
   3. Then exhale the breath, slowly and evenly, for the full count.
   4. Pause for half the count.

13 Repeat the cycle several times.

9.3 Health

14 **The cleaning breath**, which is good in itself, and which is a useful supplement to the complete breath, consists of just one cycle.

1. Slowly and evenly inhale as much as you can without discomfort.
2. Retain the air for a few seconds.
3. Then, without puffing out the cheeks, purse the lips (as if about to whistle) and *vigorously* exhale through the *mouth*, a little at a time, pausing a few seconds between each bit of exhalation, until all the air is exhaled.

15 As the cleansing breath tends to refresh one, it can well be repeated at various times during the day, as desired.

16 Two *precautions* should be observed.

17 Discontinue any breathing exercise, for a while at least, at the first sign of any physical discomfort or over-aeration. The latter may cause light-headedness and a more rapid heartbeat.

18 *Don't* do any breathing exercise in a polluted atmosphere.

913 Some Reflections about Water

1 As is generally known, our physical body consists largely of water. The physical vehicle [body] rests in watery fluid when conceived, and while carried in the womb. We are creatures of the sea, so to speak, and water is absolutely essential to our well being. *Without water we could not express in the physical.*

2 Less commonly known are some other facts.

3 A component of water, *oxygen*, contains a subtle and as yet unmeasured essence that is vital to life, an essence described by such terms as *vital life force, life force, vital energy, bioenergy, chi,* and *prana*. For this reason, water can be of decided value in any room used for quietude, reflection, or communication with spirit people [1246].

4 It is a good habit to keep a (covered) glass with a little water by the bedside, so that spirit chemists can, during the night, infuse it with elements that the body may need or in some degree lack. At times a distinctly medicinal taste will be noted in the morning.

5 Water is an effective *cleanser* of undesirable vibrations; and if there is any doubt about the quality of vibrations from clothing or furniture or other articles, the articles should be thoroughly cleansed with water.

914 A Question about Water

1 "Does water contain vital life force even if polluted?" we have been asked. It is an interesting question.

2 As everyone knows, water assumes many forms. In what is considered its normal state, it is a fluid. In its frozen state, it is ice or snow or hail or sleet. In its gaseous form, water is steam or vapor—visible or invisible. In yet another state it is mist, a visible vapor of rather fine density.

3 In *all* its various states, water retains the subtle and unmeasured substance that is vital to life. But if it is severely contaminated, as it sometimes is by impurities in pipes it passes through, or as it makes its way downhill over rocks and shale, or if it is filthy from pollution, then of course it is harmful to drink and should be avoided: While it would still contain vital life force, that force would then be more than offset by injurious, perhaps deadly, substances.

4 Recent oil spills have shown how much life—in these cases, marine life—can be destroyed when water is polluted.

915 A Cruel Misteaching about Cancer

1 Great anguish has been caused by an inexcusable *misteaching* affirmed in certain groups; a misteaching to the effect that *all* cancer originates in the mind, when ignoble feelings such as avarice, hatred, bitterness, malice, envy, jealousy, and certain types of anger, disturb mental harmony and in turn affect the body.

2 But *infants* have had cancer. So have spiritual men and women of the purest and *noblest* character. To ascribe *all* cancer to ignoble qualities is therefore *not only unjustifiable, but reckless and cruel.*

3 Of course the feelings of one's mind can never be separated from the health of one's body. Cancer *can* be caused by ignoble feelings. But to assert that *all* cancer springs from them is a grave misteaching. What is worse, the statement deeply shocks and grieves many who have witnessed loved ones suffer and perish from that disease.

4 In the 1960s and 1970s, USB *Letters* noted that a factor, if not the principal factor, causing cancer was injury to the cells, such as from blows or bruises, overexposure to the sun, excessive exposure to radiation, contact with chemicals, and possibly viruses. Also, moldy peanut butter or juice squeezed from rotten apples can cause cancer; peanuts and peanut prod-

9.3 Health

ucts are subject to infection with a common mold known as *aspergillus flavus,* which generates poisons called *aflatoxins,* one of the most potent cancer-causing agents in animal testing.

5 [Since that time, with the growth of cancer research at major hospitals and universities, the list of carcinogens has grown much longer.]

916 Not All Illness Springs from the Mind

1 Another misconception we sometimes hear taught is that *all* illness springs from the mind. That also is *not true.* (We wonder what those teachers believe about the causes of diseased animals and plants.)

2 Wise ones throughout the ages have known what the medical profession as a whole has only comparatively recently come to recognize—that mind and body may, and often do, affect each other. Certainly illness of the mind often affects the body.

3 But if a woman is bitten by a mosquito carrying the malaria parasite and contracts malaria, it is not her *mind* that has caused the disease or made her vulnerable to it. The *state* of her mind may play a part in determining how she reacts to the disease, of course; but that is all.

4 If a child is severely injured by a reckless driver, and complications and illness result, or if someone catches a contagious disease from another, it is not the *mind* of the victim that is responsible for illness to the body.

5 To ascribe all disease to the mind would be laughable if it were not so absolutely incorrect and the overwhelming cause of intense grief to some.

6 A patient's mind may *lessen* the effects of his or her physical illness; or it may *aggravate* the illness; but it does not necessarily *cause* the illness.

7 And while illness in the body sometimes affects the mind harmfully, the effect is often the reverse. Those who are cheerful and courageous during illness, those who bear ills with patience and grace, are spiritually the better, and mentally the stronger, for successfully meeting a test.

917 Other Misteachings Relating to Health

1 Some psychic publications have often asserted that if people are spiritually healthy they will be physically healthy.

2 That is just not necessarily so; and the implication is another serious error which, if accepted, acutely shocks and distresses those who ail and those who love them [see also 1314].

3   Incidentally, the corollary of the sweeping and incorrect statement quoted is *also* false, for those who are malevolent are not inevitably ill of body. In fact some of the most wicked men and women in history have enjoyed magnificent physical health.

4   Matching the error we have just discussed is the error of those who assert that *every* illness is "karmic."

5   It takes ignorance to ascribe *all* the trials and tribulations of others to past acts and actions of their own in this or previous existences.

6   What the perpetrators or perpetuators of that misteaching from both sides of life do not realize are two truths the USB emphasizes. One is that *not* all that occurs to us is the result of our *own* acts and actions. The other is that we *do* affect and are *affected* by all we meet in one way or another, in one degree or another, and for one period of time or another.

7   Those who blithely ascribe all misfortune to karma might well keep in mind another USB teaching: *to teach any untruth is to incur a debt that must be paid.* And they indeed acquire undesirable karma who by their misteachings on that subject bring grief to others.

9.4 SLEEP

918 Why We Need Sleep

1   Sleep serves two important purposes.

2   One is the rejuvenation and rehabilitation of the cells in our physical body.

3   Cytologists—biologists who deal with the structure, function, pathology, and life history of cells—tell us that almost all our cells are constantly changing, some rapidly, others over longer and varying periods of time, depending on the composition of the cells and the part of the body they are in.

4   When our objective faculties are placed in abeyance, as when we sleep, it is vastly easier for the rays and vibrations that our body needs (and can absorb from the earth itself and the atmosphere around it) to penetrate our physical being.

5   It is unfortunately true that too many people, consciously or unconsciously, by their own negative mental attitude when awake, block those

9.4 Sleep

healing rays and vibrations. In sleep, they are much more receptive to the inflow of rays and vibrations so vital to their well-being.

6   So when people say to one who is not well: "You must rest. You must relax. You must get more sleep"—they speak wisely, even if they may not understand why rest and relaxation and sleep are so essential.

7   The other reason why we need sleep is that *the real self*—that which animates one's physical body—can visit the spirit world to receive instruction, to join with loved ones, to enjoy a meeting of minds with those with whom we are spiritually akin, and, if we desire, to be of service in one way or another.

8   Those visits [1329] are often termed astral projections[2] or astral flights. But they are not always astral [1301:2]. They may be visits to the Spiritual or Celestial Realms, if we are evolved enough to belong to those realms, or if we are permitted to visit them.

919 Our Sensitivity in the Sleep State

1   We are much more sensitive in the sleep state than when we are awake. For in the sleep state we are far more alert, and events and actions are far more vivid. Many of us do much more in the sleep state than we have any conception of.

2   Some even claim to have visited Venus, or Jupiter, or Mars, or other planets. A few, a very few, *may* have actually done so; if they did, it was in their spirit [etheric] body, *not* their physical body. However, their visits—whether actual, or presented to them in a vision [706:3]—were so vivid, so real, and so completely retained in their memory, that they did not realize they had been either asleep or seeing a vision.

3   There are three things to note. One is that our physical body could not withstand the rates of vibration of other worlds. The second is that before our spirit body could embark on a journey to another planet, it would first have to be sensitized and especially prepared to withstand the various rates of vibration surrounding that planet. The third is that in our travels during the sleep state we are always accompanied by some of those who guide and protect us, even though we may not be aware of it.

---

[2] A type of astral projection, in which the spirit of a medium in an altered state apparently visits and views distant locations on earth, has become known as *remote viewing*. We term it *travelling clairvoyance* (1313:4,9).

920 Effects of Activity During the Sleep State

1 We have been asked whether a person's activities in the spirit world during the sleep state can result in physical weariness.

2 While such activities sometimes cause mental fatigue, they cannot, *in themselves,* affect the physical body.

3 However, if certain activities fatigue us during our "awake" state, those same activities during our sleep state may very well find us exhausted on awakening, because we have learned to *expect* to be affected by them in this way. In that case, it is not the activities themselves but our mind that affects the physical body.

4 The precaution that can and should be taken by those who know or believe that they are active during the sleep state, and who do not feel rested after slumber, is, on retiring, to *instruct* the subjective faculties that the physical body will be resting, and that it will be refreshed by sleep. Our body will respond. But of course it will take time, and we must be patient, for the habits of years are seldom broken overnight.

921 A Little about Sleepwalking

1 An international news service report some years ago [before 1965] opened with these words:

2 A scientific jolt has been dealt to the age-old belief that the sleepwalker is dreaming. The four scientists who thus deepened one of the deeper mysteries of the mind couldn't offer another explanation. They could only say this seemingly reasonable one is "highly questionable."

3 The report makes us once again reflect how much *more* knowledge scientists could acquire and share with humanity if they were aware of the truths of Survival and Communication, and worked humbly *with*, and learned *from*, advanced souls in spirit life. But most scientists on earth are a peculiar breed and, as we have pointed out, as a general rule are most unscientific outside their own particular fields [323:4].

4 People who walk in their sleep may do so for any of several reasons.

5 It may be to accomplish what they intended but failed to accomplish while wide awake. It may be because of the desire, conscious or unconscious, to attract attention. It may be from the wish, conscious or uncon-

9.4 Sleep

scious, to harm themselves or others. In such cases, if they themselves occupy the physical vehicle [body] that is walking, they are always guided safely back to bed by loved ones or friends on earth or in spirit life, unless they are *startled* into waking while in a perilous position.

6   But it is not always the owner of the sleepwalking vehicle who controls it while asleep. At that time, *the real self* may be away in the spirit world for one reason or another; and in some circumstances it may not be possible for spirit friends to prevent other spirits from controlling the sleeping body.

7   When a sleepwalking body falls from a ledge, or walks through a window, or uses a weapon on itself or others, it usually means that *someone else* is temporarily controlling the body with that *very* purpose in mind.

8   If, for instance, a man in his wide-awake state has the destructive impulse to take another's life, it would not be uncommon for spirit people close to the intended victim to gather about the would-be-assailant's body while he is asleep, to take control of it, if protecting influences cannot resist them, with the purpose of bringing *to* the potential destroyer the destruction he had planned for another. This drastic step, one of the ways spirit friends may take to preserve an intended victim, is usually adopted only as a last resort, when they feel they cannot protect their charge by other means: either a protective circle strong enough to repel the would-be-assailant and his cohorts, or sufficient power to turn his mind away from thoughts of harming another.

9   If a woman, for example, is under the influence of alcohol or narcotics, it is sometimes extremely easy for spirit people to control her physical body while she is asleep, and to use it for their own ends without her being aware of it. They might use it to exact revenge for real or fancied injury, or to repay a grudge, or for any of several other reasons. This happens much more often than is generally realized and many prematurely pass on to the spirit world because of such controlling.

10   Of course it is not only during the sleep state that such control can be exercised. A person in the "awake" state who is befuddled or stupefied by alcohol, or in a condition of lethargy from narcotics, is an inviting prey for unadvanced spirit people. In such cases, they may wish to control that person just to vicariously enjoy, in a fuller measure, the vibrations of alcohol or narcotics; or in other cases, to do harm.

11   (The alcoholic or drug addict has less spirit protection than others. This is because, except for our "guardian angel," those spirit people who are

particularly close to us come to us by virtue of The Law of Attraction; and those spirits who enjoy the vibrations of alcohol and narcotics would often be far from alert mentally, and therefore *not* as protecting an influence as they might wish to be.)

922 Talking In One's Sleep

1 Many people talk in their sleep, some frequently, and some rarely.

2 The thing to remember is that it is not necessarily the *sleeper* who is talking. It may be one of the sleeper's spirit guides, or someone who for one reason or another is permitted to use the sleeper's vocal cords. In some instances it may be a spirit who somehow has managed to control a part of the sleeper's physical body without permission.

3 And if it *is* the sleeper who is talking, he or she may be speaking lines in the role of pupil or instructor, or as an actor in a play.

4 So it is wise not to put too much stress on, and not to judge individuals by, what may pass through their lips during sleep.

923 A Little about Dreams

1 There are two kinds of dreams. One is the "mince-pie" or "Welsh rarebit" kind of dream—dreams resulting from physical causes such as indigestion. For when the digestive process is not working properly, it affects the activity of our mind, whether we are awake or asleep. (In the sense we discuss such dreams here, they are *not* merely as dictionaries define them: "a succession of images, thoughts, or emotions passing through the mind during sleep.")

2 The other kind of dream is the experience or experiences one enjoys when one is truly free—that is, when our physical body is asleep, and *the real self* is out of it.

3 As a rule, our recollection of those experiences is either nil, or highly distorted for any of several reasons. The distortion may occur from the effects of the re-entering of our spirit being into its physical vehicle; or because we did not clearly see or interpret what was shown to us; or because we had not instructed ourselves to fully retain the complete vision or the complete experience which was ours; or because it was *not* the time for us to retain conscious memory of what we saw, heard, and did.

9.4 Sleep

4 Even when it *is* in divine order, few indeed are those who are so keenly attuned, so sensitive, that they can usually remember exactly what they see, hear, say, or do during sleep.

5 Most of us do not remember. Sometimes because it would make us homesick [for the spirit world, our true home (1426:3)]. Sometimes because it would make us dissatisfied, unless we are serving a purpose to which we are completely dedicated. For while there is indeed much beauty on earth—something we should never forget—that beauty pales into insignificance beside the beauty of the higher spirit realms.

924 Dreams—and Droes

1 Not all interpreters of dreams agree in their interpretations.

2 To some individuals, dreams reflect clear and distinct events; to others, the reverse of what is dreamt. Thus to dream of having a bumpy air ride means, to one interpreter of dreams, that a coming plane trip will be uncomfortable; to another, that it will be smooth.

3 In any case, many a dream, as we remember it on waking, is merely a *droe*, the acronym we have coined from the first four words of a nine-word phrase: **d**istorted **r**ecollection **o**f **e**vents happening during the sleep state. (The word rhymes with go, no.)

4 It is a good idea to jot down, immediately on waking, recollections of any dream that one wishes to remember, if the recollections are clear and coherent and obviously undistorted. Many writers and composers and others are richly inspired and impressed in their "dreams" during sleep, but usually do not remember those inspirations and impressions unless they make note of them the moment they awake. For only rarely does a dream penetrate the mentality so deeply that it can be otherwise recalled for more than a few hours, or even a few minutes.

5 But there is little point in recording obvious droes, unless the same droe occurs repeatedly.

925 Some Misconceptions about Sleep and Dreams

1 Much that has been written about sleep and dreams reveals widespread misconceptions and incorrect conclusions. We touch on a few.

2 1. Some experts claim that dreams are more important to an individual than sleep. They base their conclusion on experiments showing that sleepers who are consistently awakened just as they are *beginning* to dream, become hostile, while those who are awakened after they have completed dreaming do not mind at all; and also on the fact that when dogs and cats are consistently awakened while dreaming, some die.

3 Those experts, of course, realize that dreams, in the usually accepted sense of the word, cannot occur without sleep. What they apparently do not take into account is that while a person would be greatly relieved to be awakened from a nightmare, he would naturally resent being consistently awakened from pleasant dreams, even if he did not consciously remember them—just as almost anyone, awake, would be annoyed if constantly interrupted from a delightful conversation with friends.

4 As for dogs and cats, they are in some ways much more sensitive than most people, and so would be much more quickly and severely affected by repeated interruptions of their dreaming.

5 2. Many books on dreams give a specific meaning to each of hundreds of objects, symbols, conditions, and experiences that might be noted in a dream. What their authors seldom realize is that objects, symbols, conditions, and experiences *cannot* mean the same thing to everyone, because personal interpretations will differ, depending on one's background, experiences, and past associations and memories of such things.

6 To some individuals, for instance, a serpent represents wiliness and treachery; to others, wisdom. To some peoples, white attire represents mourning; to others, rejoicing. Scores of other examples could be cited.

7 In any case, as we have said, the vast majority of our dreams are either not recollected at all when we awake, or are distorted during the process of *the real self* [our spirit being] re-entering the physical body [923:3]. We can liken an *actual* dream to reflections in perfectly still and clear water, and the *distortion* of that dream to reflections in water that is muddy and agitated.

8 3. Statements about "rapid eye movements" (or REMs) during the dreams of sleepers in monitored studies imply that without REMs a sleeper cannot be dreaming. But that is not true.

9 It is worth noting, first of all, that what occurs in dreams may and often does affect the sleeper's *physical* vehicle. Who among us has not awakened during a dream in which we were struggling with someone, to find we were thrashing about in bed? Who among us has not had the sensation of falling during a dream, and jolted oneself awake by stretching out a hand to break the fall?

10   The eyes, which are particularly sensitive organs, often reflect our eye movements during dreams. But if in a dream our gaze is fixed on a spectacle or stage some distance away, there would be no need for REMs. So there could be, and *are,* dreams without REMs.

9.5 TIME AND CYCLES

926 Some Reflections about Time

1   One thing often misunderstood is time.

2   There are some who hold that there is no such thing as *time,* as human beings understand time, and that past, present, and future are all one. *We reject this view.*

3   To accept it would be to say, in effect, that the infant, the schoolchild and the adult are one and the same at any one instant; and this obviously is not so. Or that the seed, the sprout, and the tree are one and the same thing at any one moment; which is obviously not so, either.

4   Of course "the child is father of the man," as the saying goes; but it is true only *metaphorically,* not literally. The potential of the oak exists in the acorn, and the potential of the adult exists in the infant; but between potentiality and actuality lies a vast gulf—a gulf that is bridged, if it *is* bridged, only after the succession (not concurrence) of countless events of various durations at various intervals.

5   Time itself, as measured in seconds and minutes and days and weeks and months and years and centuries, *does* exist, and is absolute [independent]. But the *way* time affects us, or the effects of time *on* us, are relative. Thus a year with a loved one may seem like an hour, while an hour of agony may seem like a year.

6   We should realize the wisdom of building, *now,* towards what we desire to *be.* For all the time we shall *ever* have, at *any* moment, *wherever* we may be, and *whichever* side of life we live in, is neither the past nor the future, but only the present—the Now. As a Blessed Soul expresses it:

7   What people call time is of very little value except for what can be accomplished in *the Now.* Some will say, "Now *is* time"; but *we* say, now is *eternal.*

8   We cannot emphasize too strongly the importance of living in *the Now*—of expressing, for good, as fully and as freely as the consciousness will permit, in *the Now*.

927 Enjoying the NOW

1   Individuals are wise who neither squander their resources nor are so overly frugal that they will not satisfy even their barest needs [709].

2   From time to time we learn of someone who lived in wretched circumstances, usually in poverty and squalor, but who, it transpired on their passing, were rich in material things that were little used either for themselves or others.

3   That is not being provident. That is being *ill*. It is a *mental* disease—such morbid fear of the future, such concern about what *may* lie ahead, that the present, *the Now*, is utterly neglected. The many little things, beautiful things, that make life glowing and wonderful to those who feel and think, rarely if ever bring joy to those possessed by unreasoning apprehension of things that may never happen and days that may never dawn.

4   There is *much* that we have to be thankful for, much that *each* day offers that can be savored and relished. The wise enjoy, with a grateful heart, all that the day brings for them to enjoy: a child's laughter, the sun and the wind, the smell of earth and green grass after rain, a brilliant sunset, the blue of the sky, the murmur of a rippling stream, a warm handclasp, the smile of good fellowship, the companionship of friends and loved ones, the flowers in the garden, and countless other delights that exist for almost everyone, rich and poor, high and low, king and commoner.

5   As we have stressed, all we have, all we shall *ever* have, is *the Now*. So it would be folly not to enjoy things of beauty that can contribute to our growth spiritually, merely because they will not last forever. And if we are wise enough to enjoy them, we can also relish them in recollection, for they can live indefinitely in our storehouse of memory.

6   The path to the mountaintop, steep though it is, need not be a cheerless one—nor was it intended to be so. It *cannot* be cheerless to anyone who has even the faintest conception of the Love and Wisdom and Goodness that are God.

9.5 Time and Cycles

928 A Little about Cycles and Human Beings

1. It has become increasingly fashionable in some schools of thought, and with many individuals as well, to refer to *cycles*—with *cycle* used in its meaning of a recurring period of time, particularly one in which certain events or phenomena repeat themselves in the same order at the same intervals.

2. They talk of a 2,000-year cycle that is drawing to a close, with a teacher appearing (as happened twenty centuries ago) at the start of another 2,000-year cycle. Or they talk of the cycle of peace and war, implying that wars *must* occur; but wars need *not* occur.

3. As we see about us, much of nature follows a cycle, one of order and regularity. The planets revolve around the sun in their own specific cycles. Eclipses of the sun occur with such regularity that they can be predicted to the minute, hundreds and even thousands of years in advance. The earth rotates on its axis daily. Day and night alternate with unfailing order and regularity, though the length of day and night is not everywhere the same. The seasons follow one another in a yearly cycle, though the seasons themselves, at any one time, are not the same in *all* parts of the globe.

4. Every time we breathe, we complete a cycle, that of taking air into our lungs and then expelling it. Our blood flows in a cycle, leaving the heart from one chamber and duly returning to the other.

5. At a certain span in their existence, many plants bear leaves, blossom, bear fruit, and shed their leaves, in cycles. The length of the cycle will vary, depending upon the plant itself, the soil, the climate, and at times man's ingenuity, but the cycle itself is unchanged. In some circumstances, in some crops in some areas, there may be *several* complete cycles a year instead of just one.

6. In addition to the cycles in nature, human beings have established some valuable cycles for their own convenience and necessity. For instance, they divide the year into 365 or 366 days and into twelve months of various lengths, each day into 24 hours, each hour into 60 minutes, each minute into 60 seconds, and each second into smaller subdivisions. There often are cycles *within* cycles, natural or otherwise.

7. But what occurs to people, generally and individually, is bound *not* to any cycle, but to what we bring about by our words, thoughts, acts, and actions.

8. Possessing, as each human being does possess, a spark of divinity, we are *not* subject to cycles, and we ourselves *determine* what our lot shall be.

9   Illumined Souls emphasize that we are our *own* prophets, and that *we* reap the harvest of our *own* prophecy. Also that *each* era is the natural result of *people's* attitudes and actions in eras *preceding*. But these things, while happening according to The Law of Cause and Effect, do *not* take place in any cycle, for we are constantly determining, by our way of life, what they shall *be;* and as *we* change, so do we change what shall *be*.

10   We are not bound to any chains or wheels, except to chains or wheels of our own making. Of course illness and other misfortunes may strike us through no fault of our own. As we have pointed out, much that happens to one may *not* be the result of one's *own* acts and actions [1410]. But we can use even illness and other misfortunes to advance spiritually —if, when unable to correct a situation or condition, we accept it graciously and courageously.

9.6 SOUND AND COLOR

929 A Little about Sound, Color, and Odor

1   Vibration, which is energy in motion, is sensed most notably as **sound** and **color**. And as everything vibrates, everything is sensed as *both* sound and color.

2   Color has sound, and sound has color. Neither can exist without the other, for *they are the same thing*. But they are perceived differently by different senses, usually the sense of hearing and the sense of sight. We may perceive either color or sound; we may perceive both; we may perceive neither. It depends upon our senses.

3   *Sound* is composed of *pitch* and *tone* [or *timbre*]. When tuned to the same pitch, there is a world of difference between the tone of a Stradivarius and the tone of the average violin.

4   Vibration is sensed in yet another way, one that seldom is as pronounced as the manifestations of sound and color. That third way, which is perceived by the sense of smell, is **odor**—which can be variously described as scent, perfume, smell, fragrance, aroma, and many other similar terms.

5   Each thing, each person, each creature, has its own particular odor, which actually is almost always a combination of odors. The odor may be so strong as to be overwhelming, or, as is much more commonly the

9.6 Sound and Color

case, so weak as to be unnoticeable to us—the range and variety of odor is astonishing, yet many animals have a far keener sense of smell than humans. Individuals may find an odor delightful and refreshing, or extremely offensive. An odor may be pleasant at one stage, and unpleasant at another. It may be pronounced at one period, and scarcely perceptible the next. But it is there nevertheless, for odor is a manifestation of vibration, just as sound and color are.

930 More about Color—and Colors

1. Some schools of thought ascribe precise meanings to various colors. Green means this, they say. Blue means that. Red, still another thing.

2. We would not generalize, however, for each primary color of the spectrum has many shades, no two of which have the very same significance.

3. We can say without hesitation that some of the deeper shades of gray, some of the darker greens and browns and reds, and black itself, usually are not "healthy." They tend to depress, or irritate, or induce a sense of restlessness. But we would not define the precise significance of the primary colors themselves, because various shades and hues of any color produce different, sometimes vastly different, effects.

4. *Shades* are gradations of a primary color; *hues*, modifications of that color. Scarlet, for example, is a hue, for it is a very bright red with a slightly orange tinge.

5. Certain shades and hues of red, for instance, are depressing, and even harmful; others are exciting and inspiring in various ways. Some of the pinks, which are pale reds, are delightful and cheerful—and to some schools of thought indicate spirituality.

6. Much the same can be said of green. Some of the darker shades and hues are most depressing. As for the lighter shades and hues, some are bilious, others beautiful and restful. (There are physicians, well aware of the healing effect of some shades of green, who instruct patients with certain eye ailments to sit where they can relax and gaze at distant trees and lawn.)

7. In general, it is a color's *shades* and *hues* that are of especial significance, rather than the primary color itself. The color, for instance, may be cool and uninspiring; but a shade of that color, or a modification of that color, may be warm and exciting.

8   There are several things worth noting about colors—and we now use the word in a comprehensive sense to include hues.

9   One is that we do not all respond in the very same way to the very same color.

10 Another is that no one reacts to any particular color in exactly the same way at all times.

11 Yet another is that while a color, in itself, may have a pleasant or unpleasant effect on us, that effect may be diminished, or heightened—and in some cases even *reversed*—if the color is beside *other* colors, or is part of an overall picture or scene. To an individual, a specific color may be unattractive by itself, yet harmonious in some surroundings; or attractive alone, but incompatible with others.

12 Colors affect us, whether or not we realize it. If we attribute any mental or physical discomfort from them to *other* things, we will make no effort to correct the real cause.

13 Personal tastes in color play an important role—in the decorative scheme of a room, for example—but it may not be wise to indulge oneself in that respect. A person may relish and enjoy certain types of art and certain combinations of colors; but if they are disharmonious, as many are, they will adversely affect him or her in some degree, mentally or physically, or both. Certainly they can cause an extremely sensitive person to become violently ill.

14 Observes an Illumined Soul:

15 Nature and the panorama of color in nature are God's handiwork, clear and beautiful. But much that people create according to *their* interpretation of what they see, distorts and confuses, to sadden the heart and soul of those who truly appreciate beauty.

16 Some consider *black* an absence of color—in contrast with *white*, which is a combination of all the colors in the spectrum. While the color white is of a highly rapid rate of vibration, many find one particular shade of it—chalk white—cold and unattractive; and fewer and fewer hospitals have white walls in sickrooms.

17 As for *black*, some of the finest spirit demonstrations take place in pitch blackness; so it is a desirable color (or lack of color) in some circumstances.

18 What gives a color its specific shade or hue? Its rate of vibration.

9.6 Sound and Color □ 931

931 A Little about Color and Music

1   There is a precise correspondence between color and music.

2   The notes in the musical scale correspond with the colors in the rainbow, which contains the entire spectrum of prismatic or primary colors. There are these correspondences:

3

Note	Color	
C	red	
D	orange	
E	yellow	Of vibrations that human beings in their
F	green	normal state perceive as *color*, red is
G	blue	the slowest rate, violet the most rapid.
A	indigo	
B	violet	

4   The sharps and flats of the musical scale correspond with *blends* of primary colors in equal parts. C sharp and D flat correspond with a blend of red and orange; D sharp and E flat, with a blend of orange and yellow; F sharp and G flat, with a blend of green and blue; G sharp and A flat, with a blend of blue and indigo; A sharp and B flat, with a blend of indigo and violet.

5   Any chord is a *blend* of colors. A harmonious chord is a beautiful blend of colors. A dissonant chord is a harsh and unsightly combination of them.

6   Music played in *one* key may affect certain people differently when played in *another* key, for a very good reason. For while the notes in a melody played in one key are in exactly the same relative positions as the notes of the same melody played in another key, the corresponding colors are quite different.

7   The same applies to chords. The notes in the chord of F, for instance, are in the same relative position as the notes in the chord of G, but the blends of colors are different.

8   People who are affected differently by a composition played in different keys inwardly perceive, as a rule quite unconsciously, the difference in the colors or combinations of colors that are expressed. Their sensitivities to colors are stronger than most people's, however unaware they may be of it.

9   The *tone* [or *timbre*] of a musical note, and the rhythm and beat of music, also have their effect. Some vocalists and violinists and other instrumentalists can shatter a goblet merely by creating a particular tone of a single note.

10 As for rhythm and beat—which are a vital part of music, as most of us know it—certain steady, even, unvarying beats can, *destroy*. That is why troops usually break step when about to cross a bridge.

11 A rousing beat stirs people's hearts. It can be the source of inspiration for upliftment, or the source of inspiration for destruction. It is a rousing beat that sends troops into battle.

12 Says a USB inspirer,

13 > Human beings have always felt a sense of rhythm, and their expression of this sense of rhythm takes many avenues—from the simple rhythm of the savage tom-tom, to the many and varied rhythms of the symphonic rhapsodies portrayed in elaborately created orchestrations in which every type of instrument is represented.

14 An awareness of the influence of chords, tone, rhythm, and beat, provide greater insight into the almost incredible power of music—a power for good, or a power for destruction. The inspirer continues:

15 > The role of music is vital in the lives of human beings. Music can calm a sea of turbulent emotions. It can also lash the tranquil waters into a raging turmoil.

16 Music can indeed inflame the quiet breast. It can overwhelm us with restlessness. It can whip us into frenzy. It can stir us to hate and cruelty. It can rob us of our courage. It can depress us and unbalance the mind. It can plunge us into hell. And it can destroy cell structure.

17 But music can also soothe the troubled breast. It can heal the mind and the body. It can flood us with repose. It can bring us profound peace. It can inspire us to love and kindness. It can imbue us with courage. It can elevate us. It can transport us to heaven.

10
The Divining Arts

CHAPTER CONTENTS

10.1 Prediction   286
    1001   Some Facts about Prophecy   286
    1002   Prophecy and Healing Are Not Divine Attributes   288
    1003   A Face and Figure in the Clouds   289
    1004   On Predictions of Approaching Disaster   292
    1005   Most Predictions Do NOT Materialize   295
    1006   A Word of Warning   298
    1007   Of Many So-Called "Saviors"   299

10.2 Astrology   300
    1008   Some Reflections about Astrology   300
    1009   Of Twins and the Stars   305

10.3 Palmistry, Phrenology, Psychometry, and Hypnosis   306
    1010   A Little about Palmistry   306
    1011   A Little about Phrenology   308
    1012   A Little about Psychometry   309
    1013   "Regression" Under Hypnosis—Some Things to Remember   310

10.1 PREDICTION

1001 Some Facts about Prophecy

1. From time to time there are individuals on earth who are especially gifted with the ability to see into the future, having brought with them a reservoir of skill in that particular form of mediumship; and by The Law of Attraction, some of their spirit friends will also possess that talent.

2. In some cases, such an earthly seer subconsciously knows the past experiences of the person he or she prophesies[1] about, and is therefore able to determine what is likely to follow.

3. In other cases, the seer voices information received from either his or her own spirit guides or from the guides of the person concerned—those who, as a result of their closeness, understand what seemingly lies in that person's future.

4. In still other cases, the seer is able to correctly read and interpret the aura of those for whom he or she prophesies. If also assisted by skilled spirit auric scientists [1311:12], the seer is usually able to predict what will *probably* happen—not only to nations and individuals, but to places as well.

5. The assisting spirit scientists may impress the seer by projecting a picture or "movie" of a future scene—which may or may not happen—or by directing a thought so that the seer will *hear* it. For clairvoyance and clairaudience[2] usually play a vital part in what the prophet or seer receives and shares.

6. There are two other important points relating to prophecy.

7. One is that regardless of how the information shared is received, the prophet or seer has some responsibility for what he or she prophesies. It is a responsibility that cannot be escaped, and one that should not be taken

---

[1] According to most dictionaries, *prophecies* are either (*a*) predictions (not necessarily divine) of the future, or (*b*) declarations (not necessarily predictions) that are divinely inspired or made by a prophet. Note that they are not at all the same thing as clairvoyance (footnote 2). The verb, to *prophesy* something, has the same two meanings, except that (*b*) may be not only by but also *as if by* divine inspiration.

[2] *Clairvoyance* is the (supposed) ability to see spirit-induced subjective visions, or to see objective spirit-world or physical-world things beyond the range of normal sight. (It is sometimes used as a general term to also include clairaudience and clairsentience.) *Clairaudience* is the (supposed) ability to hear spirit-induced subjective sounds, or objective spirit-world sounds beyond the range of normal hearing.

10.1 Prediction

lightly; so the seer should ponder well before venturing any prediction that, unwisely or incompletely made, might change the lives of others for the worse.

8   The second is to realize that prophets or seers or any other mediums, when impressed from without, are impressed by other *individuals* in or out of the physical. It is *not* God who impresses them, as they so often mistakenly assume. It was ignorance of this truth that caused much of the horrible cruelty and bloodshed chronicled in some early religious texts, such as the slaughter of entire populations. Many of those prophets, unaware of The Law of Attraction, did not realize that it was *not* God whom they heard or saw, but inspirers very much like themselves—too often intolerant, cruel, vindictive, and pitiless.

9   A lack of basic knowledge about mediumship too often continues to prevail among mediums.

10   For example, a noted individual, the channel for some remarkable spirit healing, declared that *God* told him what to do in treating a patient. He did not reflect that if that were actually the case, there would have been no failures at all; and there *were* failures.

11   A seer, well publicized for some prophecies that came to pass concerning people of eminence, has also made predictions that did *not* materialize. The explanation given was, in effect, that successful prophecies are from God; unsuccessful ones, *not* from God.

12   Another individual, famous for mediumship of high caliber, was apparently quite unaware of the mechanics of her mediumship, and wondered whether it was attributable to "secondary personalities."

13   The tragedy resulting from such lack of knowledge on the part of some who demonstrate mediumship in spectacular fashion is that their mediumship rarely leads to any understanding, or any greater understanding, of The Laws That Govern and the importance of living by those Laws.

14   It seldom makes people think. It usually does not help to make people conscious that we each possess a spark of divinity; that we are spirit beings here and now, and not just in some remote time and place; that *the real self* is indestructible; that we can, under certain conditions, commune with those who have gone on; and that the universe is governed by Law and Order.

15   The accuracy of a prophecy often depends on a knowledge of events leading up to the time the prophecy is made. *Every cause has its effect,*

and skilled minds that are aware of causes can often successfully predict what will happen unless unforeseen factors intervene.

16 We can liken it to some people on top of a steep mountain who see one car racing down the narrow spiralling road, and another car climbing up in the opposite direction. They have good reason to predict not only a collision, but approximately when it will occur. However, if the reckless driver meanwhile comes to his senses, realizes he is travelling much too fast, and slows to a safe speed, the crash may be averted.

17 The truth is that *no* prophecy is infallible, however soundly based, for unforeseen events may, and often do, change the picture.

18 Other factors in prophecy are the extraordinary power and range of thought, and the fact that many minds on both sides of life can tune in on a thought. If, for instance, an assassination is planned, the thought in the mind or minds conceiving the plan will go out into the ether—as all thoughts do—and there will be other minds (on either or both sides of life) that will consciously or unconsciously register that thought.

19 If it is only spirit people who are aware of vibrations that spell impending disaster, they may attempt to communicate that knowledge—first to those on earth with whom they are linked, and then to others. It often transpires that some on earth receive an impression of a forthcoming event, but dismiss or forget it, only to recall it after the event actually occurs.

20 A notable instance is the collapse of a slag heap in Wales in 1966, resulting in the death of scores of children. In that specific case, some spirit individuals recognized that the collapse was imminent, but, in the apparent absence of a medium through whom they could issue a clear and specific warning, they could do no more than impress a few people with what was likely to happen, and that later did happen.

1002 Prophecy and Healing Are Not Divine Attributes

1 It has been the practice in at least one school of thought to "affirm that the precepts of Prophecy and Healing are Divine attributes proven through Mediumship."

2 The affirmation is most puzzling, regardless of whether it is *precepts* or *prophecy and healing* that are affirmed to be "Divine attributes."

3 For a precept, however admirable, is not an attribute, but a commandment or direction given as a mode or rule of action or conduct.

10.1 Prediction

4   As for prophecy and healing, any study of predictions would reveal that most do not materialize, and any study of healing would show that not all are successful.

5   Many scriptural prophecies—prophecies that the people of the time expected would come to pass in *their* days—are still unfulfilled. They may never be fulfilled, whatever the basis for them at the time.

6   As for prophecies in our own day and age, anyone who keeps a record of predictions of today's soothsayers will know that most of their predictions either do not come to pass at all, or do not come to pass within the time specified. Certainly if prophecy were "a divine attribute," no correctly received and correctly interpreted prophecy would be unfulfilled. And likewise, if healing were "a divine attribute" no healing would be unsuccessful. But prophecy and healing are no more "divine" than clairvoyance, or clairaudience, or automatic writing, or any other form of mediumship or psychic phenomena: There is satisfactory and unsatisfactory expression in any field. The *only* thing divine is That which *always* manifests in *order:* the Supreme Power whose handiwork is conceived and created in goodness and wisdom and perfection.

7   By no stretch of the imagination do prophecy and healing fit that description.

8   In the following pages we record two major prophecies in our time that affected a great number of people, and we summarize the results of predictions in some recent decades.

1003 A Face and Figure in the Clouds

1   The bearers of confusion, whether malicious or merely ignorant, are indeed energetic and unremitting in their efforts. Signs and wonders, actual or promised, are a great part of their stock in trade—designed to lure people into exchanging their birthright of reason for the emptiness of blind faith.

2   From a little seaside town came accounts in 1961 of an extraordinary manifestation that would take place "by the first second of the first hour of Christmas morning 1967," purportedly by a spirit being [person] who claimed to be, among other things, "Truth Itself," "the one who creates and directs all things in the entire Universe," and "the Light, the All throughout the Universe." All would "go according to plan without any exception whatsoever."

3   These and many other statements in a similar vein were reported by one person, apparently "the sole medium" and the only person who saw and heard "the Master."

4   There were pictures of "a piece of inspirational sculpture," and a picture that "wept," and other psychic manifestations that many people, unaware of the probable explanations [1137], attributed to the self-proclaimed near-deity or deity itself.

5   Based evidently on just what *one* person claimed to have seen and heard, and the able and extensive pronouncements of another, the incidents and prophecy were widely and repeatedly publicized throughout the globe for more than six years.

6   Many individuals and groups in various parts of the world began corresponding with one another, to relay apparent corroboration that they declared they themselves had received. Many of those "corroborations" undoubtedly came from thought forms [1319:9–13] created by the corroborators themselves, and the rest by unenlightened or mischievous spirit people.

7   Men and women, some of them distinguished in their own fields of endeavor, but seemingly none too familiar with the mechanics and demonstration of certain phases of mediumship and psychic phenomena, became so firmly convinced of the appearance of a "master"—or "The Master" —and of an unmistakably divine manifestation before Christmas 1967, that they felt compelled to declare that certainty at hundreds of lectures and meetings. Scores of pamphlets on the subject, pamphlets written in obvious sincerity and conviction, were printed by the thousands and widely distributed.

8   It was stated that the purported spirit being [person] would (according to at least one group) appear "in a seemingly solid form, four to five miles [six to eight kilometers] up in the skies, appearing and disappearing, talking to the peoples," so that they would hear and "recognize" him. He would also (according to that same group) "appear on television screens all over the world, not simultaneously, but only hours apart, according to the time zone involved." A face and figure on the clouds would reveal a savior to humanity!

9   All this by Christmas morning 1967 at the latest.

10   Christmas 1967 came and went, *without the extraordinary manifestation that was promised.*

11   What is particularly sad, in our opinion, is the way a seemingly thoroughly honest and sincere but credulous person devoted time and effort

10.1 Prediction

and resources to widely spreading the "truth" so unreservedly accepted by that person. It illustrates again, if further illustration is necessary, how vital it is to exercise reason, and to always remember that a hallmark of the spiritually elevated is humility.

12 We refer to this six-year-long run of events and prophecy for several reasons:

13 — to warn against false prophets (on either side of life), some of whom are leagued with the forces of darkness that desire to so thoroughly confuse, disappoint, and disillusion the unthinking that they will refuse to consider *any* truth placed before them.

14 — to remind readers that in these days of scientific accomplishments that dwarf the imagination, it would not be such a difficult matter to project not only a face and figure in the clouds, but also a voice loud enough to be heard by literally millions of people on earth; and that powerful, unscrupulous forces bent on keeping human beings enchained in ignorance would have no hesitation in staging any possible "wonder" or "miracle" that would astound the unthinking and enslave them, or enslave them more deeply.

15 — to point out that if we let our imagination run wild, we shall see faces and figures, or other formations, in clouds, in mosaics, in foliage, in flames, in almost everything. It takes little imaging on the part of a sensitive person to see what is suggested *might* be witnessed or *might* take place.

16 — to emphasize that *no one* can absolve us from unchangeable Laws —The Laws That Govern—notably The Law of Cause and Effect and The Law of Personal Responsibility.

17 The forces of darkness know that the more they can disappoint and disillusion the unthinking, the blinder the unthinking will be to any real light.

18 One final quotation from what that "Master" is reported to have said some years ago:

19 When my medium is organized I intend to use my bank for speculation by way of lending on secured propositions, in a manner likely to create satisfactory returns, so that many operations remaining on my Earth planet may go unhindered by obvious human level restrictions.

20 There are those who have illusions of self-grandeur and self-importance on both sides of life. Fortunately, there are also those on both sides of life who recognize the needs of such individuals, and attempt to care for those needs.

21 What is puzzling is how *anyone* could credit that statement—many did—to one whom they accepted as "Truth Itself" and "The one who created and directs the entire universe."

22 False prophets unfortunately attract many good but unquestioning people, sincere people, people of integrity—people who by their obvious goodness and sincerity and integrity convince thousands of men and women who look to *others* for a way out of problems and difficulties that humanity faces.

23 What is especially lamentable is the tremendous waste of time and energy—time and energy that could be put to good use in learning and understanding some of The Laws That Govern, and then, by word and example, teaching others those Laws and the importance of living by them.

1004 On Predictions of Approaching Disaster

1 The year 1961 brought another prediction, one that affected the lives and actions of hundreds of thousands of people all over the world.

2 The fact that February 1962 would witness an extremely rare occurrence, five planets in conjunction—that is, in the same celestial longitude—was interpreted by many as a sign of momentous changes, and spawned innumerable predictions of impending disaster for humanity in that fateful month.

3 The predictions originated not only from well-meaning but mistaken souls on *this* side of life, but from (let us assume) well-meaning but mistaken souls on the spirit side of life.

4 Leading astrologers of the East and West interpreted the approaching conjunction of planets as indicating cataclysms as stupendous and terrifying as the earth had ever known; pestilences sweeping across countries and continents; earthquakes and nuclear war; the death of at least three-fourths of the world's population; and the survival of only a few chosen ones, who would be directed to build sanctuaries deep in the bowels of the earth, or on high mountain tops, and to stock them with provisions and supplies to last until the effects of the cataclysmic changes were over.

5 Newspapers throughout the world featured the prophecies of disaster, and the despair and activities (or lack of activities) of those who despaired.

10.1 Prediction

In India in particular, millions of people abandoned their daily routine of living because of the predictions of individuals they venerated.

6   Other countries were not immune from the contagion of fear. In the United States, for instance, groups of people sold their belongings, and uprooted themselves from their home of a lifetime, to journey, to "safe" places. One group was "directed" to a California town as a place of refuge; but it became a missile center, which of course would have made it a prime target in any nuclear war.

7   The dire predictions were groundless.

8   A USB worldwide *Letter* of 1961 included the following paragraphs:

9   We ask our brothers and sisters to exercise their reason on this score, as in all things. To accept without reason is to bring chaos into our lives.

10   We ask our brothers and sisters to remember how often there have been predictions of worldwide catastrophe—with the appointed time come and gone without the terrible happenings that were predicted.

11   We ask our sisters and brothers to remember that the usual explanation will be forthcoming when the predicted calamities do not occur, and when the appointed time comes and goes and the world is still very much as it is today—the catastrophe will have been averted by the prayers of the very ones who are leading so many people to the havens built and provisioned!

12   Of course there may be pestilences; we have had them in the past. Of course there may be earthquakes; we have had them in the past. Of course there may be tidal waves; we have had them in the past.

13   There may, in addition, be "fall-out" perils, triggered by design or accident; but we cannot be surprised by them if human beings delve into the forces of nature without a spiritual motive.

14   We know that any force can be used for good or bad, and that the choice is ours. And if we use great powers for destructive purposes, we must expect to pay the penalty; but the number "triggered" into the spirit world would not be in the vast proportions predicted by the prophets of doom.

15   We ask our brothers and sisters to remember that no particular good could ever come from the taking of the physical life of hundreds of millions of innocent people; that the spirit world, mighty and magnificent though its leaders are, is not equipped to cope with the influx of so many souls that would be suddenly dispatched from earth; that the terrific destruction that is predicted would not solve any problem, but only enlarge it; and that there are no select, chosen people, for all are children of a loving God.

16 February 1962 was but one in a long list of doom dates—for all through the ages there have been predictions of worldwide catastrophe, with the appointed time come and gone *without* catastrophe striking in the manner prophesied, if at all. The flood of explanations why no major disaster occurred varies, from "errors in astrological calculations" to the prayers of the very prophets of doom themselves.

17 Summer 1960 was another doom date. A USB *Letter* of that period included the following observations that on the whole are as timely now as then:

18 Despite those who predicted that the world would end during the past summer [of 1960], or that a cataclysmic war would by now have wiped out humanity, the earth still exists, and life on earth continues.

19 It is true that world tensions have mounted. It is true that we remain on the brink of the precipice. But it is also true that we still possess peace, precarious though it may be, and that we still are on the right *side* of the precipice.

20 The USB does not walk with the prophets of doom, because it is ever conscious of the magnificent power for good that lies in constructive thoughts—and such constructive thoughts have helped preserve peace, teeter though it does on the tightrope.

21 In the preserving of that peace, the power of the concentrated thought of several hundred USB supporters, focused on love and peace and good will among all peoples, has played an immense part—as of course has the thought of others who are not USB supporters but who share our ideals.

22 Let us never underestimate the power of thought of even one person. When the thought of hundreds and thousands, directed to one goal, is harnessed together, the power is truly a mighty one!

23 Illumined Souls ask us not only to continue to direct our thoughts of love and peace and harmony to all peoples, particularly to the council tables around which the leaders of nations gather, but to increase our efforts. That is what they themselves are doing.

24 They ask us to visualize what is good. They tell us that if we act as if that visualization were a reality, it will speed the creation of a comparative heaven on earth.

25 Meanwhile, while one child is hungry, while one child lacks the *chance* to live like a human being, a responsibility falls upon the rest of us. "We must share—not only our thoughts and love and prayers, but what is of a material nature."

10.1 Prediction

1005 Most Predictions Do NOT Materialize

1 Some psychics and astrologers claim an extremely high percentage of success in their prediction. Some declare that as much as 95 percent of their prophecies turn out to be correct.

2 Records kept by the USB do not support those assertions. On the contrary, our files of clippings indicate that the overwhelming majority of prediction by psychics and astrologers do *not* come to pass.[3]

3 We give excerpts from some quarterly *Letters* of the USB that from time to time summarized the results of predictions made for the second half of the previous year by "10 leading psychics," and publicized by a weekly publication with a circulation of millions. In most cases, each individual's predictions were preceded by mention of one or two that had been accurate in the past; no mention was made, however, of the many that had not materialized.

4 Here are a few, and only a very few, of their forecasts for last year [1971] that did *not* materialize. Those based on astrology are followed by asterisks.

- Queen Elizabeth would abdicate her throne.
- Princess Anne would marry in August. ***
- Paris would suffer severe floods.
- Japan would have "a year of natural disasters about or near the time of the major eclipses." ***
- England's Prime Minister would marry by the end of the year. ***
- J. Edgar Hoover, head of America's FBI, would "be out of office by the end of the summer."
- King Constantine would return to Greece.
- A truce in Vietnam would be concluded in October or November.
- Mrs. Indira Gandhi would resign as Prime Minister of India.
- Mao Tse-tung would die.
- Khrushchev would return to the political scene.
- The United States would "have further bad relations with China." ***
- A cure for cancer would be found.
- Diplomatic relations would be resumed between the United States and Cuba.
- A large jet would disappear over the Atlantic with all aboard.

---

[3] In the years since the predictions discussed here, the Internet has provided numerous references to the extremely poor success record of professional psychics predicting the future. And the Internet's free encyclopedia, Wikipedia, states that studies of astrological predictions have repeatedly shown their mean accuracy to be no greater than chance.

- There would be "a complete breakdown of the New York City subway system in the fall, resulting in numerous casualties."
- World War III would "break out by October... with Pluto going into Libra, there'll be blood on the harvest moon." ***
- The Middle East situation would be resolved. ***

5 According to many astrologers, knowledge of the exact time of birth is vital to an accurate horoscope of an individual. Certainly the precise moment of birth of some of the personalities mentioned above is a matter of record. If even in such cases predictions fail to materialize, one can imagine the "accuracy" of horoscopes of other people.

6 Three years later we wrote:

7 Unfulfilled, among many other predictions, were these for 1974:

- that Pope Paul would resign.
- that another oil embargo would "be clamped down on the United States in the fall."
- that Senator Kennedy would "go all out for the presidency."
- that then Vice President Ford would resign over President Nixon's military policies.
- that "Red China" would try to occupy Taiwan in November...
- that George Foreman would retain his heavyweight title "with a crushing victory over Muhammad Ali."
- that Russian and U.S. "hostilities" would "flare after a diplomatic mix-up."

8 Of the total of 67 predictions [for 1974], 57 did not come to pass.

9 Of the 13 predictions by two astrologers, 12 did not materialize.

10 Another year later we wrote:

11 Of a total of 54 forecasts [for 1975] at least 39 did *not* materialize.

12 Of 11 events predicted by "world-famous" astrologers, at least eight did not occur.

13 We say "at least," because the few predictions we could not readily check were given the benefit of the doubt and counted correct.

14 Among the many unfulfilled predictions for the latter half of 1975 were the following:

- that President Ford would resign, with Nelson Rockefeller assuming the presidency.
- that terrorists would steal a nuclear weapon in an attempt to hold the world at ransom.
- that North Korea, backed by Red China, would take over South Korea, with no interference by the United States.
- that Queen Elizabeth would abdicate.

10.1 Prediction

— that Pope Paul would resign.

15 The last two predictions have been made in every recent year [until 1975], and indeed have already been forecast for 1976. Of course, if the same prediction is made *every* year, the chances are much greater that it will ultimately come to pass.

16 The following year we wrote:

17 At least 60 of the 64 different predictions [for 1976] did *not* come to pass.

18 We say "at least," because three of the four results we could not readily check were given the benefit of the doubt and counted correct.

19 Among the many unfulfilled predictions for the second half of 1976 were the following:

- that Prince Charles would be lost at sea when his ship sank in a storm, but would be found alive several days later.
- that Castro would be ousted as Cuba's premier following the discovery that he had channelled huge sums of money into a Swiss bank account.
- that an outer-space civilization would warn our planet against sending certain types of vehicles into certain areas in space.
- that a gigantic earthquake would tear apart entire mountain ranges in California, revealing the biggest gold deposits ever discovered.
- that a nuclear submarine would mysteriously vanish beneath the Arctic ice cap...
- that it would transpire that United States CIA scientists had learned how to make objects vanish and later reappear.
- that Henry Kissinger would be forced to resign over secret deals.
- that one of the bloodiest conflicts in history would hit the Middle East, with Israel wiped out, and the United States involved.

20 Of the "10 leading psychics," the predictions of nine were preceded by mention of one forecast in the past that had turned out to be correct; no mention was made of the multitude of forecasts that had not materialized.

21 Considering that 25 of the 64 forecasts were about show business people whose private lives are usually public, the extremely high percentage of error is even more significant.

22 And the year after that we wrote:

23 The record last year [1977] is *sorrier than ever*... reviewing forecasts by "10 leading psychics" (including two astrologers).

24 Of 69 predictions, at least 67 were *wrong!* (The two we could not readily check were given the benefit of the doubt and considered correct.)

25   Among the numerous predictions that did not materialize were these:

— that Elvis Presley would wed a middle-aged nurse.
— that a gunman would try to kidnap President Carter's daughter Amy.
— that spacemen from other planets would land in Africa.
— that terrorists would throw Europe into turmoil by hijacking a shipment of plutonium.
— that Jackie Onassis would marry a powerful Middle East figure.
— that a Concorde supersonic jetliner would crash while landing in New York.
— that Princess Caroline would wed a famous television sports commentator.
— that the Middle East nations would dramatically reduce oil prices.
— that earthquakes would devastate Mexico, Chile, and Guatemala in July or August.

• • • • •

26   Of literally hundreds of other unmaterialized predictions in USB files, we quote just one batch, from a major news service item appearing in newspapers on December 23, 1967.

27   "Hundreds... members of a cult...believe an atomic war will kill two-thirds of the earth's population by midnight tomorrow [Christmas Eve].

28   "Earth won't be destroyed, but millions of flying saucers will land and transport earthlings who are left to outer space where their spiritual level will be raised...

29   "[The head of the cult] says his information comes from Orthon, whom he describes as leader of the galaxy that contains Earth...[and also as the 'Supreme Cosmic Being'].

30   "Many of the followers of 'the space God' have given up their jobs and left their families to be ready to leave for another planet when the time comes."

1006 A Word of Warning

1   In some years, many predictions were preceded by the statement that the psychic had successfully forecast the assassination of a prominent public figure.

2   We would emphasize that those who predict assassination may bear a great responsibility if it occurs. It could be just the spur needed to trigger the killing [1001:18]; and we would not care to be in the shoes of anyone providing that spur.

10.1 Prediction □ 1007

1007 Of Many So-Called "Saviors"

1. Now that we are in a new age—for every age is a new age [201]—we can expect so-called saviors to appear in greater numbers than ever, each proclaiming himself or herself the person destined to lead humanity out of chaos and into harmony [1413]. Many of these "saviors" feel, as their predecessors throughout the ages have felt before them, that the time has at long last come for the fulfillment of prophecies made in literature considered sacred.

2. One thing to bear in mind is this: Many of the prophecies, at the time they were announced, were made for the express purpose of keeping the multitudes under control. And when we hear, as we do every little while, of an "avatar" or "savior" making his or her appearance to "fulfil" something that was foretold in the long ago, in reality it is usually only *in order to keep order*—as that particular "avatar" or "savior" *believes* is order.

3. Most of these so-called saviors have been (or are) well and thoroughly versed in ancient prophecies; and with the desire to place themselves upon a pedestal, they have gone forth (or go forth) to preach their gospel, gathering about them many, especially those who will not think for themselves. But:

4. — They have *not* taught (and do *not* teach) that each of us is our own savior.

5. — They have *not* taught (and do *not* teach) that we are our *own* prophets, and that *we* reap the harvest of our *own* prophecy. That is THE LAW.

6. — They have *not* taught (and do *not* teach) that there is no need for any prophecy to be fulfilled in order for people to save themselves.

7. How many times, in our very own lifetime, have we known of one leader after another who has come forward, preached his or her gospel, announced that something was shortly to happen, usually along the lines of ancient prophecies, and declared in effect: "*I* have come! *I* am the answer to the prophecies of old! I say this! I say that! Come with *me* to a high place! Come with *me* to a low place! Come with *me* to the seaside! Come with *me* to the mountain top! *I* shall protect you! I am divinely inspired! I am divinely sent!"

8. And just as many times have such leaders failed their followers. (With of course the usual explanation: the calamities *they* had predicted were averted because of *their* prayers.)

1007 □   Chapter 10 *The Divining Arts*

9   How many lives have been adversely affected throughout history because of false prophets and false saviors attempting to fulfil prophecies made, or prophecies misinterpreted, or prophecies *mis*prophesied in the first place as far as the reckoning of time is concerned?

10   So-called "avatars" and "saviors" thrive in troubled times. And each era, to those in that era, *is* a troubled time. What we should remember is that each age is what people have made it. In other words, *each* era is the natural result of *people's* attitude and actions in eras *preceding*.

11   For The Law of Cause and Effect applies not only to individuals, but also to peoples, nations, and humanity as a whole.

12   Of course, having free will, people in each era can initiate the cause of *new* effects. And people can rise above their environment. Thus each of us can contribute, for good or ill, and in greater or lesser degree, to both our *own* age and the ages that follow.

13   We should remember one other thing too. If "God" willed destruction for us, not all the powers and prayers of humanity could avert it; and those who think they could save their earthly body, would find it makes little difference where they go.

10.2 ASTROLOGY

1008 Some Reflections about Astrology

1   We have often been asked for our views on astrology, particularly with respect to the value of *horoscopes*; the degree of influence, if any, exerted upon the lives of individuals by the relative positions of the sun and planets at the time of their births; and the varying influence of those heavenly bodies, as their positions change, on people's day-to-day lives.

2   Such interest is understandable; for astrology, a subject about which thousands of articles and volumes have been written over the centuries, is now enjoying extraordinary popularity. Of course we cannot touch on it more than briefly in a few pages. But we can provide, in simple terms, a few facts for sisters and brothers to reflect on, to aid them in reaching their own conclusions.

3   From ancient times, there have been those who believed that the immense sky is the source of all life, with all energy emanating from heavenly bodies, whose relative positions at any time determine the direction, amount, and nature of their energies at that time, to varyingly influence

10.2 Astrology □ *1008*

people born under different "signs." The study that assumes and professes to interpret the influence of those heavenly bodies is *astrology*.

4 For several thousand years—until 1781—astrology was never based on more than seven bodies: the sun, the moon, Mercury, Venus, Mars, Jupiter, and Saturn. Uranus was discovered in 1781, Neptune in 1846, and Pluto in 1930. After each discovery, astrologers of the day devised an interpretation of the influence of the newly-discovered body, and those interpretations have come to be accepted by astrologers generally. [Since this was published in 1971 more bodies orbiting our sun have been discovered, including one larger than Pluto (1301:n4), and Pluto has been "demoted" from being a major planet.[4]]

5 Let us consider a few points.

6 1. The USB emphasizes that we affect all we meet, and are affected by all we meet, in one way or another, in one degree or another, and for one period of time or another. The effect may be so trifling as to be imperceptible, or it may be pronounced. It may cause barely a ripple in our emotions, or it may affect us strongly, even violently. It may last only a fraction of a second, or it may last more than a lifetime and accompany us into the next realm of our existence [1410:3].

7 Thousands of *things* of course also affect us in varying degrees. The pygmy in the jungle starts out in vastly different surroundings, conditions, and circumstances than the individual in a major metropolitan city. In too many countries, the color of the skin unfortunately still affects one's freedom or opportunities. Lack of religion, or religion itself, orthodox or unorthodox, almost always affects one's early life, especially in a child's formative years, with its influence sometimes lasting an entire lifetime or longer. Whether one's family is rich or poor in the things of the world, or in the things of the spirit, also affects the individual. So does parental love and wisdom, or lack of them. We could cite many other influences.

8 Climate strongly affects many people. Some thrive only in abundant warmth and sunshine, others in cooler climes. Some are extremely susceptible to atmospheric changes and variations in altitude. The quality of the air we breathe, and the amount of oxygen in the air, affects all of us.

---

[4] In August 2006 the International Astronomical Union voted to reclassify Pluto from major planet status to the new designation of *dwarf planet*, along with a few other similar bodies (1301:n4) and many more prospective ones. After June 2008 certain dwarf planets are also known as *plutoids*.

2. We know that the sun plays a vital role for us who live in physical [earthly] bodies, for its rays provide the earth with heat and light, which are responsible for many of the phenomena of nature in our world.

(The sun is the only real star in our solar system, but astrology regards the planets as stars also.)

We know that the moon, too, affects the earth. It reflects light from the sun. It affects the tides. It affects some humans and some animals. From all evidence, there is more romance and more arson during the full moon than at any other time. But are these effects at all significant compared with the effects of such influences as race, color, creed, nationality, wealth, poverty, dwelling place, and other circumstances?

3. At its farthest position from the earth, the moon is not even 253,000 miles [407,000 kilometers] away. The other known planets in our solar system are either millions or thousands of millions of miles [kilometers] away. *Venus,* the nearest planet to us except for our satellite the moon, is never closer than some 26,000,000 miles [41,800,000 kilometers; at least 100 times farther than the moon]. *Pluto,* [until 2006[4]] generally considered the outermost planet of our solar system and the second farthest planet from us, is never closer than some 2,600,000,000 miles [4,180,000,000 kilometers; 100 times farther than Venus]! If we also consider that Venus is smaller than the earth, and that Pluto is less than one-hundredth the size [volume] of the earth, would it not be stretching the imagination to believe that they could in *any* notable degree affect our lives?[5]

One could as well believe that the earth and its people significantly affect other planets. (We know that some people assert that we can and do affect the sun; but as we have pointed out, human minds cannot affect the orbit of the earth itself, let alone change the sun's appearance one jot, or alter its orbit one iota [816:2–5]).

4. According to early 1971 estimates, there were 3,690,000,000 people in the world [see 821; we will double before 2020]. That means that on the average there were then some ten million people with the very same birthday for each of the 365 or 366 *dates* of the year—January 1st through December 31st. Who could assume that the lives of any ten million people with the same birthday would follow a markedly similar pattern,

---

[5] Besides our own Moon, other planets in our solar system have moons. Six such moons, orbiting Jupiter, Saturn, and Uranus, are nearer to us and larger than Pluto. Four of them are larger than the Earth's Moon and two of them are larger than Mercury. One may wonder why such bodies do not feature in astrologers' calculations.

10.2 Astrology

even without the variety of conditions and circumstances that we know *do* affect individuals?

15   To narrow it further: Of any ten million people having the same birthday [in 1971], there were on the average more than 7,000 people born during each particular *minute* of that particular 24-hour date. Is it reasonable to assume that their lives will closely parallel one another's despite differences in race, religion, gender, color, dwelling place, and educational and other opportunities?

16   5. Who has not known of twins, born within a few minutes of each other, and living all their lives near each other, whose work, interests, and manner of living had little in common? (We exclude identical twins, some of whom for various reasons, not astrological, live singularly similar existences.)

17   6. While there are many things that can affect the life of an individual, there is nothing that *necessarily* rules and regulates it. History abounds with instances of people who have triumphed over every imaginable condition and circumstance such as poverty, prejudice, illness, blindness, deformity, adversity, and one misfortune after another.

18   Are not such conditions and circumstances immensely more powerful than any "influence" of planets millions or thousands of millions of miles [kilometers] away could possibly be?

19   7. As for *horoscopes,* interest in them is so phenomenal that there are literally thousands of daily papers all over the world that contain a column of predictions and advice for the day for people born under various "signs." There has been commercially-sponsored *dial-a-horoscope,* with each sign of the zodiac having its own telephone number, and with callers receiving "their lucky words, colors, and numbers for the day."

20   Many newspaper columns often include advice that would usually benefit anyone on any day. Many others are amusing, if regarded purely as entertainment. But can anyone believe that heavenly bodies will indicate the afternoon of a specific day as the best time for a new hairdo, or the most appropriate day or days for replenishing a wardrobe?

21   The answer, regrettably, is "Yes;" for polls reveal that there are millions of people who lean upon daily or monthly horoscopes to such an extent that they will take no step unless their horoscope is "favorable." In effect, they abdicate their own judgement and initiative. Is this not an abandonment of "personal responsibility, from which no one, anywhere, at any time, under any circumstances, is, if normally capable of reasoning, exempt"? [404].

22 Would not a life lived according to horoscopes lack richness and experience? Would it not be likely to deprive an individual in a physical body of those opportunities and experiences that are available only on earth, or of the chance to learn any needed lesson that can be learned here and here only, and that sooner or later must be learned? [1424].

23 8. Astrology can sometimes be especially harmful when used as a vehicle for prophecy. To prophesy, for instance, that so-and-so would be in danger of assassination at such and such a time, is to add strength to the thought, which can then travel farther, for more people in or out of the physical to pick up and mull over—and sometimes act on [1006]. Thoughts are indeed powerful, whether constructive or destructive, let us not forget.

24 [Is it not likely that spirit people will try to impress horoscope interpreters, just as they do diviners using other methods? (1011:8, 1012:8–9, 1013:6,8)]

25 9. The precise roles that most heavenly bodies play in the scheme of things is something we do not profess to know—other than they provide further evidence of The Magnificent Power that enables the universe to *be* and to move in an orderly, mathematical fashion. No wonder some wise ones of olden times referred to that Power as The Great Mathematician.

26 We might well ask some other questions.

27 — If a Caesarean operation were performed earlier than necessary, or if labor pains were induced prematurely, so that a child would be born under a different "sign" than would normally be the case—could one reasonably assume that its entire life pattern would be altered?

28 — Is not *gender* of far greater significance to individuals than any planet millions or billions of miles [kilometers] away could ever be? With rare exceptions, have not women always had far fewer opportunities than men, and in almost every field of endeavor, even when born at the very same time and place?

29 Even among some supposedly civilized peoples today, are not women still regarded merely as chattels, and punished far more severely and brutally than men for the very same offenses?

30 With comparatively few exceptions, people have always tried to avoid some of their responsibilities, little realizing that no responsibility can be

10.2 Astrology

forever evaded. Too many depend on horoscopes, and believe their stars are to be blamed if things go wrong. Or that spacemen from other planets will come and carry them off to an easier life elsewhere. Or that a savior will assume their burdens and absolve them from sins of omission or commission.

31 But no one can journey far along the path of spiritual progress until he or she consciously or unconsciously realizes and accepts and lives by certain truths: that we ourselves are *responsible* for what we say, think, and do; that we are the product of all that we have been; and that *we are our own saviors*.

32 For ourselves, we subscribe to the words of Shakespeare's Cassius[6]:

33 "The fault, dear Brutus, is not in our stars,
But in ourselves....."

1009 Of Twins and the Stars

1 A study (by a chronicler of human genetics) of more than 1,200 twins confirms a teaching of the USB: that the time of birth and the relative positions of the planets of our solar system at that moment, do *not* govern the character, lot, or interests of an individual.

2 One twin may be generous, the other stingy. One may possess musical genius, the other no ear for music at all. One may show love and compassion for follow human beings; the other, animosity and pitilessness.

3 Identical twins of the same sex, developed from a single fertilized egg, are exactly the same in countless details *physically*, with normally no variation in *hereditary* tendencies, because their genes, the units of heredity, are identical in every respect.[7]

---

[6] William Shakespeare, 1564–1616, English playwright, poet, and dramatist; in *Julius Caesar*, c1599, Act I, Scene ii.

[7] More recent findings suggest that about half of all identical twins experience one or more of the following: being "mirror" identical twins, having had placenta problems (TTTS), or having a preterm delivery. A fraction of these cases may experience lasting disabilities or other results (many not mental) which could affect their behavior and cause identical twins to differ. But examples are often reported of healthy young identical twins living together with quite different initial inclinations. (Early-stage research into epigenomes, which appear to control a higher or lower activity of the genes, is finding that these "chemical switches" cause differences that develop with age, particularly if the twins live apart.)

1009

4   But as the study we refer to confirms, the mental traits of identical twins may be very dissimilar, as dissimilar as those of singleton siblings, a fact that perplexes parents of identical twins that are outwardly so remarkably alike. It is of course no puzzle to those who know that we are the product of all that we have been, and that our physical bodies are *not* us but only the vehicles we inhabit for a while.

5   We can liken the physical bodies of most identical twins to two violins identical in every detail, played by different violinists: The music evoked will rarely be exactly the same.

10.3 PALMISTRY, PHRENOLOGY, PSYCHOMETRY, AND HYPNOSIS

1010 A Little about Palmistry

1   Palmistry is another popular subject about which a great many volumes have been written.

2   Strictly speaking, palmistry (or chiromancy) is the "art" or practice of telling fortunes and interpreting character by the lines, markings, and configurations of the palm of the hand.

3   Its twin "art" is chirognomy, which professes to interpret the significance of the shape of the hand and fingers.

4   However, like some famous palmists of the past, virtually all so-called palmists of today practice both "arts," and for this reason many professionals in the field prefer the phrases *hand analysis* or *hand reading* to the word *palmistry*.

5   There are several things to bear in mind about palmistry.

6   It is only one of the *many* tools that some who are mediumistic, whether they know it or not, consciously or unconsciously use in tuning in with their spirit associates, of whom they may or may not be aware. There are palmists who know well the truths of Survival [of physical death] and Communication [with spirit people], but do not acknowledge them for one reason or another. And some of them, especially those with the ability to see into the future, and who by The Law of Attraction are linked with spirit people possessing the same talent, have at times been extraordinarily accurate in their predictions.

10.3 Palmistry, Phrenology, Psychometry, and Hypnosis

7   There are tea-leaf readers, coffee-grounds readers and card readers who are also sometimes successful in predicting the future. But it would be difficult for the thinking person to accept that the tea-leaves or coffee grounds or arrangement of cards could, *in themselves*, indicate anything about a sitter's prospects. It would certainly be infinitely easier for spirit people to influence a reader mentally, than, in a few seconds, to arrange tea-leaves, coffee grounds, or cards into specific patterns that might suggest what lies ahead.

8   Similarly, a prediction by a palmist that comes to pass is *not* because of any lines or markings in a palm, but by the palmist's conscious or unconscious reservoir of skill in prophecy, a particular form of mediumship, augmented by the skill of spirit associates.

9   The length of the "line of life," for example, may have the same meaning to most palmists. But there are people with a short line of life who reach a ripe old age, and others with a long line of life who are cut off in the flower of their youth. Certainly the millions of young men who were killed in various wars in the 20th century alone did not all have a short line of life.

10   — The palmist who is mediumistic will receive, and if talented in that direction will correctly interpret, the vibrations of a sitter, for the palmist is at least partly in the sitter's aura when studying his or her hand.

11   — The lines, markings and configurations in the palm mean no more than those anywhere else on the body. And not all palmists interpret them in exactly the same way.

12   — Neither palmistry nor astrology is the science its adherents claim for it. Besides this, the two have little in common, although the names of planets are used for various "mounts" and "rings" and "plains" in the palm of the hand.

13   — A danger with palmistry, as with other kinds of fortune telling, is that the expression of negative ideas may affect sitters to the point of causing them to act as they would not otherwise act.

14   Three of many teachings that the USB repeatedly emphasizes should be borne in mind, are:

1. We are the product of all that we have been.
2. While we may inherit *physical* characteristics and susceptibilities, we do not inherit mental traits, because our mentality is part of *the real self*, the product of all that we have been.

3. *Not* all that occurs to us is the result of our *own* acts and actions.

15 *These* are some of the governing factors in our lives, not the lines, markings, and configurations in the palm of our hands or anywhere else.

16 In substance, there is little in palmistry, although many practitioners in this field are honorable people who honestly believe what they interpret.

1011 A Little about Phrenology

1 Phrenology is the theory or analytical method based on the idea that an individual's character and mental faculties are indicated by the shape and protuberances of his or her skull.

2 We do not subscribe to this idea, for several reasons.

3 An inspirer reminds us that the shape of the skull is not infrequently altered during its passage through the birth canal. Even if the formation of the head is perfect in the womb, the bone structure may not be sufficiently firm to be unaffected by any constriction in the canal or by implements that may be used to aid delivery. But any changes in the configuration of the skull would rarely affect an individual's character, certainly not immediately, however much they might limit the expression of it, or the expression of his or her faculties and abilities.

4 In any case, as we point out elsewhere, inclinations and propensities are neither altered nor eliminated just because the *means* to express them may be absent [618:3–4].

5 All that we inherit—usually from our parents or grandparents—are *physical* strengths and weaknesses, and *physical* structure and appearance, including the structure and appearance of the skull if it is unaltered in the birth canal.

6 We do *not* inherit character or faculties from anyone. Of course our character may be tested, and our faculties and abilities encouraged or discouraged, by our environment, particularly that of our home and family.

7 No so-called "accident of birth," or accident during birth, can in the long run much affect *the real self*, that animates our physical body while we live in it.

8 Some phrenologists do reach correct conclusions of the character and mental faculties of others. However, this is due not to any sensitivity in their fingertips as they touch the skull, or to their measurements of a skull's configuration, but to impressions they receive, as a rule quite

10.3 Palmistry, Phrenology, Psychometry, and Hypnosis□ 1012

unconsciously, from their spirit associates, of whom too often they know little or nothing. Such phrenologists are usually psychic, whether or not they realize it.

9   Of course in most cases the impressions come in the first place from the spirit guides of those being "phrenologized."

10 We have said that there is little in palmistry although many practitioners in this field are honorable people who honestly believe what they interpret [1010].

11 We can say the same about phrenology and phrenologists.

1012 A Little about Psychometry

1   Psychometry is defined in some dictionaries as the supposed faculty of divining knowledge about an object, or about a person or persons connected with it, by contact with or nearness to the object.

2   *We* define psychometry as the process by which a medium, viewing or holding or touching an object, is able to obtain and relate information about it, or about some of those who are or have been associated with it.

3   Vibrations of a person who handles an article often, or who has been close to it for any length of time, will cling to that article for a while at least, and in some cases for scores of years or longer. Much depends on the duration and degree of the contact.

4   A ring or jewel that a person habitually wears, for instance, will contain not only more vibrations but more powerful vibrations of its possessor than a trinket that is rarely worn.

5   What puzzles many is how an object, for example, that has been long submerged in the ocean, may still be "read" by a psychometrist, especially in view of the fact that water is a great cleanser of vibrations.

6   But there is a simple and correct explanation for the overwhelming majority of such cases: A sitter's spirit guides who have acquired knowledge of the object, or who are accompanied by beings familiar with it, *impress* the psychometrist—either directly, or indirectly through the *psychometrist's* spirit guides.

7   There *are* times when psychometrists instinctively feel something, correctly, about an article. There are also times when they sense and accurately interpret an article's vibrations.

8   But in most cases, spirit people are the providers of such information.

9 Here, as in too many other matters, not enough credit is given to spirit people who help so many of us in so many ways.

10 To those who feel how incredible any psychic phenomenon is, we quote an Illumined Soul's words: "*All* nature is incredible."

1013 "Regression" Under Hypnosis—Some Things to Remember

1 Because of the increasing interest and the many conceptions about "regression" under hypnosis, we touch on several factors that may operate in "regression," so that readers may not be misled by well-meaning but uninformed practitioners or writers.

2 *Hypnosis* is of course an artificially-induced state resembling sleep, characterized by heightened susceptibility to suggestion.

3 *Regression* is the act of going back to a previous place or state.

4 But as we shall see, what is regarded as "regression" under hypnosis may not be the "regression" of the person (subject) hypnotized, or the regression of anyone at all!

5 Hypnosis, wisely and skillfully applied, has its place. Among other things, it sometimes induces easier or even painless childbirth. It often frees individuals from phobias of one sort or another, such as the fear of travelling in planes, the fear of complete darkness, the fear of heights, and the fear of enclosed or narrow spaces. And it frequently aids in changing undesirable habit patterns.

6 As far as "regression" under hypnosis is concerned, however, the results and conclusions are often questionable. The following points should be noted well.

7 — If a subject, while under hypnosis, is given the suggestion or command to obey *only* the voice of the operator (as the hypnotist is commonly called), that is what the subject will *usually* do *if* the operator is powerful enough. But the operator *also* may be, consciously or unconsciously, under the control of others—a possibility that should not be overlooked.

8 — A subject under hypnosis is as a rule exceedingly susceptible to suggestions and commands from other minds, on either side of life. So the subject will generally obey such suggestions and commands, and will usually freely *relay* opinions or narrations of others —*seemingly as his or her very own.*[8]

10.3 Palmistry, Phrenology, Psychometry, and Hypnosis

9   The other mind or minds could be that of the operator, or the operator's spirit associates, or, if the operator is not powerful enough to prevent it, spirit friends of the individual under hypnosis, or momentarily intruding spirits, desirable or undesirable, seizing the opportunity to present *their* accounts, real or imagined.

10   In other words, many a person under hypnosis is in a sense an open line which almost anyone can use. In effect, he or she becomes, *temporarily*, a trance medium—but as a rule *without* the skilled spirit associates that surround and that normally can *protect* the usual trance medium from the intrusion of undesirables.

11   — While many narrations related under "regression" are true accounts, they are not necessarily the accounts of the person "regressed." A narration may be accurate in every detail, including the language of the time and place "regressed" to, and dates and events and descriptions that investigation will verify, and still be the narration *not* of the person under hypnosis but of someone else.

12   We know that there are many people who have been in spirit life for centuries who for various reasons do not realize they are no longer in their physical bodies; and they, as well as some who *do* know they have passed on, continue to dwell mentally on the conditions of their earthly life at the time of their passing. They would have little difficulty in presenting an accurate picture of their times, except perhaps for a few minor inaccuracies such as anyone might unwittingly relate in recalling events even just a few weeks old.

13   — It is sometimes disastrous for "regressed" individuals to learn of particularly bad or violent roles they played or come to *believe* they played.

14   If they did not actually play those roles [but did not know this], they could become afflicted with an unbearable sense of guilt—for wrongs they had *not* committed.

15   And if they *did* actually play those roles, it could still be a violation of the spiritual Law against acquainting anyone with more than he or she can *comfortably* understand; and those who break that Law incur a debt they must eventually pay.

---

[8] The USB's American medium, who was exceptional and widely-experienced (Intro:18), told me that the best mediums usually cannot tell *who* is relating the information being given by a subject under hypnosis. –Ed.

16 — We have pointed out the harm that too many practitioners in various branches of medicine, notably psychotherapy and psychiatry, cause by their unawareness of certain truths [909:2]. We can say the same about hypnotists. A little knowledge is often far worse than no knowledge at all.

17 — The USB stresses that there are at least as many levels of spirit individuals as there are of people on earth; and those levels include the ignorant, the malevolent, and the merely mischievous. It is not difficult to imagine the "field day" some of them could enjoy through many persons under hypnosis.

18 — If any account during "regression" purports to show a change in gender, as many accounts do, it is proof that the account is not that of the individual "regressed," but of someone else—usually someone with whom the individual had been very closely linked. For whether or not one believes in pre-existence (existence before present life on earth), an individual's gender [of *the real self*] does *not* change [1321:13–15].

19 Contrary opinion on this score may spring from unawareness that the various bodies that make up the spirit [etheric, counterpart, subtle, beta] body are in every respect replicas of the physical body in its perfect state, except for their more rapid rates of vibration [1310:4,17]; that most dreams that are remembered at all are distorted in the recollection [923:3]; and that unusual masculinity or femininity is most often the result of overabundance or insufficiency of certain genes, the units of heredity.

20 Would that other aspects of the reality and actual roles played in incidents narrated during "regression" were as easy to determine.

21 We stress two things in summing up.

22 One is that what is said by those "regressed" under hypnosis is not necessarily said by *them* or about *themselves*, and that information then given, regardless of who presents it, is not necessarily correct.

23 The other is the warning the USB continually sounds: *Weigh well the words of anyone*—on either side of life.

The Spiritual

11
Phenomena

CHAPTER CONTENTS

11.1 Types of Unorthodox Healing		**317**
1101	The Healing Arts	317
1102	Four Phases of Unorthodox Healing	317
1103	Trees and Healing	318
1104	On Acupuncture and Other Healing Methods	319
11.2 Methods of Unorthodox Healing		**320**
1105	Some Points to Remember about Healing	320
1106	A Little about the Mechanics of Healing	320
1107	The Mechanics of Absent or Distant Healing	322
1108	Some Other Points Relating to Healing	323
1109	On the Meaning of "Magnetized"	324
1110	Suggestions for a Healing Circle	325
1111	Healing, and Prayers for Healing—Some Things to Remember	327
1112	Temperatures Felt During Healing	329
1113	Why Some Are Healed and Others Are Not	329
1114	Virus Infections—and Healing	330
1115	Reflections on "The Great Unseen Healing Force"	331
11.3 About Healers		**331**
1116	Healing and Spirituality	331
1117	On Choosing Healers	332
1118	On Seeking Help from Several Healers	333
1119	The Greatest Gift	333
1120	Reflections on: "Physician, Heal Thyself"	334

continued...

11.4 Materialization and Plasms — 335

- 1121 Protoplasm, Ectoplasm, and Some Other Plasms — 335
- 1122 A Little More about Ectoplasm — 336
- 1123 Some of the Mechanics of Materialization — 338
- 1124 Explanation of a Phenomenon: NOT Mind Over Matter — 339
- 1125 On Certain "Marvels" — 341

11.5 Other Phenomena — 342

- 1126 The Senses of Déjà Vu and Déjà Dit — 342
- 1127 A Little about Stigmata — 343
- 1128 A Little about Dowsing — 344
- 1129 A Little about Apports and Apporting — 345
- 1130 Spirit Scientists and Psychic Phenomena — 346
- 1131 Phenomena and Law — 347
- 1132 A Little about Genius — 347
- 1133 A Little about Exorcism and Obsessions — 349
- 1134 Some Reflections on Glossolalia, or Speaking in Tongues — 352
- 1135 A Simple Explanation of Some Achievements by Animals — 353
- 1136 Reenactment of Battle Scenes — 354
- 1137 Some Misunderstood Psychic Phenomena — 354

11.6 Psychic Experiences — 356

- 1138 A Little about the Psychic Centers — 356
- 1139 On the Chanting of Certain Sounds and Mantras — 357
- 1140 A Little about Meditation — 357
- 1141 On the Use of Drugs to Stimulate Psychic Experiences — 361
- 1142 A Word of Caution — 364

11.1 TYPES OF UNORTHODOX HEALING

1101 The Healing Arts

1   Other than the traditional healing arts practiced in the medical and allied professions, many members of which are truly dedicated to humanity and seek only to serve others, there are four main manifestations of unorthodox healing arts [also called *spiritual healing* (but see 1102) and *alternative healing*].

2   It has become the practice in some quarters to deride the work and efforts of those practicing unorthodox healing. We don't.

3   When more and more earthly physicians know and avail themselves of the experience and knowledge of advanced spirit collaborators a great deal of what is now standard practice in the medical and allied professions will be gradually superseded by other techniques. But the time is not yet, as far as much of their work is concerned.

4   Many unorthodox healers, including those who do splendid work in their field, have little idea of either the various *types* of healing or the actual *mechanics* of healing. Nor are all aware of the host of skilled spirit specialists without whom innumerable "miraculous" healings would not be possible. [Clearly many such healers are mediums, 1116:1.]

1102 Four Phases of Unorthodox Healing

1   There is much confusion about different kinds of unorthodox healing, certainly at least in the terms used. "Spirit healing" and "spiritual healing" are often used interchangeably, for example, although they are not the same thing.

2   A USB inspirer has clarified and described the four main forms: *magnetic healing*, *mental healing*, *spirit healing*, and *spiritual healing*.

Magnetic Healing

3   Some people have a superabundance of magnetic curative essence, manufactured within their physical [earthly] bodies. When they enter the auric emanation of someone who needs relief from a physical condition, there exudes from their being—usually from their fingertips or from any of the orifices of their body—a magnetic curative essence that gravitates to the part of the patient's body that needs rehabilitation, when mentally directed there.

4 Such healing is *magnetic healing*—which may or may not be permanent, depending on whether enough of the healing essence is absorbed, and on whether the patient is mentally receptive.

Mental Healing

5 Mental healing is the conscious directing of the flow of vital healing force [essence, energy] either to one's own body or to those at a distance.

6 In the latter case, it is often called *absent healing*. We much prefer the term *distant healing*.

Spirit Healing

7 Spirit healing takes place when a spirit guide enters the auric emanations of a medium and uses the physical vehicle of the medium to heal another person.

8 Many of our spirit friends continue to work along the lines they practiced on earth. Thus a spirit who was an osteopathic physician on earth, might manipulate the medium's hands.

9 If the spirit friend was a diagnostician, he or she might diagnose, using what we could call X-ray clairvoyance to see what was wrong. If trained to heal, the spirit friend might then also be able to correct the condition.

10 A healing channel [medium] sometimes is the instrument for many spirit healing workers, each skilled in a different field, and each contributing to the over-all work of the team [or band].

Spiritual Healing

11 Spiritual healing takes place when one or more spirit people heal the patient directly.

12 In other words, in spiritual healing there is no earthly channel or intermediary used.

1103 Trees and Healing

1 "Is it indeed possible to draw strength from trees? And do they actually respond to gratitude and affection?"

2 The answer to both questions, which we are often asked, is "Yes."

3 People can get strength and energy from trees, just as they can from walking, especially if barefoot, along the seashore [or on wet grass]. For in trees, as at the seashore, there is water. And the oxygen in water contains a subtle and as yet unmeasured substance that is vital to life, an

11.1 Types of Unorthodox Healing

essence described by such terms as *vital life force, life force, vital energy, bioenergy, chi,* and *prana*.

4   If a tree's roots are deep in the earth, the energy—flowing from the soil through the roots to the trunk of the tree, and from there to the branches and leaves—will often carry not only water, but other essences conducive to healing. So unless an individual is allergic to the bark or leaves or pollen of any particular tree, touching it could be very beneficial.

5   As for trees responding to expressions of affection and gratitude, this is also true with respect to other growing things in Nature—plants and animals both.

6   Several things should be considered in deciding how long we should put our hands on a tree at any one time: the area we happen to be in; the climatic conditions; and our degree of receptivity. Too long a contact with a tree, like an overdose of medicine, could be injurious; so the contact should be brief, at least to start with. Later on it can be gradually extended as long as no harmful effects are noted.

1104 On Acupuncture and Other Healing Methods

1   The USB's repeated emphasis that we can learn from history applies to every human endeavor, not excluding the healing arts.

2   In Western countries, interest in acupuncture began to surge some years ago as a result of impressive testimony of people in high places who had witnessed its application and effects.

3   Acupuncture is one of many ways of relieving or releasing excessive pressure in certain parts of the body [B09:30–33]. Acupuncture of course also serves as an anesthetic to produce general or local insensibility to pain or other unwelcome sensation. With acupuncture as an anesthetic, patients remain in full possession of their faculties and converse freely during an operation, can often get down unaided from the operating table within a few minutes after surgery, and suffer little or no unpleasant aftereffects of any sort. In fact, unless the stomach or throat or mouth is being operated on, patients can usually even *eat* during surgery.

4   Acupuncture has been successfully employed in China for well over 4,000 years, but it is only in comparatively recent times that the western world has begun to pay it the attention it deserves.

5   Some other Chinese remedies that have proved their worth for thousands of years are herbs, massage, and moxibustion—treatment by means

of flammable substances placed on the skin at acupuncture points and burned to produce stimulation by heat.

6 There is indeed much in medicine, as in other fields, that we can learn from a study of other countries and other eras; for in every age there have been great souls on earth with one purpose—to share knowledge and wisdom possessed by themselves or their spirit mentors.

7 Of course acupuncturists, like those in other professions, vary widely in ability; and other things being equal, the results from acupuncture will vary with the degree of skill of the acupuncturist.

11.2 Methods of Unorthodox Healing

1105 Some Points to Remember about Healing

1 It is love that inspires Illumined Souls to share their light with us. It is love that inspires one to serve others. And it is love that can remarkably speed the healing process.

2 In mental and spirit healing [1102] it is particularly important to send out love to the patient.

3 It is also important to visualize the patient as whole, perfect in every cell. The Law of Life provides intelligence to each and every cell of every being; and if the patient is receptive and imposes no barrier, the cells in his or her body will usually respond intelligently to the healing flow directed to them.

4 Color also plays, or can play, a great part in healing, for different conditions respond best to different colors [930:6,13]. Visualizing the most appropriate ray of color to direct to the patient is therefore of great value.

1106 A Little about the Mechanics of Healing

1 Healing is not as simple as it seems.

2 Most of the uninformed—among them many healing channels themselves—think that all "healers" have to do is to place their hands on [or near] a person [the so-called "laying on of hands"[1]], to bring about a cure; or to raise their arms with the palms of their hands facing an audience, for a supply of healing essence to originate from their being and flow to those in need. But it just does not happen that way.

11.2 Methods of Unorthodox Healing

3   Even in private healing, where patients are treated one by one, alone —and where, by the way, the vast majority of *lasting* cures are accomplished—there are at least several members in a healer's spirit team including diagnosticians, physicians, scientists, and chemical engineers, and they play an important and vital role in the alleviation or cure of ills. Among their other duties:

4   — They help to raise the rate of vibration, so that healing may be more easily accomplished.

5   — They extract from the atmosphere, and from articles in the environment, or bring in from the outside, chemicals that the patient lacks.

6   — They regulate the flow of healing essence or essences, so that the patient receives no more than he or she can comfortably absorb.

7   — They try to induce the patient to relax, or relax further, so as to be more receptive to the healing flow.

8   (Water, as we have mentioned before, is a great cleanser of vibrations [913:5]; that is why some who heal by the "laying on of hands" take pains to rinse their hands before and after treating any patient.)

9   In healing demonstrations before large crowds, the number of behind-the-scenes spirit workers is at least double the number of people present in the physical. The spirit host will include those who understand the needs of their individual "charges," and who often will arrange an exchange of healing essences—the surplus of any essence of which individuals have more than enough, for a supply of essence of which they have less than enough. The exchange of healing essences is arranged between the spirit teams of the patients themselves, and not by the healer or the healer's spirit team.

10   At large gatherings, and sometimes even at small ones, less-than-highly-evolved spirit guides of less-than-highly-evolved individuals may try to "raid" certain chemicals from even those who have no overabundance of them, instead of trying to arrange a satisfactory exchange of essences. If a person at such gatherings suddenly feels drained of energy, it may be because his or her own spirit friends have been unsuccessful in preventing a raid [1244].

---

[1] A form of "laying on of hands" known as *Therapeutic Touch* (TT) has been accepted by modern medicine. First demonstrated by its ability to raise hemoglobin levels, it has been taught to thousands of healthcare professionals and nurses and used in many hospitals. This has been followed by a similar energy therapy called *Healing Touch* (HT).

11   Some healers who demonstrate before immense crowds do truly excellent work, humbly, spiritually, and without fanfare.

12   Others, however, and notably some with a flair for theatrics and with a dramatic or melodramatic evangelical fervor, real or assumed, make a "production number" of their demonstration, which as a rule is exceedingly well planned in every respect and to the very smallest detail—all designed, in many cases successfully, to stir mass hysteria and mass enthusiasm on the part of the audience, some of whom may in consequence feel better, for the moment anyway.

13   Those healers usually claim, or at least give the impression, that they themselves direct or project the flow of healing, which is not true, regardless of where or from whom they claim the healing comes. They usually insist that "faith" is necessary, which is not true, either. And they often assert that if a person is not healed it is because he or she lacks faith, which is also not true. (Too often, by the way, that "faith" is measured by the amount contributed to the cause. Which is all rather sad.)

14   We dial a number on the telephone and reach someone, who may be next door or a thousand miles [kilometers] away. Little do most people realize the intricate process that makes such wonderful communication possible.

15   We can say the same about healing.

1107 *The Mechanics of Absent or Distant Healing*

1   There are many methods of distant healing, which, by the way, is not accomplished as some believe, purely by thought. However, thought is the *means* of setting distant healing in motion: It is the first step, and an invaluable one, in the healing process. For on earth, thoughts are not things, but the magnificent power behind things—the power that brings things into expression. [206:2].

2   Subtle and invisible substances vital for healing, such as cosmic rays, chemicals, and essences, are all abundantly available *in the atmosphere* —which, by the way, contains not only much that is constructive, but much that is destructive.

3   The *mechanics* of distant healing begin when a healer directs a healing thought or a healing prayer (which is intense and concentrated thought) to or for a patient, at the same time preferably *visualizing* the patient in glowing health. Skilled spirit chemists and chemical engineers, as a rule members of the healer's team, then extract from the atmosphere and transport or relay what the healer's spirit medical specialists believe the

11.2 Methods of Unorthodox Healing

patient needs. And if the patient has no conscious or unconscious mental block or negation to bar its passage through his or her aura, it will be delivered, and the intelligence in each affected cell will absorb or try to absorb it.

4   Alternatively, the healer's spirit healing team may mentally advise the patient's spirit friends to extract certain substances from the atmosphere for their charge. If they cannot do so, or cannot extract enough of what is needed, some of the healer's team will join them either to do the job themselves or to help in doing it.

5   In some cases, the healer travels in his or her spirit [etheric] body to the patient, and takes part in the healing.

6   Another method, not uncommon, is for skilled members of a healer's spirit team to impregnate a handkerchief or scarf or some other articles with healing essences before it is sent to a patient to hold or keep in bodily contact for a time [1109:3].

7   Still another method is for the healer's spirit healing team to perform a *spirit* "laying on of hands," so that the patient may directly absorb needed curative substances that the spirit team has extracted from the atmosphere, or from growing things or colorful articles in the patient's surroundings.

8   It is plain that while there are various methods of distant healing, in most cases it is the subtle invisible substances in the atmosphere that are the curative agency.

9   And as those substances are usually absorbed into the body by inhalation, those needing relief from physical ills should breathe as slowly and deeply as is comfortable for them during prearranged periods when healing is directed their way.

10   The subtle invisible substances we speak of play an important role in other forms of healing also. It is always the case in *spiritual healing*, very often the case in *spirit healing*, and sometimes the case in *magnetic healing* if the healer's spirit team considers those substances necessary and knows how to extract them from the atmosphere.

1108 Some Other Points Relating To Healing

1   When we ask spirit healers to heal or visit someone for the first time, we should mention not only the name but the full address of the person needing aid. In most cases it would help them to reach the person much

more quickly, for there are innumerable instances of hundreds and sometimes even thousands of individuals having the very same name.

2   If we know or suspect the condition that needs relief or cure, we should mention it to the spirit healers. It might facilitate their investigation and diagnosis.

3   There is no need, however, to suggest treatment for the condition. They will know what to do, and will solicit the aid of specialists if necessary.

4   There is *no* set number of spirit healers in a healing team; there could be one, or fifty, or more, depending on many things. In any case, it is better to have one skilled physician or chemist than a score of far less competent ones. What is paramount is skill, the ability that comes from such things as knowledge, practice, and aptitude.

5   Whether one should say a healing prayer each day for patients, or ask for continuous help for them for a certain period, depends on the routine established between healers and their spirit co-workers.

6   We know that many individuals and organizations make it a point to state, at each healing session, the names of all on their current healing list, and to pray for their recovery.

7   Others find it enough to just once express the need for healing for any person. However, it may comfort friends and relatives of those who are ill to hear the names mentioned at a healing session, and if they then visualize their dear ones in radiant health, it may help—always provided, of course, that the ill do not consciously or unconsciously create a wall around themselves that the healing flow cannot penetrate.

1109 On The Meaning of "Magnetized"

1   "When it is said that something or someone is magnetized," people have often asked us, "just what exactly is meant?"

2   When this word is used in connection with psychic phenomena, its meaning has little in common with definitions in standard dictionaries.

3   When a *thing* is "magnetized," it is impregnated with an essence or essences that make it more conducive to phenomena. A handkerchief, for instance, if magnetized by a healer—by, let us say, holding it for a while—will be impregnated with healing essences that may heal or aid in healing someone else who later holds or carries the handkerchief. The

11.2 Methods of Unorthodox Healing

magnetization of things may last for an indefinite time, from a few moments to many months or longer.

4   When *individuals* are magnetized, and as a result sensitized, many changes, sometimes profound ones, take place in their physical bodies. It may be in their actual physical appearance; or in their countenance, which may for example be made brighter or gloomier than usual; or in their circulation; or in several other ways; or in a combination of ways, including the activation or stimulation of their psychic centers [1138].

5   In most cases, individuals who are magnetized feel a sense of well-being and receive an inflow of thought from one or more minds, whether or not they are aware of that inflow; and if their psychic centers have become sufficiently receptive, they may then be *conscious* of psychic phenomena.

6   We can expect any "quickening" of an individual's bodily or mental processes to bring greater attunement with those out of the physical, who of course project to us from bodies of a more rapid rate of vibration. But that greater attunement, and the demonstrations that may result from it, are not necessarily of a spiritual nature or helpful to uplift in any way, a fact we would emphasize.

7   For while it is *spirit* individuals who determine the type and nature and level of such demonstrations, it is *we* who almost always determine the quality of our spirit visitors. For by The Law of Attraction, "the greater our spirituality, the nobler our character and ideals and aspiration and efforts, the higher is the caliber of those spirit friends who come to us as guides and teachers"—or in other capacities, such as spirit chemists and scientists who may "magnetize" us.

8   It is important to realize that *we* in effect select the level of our "magnetizers." Those who frequent and enjoy low places where unevolved beings on both sides of life are likely to congregate, and those who delight in things that are far from spiritual, can hardly hope to be magnetized by forces of an elevated nature.

1110 Suggestions for a Healing Circle

1   With many people desiring to take part in a distant healing (or absent healing) circle, we offer a few suggestions on the subject.

2   We emphasize that these suggestions describe only one method (a method many have successfully followed), and that a circle should consider any changes its own spirit friends advise.

3   There are many healing circles that accomplish much good although their methods differ.

4   1. For the best results, *harmony* in the group is essential, something we cannot over-emphasize. Better a few members *and* harmony, than many members without harmony.

5   2. A little appropriate music before the healing session commences may be helpful [1245]. We ourselves do not recommend music during the session because it may detract from any concentration and visualization necessary.

6   3. Start the actual session with a short and simple prayer, which could well include thanks for the blessing of life, and for the presence of especially-selected skilled spirit helpers who share the desire of the circle to cure or alleviate the ills of others.

7   Pray that those in need will be receptive to the healing flow and absorb it, and that *their* spirit friends will understand and help to regulate the reception and absorption of that flow.

8   There is no need to dwell on God's virtues—as some feel they should do.

9   4. Limit the healing session to fifteen or twenty minutes to begin with —including preparations for being comfortable and relaxed; the opening prayer; the recital of the name, address if known, and need of each person for whom healing is sought; a period of quiet; and a closing prayer. When the healing circle is well established, the period may be gradually lengthened, particularly if spirit friends suggest it.

10   (The suggested limitation is of course for the circle as a unit. There is nothing to prevent individual members, during their own quiet periods, from directing healing to anyone.)

11   5. An alternative is to recite, one by one, the name, address, and need of individuals requiring help, with all members of the circle concentrating on the person named for say twenty to thirty seconds. It is difficult to hold a thought for more than a few moments; in any case the *intensity* of a thought is more important than its duration, other things being equal.

12   6. Visualize the patient completely well. If it is the patient's arm, for instance, that needs relief, *visualize* that arm in perfect health, moving freely without discomfort.

13   7. Another alternative is to merely recite a list of the names, addresses, and needs of those afflicted, and leave it to spirit people present to do the rest. This is common practice when the list is a long one.

11.2 Methods of Unorthodox Healing

8. It may help patients to know just when the healing circles sits; and if they will at that time relax and breathe slowly and deeply, it will facilitate the healing process. Advise them to visualize an inflow of healing essence, being delivered to the tips of their toes and then all the way up to the top of their head, and to pause for a few breaths at any spot particularly in need.

9. Conclude the session by thanking those spirit friends who are in attendance, and rejoice as if the healing has been accomplished. The vibrations of rejoicing are powerful, and can be put to good use.

10. Subdued light during the healing session is conducive to a relaxed atmosphere, concentration and visualization, and freedom from distractions.

11. Have a glass of fresh water beside each healing member. As the water will be "magnetized" by spirit friends, it will usually refresh anyone who drinks some of it if fatigued or "depleted" during the session. Drink the rest at the end of the session.

12. Small portions of seven vital elements [1246:4] would be useful in the healing room, for spirit friends to use for members of the circle who lack a sufficient supply.

13. Request patients on the healing list to send a brief progress report at regular intervals, say every three or four weeks—or more often if they wish. If they do not report, or stop reporting, you may assume they no longer need help.

(If a patient *attends* the healing session, the "laying on of hands" [1106:2] may provide greater help. It is advisable not to touch certain parts of the anatomy; in such cases, hands should be placed on the patient's head [D12].)

1111 Healing, and Prayers for Healing—Some Things to Remember

For a clear picture of the relationship between prayer [522:3] and healing, several things must be understood.

The first is that when we pray to the God of our understanding, we should not assume, as almost everyone assumes, that we are praying to the very *same* God of everyone else's understanding. That is just not so.

The higher our spiritual consciousness—that is, the higher we have evolved spiritually—the higher our conception of God. There are literally millions of different conceptions of God; and it is to these different conceptions of God that different people pray.

4   Many spirit people can "tune in" to an earnest prayer, which is an intense and concentrated thought expressed silently or aloud. Among them may be some with the skill and ability to accomplish what is prayed for. But usually our own guides and spirit friends pass our prayers along or upward. It is as if our prayers climb a ladder until they reach their destination. If, as often happens, our own spirit associates can relieve or cure a condition, there is of course no need for our prayers to travel farther.

5   Another point to remember is that an affliction or tendency to an affliction that we are *born with* is much more difficult to cure or arrest than that same affliction acquired later.

6   One might say, as many do: "Why pray for healing at all? Having all-wisdom, God *knows* our problems and our needs."

7   It is true that God (or our conception of God) does know our problems and our needs. But God is a God not of caprice, but of Law; God *expresses* through Law, let us never forget. When we ask, when we pray, we set a Law in motion; and a prayer for healing, whether for ourselves or for others, is a request for aid from those skilled in the particular field of healing needed.

8   There are spirit specialists in different fields of healing, just as there are specialists in different branches of medicine on earth. But of course they have other duties and responsibilities also, and instruction to receive if they wish to acquire further knowledge. So apart from those on earth with whom they may be linked by the Law of Attraction, they occasionally attend others, assuming they have the time, usually only when *asked*—either by the sufferer, or by the sufferer's friends on either side of life.

9   Still another point to bear in mind is this: Whether on earth or in spirit life, we assume great responsibility if we venture without invitation into a situation that is not our direct and immediate concern. We are responsible for what we think, say, and do; and what we say and do, unasked, with respect to others, is a still more serious thing. Many on earth have learned the wisdom of refraining from giving counsel on certain matters, or taking part in certain activities, unless invited to do so. So of course have many spirit people.

10   We would stress another point. In itself, the mere petition or prayer neither brings healing to us, nor prepares us to be receptive to it. But by setting a Law in motion, it invites others to help us if they can, and, if

11.2 Methods of Unorthodox Healing

they cannot, to relay the plea to those who *can*, provided the circumstances are favorable.

11   Another thing to remember is that in prayer one usually is quiet; and to be quiet is a step towards being receptive. Of the millions who pray, however, too many pray in desperation; and in that very desperation is a tenseness and a tightness that may prevent them from absorbing much of the healing essence directed to them. Mental attitude is most important in prayer; and when one prays with expectation and a joyous anticipation of the result, one is more receptive to what is available.

1112 Temperatures Felt During Healing

1   We have been asked whether cold hands are a handicap to anyone who heals by the "laying on of hands." The answer is "No."

2   While a patient may feel any physical coldness (or warmth) of the healer's hands, that coldness or warmth will not affect the flow of healing essence directed through the healer, or that comes from the healer. Nor will it affect the coolness or warmth of the healing essence itself.

3   During the "laying on of hands," one patient may feel a warm or even intensely hot flow; another, a cool or even intensely cold flow, even though they are treated by the same healer for the same condition. There are several reasons, or combination of reasons, for this.

4   The body chemistry of one patient may be different from another's. The patients may not be equally sensitive to the temperature of the healing essence. The flow may be directed by different spirit associates of the healer; for there often is not just one spirit healer in a healing team, but several, as we have said, and in some cases many.

1113 Why Some Are Healed and Others Are Not

1   When healings do *not* take place, whether unorthodox or orthodox, it is usually for any of three reasons.

2   One is that it may be *necessary* for some individuals to endure certain afflictions, for reasons which they may or may not fathom at the time, and which we will not go into here.

3   Another is mental block or negation on the part of some patients, creating barriers that healing essences cannot penetrate.

4   The third is that the conditions may have reached the point where they are beyond correction.

1113 ☐

5   "Faith" by patients is not essential, though it is helpful. What *is* important is that they be "open"; they will then be more receptive to the healing essence that comes their way from those who know how to project it—regardless of whether patients have faith or not.

6   There are innumerable cases of people cured by mental healing who did not even know it was being directed to them. As long as they are open and receptive, consciously or unconsciously, and can thus *receive* what is available to them, the healer (expressing heartfelt love, and visualizing perfection in every cell) may be able to help them.

7   Mental block or negation often prevents marvelous healing from taking place. So it is good, if needed, to instruct patients on proper mental attitude.

8   The medical profession has many additional considerations to take into account, [all of which depend on medical and physiological issues that are unique to medical science on earth].

9   Regardless of whether the healing is orthodox or unorthodox, it is clear that *not* all patients will at *all* times respond in the *same* way to the *same* treatment for the *same* illness.

1114 Virus Infections—and Healing

1   Destructive elements in the atmosphere include viruses, disease-producing agents smaller than bacteria—in fact so small that they are not always visible or distinct even under high-powered microscopes.

2   The earth's atmosphere is full of viruses, which we may absorb merely by breathing. And once such microscopic life finds a suitable lodging place in the human body (or elsewhere), it sets up housekeeping, so to speak, and is almost always a most stubborn and tenacious intruder to oust or destroy.

3   What will sometimes expel the unwelcome guest is something that it finds unbearably distasteful; but because of the thousands of different viruses that exist, it is rarely possible to prescribe the substance that would be effective against any particular condition without first knowing the specific virus that is causing trouble. Without that knowledge, any successful treatment would be a matter of sheer chance.

4   It is for this reason that spirit physicians, like those on earth, find our virus infections so difficult to cure.

1115 Reflections on "the Great Unseen Healing Force"

1 It is customary among certain survivalists [who believe in survival of physical death] to "ask the great unseen healing force" for relief from all ailments and infirmities. But there is no single healing force, seen or unseen, that can cure all ills.

2 There are, however, various healing essences, chemicals, and rays, which singly or combined with others, may be effective in one or more specific conditions; and under the right circumstances, they will either remove the *cause* of a condition, or *arrest* the condition, or alleviate or end the pain and discomfort *resulting* from the condition.

3 Many individuals on earth are channels for spirit specialists expert in their own particular fields in restoring health. Some are especially proficient in alleviating the pain from a slipped disc, or in completely curing the condition; some, in unlocking stiff joints; some, in relieving or ending migraine; some, in dispelling the pains of arthritis; some, in curing cancer, and so on. There may even be a few channels for healing all kinds of ills, for all we know.

4 But while there is *no* panacea, no "great unseen healing force" that can cure *all* ills, the mere asking for help, regardless of *who* or *what* is prayed for, is often the prelude to relief, as we have pointed out [1111:7].

5 There is vastly more involved in healing than merely asking a mythical "great unseen healing force" for aid.

11.3 ABOUT HEALERS

1116 Healing and Spirituality

1 The USB points out that spirituality [608] is not necessarily related to mediumship, any more than it is related to other gifts such as painting or music or writing. Or, we would add, healing, some types of which are forms of mediumship.

2 We also point out that the more spiritual we are the greater the channel we can be for healing, if that is our avenue of service. But while spirituality will impart a nobler quality to healing—as it will to any other endeavor—it is still not essential to it.

3 The evidence is abundantly clear to those who note the contrast between the personal caliber of some healing channels and the cures accomplished through them. Some of the cures have been so incredibly remarkable as to border on the "miraculous," despite channels or controls who are far from admirable in character and far from advanced spiritually.

4 However, we of course bless them for the good they do, and deplore their actions only when they use healing, as some do, to implant fear and misteaching into those whose ills they help to remove or alleviate.

1117 On Choosing Healers

1 We have been asked whether those at a meeting who need healing should be directed to whatever healer is available, or be allowed to wait for the healer they prefer.

2 As we see it, three points are involved. One is the individual's freedom of choice, which should not be interfered with as long as it harms no one. For this reason, we feel that people should be free to wait for the healer of their choice, just as they should be free to go to the doctor or dentist or lawyer of their choice.

3 The second point is that good conditions—and certainly a happy frame of mind on the part of patients is one of them—are important in healing. We know the part the mind may play in illness and in recovery; and if patients fret because they cannot be attended by the healer they desire, it will not speed their recovery, for most certainly they will not be as consciously receptive.

4 The third point is that if healers are understanding and truly selfless, they will not be jealous or put out if patients prefer other healers. On the contrary, they will rejoice if patients can be attended by the healer of their choice. They will rejoice even more if patients are healed, *regardless* of who is the channel for the healing. And they can, if they are not at the moment treating anyone, direct healing thoughts to a patient ministered to by another.

5 When there is a specified time for healing and more than one healer, it is good to announce exactly how long the period will last. Some patients, realizing there may not be time for them to visit the healer they prefer, will then go to another, without the same degree of frustration and disappointment they might otherwise feel.

11.3 About Healers

1118 On Seeking Help from Several Healers

1 There are some who teach that it is unwise to seek help from more than one healer at any time, especially for the very same condition, their theory being that the healing vibrations from or through different healers would counteract or nullify one another's. We do not agree with this teaching.

2 Even if many healers treated the same specific condition of a specific individual, their efforts would not negate one another's. The patient could very well obtain a certain amount of relief from each healer. Then, too, the power from or through one healer might be enough to *start* a flow of healing essence or essences needed, but not enough to *maintain* that flow, in which case healing essence from other sources would be desirable and welcome.

3 In any event, the flow from or through several healers should not harm a patient, who should absorb only what can comfortably be absorbed—for the flow of healing essence is well regulated, either by those in the patient's own spirit team if they are skilled in that respect, or, if they are not, by spirit experts they can call on, or by the patient, consciously or unconsciously.

4 We should be aware that there may be several spirit physicians in a healer's team, each with his or her own specialty of knowledge and skill, just as there usually are among any group of doctors on earth, for there is specialization in medicine in the spirit world as well as on earth. And just as doctors on earth often consult one another, so do spirit doctors, who will seek the help of others if they feel that a patient is not progressing, or not progressing rapidly enough.

1119 The Greatest Gift

1 Healing plays an important part in the USB's work, as do other spiritual and psychic gifts. There is room and use for all, each in its own way.

2 It is unfortunate to find some exponents of healing describe it as the greatest gift, and as the gift that furnishes the greatest proof that we are spirit here and now.

3 Some healing, as we have shown, can be accomplished without spirit help—and by that we mean the help of those not in a physical [earthly] body. For of course we are all "spirits," no matter which expression of existence we are in.

4 In any case, for some to say that healing proves we are at least part spirit "because spirit heals us," is puzzling. It could be said, with equal

logic, that we are at least part penicillin if penicillin cures us—or part anything else that brings relief from discomfort.

5 *The greatest gift one can possess is what helps uplift and spiritualize[2] others, and awakens them to the spiritual realities of life and to the God within them.* [101:10–11].

6 The greatest gift we can possess is what makes others conscious that we each possess a spark of the divine; that we are spirit here and now, and not just in some remote time and place; that *the real self* is indestructible; that death cannot separate those who love; that we can commune with loved ones who have gone on; that the universe is governed by Law; that God is a God of Love and Wisdom, of Law and Justice, and is That Which Is All-Good; and that because all human beings [on *both* sides of life] are God's children, this means we are *all* spiritual sisters and brothers without exception.

7 Whatever reveals *that* to an individual is, as far as *that* individual is concerned, the greatest gift we can possess.

8 Unfortunately, healing seldom falls into that category, except where healers make a point of using it to introduce the truth of Survival [of physical death] and other realities. Otherwise people visit healers as they visit medical doctors—for relief or cure, without it in the least affecting their philosophy or knowledge or way of life.

1120 Reflections on: "Physician, Heal Thyself"

1 As we have pointed out, sayings repeated again and again over a long period of time are generally accepted without question by the unthinking —even though the sayings may contain little truth. They are also endorsed by some who usually weigh all things well before accepting or rejecting them.

2 One of those sayings is the admonition: "Physician, heal thyself."

3 Repeated so often and for so long, in fact for at least twenty centuries, its implication—"If you can heal others, surely you can heal *yourself*"— is assumed by many to be correct. *But it is not.* If it were, very little healing of any sort would be accomplished.

4 In orthodox healing, there are thousands upon thousands of physicians who restore others to perfect health but are not in perfect health themselves. We see that all about us.

---

[2] In discussion, Michael mentioned that spiritual teachings have the *potential* to spiritualize one.

11.4 Materialization and Plasms

5   As for unorthodox healing, we have explained why some are healed and others are not [1113]. In any case, it would be rash and uninformed to assert that no one who is less than completely well in body can be a clear and pure and noble and satisfactory channel for healing essences to flow through to another individual.

6   Two questions arise. Why should a *healer* not be free from discomfort? Why should *any* pure and noble soul suffer pain? The answers may be clear if we reflect upon a few facts.

7   One is that just as patients may need healers that are suitable channels through which they can receive a flow of the specific healing essence or essences required, so may healers themselves need suitable channels through which the specific healing essence or essences *they* require may flow to them.

8   Another is that while mental (which includes spiritual) qualities are not inherited, physical susceptibilities and conditions often are. So no matter how evolved individuals may be, they should not be expected to be free from all hereditary ailments. Those hereditary ailments, by the way, are not necessarily designed to test them, nor are they necessarily theirs because of karma. They may be theirs merely because they are in a specific family unit that they may have joined to provide example and inspiration in one or more of several ways—to show, for instance, that one can graciously and courageously endure ills that cannot be corrected; that one can meet adversity well; that one can rise above one's surroundings, or create new ones; that one can live spiritually even in the humblest circumstances; and, sometimes, that one can be a light in the darkness.

9   Another fact to remember is that more highly evolved souls tend to be less comfortable (than others) in a physical body, which they consciously or unconsciously realize is not their natural dwelling place.

11.4 MATERIALIZATION AND PLASMS

1121 Protoplasm, Ectoplasm, and Some Other Plasms

1   **Protoplasm**—the living matter of all vegetable, animal, and human cells and tissues—is the basic substance of all plasms—the various plasms which, when *combined* with certain chemicals that spirit chemists bring from their side of life, make various types of spirit manifestation possible.

2   Protoplasm is visible under a powerful microscope.

1121 ☐   CHAPTER 11 *Phenomena*

3   ***Ectoplasm*** is a condensed and easily visible form of protoplasm—or *part* of a form of protoplasm, to be more accurate; for it is composed of only the outer layer of the protoplasmic cell, and not of the entire cell.

4   Ectoplasm is almost invariably white or whitish, but that of highly spiritual people may appear in such colors as pink, rose, lavender, or purple.

5   In materialization [1123] in which spirit people are garbed not in the usual white robe, but in either everyday clothing or splendid colorful regalia with bright and shining jewels, the colors necessary for the various hues are extracted from sources at hand—the garments of the medium and sitters, the drapery and carpet and other furnishings, and any flowers present. This is done by spirit chemists [1130:4] especially trained in the work of molding and fashioning ectoplasm [for materialization and for other demonstrations also].

6   ***Teleplasm*** is the plasm used to reproduce audible sound.

7   ***Duoplasm*** is the plasm used when a spirit person [or creature] is seen but not heard.

8   ***Bioplasm*** is the plasm used when a spirit person is both seen and heard.

9   ***Microplasm*** is the plasm used either to transport the spirit [etheric] body of the medium away from the scene, or to block out any interference (conscious or unconscious) from the medium's own mind, so that a full and free flow of communication is possible.

10 (During trance, the medium's spirit body is usually close by, unless it is away on a special journey planned by the "controls" [1232:1])

11 One of the advantages of a circle [of "sitters," 1242], always assuming it is harmonious, is that it is much more likely to provide enough of the various plasms needed for various types of manifestation. That is because not all of us possess the same plasm or plasms, or in the same degree.

12 Some gifted mediums can themselves supply all the plasms needed for different demonstrations, but a good "battery"—someone that can provide additional plasm or plasms—is always welcome.

1122 A Little More about Ectoplasm

1   Ectoplasm plays a vital role in many psychic phenomena.

2   It usually emanates from the physical body in *waves*. At sittings or circles (séances) held in the dark or in subdued light, the semi-fluidic substance, which is then more often visible, may be molded by skilled spirit chemists into rigid rods, often with finger-like endings. With these

336

11.4 Materialization and Plasms □ 1122

rods, which they can easily manipulate, they can *move* objects about, or *suspend* objects, notably the "voice box"—the artificial larynx they construct for spirit communicators to use in speaking instead of the medium's vocal cords [1218].

3   There are scores of thousands of people who have witnessed demonstrations in which ectoplasmic rods play successful roles, including the common one of causing a "trumpet" to gently caress a sitter's face.

4   Light is usually harmful to ectoplasm, and the switching on of bright light will normally cause ectoplasm to instantaneously return with lightning-like force into the physical bodies from which it emanated. There are many cases of severe injuries, and sometimes even death, to mediums, from whom as a rule most or all of the ectoplasm is drawn at circles, when bright light was suddenly switched on.

5   But—and this is a *big* but—there are some spirit chemists who, by adding certain chemicals, can and do fashion, around ectoplasm and ectoplasmic rods and other formations, a protective sheath against light rays. The chemicals may include not only those temporarily withdrawn from individuals in the physical and from furnishings and apparel, but chemicals of a more rapid rate of vibration brought from the *spirit* world.

6   It is due to such protection there are so many well-documented cases of "paranormal" movement of objects, including the levitation of people, in full light, even the light of the noonday sun. There is abundant, unimpeachable testimony that a world-famous medium of his day, Daniel Dunglas Home [pronounced Hume] (1833-1886), was levitated time and again in broad daylight—once to float horizontally out of one window of a [third floor] room and return through another! And it is a matter of record that during Abraham Lincoln's presidency there were many manifestations in the White House of psychic phenomena, including the levitation of a grand piano [in full light; see also 1206:8].

7   Such demonstrations, which still occur more frequently than is generally imagined, and certain others such as "table turning" or "table tipping," are usually (but not always) accomplished by spirit fashioning and use of ectoplasmic rods, sheathed when necessary for protection against light. Much of the work of poltergeists is also accomplished by means of ectoplasmic rods, very often constructed from the ectoplasm of children who have reached the age of puberty, whether or not the children are at the immediate scene at the moment, as we explain elsewhere [1133:31].

8   Ectoplasm is also used in some cases of automatic writing.

1123 Some of the Mechanics of Materialization

1. Materialization is a far from simple thing. In fact it requires more study and effort than any other form of psychic phenomena, which is why it is so rare.

2. Materializing spirits are mainly responsible for molding ectoplasm into a recognizable likeness of themselves, but of course they are vastly aided by the medium's spirit collaborators. These collaborators provide added chemicals and ectoplasm brought from the spirit world for use if needed, which is almost always the case, because it is seldom indeed that the chemicals and ectoplasm furnished by the medium and sitters are enough.

3. Spirit people who rarely materialize must usually be content with having just their hands and faces, and sometimes only their faces, recognizable. In such cases, which make up the overwhelming majority, spirit chemists need to take pains only on that score, and fashion the rest of the ectoplasm into folds resembling the garb of the desert Arab.

4. It is usually the spirit [etheric] body—a replica of the former physical form—upon which ectoplasm is molded to make materializing spirits appear as they did on earth. This is because memory alone is seldom dependable enough in fashioning a likeness that sitters would recognize, especially if many years have gone by.

5. Spirit people who wish to materialize fully and completely must learn all that they need to know for perfect materialization, and they go to spirit schools of higher learning for instruction in that form of phenomena. They themselves usually supply most of the [spirit] chemicals and ectoplasm needed for perfect manifestation [see 1121:1].

6. They are the only ones who can appear to us *exactly* as they did on earth—not only in form and features, but in personality, and in attire, footwear, and colorful regalia and jewels, and with whatever objects (such as musical instruments) they may wish to show.

7. For in the spirit realms, as on earth, nothing is achieved without aspiration and effort.

8. In materialization, as in all other psychic phenomena, the attitude of the sitters plays a most important part in determining what results are obtained. The medium's health is another factor. So are climatic conditions.

9. One caution. There are times when *impersonations* occur during materializations, just as they sometimes do in other demonstrations. It is important for the sitter to be aware of this.

11.4 Materialization and Plasms

10   Although their appearance at about the time they passed on is often the one they remember best, materializing spirits seldom find it difficult to appear as they were at any earlier period.

11   They can see old photos of themselves in the possession of friends and relatives on earth, to refresh themselves on how they looked, or study any copies they themselves own of photos that were taken on earth. For it is not unusual for spirit people to possess photos, especially of those taken with people they continue to cherish.

12   They can consult other spirit people, family members and friends, about their appearance at a certain age.

13   They can tap their storehouse of memory, or those of their spirit friends, to recall how they looked at any particular time.

14   Of course it would be easy to show themselves with any misformation of body that a sitter would recognize, such as a missing arm or leg, or any prominent facial feature or mark; but those are not too common.

1124 Explanation of a Phenomenon: NOT Mind Over Matter

1   Around the early 1970s, much more than the usual nine-day wonder was aroused by a young man who seemingly could bend or break metal objects simply by touching them or passing his hand slightly above them. On television and in the press, and wherever he demonstrated that phenomenon, there was much speculation about an ability that mystified even its possessor, who admitted he knew nothing about the *why* of it, but believed that beings on other planets were channelling their energy through individuals like himself.

2   What is surprising, though, is that many psychic publications seemed to have no idea of the explanation of the phenomenon, although the young man himself unwittingly offered a clue in stating that it occurred only when *other* people were present.

3   The explanation is this: manipulation by spirit people of ectoplasmic rods, which can penetrate *through* glass or other barriers; and the "battery" of power provided by others [and spirit scientists' ability to alter molecular structure of objects, i.e., to "soften" them].

4   Although he was unaware of the fact, the individual we discuss was a *medium*, and he possessed a comparatively unusual form of mediumship; but he obviously needed a "battery" [1121:12] for the type of demonstration for which he became noted.

5   In his case, as in the case of many other individuals who it is mistakenly believed affect objects by the power of concentration, the results are *not* achieved by mind alone.

6   We emphasize this: the combined minds—and minds *alone*—of a billion people would not move a mountain or even a pin or a piece of paper one inch [a centimeter].

7   Literally hundreds of people, notably the very young, have since duplicated the seeming "ability" to easily bend or break metal objects; to set long-silent clocks and watches starting again; and to commit other mystifying phenomena—all *apparently* without the application of material force. It recalls the popularity of table-tipping at the start of the 20th century; except that spirit power was then *recognized* as the vital ingredient of psychic phenomena—*which indeed it still is.*

8   There are many individuals, on both sides of life, who by accident or design are engaged in diverting people *away* from Truth.

9   Some deliberately *confuse* rather than enlighten. They purposely *misinform* rather than inform. They wilfully promote *ignorance* rather than understanding.

10 Others, in no way evil or mischievous, delight in arousing astonishment and wonder, and the speculations that follow.

11 They had perfect opportunities to do so during the miscalled "mind over matter" demonstration on television by the gentleman we refer to. Hundreds of television viewers in their own homes found not only cutlery, nails, keys, and other articles bending or twisting during his performance, but also the functioning of watches and clocks that had not run in years. Some radio transmission devices were temporarily put out of commission.

12 The demonstration led to speculations, ranging from the supposition that it was this man's *power* being evidenced all over the land, to the theory that it meant a revolution in science!

13 The actual cause was the tapping by various spirit individuals of the mediumistic powers some of the television viewers possessed, whether they knew of them or not; and the ability of some spirits to easily and with remarkable speed alter the molecular structure of objects and sometimes even of living things. We mention a few examples of the latter elsewhere [1129].

14 Three things should be noted:

15 Marvelling at "wonders" will not furnish the explanation of them.

11.4 Materialization and Plasms

16 It is doubtful whether those "wonders" serve any useful purpose whatever.

17 Only those who know something of spirit skills and the *mechanics* of spirit demonstrations can understand how such psychic phenomena as we have described take place.

1125 On Certain "Marvels"

1 The ability to walk barefoot on the smoldering remains of a fire without suffering injury of any sort is one of many "marvels" that excite amazement.

2 Whatever the explanations of this phenomenon, and there are several, one thing is especially worth noting: with rare exceptions, those who supervise or direct the proceedings are *mediums*, each with a spirit team that includes chemists highly skilled in providing protectively sheathed ectoplasm around the feet of the firewalkers.

3 Some who take part in the fire-walking rite or ritual—which is what it usually *is*—prepare themselves by developing and entering a state of consciousness that makes them unaffected by heat.

4 Some enter a deep trance state in which a spirit individual takes over.

5 Some are in an ecstatic condition in which they *literally* do not feel pain or discomfort. In that condition they would feel no pain even if their flesh were pierced or partly destroyed by acid.

6 Certain herbs and other plants act as an anesthetic when massaged into the flesh, making it temporarily immune to intense heat, in which case protectively sheathed ectoplasm would not be needed. Such immunity is of course more rapidly achieved by those who always go barefoot and whose soles are therefore exceedingly tough.

7 A noted medium in the U.S. Pacific Northwest had [in 1974] the "gift" not only of handling live coals without sustaining burns, but of seemingly communicating that immunity to others as long as they were in his presence. Here again, protectively-sheathed ectoplasm is the explanation. One of his guides, by the way, was a most famous medium of an earlier time who possessed that very same "gift" when on earth.

8 Some individuals, after years of preparation, can sleep or lie for hours on a bed of nails without injury.

9 Others, in a state of induced catalepsy, can lie between two objects—their head on one, their feet on the other—and remain rigid and impervious to heavy weights or pounding on their body.

10 Others can thrust long hatpins or needles through their cheeks without drawing blood. Here the flow of blood is controlled, either by themselves or by others from one or both sides of life.

11 In almost all cases such as we have mentioned, and whether or not protectively sheathed ectoplasm is involved, the help of skilled spirit chemists is essential.

12 But however spectacular such demonstrations may be to those who do not understand how they take place, and whatever the degree of wonder they evoke, they do not necessarily denote any spirituality among those taking part.

13 For *in themselves* those "marvels" do *not* help uplift or spiritualize people. *In themselves* they do *not* lead to a nobler way of life, or an understanding of The Laws That Govern, or an appreciation of the Love and Wisdom and Justice and Goodness that are God.

11.5 OTHER PHENOMENA

1126 The Senses of Déjà Vu and Déjà Dit

1 Many individuals have experienced the sense of ***déjà vu*** (the French for *already seen*), which psychologists define as the illusion of having previously experienced something actually being encountered for the first time.

2 To those familiar with psychic phenomena, however, a more accurate definition is the feeling or conviction of having previously experienced something that is being encountered—for that feeling or conviction is seldom an illusion.

3 There are several explanations for the sense of déjà vu.

4 It could spring from an *actual* event in which the individual had indeed played a part.

5 It could be the response to the [simultaneous] relaying or relating of a scene or event in which either the individual, or a close companion or companions, had been present. In the latter case, we can liken the individual to a medium in trance, whose speech and actions are then usually *not* the medium's own, but those of someone in temporary control.

11.5 Other Phenomena

6   Many of us have heard someone exclaim: "I *know* I've been here before! I *know* it!" There are countless instances of people describing the interior of a home before entering it presumably for the first time, or describing what lay around the bend of a road they were presumably travelling for the first time. In such cases, the sense of déjà vu may arise from a visit during the sleep state; from a sudden recollection of a visit during another existence; or from unconsciously receiving the impressions of *others* (on either side of life).

7   The sense of ***déjà dit*** (the French for *already said*) is also not uncommon. What may particularly puzzle an individual experiencing that sense, is that the fragment of conversation that seems so familiar sometimes appears trivial—*too* trivial to be so clearly and unmistakably recollected.

8   The explanation may be that it was not trifling at the time it originally took place, especially in the context of the *entire* conversation of which it was a part, or it would not be so vividly recalled. Or the conversation could have taken place during the sleep state, or been read, or heard, and somehow impressed itself on the consciousness.

1127 A Little about Stigmata

1   Many wrong conclusions are reached by people who are unfamiliar with the mechanics and demonstration of psychic phenomena. And few phenomena have aroused such wonderment and misconceptions as certain *stigmata*—those marks resembling the wounds of the crucified body of Jesus, and considered by many to be supernaturally impressed on the bodies of certain individuals, usually, but not always, those in some religious groups.

2   Stigmata may occur as the result of a person's conscious or unconscious *craving* for their appearance. (We have pointed out that, on earth, thoughts are *not* things, but the magnificent power *behind* things—the power that *brings* things into expression [206:2].) Stigmata may be the result of the work of spirit chemists who when living on earth possessed, and now *continue* to possess, extraordinary religious fervor about certain convictions—a fervor they will do *all* they can to excite in others. Stigmata may arise from a combination of both circumstances, in which case it is much easier for them to appear.

3   We point out elsewhere that the subjective mind, which has greater scope than the objective mind but does not reason, obeys the objective

mind; that the subjective mind can be likened to a receiving set; and that once a habit pattern is formed, as in the action of the heart, lungs, and digestive system, the subjective faculties (which are the subjective mind in action) will make every effort to see that the habit pattern continues [1231:4–8].

4   To put it another way, many things that *begin* from, and as the result of, conscious effort or direction, become in time automatic, functioning as and when required or desired.

5   Of the abundant evidence on that point, two examples will suffice. It has become the habit of millions to reach for the light switch the moment they awake in the morning, without first thinking: "I must turn on the light." It has become the habit of tens of millions of drivers to put a foot on the brake pedal when approaching an unmarked intersection, without first thinking: "I'm coming to a crossing; I must slow down."

6   In the same way, once stigmata have appeared, they become more easily manifested with each reappearance. The habit pattern becomes more and more firmly established in the cell structure; and even though the cells themselves are constantly being replaced, the habit pattern established by the subjective faculties continues. Eventually, the stigmata will easily appear and disappear, either at the conscious or unconscious *wish* of the individual on whom the marks occur, or at spirit command to the individual's subjective faculties.

7   Stigmata provide yet another example of things that appear mysterious and unfathomable until the light of knowledge is turned upon them.

1128 A Little about Dowsing

1   Dowsing is the faculty some people possess of finding underground water, minerals, or precious stones by the use of what is called a dowsing or divining rod—frequently a forked (roughly Y-shaped) stick, often of birch.

2   The dowser works by holding the two forks of the stick, one fork in each hand, while walking, the stick sometimes twisting strongly downward when it is above what is sought. The action of the rod is almost always automatic, quite independent of the dowser's will, indicating that some degree of mediumship or psychic sensitivity is required.

3   This is confirmed by the fact that while some people using a dowsing rod by themselves will find it does not respond even if what they seek is

11.5 Other Phenomena

present, it *will* often work for them when a successful dowser places his or her hands on their shoulders or on their hands holding the rod.

4   The dowser's spirit companions play an important part in the work, manipulating the dowsing rod by means of protectively-sheathed ectoplasm.

5   Another point is worth noting. By The Law of Attraction, the spirit helpers of a farmer (for example) will include some who recognize farm needs, of which water is often a major one, and who try to help secure those needs in one way or another.

1129 A Little about Apports and Apporting

1   Derived from the French verb *apporter*, to carry or fetch, the word *apport*, strictly speaking, applies to any material thing that spirit people transport from one place to another.

2   Most people who know something about psychic phenomena, however, think of apports as material objects that spirit people, *during* circles or sittings (séances), bring in from outside. Usually it is at circles held in low light or no light at all; for in most cases bright light prevents demonstration of apports, as it does with some other types of phenomena [1122:4].

3   That apports arouse amazement, fascination, and speculation, is hardly surprising. The phenomenon seems especially remarkable when exotic fresh fruit or flowers, or live birds, are brought into a room during a circle, or when something impossible to bring into the room by normal means, because of its bulk, is discovered to be present when the lights are switched on.

4   Apporting is possible only because there are spirit people who not only understand the molecular structure of material objects, but know how to reduce them in size, disassemble them, and reassemble them.

5   A Blessed Soul tells us that apporting often involves both the disassembling and reassembling of objects—or as some term them, the dematerializatian and rematerialization of them. He says:

6   If an apport has to pass through another solid object as it is carried on its way, its structure and rate of vibration must be changed to the precise condition and degree that will enable it to be easily and instantly passed *through* that object. The apport is then reassembled into its normal state, unless there are other material objects through which it must also pass.

7   In some cases, an apport's structure and rate of vibration may have to be altered *several* times before it can be brought to its destination. As an illustration, let us consider a jewel in a safety deposit box in a compartment in a vault in a bank. The jewel's structure and rate of vibration would have to be changed before it could be removed from the safety deposit box; changed again, to remove it from the compartment; changed yet again, to remove it from the vault, unless the vault were of exactly the same material as the compartment; changed again, to remove it through the bank's windows or door; and at least once or twice more before it is brought into the room where the circle is meeting.

8   The Blessed Soul continues:

9   The process is somewhat different when a living creature such as a bird is apported from the garden, let us say, and is presented, still warm, still fluttering, to sitters. In such cases, an ectoplasmic sheath is placed around the bird's physical [earthly] body, to protect it from shock while its structure and rate of vibration are altered to enable it to be passed safely through the wall or door or window of the meeting room.

10   There are spirit people who can easily pass a bird's spirit [etheric] body through a material barrier; but in some cases they consider it desirable to, for a split second, *separate* the bird's spirit body from its physical body—still linked together, however—while they pass them through.

11   Much depends on the kind of *structure* to be penetrated, the size of the *creature* to be passed through, and the type of *energy* that must be used.

12   What is quite incomprehensible to us is the *speed* with which expert spirit scientists and chemical engineers can apport objects. We are told that apporting involves factors far beyond our ken, far beyond the knowledge of scientists on earth today, and far beyond our present vocabulary to describe.

13   But at least we can understand *what* is done, even if we cannot understand just *how* it is done.

1130 Spirit Scientists and Psychic Phenomena

1   Most people know too little about the tremendous work of spirit friends before and during successful demonstrations of psychic phenomena.

11.5 Other Phenomena

2   Most books on psychic phenomena make little or no mention of the invaluable behind-the-scenes work of various spirit groups, spirit scientists and spirit chemists in particular.

3   **Spirit scientists** are those who engage in any of the fields of scientific research in the spirit world. They also help to make certain spirit demonstrations possible.

4   **Spirit chemists** usually are chemical engineers who confine their activities to preparing a medium's physical body to absorb more of the vital chemicals needed in producing fuller and more complete and satisfactory manifestations of phenomena.

1131 Phenomena and Law

1   All spirit manifestations occur only according to Law—and not contrary to Law, whether or not we understand it.

2   It is unfortunate that many honest and sincere people accept a demonstration as miraculous because they do not understand the *operation* of a specific Law in action. In that lack of understanding, they reach conclusions that eventually bring disappointment and disillusionment—not only to themselves, but to others who accept those conclusions as truth.

3   What is worse, if they declare or publish those conclusions as *truth*, they sow the wind and will reap the whirlwind, whatever their motives. For as we repeatedly stress, we are *responsible* for what we teach; and to teach *any* untruth is to incur a debt that must be paid.

1132 A Little about Genius

1   Genius is of course the exceptional capacity for "creative" and "original" work in such endeavors as music, painting, writing, medicine, the sciences, and teaching in all fields. We place the words *creative* and *original* in quotes because, as the USB emphasizes, one accomplishes nothing of worth by oneself.

2   Most individuals on earth are here to develop one or more facets of their being. A few others, however, are here to improve a facet that is already extraordinarily polished; this explains some cases of genius.

3   In other instances, genius results from the "overshadowing" by a spirit being who is remarkably advanced in one or more fields. In other words,

the earthly genius is an *instrument* for that spirit, whether or not he or she or others recognize the fact.

4 Sometimes geniuses are on earth not to develop or increase their ability in their fields, but to display their talents for the enjoyment and benefit of millions.

5 We know that like attracts like; and the more evolved we are in any field, the more do we attract those spirit people who are evolved to the same degree or greater in that field. An Illumined Soul adds:

6 What is too rarely realized, however, is that the genius also attracts many spirit people who draw close to him or her *not* to serve, but to *be* served—not only those who contribute to the perfection of the genius's expression, but a vast host who plead and even clamor for an opportunity to see or hear, and if possible to understand, that expression.

7 Among them will be some who, upon returning whence they came, will share with others, on both sides of life, the nuggets they have gathered. Those who work with mediums on earth may share their acquired knowledge *with* their channels, and *through* their channels, and even directly impress still others with whom they are spiritually attuned.

8 Throughout the ages, geniuses on earth have made enormous contributions to spirit people *also*—a fact seldom if ever recognized. For every single soul on earth who derives knowledge and pleasure from the art of a genius on earth, there are scores of souls in spirit life who do so too.

9 Another point of interest is this. Many who are aware of the truth of Survival know that people on earth often visit the spirit world during the sleep state, for one or more of several reasons. But what is *not* usually known is that many people on earth, during their sleep state, are privileged to see and hear a genius on earth at work.

10 The surgeon in San Francisco, for instance, asleep at three o'clock in the morning, may witness an operation by a surgical genius in London at that very moment, eleven o'clock in the morning London time. In the same way, a surgeon asleep in London at eleven o'clock at night may observe the skill and artistry of a surgeon at three o'clock in the afternoon, San Francisco time. Similarly, those with neither the funds nor the time to attend a performance by a musical genius in another part of the world, may, during the sleep state, attend that performance.

11.5 Other Phenomena □ 1133

11   If there is a need, conscious or unconscious, or if we express a sincere and intense desire for greater beauty and enlightenment, spirit friends will usually escort us during our sleep state to a place where we can find them, on either side of life—although for various and very good reasons we seldom consciously recall the experience on awaking.

12   One thing is plain. That marvel, the genius, delights and instructs many more souls than he or she has any idea of.

1133 A Little about Exorcism and Obsessions

1   Exorcism became a very popular subject in the 1970s because of two things.

2   The first was a novel (later made into a movie) about a young girl who is "possessed" by an evil spirit, from whom she is finally free when it is provoked into switching into the body of an exorcist, who then plunges through a window to his death—and presumably the death of the obsessor also!

3   The second, not fictional, concerned a man who, subjected to a night-long exorcism in a vestry, apparently was transformed from a loving husband into a maniac who murdered his wife.

4   **Exorcism** is of course the use of ritual commands or religious or solemn ceremonies to expel an unwelcome and undesirable spirit person who is possessing the body of someone in the physical.

5   Because much if not most that is written on the subject is quite inaccurate, we relate a few facts.

6   — *Possession* and *obsession* are terms that are often used interchangeably; but while possession may be good or bad, depending on circumstances, obsession is always bad. We prefer to say **possession** when people, usually mediums, invite or *allow* a spirit person to temporarily occupy their physical bodies and use their vocal cords; and **obsession**, when low or degrading spirit people are in control.

7   — Not all spirit people who assume control of individuals without their permission are bad. Some are merely simple and unevolved, with no desire to harm or annoy anyone; sometimes they do not even *realize* they are occupying a physical body. Competent mediums and rescue circles [1228:6] seldom have much difficulty in persuading such spirits to leave a physical body.

8   Exhortations, commands, and curses, no matter in what tongue they are couched, have *little* effect on truly hardened obsessing evil spirits,[3] except in some cases to amuse or anger them.

9   To oust such obsessors requires the skill of powerful, highly evolved spirit guides, who at times have to use actual force to achieve their purpose. Usually, there is also need for the help of especially selected individuals in the physical, as a rule mediums suitable for the task.

10   — Those who are aware that there is no death or annihilation for any individual, on either side of life, know that no "transfer" or "switching" to another physical body *of any sort* will destroy obsessing spirits, regardless of what is related or implied in fiction or in literature considered sacred.

11   — Some claim, wrongly, that the only way to dispel an obsessing spirit is to first somehow induce it to "transfer" into the body of a medium, and then rely on enlightening conversation to persuade it to withdraw. This may work with an unaware but well-meaning spirit, but an *evil* spirit will not so easily surrender possession of a physical body it comfortably controls.

12   — Others claim, also wrongly, that it is not possible for a person to become unwillingly obsessed. *That is just not so.*

13   "A Little about Sleepwalking" [921] mentioned several causes of unwanted possession, and emphasized that it is much more common than is generally realized.

14   — Electrical shock treatment will sometimes expel an obsessor, for while a possessor or obsessor occupies a physical body he or she is sensitive to any pronounced spasm or convulsion or other violent disturbance experienced by that body. It should be noted that an

---

[3] Some religious traditions have promoted a fear of spirit people. Certainly there are scriptural warnings about taking precautions with spirits, just as we should with certain people here on earth. But there are also many scriptural instances of communication with spirits, including those with spirits that are fully materialized (1123). The only scriptural condemnations of communicating with spirits occur in early writings of the Israelites. Scholars explain that these condemnations were written when the early Israelites were fiercely defending their belief in one God while surrounded by polytheistic cultures that believed in various spirit gods. Their condemnations are hyperbole from less educated times, frequently belonging to superstition and magic; they cannot be understood today literally, but only when cultural contexts are translated from one historical period to another.

11.5 Other Phenomena

obsessor usually responds to the physical body's reaction to the electrical impulses, rather than to the impulses themselves.

15   (A related note of interest: A spirit communicator using the vocal cords of a deep trance medium may be *expelled* from the medium's body if the medium has a spasm of coughing or sneezes violently. This happens quite often.)

16 — Electrical shock treatments, which may be successful for varying periods, should be most carefully and skillfully applied by highly qualified medical personnel, to reduce the possibility of damage to cell structure.

17 — Obsession is a not infrequent cause of what is [incorrectly] considered to be insanity, a fact we wish more physicians and psychiatrists were aware of. Again we say how much humanity would benefit if *more* physicians knew the truths of Survival [of physical death] and Communication [with spirit people], and consulted and worked humbly with skilled colleagues in spirit life.

18 How can one protect oneself against obsession?

19 A few things should be noted.

20 — Those with a deep desire for spirit communication or spirit demonstration of one sort or another are particularly susceptible to obsession if they are gullible enough to *unquestioningly* accept all that is brought *to* them or *through* them by any spirit person. As there are at least as many levels of consciousness among spirit people as there are among people on earth, one would be wise to visit a medium or two of unimpeachable repute and integrity to check on the identity and caliber of spirit communicators who wish to use one as a channel, particularly if they claim to be noted or exalted figures of the past or suggest that one is of great spiritual elevation.

21   To fail to do so is to risk opening the door to anyone and every spirit person who wishes to come through, which is certainly far from wise.

22 — Some potential mediums are especially susceptible to obsession until and unless they acquire a capable team of protectors. At puberty, some children are also extremely susceptible.

23 — It is well to abstain from excessive amounts of alcohol or drugs, and to avoid places where they are the main attraction.

1133 □

24 — Contrary to a popular view, the mere prayer for a circle of white light or other protection is seldom sufficient to secure it. Nor will mere affirmations or mantras, however often repeated, provide it.

25 However, a group that meets in harmony and with pure and selfless motives, will, by The Law of Attraction, draw spirit people of like nature and thought; and *they* will, if needed, enlist the aid of others in establishing a circle of light that uninvited or undesirable entities would find most difficult to penetrate.

26 This also applies to individuals who "sit" alone [for communion with spirit people].

27 In both cases, the latter especially, the right mental attitude is of the utmost importance in helping to prevent obsession.

28 Why are some children at puberty so easily obsessed?

29 Because at puberty the reproductive organs—one of the seven psychic centers that we discuss [1138:3]—generate an abundance of powerful, often explosive, energy, an energy that is sometimes used by unadvanced or bad spirits to obsess a child.

30 Much more frequently, however, it is manipulated by *poltergeists:* unevolved or mischievous spirits who cause confusion or alarm or terror by creating noises and disturbances, tossing objects about, or causing other phenomena that most people do not understand.

31 The particular energy from a child's reproductive organs at puberty may so pervade a home that it can be used by poltergeist even when the child is not present.

1134 Some Reflections on Glossolalia, or Speaking in Tongues

1 In more recent times there has been interest among some people in *glossolalia,* or *speaking in tongues*—the chief characteristic of which is the incomprehensible speech uttered by an individual or group of individuals in certain forms of worship.

2 It is far removed from the *scriptural* speaking in tongues with which it is frequently compared. For in scriptural days, anything spoken through a medium in a language the *medium* did not understand was usually quite intelligible to at least one or more people present [and this is called xenoglossy].

11.5 Other Phenomena

3   These days, however, speaking in tongues is almost invariably a meaningless jumble of syllables uttered during frenzy or "ecstasy" bordering on hysteria, a hysteria that quite often is contagious. What flows nowadays from the mouths of those speaking in tongues is mostly a succession of sounds that could be expected from unprogressed spirits who when on earth belonged to an uneducated and extremely primitive tribe or people—a tribe or people who, possessing little language, used those very same sounds to make their needs and desires known to one another. In hysteria, of course, the door is often wide open to anyone; and primitive practices would attract *primitive* spirits.

4   What purpose is served by speaking in tongues if what is uttered is not understood, or not translated into anything *meaningful?* There are individuals, it is true, who are stimulated emotionally by it; but is that stimulation any different from what some people experience during, say, a mammoth "rock festival"? Does it increase anyone's knowledge or spiritual values?

5   Glossolalia, or speaking in tongues, is also known as *the gift of tongues*. In such circumstances as we have mentioned, it is not, in our opinion, a gift to be desired.

1135 A Simple Explanation of Some Achievements by Animals

1   Time and again we hear reports of animals, inadvertently left behind during a trip, travelling hundreds or even thousands of miles [kilometers]—across deserts, mountains, and rivers—to rejoin their owners, even when the latter have moved to places their pets have never seen.

2   Many theories have been advanced for such achievements, but we have yet to note the most common reason—that the animals were successfully impressed and directed by spirit people aware of the grief caused by the separation: guides of the family that loved their pets, or family members formerly on earth that pets would recognize and obey.[4]

3   Most animals are intelligent, and many are more psychic than most humans.

---

[4] In discussing this topic, Michael mentioned that it is also possible for some spirit friends to apport the lost animals.

1136 Reenactment of Battle Scenes

1. There are people who have witnessed visions depicting the reenactment of battle scenes that took place hundreds of years ago. It is something that puzzles many.

2. Any of several explanations may apply.

3. In some cases, people visiting a former battlefield may tune in to a "picture" projected to them by one or more minds of those on either side of life—those who know the details of the battle from having read about it or having taken part in it.

4. In a few instances, individuals whose study has familiarized them with what took place will conjure up the scene in their own minds. They may then witness the actions of the thought forms [resembling spirit people] they themselves create, and not necessarily an exact reenactment of the actual event. (As we point out elsewhere, thought forms can only say and do what their creators consciously or unconsciously *desire and expect* them to [1319:9–13].)

5. In most cases, however, the explanation is this: Some of those slain in battle are still so possessed by bitterness and the desire for victory that they are not conscious of anything else—even the fact that they no longer are in the physical—and they *continue* to enact and reenact the last earthly experience they recall. Time means nothing to them, and they remain as yet unteachable—still unaware that they have passed on to spirit life, that the battle they were engaged in has long been over, and that other and happier experiences and opportunities await them if they will only release their grip on the past and the feelings that overwhelm them.

6. They were of course met when they passed on—*all* souls are—but not everyone realizes it at the time, for one reason or another.

1137 Some Misunderstood Psychic Phenomena

1. The less one knows about the mechanics of psychic phenomena, the more one marvels at them, and the more is one inclined to ascribe them to God or to someone exceptionally close to God.

2. The truth is that *all* psychic phenomena occur from the use of one or more laws of which most people know little or nothing. So however extraordinary and wonderful the phenomena may be—as indeed many *are*—they are *not* miracles in the generally accepted sense. And most people, who have investigated them with an open mind, accept the fact that psychic phenomena are almost always caused by those who live in the *spirit* side of life.

11.5 Other Phenomena

3   We reflected on this when we heard about a "miracle" that has brought visitors by the hundreds to the scene: blood, reportedly analyzed as actual human blood, flowing from time to time from the eyes of a portrait. The explanation is simple (as most explanations are to those who are aware of them): skilled spirit chemists precipitating from the portrait's eyes minute quantities of blood extracted from those living in the area or visiting it.

4   As we have pointed out, some spirit people who retain the consuming and overwhelming religious fervor they possessed on earth, will do anything they can to excite that same religious fervor in others—even to the extent of perpetrating what they *know* many will regard as "miracles."

5   Two phenomena that impressed many people [see also 1003] are worth mentioning: a bird that sometimes perched seemingly in the air, and a figurine that occasionally "wept."

6   Regarding the first, the bird undoubtedly perched on an ectoplasmic rod, which if protectively sheathed, *would* successfully withstand light [1122:5].

7   The second was plainly a case of skilled spirit chemists extracting water from the atmosphere or some other source and precipitating it from the figurine's eyes. (Such cases are not uncommon.)

8   Two other interesting, well-documented, and, to many, puzzling cases of phenomena—not, however, designed to mislead anyone—received wide attention when chronicled at the time and whenever discussed since.

9   One is of a farmer who everyone said "had a way with bees." When he died, and the cortège arrived at the grave, they found the area swarming with bees—on the floral wreaths, a nearby bush, and over the grave itself; but the bees molested no one.

10 The other is of a huge dog that terrorized a rural neighborhood by frightening sheep and killing poultry, and that disappeared into thin air when chased by farmers. A famous journalist, described as "a ghost chaser," was finally engaged; and the next time "the ghost dog" was observed, the investigator sped to the scene, accompanied by two highly trained police dogs. The journalist himself witnessed no other animal, but the police dogs barked and attacked a seemingly "empty space to begin a snarling, tooth and claw dog fight." When it ended, one police dog stood in apparent triumph; "the other police dog lay dead—killed by a ghost it could not subdue."

1137 ☐

11   The explanations for the two cases are simple. In the first, the farmer had indeed "had a way with bees"; and some insects, like many animals, are psychic; and the bees were present in a silent tribute to the spirit presence of someone they had long known and liked.

12   In the second case, one police dog must have died of fright, for it could not have been physically injured by an unmaterialized creature. The second police dog apparently managed to scare the spirit dog away; it could not have "killed" the spirit dog, as the narrative implies it did.

11.6 PSYCHIC EXPERIENCES

1138 A Little about the Psychic Centers

1   The psychic centers—or "chakras," as some call them—are especially sensitive regions in the physical [earthly] body that serve, among other things, as what might be described as *receiving centers* and *storehouses* of vital life force [913:3]. (In our opinion, *psychic centers* is the more descriptive term.)

2   We usually receive this vital life force when we breathe air into our lungs. From the lungs, the blood stream carries this subtle substance, this vital energy, to the psychic centers, and to every other cell and organ in the body.

3   The seven psychic centers, or regions of particular receptivity, are: the center of the forehead, the top of the head, the back of the head, the base of the spine, the reproductive organs, the solar plexus, and the throat.

4   Proper breathing exercises will stir the psychic centers to greater activity, thus making us [temporarily] more receptive, consciously or unconsciously, to spirit impressions and manifestations, including communication. One simple exercise we can recommend is this:

    1. Inhale steadily and deeply, filling the lower part of the lungs.
    2. Retain the breath.
    3. Exhale slowly and evenly.
    4. Pause.

5   Perform the cycle seven times, inhaling and exhaling through the nostrils, and doing each of the four phases of the cycle to a count of seven.

6   Then, breathing deeply and slowly, try to center your consciousness on the psychic centers—one center at a time, of course.

11.6 Psychic Experiences

1139 On the Chanting of Certain Sounds and Mantras

1   Of all the sounds known to humanity, the most powerful is the sound *aum*, often misspelled *om*, and almost always mispronounced. Rarely is *aum* correctly pronounced—as *one* syllable, with the *au* having the sound of the *ow* in *how, now, town*.

2   To chant *aum* or any other powerful sound a few times, either aloud or silently, is useful in some circumstances, such as at the beginning of a circle, a healing session, or a period of meditation; for chanting certain sounds may serve at least two purposes. It may increase the rate of vibration around us, thus making it easier for spirit guides of more rapid rates of vibration to draw closer to us or to interact with us in one way or another, if they wish. It may stimulate our psychic centers, so that we become in some degree conscious, or more conscious, of normally unseen, unfelt, and unheard activity about us; and if what we are then aware of is elevating or exalting, it may raise our level of consciousness for a while.

3   But the mere chanting of certain sounds will not permanently increase our rate of vibration one iota, or make us one jot more spiritual. Neither will any mantras—words or formulas recited or sung—no matter how often repeated, or whatever the hypnotic effect on an audience or the chanters themselves.

4   Only by consciously or unconsciously living in greater measure according to The Laws That Govern (or THE LAW), can we raise ourselves one rung higher on the ladder of spiritual progression [1425:1].

5   Melodious tonal quality is important if the chanting of certain sounds is to have any beneficial effect. We can say about chanting sounds what we say about singing at circles [1242:16]: "...but songs are often sung so badly, or sung so slowly, that they *lower* the vibrations instead of raising them."

1140 A Little about Meditation

1   For various reasons, a great deal has been and is being spoken and written and taught about meditation. It has become a subject with an abundance of instructors in various schools of thought—as so often happens when there is a surge of interest in any field, in this case the search by millions of people, notably the young, for *something* that will help them cope with the multitude of problems, conditions, and turmoil of the times.

2 Certainly existence in this day and age, although in some ways much easier for the average individual that in many other periods, is far less simple now, resulting in some problems that rarely occurred in the past.

3 *Meditation*—and we use the term not only in its major dictionary meaning of reflection, contemplation, or extended thought—*is difficult to define;* for it is a personal, intimate process varying not only with the sundry schools that teach it, but with the individuals who practice it. But whatever form it takes, successful meditation relaxes, exhilarates, or refreshes the individual.

4 Meditation is too vast and many-sided a subject to cover more than briefly in a page or two, but we can summarize a few facts.

5 Meditation may be a reaching *outward;* or a reaching *inward;* or a receptivity that draws us closer to an attunement with what many call the still, small voice; or a state of demanding nothing, seeking nothing for oneself, and desiring nothing but to be used in some way for some good by some power greater than oneself.

6 But except for those teachers who accept and declare and are grateful for the truths of Survival and Communication [with spirit people], *no* mention is made of another and most important reason for meditation: greater rapport with, and occasional manifestation by, loved ones and others in spirit life with whom we are linked [1231:9].

7 There are individuals who can achieve a state of meditation simply by taking a few deep breaths, or by one or two breathing exercises. Some schools of thought consider *concentration* a prerequisite; others, a *blankness* of mind. But concentration makes it difficult to relax; and it is almost impossible, if not indeed *entirely* impossible, *not* to think of anything consciously or unconsciously.

8 Some schools stress the soothing strains of soft, inspirational compositions: music to meditate by, so to speak [1245].

9 An Illumined Soul points out:

10 No *one* path to meditation, and no one *form* of meditation, are suitable for all people, and so all individuals must determine for themselves what path and form are best for *them.* And the path and form that are best for them at *one* time, may *not* be the best for them at another.

11 Some students receive their "own" mantra—usually a sound or sounds quite unintelligible to them—to repeat over and over again, silently or aloud, as an aid to meditation; a mantra to *consciously* reaffirm if they find their minds have been wandering, as naturally quite often happens.

11.6 Psychic Experiences

The mantra, which individuals are as a rule instructed not to divulge to anyone else, is given to them by their "teacher"; but almost any abracadabra of the individual's own choosing would be just as effective, and would cost them nothing. (In 1976 some teachers charged up to $125 for a "personal" mantra!)

12 Some schools ask students to take a topic or word or phrase and meditate on it, in the sense of contemplating or reflecting on it. Others take a petal or a jewel or some other things, not necessarily to concentrate on it, but to divert their mind from other things or other thoughts; and in the process, some *do* reach a state of relaxation.

13 The Illumined Soul goes on to say:

14 We do not criticize the practice of meditation. In fact we favor it for most people, just as we favor anything else that tends to make an individual aware, or more aware, of the many blessings and opportunities that life on earth provides.

15 Meditation can be a beautiful experience for many, if it is practiced in *moderation*—just as attunement and spirit communication can be with the same provision.

16 If meditation or attunement or spirit communion is practiced under the influence of alcohol or mind-altering drugs, however, the results can be, and often are, tragic.

17 We explain elsewhere that when our objective faculties are placed in abeyance, as in sleep, it is vastly easier for desirable rays and vibrations to penetrate our physical body and help to bring harmony to cells that need it [1231]. When we "enter the silence," our objective faculties are also less active than usual, so that we may become more receptive to desirable influences.

18 Of course we may then become also more open to influence from other minds, of beings on both sides of life, but not more so than in any other approach to the unknown.

19 Some other points are worth noting.

20 — Despite claims to the contrary, successful meditation does *not* depend on asceticism, abstinence, continence, or renunciation of the normal pleasures of life. As we have more than once emphasized, the physical body has its needs, and those needs should be met if it is to be a temple as worthy as possible of the spark of the divine that inhabits it while we live in the physical.

21 — Changes within the physical body take place during meditation: as a rule, there is less oxygen inhaled, less carbon dioxide exhaled, a slower heartbeat, and a slower rate of breathing, among other things. (The same changes occur during normal rest and relaxation.)

22   Certain breathing exercises, however, may produce the opposite effects. One is over-aeration, which sometimes causes light-headedness and a more rapid heartbeat.

23   The bodily changes during meditation are of course brief; and when meditation is over, bodily functions return to normal after a time.

24 — With practice, a state of at least temporary tranquillity may be achieved by meditation. But contrary to extravagant claims, meditation does not lead anyone to "God" or "the source of thought" or "the unlimited reservoir of energy and creative intelligence." Even if it were humanly possible to achieve such heights, they would *not* be so easily attained.

25 — As for reaching "cosmic consciousness," which some assert is open to those who meditate, we have pointed out that cosmic consciousness or the cosmic pool or the cosmic sea or whatever other similar terms are used, is composed of *all* thought: thoughts from everyone, everywhere, on both sides of life, good thoughts and bad thoughts, positive thoughts and negative thoughts, constructive thoughts and destructive thoughts. So "cosmic consciousness" is not necessarily desirable: Much depends upon *what* thoughts and *whose* thoughts are received or reached.

26 — Some teachers state that the goal of meditation is the ability to perceive "the essential nature of any object; the basic, underlying state of existence"—whatever that may mean. How one can perceive "the underlying state of existence" of, say, a table, or a filing cabinet, or a rose, or a squirrel, or an automobile, is hard to imagine. But some claim that they reach that state of knowing. They cannot describe just *what* they know; they just *know!*

27 — Like short naps, short periods of meditation, once or twice daily, can be of great benefit. But meditation, unlike short naps, may be harmful to the immature or gullible or ill.

28   Then, too, in some cases meditation or the preparation for meditation causes dizziness, a buzzing in the ears, or other physical discomforts. So it is not for everyone.

11.6 Psychic Experiences

29 — The overcoming of inhibitions, which some consider a valuable product of meditation, is not necessarily a good thing: Much depends on the *nature* of the inhibitions.

30 Some inhibitions are useful, some are vital. Certainly a world without inhibitions would soon become a world of lawlessness and anarchy.

31 — Many so-called meditation techniques come from countries sadly lacking in care or concern for their people, with squalor and disease a way of life for the multitude.

32 — Meditation too often serves to induce passivity in relationships, and resignation to conditions that can and should be corrected. In such cases, meditation is not only of no help to individuals, but an actual hindrance to their development.

33 All in all, however, meditation has much to recommend it, always remembering that it should not be a retreat into an ivory tower, but a girding of the loins in the battle of life.

34 Meditation should never be a *substitute* for living, but an aid towards a nobler, more *spiritual* existence.

1141 On the Use of Drugs to Stimulate Psychic Experiences

1 There are probably very few people today who have not read about what some call "psychedelic drugs"—particularly those that are popular because they are easily and inexpensively made. Many young adults have taken such drugs, some for stimulation, others for the "mystical experiences" that they have been led to believe may follow.

2 They have been encouraged by the advocates of psychedelic drugs, many of whom assert that the drugs furnish an introduction to reality and expand the mind.

3 In almost all instances, however, the drugs provide not an introduction to reality, but *a retreat from reality*.

4 And instead of expanding the mind, the drugs usually just leave the mind completely unprotected against all influences—in many cases the comparatively unevolved minds of others (on either side of life).

5 The drugs provide an open door to many delusions, including delusions of superiority and invincibility that sometimes result in the death or injury of the drug users themselves or those who cross their path. We shall never know how many drug users die by walking blithely and fearlessly into motor traffic under the delusion that nothing can harm them; or drive

recklessly because of the impression that they are immune from hazards; or step off rooftops in the belief that they can fly; or dive through windows in the feeling that they are beyond The Law of Cause and Effect; or kill or injure others under the compulsion to do so.

6   In these cases, we would emphasize, it is not the drugs in themselves, but the delusions they give free rein to, that are responsible.

7   There are many drugs that are used to induce psychic experiences. Among the commoner ones is mescaline, which is derived from a variety of mescal cactuses, of which perhaps the best known is peyote. Some Native North American tribes have for centuries used peyote for ceremonial purposes, chewing the button-like tops for their stimulating effect.

8   There have always been those who feel that a hastening process to the approach of psychic experiences is desirable. So people in various eras discovered and used growths in nature that are conducive to dulling certain sections of the body and exhilarating others.

9   We would not say that such use is good or bad; but in our opinion, any exhilaration or stepping up of certain bodily processes should be a *natural* development.

10   Our bodies usually react unfavorably to artificial stimulation of the psychic centers. So although drugs are used for this purpose in many parts of the world, and among many peoples, we do not recommend the practice.

11   Some advocates of the use of psychedelic drugs assert that these drugs spiritualize a person. We do not agree with this claim.

12   One's *life* spiritualizes, if one lives it *spiritually*. In most cases one is not spiritualized as the result of psychic experiences.

13   Spirituality is not necessarily related to psychic experiences or psychic attributes, any more than it is related to talents such as painting or writing or music.

14   While the partaking of psychedelic drugs often stimulates the psychic centers, the effect is only temporary. And the reaction frequently causes acute discomfort—fortunately not too lasting—from spasms of the stomach, for instance, or from a change in pace of the digestive tract.

15   Many of the psychedelic drugs are apparently not habit forming. Certainly we know of no one who would consider the usual aftereffects pleasant enough to enter into many periods of experimentation with the drugs.

16   Some say that the sensation created by the drugs brings them a closer realization of their association with all else in the universe. The fact is,

11.6 Psychic Experiences

however, that one reacts either according to the stimulation the drug provides, or according to what one has been led to believe one may experience. For under the influence of certain drugs one is particularly susceptible to suggestion, even to suggestions made *before* the drug is taken.

17 That is why many see or hear or feel or sense what reading or teaching has led them to believe they may see or hear or feel or sense. It is often a sort of self-hypnosis, what they experience being presented from the recesses of their own minds. Or it could be presented by other minds, on either side of life [613:3–4].

18 Some say that under the influence of the drugs they see *beyond* the normal sense of vision. If they do, they see a part of the spirit world, whether or not they recognize the fact.

19 Some say that the drugs provide them with a sense of *knowing*. Knowing what? "Knowing" is one of the many imprecise terms, employed by several schools of thought, that are open to widely different interpretations.

20 Some say that the drugs make them aware that they are especially selected ones, privileged to see beyond all that *is*. One cannot see beyond all that is, for beyond that would be—*nothing*.

21 Some say that in taking the drugs they find God. People who make that statement should search their own consciousness for their personal interpretation of God—for *that* is what they will find, nothing more, and nothing less. For what is God, to each of us, but our *personal* view or thought of That Which Creates and Expresses in and Controls the Universe? The opinion differs with each individual: The more spiritually evolved we are, the higher our conception.

22 If one thinks God is *perfect peace*, one may sense perfect peace when one's psychic centers are stimulated by the drugs.

23 If one thinks God is *being*, one may then experience a sense of being.

24 If one thinks God is *knowledge*, one may then experience a sense of knowing. One will not know *what* one knows, or *how* one knows; one just *"knows."*

25 One may feel one is a part of the rhythmic pulsation of the universe, as of course one is, and as of course everyone else is too—as of course is *everything* in what we call our universe. One may become a little more conscious of it then, for the moment.

26 The puzzling thing is that so many expect, by lying down on a pallet and absorbing the stimulating essence of a root, a herb, a growth in nature, to become at one with all there is.

27 For a while, perhaps, they may believe that they feel that. And then comes—reality, often accompanied by great discomfort in body.

28 God is not reached by the waving of a wand, or by the mere partaking of a drug.

29 Says an Illumined Soul:

30 I do not know of *any* road to God but the path of love and service to our fellow travellers. And I have yet to find a simple method of reaching the heights of expression that bring perfect at-one-ment, conscious or unconscious, with all that is.

31 The psychedelic drugs may produce, in some people, a state of exhilaration surpassing all that they had yet experienced. "This is life!" they feel. "This is the ultimate in expression! This is the mountain top!" And then, too often, when the effects of the drug have disappeared, they plunge into the depths of despair. The same Illumined Soul also says:

32 We much prefer the slow and steady climb, and fulfillment, to the rapid ascent precariously held, then loosened and lost.

33 The path to the mountain top is never easy, the USB emphasizes time and again. There are many steps to take, painstakingly, one step at a time, most of the way with a burden on one's back—a burden one has learned to bear gracefully, graciously, gratefully, and courageously.

1142 A Word of Caution

1 There are some people who freely relate their psychic experiences to others.

2 While it may or may not be unwise to mention them to family members who are blind to everything that orthodoxy rejects, it might be *disastrous* to relate them to anyone in the medical field who has little knowledge of Survival [of physical death], Communication [with spirit people], and the reality of psychic phenomena in general.

3 Many individuals now confined to mental asylums (however euphemistically renamed) were committed there because their actual experiences of hearing spirit voices or seeing spirit people were regarded by medical personnel as hallucinations and evidence of severe mental disorder.

4 It is something to bear in mind.

12

Survival and Communication

CHAPTER CONTENTS

12.1 Survival		**367**
1201	On Survivalists	367
1202	A Note on Some Sceptics	367
1203	An Attitude to Avoid	368
1204	On Grief at Losing Loved Ones	368
12.2 Mediums		**369**
1205	Of Psychics and Mediums	369
1206	Mediums and the Mechanics of Mediumship	370
1207	Mediums and Mediumship	371
1208	Some Essentials of Good Mediumship	372
1209	Of Books and Mediums and Authors	373
1210	Errors of Some Communicators and Some Mediums	374
1211	On Exploring Various Mediums	376
1212	"Spirit Says..."—a Misleading Term	376
1213	Mediums and Their Former Guides	377
1214	"Gifts of the Spirit"—and Remuneration	378
1215	Could Devices Replace Mediums?	378
12.3 Mediumship		**380**
1216	Developing the Gift of Mediumship	380
1217	Is Mediumship Inherited?	383
1218	Direct Voice and Independent Direct Voice	384
1219	Diet and Mediumship	384
1220	Use and Misuse of Mediumship	385

continued...

12.4 Spirit Guides and Spirit Friends — 387

- 1221 A Little about Spirit Guides — 387
- 1222 We Are Never Alone — 389
- 1223 On "Commanding" One's Spirit Guides — 390
- 1224 We Owe Our Spirit Friends the Same Courtesy We Owe Others — 391
- 1225 What We Mean by "Illumined Souls" — 392
- 1226 Today, Truly Great Souls Issue No Commands — 393
- 1227 A Little about the Native North Americans — 394
- 1228 How Spirit People See — 395
- 1229 Some Thoughts about "Rays" — 397
- 1230 Weigh Well the Words of Those in Spirit Life — 397

12.5 Communication — 400

- 1231 Our Mind and Our Faculties — 400
- 1232 Some Factors Affecting Spirit Communication — 401
- 1233 Spirit "Standbys" — 404
- 1234 Three Points Relating to Spirit Communication — 407
- 1235 The Message—and the Giver of the Message — 409
- 1236 Variety in Communication — 409
- 1237 Variety in Ways Spirit Guides Impress Us — 411
- 1238 On Some Tardiness or Failure of Spirit Friends to Communicate — 411
- 1239 When the Living Appear as Spirit People — 412
- 1240 A Note about ESP — 413
- 1241 Apparent Precognition of USB Teachings — 413

12.6 Home Circles — 414

- 1242 Home Circles and Mediumship — 414
- 1243 Some Helpful Measures before and during a Circle or Sitting — 417
- 1244 A Protective Measure — 418
- 1245 Music—and Healing, Quiet Periods, and Circles — 418
- 1246 Of Value in Rooms Used for Circles or Quietude — 419
- 1247 Cheerfulness in Sittings and Sickrooms — 420

12.1 SURVIVAL

1201 On Survivalists

1   A great many systems of beliefs include *survivalists:* those who believe or know that we all survive the change called death.[1] [Note that Survival does *not* necessarily imply reincarnation.]

2   Not all survivalists, however, are aware of the reality and normalness of spirit communication.

3   What is lamentable is that, among the millions who accept these truths, many are much more articulate and emphatic in *disagreement* about comparatively unimportant points, than in sharing and publicizing what they all accept.

4   What is sadder still is the number of survivalists who have little conception of, or interest in learning about, the magnificence and perfection of The Laws That Govern and other truths far *more* sublime than those of Survival [of death of the earthly or physical body] and Communication [with those in spirit life].

5   Two others points are worth noting.

6   Except for their awareness of continuing life and the fact of spirit communication, many survivalists are no more universal in their thinking than members of hundreds of other organizations.

7   Some survivalist groups have replaced their early simple and clear principles with less simple and less clear expressions, and have added principles that do not survive the scrutiny of reason.

1202 A Note on Some Sceptics

1   Where Survival and Communication are concerned, there is in this day and age little excuse for the sceptic.

2   For evidence is so abundant, so varied, so *overwhelming*, so confirmed by people in all walks of life in all countries, that the thorough and impartial investigator cannot long be unconvinced.[2] Others, as we point out elsewhere, will support *any* hypothesis, however fantastic and implausible, rather than acknowledge that life *continues*, and that we can, under the *right* conditions, have sweet communion with those who have passed on to the spirit world [B05:5].

---

[1] Some people who believe in an afterlife refer to life on earth (in physical bodies) as life "in the flesh." And some refer to the spirit world and life there as "beyond the veil" or "the other side."

3   The average sceptic of Survival and Communication is like a woman who confines herself in a dark and windowless room and asserts that there is no light; or like a man who denies the existence of the Pacific Ocean because he himself has not sailed on it, or the existence of Antarctica because he himself has not set foot on it.[3]

1203 An Attitude to Avoid

1   Some survivalists look down on those who do not know the truths of Survival and Communication. Let us never fall into that error. Says a Blessed Soul:

2   > We do not look upon those who do not yet possess the vision, as being lost, soulless, condemned, or doomed. No! We look upon them as our sightless sisters and brothers, and we try to lead them to the light.

1204 On Grief at Losing Loved Ones

1   It is the fashion in some circles aware of Survival to criticize those who weep or grieve in any other way when loved ones pass on to spirit life, and to attribute that grief to selfishness. Immoderate and excessive grief is of course unwise. And it distresses spirit friends and relatives to see their loved ones overwhelmed by sadness. But it would be most *unnatural* for anyone not to be saddened by the passing of someone dear, even when it brings release from a long and painful illness.

2   If those we are fond of move to another town, do we not *miss* them? Do we not miss them still more if they move to a distant country? We

---

[2] Types of afterlife evidence that clearly require mediumship include physical phenomena, such as materializations and independent direct voice, and mental phenomena such as clairvoyance, clairaudience, remote viewing, proxy sittings, cross-correspondences, and speaking in unknown languages. Types in which the need for mediumship is less apparent include instrumental trans-communication (ITC), electronic voice phenomena (EVP), poltergeists, and laboratory experiments with psychics. Types of evidence that do not appear to need a medium include apparitions, deathbed visions, near-death experiences (NDEs), out-of-body experiences (OBEs; see 1313:n8), dreams, hypnosis, past-life regressions, and the ouija board.

[3] It has been reported that most of the best known of these sceptics have *no* scientific background, and that practically none of them have had *any* experience in psychic or paranormal phenomena.

can rejoice over new experiences and opportunities that are theirs and *still* miss their presence. For communication by mail or phone is not the same as close companionship and nearness.

3 Still greater is the sense of separation when the departure is to an altogether different expression of existence; and the person who then does not grieve in the slightest cannot, in our opinion, possess much affection, tenderness, or sentiment.

4 As for tears, to think that it is weak and unmanly to weep is to betray ignorance, for indeed is there "a time to weep, and a time to laugh; a time to mourn, and a time to dance." It is only excessive or morbid emotion that is harmful. Certainly tears *do* bring relief to a heart that is full to overflowing—whether that fullness is inspired by tragedy, or loss, or rejoicing, or spiritual ecstasy, or a profound and overwhelming realization of The Goodness That Is God.

12.2 MEDIUMS

1205 Of Psychics and Mediums

1 The difference between psychics and mediums is not always clearly recognized.

2 A *psychic* is a person [on earth] who is sensitive to forces or influences of a seemingly supernatural nature.

3 A *medium* is not only a psychic but, much more *importantly*, a channel used by spirit people to communicate with people on earth and to help in making some other psychic phenomena possible.[4]

4 While *all* mediums are psychic, *not* all psychics are mediums. It is something to bear in mind. And while almost everyone is psychic in one degree or another [1216:2], comparatively *few* individuals have potential mediumship [1210:10].

5 There are other significant differences.

6 — A major one is that while almost all mediums know and acknowledge the truths of Survival and Communication, most psychics either do *not* know them or, if they do, *fail* to acknowledge them for one reason or another.

---

[4] More recently the term *psychic medium* has appeared, presumably to help explain the term *medium* to those unfamiliar with it.

7 — The psychic centers [1138] are far more developed in the average medium than in the average psychic, and mediums are consequently far more sensitive to vibrations of any sort, physical as well as non-physical.

8 — Most mediums can usually tell whether a thought or impression comes from a spirit person or from someone on earth. Most psychics cannot.

9 — Too many psychics, unaware of the fact that we receive thoughts and impressions from others on earth and in spirit life, believe that either God or they themselves are the source of all they proclaim. Certainly their rate of error is proof enough that the former is absolutely *not* the case.

1206 Mediums and the Mechanics of Mediumship

1 Not all mediums are aware of the *mechanics* of mediumship or the *extremely variable nature* of mediumship. It is unfortunate.

2 A notable example is D. D. Home [1122:6], a most versatile and truly superb medium of the 19th century, and an individual of unimpeachable integrity and character. Unfamiliar with the variability of mediumship, however, Home was inclined to attribute to fraud anything that differed from his own.

3 A prominent medium of the 1970s, whose materialization séances[5] took place in the light, was quoted as suggesting that materializations that take place in the dark are the work of charlatans.

4 These two mediums were quite unaware that ectoplasm, which is *vital* to materialization, is vulnerable to bright light *except* when skilled spirit chemists form a protective sheath around it [1122:5].

5 However able they are, not all musicians play the very same *type* of instrument, of course; and not all musicians who *do* play the same type of instrument play with the same skill or effect. The *quality* of their individual instruments also affects their performance.

---

[5] Meetings for the purposes of seeing physical spirit phenomena (supernormal manifestations) and for two-way (conversational) communication with spirit people, requiring the presence of a medium, in former times were usually called *séances*. The word *séance* is derived from the Latin and French for "to sit"; it means a sitting, meeting, or session. More recently the term seems to be becoming less popular and less used; instead *circle* or *sitting* is usually used. As with séances, sittings may be private sittings or group sittings. Circles and group sittings may have other purposes besides the two mentioned for séances, including healing, prayer, developing mediumship, developing healing ability, and spirit "rescue" (1228:6).

12.2 Mediums

6 Similarly, the spirit chemists in one medium's team [or band], however able they are, may not be as expert in a particular form of mediumship as those in another medium's team. And even if they were, the results could vary. For a major factor in psychic phenomena is the *extent* of the chemicalization and development of the medium's psychic centers, which at least partly determine his or her type or types of mediumship and the degree of that mediumship.

7 While mediums should expose the fraudulent in their field, they should not recklessly prefer charges. They should not assume that only what parallels *their* own mediumship is genuine, an error they are apt to commit if unfamiliar with the mechanics and variations of mediumship.

8 Incidentally, neither of the two mediums discussed have matched one phenomenon of James J. Dickson, a noted California medium who returned to spirit life in 1956. Such was his degree of mediumship in his field, and such the ability of the skilled spirit chemists in his team to protectively sheath ectoplasm, that the materialized form of one of his guides would sometimes meet and greet expected visitors in the street in broad daylight, take them by the arm, and usher them into Dickson's home!

1207 Mediums and Mediumship

1 To those who think about it, the existence of mediumship is part of the abundant evidence of the Love and Goodness that are God.

2 For mediumship removes the terror of the tomb, the dread of death, and the fear of the future. It proves that those who leave the physical world are still *alive;* that they are *not* parted from us by an unbridgeable gulf; and that, on the contrary, they are sometimes closer to us than ever before.

3 Water is seldom purer, however, than the channel through which it flows, or the vessel into which it has been poured. The same can be said with respect to communication and mediums [1208].

4 As with almost every other group, mediums vary widely in skill, in character, and in integrity.

5 We say this emphatically—and it is a cardinal teaching of the USB:

6 The medium who is highly developed in his or her mediumship, and who is *also* truly spiritual, is a pearl beyond price.

7 Without pure, selfless, *spiritual* mediums, much that Illumined Souls share with humanity could not be presented, and to those mediums the world owes much.

8   There is, unfortunately, a scarcity of such instruments [mediums]. But with their burning desire to help humanity, and to attempt to divert it from the path of destruction, Illumined Souls do not confine themselves to only those who are *worthy* of their presence, but, wherever it is possible, they share their wisdom with and through other individuals also, directly or (as is usual in such cases) indirectly [using standbys, 1233:3, or relays, 1215:9].

9   Wherever the need is great enough, there beings from the higher spirit realms will appear, to demonstrate in one way or another, even if the channel leaves much to be desired. It is then a far from pleasant experience for them, but one they willingly assume, dedicated as they are to their purpose.

10 We wish that more mediums understood this. We wish that more mediums realized that the greater their spirituality, the better they could serve as channels for elevated spirit souls—always provided of course that their psychic centers are sufficiently sensitive.

1208 Some Essentials of Good Mediumship

1   Good mediumship is essential to prove Survival and Communication. Therefore it is also essential that mediums always strive to maintain [and monitor—in themselves and others—] high standards of mediumship [D25:3–7].

2   To serve on *higher* levels, mediums also need to be humble, open-minded, and universal [D25:8–9].

3   Noble qualities—of which spirituality [608] is by far the most important—are more essential in mediumship than in any other field. For it is the *qualities* of a medium that determine whether communication will be free and unfettered, as it can and should be, or whether only an elementary level of communication is possible.

4   And it is a fact that spirituality is not necessarily related to mediumship, any more than it is related to other gifts such as painting and music and writing. (Excellence in mediumship, like excellence in any other field, does not in itself indicate excellence of *character*.)

5   If a medium is *truly* spiritual, the doors may then be flung wide for revelations of truth and beauty almost beyond our imagination—even more sublime than the truth and beauty of Survival.

12.2 Mediums

6 We must never forget that the limitations of communication are set not by spirit inspirers, but by the instruments that they use [1220:7].

7 Good mediumship includes being rigorously truthful about the messages and the sources of the messages that mediums relay [D25:10–13].

8 Unfortunately, some mediums have wilfully twisted truth for their own ends, deliberately creating the impression that the progress or retrogression of our guides and loved ones depended on *our* actions—the wisdom or unwisdom of which they, *the mediums*, could alone determine. It is a subtle and often successful way of enslaving those who are anxious to help their dear ones, and who believe that those mediums best know what should be done in that respect.

9 The best protection against such misteaching is the exercise of reason.

1209 Of Books and Mediums and Authors

1 The parade of books on psychic matters is seemingly endless. Alas, most of them leave the reader little more informed, and vastly more confused. Sometimes this is true even when mediums themselves are the authors.

2 Some of those mediums have no idea how they came to possess their "gifts of the spirit," and no inkling of the many spirit souls who make it possible for them to express those "gifts." We are not concerned with such mediums here.

3 What we *are* concerned about are those mediums who *know* how much they owe to spirit helpers, who *know* they are as a rule merely relaying what is presented to them in one way or another—but who nevertheless choose to ascribe their talents to an ability to directly tap a mythical collective unlimited source of supply. Some of these mediums find it immensely more profitable, financially, to arouse amazement and astonishment and admiration for their abilities and themselves, than to teach either the *facts* about the faculties they display or the *truth* that can set people free.

4 The greatest sin of such mediums is that they divert people *away* from truth, instead of pointing the way *to* truth.

5 Mainly interested in puffing themselves up, too many such mediums and authors neglect golden opportunities to awaken or increase humanity's understanding of The Laws That Govern. They share little of worth, for their teachings abound in error. Some of them lead one nowhere, except to their own coffers. They praise the founder and leaders of every cult

and group, so that those cults and groups will provide them with larger and more receptive audiences. They out-orthodox the beliefs of the orthodox, or at any rate the *assertions* of those beliefs, so that they may capture a still wider market for their wares. Some of these mediums wilfully and knowingly disclaim or deny their spirit helpers. They perpetuate or propagate error, if it is lucrative to do so.

6 Individuals who misuse their powers to place themselves upon a pedestal, and those who more securely enthrone error in the minds of others because it is profitable to do so, would do well to realize a truth the USB emphasizes:

7 > To teach *any* untruth is to incur a debt that must be paid. To *wilfully* and *knowingly* teach it, is to incur a *greater* debt. And for *each* seeker who is taught the untruth, a *separate* debt is incurred. That is the Law.

8 We recognize that there may be some good in most teachings, and that there is more than one path that leads to the mountaintop. But we cannot be silent about the encouragement of people along paths, or *to* paths, that lead to a precipice—the precipice of *salvation through others*, the precipice of *no personal responsibility*.

1210 Errors of Some Communicators and Some Mediums

1 Some spirit communicators have promised much too much, much too soon, to far too many, thus inspiring sitters to devote time, enthusiasm, and energy that often could have been put to far better use. They dangled the bait of eventual clairvoyance, clairaudience, automatic writing, or some other form of psychic phenomena, even when they knew that the process of properly chemicalizing the psychic centers to the degree necessary for satisfactory mediumship was not likely to be completed.

2 And some spirit communicators, to bolster their own ego or the ego of unthinking sitters, even proposed aims for the latter for which they were quite unsuited, and projects that served no useful purpose whatever.

3 One sitter was directed by his "guide" to take some soil from his native land and mix it with earth in the corresponding latitude and longitude half way across the world, only to discover later that the corresponding point was in the Atlantic Ocean!

12.2 Mediums

4   Some sitters were told *by* or *through* mediums that they would die in such and such a year. None of those particular predictions came to pass, but one can imagine the shock, anxiety, and distress of the sitters and their families, especially during the "fatal" year.

5   Some mediums have also not been above reproach. They attracted attendance in "unfoldment [mediumship development] circles" by promising the moon to those who attended. Some have had as many as 20 or 30 students at a weekly class, sometimes with a private sitting for each student once a week, all for a fee.

6   We do not condemn fees; as we make clear, we hold that mediums are *entitled* to adequate remuneration for their work, just as people in other professions are [1214]. But it is less than noble for people in *any* profession to perform and charge for services that they know are worthless, or virtually worthless.

7   We should beware of mediums who state that people can develop, in a few sessions with them, some specific form of mediumship such as clairvoyance, trance, or the ability to give "life readings"—or whatever form of mediumship is especially popular at the moment.

8   Some "students" have faithfully travelled great distances each week, even in the severest weather, for as long as twenty years and more, to "develop" a faculty that the medium knew from the start, or must have known before long, could not amount to much. For while we may all have some degree of potential in almost any field, it is not necessarily a potential of excellence or anything remotely close to excellence.

9   It is wrong to mislead people into expending time and effort on anything in which they plainly cannot become more than mediocre at best. Often from the desire for monetary gain, but sometimes merely from ignorance of the *mechanics* of mediumship, it has been the fashion to tell individuals that they have promise of mediumship if taken in hand. But *what* degree, if any, of *satisfactory* mediumship?

10   It is certainly not true that *anyone* [during this lifetime] can be an *acceptable* medium in the generally accepted sense. *Not* everyone can be that, just as not everyone can be an expert mathematician, or an eminent physician, or a magnificent pianist, no matter how long and earnestly one may strive.

11   The medium we respect is one who makes no promises to anyone; who is conservative in estimating the potential of students; who keeps classes

small, so that all students have ample opportunity to demonstrate their abilities; and who affirms that all sittings, his or hers included, are experimental, with no guarantee of demonstrations or manifestations.

1211 On Exploring Various Mediums

1 Those who prize Truth above all else [304] should break the chains that bind them to any medium who tries to enslave them, who directly or indirectly discourages them from going to other mediums, often by speaking disapprovingly of "shopping around." Seekers after Truth *should* "shop around." They must be free, as free as the air they breathe. They must allow no one to chain them or bind them in any way.

2 Some people, overly grateful to a medium who proves Survival to them, sacrifice their reason and blindly accept everything that that medium tells them. They make a great mistake, which can seriously retard their spiritual development.

3 Of course we should, for example, be grateful to one who saves us from drowning. But if that meant surrendering our reason and automatically accepting everything our rescuer said, we would be better off drowned.

1212 "Spirit Says..."—A Misleading Term

1 The phrase "Spirit says" too often prefaces statements by some who know of the truths of Survival and Communication. Especially when expressed by mediums, writers and speakers, it gives a nice ring of authority to whatever comes after, so that many assume that what follows is necessarily true—and too often it is not.

2 It is a phrase, therefore, that should be sparingly used or, better still, omitted altogether. Far better to *name* the spirit person or group who has made a statement, or otherwise to use such phrases as "Some spirit people tell us…" or "Some spirits say…"

3 As we emphasize, the mere passing to another realm of existence does not automatically endow anyone with greater virtue, knowledge, wisdom, or spirituality, and it would be folly to accept anything merely because "Spirit says" so.

12.2 Mediums

1213 Mediums and Their Former Guides

1. Some people are puzzled by the fact that they never hear of mediums mentioning, on returning at a sitting after passing on to spirit life, that they have met or seen or spoken to the guides whose channels they had been; and they wonder whether mediums *do* actually meet them.

2. We can say this: Mediums who return to spirit life are most assuredly greeted and welcomed by the guide or guides they had served on earth—and of course by others also.

3. As to why so few if any *mention* their former guides, it may be for either of two reasons.

4. The first is that they may assume that everyone takes it for granted that they have met them.

5. The second is that they may desire to be remembered for *themselves*, and not as the channels for *others*. Personal pride too often prevails, as it does with too many mediums on earth. And if departed mediums desire to be regarded as *the* important element in past communication, with no wish to share any "glory" with their former guide or guides, they would be little inclined to say: "Of course I've met so-an-so, who served you so well all those years."

6. Some mediums are not really spiritual or humble, despite the facade they present to the public.

7. Some other points:

8. — When mediums' stay on earth comes to an end, their guide or guides usually feel that they have completed their service through those channels, and that they are free, as of course they are, to enter other avenues that interest them. They would naturally greet and welcome those with whom they had long been linked, and perhaps see them from time to time, but the close relationship is in most cases ended.

9. — Some mediums, especially those of high spiritual stature, may have no further desire to communicate with people on earth, even with individuals they may have served for decades. Having fulfilled their term of service as mediums, other interests beckon, and they see little point in reopening a door that has closed.

10. — Of course the medium who had great pride in being the leading figure in a group or organization, of dominating all its activities, and of being in a sense worshipped by it, will usually wish to remain

1213 ☐   CHAPTER 12 *Survival and Communication*

11   on a pedestal. And what better way exists than by attending sittings or circles and *continuing* to run things from the spirit world?

Those on earth who found reflected "glory" in being close to such a medium, would encourage that medium to demonstrate or express in one way or another, to bolster their *own* positions of authority in the group.

1214 "Gifts of the Spirit"—and Remuneration

1   We are surprised by the number of people who feel that mediums should not be recompensed for their work. There should be no compensation, many say, for the exercise of "gifts of the spirit."

2   There are two errors in that thinking, in our view.

3   For one thing, any talent, any ability, in *any* field, mediumship included, is not a "gift" in the sense of having been *bestowed* upon the one who expresses it, for talent or ability *cannot* be bestowed upon another; it has to be *earned*, usually over a long period of time, as we reckon time.

4   For another thing, while some mediums are financially in a position where they need no remuneration for their services, many others are not so fortunate.

5   We should also remember that mediums who can devote full time to the spiritual needs of others, can serve *many* more people than mediums who have to earn their daily bread in another occupation.

1215 Could Devices Replace Mediums?

1   There are those who believe that devices will be invented that will replace mediums. Surprisingly enough, their belief has been well publicized by a few psychic publications, edited by individuals who should be familiar with the *mechanics* of mediumship.

2   To those who ponder over the matter, several points may come to mind.

3   1. The first is that psychic phenomena, including communication with those in the spirit world, are determined by people in the *spirit* side of life. They are not at the command of those who head scientific laboratories on earth, or of anyone else on earth.

4   Much coverage was given to a few people who, after the better part of a year of daily experiments of sitting quietly and asking questions while a tape recorder ran, apparently were *finally* able, on playing back their

12.2 Mediums

most recent tapes at increased volume, to hear what it is claimed are spirit voices [known as Electronic Voice Phenomena (EVP) and as a type of Instrumental Transcommunication (ITC)[6]].

5   Assuming that to be correct, what seemingly has passed unnoticed and unrealized is that no results were obtained until the experimenters developed a certain degree of mediumship for a certain type of phenomenon —in this case one that requires enough energy to build an ectoplasmic "voice box" for independent direct voice [1218].

6   If mediumship had *not* been necessary, and was *not* developed during those many months, why were spirit voices heard only after a long span of time, and not from the very start?

7   2. Among various devices used today for communication between people in the physical are the telephone, videophone, [various recorders, computers,] radio, and television, and questions and answers are of course commonplace over them. Would anyone sceptical of the overwhelming mass of evidence of Survival and Communion with loved ones accept voices over similar devices as being the voices of people *not* in the physical? Is *any* device likely to convince such an individual of these truths?

8   The scoffers who will not accept the abundant evidence of scores of thousands of people, among them scientists of immense stature and unimpeachable repute and integrity, who have talked at length with materialized spirit people, and even *embraced* them, and then seen the materialized forms dissolve and disappear before their very eyes—would such scoffers accept voices over any device as coming from *another* expression of existence?

9   3. We emphasize three facts that are relevant here: Mediums also serve in the spirit world, to relay communication between people of vastly different levels of consciousness; the spirit realms are just as

---

[6] Police and law courts are sometimes required to determine whether two different recorded voices are of the same person. In an interview published in 2004 in the *ITC Journal* (Vol. 19, pp. 40-47) a national expert on human voice recognition stated that given sufficient length and quality of recording it is possible to identify numerous characteristics of the speaker's speech organs. These include dimensions, tissue densities, air pressure, and any structural malformations of the vocal cords, larynx, and nasal cavity. If comparing these characteristics from two different recordings indicates the same speaker with a probability of 95% or more, he said this is acceptable proof in Italian law courts that they were spoken by the same person. In this way, he stated, about ten EVP voices have been established to be undoubtedly the same as that person's voice when alive. In some of the cases the probability was 99%.

"solid" and "real" to those who live in them as things on earth are to us; and most if indeed not all of our inventions for good were conceived *in the spirit realms*.

10   Considering these things, would not devices have been already invented and used in the spirit world for communication between different realms, if it were possible to do so, and if it was felt they would be an improvement on mediums?

11   The fact is that mediumship is *vital* for the majority of people on earth who are not able to directly communicate with spirit people. Mediums are as *essential* to communication as oxygen is to water.

12   Of course, just as water may be pure or impure in varying degree, so too with mediumship. But mediumship is *indispensable*.

13   We do not say that people will never devise exceedingly fine instruments or devices that may *aid* the process of such communication. But we do say that without mediums, *no* such communication would be possible.

12.3 MEDIUMSHIP

1216 Developing the Gift of Mediumship

1   An Illumined Soul tells us:

2   All God's children have the powers of the spirit to some extent—dormant within them—which can be brought out and developed... But (they) must remember that it is indeed essential that they are patient and persevering, not expecting miracles.

3   To those who sit for development of mediumship, with the genuine desire to serve, few things are as puzzling as the often seemingly complete lack of progress in that direction. There are many reasons for this.

4   The subject is a vast one—too vast to be completely covered in even a hundred pages—so that we can only touch on it briefly.

5   To begin with, while we all possess gifts of the spirit in some form or another, we do not possess them in the very same degree. Much depends on our development in those respects. Much depends on *why* we are here on earth.

12.3 Mediumship

6   We are like icebergs, by far the greater part of us hidden below the surface—and only revealed, if at all, after much exploration [606].

7   We may be here to develop one or more particular facets of our being, in which case other facets often lie dormant and submerged.

8   We may not be here to serve as mediums in the sense many survivalists understand the term: those sensitive enough to be channels for direct or indirect communication from spirit people to people on earth, or between them.

9   Another thing is that *different* gifts of the spirit require *different* chemicals within an individual for satisfactory manifestations to take place. It usually takes many years for spirit workers who are close to us to so chemicalize and activate the psychic centers [1138] in our physical [earthly] body that we become conscious of what is directed to us by spirit people. But we are at times impatient; and impatience is a great barrier to development.

10 It is strange. We accept the fact that it requires years of effort—day in, day out, several hours each day—for one to become a skilled violinist, or ballet dancer, or electrician, or scientist, or physician.

11 Yet when it comes to things of the spirit, things of a much higher rate of vibration, some expect to achieve success in a short time just by sitting alone or in a circle for an hour or two each week!

12 To think about it is to realize how blessed we are—and how marvelous and almost incredible it is—to have *any* contact, direct or indirect, with those on the other side of life.

13 That blessing is ours only because of the many willing workers in the spirit world who band themselves together in love and harmony, in a multitude of activities, and sometimes for *decades*, in the hope of making an individual on earth a clear channel for spirit communicators. Too few realize the tremendous work and preparation by spirit collaborators before demonstrations *to* us, or *through* us, are possible.

14 And too often, just when their endeavors begin to bear fruit, those on whom they have lavished so much time and effort and attention turn aside from things of the spirit; or, instead of so living and preparing themselves that they can become channels for truly great souls, are content with the *beginnings* of mediumship, sometimes for purely selfish ends. It is enough to make the angels weep.[7]

---

[7] After the blossoming of mediumship in the 1850s, conditions for its development may have begun to decline with the appearance of electric lighting (1890–1910) and radio (1920s), and probably continued during the two world wars (1914–1918, 1939–1945) and with the advent of television (1940s). This decline further increased as

15   We would make it as clear as we can that regular circles *can*, and often *do*, accomplish much good, regardless of whether anyone in the circle sees or hears or feels or senses spirit people or phenomena.

16   For whenever any group—or individual, for that matter—sits in love and harmony and the desire to serve, a place and a power are provided for unseen ones to use for good, which they do, in many, many ways.

17   Another barrier to development arises when sitters have their minds set on the precise gift of the spirit they desire—which may *not* be that for which they are best suited and can best be prepared. They thus block their own progress. The best thing those who seek development can do is to sit without any preconceived ideas, and only with the desire to be used in the way or ways in which they can best serve.

18   Still another point to remember is that whether or not one is a "born" medium, it takes years of unremitting effort and patience and perseverance for even the most spiritual person to become a pure channel for illumined beings. There is no royal road to mediumship—especially for those who wish to be worthy instruments for beings of high spiritual stature.

19   There *are* instances where individuals have gone into trance, for instance, and shown excellent mediumship during their very first sitting in a group. But for each such instance, there are at least a thousand cases of people sitting in "development classes" for a decade or more without developing *anything* resembling satisfactory mediumship of any kind.

[7 cont.] women entered the work force during World War II, life became more fast-paced and pressured, and two working parents then became the norm.

These changes undoubtedly made it much more difficult for budding mental mediums to dedicate the many years of preparation time needed to develop to the impressive levels and high standards attained by renowned mediums of former generations. Many of those former, highly-developed mediums, through deep trance or independent direct voice mediumship, made possible direct, highly evidential, and extended spirit discourses and conversations with spirit loved ones, friends, and teachers. Many also gave repeated demonstrations to large audiences, and allowed themselves to be intensively investigated.

Further disadvantages for most modern mental mediums are that they have not had access to the high standards of training given to and by such accomplished predecessors, and it is now much harder to find dedicated sitters to support their development.

12.3 Mediumship

20   The rare instances we mention are usually either of those "born" with the faculty of mediumship—which they had expressed in the past—or the sudden blossoming of it after many years of effort by their spirit helpers to sufficiently chemicalize and sensitize the channel's psychic centers.

21   As we have suggested, a person may be a medium in *other* respects than in its most common meaning. She may be a medium, *usually quite unconsciously*, if she is sensitive, whether she knows it or not, to impressions that come from spirit people, and if she transmits those impressions to others or enables them to benefit from them.

22   The surgeon whose hand may be guided or assisted by a spirit colleague, skilled in surgery, during a particularly delicate operation; the teacher or speaker who finds previously unformulated ideas pour into his mind or flow from his lips as he addresses others; the healer who uses a force other than that from her own body to alleviate a patient's ills; and the writer who, when he takes up his pen, discovers a torrent of thoughts and words that surprise him—*all these too, and many others, are mediums.*

23   In some cases, especially with professional people, they are also in fact *colleagues* of the spirit people who may work through and with them, and their work is a *joint* endeavor, whether they know it or not.

1217 Is Mediumship Inherited?

1   Is mediumship *inherited?* This question is often asked—and often answered incorrectly.

2   Let us consider two of the many factors that make for satisfactory demonstrations of mediumship.

3   One factor is the activation of the seven psychic centers [1138]. As these centers are part of the *physical* body, their degrees of sensitivity may be, and usually are, inherited, just as *other* physical characteristics are inherited. It is a matter of genes, the units of heredity carried in chromosomes.

4   If the psychic centers are already quite sensitive through heredity, it obviously is easier to become more receptive; and if the degree of inherited sensitivity is great enough, there may be little or no need for measures to stimulate the psychic centers further. There are recorded cases of top-flight mediums who did nothing, at least consciously, to either develop or expand their psychic sensitivity.

1217 □

5 The second factor is the *faculty* of mediumship. As the USB emphasizes, each of us is the product of all that we have been—and that product, *the real self,* of course includes the faculties we bring with us to earth, whether or not we use them here. In many instances, one of those faculties is mediumship.

6 However, just as a violinist's skill is shown to better advantage when using a fine violin, so is a person's mediumship shown to better advantage when he or she has highly sensitive psychic centers. And just as the violin is an avenue of expression for the *skill* of the violinist, the psychic centers are an avenue of expression for the *faculty* of mediumship.

7 Even if an Amati or a Stradivarius remained in a family for generations, it would not mean that all who possessed it could play it equally well, or indeed play it at all.

8 It is plain that although the avenues of expression for a skill or faculty may be handed down, the skill or faculty itself is *not*.

9 To the question then, "is mediumship inherited?", the answer is "No."

10 (A sympathetic and harmonious environment is of course helpful in unfolding or developing *any* faculty. If, for instance, a child grows up in a home where good poetry or good music or good sculpture is part of the setting, its own talents, if any, in those fields will be stimulated and fostered. The same with mediumship.)

1218 Direct Voice and Independent Direct Voice

1 **Direct voice** is the term used when spirit communicators speak through either the vocal cords of the medium, or a "voice box" constructed in the atmosphere by skilled spirit chemists and scientists.[8]

2 **Independent direct voice** is a specific term for the latter method.

1219 Diet and Mediumship

1 We are often asked whether diet plays an important role in developing spiritual qualities or in the development of mediumship.

---

[8] These methods of communication, and the former in particular, are also popularly known as *channelling*; there are many other forms of mediumship besides these two.

12.3 Mediumship

2. *The answer is No*—certainly not as far as normal, everyday diets are concerned.

3. At no time does diet have any effect on *spiritual* qualities. It does not create or expand them, or reduce or destroy them.

4. As for mediumship, normal everyday diets only influence it if they affect the *health* of a medium. In that event, the *quality* of the mediumship suffers and it becomes more difficult for *advanced* souls to work with it.

5. There are certain fruits and plants of the soil, and products from those fruits and plants, that, if ingested, tend to induce psychic experiences, and in some cases to facilitate mediumship.

6. We have touched on this [1141]; and as we have said, we do *not* recommend them, because our bodies usually react unfavorably to artificial stimulation of the psychic centers.

7. As far as ordinary foods go, the type of food has nothing to do with mediumship. So we can expect to find, and do find, vast differences in diet among mediums of the highest caliber and spirituality.

8. In any case, as has been well said: "It is not that which goeth *into* a mouth that defileth, but that which cometh *out.*"

9. In the main, the quality of mediumship depends largely on our physical condition, our mental attitude, our receptivity, and the development of our psychic centers—*not* on our diet.

1220 Use and Misuse of Mediumship

1. Mediumship is unquestionably one of the greatest talents that a person can possess; but unless it is accompanied by spirituality, it is a doubtful blessing.

2. What is harmful is not the use, but the *misuse*, of any force; and psychic power—like fire, electricity, and atomic energy—can be used either for good or for bad. The choice is ours.

3. Apart from fraud—which is perpetrated by a few practitioners in almost every field—many mediums too often restrict their psychic force to the trivialities of an elementary level of communication.

4. Proof of Survival is of course vital and important. It is a first step, and a most important step, to Truth revealed through mediumship. But it is only a *first* step; it is by no means the entire journey—a journey of almost unimaginable beauty.

5   Another thing to remember is that the desire for power—control or command over others—is expressed in many fields by many people, including a few unscrupulous mediums who, behind a facade of humility, suggest or imply that they are the repository of wisdom available to few if any others [B03:2]. That "wisdom," unfortunately, is usually a hotchpotch of errors compiled from various sources and augmented by some original, deliberate misteachings.

6   An Illumined Soul says:

7   > We must remember that the limitations are set not by us, but by the instruments we use. And if the instruments that we use are open in their heart and mind, free in their heart and mind and spirit, if they can put themselves in the background... if they can be humble and know they are in the world to serve God and humanity, then indeed it is possible for us to do great things.

8   Another sums it up succinctly.

9   > We realize that mediumship properly used in the right way can be a tremendous blessing and boon to humanity. But... it can also be used to *enslave* people.

10   As far as fraud is concerned, it is a fact that from time to time there are mediums who prostitute the very Truth they profess to serve. In the United States some decades ago, there was complete and overwhelming proof of the most heartless fraud at "materializations" at a world-famous Mecca of mediumship. England too, has had its share of mediums who prey upon the public. So have other countries.

11   That the number is not greater is at least largely due to those psychic publications that expose such malpractice as soon as they are aware of it.

12   In any case, the ranks of charlatans and rogues are insignificant compared with the great majority of mediums, in the public eye or in unpublicized home circles, who are in every way beyond reproach [B04:6–9].

13   Despite their recognition of the wrongs that some mediums do, Illumined Souls do not condemn them. Again and again they say: "We do not condemn *any* soul." In their gentleness and compassion, their main feeling is sorrow for those who fail to use their psychic force for good only. One of them has said:

14   Some of the instruments that we have used or endeavored to use, in many respects though we have great regard for them, nevertheless have failed us, and in consequence have failed *themselves* which... is even more to be concerned with. For we are saddened to see those who have the power of the spirit upon them neglect their duties in regard to the things that they have to do.

12.4 SPIRIT GUIDES AND SPIRIT FRIENDS

1221 A Little about Spirit Guides

1   Whether or not we are conscious of them, whether or not we *know* about them, not one of us is without *spirit guides:* spirit people who touch our lives for varying lengths of time for various purposes.

2   Most people on earth have little idea how *many* spirit people may be ministering to them. Even those who are aware of the truths of Survival and Communication rarely have any conception of the number of souls who may touch their universe for one reason and another—to guard and guide, to inform, impress, and inspire, to encourage and strengthen, and to help develop and improve some of the facets of their being.

3   For each of us has many "sides," some of which we may not even be remotely aware while on earth. We are like icebergs, by far the greater part of us hidden below the surface.

4   Our spirit helpers and collaborators may speak to us or be silent. They may be sensed or unsensed, seen or unseen. Some may be with us from the moment we first draw breath, others from time to time for varying periods. Some we may never be aware of until we return to spirit life, if then.

5   Some survivalists believe that a person has only *one* spirit guide. But as Illumined Souls tell us, average people on earth, whether or not they are aware of it, each have about a dozen spirit souls who are close to them, assisting or trying to assist them in one way or more.

6   Contrary to some common misteachings, there is *no* limit to the number of spirit souls who may link themselves with us. Advanced ones who are on earth for a great purpose may have several score, or more, of spirit associates. Others of course will have far fewer.

7   What is surprising is that many who often speak of "my guide," neither know nor try to find out the guide's *name*.

8   Each of us has, among our guides, someone commonly referred to as "a guardian angel," though guardian angels rarely come from celestial realms. Theirs is the responsibility of watching over us from birth to death, of endeavoring to bring light or greater light to us, and of trying to turn or keep our mind on things that are good and godly. Guardian angels are always *good* spirit people who have undertaken that task of service.

9   How disappointed many of them must be to see their charges doing so much that were better not done, saying so much that were better unsaid, and thinking so much that were better unthought. It must comfort them to know, with their truer perspective of time, that the "three score years and ten" that we are their charge is scarcely a flash in eternity.

10 Apart from our "guardian angels," who are almost always more evolved than their charges, most of the spirit people who are close to us come to us by virtue of The Law of Attraction. As we progress to a higher level spiritually, we attract others on *that* level, and also some from still *higher* levels who draw close to teach or inspire us.

11 But while like attracts like, our spirit friends and guides do not as a result come *only* from those who are on *our* level of consciousness; if that were so, few of us would receive inspiration of a much *loftier* nature. Fortunately, because of The Law of Service, each of us is usually *also* attended from time to time, and for varying periods, by those from higher levels of consciousness than our own who endeavor to inspire us to greater and nobler effort.

12 We should remember well that we ourselves largely determine the caliber of those spirit people who come to us.

13 We should not worship our guides or blindly accept all that they say. Nor do those on a high level of consciousness accept any worship or adulation, or desire unthinking acceptance of their teachings and philosophy. But with time and close acquaintance, we may come to have great love and affection for them, a profound gratitude for all they do, and an ever greater realization of their importance in our scheme of things [206:7].

14 We should remember, too, that they serve us but are not our servants, despite what some people in their ignorance assert.

15 We are sorry to note how many people instantly and unhesitatingly accept *anything* their "guide" or "guides" tell them. "My guide says this..." they remark, as if that settles the matter for them once and for all.

12.4 Spirit Guides and Spirit Friends

They would do well to remember that to be on the other side of life does not automatically give one wisdom, understanding, or the gift of instruction. There are at least as many levels among spirit people as there are among "mortals."

16   We note another thing: The *more* advanced individuals are in the spirit world (or on earth, for that matter) the *less* do they wish anyone to accept their philosophy and teachings except from profound inner conviction produced by reason [310:4].

17   We know of some deservedly respected guides who have shared much truth with humanity—and also much error! Well meaning though they are, they are still not completely rid of misconceptions they have long cherished or misteachings they have long accepted.

18   Whether on earth or in spirit life, both the *closed* mind and the *credulous* mind are barriers to greater enlightenment, greater understanding, and greater spiritual progress.

19   Good and helpful spirit people come to us because of a selfless desire to serve. Serving us selflessly, they progress spiritually—just as *we* progress spiritually when we serve others without thought of reward.

20   They do not work out their problems through *us,* any more than we work out our problems through *them* [705].

21   Enlightened guides, like other evolved souls, come to inform and inspire us. They come to encourage and strengthen us spiritually. They come to remind us of the laws of God, a God that is all-love, all-wisdom, all-justice. They do *not* come to do our work for us, or to deprive us of the trials and tests which, well met, develop our character and enable us to advance to higher spiritual levels.

22   They do not command us to do this or that. They do not demand compliance with their suggestions, or unthinking agreement with their wishes and beliefs. They do not suggest that we complete projects they had left unfinished. And they do not ask or expect more respect than they merit.

1222 We Are Never Alone

1   We have noted that each of us on earth has numerous guides, that they minister to us in numerous ways, and that they may be with us our entire lives or for varying periods, whether or not we are aware of it [1221:2–5].

1222 — CHAPTER 12 *Survival and Communication*

2   Indeed we are *never* alone. It is a truth that should make the heart sing, and the soul rejoice. It is a truth that should help us to shoulder our burdens and responsibilities with greater willingness, greater enthusiasm, greater courage—and greater happiness. For any burden or responsibility is less heavy when we *know* others walk beside us.

3   There are some people who are horrified at the idea that they are never alone, that all they do is known to spirit people, and that they have no privacy (or so they *think*) at any time and under any circumstances. A few have therefore left movements that teach the closeness of spirit associates.

4   Two important things should be remembered.

5   One is, that spirit people *are* close to one whether one is aware of them or not, whether one believes in their existence or not, whether one welcomes them or not.

6   The second is this: If one is rude and uncouth and inconsiderate of the privacy of others, so in the main will be the caliber of one's spirit friends; if one is courteous and delicate and considerate of the privacy of others, so will one's spirit friends be, and they will not intrude when their presence is not desired.

7   One other point should be noted: Spirit guides and associates are in no sense of the word "spies." If at a demonstration they show that they know what someone has thought or done, it is usually only to give *proof* of their closeness—proof that provides joy and exhilaration to those who have not known that there is no death to the spirit, that life continues, that communion is possible under the right conditions, and that there is no separation between those who truly love each other.

1223 On "Commanding" One's Spirit Guides

1   We have observed that not all mediums and "teachers" possess much knowledge or wisdom. Or common courtesy, we would add.

2   There are a few mediums and "teachers" who counsel students to *command* spirit guides to do this or that—to heal their charges or others to whom healing is directed, for example.

3   It is sad—the number of mediums and "teachers" who do *not* teach and exemplify the virtue of politeness.

4   Fortunately for some students who follow the misguided advice, their spirit guides will, if compassionate and understanding, continue to serve

12.4 Spirit Guides and Spirit Friends □ 1224

them—*despite*, and not *because* of, the ignorance revealed by discourtesy—just as parents continue to take care of infants too young to understand or show good manners.

5 Other guides, however, especially those who have not volunteered or been selected to serve an earthly charge for any specified time, may decide to just wash their hands of such a person issuing commands, which would be quite understandable.

1224 We Owe Our Spirit Friends the Same Courtesy We Owe Others

1 We have mentioned how disappointed many "guardian angels" must be to see their charges doing so much that were better not done, saying so much that were better unsaid, and thinking so much that were better unthought.

2 How disappointed, also, they and other spirit friends must be when any of us, sometimes from thoughtlessness, fail to realize we owe them the same courtesy and respect that we show, or certainly *should* show, our friends on earth.

3 To many of us, it is our *spirit* friends who are our true family, far more real and precious than our so-called flesh and blood.

4 To others, spirit friends are remembered only when help is needed, or when there is nothing or no one else of interest at the moment. They sit only when it suits them, accept inspiration without a word of thanks, and cancel a set period of meditation—which is an appointment with spirit friends—without a word of notice or excuse. And then they wonder why any of their spirit friends, feeling that further association is futile, eventually withdraw. (All may do so, of course, except "guardian angels"—they who have either been assigned to the task or volunteered for it for some reason. *They* do not leave.)

5 Our spirit friends have enough work to do in their own spheres, and cannot always be at our side at a moment's notice, unless the relationship is a particularly close and beautiful one. However, they generously alter their schedule to suit ours, if we sit regularly at a set time, whether it is every evening, or once a week, or twice a month, or whatever suits *us*.

6 If for any reason it is not convenient for us to sit at the appointed time, we have only to tell them, as soon as possible, either silently or aloud. In their wisdom and understanding, they know that many things may arise to keep us from our appointment with them: sudden visitors, telephone

calls that we cannot quickly end, unexpected work that must be done, or other things. But we can at least express our regret, and let our spirit friends know that the sitting must be either deferred for a while or cancelled altogether.

7   Even some mediums, who should know better, are guilty in this respect. Some even act as if their spirit associates were servants to be ordered about. They don't, for instance, *ask* them to please visit someone, they *send* them.

8   We must never forget this: our spirit friends serve us, but they are *not* our servants. (In any case, we should of course treat *everyone* with respect and consideration, servants included.)

1225 What We Mean By "Illumined Souls"

1   Among those who live in the higher levels of the Celestial Realms [1301:2] are some who are qualified to enter the [even higher and brighter] Kingdoms but who defer that step so that they may continue to have clear, *unrelayed* communication—almost always in direct voice or independent direct voice sittings—with those on earth with whom they are closely linked in love or great endeavor; for it is most difficult for residents of realms *beyond* the Celestial to have such communication. We consider such individuals, and of course those who actually live in the Kingdoms, *Illumined Souls*.[9]

2   When *we* use that term, however, [and the term *Illumined Inspirers*], we refer specifically to those who are also the founders and inspirers of The Universal Spiritual Brother&Sisterhood; in other words, the spiritual leaders[10] of this movement to uplift and spiritualize humanity, to awaken all people to the spiritual realities of life and to the [spark of] God within each of them, and to once again present Truth simply and clearly. [See also 316:5–6, B02:7.]

---

[9] See also Pref:5, 101:5, and 102:4. Followers of the USB on earth sometimes refer to them as Great Souls, Enlightened Ones, Exalted Beings, and Advanced Souls. Michael often called them Illumined Ones. Others use terms like Ascended Masters, angels, and Beings of Light. The ancient Hermetic philosophy (313) frequently mentions the teachings of "the Illumined."

[10] Michael often referred to the pre-eminent of these illumined leaders as his spiritual father. This leader was a frequent reviewer of the draft USB *Letters*.

12.4 Spirit Guides and Spirit Friends

1226 Today, Truly Great Souls Issue No Commands

1. "Other times, other manners" goes the old saying.

2. In less advanced stages of human progress, when the exercise of reason was far less common than it is today, when people generally were mentally and spiritually much less developed and could as a rule be controlled only or mostly through force and fear, there was a compelling need for great prophets and leaders to *command*. Such was the way of life at the time, and such the general ignorance of people, that commandments were necessary.

3. If Moses, for instance, had merely *suggested* or *advised* or *recommended* the ten principles for righteous living, his people as a whole would have ignored them—as many did anyway, time and again. Forcefulness was essential then, and what could have been more forceful at that time than a *command*—a "thou shalt" or "thou shalt not"? There was an imperative *need* for "thou shalts" and "thou shalt nots" if the children of Israel were to survive as a people, and not be absorbed by their neighbors.

4. People who reason do not usually need commands to control their actions. And while there are still hundreds of millions of people on earth who do not exercise their reason to the extent they should, or could, particularly in some fields, humanity as a whole has advanced in that respect: It *does* use a portion of its reasoning faculties, certainly to a greater degree than ever before.

5. Thus people of *today* are in need not of those who would command, but of those who lead by *teaching* The Laws That Govern and *living* by those Laws. So—*today*—truly great souls never command us to *do* this or that, or to *refrain* from doing this or that.

6. The millions who, like their parents before them, are steeped in traditions that dominate their life, will not understand this. To them, *any* "thou shalt" or "thou shalt not" in literature considered sacred is one that must be obeyed blindly by one generation after another, with punishment far worse than death for those who do not heed it.

7. We need not concern ourselves with "thou shalts" and "thou shalt nots," except to so live that they are never necessary.

8. One of the aims of the USB in sharing our teachings and philosophy is to free people from all "thou shalts" and "thou shalt nots." We place *a way of life* before them, with no commandments, *no* orders, *no* discipline other than what their conscience dictates or their reason embraces, and *no* rules of conduct so long as their actions injure no one.

1226 □   Chapter 12 *Survival and Communication*

9   We know that a "thou shalt" or "thou shalt not" *does* influence those who cannot reason, or will not reason, or are afraid to reason. But it has little or no effect on those who stoutly defend their own rights—and better still, the rights of others.

1227 A Little about the Native North Americans

1   No more honorable and spiritual a race has existed on earth than the Native North Americans (also called by some North American Indians), until so-called civilized white people entered their domain, robbed them of their lands, broke faith with them a thousand times, slaughtered their people, and introduced them to instruments of death and destruction.

2   On the whole, textbooks and television do grave injustice to a noble people who worshipped one God ("The Great Spirit"), who regarded all people as sisters and brothers, who knew the truths of Survival and Communication, who spent part of each day communing with the spirit side of life, and who lived lives of simplicity and spirituality far beyond the understanding of those who found their heaven in material possessions.

3   Betrayed, placed in stockades, abused in many ways, the treatment of the Native North Americans until recent times is the great shame of a great nation.

4   The Native North Americans had a sense of responsibility and a degree of tolerance not found in many others. And from the spirit world, they still display an extraordinary tolerance and understanding, even of those on earth who, in their ignorance, mistakenly feel they are inferior, and reject them. For among those who know of Survival, who know of Communication, who know of spirit guides, there are some who are reluctant to consider the advice of a spirit Native North American, or to accept one in their team.

5   It is a sad commentary on the state of consciousness of such people—rejecting those who devote their lives to love and service, those we should rejoice to welcome into our circle of friends. But where the door is closed to them, Native North Americans work silently, unrecognized, unheralded, and certainly unappreciated, still serving, still showing an understanding and compassion that only the great of soul possess, to help even those who in their ignorance do not accept them.

6   The *rejecters* are the losers. For Native North Americans provide love and companionship and joy to those who recognize their worth and value

12.4 Spirit Guides and Spirit Friends

their friendship.

7 Many an Illumined Soul whose own astral body had returned to the elements of the astral plane, and who now wishes to speak *directly* to those on earth, uses the astral body of a Native North American to do so. This is because the purity of the Native North Americans of yesteryear makes their astral bodies comfortable vehicles of expression for spiritually elevated souls.

8 Native North Americans in spirit life often have another burden to bear —the limitation in the mind of some mediums and sitters that compels them, if they wish to communicate at all, to speak in such language as: "Me speak to paleface" and "Me bring heap big power."

9 We have heard the very same Native North Americans, when able to converse without the mental limitations consciously or unconsciously imposed by others, speak in language of such content and beauty as to make one weep. But Native North Americans, noble of spirit, accept those limitations, unfair though they are, if by a word or thought they can in some way serve an earthly charge.

10 The story of the Native North Americans provides a distressing example of what can happen to a people as a result of the greed, and lust for power, of others. It is a striking instance of people's inhumanity to others.

1228 How Spirit People See

1 An article in a psychic periodical contains the following sweeping statements: "It must always be realized that the spirit people do not see us as we, on this plane, see each other. They are cut off from the physical sphere to the extent that people and objects are no longer visible to them."

2 Those assertions are quite incorrect.

3 We have no doubt that they are *unintentional* misteachings, and we discuss them because those *accepting* such misteaching will be handicapped in various ways when they return to spirit life.

4 If some spirit people do not see us as we on earth see one another— that is, see our outward *physical* appearance—it is because they do not realize that the spirit [etheric] eye *can* see a physical [earthly] body just as clearly as the *physical* eye sees it.

5 They were accustomed while on earth to seeing with their physical eyes only; and if they had been convinced that spirit individuals *cannot* see people on earth or material objects with their spirit eyes, they may

not be conscious that they actually *do* see them [known as spirit blindness]. *Such is the power of thought*—which is immensely more potent in the spirit world than on earth [1323].[11]

Circles, and "rescue circles"[12] in particular, furnish abundant and irrefutable evidence that the spirit eye *can* see as clearly as the physical eye. Those gatherings are frequently attended by spirit people who are unaware that they have left the physical. Those who had firmly believed that the "dead" remain in their grave until the trumpet sounds on a resurrection day, may not *know* that they are in another expression of existence. (Note, again, the power of thought.) They ask why their family and friends no longer seem to see or hear them, although *they* can see and hear the *others*—and they *prove* it by correctly relating what they have seen and heard.

Until they realize that they have "passed on," and that their spirit body is just as useful to them as the physical body they formerly possessed, they will remain in a state of perplexity and stagnation and confusion, as many do for scores or even hundreds of years.

How much suffering would be averted if simple truths were clearly and correctly understood, and clearly and correctly shared!

(For another example of how *thought* can affect those who leave their mortal frame while unaware of the truth of survival, there are innumerable instances of spirit people who could not see a spirit arm or leg because they had, while on earth, lost the corresponding physical limb. They had to be led to realize that they had passed on to the spirit world, and that they were now whole in body [1310:18], before they could become *conscious* of that wholeness.)

---

[11] Another example: Students of OBEs (1313:n8) report that many of us spend our out-of-body sleep time (about one-third of our earth lives) lying in a dormant condition a few inches above our physical bodies. This is undoubtedly due to the far greater power of thought in spirit life, and our intention when going to bed to get rest and relaxation. In fact it is usually only our *physical* bodies that need rest; our consciousness in our spirit bodies could instead use this time for spirit travel, learning, or service, etc.

[12] In a "rescue circle," a medium and sitters cooperate with a spirit team to try to help "lost" spirit people who usually do not realize (very often stubbornly) that they have departed this world, and/or have other misconceptions (324) that are severely hampering their progress in the spirit realms.

12.4 Spirit Guides and Spirit Friends ▢ 1230

10   Clearly it is important to enter the spirit world with as few misconceptions as possible [particularly regarding the afterlife].

11   Incidentally, advanced spirit people see not only our outward physical appearance, which is what we on earth normally see of one another; they see our aura too [1311]. Of course some mediums and psychics on earth also see our aura.

1229 Some Thoughts about "Rays"

1   There are people who say that their guides come "on a gold ray" or an orange ray or a ray of some other color. Such a description should be taken as a figure of speech—and not literally, as some who are not too familiar with the aura take it.

2   For while there are those who believe that a spirit guide is actually *propelled* on a ray—hence the expression quoted—in fact the ray *emanates* from the guide's *own* person, *from his or her aura* [1311].[13]

3   The average aura, which of course is ever in a state of change, normally contains several shades and hues, of which one could well predominate—gold or green, or blue, or scarlet, or whatever else it may happen to be. It is usually a *portion* of the predominant color engulfing a spirit person that the medium and sitter see, if they see it at all. Says a Blessed Soul:

4   > Around individuals, whether in the spirit world or in the physical, there is immense activity and variation in the colors and patterns in the aura—revolutions within revolutions, cycles within cycles, formations within formations, with variations in design, some geometrical, some not. But in many cases *one* color will for the moment be particularly outstanding.

1230 Weigh Well the Words of Those in Spirit Life

1   Some who come from the spirit world are instrumental in bringing or adding confusion to people's minds, often because of their desire to persuade others to their own narrow beliefs. They still think limitedly,

---

[13] It would seem to be much clearer and more accurate if, for example, we said that a guide comes "with a gold aura" or "with a golden light" instead of "on a gold ray."

usually only of the lands they once lived in. They have not outgrown prejudices of race and color and creed. They are still far from universal in their outlook.

2 What a contrast with Illumined Souls, who know that *all* are children of a loving God, and that *all* possess a spark of the divine, no matter what the color of their skin, the faith they were born in, the land they live in, or the views they believe in.

3 We should always remember that those who pass on to spirit life do not instantly change in their thinking, or in their character. In many instances it takes years, or centuries, and occasionally even thousands of years, for some of them to attain higher levels of consciousness.

4 So we should weigh well the words and sentiments of those who come to us from the spirit world, just as we should the words and sentiments of those who live on earth [208–209].

5 We should love them, as we should love those on earth. We should recognize the spark of the divine within them, as we should the spark of the divine within those on earth. But we should not attribute any wisdom or knowledge or understanding to them merely because they are on the other side of life.

6 During large numbers of group sittings (séances) attended over the years, USB leaders have occasionally heard spirit speakers whose sentiments and expressions revealed how sadly unenlightened they were.

7 Some spirit guides request or demand the carrying out of missions that are of little value, or that involve time and effort that could be put to far better use [1210:3]. They may do this for any of several reasons: to satisfy their own desire to accomplish something that they consider of value; to complete a program they had started but did not finish; to satisfy their personal longing to remain in the minds and lives of those they had known on earth; to show that a thing can be done, whether of value or not; or to induce in their "charges" that sense of importance that some feel when they perform an assignment.

8 It is only *undeveloped* people, on either side of life, that demand that we do whatever they tell us, or that we accept whatever they give us. We should shun them resolutely.

9 The more advanced that spirit people are, the greater is their humility, and the more insistent is their advice to accept only what our reason and inner self unreservedly embraces. Not for an instant would advanced

12.4 Spirit Guides and Spirit Friends

beings interfere (even if they could) with the freedom and free will that are the right of every soul.

10 There are many instances of spirit communicators misinforming the credulous on earth. Their misinformation, whether deliberate or springing from ignorance, has often been featured in some "new age" periodicals that indiscriminately accepted and published almost anything that came from anyone no longer living in the physical.

11 Two examples are worth mentioning here.

12 One concerns a woman who, according to newspaper accounts some years ago, died after a fast of sixty-six days. The fast was said to have been "a scientific experiment for peace" conducted on the instructions of "space people."

13 Later, in a purported spirit communication from her, she is said to have undergone "agony"—"like physical pain"—until adjusted to "cosmic daylight." It was claimed that she had acted on earth as an instrument [medium] of a host of "Masters," several of whom were named.

14 There is *no* agony of any sort for anyone of spiritual elevation who passes on, *no* pain from "cosmic daylight" (whatever that may be) or anything else.

15 Regarding the host of "Masters," we *know* that at least two of those named did not, and would not, use such a channel.

16 In another case, it was declared that a statesman's "negative karma" was erased on his passing, and "his debts were forgiven him," because of the "feelings of sorrow and compassion" of others.

17 As for erasing anyone else's karma, we repeat one thing the USB emphasizes: We are, each one of us, our *own* savior. No one—and not thousands or millions or billions of souls—can absolve us from The Law of Cause and Effect, or remove *any* conditions facing us in spirit life as the result of our own acts and actions.

18 We should not only weigh well the words of those in spirit life. We should bear in mind that we cannot escape responsibility for what *we* freely do, no matter *why* we do it.

12.5 COMMUNICATION

1231 Our Mind and Our Faculties

1. Mind expresses itself in many mysterious ways.
2. It expresses itself *in* a physical body, and *out* of a physical body, but *always through a brain*.
3. In the physical body, our mind or mentality consists of two parts—the objective mind or mentality, and the subjective mind or mentality. Between them, the objective and subjective minds, which have different functions, control the entire body.
4. The objective mind, which is our will, is that part of the mind that directs activity. It is the *reasoning* part of the mind. It also directs the subjective mind, which has greater scope than the objective mind but does not reason.
5. The subjective mind is responsible to the objective mind, which it obeys. But once a habit pattern is formed, the subjective mind *can* function, and usually *does* function, without the continuing command of the objective mind.
6. Our objective faculties—the objective mind in action—control the operation of our physical cell structure. They control the five physical senses of touch, smell, taste, hearing, and sight. When we reach for something, or grasp something, or hear or see someone, or savor food, or inhale the fragrance of a rose, we are using our objective faculties.
7. Our subjective faculties—the subjective mind in action—control the various organs of the body (such as the heart, lungs, and digestive system) that operate according to a habit pattern.
8. The subjective mind is also the *receptive* part of our mind. We can liken the objective mind to a transmitter, the subjective mind to a receiving set.
9. If we remember this, we can see the importance of placing the objective mind in abeyance when we meditate or sit for communion with spirit friends. Only then can what we receive come through comparatively clearly, unimpregnated with our own ideas. Only then can we be more fully open to the minds of spirit friends.
10. When our objective mind is placed in abeyance, those other minds do not have to battle it, and can therefore project their thoughts to us not only much more easily, but usually in a far clearer and purer fashion.

12.5 Communication

11   Of course when we meditate or sit, we are also open to thoughts of those who live in the physical. But wherever thoughts come from, those on a level lower than our own level of consciousness will be rebuffed by our aura.

12   It is our subjective faculties through which we receive inspiration—whether it comes in a sudden flash, or when we sit receptively in silence, or in other ways.

13   A USB inspirer has said:

14   There are those sensations, and there are those emotions, that defy the spoken word. And only in the silence—in the blessed silence—do we actually realize the potency of the *unspoken* word.

15   Some psychologists touch on the receptiveness of the subjective faculties when they suggest playing records of instruction or direction while the patient sleeps. That procedure, by the way, would be vastly more successful if the patient consciously and forcefully *directed* his or her subjective mind to listen and absorb and obey what it hears while physically asleep.

16   We have pointed out that mental healing is the conscious directing of the flow of vital healing force either to one's own body or to those at a distance [1102:5]. We can see now how we can assist in changing the habit patterns of cells that need rehabilitating, and how we can, by our mental attitude, be open and receptive to the energies directed to us by others (on either side of life).

1232 Some Factors Affecting Spirit Communication

1   At least four minds are involved in and may affect spirit communication. These are the minds of the communicator, the medium's control or controls [guide(s) temporarily controlling the medium], the medium, and the sitter. The receptivity and personal interpretation of all the minds involved, the would-be communicator's knowledge, or *lack* of knowledge, of the procedures of communication, and the mental attitude of the sitter or sitters, can be important factors. Even if these four minds present no barriers to spirit communication, there are many other factors that may affect it:

2 — the mind of an interpreter [1325:7], if translation is needed;
3 — the minds of any relays [1215:9] that may be needed;
4 — the mind of a standby [1233], if needed;
5 — the physical health and vitality of the medium and the sitter;
6 — the degree of skill of spirit chemists in preparing the medium's physical body to absorb any vital chemicals needed for full and satisfactory demonstration;
7 — climatic conditions, which greatly affect communication, sometimes preventing it altogether;
8 — the difficulty some spirit communicators have in adjusting to a rate of vibration different from that to which they have become accustomed;
9 — any intense desire of a sitter to hear from *specific* individuals. This often prevents or hinders them from moving a sufficient distance from the sitter to approach the medium or the medium's controls;
10 — the fact that not all mediums can be successful with all sitters, or always successful with even any *one* sitter;
11 — the difficulty highly advanced spirit people find in communicating through any medium who is none too spiritual, although they will, if the need is great, make every effort to successfully do so; and
12 — the difficulty advanced souls have in expressing their spiritual concepts in earth languages. As an Illumined Soul says:

13 > In the transmission of the power of the spirit world into the words of the physical, much must be lost. We are restricted when we have to convey, in words, things that are of themselves of such spiritual context and nature.

14 Other circumstances also play a part.

15 — Unless well experienced in communication, spirit people often must not only prepare and *rehearse* what they wish to say to someone they know or hope will be present at a sitting, but also must *concentrate* on it so as to remember it when given their opportunity to speak. That concentration frequently makes them quite oblivious of anyone or anything except the person they are particularly anxious to speak with, and what they wish to say. We can liken them to amateur actors—and some professionals too, for that

12.5 Communication

matter—waiting in the wings for their cue to enter, meanwhile concentrating on their lines and the actions ("business") that will be required of them.

16 — Each time a different spirit communicator takes his or her turn to speak, there is almost always a change in the rate of vibration. There would usually be further changes in the rate of vibration when the same communicator speaks to other sitters.

17 — The power available at any sitting is not unlimited. (How often have we heard spirit friends at a sitting say: "The power wanes.") And when the medium's guides and controls are versed enough to explain beforehand that time and power must be rationed, especially if there are many spirits who wish to speak, spirit communicators realize the wisdom of not dissipating their energies and concentration.

18 — Communication in a non-private sitting may also be affected by the minds of other sitters, some of whom may be impatient to converse with their own friends, and who may consciously or unconsciously direct a barrage of thought to the speaking communicator to hurry and finish conversing. It is unfortunately true that not everyone shows courtesy and consideration for others, and these qualities are sometimes as lamentably absent at group sittings as they often are elsewhere.

19 — Some spirit people will push their way to the front and clamor for the attention of the medium or the medium's controls. By The Law of Attraction, a gentle and courteous person on earth will have gentle and courteous spirit friends who would not descend to such unmannerly behavior.

20 — In some instances, spirit people will not make themselves known to a medium or the medium's controls if for any reason they consider it *inadvisable* for their charges to continue to visit that medium. In such cases, they will not make their presence known at a demonstration, public or private: They will attend it, if they do, only to try to *protect* their charges from undesirable influences of one sort or another.[14]

---

[14] We discuss helpful procedures and measures that sitters and mediums can use and take before and during communication periods, in Topics 1138–1140 and 1242–1247.

1232 □   Chapter 12 *Survival and Communication*

21   Sitters may be puzzled when spirit friends or relatives (with whom they had been very close) are quite unconscious of their presence at a group sitting. It is a situation that is not uncommon, but it can be corrected.

22   — A sitter can usually help a spirit communicator to recognize his or her presence, if the communicator is speaking to someone else, simply by addressing the communicator. (Incidentally, the tonal quality of one's voice may *add* to the power available for communication.) Or the person on earth who is conversing with a spirit individual can help by saying some such thing as "Do you know who is sitting on my left?" or "so-and-so is here."

23   — Not infrequently the spirit communicator has to be helped by the medium's controls. They may, for example, point out that several friends and relatives of a spirit girl are present, and ask her whom she would especially like to talk with. And she may reply: "My mother is here. May I speak to her?" and yet be quite unaware that her father is also there.

24   — Many spirit people, in their eagerness to converse with a loved one, may momentarily have what may be described as *tunnel vision*—a drastically narrowed field of vision, as in looking through a tube—and no peripheral (or side) vision at all.

25   We emphasize that spirit communication is a most complex and delicate process, with very much more behind-the-scenes activity than is generally recognized. That we have *any* communication at all, the *extent* of that communication, and sometimes the almost incredible *degree* of communication, are wonders indeed.

1233 Spirit "Standbys"

1   Despite the volumes that have been written on spirit communication, there are many things that continue to puzzle the average sitter. One is the fact that communications from several different spirit people during any of various types of sittings—for instance, an independent direct voice sitting [1218]—may be spoken, or appear to be spoken, in the very same voice.

2   There are several reasons for this—and here we discuss them only as they relate to mediums of absolute integrity.

12.5 Communication

3   One reason is that a medium's spirit team may include a *standby*—a skilled communicator who speaks for spirit people who have not mastered the techniques of voice communication through a medium. Those techniques, by the way, are often more than ordinarily difficult for those who knew nothing of spirit communion while on earth, particularly those who scoffed at the very idea, in which case it is not unusual for some conscious or unconscious resistance to the idea to linger in their mentality. The main requirements of a standby are speed and skill in correctly receiving and relaying the actual words or impressions of would-be communicators.

4   If the medium's spirit team lacks a regular standby, someone in the team will usually assume that role if necessary. There are times, however, when an "outsider," as a rule someone who knows the would-be communicator well, is permitted to play that part, if cleared by the doorkeeper [1242:24–26].

5   The standby may receive the mental impressions of a would-be communicator and express those impressions aloud; or the standby may repeat, word for word, what the would-be speaker mouths but is inaudible to anyone on earth, except perhaps some clairaudient sitters.

6   A second reason is that the spirit communicator may not be present at the sitting. In that case, the communicator's thoughts or words are relayed, either directly or through a chain, to the standby who gives voice to them. Such is the speed of thought, as we have mentioned [206:5], that a sitter's words can be relayed to a far-off communicator and answered in virtually the same instant.

7   A third reason is this. The "voice box" [1218]—the independent vocal cords—is constructed from various kinds of plasms, contributed by the medium mostly, and (consciously or unconsciously) from sitters from whom they can be temporarily borrowed without physical strain, plus of course the chemicals brought by spirit chemists and scientists who play a silent but invaluable role in every type of communication. If the spirit speakers are untrained or unskilled in using the constructed vocal cords easily and satisfactorily, their voices are quite likely to sound alike, sometimes very much like that of the medium, from whom so much energy is drawn.

8   Standbys serve a useful purpose, but some of them overlook, or do not know of, or for other reasons ignore, procedures that contribute to a satisfactory sitting.

9 — Standbys should make it clear from the outset that they are *relaying* a communication, not originating it.

10 — They should question the spirit communicator, and *not* the sitter, about any relationship between them. Such information could be most evidential and of immeasurable value, especially in a sitter's first visit to any particular medium.

11   For a standby to tell a sitter something like: "I have Anne here. Who is she?" is, to our way of thinking, quite unacceptable. It would be far better, though still not the best procedure, to say: "Anne is here. She says that..."

12 — Except in rare cases where offensive language is used by spirit communicators, standbys should relay the *exact* words they receive. They should realize that the level of consciousness of any spirit individual whose words they relay may not be on the same level, or even close to the same level, as the sitter's. They should *not* alter the language of the spirit communicator to conform to their view of the caliber or terminology of the sitter.

13 — As there are at least as many levels of consciousness among spirit individuals as there are among people on earth, standbys may be wise or ignorant, reliable or unreliable, modest or pompous, humble or proud, truthful or untruthful. The discerning sitter, knowing this, will not blindly accept anything merely because "Spirit says so" [1212].

14 — Some spirit standbys, like some other spirit people, retain extraordinary fervor about certain policies and convictions, right or wrong, and will do anything to excite or intensify such fervor in people on earth. We should remember that enthusiasm and an ability to articulate are no promise or assurance of worth; in fact they are often the stock in trade of the unscrupulous on either side of life.

15   (There are also other types of psychic phenomena in which spirit standbys play one part or another, if needed.)

16 On this subject a USB inspirer has said the following:

17   Many and varied are the levels of communication, and many and varied are the *areas* on each level of communication.

18   To those who seek spirit communion, much can be brought to bring joy into their life, a light into their eyes, a song into their heart. And yet—some find sittings a barren experience, not

12.5 Communication

because they expect too much, but because of the lack of understanding shown by the medium's controls, standbys included.

19 They who do not question, they who are not analytical, they who have been led to believe, *wrongly*, that *any* expression from a spirit speaker is an authoritative and final one—*they* are often misled or misguided. Only those at a sitting who have their eyes wide open, so to speak, who realize that all cannot *always* be as they wish or expect it to be, can separate the wheat from the chaff, or indeed recognize if there is any wheat at all!

20 We do not criticize or condemn standbys who for any reason do not follow the procedures we recommend. We pray for more light for them, a greater expansion of their consciousness, and a desire on their part to share only what is pure, only what is noble, only what is holy, and only what is true.

21 Mediums would do well to impress sitters with the fact that *every* communication period is an experiment, regardless of the type of phenomena expected. They should also present a clear description of what may take place. It is especially important that they tell newcomers to the "supernormal" of what is *likely* to happen.

22 In many instances where sounds are heard during sittings, such as the whir of motors or the ringing of bells that are not actually present in the room, it should be made clear to sitters that they have heard *simulated* sounds, and that it takes skill on the part of spirit demonstrators to produce them.

23 Education of sitters and students on these and other points would clear up some demonstrations at sittings that puzzle not only the newcomer, but many who have attended sittings for years.

24 All in all, sitters obviously would be wise to judge a communication not by the tone of the (apparent) spirit communicator, but by its *content*.

1234 Three Points Relating to Spirit Communication

1 Personal interpretation is part of our mentality, no matter who or where we are, or whether or not we live in a physical body.

2 In the great majority of cases, what exalted beings share with people on earth does not come to us directly, but is relayed through many souls [1215:9, 1232:1–4]. The personal interpretations of those in the "relay"

may sometimes so color and distort a communication that it bears little or no resemblance to the original by the time it reaches its destination.

3 The *recipient's* personal interpretation must also be considered, whether or not a communication is altered in transmission.

4 Spirit communicators who are less than highly evolved, in their desire to impress, sometimes assume the identity of a person of distinction or importance. So it is wise to judge, by the light of reason, all that is presented by *anyone*. As Illumined Souls tell us:

5 Do not consider our *names* in weighing what we share, and do not unthinkingly accept *any* teachings and philosophy. Judge all teachings and philosophy, old and new, on the teachings and philosophy themselves!

6 Remember, there are *many* false prophets, on both sides of life. Remember, too, that there are spirit people who *impersonate* great souls, to better impress their own teachings and misteachings on the unwary and unreasoning.

7 *Especially* beware of people (on *either* side of life) who claim to possess supreme power or to be the *sole* fount or representative of Truth. For as we know, the more advanced the being, the more *humble* is that being.

8 Errors may occur even in "authoritative" works of earnest and sincere writers.

9 A famous book, considered a masterpiece on its subject, quotes some spirit individuals as renouncing their denial (made when on earth) of the truth of spirit communication. Which is understandable. But at the same time they are quoted as also renouncing other views that *were*, and *are*, correct! Because they were told by someone that their opinion on communication had been incorrect, and they then confirmed it by their own success in communicating, they apparently fell into the error of blindly accepting everything *else* that he told them.

10 This emphasizes the fact that anyone, on either side of life, may be correct in some things but not in others. It is something the seeker of Truth should always remember.

12.5 Communication

1235 The Message—and the Giver of the Message

1. We often hear that what counts is the *message*, not who gives it. The message *is* more important, without question.

2. But *who* gives it is *also* important, for it could impel us to weigh the message well. If we *know* that a message is from someone whose opinions we have come to respect, or from some great soul on earth or on the other side of life, we are much more inclined to ponder over it.

1236 Variety in Communication

1. It is occasionally claimed that this or that form of mediumship, or this or that type of trance, or this or that method of communication, is the best of its kind for the age we are in.

2. There is no "best" for the age in those respects. All forms and types and methods have their use and their place, depending on conditions and circumstances.

3. The *forms* of mediumship, if any, and the degrees of *ability* in those forms, depend largely on the extent to which the psychic centers have been activated and chemicalized.

4. Incidentally, there is often much difference between the form of mediumship we may *desire* to possess, and the form for which we have the greatest *potential*. The only individuals who can with any certainty say anything about our latent powers (if any) are those spirit friends who take part in developing our psychic centers (sometimes for many years before we are *aware* that there is such a thing as mediumship), and even *they* often cannot tell in advance.

5. Some assert that light trance is better than deep [or full or "dead"] trance. The assertion is puzzling, as in many cases the *reverse* is true, although *both* types can be, and are, of value.

6. In light trance, mediums are in one degree or another *conscious* of what is expressed through their lips; in deep trance, they usually are not.

7. The medium's *mind* may affect what is said—except during deep trance, and *provided* enough microplasm [1121:9] is available and is used to transport the medium's spirit [etheric] body away from the scene, or to block out any interference, conscious or unconscious, from

the medium. It is only then that the communication *cannot* be colored by the channel.

8 (Of course there may still be the consciousness of the medium's *controls* to surmount or pierce—especially if their views are different from the communicator's.)

9 Another advantage of deep trance mediumship is the greater freedom it affords communicators to discuss matters of a personal or private nature. As they need not then be subtle about what they wish to say, there is less likelihood of a sitter misunderstanding them, or not understanding them at all.[15]

10 As for *methods* of communication, USB inspirers tell us this:

11 When there is a *need*, those spirit friends who are close to us will use every and any available method to successfully communicate—even *the Ouija board*, which we would not ordinarily recommend, because it may respond too easily not only to a sitter's *own* mind, but also to the manipulation of mischievous or deceiving spirit people. But good communication *is* possible through it; and we know of instances where earthly lives have been enriched and gladdened by Ouija board communications presenting perfect proof of survival and the fact that spirit loved ones will seek *any* avenue to make themselves known—which is why we oppose the banning of Ouija boards.

12 *All* varieties of spirit communication do indeed serve a purpose.

---

[15] Direct communication with spirit people when the medium is unconscious, as when in deep trance (through direct voice and sometimes through independent direct voice, 1218), is probably preferable only when the sitter is convinced of the reliability and integrity of the communicators, or of the high spirituality of the medium. This is because when a medium is not sufficiently spiritual, and his or her spirit guides do not provide sufficient protection, it is possible in these cases for mischievous or malevolent spirits to misuse the channel without the medium's knowledge. For spirit communicators that the sitter did not know during a former life on earth, it could take quite some time to be properly convinced of their integrity. A highly *spiritual* medium will have spirit guides who prevent undesirable spirits from gaining access to their medium; spirit communicators who are of high spirituality and integrity will normally require a highly spiritual medium to work with (1232:11).

12.5 Communication

1237 Variety in Ways Spirit Guides Impress Us

1   Different spirit guides may have vastly different ways of impressing their earthly charges. So what may have a particular and definite meaning to *one* individual on earth, may have quite a *different* meaning, if any, to others.

2   To one person we know, a dream of teeth being extracted is an unfailing indication of approaching illness or accident to someone dear; to others, nothing but momentary discomfort during the dream.

3   For one medium, spirit guides may block out perception of the aura of a person they believe is about to die. It is their way of impressing their channel with their belief. But none of us can actually lose our auras, whether or not they are visible to others.

4   Such symbols are at times used to convey ideas in the spirit world, as on earth. But as we have noted, symbols, particularly pictures, may be interpreted differently by different people; and the more stages there are in any relayed communication, the greater is the possibility, especially if the communication is conveyed by *symbols*, of the message received at its destination being quite different from the message originally sent.

5   We are all different individuals, with different groups of spirit guides who impress us in different ways. Indeed does The Law of Variety, as we have more than once pointed out, operate *everywhere* and on *all* levels of expression.

1238 On Some Tardiness or Failure of Spirit Friends to Communicate

1   Many people have been puzzled when close friends who pass on (return) to spirit life do not quickly keep a promise to make contact through a medium.

2   There are several possible explanations for tardiness or failure to communicate.

3   One is that many who return to spirit life are so thrilled with being reunited with loved ones who have preceded them, or find such delight (if they have earned it) in experiencing beauty beyond their wildest imagination on earth, that they for a time completely *forget* the world they have left.

4   Another is that there is little or no awareness of *time* in the spirit world, as we reckon time on earth. As we point out elsewhere [1328:1], in those realms it is *events*, especially events of great significance, that are the reference points. And furthermore, the absence there of alternating day and night makes for less awareness of the passage of time.

5 If individuals experience a long and painful illness immediately before passing on, it may be many months (as *we* reckon time) before they are free from it mentally. Their spirit bodies would be perfect in every way as they always are; but if their minds or mentalities had long been immersed in their illness, it would be most unusual for them to quickly realize that they were rid of all bodily ills. In fact it is not uncommon in such cases for individuals to think for a while that they are merely *dreaming* that they are well or that they have been reunited with loved ones.

6 There are also other things to consider.

7 Even if spirit friends and loved ones intensely desire to make their presence known to sitters, they may be unable to attract the medium's attention, for any of several reasons. In any case, sittings are often so crowded with spirit people eager and anxious to reach their earthly friends that only a comparative handful can be served.

8 Then, too, some intending spirit communicators may find that the mediums their friends on earth visit are not suitable or comfortable channels for them, for one reason or another. They may discover what many of us on earth have discovered: We have varying degrees of success through some mediums, and no success at all through others, depending on any or many of various conditions and situations prevailing at the time [1232].

1239 When the Living Appear as Spirit People

1 Sometimes sitters become disillusioned and disappointed with mediums, even those of the highest integrity, if the mediums or the mediums' controls announce the spirit presence of people who are still living on earth.

2 But those people could very well be present in their spirit bodies.

3 We cannot too strongly emphasize that it can be most difficult for a medium or a medium's spirit co-workers to tell whether a visitor is a spirit person or someone still living on earth and attending in their spirit body —for all are "spirit" when they appear in this fashion, and they appear in precisely the same way.

4 Much heartache would be avoided if sitters were informed that such occurrences are possible, and could happen sometimes for one reason or

12.5 Communication   □ *1241*

another. In the case of a mother, for instance, who was concerned about her children, it would be quite natural for her to journey in her spirit body to them while she was resting or asleep.

1240 A Note about ESP

1   ESP is defined as "extrasensory perception; perception or communication *outside of normal sensory activity*." (The emphasis is ours.) It is a good definition; but the term is unfortunately often applied to include perception of, and communication from, spirit people *regardless* of how they make themselves known.

2   In a great many cases, however, perception and communication are of course not "outside of normal sensory activity," but *within* it. At a materialization sitting, for example, we see materialized spirit people with our *physical* eyes; we hear them with our *physical* ears; we touch them with our *physical* hands. And when at sittings or in our everyday lives we are enchanted by an exquisite fragrance brought by spirit friends, we are conscious of it through our *physical* sense of smell.

3   There are many other examples that could be cited.

1241 Apparent Precognition of USB Teachings

1   More than a few people have told us that they sometimes became aware of USB teachings and philosophy *before* they received the quarterly *Letters* containing them—either from a sudden inner knowing, or from what their own spirit guides told them.

2   We were not surprised.

3   In the early years of The Brother&Sisterhood on earth, its inspirers explained that when a sitting was scheduled in USB headquarters, for spiritual discussion with Illumined Souls, a vast spirit assemblage gathered in scores of concentric circles around us, eager to hear those of such high spiritual stature.

4   Many listeners would nod in approval. One or two sometimes shook their heads in disagreement. Others appeared reflective. But all hung upon the words they were privileged to hear; and those who were able to directly or indirectly *impress* their earthly charges with what they accepted, sooner or later did so—unless their charges had *also* attended the sitting. (As we have pointed out, many people on earth, during their *sleep* state, travel to places on earth as well as in the spirit realms, in their search for beauty and enlightenment.)

5 It is not unusual, by the way, for spirit groups to remain long after a sitting is concluded, animatedly discussing the teachings and philosophy they have heard.

12.6 HOME CIRCLES

1242 Home Circles and Mediumship

1 Home circles are quite common among survivalists, and there are literally many thousands of small groups throughout the world that meet regularly for one worth-while purpose or another: to direct healing to those in need; to pray for peace and good will among human beings; to hold communion with loved ones in spirit life; to experience [physical] spirit phenomena; to develop latent mediumship; or for spirit "rescue" [1228:6, 1322:3].

2 With no desire for publicity of any sort, and usually known only to friends, home circles do much good, including the occasional fostering and development of mediumship of high caliber and spirituality. That accomplishment sparks many requests for the best way of starting a home circle with that aim in mind.

3 We know of no method that would be best for *all* circles, but we can recommend one that has been singularly successful. We emphasize that it is only one of several methods, and those who adopt it should observe any reasonable changes that their own guides and controls [1232:1] may suggest. For what works for one person or group might not necessarily work well for others. And of course no one better knows what is best for us than those spirit friends who have been close to us for many, many years.

4 For the finest results, it is necessary to have sitters [circle members] who are in harmony with one another, who are humble and selfless and *patient*, who will sit with no material motive in mind, and with just one desire: to be channels for good.

5 In some instances, a few of the original members will need to be replaced before a completely satisfactory circle can be established.

6 Members of the circle should be *spiritual*. For many spirit people who attend will do so because of The Law of Attraction. The more selfless

12.6 Home Circles ☐ 1242

and noble our aims, the more advanced will be those who appear; the less selfless and noble our aims, the less advanced, as a rule, will our visitors be. And despite what some people teach, prayers for protection are not sufficient in themselves to guard us from unwelcome ones. Our strongest and most effective safeguards are our character and the way we live, if of a high enough level.

7   It is usually better if the circle is under the direction of someone well versed in psychic phenomena.

8   Some further pointers.

9   — Sit at the same time of day, and the same day of the week; and those spirit people who are attracted to you will try to attend regularly. They have interests on their own side of life too, of course; but with the usual kindness of considerate souls, they will, if possible, rearrange their plans to suit yours if a fixed time is set.

10 — From five to seven people, preferably seven, make an ideal circle, as far as numbers are concerned; but it may be larger or smaller, as you wish. If possible, have an equal number of men and women (other than the individual in charge), seated alternately.

11 — Until a circle is chemically and spiritually established, it is wise not to seat relatives—such as a mother and daughter, or husband and wife—next to each other: This will tend to prevent concentration of psychic power in any one spot. (Of course this precaution is not necessary at group sittings with a skilled medium.)

12 — Sit in subdued light, preferably a rosy light. (White light hampers some manifestations, and you may not know at the outset what form of mediumship you or others in your group may be blessed with.)

13 — Sit in a relaxed and restful position, hands on your lap but not touching each other, and, only if you find it comfortable, with the palms up.

14 — Open with preferably an informal prayer by someone [521:12], or with a well-known prayer that can be recited in unison. It need not be long, for it is a prayer's sincerity and intensity that matter, not its length.

15 — Then, if you wish, ask for healing for those who need it, mentioning them by name.

16 — There is no need to sing. We know that some teachers recommend singing, but songs are often sung so badly, or sung so slowly, that

they *lower* the vibrations instead of raising them. Use your own judgement on this score, however, based on the voices in the group.

17 — After the opening prayer [and healing and singing, if any], sit in silence, with the mind closed as much as possible to all material things, and with your heart filled with love and harmony and the aspiration to serve God. This is not easy to do, and material thoughts will probably intrude from time to time; but *consciously* displacing them with spiritual thoughts will make intrusions fewer and fewer.

18 — If a spirit voice addresses you, respond at once. Other than that, wait until the sitting is over before commenting on anything you have seen or heard.

19 — Sit no longer than half an hour, to begin with. Once your guides and controls make their presence known, however, leave the length of the sitting to them.

20 — Close with thanks for having had the opportunity to sit together, with appreciation for those spirit friends who were present, and with the assurance that loved ones were around you.

21 — When the sitting is over, then (and only then) discuss what you have felt or experienced.

22 Even if no manifestations occur—and it sometimes takes months or years to get results—you should emerge from sittings spiritually refreshed. For no one should be other than improved after seeking only what is good, and desiring only to serve.

23 If anyone in the circle shows potential deep-trance mediumship [1236:5–9], a skilled medium should be present from then on. There are good reasons for this precaution.

24 One is that it would be most unwise for a person with such potential to be "open" without a trained spirit "doorkeeper" on hand to prevent undesirables from entering. Just as it takes time for potential mediums to reach a high level of performance, so too with doorkeepers: If they are not experienced in that role, they may not be fully competent to screen those who would control their channels, or to engage in "dual control" when another spirit person wishes to speak through a channel but falters in the attempt.

25 Only thoroughly able mediums can be certain whether doorkeepers are ready to perform their duties without aid, and whether potential mediums can safely enter the deep-trance state.

12.6 Home Circles

26   Doorkeepers are normally the first to use their medium at sittings. If they are fully trained and capable, no one else will speak through their medium without their permission, and then only if the medium is completely protected from all undesirable influences.

27   Prayer alone is *not* enough to guard an inexperienced medium who "opens up" before a trained doorkeeper is there to screen those who would use the "open door."

1243 Some Helpful Measures before and during a Circle or Sitting

1   Before going to a circle for any of the purposes we have mentioned, or to any sitting held by a deep-trance medium, we should be most careful where we go and whom we meet in the immediately-preceding hours. A sitter who spends this time in taverns or bars or gambling dens, for instance, or any other place where far from advanced spirit people are likely to hover, is likely to attract and be accompanied by one or more of those spirits upon leaving. And if they gather enough strength during a sitting or circle to break through and become troublesome, they may try to satisfy any cravings for revenge, or passion, or cruelty, or mischief, or any other thing that *we* consider undesirable. (In their own eyes, we should remember, they would only be doing what they think they are *justified* in doing.)

2   It sometimes requires many spirit helpers to keep a circle or sitting protected from intrusion, even in normal circumstances. It is more difficult when strangers sit, and often still more difficult if sitters have had unwholesome contacts earlier. Sitters bring their own conditions to a sitting, let us bear in mind; and we owe it not only to ourselves and other sitters, but to those spirit friends who so generously serve us, to do nothing to attract undesirables.

3   Mental alertness is an asset during a sitting or circle, for it not only makes a sitter more aware of what goes on, but it helps to raise the vibrations.

4   We can be passive and receptive, and still alert. Daydreaming and relaxing to the point of almost falling asleep are not at all helpful. Of course it is usual for those on the verge of trance to feel drowsy—but that is another matter altogether.

5   A USB inspirer [and a very experienced spirit control] offers the following observations on this latter subject. We stress that her method is only

one of several, even though we fully and completely endorse what she says.

6   Communication depends, *among other things*, upon receptivity of the psychic centers—psychic centers we *all* possess. *Passive* receptivity of the sitter is of course helpful, and in fact *important;* but we do *not* share the view of the usual development circle that sitters should go mentally blank and say aloud what they *think* they see or feel or hear. It is not how *we* would conduct a development circle...

7   Mental activity is desirable *before* a sitting for development, mental alertness *during* the sitting.

8   We recommend lively discussion *before* a development sitting, because it will attract entities of an acceptable caliber.

1244 A Protective Measure

1   The solar plexus is usually the most sensitive of our psychic centers.

2   So if we fear or feel a depletion of energy or an inflow of undesirable vibrations, we would do well to fold our arms across our chest. Crossing our ankles would also be helpful.

3   Both actions tend to bar the door to unwelcome inflows or poaching of our energy.

4   A silent prayer to our spirit friends for aid sometimes brings immediate recovery of lost power.

1245 Music—and Healing, Quiet Periods, and Circles

1   Music can play an important role in healing, in quiet periods, and in circles devoted to one or more purposes.

2   In healing, appropriate music often makes for a greater sense of receptivity to both healer and patient, and for fuller attunement between the healer and spirit collaborators. It can help to relax the patient physically and mentally, to more fully receive and absorb the curative flow.

3   Music is often helpful before or during quiet periods, and before or while sitting for development of the psychic centers—provided it is of a type conducive to receptivity and relaxation. But it is usually *better* to

12.6 Home Circles

have music only *before* such periods, as most people cannot block it from their consciousness during the periods themselves.

4 The *kind* of music is also most important. Draggy, dreary, and funereal music, for example, are unwelcome, for they *lower* the vibrations.

1246 Of Value in Rooms Used for Circles or Quietude

1 We have noted that the oxygen in water can be of decided value in any room used for circles or sittings, or for quietude, reflection, or meditation [913:3].

2 During a home circle or sitting, where some of the vital energy of the medium or the sitters may be drained for one reason or another, skilled spirit chemists can use the water to restore any depletion of energy. They can also use it to disperse unpleasant vibrations.

3 Oxygen is not the only useful element. Skilled spirit chemists can put several others to good use also—to replenish physical [earthly] bodies that do not contain enough of those elements, and to make some types of manifestation less difficult. It is naturally more convenient for spirit chemists to extract needed amounts of substances from what is within reach, than to extract minute particles at a distance and bring them in.

4 The following are especially valuable to have at hand: a little *sulphur*, a little *magnesium*, and a little *potassium*—they can be obtained at a pharmacy; a bone or piece of chalk, for the *calcium* they contain; some salt, for the *sodium;* a little bleach, for the *chlorine;* and a book of matches, for the *phosphorus*. These are seven principal elements that the physical body requires in sufficient amounts for normal well being. Your own spirit friends may suggest additional elements if they feel that you need them.

5 Also useful are a growing plant, a dish of earth, or both, as they contain chemicals that spirit chemists can use if needed; and if the furnishings are not colorful, several vials of water of various and vivid colors (in addition to the plain water).

6 Except for the plain water, which should always be fresh, the things mentioned will seldom have to be replaced. Incidentally, one can usually benefit from drinking the plain water when a period of quietude and reflection is over—and we recommend it unless your own spirit friends, for some reason or other, counsel otherwise in your case.

1247 Cheerfulness in Sittings and Sickrooms

1. More often than not, the spirit team of a trance medium includes a child who can provide lightness, brightness, and joyousness—things that can contribute much to the success of a circle or sitting. For children aid in dispelling undesirable conditions that interfere with and sometimes even *prevent* communication: tension; nervousness; anxiety; overeagerness; and fear on the part of newcomers or inexperienced sitters.

2. The infusion of lightness and brightness and joyousness, an infusion which in some circumstances requires much effort, is conducive to successful communication: Anything that helps to dissipate grimness and apprehension, and anything that helps sitters to relax, raises the rates of vibration at sittings, thus making it easier for spirit loved ones and others to appear.

3. Those sittings that are reunions with loved ones should be *joyous* occasions, and so it is important to start them on a note of cheerfulness. As we have said, the vibrations of rejoicing can be used by spirit friends towards a desired purpose.

4. The same infusion of lightness and cheerfulness should be shown by visitors to a sickroom—even if the heart is heavy at such times, as often it is bound to be. For vibrations of a visitor's distress or apprehension not only may be sensed by the ill, to heighten their own concern, but they may actually hinder the endeavors of spirit ministering ones to cure, alleviate, or arrest a condition.

13
Spirit Life

CHAPTER CONTENTS

13.1 The Spirit World — 423
- 1301 The Earth and Its Spirit Realms — 423
- 1302 The Music of the Spheres — 425
- 1303 Of Earth and of Spirit — 425
- 1304 What W<small>E</small> Mean by a Group Soul — 425
- 1305 Of Some Karma—and "Grace" — 426
- 1306 There Is No Need for Spirit Duplicates of Everything on Earth — 426
- 1307 Answers to Some Questions about Spirit Life — 428
- 1308 On the Fate of Animals — 430

13.2 Our Spirit Makeup — 432
- 1309 We Retain Replicas of the Physical Body in Its Perfect State — 432
- 1310 The Various Bodies We Possess — 433
- 1311 About the Aura — 435
- 1312 The Akashik Records – the Book of Life – the Cosmic Memory – Etc. — 440
- 1313 On "Bilocation" — 441
- 1314 Illness Does N<small>OT</small> Start in the Spirit Body — 443

13.3 Spirit Existence — 444
- 1315 When Does an Individual Enter the Physical? — 444
- 1316 A B<small>END</small> in the Road — 444
- 1317 A Three-Day Waiting Period? — 445
- 1318 Reflections Relating to Our Path of Progress — 446
- 1319 Some Facts about Astral Bodies and Thought Forms — 447
- 1320 No One Is Ever Destroyed — 450
- 1321 A Little about Twin Souls — 450

continued...

13.4 Living in the Spirit World — 452

1322	Everyone Is Met When Passing On to Spirit Life	452
1323	A Major Use of Thought in Spirit Life	453
1324	There IS Speech in the Spirit World	454
1325	The Importance of Vocabulary in Spirit Life	455
1326	Humor—and the Spirit Realms	458
1327	Titles in Spirit Life	459
1328	Time in the Spirit World	459
1329	Travel in the Spirit Realms	460
1330	A Little about Children in the Spirit World	462
1331	Some Facts about Earthbound Spirit People	464
1332	Some Facts about Suicides	465
1333	In Spirit Life, We Do Not Always Meet Those We Wronged on Earth	466

13.1 THE SPIRIT WORLD

1301 The Earth and Its Spirit Realms

1 The spirit world or spirit realms, which are all around and about us, consist of *all* the spheres or planes (corresponding to *levels of consciousness*) occupied by those who do not live in a physical [earthly] body.

2 Those spirit realms—Etheric Realms or Etheria are terms[1] some use—include, in ascending order of more rapid rates of vibration, the Astral Realms, the Spiritual Realms, and the Celestial Realms.[2] Beyond the Celestial Realms are still higher realms and levels of consciousness that some refer to as Kingdoms.

3 There are a great many spheres or planes (and levels of consciousness) within each realm, with each sphere or plane gradually and almost imperceptibly blending or merging with one of a slightly *less* rapid rate of vibration and with one of a slightly *more* rapid rate. It is the same with the realms themselves.[3]

4 We can liken the various spirit realms, and the spheres or planes *within* each realm, to the bands of colors in a rainbow, the bands gradually interpenetrating or intermingling at their edges, although from afar they appear quite separate and distinct.

5 Within the various realms, the change from one sphere or plane to a higher one is so gentle, subtle, and gradual, that travellers will rarely notice it until they begin to feel slightly uncomfortable—just as those who live in the lowlands on earth may suddenly find themselves breathing with difficulty while climbing a steep hill or mountain for the first time.

6 Many people consciously or unconsciously limit what they themselves cannot or do not fully understand. For this reason some teach, and many others accept, various misconceptions about the *number* of planes and spheres in the spirit realms.

---

[1] Some also use *etheric* in terms like etheric body and etheric duplicate.

[2] To explain recent discoveries at sub-atomic levels, research physicists now find they must develop theories of existence in multiple dimensions.

[3] Some survivalists (believers in survival of physical death) speak of the "Astral plane" and also of the "earth [physical] plane."

7   One of the common misteachings is that there are seven spheres, each composed of seven planes. Some teachers even ascribe different colors to the various spheres, and to the planes within each sphere. In actuality, however, there is *no* limit to the number of planes or spheres in the spirit realms, for those planes or spheres correspond to levels of consciousness (and vice versa), and there is no limit to the expansion of our consciousness. An Illumined Soul has said:

8   The *people* make the plane, *not* the plane the people.

9   It is conceivable, by the way, that *one* individual could be the only person on a plane; but with the billions upon billions of souls in spirit life, that is scarcely likely.

10 The earth and its spirit realms form *one unit*, with the earth being not only a proving ground, but a place that provides certain experiences and opportunities (for good or bad) that are not available elsewhere in the unit [1424–1425].

11 In fact *each* planet in our solar system has its *own* spirit realms, including those planets that people on earth have not yet "discovered,"[4] with each unit of planet and spirit realms having its own spiritual leadership [706:5].

12 Another Illumined Soul has said:

13 People may build barriers. People lacking awareness may consider other worlds to be far removed [in relationship], even if they believe they exist! But there is only one life, which is continuous, irrespective of time or place. All the spirit realms and earth are one—including the planets, for many inhabit them.[5]

---

[4] Since this was first published in 1975, at least five other bodies orbiting our sun have been discovered, of which one, named Eris, is a little larger and of greater mass than Pluto. See also 1008:n4.

[5] The scientific concept that everything is connected (206:n3) may be seen as agreeing with this.

13.1 The Spirit World

1302 The Music of the Spheres

1 "The music of the spheres" means different things to different people.

2 Illumined Souls tell us that the music of the spheres is composed of the rates of vibration that make up the higher spirit realms; that it is indescribably beautiful, and like no other sound; and that it is full and complete, magnificent in its chords and harmonies, and in every other respect.

3 Each one of us can attempt to describe only our *own* experience of that heavenly music. And even our own understanding of it will change from time to time, as we evolve spiritually, or as we are privileged to become more conscious of it.

1303 Of Earth and of Spirit

1 Some survivalists [people who believe in survival of physical death] have taught that "the best imponderable emanations of the earth gravitate to what we call the spirit world and help to form its substance."

2 That is absolutely not so.

3 No emanations of the earth gravitate to the spirit world. And nothing of a *physical* [earthly] nature can form or help to form *spirit* substances. While spirit energy or spirit substances may pervade and animate something *physical*—a classic example is *the real self* inhabiting and animating a *physical* body—nothing physical can pervade or animate any spirit thing.

4 There is an immense gulf between what is of earth and what is of spirit.

5 That, by the way, is why there is a much vaster difference between the physical and spirit [etheric] body than there is among the numerous vehicles [bodies] that make up the latter [1310:1–9]. That is also why the release from a physical body is so often a lengthy one, sometimes taking *years*, while the sloughing off of a spirit body may take place during a brief sleep or with no sleep at all.

1304 What WE Mean by a Group Soul

1 With the term "group soul" meaning different things to different schools of thought, we give the USB's interpretation: a group of individuals united in a common purpose.

2   Members of a group soul, as we define the term, would not differ too much in their rates of vibration, and, in their common purpose, would *complement* one another in many and various ways.

3   We can liken a group soul to a bouquet of flowers, *each* bloom an expression of loveliness in its own right, *each* contributing to the greater beauty of the whole bouquet—and *each* at the same time losing *nothing* of its own special charm.

1305 Of Some Karma—and "Grace"

1   Can karmic debts acquired on earth be paid in spirit life? *Some* karmic debts, yes; but not all.

2   If a spirit man had maimed someone while on earth, for instance, and had come to genuinely regret his action, he could not only direct healing thoughts to his victim, but he could also make the effort to learn *how* to cure or alleviate the injury, or to *assist* others in doing what can be done in that respect.

3   If a woman had robbed someone of money or possessions, to give another example, and was truly sorry for it, she could try to inspire her victim, or the family of the victim, with ways and means of *recouping* that loss.

4   In cases such as these, karmic debts are paid if there is sincere repentance, and if the desire to undo wrongs springs *not* from fear of retribution, but from realization of the error and a profound desire to make amends.

5   As for "grace," there is *no* grace in the theological sense of "the freely given, *unmerited* favor and love of God." That would be quite irreconcilable with a God of Love and Wisdom, of Law and Justice, and That Which Is All-Good [1415].

1306 There Is No Need for Spirit Duplicates of Everything on Earth

1   Ignorance is the mother of misconceptions, the USB emphasizes. And among the countless widespread misconceptions and misteachings that ignorance has spawned are these: that each and every *thing* on earth has a spirit [or astral or etheric] counterpart—or, let us say, *a spirit [world] duplicate*, to phrase it more precisely; and that spirit children who visit us may take the spirit duplicate of any earthly toy they like.

13.1 The Spirit World

2   Let us reason a moment.

3   What would be the point of having a spirit duplicate of the hundreds of billions of articles that are manufactured each year on earth? What *possible* use would there be in the spirit world for a spirit duplicate of every pin, every lock, every book, every leaflet, every watch, every cake, every piece of tissue, every furnace, every thermometer, and thousands of other things that are manufactured on earth? And what would happen to any *assumed* spirit duplicate of any earthly article that was consumed or destroyed?

4   If each sheet of paper had a spirit duplicate, what would happen to that duplicate if the sheet were burned to ashes? What would happen to the duplicate if the sheet itself were *written* on? What would happen if the sheet became part of a bound *volume*? Would the volume have its *own* spirit duplicate? Would the sheet's spirit duplicate float about in the spirit world, or would it somehow automatically gravitate to its proper place among the spirit duplicates of the *other* sheets in the volume?

5   Would the *individual* spirit duplicates of the wheels, tires, cab, windshield, and other parts that make up a truck, automatically fuse into a spirit duplicate of the *assembled* truck? What would happen to *that* duplicate if a *material* wheel were removed or damaged?

6   If a spirit child liked a toy locomotive on earth and took away its alleged spirit duplicate, what would happen later if another spirit child liked the same toy? If the toy locomotive on earth was afterwards coupled to a string of railroad cars [carriages], would the spirit duplicate of the train be incomplete? Or would the spirit duplicate of the locomotive suddenly vanish from the possession of the spirit child in order to join the spirit duplicates of the cars?

7   The fact is that there is *no* spirit duplicate of *anything*, although any creature that lives in a physical body, human or otherwise, has a *spirit body*, which is something else entirely.

8   Another thing to note is that the beauties of the higher spirit realms—whether of landscape or color or architecture or painting or music or anything else—far surpass the beauties of earth. What purpose would there be in having a replica of anything *inferior* when something immensely *superior* is at hand?

9   There are of course countless things that are found on both sides of life—such things as homes, gardens, scenery, and schools and halls of learning, for instance—but in every case the quality is far superior in the higher spirit realms.

10 However, if for any reason spirit people wanted to review things on earth—such as inconsequential books, let us say—they could review actual copies of the book on earth, if they knew how to go about it, or they could peruse spirit-reproduced copies in a few moments by someone skilled in that process.

11 Children are children, wherever they are, and almost always want and need playthings. And spirit children very often *do* receive exact replicas of earthly toys that delight them. But the facsimiles are molded of *thought* [1323]. In spirit life, as we explain, thought is not only the magnificent power *behind* things, but the actual stuff of which things are made. And there are many individuals in the spirit world who devote themselves to manufacturing clothing, toys, and other articles that spirit infants and young children may need or like but cannot make themselves.

12 We do not say that there are no spirit *prototypes* of many things on earth. There are, but they are not "counterparts" or "duplicates" of them.

13 Some spirit prototypes such as schools, hospitals, homes, gardens, and operas serve a useful purpose on *both* sides of life. Other spirit prototypes are conceived by spirit people for use on earth only; and those conceptions, sometimes accompanied by drawings or spirit models, or both, are the inspiration for some of humanity's greatest "inventions."

1307 Answers to Some Questions about Spirit Life

1 Because of their general interest, we quote some questions put to us, and our answers.

2 1. "The USB teaches that things in the spirit world are as real and solid to spirit people as things on earth are to us. What would happen if someone hurled a spear at another, or severed a limb with a sword?"

3 Nothing serious.

4 Spears or swords or any other weapons could only affect spirit people if they *thought* they could, and even then they would pose no real problem. For they, or other people, could either *think* the weapons away, or pluck the spears from their bodies, or put the severed limbs back in place.

5 The spirit [etheric] body of an individual *cannot* be harmed in any way. Of the various bodies a person possesses, only the *physical* vehicle

13.1 The Spirit World

can be impaired. However, it is not uncommon for spirit people unaware of this truth to suffer great anguish from the belief that the spirit body is or *could* be damaged—until they learn that nothing and no one can injure a spirit body.

Thought governs the spirit world to a degree that few on earth realize.

2. "What happens if a spirit animal is hurt?"

It would be attended by spirit people devoted to the care and welfare of creatures.

3. "What is inside a spirit body?"

Exactly what is inside a physical body, but of much finer substance [1309].

4. "Do spirit hair, fingernails, etc., steadily grow, as on earth, thus requiring periodic attention?"

They grow if individuals *expect* them to.

5. "What happens when two spirit objects, such as 'wood' or 'stone,' collide? Would they bruise or shatter or splinter?"

They might. But spirit people could, by the power of thought, promptly restore them to their previous condition.

6. "Is it mechanically possible to drill holes in spirit materials?"

Yes. But it is much simpler to use the power of thought to construct holes *directly* than to use that power to construct a drill and then manually operate it.

7. "What does a spirit person feel if she accidentally bumps into an object?"

Nothing, unless she *expects* to feel pain or discomfort from the contact. But she could throw off that feeling at once.

8. "What does a spirit person feel if another grips his hand too firmly?"

Here too nothing, unless he *expects* discomfort. Of course he could sense any warmth or sincerity in a handclasp, just as *we* do.

21   9. "Why do first reports from individuals who have passed on to spirit life so often mention 'guided tours' for the new arrival and the discovery of the spirit homes they have built for themselves?"

22   It is perfectly natural for new arrivals in the spirit world to be shown the surroundings that will be theirs for at least a while, and it is a courtesy they welcome.[6]

23   The latter part of the question reveals a common misconception; for despite what many teach, people do *not* build their spirit homes while they are still living on earth. A Blessed Soul says:

24   What people prepare for themselves, while on earth, is not actual *dwellings* in the spirit world, but individual entries to areas or planes (levels of consciousness)—the exact *level of consciousness* that each achieves on earth and so will automatically gravitate to in the spirit realms [1301], though not always at the very instant of passing.

25   One may first go to a lower level to meet and be reunited with any loved ones who would not be comfortable in the level one will be occupying.

26   If a long or painful illness preceded one's passing, one would usually need a period of adjustment or convalescence in one of the many rest homes or hospitals in the Astral Realm. (There is no need for such facilities in higher realms.)

27   Another consideration is this. Even if it were possible, while on earth, to build an actual spirit dwelling for oneself, it would in almost all cases be pointless: For if over the years one's level of consciousness changes frequently, as is usually the case, one would, *as* frequently, have to start rebuilding. It would be a waste of time and effort.

1308 On the Fate of Animals

1   There are many misconceptions about the fate of animals. Do they, as some teach, return or become part of "a group soul"?—which such teachers interpret as a huge mass of energy without identification, one in which all individuality is obliterated and lost. Or do they, as some others

---

[6] Upon further questioning in 1979, Michael told me that the power of thought is so strong that it blocks off memories of our nightly visits to the spirit world while living on earth.

13.1 The Spirit World

teach, evolve to a state where they eventually live in a human physical body?

2   To both questions, the answer is "No."

3   Animals do *not* lose their identity and individuality; and when their earthly life is over they continue their existence in the spirit world, just as people do. There is abundant and incontrovertible evidence of this in sittings and circles, where pets return to make their presence unmistakably clear; in clairvoyant and clairaudient descriptions of pets and their activities; and in the accounts of many spirit people who relate that on returning to spirit life they were met and welcomed by cherished pets, including those that were their companions during their childhood.

4   Animals retain their *individuality*, and they can and do progress in the spirit world, but they cannot exist and express in a range of rates of vibration other than their own: *Nothing can.*

5   And like people, animals also retain their *form*, which of course is then a spirit [etheric] one, in every respect a replica of the physical one in its perfect state. Those spirit bodies are as real and solid to people in spirit life as the earthly bodies were to people on earth.

6   Animals, domesticated or undomesticated on earth, frequently live in quite high spirit realms of expression.

7   Highly advanced spirit bings often visit realms of less rapid rates of vibration to mingle with people living there. They do the same for pets they love. For the love tie is the greatest tie of all.

8   A misteaching based on yet another—the misteaching that *we* are part of God [503]—is that we can transfer *divinity* to creatures in the animal kingdom, so that they will eventually return to earth as human beings.

9   However, as we have mentioned before, the infinitesimal spark of the divine that we are blessed with [and that animals are not, see 808:12] does *not* invest us with all the powers or attributes usually associated with the Deity.

10   Nor have human beings ever been animals, as some teach.

11   Many misconceptions arise from unawareness of two Laws discussed in Chapter 4: The Law of Variety and The Law of Vibration.

13.2 OUR SPIRIT MAKEUP

1309 We Retain Replicas of the Physical Body in Its Perfect State

1   Thousands accept the common misteaching that individuals progressing through the spirit realms discard many of the parts of the body for which they had so much need on earth—among them the larynx, the digestive system, and the reproductive system.

2   But *every* part of our body for which we have use on earth has a use in the spirit world also, quite apart from its value in providing a means of recognition.

3   While the digestive system, for instance, would not and could not be used in the spirit world to digest food as we know food on earth, it has and does serve a purpose: the absorption of vital essence found in the atmosphere of any particular realm, for perfect expression of the vehicle *for* that realm.

4   As for the larynx, the higher the realm of existence, the more can communication be conducted by *thought*. But communication *can* be conducted more leisurely, if desired —and it often *is* desired—by *voice* [1324]; and here the larynx is essential. (Of course the tonal qualities of sounds in higher spirit realms are of different rates of vibration than the tonal qualities of sounds on earth.)

5   Similarly, there is use for every other part of the body that is of value in one way or another on earth.

6   Apart from all this, however, the indissoluble triune that each of us is—soul, spirit and mind [602]—requires a vehicle of habitation in the spirit world if it is to be, as it *is*, more than just a vague, misty, formless thing. What better or more comfortable vehicle than one of the replicas of the physical body in its perfect state? [1310].

7   One could say that legs and arms are not necessary to provide a vehicle for a triune of soul, spirit, and mind; those on earth who have lost both legs and both arms prove that conclusively. The same could be said about ears, eyes, and hair, for that matter. But we would be quite unable to recognize beloved ones and others, on either side of life, by sight, if they did not possess the familiar features and appearance we are used to. Likewise, in many cases, spirit people would be unable to recognize one another without those features, unless and until they became familiar with one another's "light" [1311:6].

13.2 Our Spirit Makeup

8   We must remember that we look for what we *expect* to find. If we expect to see certain people, certainly we expect to see them with all we associate with their appearance—including arms, legs, torso, head, and features. And all those parts and features *are* there for us to see.

1310 The Various Bodies We Possess

1   In the long journey of progression, we occupy more than five bodies—*physical [or earthly]*, *astral*, *psychic*, *spiritual*, and *celestial;* and after these, still others.

2   We possess *all* these bodies while on earth. *All* of them are dwelling places for *the real self*, with the habitations becoming increasingly fine—that is, of a more rapid rate of vibration. At all times, our outermost body is the one in which we are most comfortable, most at home in, and which, as a rule, is the only one we are aware of then.

3   The **physical body** is the outermost and the grossest [lowest rate of vibration], and grosser bodies always completely envelop finer ones.

4   All the various bodies that we still retain at any time, other than the physical body, together constitute what is sometimes called the *spirit [etheric] double* or (the term we prefer) the **spirit body** [or etheric, incorporeal, counterpart, subtle, or beta body]. *The real self* always remains in the spirit body.

5   The **astral body** is slightly less dense in structure than the physical body a person occupies on earth. Spirit people who live in a rate of vibration close to that of the earth use astral bodies.

6   When they progress and reach the upper planes of the Astral Realms [1301:2], they discard the astral body and inhabit their **psychic body**, which is only slightly less dense than the astral.

7   When they advance to the stage where they leave the astral planes and enter the Spiritual Realms, they discard the psychic body and inhabit their **spiritual body**.

8   When they advance still further, and leave the Spiritual Realms for the Celestial, they discard the spiritual body and inhabit their **celestial body**.

9   And when they enter still more exalted realms, which some term *the Kingdoms*, they inhabit bodies of even finer rates of vibration.

10 Those who come to us at home circles or sittings usually use an astral body at the time, for reasons of comfort. But that is not always necessary.

11 Under right conditions, and especially when the medium and the sitter or sitters are highly spiritual, communicators from the Spiritual or Celestial Realms can, if they wish, use their spiritual or celestial bodies. The choice is theirs.

12 It is important to remember that the spirit body does *not* envelop the physical body, as some survivalists mistakenly assert, but is *enveloped* by it. Misconception on this point causes much confusion with the aura, as we shall see shortly [1311, 1314:3].

13 When we are awake, the spirit body is almost always *within* our physical body.

14 When we are asleep, the spirit body usually either goes on a journey—it can travel immense distances, and rapidly—or it stays close by, *outside* our physical body, from which it has withdrawn, generally from the top of the head.

15 When our spirit body is seen elsewhere, it is as a rule when we are asleep. But some people can *consciously* project their spirit body while they are awake.

16 The spirit body is connected to the physical body by what is called "the silver cord." It is when that cord is severed that "death" takes place.

17 Except for its more rapid rate of vibration, the spirit body is in every respect a *replica* of the physical body in its perfect state [1309].

18 It is free from scar or blemish of any sort, regardless of how scarred or maimed the *physical* body may be. But spirit communicators sometimes simulate or discuss such imperfections so that they may be easily recognized.

19 The spirit body is whole in every respect, even though some spirit people may see their own spirit bodies as they last saw their [imperfect] *physical* bodies [1228]. Likewise, as a result of misteachings that some had absorbed, they may "see" some other spirit people in the grotesque and misshapen forms they had *expected* those others to possess because of the lives they had lived on earth. Thought is indeed powerful [especially in spirit life]!

20 In the *lower* realms of the spirit world, it is people's *auras*—and *not* their spirit bodies—that are far from beautiful.

21 The fact that the spirit body is a "duplicate" of the physical body is disturbing to some, who take it to mean that their outward appearance in the

13.2 Our Spirit Makeup

spirit world will always be an exact likeness of their outward appearance on earth.

22 That is not necessarily so, however.

23 Just as water assumes the shape of the vessel into which it is poured, the spirit body, which is remarkably elastic, assumes the shape of the physical body that it occupies. However, in the spirit world, where thought is not only the magnificent power behind things, but the actual stuff of which things are made [1323], those who know *how* to do so may, if they wish, by the power of thought change their appearance to suit themselves—providing of course, that they have earned the right to do so. They can, for instance, change their size, or the color of their hair, or the shape of their eyes, or any other feature. Of course they may not be recognized by others, certainly not at once, if alterations are numerous; for this reason, few spirit individuals opt for radical changes.

1311 About the Aura

1 The *aura* is the magnetic field of energy that *emanates from and envelops* people, creatures, and things—*all* things.

2 Everything, regardless of its size or nature, [on both sides of life,] has an aura, a magnetic field of energy—what some schools of thought term an *odic* field or *electromagnetic* field, [or a *biofield* for living things].

3 The aura follows the shape or form of what it emanates from and envelops.

4 A person's aura has colors, and where the colors blend or mingle, it has hues. These colors and hues, and the size of the aura, vary with each individual and with time.

5 Part of the human aura—the outer part—consists of what might be called a protective "film," more or less oval in shape, whose purpose is to prevent (or try to prevent) auras that are not in harmony with it from entering and melding with it.

6 It is a *portion* of this protective film that is often recognized as a "light" during sittings and circles, and of course at other times also. The light varies not only in brightness and color and shape, but in size, ranging from a pinpoint to a huge ball.

7 The aura is usually invisible to people on earth, except at times to some clairvoyants. And not all who see the aura are able to read and interpret it correctly.

8   The width of the human aura varies from a few inches [centimeters] to many feet [meters], depending upon the development of the individual. [The auras of Illumined Souls are the largest, and brightest.]

9   The size and colors and hues of our auras are in a constant state of flux, ceaselessly changing as they instantly display our condition and everything we say and think and feel and desire [1229:4]. Minute changes are of course usually imperceptible even to the clairvoyant, and are apparent only to the highly trained auric scientist, on either side of life (there are not many on earth).

10   Our auras record the sum total of what we have been and what we are—our character, our personality, our mental (which includes our spiritual) levels, our present state of consciousness, in fact *everything* about us.

11   We may lie to other people. We may conceal our thoughts and emotions from them. But to those who can see and read it, one's aura tells all; and to advanced spirit people, one is an open book.

12   The full and entire existence of an individual (as he or she has lived it) is recorded in one's aura, which can be read in detail by expert spirit auric scientists only—although there are those on earth who claim they can do as much. (We can liken a spirit auric scientist to a radiologist on earth who impersonally examines and interprets medical X-ray photographs.)

13   Incidentally, when we pass on to spirit life, it will be a spirit auric scientist who reveals our past to us, to the degree this is permitted. For contrary to common misconception and common misteaching, it is seldom that those who pass on become completely familiar at once with *all* aspects of their existence. That would in most cases be highly unwise, for various and very good reasons; and whether we are on earth or in the spirit world, THE LAW allows only those revelations that can be comfortably understood.

14   Our present state of consciousness, our mental level, our spiritual level, our state of progression, are all revealed in the shades of color, or combination of colors, in the aura, and by the size of the aura.

15   So, too, is our physical condition; and one way skilled [usually spirit] diagnosticians can tell whether there is discomfort or disease in our physical body is by noting the *colors* in the aura that envelops us—*the general aura*, let us call it. The vibrations of illness are quite different from the vibrations of health.[7]

13.2 Our Spirit Makeup

16 Skilled diagnosticians can also detect the specific discomfort or disease by the colors of the specific auras of the organs or cells affected; for those organs and cells, like everything else, have their own auras.

17 Some clairvoyants are blessed with what is called X-ray vision. In that case, whether or not they see the colors in an aura, they see the body as it would appear in X-ray film—with blotches or darkness revealing areas where the flow of vital energy is not being properly absorbed, thus causing disharmony in those areas.

18 Because of its extreme sensitivity, the aura attracts, repels, or melds with other auras—auras of things, and auras of individuals and creatures on either side of life.

19 When we feel strongly attracted or repelled by someone, it is usually our unconscious response to the reaction of our aura to *another's* aura.

20 When the spirit body travels, as it often does in the sleep state or during trance, it is accompanied (and enveloped) by a portion of the general aura. However (and there are any number of misteachings about this), there are *no* distinct and separate auras for the various components that make up the general aura, call those components what we will. *It is one aura.*

21 The portion that accompanies the spirit body when it travels is not completely separated from the rest of the aura, but is attached to it by the silver cord [1310:16].

22 When we make the change called death, the spirit body is accompanied by the general aura except for the part that emanates from the *physical body*. That part *remains* with the physical body; and as the physical body returns to the elements, its aura is broken up into auras of the various elements themselves.

23 As everything has an aura, the things we eat and drink have their own auras too. The aura of what is extracted and absorbed by our digestive system becomes a part of the aura of the cells that eventually assimilate, for a time, what has been extracted and absorbed; and to the extent that it affects our physical condition, it is displayed in the general aura. So there is some basis for the statement that we are what we eat—just as there is for the statements that we are what we think, we are what we feel, and so on.

---

[7] There are also reports of instruments that have been used to identify health problems apparently from the aura (*see also* B09:29).

24   If the aura of what we eat does not blend too satisfactorily with the aura of the cells that normally would assimilate it, or if it is incompatible with or rejected by the aura of those cells, it is reflected by an upset condition of some sort, or by discomfort or pain here and there.

25   That is *one* cause of allergies—the *incompatibility* of one aura and another, in this case the aura of the cells and the auras of certain solids and liquids.

26   Some believe that there is a relation between spiritual sensitivity and allergy sensitivity. But there is none.

27   Spiritual sensitivity is mental. Allergy sensitivity is physical.

28   Allergy sensitivity—and psychic sensitivity too, for that matter—may be inherited; but not all members of a family will necessarily inherit them, or inherit them to the same extent.

29   Of course sensitivity, *in itself*, is not always distressing or unfortunate. If one is sensitive to what is lovely or fine or noble—like an exquisite flower, a magnificent sunset, a beautiful thought beautifully expressed, or a truth—*that* sensitivity brings exhilaration and joy. It is a desirable sensitivity.

30   As for the control of allergies, we could, by regular and continuing direction and command, *educate* cell structures to become either less sensitive or more sensitive, depending on our need or desire at the time.

31   But in the case of sensitivity, say, to pollen, which causes so much distress to so many, it would take so long, and require such effort to educate the cells to be less sensitive, that it is hardly worth while—especially when serums (injections) usually bring relief in a comparatively short time, and with little or no effort on the part of the sufferer.

32   One of the effects of injections is to produce antibodies that build or create, in the body, immunity to what it is sensitive to. Each and every cell has *intelligence*, as we have emphasized, and it is the *intelligence* in the cells that puts injections to work. As old cells become immunized, and as new, immunized cells replace older or affected cells, the body becomes more or less immune to what formerly disturbed it.

33   This is because the aura of immunized cells, which of course is different from the aura of susceptible cells, will not violently reject, or too greatly resent, the aura of what the body once found so incompatible or repellent.

13.2 Our Spirit Makeup

34   As one's aura tells all—including one's mental level (which includes one's spiritual level), one's state of progression, and one's physical condition—there is not just one rate, but *many* rates of vibration in a person's aura.

35   It is the *total* effect of the various rates of vibration in one aura, and the *total* effect of the various rates of vibration in another aura, that determine whether the auras are compatible, and the degree of compatibility or incompatibility.

36   In some cases, while most of the rates of vibration in one aura may be harmonious with most of the rates of vibration in another, there may still be a jarring or discordant note. How often do we hear someone say, in effect: "I *like* so-and-so, but *something*—something I can't quite put my finger on—prevents me from drawing as close as I would wish to."

37   It usually means that *somewhere* in one aura are vibrations reflecting thoughts and views that at that particular time are in sharp conflict with thoughts and views reflected in the other.

38   To summarize the compatibility of auras, whether they are or are not in harmony depends on many factors. There can be harmony in certain respects, and not in others; at certain times, and not at others. One's aura will vary at any precise moment with one's mood, one's physical condition, one's state of consciousness, and one's attitude. For this reason, one aura will not always be in the same degree of harmony or disharmony with another aura.

39   An understanding of how auras may react on one another makes it clear how *essential* it is to have harmony in groups that meet for any special purpose—especially in groups directing a service to others, or attempting to practice or develop psychically or spiritually.

40   Only if there is *harmony* in a group aura can that group achieve much of value.

41   If a group is harmonious, it will attract many more spirit people with not only the desire but the ability to serve, and this will add to the power of the group as a whole.

42   A common misteaching is that the various bands of color in the aura represent or emanate from different "bodies"—"the emotional body," "the desire body," "the mental body," "the spiritual body," and so on. This misteaching sometimes springs from confusing the bands of the aura with the spirit body, which some people erroneously believe surrounds the physical body. We discussed this misconception recently [1310:12].

43   The aura *does* have bands of colors and, where the colors blend or mingle, hues. But the number of bands is not the same in the auras of all people, and may vary from one individual to another—and even in the aura of *one* individual—from one time to another. To assert, then, that this band of color or hue represents "the emotional body," or that that band of color represents "the desire body" or some other "body," is clearly incorrect.

44   We have already noted that emotions, desires, and our spirituality if any, are all *part* of our mentality or mind [604:7]. They do *not* exist in separate compartments. And they do not exist *away* from the mind, but *in* the mind.

45   There are many other misconceptions about the aura.

46   One writer declares that anybody about to die has no aura. And adds (we change the tense): "When nature withdraws the colors from the aura, the person shortly after always dies."

47   Both statements are quite inaccurate.

48   The writer quoted describes two instances to support these misteachings. In one case, an investigator saw no aura about a woman the day before she died. In the second case, a medium saw no auras surrounding people who met death a few seconds later. It is possible that the spirit guides of the investigator and medium blocked out *perception* of the auras in those cases, as a sign that they, the guides, foresaw impending death. But whether or not this is the explanation, the blocking out of anything does not mean it has ceased to exist, but only that it may no longer be as readily perceived, or perceived at all.

49   For no one's aura can be destroyed. It may be changed, yes; we know it is in a constant state of flux. But removed or annihilated, *no*.

1312 The Akashic Records – the Book of Life – the Cosmic Memory – Etc.

1   It is sad but true that in too many fields the simple facts are seldom presented *simply*. The aura is no exception.

2   Notable examples are the terms and descriptions purporting to relate *how* and *where* the impartial record of an individual is preserved, and *how* one is reminded of that record when one returns to spirit life.

13.2 Our Spirit Makeup

3 Many speak of the Akashic Records, the Book of Life, the Book of Remembrance, the Great Memory, the Memory of the Universe, the Cosmic Record, the River of Life, the Tapestry of Life, and other similar and often imposing titles. And among some strange assertions made is the statement that thousands of miles [kilometers] above the earth is a great belt on which is indelibly noted every thought and word and deed of every individual who lives or has ever lived on earth.

4 The facts, however, are either *unknown* to most "authorities," or in *their* opinion seemingly too simple, clear, and undramatic to portray as they actually are.

5 Too many confuse the *methods* of revealing a record with the *record itself*—a record that is contained in the aura [1311:12].

6 For there are various spirit-world methods of presenting that record (to the extent permitted) to new arrivals—other than to the very few individuals who for good reason can read their own aura.

7 And just as a highly gifted tutor on earth selects the teaching method best suited to the student, so does a highly gifted spirit auric scientist select the method of revelation best suited to the individual to be informed. The method might be a book, for the individual to read page by page. Or a spoken account. Or a "movie." Or a series of slides depicting significant events in the individual's past, however trivial some of them may have seemed to him or her at the time. Or any of several other methods. Or a combination of two or more methods. (Those presentations would of course be of a finer rate of vibration than similar presentations on earth; but they would be just as "solid" to spirit individuals as their like would be to people on earth.)

8 But regardless of the *form* of presentation, the full and complete record of an individual is in the *aura*.

1313 On "Bilocation"

1 In some circles there is frequent mention of *bilocation:* the [supposed] state of being, or the ability to be, in two places at the same time.

2 Most of the conclusions on the subject are obviously based on unawareness of either the spirit [etheric] body or its capabilities.

3 It is not uncommon for individuals under anesthesia to find themselves floating above their physical body, seeing and hearing what goes on.

There are too many thoroughly documented cases of this phenomenon to doubt that it happens.

4   Another phenomenon that has been abundantly demonstrated is what is called *travelling clairvoyance* [remote viewing]: describing what at the moment is taking place elsewhere, sometimes hundreds or thousands of miles [kilometers] away.

5   Still another is that of people on earth, musing or lost in reverie, finding themselves conversing with others on earth some distance away, and being recognized by them—with normal communication subsequently confirming details of the visits.

6   If we reflect in the light of what we know about the spirit body we will realize that there is *no* bilocation in such cases, and that bilocation is an *impossibility*.

7   We have pointed out that *the real self* always resides within our *spirit body*, which, when are in the wide-awake state, is as a rule confined within our physical frame. When we sleep, the spirit body usually goes on a journey, or it stays close by, outside our physical body.

8   — When anesthetics, besides producing insensibility to pain or other sensation, induce deep sleep, the spirit body usually retires from the physical body for a while, and *the real self* often notes what is happening *to* and *around* our physical body; but we rarely remember it on returning to normal consciousness.

9   — In one method of travelling clairvoyance, one or more of the medium's spirit guides are away and back in a trice to describe or present a picture of what they have seen elsewhere. In another method, a guide temporarily controls the medium's physical body, while *the medium's real self* travels in his or her spirit body to a place, observes it and returns, to either relay a description through the controlling guide or to present it directly.

10   — As for people on earth who suddenly find themselves visiting *others* on earth, it is merely one form of what some term an OBE, OOBE, or out-of-the-body experience. We of course recognize it as an out-of-the-*physical*-body experience.[8]

---

[8] Some also call OBEs astral travel or projection of consciousness. There are people and organizations on earth that research OBEs and teach others how to develop the ability to experience them, for the purposes of travelling, learning, and giving service in the spirit realms (other dimensions; see also 1329), interacting with spirit people, and remembering their experiences after they return to consciousness in their physical bodies.

13.2 Our Spirit Makeup

11   In the various cases we have discussed, as in others of a similar nature, *neither* the physical body *nor* the spirit body was in two places at once: They were in *different* places.

12   With the spirit body usually out of the physical body during sleep (and also during some other states), there are literally hundreds of millions of instances each day of the two bodies being in *different* places, connected of course by the incredibly elastic silver cord [1310:16]. But *neither* body is ever in *two* places at the same time.

13   Nothing is.

1314 Illness Does NOT Start in the Spirit Body

1   Some survivalists state that illness starts in the spirit [etheric] body, and that the spirit body must be healed before a physical or mental condition can be cured.

2   That is just not so.

3   This results from mistaking the aura for the spirit body. For as we have stated, our aura *surrounds* our physical [earthly] body and represents its condition, as it represents everything else about us—our character, our personality, our mental (which includes our spiritual) levels, in fact the sum total of what we are. Obviously we cannot change anything by altering its *representation*, which in essence is what the aura is.

4   In any case, as we have also pointed out, the spirit body does not envelop the physical body, but is almost always *within* it when we are awake. And the spirit body could not be cured because, as we have explained, except for its rate of vibration, it is a replica of the physical body in its *perfect* state [1310:17].

5   Incidentally, some spirit surgeons go through the motions of operating on what many people *think* is a surrounding spirit body. It may be good showmanship and impress patients who know no better, but any actual surgery or cure or alleviation of *physical* ills is performed on the physical body itself, and *only* on the physical body.

13.3 SPIRIT EXISTENCE

1315 When Does an Individual Enter the Physical?

1 There are many and varied opinions as to just when an individual—the indissoluble triune of soul, spirit, and mentality [or *the real self*; 602]—enters a physical body. Some say it is at the moment of conception. Some say it is about three months later. Some say it is at the quickening, when the child in the womb begins to show signs of life. Some say it is just before or during delivery.

2 Any of these opinions may be correct, depending on the circumstances, for there is *no* set time for that important event. The moment of entry, which depends on many things, ranges from the moment of conception to just before or even *during* delivery. In some cases, an advanced being may direct and guide the progress of the embryo and fetus until he or she decides to enter it, but this is certainly far from common.

3 What is important to remember is that the entry takes place according to *Law*, within the latitude enabled by Law, and that there are many spirit people who assist in the process. (Of course they assist not only in this respect, but in helping to preserve the life of an infant or child during its early years when it cannot take care of itself: Without spirit aid, that life would seldom long survive on earth.)

4 A similar variation, by the way, may occur after death. A young infant or child will usually grow and mature in the spirit world just as it would on earth. But highly advanced beings revert quickly to their maturity, unless for some special reason they do not wish to do so. Of course in manifesting themselves to those on earth whom they had known, they would present an appearance and a *content* of speech that would be familiar and recognizable.

1316 A BEND in the Road

1 In their later years on earth, too many people assume that they approach the *end* of the road.

2 Unaware that there is no death, no annihilation of any individual anywhere at any time, they little realize that they are merely drawing closer to an important *bend* in the road—beyond which bend lie the spirit realms, with experiences and opportunities of almost unimaginable beauty for those who have earned them.

13.3 Spirit Existence

3   Our journey through existence is an endless one, with a multitude of bends in a road that winds on both sides of life. On earth, "birth" and "death" are the major bends; but usually there are many other bends also, including those that lead to childhood, adolescence, adulthood, occupation, and old age.

4   It is important to remember, on both sides of life, that we are the product of all that we have been; that we are ever in the process of *becoming;* and that each of us determines, by our way of life, whether a bend in the road leads towards the depths or towards the heights: whether it leads us back to a valley; or close to a precipice where, if we fall, we must sooner or later pick ourselves up and slowly, painfully, and laboriously renew the climb; or to a mountaintop where we may rest, refresh ourselves, and prepare to make our way to another and higher peak.

5   If we live according to noble conceptions of what is good and godly, if we live according to THE LAW, we can approach each bend in the road with less apprehension, knowing that nothing can halt our upward climb for long.

1317 A Three-Day Waiting Period?

1   From time to time we hear the teaching that the spirit [etheric] body remains attached (by "the silver cord") to the physical body for about seventy-two hours after death, and that if burial or cremation takes place within that time the spirit body may suffer pain or injury. That is just not so.

2   Few if any would claim that there is pain or injury to the spirit body when a physical limb is amputated, even though a person always suffers some degree of shock at such a time. And of course there is no pain to the spirit body then—or at any other time.

3   If spirit people "feel" any heat or shock when their physical vehicle is buried or cremated before three days go by, it is only because that is what they had been led to *expect*. This is another illustration—we mention others—of the need to enter the spirit world with as few misconceptions as possible.

4   Let us think for a moment. There have been literally tens of thousands of cases in the last hundred years alone of sudden and *instant* severance from the physical body. When that body is in a split second blown to bits—as it is in some explosions, bombings, plane crashes, and automobile accidents—the spirit body is instantly severed from the physical body it had inhabited. But while there may be a little shock to the *mentality* of the individual, there is no pain or injury to the spirit body itself. In fact in most of such cases, the victims are for the moment quite *unaware* that they have left their physical body!

⁵ Another point to consider is that it is the custom of some peoples, especially in those hot climates where there is little or no refrigeration, to dispose of the body of the dead within twenty-four hours. We know of no case of any complaint of pain or injury to the spirit body of anyone who had accepted the custom, and who therefore did *not* expect disposal of his or her body to be deferred.

⁶ In addition, an inspirer says:

⁷ Regardless of how individuals lose their mortal frames, and no matter if they think they are alone, they are *not* alone. For even in sudden and unexpected tragedies where there is great loss of physical life, from all directions come devoted spirit souls who are ready and willing and able to aid people who have left their physical bodies, whether those bodies are intact or completely disintegrated.

1318 Reflections Relating to Our Path of Progress

¹ The USB emphasizes that not all healers or mediums are spiritual, or founts of knowledge. Many do not know much about the nature of existence beyond life on earth, or even about the mechanics of their very own "gifts."

² We should bear these things in mind when contemplating such assertions as those by a well-known medium that spirit individuals "no longer cling to personal identity" and eventually become so "purified" as to be "absorbed into the God force and returned to whence" they came.

³ Those views are *not* correct.

⁴ It is puzzling how anyone can declare that we come *from* God and return *to* God. Others put the same idea in another way: They speak of "involution" and "evolution"—descending from perfection into imperfection, and then slowly, tortuously, and laboriously making the long journey back to perfection.

⁵ But why should what is already *perfect* need the experience of being *imperfect?* And is not perfection the *goal* rather than the *beginning?*

13.3 Spirit Existence 1319

6   There are individuals who somehow cannot or will not realize that the Force or Power or Being that we call God is the *Creator*, and that only a *spark* of the divine is within us; and lacking such understanding, they picture God in their *own* image.

7   But as we emphasize, the individual who thinks and reasons about this finally concludes that God cannot be limited or circumscribed by our mentality [506:1–2].

8   It would be wiser to realize that there are certain things that must remain beyond our comprehension, certainly at least while we are living on earth, and perhaps long, long after, than to glibly make statements that show little knowledge and less reason.

9   As for personal identity, we do *not* lose our individuality when we return to spirit life. On the contrary, we *retain* our individuality, which is *the real self*—our entire consciousness, the triune of soul, spirit, and mind that we are, as we define these terms. In fact our individuality is not merely retained; it is *expanded* as we progress.

10   Another thing, by the way. We do *not* tend to become identical, however far we progress; for The Law of Variety operates *everywhere*, and on *all* levels of expression. Were it not for that Law, existence in the spirit world would be comparatively drab, and not as it actually is: fuller, richer, more varied and colorful and glowing and beautiful the higher we advance.

1319 Some Facts about Astral Bodies and Thought Forms

1   Much has been said and written about souls floating about in space because of sins of omission or commission while on earth.

2   There is *no* such thing.

3   When we pass on, we gravitate to the precise spot in the precise plane that we have prepared for ourselves by all we have done or not done while on earth—so perfect is Justice, as is every thing else that is of God, of course.

4   Misunderstanding of astral bodies—or "shells" as some term them—is responsible for much error in what is said, written, and taught.

5   We have mentioned the various bodies we possess while still living on earth; the fact that we use, as our outermost body, the one most comfortable for us in the plane we live in; and the fact that we discard them one by one as we advance to higher rates of vibration [1310:1–9].

6 Once discarded, the astral body gradually disintegrates—unless the person who had inhabited it mentally kept it intact with an eye to future use, such as returning in it to converse directly with loved ones, or using it to relay communication through. The astral body remains intact just as long, and only as long, as its one-time occupier directs.

7 Many great souls have no desire to return to the atmosphere of earth, and would not maintain contact with it if direct contact was all that was possible. Fortunately for us, however, they can maintain indirect contact with earth through their astral body, *to* which, and *through* which, they can project their thoughts and words.

8 Like a medium's body, the astral body is sometimes permitted to be controlled by others besides its original inhabitant. The reason is this: Only those who know the value of the astral body preserve it on advancing beyond the astral plane. In other cases, it returns to the elements of the astral plane, after which it cannot be reconstituted—just as the physical body, once returned to the elements of the earth, cannot be reconstituted.

9 There also exist *other* shells, shells that are often mistaken for astral bodies, those other shells being *thought forms* created [usually] by the minds of those who live on earth.[9]

10 Thought is indeed power—the power that *brings* things into expression [206:2]. And millions of worshippers on earth create, by the very intensity of their thoughts, thought forms of those they worship. Those thought forms provide great comfort to such people, who are quite unaware that they themselves have created them.

11 While spirit people can use the astral bodies they once occupied (or others, if permitted) to project their thoughts, they *cannot* use the thought forms created by those who live on earth, because such forms are controlled by their *creators*. For when individuals on earth create thought forms, they also create (within their own minds, usually quite unconsciously) what the thought forms will project or say to them.

12 That is why, in the case of "visions" of what are not astral bodies but thought forms, the individuals on earth see and hear precisely what they wish to see and hear.

13 Too often, people are their own worst deceivers.

---

[9] In answer to a question, Michael told me that spirit people can also create thought forms; but people on earth can only see the thought forms that they *themselves* have created. He also said that spirits tell the difference between spirit people and thought forms by the aura.

13.3 Spirit Existence

14 Thousands of people in different parts of the globe may at the very same instant "see" the very same person they worship—but in, almost every case (or every case but one) they will be seeing the thought forms that they themselves have created.

15 Another thing to note is that we do not change mentally by the mere passing into a different expression of existence. And spirit people who were, while on earth, of intense religious fervor, will, unless of great integrity, often produce or try to produce appearances that will excite the same religious fervor in others. They think, in their error, that the end justifies the means; but that of course is not so.

16 Thought forms [like discarded astral bodies] disintegrate only when the mental force that creates them either declines in intensity or is directed to another idea or creation. As long as the mind holds the picture, so long will the thought form exist.

17 The possibility or likelihood of thought forms is something that anyone who "meditates" should be ever conscious of—especially if a prominent or glamorous role is depicted for one, or if one's "communicators" claim great spiritual power or elevation. In such cases, one should make every effort to have a sitting from time to time with a medium or mediums of unquestioned ability and repute, to try to learn whether the impressions one receives actually come from spirit minds or from creatures of one's own creation.

18 If the impressions *are* from spirit minds, there may be need then to try to ascertain whether they are who they claim to be, or deceivers of one sort or another.

19 In all cases, however, as the USB repeatedly cautions, we should weigh well the words of most people on *both* sides of life, before accepting anything. There are too many mischievous spirit people who, like naughty children, deceive others for the fun of it. What is far worse, there are forces of darkness whose aim is to so disillusion the credulous and unthinking, and some of the thinking as well, that they will turn away in discouragement from *anything* that purports to come from the spirit world.[10]

---

[10] Some speakers and writers state with conviction that they have experienced strange but intelligent life-forms, for example like trolls, from other dimensions of life. Since no mainstream descriptions of the spirit world mention such creatures it is most probable that those experiences were either of thought forms, or of the work of mischievous or malevolent spirit people, many of whom continually strive to mislead people and divert them from the truth (1124:8–10).

1320 No One Is Ever Destroyed

1. Too often we read that a day of reckoning, a day of judgement, comes for every individual, with destruction and annihilation of those who have lost the path.

2. That is quite untrue.

3. For an indissoluble part of each eternal *real self* is a spark of the divine [601:2]; and a spark of the divine can never be destroyed.

4. Of course each day is, in a sense, a day of reckoning, a day of judgement, for each and every one of us, "mortal" and "angel" alike, in that we are constantly sowing the seeds of what will *be*. But the doors to spiritual progress are never closed to *anyone*.

1321 A Little about Twin Souls

1. A great deal has been said and written about *twin souls*. Much that is expressed, however, is more fanciful than true, and so we present a few facts on a most intriguing subject. Those who accept these facts will recognize some common misteachings for what they are.

2. Twin souls is a term used for the two halves of one soul—using *soul* in the sense of *a human being; a person* (and not in the USB's usual meaning of the spark of God within each individual).

3. For some purpose or purposes unknown to us, *all* souls were at one time divided into *two*, to go their separate ways for varying spans of time before eventually reaching the stage where they can reunite for good.

4. There are many conjectures as to why such division or separation took place, but they remain just that: *conjectures*. When Illumined Souls of almost incredible wisdom and spiritual elevation do not know the reason or reasons for it, we can resist the theories of those of lesser stature.

5. We have said on another subject: We *know* that *we are;* this we *know*. We know, too, *what* we are. But *why* we are, or *how* we are, this we do *not* know.

6. Similarly we can say: We *know* twin souls *are;* this we *know*. But *why* they were divided, or *how* they were divided, or *when* they were divided, this we do *not* know.

7. There are certain things that must remain beyond our comprehension, certainly at least while we are living on earth, and perhaps long, long after. But while we do not know the *why* or *how* or *when* of twin souls,

13.3 Spirit Existence

we can know *some* things about them, including the lasting and rapturous reunion that it is possible for them, *in time,* to achieve.

8   In describing The Law of Affinity, we noted that it is, in a sense, the finest distillation, the purest essence, of The Law of Attraction. For while we may attract or be attracted to many, we have only one *affinity*—our twin soul, whom few of us meet on earth.

9   People often say they have, or feel, an affinity with someone, when it is actually just an attraction to someone—a vastly different thing.

10   The Law of Affinity is definite: *one* has an affinity to *one*—and *only* one.

11   — It is not unusual for twin souls to accept different pathways for literally ages. They may not meet even if they *both* live on earth. And unless at least one of the pair is aware of its eternal tie to another, and thus naturally longs and reaches out for the other, they may not meet even if both live in the spirit world.

12   When either or both twin souls are *conscious* of their unique relationship, they are much more likely to meet—either during sleep state, if both live on earth, or during the sleep of one, if the other is in spirit life. Of the comparatively few twin souls who *do* meet on earth, not all recognize each other as such, or even know about affinities or the special relationship between affinities; but their companionship is in almost all cases a harmonious and happy one.

13   — Of each pair of twin souls, one member is *male*, the other *female*. Each *retains* its gender, which does *not* change while they are divided.

14   We can see why some who do not understand the structure of the spirit body, or the facts about twin souls, may believe that an individual's soul gender can change. This misconception, by the way, is sometimes based on dreams by individuals who little realize that most dreams either are not remembered at all, or are *distorted* in the recollection.

15   — Some teachers associate wisdom with the male twin soul, and love with the female. We do not. For *both* halves of one soul may possess these desirable qualities in varying degrees; and by no means is wisdom the prerogative of the male, or love the prerogative of the female. Ignorance on these points, incidentally, often strengthens the misbelief that one's gender can change.

16   In this connection it is interesting to reflect that *love* and *wisdom* are twin attributes that Illumined Souls ascribe to God, which attributes of course are revealed in countless ways to many who think about this.

17   — It is rightly said that the only perfect marriage is the marriage of twin souls—provided, we would add, that both are highly evolved and more or less of one mind. Twin-soul marriages are rare on earth, because so few meet their other halves here; but the rich and rewarding companionship of like minds is almost always possible, and should be sought. The harmony from such companionship will inspire most individuals to greater spiritual heights than they could reach alone.

18   — When twin souls reach the point where neither needs any of the experiences and opportunities that earth alone offers, they may, if they wish, become reunited, permanently this time, as *one soul*. The fusion of twin souls is an exceedingly delicate, long, and intricate process—but a glorious one!—that is completed only in realms beyond the Celestial, however much earlier it may begin.

19   The love between twin souls of profound spirituality is truly the *great* love, the romance magnificent, the passion sublime—dwarfing all other loves, beautiful and wonderful though some of those other loves are.

20   Can there be a greater incentive to evolving as rapidly as we can, than the knowledge of an affinity and the matchless love that only twin souls of high spiritual stature can experience?

13.4 LIVING IN THE SPIRIT WORLD

1322 Everyone Is Met When Passing On to Spirit Life

1   Every soul that passes on to the spirit world is received there, *without exception*. It may be by one spirit helper, or several; by loved ones, or those specially trained to receive newcomers, or both.

2   Of course the level of consciousness of the individuals received may be such that they do not realize they are being met, especially if they have been catapulted into spirit life suddenly. They may be taken to spirit hospitals, or to spirit homes of rest and repose, and be quite unaware of

13.4 Living in the Spirit World

it—just as victims of accidents in our own world may be in a coma for days or weeks or months, and have the care of doctors and nurses, without having the slightest realization of the ministrations they receive.

3 Some who pass on to spirit life cannot, because of their spirit blindness [1228:4–5,9], *see* the light of those who would minister to them, and teach them, and show them that they no longer remain in a physical body. It is in such cases that some "rescue circles" do so much good. By conversing with people on *earth* who are visible to them at these circles, such spirits can often be made to realize that they no longer are in the physical, and that they nevertheless still *live*. They are then usually much more receptive to other spirit people who wish to help them.

1323 *A Major Use of Thought in Spirit Life*

1 In the spirit world, thought is not only the magnificent power *behind* things, but the actual stuff of which things are *made*. In other words, there it is *of* thought itself that all is built. All the visible things in the spirit world, such as the magnificent edifices, beautiful scenery, exquisite gardens, and other lovely things that many spirit people tell us about, are created *of* thought—in many instances only by the united effort, directed to one purpose, of several hundred or even several thousand souls.

2 But it is *not* enough to just "think" a thing for it to exist, as many mistakenly believe.

3 For one thing, one must know or learn not only *how* to retain the visualization of a desired object—how to *hold* the picture in one's mind—but how to at the same time sufficiently concentrate and mold or amalgamate thought to *construct* that object. Not everyone can do this at first, of course.

4 For another thing, no spirit person can create anything he or she has not merited. Those who live, for instance, in the lower levels of the spirit world, levels where all is dark and dismal, cannot create sunlit gardens or mansions for themselves, regardless of their desires or their powers of concentration. For nothing can be constructed, let alone endure, in any spirit plane unless the atmosphere of that plane is suitable for it; and in a plane whose occupants had led earthly lives that were anything but spiritual, and whose minds remain full of ignoble and destructive thoughts, the atmosphere is necessarily of such a nature that nothing of

beauty and delight can be created in it, no matter how powerful the mentality of its inhabitants.

5   Such is the Love and Kindness that is God, however, that the moment any occupants of the darker realms realize and regret past errors and wish to make amends for them, or sincerely plead for a chance to improve themselves spiritually, "angels of mercy" [from higher realms], who have voluntarily chosen the mission of helping those in darkness, will make their way down to them to aid them and guide them towards the light [103:7]. And as they reach higher and higher levels of consciousness, the more will they be able to create and enjoy things of worth.

6   But even when an individual or a group of individuals has earned the *right* to create a desired object, the process is by no means an instant one. It is not enough, for example, to just "think" of a house for a house to appear. One must have a clear and complete picture of that house in one's mind—the size, the shape, the color or colors in it, the number of rooms, the type of floors and windows, and the hundreds of other details of architecture, design, and ornamentation. The house must be constructed as outlined above, but piece by piece, area by area, room by room, and so on. It takes time and effort.

7   We emphasize two points that many who know of the truth of Survival [of physical death] still find hard to grasp.

8   One is that things in any spirit plane are just as *real*, just as *"solid,"* to those *in* that plane as similar things are to people on earth.

9   The other is that in the higher spirit realms there is unimaginable beauty —far surpassing the beauty of anything on earth.

1324 There Is Speech in Spirit World

1   Some popular books, written by individuals who have contributed much to spreading the truths of Survival [of physical death] and Communication [with spirit people], nevertheless contain several errors, notably the misteaching that communication in the spirit world is conducted *only* by thought.

2   *That is just not so.*

3   And most of those who leave life on earth with the conviction that there is *no* speech in the spirit world, find that as long as they retain that misconception they can neither *speak* to others nor *hear* what others say.

13.4 Living in the Spirit World

4 On the other hand, those who know nothing of Survival and suddenly find themselves in spirit life, usually will converse quite naturally and normally with others, the moment they are conscious of them.

5 How could we expect a newcomer to the spirit world, untrained in the skill of communicating by thought alone, to suddenly possess that skill? It would be still more to expect of infants and very young children, and those who had been unable to speak on earth.

1325 The Importance of Vocabulary in Spirit Life

1 As we repeatedly affirm, to be on the other side of life does not automatically give one wisdom, understanding, or the gift of instruction, and we constantly urge seekers of Truth to weigh well the words of *anyone*, on either side of life.

2 This advice bears repeating, because psychic publications frequently report two "teachings" from "spirit friends"—teachings blindly accepted by too many on earth: that speech is "wholly unnecessary" in the spirit world, and that that world has "a universal language... *thought*."

3 Both assertions are quite incorrect.

4 For a *language* is fundamentally a body of words common to a group, community, people, or nation. And while thought is *not* that, thought is almost invariably expressed in *words*, silently or aloud.

5 In fact in almost all cases, here or in spirit life, we *think in words*, or language. We think in a language we *understand*. And as a rule, it is the *words* we consciously use in speaking, or unconsciously use in thinking, that form the basis of communication, whether on earth, or in the spirit world, or between one side of life and the other.

6 So despite what some assert, it is obviously not enough to just "think" in order for others to *know* what we think. If the thought is to be understood by others, it usually must be expressed in *words*, and in a *language* that they either know or that they have translated by interpreters.

7 There are many skilled linguists in spirit life who serve as interpreters, just as there are on earth. There, as here, it is an honorable calling.

8 What needs no language is thought that is revealed by menacing motions, signs of pain or discomfort, certain gestures, some facial expressions, and some body movements.

9   We wonder how those who maintain that all communication in spirit life is conducted by thought alone [without using a familiar language], would communicate such [USB] teachings as:

10   Think, and accept. Think, and reject. Think and suspend judgement. But *think!*

11   Correct what *can* be corrected. Accept *all* else gracefully, graciously, gratefully, and courageously.

12   One thing we can say with finality: There is *no* finality!

13   We wonder how they would communicate such sentences as:

14   Plankton is the aggregate of passively floating or drifting organisms in a body of water.

15   Viruses are ultramicroscopic, infectious agents that reproduce only in living cells.

16   A nucleotidase is any of the class of enzymes that catalyze the hydrolysis of nucleotides into nucleosides and phosphoric acid.[11]

17   Even if these sentences were *spoken*, anywhere, to someone face to face, so that there could be *no* doubt of exactly what was said, how could *anyone* understand them who did not know the meaning of such words as *aggregate, organisms, ultramicroscopic, enzyme, catalyze, hydrolysis, nucleotides,* or *nucleosides?*

18   Could we expect spirit *infants* to grasp their meaning? Or even every adult?

19   Does not the belief that language is "wholly unnecessary" in the spirit world suggest that *all* who enter it become instantly and automatically all-understanding and all-knowing?

20   As for those who say, as some do, that everything can be *visualized* for transmission by thought, we would ask these questions: How can one visualize *viruses?* Or *distinguish*, in visualization, *one* type of virus from another? Or visualize a nucleotidase, even if one knows what it is?

21   Let us reason further.

22   We have emphasized that in almost all cases we think in words, or language.

---

[11] A favorite remark of Michael's on this subject was to wonder how they would convey "to buy a pig in a poke," especially to someone who does not speak English.

13.4 Living in the Spirit World

23   *Thought*, which is mind in action, has *vibration*, and therefore is sensed as *sound* (among other things). In communication by thought, receivers will consciously or unconsciously "hear" the sounds of the words transmitted, but their *understanding* of those sounds will as a rule vary with their education and the languages they know.

24   Take, for instance, the sound of the English words *see* and *sea*. On either side of life, a French speaker could comprehend that sound as meaning, among other things, *so, so much*, or *if*. An Italian, as *yes, himself*, or *themselves*. An English speaker, as any of more than a score of meanings, including *ocean; a large lake or landlocked body of water; a large wave; perceive; view; recognize; meet and converse with; match (a bet); consider;* and *the jurisdiction of a bishop*.

25   Another example. The English *book*, the French *livre*, and the Spanish *libro* mean the very same thing. But they have different sounds; and whoever hears one of them would have to know something of the language spoken or projected to understand what is meant—unless an interpreter is present to translate it.

26   The English words *write, rite, right*, and *wright* have the very same sound. How could anyone who hears that sound know *which* word is meant unless it is in context with sounds of *other* words?

27   One thing more. In the spirit world there are a great many levels of instruction and education. There are innumerable occupations. There are meetings and social gatherings. There are scores of games that children play. There is a rich variety of entertainment, including operas.

28   Can one imagine *any* of them, or *all* of them, taking place without any *words* being spoken?

29   It should be plain that, with rare exceptions, *language*, and knowledge of the *meaning* of words in that language, is essential to expression and comprehension *anywhere*, regardless of whether words are spoken, written, presented in Braille or sign language, or projected by thought.

30   It follows that the greater our stock of words and understanding of the meaning of those words, the more ably we can clearly convey, relay, or receive communication of any sort, including communication by thought —wherever we are.

31   We would be wise to return to spirit life with as descriptive and useful a vocabulary as possible.

1326 Humor—and the Spirit Realms

1. We have emphasized that the beauty of the higher spirit realms is breathtaking; that contrary to much misteaching on the subject, there is use for every part of the spirit [etheric] body, which is a replica of the physical body in its perfect state; that there *is* speech in the spirit world, despite what some "teachers" assert; and that love and affection and beauty play ever more important roles in the scheme of things as one advances.

2. It is not a silent, ever colder, grimmer existence for the evolving individual, but an expressive, ever warmer, more beautiful one.

3. Some on earth are aware of this. Not all of them, however, realize that a sense of humor is a *characteristic* of spirit people of truly high spiritual stature.

4. A sense of humor includes humor and wit, both of which refer to the ability to perceive or express what is clever or amusing. But while *humor* consists mainly in recognizing, appreciating, or expressing what is diverting, funny, or absurd—all in a kindly way—*wit* is the ability to perceive a resemblance between things that are really unlike, and to express it quickly, briefly, sharply, and, above all, entertainingly.

5. Of course in the higher spirit realms, wit and humor are never used to disparage, ridicule, embarrass, or disconcert anyone, an inspirer tells us. He goes on to say:

6. > A sense of humor is most important, as it is conducive to laughter, merriment, and joyousness. And when laughter, merriment, and joyousness fill one's being, it is easier to rise to a higher level, because they increase the rates of vibration.

7. > The individual who does not enjoy a witty remark, or a story or experience of a humorous nature, lacks much that makes for one's perfect expression.

8. The higher spirit realms, we repeat, are *not* cold and still and colorless, but warm and vibrant and rich in color. Occupants of those exalted realms are not engaged solely in serious and deep study, inquiry, and service. No! There is room—in fact in those high spheres there must by their very nature *be* room—for happiness and lightness and brightness; and a sense of humor contributes to them all. We can indeed say:

9. > Humor is the leaven
> Without which heaven were not heaven!

1327 Titles in Spirit Life

In a communication from the spirit world in 1956, an eminent spiritual leader on earth of the early 1900s had, among other things, this to say:

> Over here there are no religious titles. There are no kings, no queens, and no nobility. Here we are only noble of the spirit, noble of the soul. Here we are all one in spiritual truth and realization. Here there are no barriers between people.

Similar remarks have been made by many others. But such observations are true only of the *higher* spirit realms.

In less advanced spheres, many who had ruled or held high position on earth delight in *retaining* their earthly titles, and many others find reflected glory and importance in paying homage to them. In such spheres there usually *are* barriers between people.

On earth, it is those in power and authority who confer titles on the rank and file. In the higher spirit realms, the reverse is true: It is the rank and file that confers titles, bestowing them on those they look up to, those they love and esteem for their wisdom and spirituality and nobility of purpose or achievements. In those realms, such titles as Mentor or Blessed One or Revered One or Illumined One are terms of profound respect or affection, terms not easily earned.

Incidentally, people of honesty and courage such as the spiritual leader quoted do not hesitate to acknowledge their errors when they discover them. It is a sign of the integrity that characterizes great souls.

1328 Time in the Spirit World

While we on earth need to watch the time for many reasons, there is little or no awareness of time, as *we* measure and understand it, in the spirit world. There it is *events*, especially events of great significance, that are the reference points.

Those who on earth are always conscious of the time, will *remain* conscious of it when they pass on (return) to spirit life—until they realize that time (as they have known it) is useless to them, and discard that conception, just as they will discard some other conceptions. Some spirit people use a calendar or clock, or both, to help them adjust their activities to those of loved ones on earth, to remind them to be with them

1328 □   Chapter 13 *Spirit Life*

on special occasions, or to visit earth at any particular season that enchants them. When they fully adjust to spirit life, however, they will realize that such devices are not really necessary.

3   Anyone on earth fortunate enough not to have to be a slave to the clock would do well to live as much as possible *without* regard to time, in preparation for spirit life and a timeless existence.

4   How do residents of the spirit world know just *when* a spirit activity will take place, if there is *no* awareness there of time as we reckon and understand it?

5   As with things on earth, things in spirit life start with an *idea*. Spirit impresarios who have the idea of arranging a concert, for instance, will advertise or publicize it by "broadcasting" the thought—a thought that is relayed by one or more minds to many other minds, who in turn relay it to still other minds, and so on and on and on; so that it is not long before all or almost all those in a realm become aware of what is planned.

6   The "broadcast" may list the program; state who will conduct it; name the soloist and choral group if any that will take part; and provide other informative details. There is no smugness: no assumption that the offering would be of delight to all.

7   It will usually conclude with the reminder that a notice will be "broadcast" just before the concert is about to commence. The notice would instantly reach everyone interested—such is the incredible speed of thought, as we have more than once emphasized.

8   While, in the higher spirit realms at least, only *accomplished* musicians would take part in a concert, a rehearsal, if desired for any reason, would be held immediately before the actual performance.

9   The audience would consist of all who wish to attend who can comfortably do so. Those familiar with the mechanics of travel in the spirit world could reach the scene in the twinkling of an eye.

1329 Travel in the Spirit Realms

1   We have pointed out that during sleep we may travel to the spirit realms for one or more reasons, most usually to receive instruction (or, in some cases, to *teach*), or to visit loved ones including those with whom we are *spiritually* akin. (We prefer the term "spirit flights" [or "etheric flights"]

13.4 Living in the Spirit World   □ 1329

to the more commonly used "astral flights," because many flights visit realms higher than the Astral [1301:2].)

2   We may also travel in our spirit body to meet people who are living on earth, and who sometimes remember our visits and even our *appearance*.

3   Though we rarely remember it, we are accompanied by at least one spirit person during a spirit flight.

4   A too common and surprising misteaching by many, on both sides of life, is that those living in the spirit world need only to *think* of being in another place to be instantly and automatically there.

5   That is just not so.

6   Thought alone is *not* enough: One must know the *mechanics* of such incredibly speedy movement. Just as almost all infants on earth need help in their first attempts to walk, so do almost all new arrivals in spirit life need help in learning how to transport themselves in a trice from one place to another. Some spirit people may aid new arrivals by, for instance, taking them by the arm, proclaiming a destination, and exclaiming: "Away we go!"

7   But that in itself is not sufficient. Spirit people must know not only precisely *where* they wish to go, but the *precise direction and path* to take. For in the spirit world there are many places with the very same name—just as there are on earth, where to cite a few examples, we have at least six Londons, at least three San Franciscos, many inland bodies of water called Long Lake, more than a dozen Woodstocks, and not less that six Yorktowns.

8   When spirit inhabitants wish to be in a certain place in the spirit world or on earth, they obviously cannot just *think* "Woodstock," for example, to *be* in Woodstock. *Which* Woodstock? And *what* path and direction must be taken to reach it?

9   We have been asked: What clothing do we wear on those flights? And who provides it?

10   As to what we wear, we usually travel in the attire that is customary in the part of the world we live in.

11   As to how the clothing is provided, it may be in any of several ways.

12   The spirit body, which is remarkably elastic, as we have mentioned, can be molded to look as if it is garbed in a robe or any other garment desired. People about to take spirit flights can do the molding themselves, if they know how. If not, skilled spirit chemists will either do that for them, or provide a garment made out of the atmosphere by the power of thought.

13 Two other things should be noted.

14 Not all spirit people have evolved to the point where they merit the privilege of travelling by the power of thought. Those who gravitate to dark and dismal regions because of the way they lived on earth, do not have that privilege; it becomes theirs only if and when they radically improve in character and aspiration.

15 Even those living in realms of light cannot always go everywhere. They would be uncomfortable in planes of much more rapid rates of vibration than they are accustomed to; but they can enter some of those places, usually for just a spell, and only if they are assisted by inhabitants of those or higher planes.

16 THE LAW is perfect. Spiritual progress is *earned*—earned to the degree that we acquire and *apply* spirituality and *knowledge* of The Laws That Govern [1425].

1330 A Little about Children in the Spirit World

1 We have often emphasized the wisdom of weighing well the words of anyone, on earth or in the spirit world. Well meaning though most people may be, too many judge things from limited knowledge and experience, and then fall into the error of generalizing from specific instances.

2 Such thoughts arose when we learnt of two assertions in a psychic publication, attributed to a spirit teacher, but lacking needed details. One assertion is that when parents and children pass on to spirit life at the same time, they do *not* live together, because the children go to "a special place in the astral." The other is that a mother whose children have preceded her to the spirit world will, on her passing, find them just as they were when they lived on earth.

3 There is inaccuracy or incompleteness in both those assertions.

4 For as a rule—we exclude cases where children have lived in terror of cruel or unloving parents—a family that passes on all at the same time remains intact in the spirit world, at least for a while. It would be cruel and inhumane to permit children to suddenly find themselves among strangers, separated from those they had known and loved. Nor would it please their parents.

13.4 Living in the Spirit World

5   Of course many family units in spirit life, like many on earth, consist of individuals with a variety of needs, interests, attitudes, and levels of consciousness. And *eventually*, of course, members of a spirit family may go their individual ways (just as happens on earth). They separate if there is a desire to do so—usually with the friendliness and good will that come with knowledge and understanding and the realization that they can meet when they wish.

6   Children without parents in the spirit world are cared for by any of several classes of people, depending on circumstances: There is no hard and fast rule. Whenever possible, and provided the atmosphere is one of love and kindness, they are placed where they can see a familiar face—that of an aunt or uncle, or grandparent, or older brother or sister or cousin, or some other close and dear relative or family friend—so that they will not suffer the frightening feeling of being only with complete strangers. If that is not possible, they are placed with others who will love and care for them: those who need the experience of looking after little ones in order to progress, or those who volunteer and are thought suitable for the task.

7   With children who are not old enough to remember, the need for a familiar face does not arise. But in all cases, those who show signs of not being thoroughly satisfactory guardians are replaced, to receive another opportunity later when better qualified.

8   Spirit children do *not* live in any special place in which adults of varying ages are excluded. As on earth, that would make for a narrow existence, hardly conducive to well-rounded development. Nor are they isolated from all earthly experiences. For from time to time, accompanied always by ministering ones, they visit the family and friends they have left behind; they attend schools on earth, to see and know what children in their native lands learn and do; they are present at festive occasions such as family reunions, parties, and picnics; and they are often taken to earthly events that are joyous or educational.

9   They are shielded from the agony of seeing fatal tragedies on earth, and they are not taken to areas in the spirit realms where the victims are brought. But in their visits to their native lands they sometimes do see and keenly feel—more than many on earth do—the heartbreaking lot of children in some parts of the world.

10   All in all, however, and quite *contrary* to misteachings on the subject, spirit children are *not* divorced from the realities of life on earth. In fact in many cases they are more aware of those realities than they would have been if they had remained on earth.

11   As for how spirit children appear to parents who join them later, it depends on the degree of knowledge the parents possess about life in the spirit world.

12   We know that while loving parents, during the sleep state, may visit their children in the spirit world, they rarely if ever remember those visits on waking. So the memories they almost invariably recall are the last earthly experiences and appearance of their children—for instance as infants, or as little boys and girls. If parents do *not* know that children grow and progress in spirit life, *that* appearance, the appearance they *recall*, is what they will *expect* to see, and is what will be *arranged* for them to see—until they realize that their children must have changed in the intervening years.

13   But parents who while on earth understand that children mature in spirit life, would *not* expect to find their children as they last knew them on earth, and would not be shocked or surprised to find that a child had become an adult. The wells of memory of their sleep state visits are unsealed, so that the child, now grown, is no stranger to them.

1331 Some Facts about Earthbound Spirit People

1   Spirit people may be earthbound for any one or more of a number of reasons, some of which are given below. The important thing to remember is that *earthbound spirits are not necessarily criminal in nature.*

2   An earthbound spirit may be one: who clings tenaciously to what gave her happiness on earth; or who has no wish to be free from the ties that bind him to earth; or who, because of her level of consciousness, does not see and understand the truth of spirit life, or if she does, still craves earthly pleasures; or who does not realize that he is out of the physical body; or who, even after she is taught and knows that she is free from the vibrations of earth, continues to desire to feed her body in a way that will give her satisfaction; or who, while of sound mind, had taken his own life in order to escape his obligations—*so he thought*. In the long run, of course, there is *no* escape from our obligations.

13.4 Living in the Spirit World

Those who take their own life because of despondency or derangement, or because of obsession or possession by undeveloped spirit people, can be helped by our prayers, which are as beacon lights to them. They eventually learn that they have not resolved their problems, which must still be met. They are not tied as securely to earth as other suicides, if at all.

1332 Some Facts about Suicides

A widespread misteaching about the fate of suicides has caused great anguish to many who are aware of survival, and who know of dear ones who have perished by their own hand.

In article after article, and from one platform and another, people have stated that *all* suicides are earthbound until "the normal appointed time" for their passing, meanwhile remaining in darkness and suffering the torments of the doomed.

But that is just not so.

What happens to those who take their own life is determined by circumstances. And for that reason, no blanket statement should be expressed —certainly not an inaccurate one that causes such intense grief.

Motive, as always, is a factor, though by no means the only factor on the scales of justice. And there is a vast difference in motive between the man who takes his own life in order to escape his obligations, and the woman who, distraught by the tragic death of her husband and children, puts an end to herself.

Could a God of Love and Wisdom and Justice dispense the *same* judgement to both?

We [on earth] establish special places for those who are deranged, and try to give them the care and attention they need. *We* don't hold them to be responsible for their actions to the same extent as those we consider completely sane.

Could a God of Love and Wisdom show *less* compassion and understanding than *we* show?

Suicides may be completely earthbound. They may be tied to earth to a certain degree only. Or they may not be tied to earth at all.

Much depends on their motive, on their sanity, and on the sum total of their entire life—*not* on just the final act alone.

1333 In Spirit Life, We Do Not Always Meet Those We Wronged on Earth

1 It is commonly taught that those who deliberately mislead others on earth, or harm or injure them in any way, *always* meet them later in the spirit world to seek forgiveness. *But that is not so.*

2 For one thing, victims living in far higher realms than the realms of the abusers, may have *no* inclination to visit lower realms even for a moment. They could, it is true, receive thoughts or apologies directed to them, if correctly relayed, but they may have reached the stage where the earthly experience no longer affects or interests them, in which case they may neither remember nor care to recall the incidents.

3 For another thing, abusers may not feel that they had committed a wrong, and then of course they would have no reason to seek forgiveness.

4 Victims could not forgive anyone, anyway, however much they could overlook wrongs. For as we point out, it is *not* in our power, or anyone else's power, to forgive others (in the meaning of cancelling a debt) [1415]. Nothing anyone else could do can prevent the harvest of good or ill that individuals reap from what they say, think, and do.

5 As for the many false prophets and teachers and others who in one way or another have deceived thousands and sometimes even millions of people, it obviously would not be possible for them to meet *each* individual who suffered because of them. In such instances, one way of showing remorse for their actions, or repudiating views they had expressed, is by proclamations posted in key places where their victims were (or are) likely to congregate on arriving in the spirit world.

14

Spiritual Progress

CHAPTER CONTENTS

14.1 Spirituality — **469**

   1401 Quotations and Thoughts on Spirituality by Our Inspirers 469
   1402 The Good and the Spiritual 469
   1403 A Note on Spirituality 470
   1404 Consideration for Others—a Spiritual Quality 470
   1405 There Is No Such Thing as "A Spiritual Bank Account" 471
   1406 Can One Regress Spiritually? 471
   1407 The Importance of Spiritual Development 472

14.2 Challenges — **472**

   1408 The Uses of Adversity 472
   1409 Perfection on Earth? 474
   1410 NOT All That Happens to Us Is the Result of Our Own Acts and Actions 475

14.3 Responsibilities — **476**

   1411 "Am I My Brother's and Sister's Keeper?" 476
   1412 The Garden and the Gardener 477
   1413 "Saviors"—and Annihilation 478
   1414 About "Leaving It to Spirit" 479

14.4 Forgiveness — **480**

   1415 Some Reflections about Mercy, Forgiving, and Forgetting 480
   1416 On Overlooking Faults and Wrongs 481

14.5 Enlightenment — **482**

   1417 Enlightenment 482
   1418 On Pondering over These Teachings 482
   1419 No One Is a Focal Point for All Light 482

continued...

14.6 The Path — 483

1420	The Path to the Mountain Top	483
1421	Excerpts on Spiritual Progress	484
1422	Closeness to Spirit Inspirers	485
1423	No One Can Walk the Spiritual Path for Another	485
1424	Some Lessons That Can Be Learned Only on Earth	485
1425	Knowledge, as well as Spirituality, Is Essential for Progress	488
1426	On Fighting the Good Fight	488

14.7 The USB View — 489

1427	The Dawning	489
1428	The USB Path	489
1429	For the Sower of Seeds	489
1430	Some USB Accomplishments	491
1431	The Greatest Need	491
1432	A Vision of Illumined Souls	492
1433	In The Brother&Sisterhood	492

14.1 SPIRITUALITY

1401 Quotations and Thoughts on Spirituality by Our Inspirers[1]

1 When people cease to live simply, they lose their perspective of what is spiritual [608].

2 The greatest quest is the quest for Truth; the greatest conquest, the conquest of self.

3 The wiser we become, the more we realize how *perfect* is Justice.

4 *Humbly* ask, and ye shall receive—spiritually. *Truly* seek, and ye shall find—spiritually. *Firmly* knock, and the door shall be opened—spiritually.

5 To live *spiritually* in a material world—*that* is the great achievement, *that* is the great victory, *that* is the great conquest.

6 It is *spiritual* people who make their way to the mountaintop—whether their skin is brown, or red, or yellow, or black, or white. The outer garment is no indication of the soul within.

7 In the long climb upwards, each individual grows in realization: from *denomination* to *interdenomination;* from interdenomination to *non-denomination;* and from non-denomination to *universality*.

8 Only as one thinks—constructively—does one grow.

9 A spiritual being expresses love as well as beauty. A spiritual being expresses the light of The Most High.

1402 The Good and the Spiritual

1 The difference between the good and the spiritual is motive, or lack of motive.

2 Whatever their motive or lack of motive, those who serve in *any* way usually do good to those they serve. People *do* good if they serve others, whatever their reason. However, if it is with the idea of personal gain or glory, the action is not spiritual.

3 Good people are not necessarily spiritual, but spiritual people are always good.

---

[1] See also Topic 608.

1403 A Note on Spirituality

Many are puzzled by the fact that some who profess to be spiritual, and who repeatedly emphasize the need for spirituality, little hesitate to take unfair advantage of others—even their friends and business associates—if by so doing they can gain materially. If it suits their purpose, they are not reluctant to violate the *intent* if not the letter of an agreement or understanding.

There are two things to remember here. One is that talk is cheap, perhaps the cheapest thing on earth. The other is that "handsome is as handsome does," as the old saying goes, and spirituality is evidenced less by words than by deeds. The *truly* spiritual will not knowingly do anything that borders on or remotely resembles craftiness.

Nothing is ours unless we apply it, the USB emphasizes. And whether it is integrity or spirituality or any other quality, we do not possess much of it if we do not express it in our daily life at every opportunity.

An inspirer has said:

> Truly spiritual people do not proclaim to all within the sound of their voice that they are spiritual. Nor is there need to do this. Their spirituality, if any, and the degree of that spirituality, will—to those who have eyes to see—be evidenced by their way of life, and in the ways they express themselves in all things, great and small.

1404 Consideration for Others—a Spiritual Quality

It is upsetting to see the littering of streets and highways and parks, the abuse of rest rooms, the taking of excessive space in parking vehicles, the marring of surroundings designed for the enjoyment of all, and the habitual discourtesy of many individuals in their daily lives. For such failings reveal a lack of regard for the rights and feelings of others—and consideration for others is a quality without which no one can be far evolved *spiritually*.

Much of the fault lies with those parents who show no regard or politeness to each other or to others, and who, by their general language, demeanor, and behavior set a lamentable example to their children.

What is needed more than ever is education, which includes discipline, which means strict enforcement of rules and ordinances enacted by a community or group of communities to preserve cleanliness, beauty of surroundings, and comfort for its members.

14.1 Spirituality

4   The experience of even so-called "backward" peoples proves that authorities *can* protect society from the actions of the inconsiderate if the desire to do so is strong enough.

1405 There Is No Such Thing as "A Spiritual Bank Account"

1   It is disturbing to note that there are those who teach that one can open "a spiritual bank account," add to it from time to time, and "draw against it" in case of need.

2   For this is a *grievous* misteaching. To draw a comparison with a material bank account is bad enough. To help give others a false sense of security that "a spiritual bank account" suggests, is worse.

3   To do *anything* with the express purpose of being rewarded spiritually, is to automatically fail in that respect, even if others gain from it. A man may for example, establish a center where he presents one or more facets of Truth, and from which visitors may benefit spiritually. So will he, too, if his motive is *selfless;* but if his aim is acclaim from the multitude or a spiritual jewel for himself, he will be disappointed.

4   To give with the expectation of getting, to do anything with the expectation of being rewarded, is not selfless. That is why, incidentally, we cannot subscribe to two of the closing phrases of an otherwise admirable prayer attributed to Francis of Assisi.[2] Those two phrases are: "for it is in giving that we receive, it is in pardoning that we are pardoned."

1406 Can One Regress Spiritually?

1   The answer is "Yes," it is indeed possible to do so. We can advance or retrogress in *any* facet of our being. We can advance in some facets, and retrogress in others. Overall, we can progress; we can, as often happens, remain for a spell on a spiritual plateau while we absorb what we have received and what we are receiving; or we can slide back.

2   But we cannot retrogress *below* the species of expression we belong to, despite some misteachings on the subject. We cannot retrogress *below* the specific range of vibrations that enable us to be human beings [414:9–13].

---

[2] Francis of Assisi, 1182–1226, born Giovanni Bernadone, Italian preacher, mystic, founder in 1209 of the Franciscan Order, sainted.

1407 The Importance of Spiritual Development

1. Illumined Souls emphasize the importance of *spiritual* development. One of them has said:

2. > These things that one so often refers to as development—remember there are *many* forms. There are many who are psychically developed, and excellently so; but there are few... who are *spiritually* developed. And it is *this* that matters to us. And it is *this* alone that makes possible the contact between us... Remember... that it is *this* that matters. Not the psychic force so much, important though it must and will be in our work. It is the *spiritual* force.

3. The USB stresses that among the highest forms of development is the mental attunement with great souls that comes to those who by their lives show their *worthiness* of that attunement. They may be unaware of that attunement, but it is real, nevertheless, if what they do and say and think is godly, if they are humble and sincere and serve selflessly in the way or ways that are at hand.

4. Among the spiritual things we *can* do, is to sit in the silence, with love and peace in our heart, and be *used* for *good*, if we ask it humbly and from the depths of our being. Enlightened spirit friends *will* use us then to bring light to those in darkness, or to those tied to earth for one reason or another. Advanced souls *can* use us then to heal others in mind and body, if they so desire; for we cannot be spiritual without being a channel for good, and the greater our spirituality the greater can we serve in that respect.

14.2 CHALLENGES

1408 The Uses of Adversity

1. *How* we respond to things, and not things themselves, is what is important to us. For *how* we respond to things—whether we use them as milestones or millstones along the way—determines whether we advance or fall back spiritually.

2. We can be bruised on the rocks, pick ourselves up, and resume the climb. Or we can be bruised on the rocks, relinquish the climb, and retrace our steps to the valley below.

14.2 Challenges   □ *1408*

³ Experiences can impoverish us or enrich us, embitter us or mellow us. *The choice is ours.* As an Illumined Inspirer puts it:

⁴ Many travel the pathway of disillusionment, the pathway of broken dreams. Some who travel that pathway become stronger of soul, richer of soul, more understanding of soul, more compassionate of soul.

⁵ It will give us strength if we remember that the mountaintop is never reached in one bound; that what to *our* eyes seems perfection is never achieved in just a few score years; that heaven and hell are states of mind, states of our own making; and that all the great prophets, teachers, seers, and enlightened spiritual leaders of the ages encountered sorrow and hardship and difficulty during their stay on earth.

· · · · ·

⁶ Adversity is one of the greatest tests we meet on earth. It is a test of our character, of our principles, of our spirituality. An Illumined Inspirer has said: "The earthly life is a testing ground of the soul." If we can be highly spiritual in a material world, we prove our spirituality and our worthiness to advance to higher spheres.

⁷ For contrary to what is often taught, we do not automatically gravitate to a "summerland" when we leave this earth. Only if we have *earned* it do we advance to a plane higher than earth itself [1319:3].

⁸ Adversities indeed provide us with opportunities to prove our worth. This does *not* mean that we should seek or invite illness or unhappiness or tragedy or the loss of dear ones. It does *not* mean that we should squander our possessions; or deliberately live in poverty or squalor; or, as has happened in some parts of the globe, maim ourselves physically for one reason or another. (The last, by the way, causes spiritual *retrogression.*)

⁹ But it *does* mean that we should live as nobly and as bravely as possible under *all* circumstances.

· · · · ·

¹⁰ It is important to realize that no one can escape or resolve *all* problems. Not even the great spiritual leaders of the ages could do so. However, they overcame the problems they could, and lived with the rest bravely, cheerfully, and without bitterness. As an Illumined Soul counsels:

¹¹ Correct what *can* be corrected. Accept *all* else gracefully, graciously, gratefully, and courageously.

12   To do so is to reveal spiritual strength—which is the right mental outlook and the ability to take in stride what each day has to offer, so-called good and so-called bad alike. Spiritual strength can come from what we have learned from experience; and *this* life—our life on earth—*is* in almost all cases one of experience. It was not intended that we should be able to dispel distasteful situations in an instant by drawing upon our inner resources; but if those inner resources include spiritual strength, we can respond with a greater measure of tranquillity, or a measure of comparative tranquillity, to all that comes our way.

13   Challenge is necessary in our lives, for many reasons; and the challenges presented by problems provide us with opportunities to grow in stature spiritually and to raise the level of our consciousness.

1409 Perfection On Earth?

1   We have been asked whether anyone is expected or required to be perfect. The answer is *"No."*

2   Of course we should *try* to live by The Laws That Govern, to the extent that we consciously or unconsciously understand them [1425:1], but we cannot hope to be without faults and frailties while in the physical on earth.[3] It would be too much to expect of anyone—certainly at least where there are many different levels of consciousness, many conflicting vibrations, and many temptations of every sort at almost every turn. In any case, the earth is a *proving ground*, let us not forget [846:3, 1408:6], and we may be tested often, whether we wish it or not, or whether we are conscious of it or not.

3   We have comforting assurance from truly Illumined Souls of an almost incredible elevation spiritually, who tell us:

4   We do not expect perfection from *you*—or anyone else in a physical [earthly] body—because *we* are not perfect...

5   It is not possible for anyone on earth who mingles with other people to always avoid "unworthy" thoughts or impulses, for those thoughts and impulses surround us on all sides, and often penetrate our auras, even if only for a moment.

6   As far as "unworthy" impulses are concerned, if we are not able to completely block them out, we can at least *resist* them [728:6–7].

---

[3] Our faults include misteachings we have accepted along the way, which are barriers to our progress and so need to be unlearned (208:2).

14.2 Challenges

7   And regarding "unworthy" thoughts, which abound in the atmosphere and crowd upon us—or which sometimes arise within us—the easiest way to remove them is to consciously *replace* them with noble ones. With practice, this will become second nature to us.

8   The secret, then, is to *resist* unworthy impulses, and to *replace* unworthy thoughts with lofty ones.

9   Instead of nurturing hatred for those who abuse us, for instance, we can, while with dignity refusing to take that abuse, pray that light will enter their universe. And instead, say, of coveting what belongs to another and to which we have no right, we can reflect upon the worth and beauty of what we *do* possess.

10   The road to the mountaintop is never an easy one, we stress. But even if we fall back one step for every two we advance, we still make headway, and our upward climb cannot be halted if we truly desire and make the *effort* to reach the peak. And while we cannot be perfect on earth, we *can* be highly spiritual in a material world and thus demonstrate that there are *no* lessons, of those available only on earth, which we *still* need to learn [1424].

1410   NOT All That Happens to Us Is the Result of Our Own Acts and Actions

1   The Law of Cause and Effect is well known: As we sow, we reap. As we plant, so is the harvest. Each thing we say or think or do brings its inevitable result.

2   But that Law is misunderstood by many, who assume that *all* that happens to individuals is the result of their own acts and actions. That is just not so.

3   Indeed no one is an island unto oneself. And indeed we do affect all we meet, and are affected by all we meet, in one way or another, in one degree or another, and for one period of time or another. The effect may be so trifling as to be imperceptible, or it may be pronounced. It may cause barely a ripple in our emotions, or it may affect us strongly, even violently. It may last only a fraction of a second, or it may last more than a lifetime and accompany us into other realms of our existence.

4   A man who commits suicide, for example, by blowing up the plane on which he is a passenger, affects not only himself, but others. And only a very unthinking person would assume that everyone else on that plane had merited death in that precise time and fashion.

5   If there are *innocent* victims of our actions, The Law of Compensation makes up for what they suffer through no fault of their own [408].

6   The Law of Cause and Effect and The Law of Compensation together form The Law of Justice, and because of this Law there cannot be *any* injustice *in the long run*.

7   We should make no mistake about this: Much that happens to individuals may *not* be the result of their own acts and actions.

8   However, as the USB stresses, it is not things in themselves, but the way we respond to them, that is so important to us. Each circumstance, each condition, so-called good and so-called bad alike, provides us with the opportunity to grow in stature spiritually. If we graciously accept a condition that cannot be corrected without causing harm to others, we advance a step. Greater is the advance if we overcome the condition—provided that we do so in a *spiritual* manner.

9   If we overcome the condition by trampling on other people or taking advantage of them, we not only fail to advance spiritually, but we *retrogress*.

10 Many people, by the force of their personality, make their way to the forefront of a movement, and acquire the reputation of being "spiritual"—in some cases only because their admirers do not know of the victims used as stepping stones in the climb to prominence.

14.3 RESPONSIBILITIES

1411 "Am I My Brother's and Sister's Keeper?"

1   An age-old question—"Am I my brother's and sister's keeper?"—is often quoted, with the response assumed to be in the affirmative.

2   But the correct answer is: "No, we are *not* our brother's and sister's keeper; we are our brother's and sister's *brother* or *sister*."

3   We are sisters and brothers because each one of us possesses a spark of divinity within us, the spark that makes us children of a living and loving God. And as sisters and brothers, we should walk beside others in need, encouraging them along the path, inspiring them to grow in stature and in strength spiritually, and, if need be, sharing their burden for a while if they become too weary to bear it alone [704].

4   But we should not deprive them of the opportunity to make their own way to the extent they can. We should not deprive them of those experi-

14.3 Responsibilities

ences and lessons that they can find and learn only on earth [1424]. We should not deprive them of the dignity and sense of worth that come to those who do their best to make their own way, who take pride in craftsmanship in their occupation, however humble, and who do all they can to be no charge upon others.

5 As we have stressed, we *should* help those who cannot help themselves, or cannot help themselves sufficiently—the aged and infirm and ill and unemployed.

6 There are, unfortunately, many who for one reason or another are quite incapable of attending to even their simplest wants, and who need help almost every moment of the day. But we are still *not* their keeper, but their brother or sister. We are our brother's and sister's *brother* or *sister*.

1412 The Garden and the Gardener

1 The gardener is responsible for how the garden grows, and so for the health and growth of all the plants in it. Many are the gardener's tasks, from pruning to uprooting weeds. When needed, the gardener provides moisture and nutrients, adjusts amounts of light and shade, and protects plants from wind and frost.

2 The gardener has much to tend—flowers, vines, bushes, trees, lawn, and shrubbery. And many are the virtues and qualities a good gardener possesses: patience; thoroughness; tenderness; knowledge of what *each* plant requires for full expression of its beauty; and love for all growing things, even those that, with a heavy heart, he or she *removes* from the garden to prevent harm to others.

3 It takes time and effort to bring a garden to its fullest beauty. It means that each plant in the garden must have attention, the specific attention vital to its growth. It means that when any plant begins to crowd out others, it must be either cut down or transplanted in a more spacious area in the garden. Only in this way will each plant receive its just share of sunlight and nourishment.

4 In the garden that is the USB, there are many plants, many beautiful expressions of nature. Everything possible is done to preserve them; and with diligence and great care are they nurtured, so that they may continue to gather strength and sustenance from the soil and the atmosphere. Everything possible is done to prevent weeds from choking them or stifling their growth; weeds are plucked out by the roots.

5   Everything possible is done to make sure that the USB garden *remains* a place where all but undesirable growth may reach out in any direction for sustenance.

6   In the garden that is the USB, there is ample room for all growing plants that do *not* seek to stifle or destroy others, and that do *not* seek to monopolize the sunlight.

7   The garden grows; and as the garden grows, greater are the duties of the gardener.

1413 "Saviors"—and Annihilation

1   Particularly during the 1960s [with their widespread prediction scares; 1004], there have been statements that beings from other planets will visit earth [706]—either to save us all, or to carry away to safety those who should be saved, leaving the rest to perish.

2   Whether such proclaimers express their *own* views, or the views of those for whom they are channels, one thing is clear: It is personal interpretation entering the entire scheme of salvation.

3   The question naturally arises: *Who* is to determine the fate of others?

4   Says an Illumined Soul:

5   There is not *one* of us who can judge for another which shall remain, and which shall go; which shall suffer, and which shall be made whole; and which shall take the high road, and which shall take the low road.

6   The individual *alone*, by his or her way of life, determines the niche he or she shall fill. *Not* one group. *Not* one individual. *Not* one mentality—and I include myself.

7   When one hears that from some far-distant sphere comes a world savior, remember this: You as an individual are your personal savior. And only according to *Law* are we placed where retribution takes place, and compensation, and effect. These are automatic Laws.

8   Do not look for an individual from outer space, garbed in outlandish garment, to suddenly fly into your atmosphere to free you. *You* are your *own* savior!

9   It is strange how many always look for *someone else* to do things for them, to release them from personal responsibility, and yet at the same time insist, quite properly, on their right of personal interpretation. They

14.3 Responsibilities

state over and over again that they realize that they themselves are responsible for all that they do, but they still seek *someone else* to bear their burdens. And not content with that, they prescribe just *how* the burdens should be borne!

10 Many feel that *annihilation*—in its meaning of extinction, or reduction to nothing—is the fate of those who do not walk a particular path. But eternal life is the lot of *all* individuals: It is something we cannot escape, even if we wished to [1320:3].

11 In the same sense of the word, there is no annihilation of the *physical* body either. It merely returns, in time, to the elements of which it is composed, once what animates it leaves it.

12 Not a *single* thing can be reduced to nothing. Changed, yes. Transformed, even beyond recognition, yes. But annihilated, *no.*

13 There *are* times when spirit individuals may for good reason be placed in a condition of dormancy or hibernation; and we can see how personal *misinterpretation* of this condition could lead to a belief in annihilation.

1414 About "Leaving It to Spirit"

1 Too many people, faced with any problem, even the simplest, sometimes with just the problem of doing or not doing something, "resolve" the matter by "leaving it to spirit [helpers, authorities?]."

2 As a rule, they accomplish little by such a philosophy, and miss splendid opportunities to grow in stature by courageously coming to grips with problems, deciding what to do, and doing it.

3 Our spirit friends can be, and often are, of enormous worth to us. But as the USB teaches, they—those of them who are enlightened, that is—come to inform and inspire us. They come to encourage us and strengthen us spiritually. They come to remind us of the laws of God, a God that is all-love, all-wisdom, all-justice. They do *not* come to do our work for us, or to deprive us of the trials and tests which, well met, develop our character and enable us to advance to higher spiritual levels [1221:21].

4 They may from time to time offer suggestions, and even relate experiences to illustrate a point; for as we teach, people may learn not only from their own experience, but from the experience of others [860]. But enlightened souls will not make decisions for us, or resolve problems that *we* should resolve.

5   Of course the picture is quite different where *unenlightened* souls are concerned. The bossy and meddlesome in the spirit world (as on earth) will try to run the lives of others. They relish nothing better than people who make no decision of their own, who take no step without consulting them, who accept nothing without their corroboration. Of course anyone on earth who depends on them to that degree eventually learns that valuable time was lost, and valuable lessons unlearned.

6   Just as loving ones on earth will do what they *properly* may for those who are unable to, so will enlightened souls in spirit life do what *they* properly may to help us. But while they may open a door for us, or point to the door, we *ourselves* must make the effort to go through the open doorway, if we are to lastingly benefit from a situation.

7   It is good to pray for strength and inspiration to live each day, and care for the problems of each day, as well and as wisely as we can. Often it is also good to consult others, remembering always that it does not lessen our responsibility in the slightest. But we should try to do all that we consciously know how to do, and can do, before seeking more than normal aid from others on earth or on the other side of life.

8   Certainly we should not just "leave it to spirit."

14.4 FORGIVENESS

1415 Some Reflections about Mercy, Forgiving, and Forgetting

1   Quoted for centuries is a famous line that millions of people accept without question: "To err is human; to forgive, divine."

2   This thought is beautifully expressed, but it is not completely true.

3   To err is indeed human. But to forgive is *not* divine: it *cannot* be. Neither is mercy. For forgiveness and mercy suggest a capriciousness and an inconstancy that are quite irreconcilable with a God of Love and Wisdom, of Law and Justice, and That Which Is All-Good. Spiritual laws, which are part of The Laws That Govern, apply to *everyone, everywhere, always*. While there may be countless exceptions to some laws created by human beings, there are *no* exceptions to The Laws That Govern.

4   However, far more sublime than mercy or forgiving could ever be are the love and wisdom revealed by The Laws That Govern. In the divine scheme of things, every cause has its effect; and for each of our errors of omission or commission we pay, and pay in full, sooner or later. But once

14.4 Forgiveness

we have paid a debt, that part of the slate is wiped clean, for us to again write what we wish on it, free from old scribblings and errors—although the memory of past errors may linger with us, consciously or unconsciously.

5   (Of course the debt is greater when committed, wittingly or unwittingly, by those who know right from wrong, than when committed by those who do not know the difference.)

6   Mercy is a human quality, an excellent quality if wisely exercised. Unwisely exercised, however, it may open the door to further ills, for many criminals who are prematurely released repeat their offenses or commit graver ones.

7   Incidentally, to exercise *unjustified* mercy to offenders is to assume a degree of responsibility for any further offenses they commit—something not everyone realizes.

8   We can be understanding. [We can cease to hold anything against them.] We can try to rehabilitate the weak and errant. But it is not in our power, or anyone else's power, to *forgive* others (in the meaning of cancelling a debt). For nothing that anyone else could do can prevent the harvest of good or ill that individuals reap from what they say, think, and do.

9   As for *forgetting*, nothing is ever forgotten to the extent that it cannot under the right circumstances be recollected. But in the fullness and goodness of time, and especially as we evolve, things that greatly pain and grieve us lose their power to affect us deeply, or to affect us at all; so much so that, looking back over the span of even just a few years, we sometimes wonder why we were previously so distressed.

10 But while it is not for us (or anyone else) to forgive, and truly impossible to ever completely forget, there are several things we can do. We can rise above vindictiveness. We can rise above hatred. We can rise above personalities, even while we can, and should, resist injustices and wrongs. We can bless all souls—*all* souls—and pray that light will enter where there is darkness.

1416 On Overlooking Faults and Wrongs

1   Though it is not in anyone's power to forgive another (in the meaning of cancelling a debt), there is much that we can well *overlook* [or cease to hold against another] in our day-to-day existence.

2   A person *does* grow in stature spiritually if he or she *within reason* overlooks the faults and foibles and frailties of others, and in some instances even the *wrongs* they commit.

3 But what one may properly overlook as an *individual*, is rarely what one may properly overlook as an *agent or representative of others*.

4 As an individual, to overlook faults and wrongs may or may not indicate strength. As an agent or representative of others, it indicates weakness and gross neglect of responsibility.

5 More than a few of the disturbing conditions society faces today are the result of such neglect on the part of many who hold positions of authority and responsibility in various fields. Those who fail to fulfil their responsibility do not advance spiritually; on the contrary, they regress. For in the long run there is no "getting away" with anything, despite what some mistakenly believe.

14.5 ENLIGHTENMENT

1417 Enlightenment

1 *Enlightenment* is freedom from ignorance, prejudice, or superstition. It is a comprehensive term that embraces both *fact* and *truth*.

2 Of course nothing provides greater enlightenment than truth, the greatest light of all.

1418 On Pondering over These Teachings

1 What the Illumined Inspirers of The Brother&Sisterhood present here in the way of truth are kernels, so to speak—kernels that expand as we think about them, kernels that may be developed into talks and articles that will help others [D27:9–14]. And we shall often find, as we ponder over these kernels, a flood of inspiration and revelation streaming into our consciousness.

1419 No One Is a Focal Point for All Light

1 We should not blindly accept the words of anyone on earth (in addition to anyone in spirit life). Many individuals make extravagant claims about themselves or others; and however preposterous the claim, some will believe it.

14.6 The Path □ *1420*

2   Even those who assert they are the Deity will not lack followers—as we discuss a little more fully elsewhere [B02:2–4]. Common sense is *not* too common!

3   From time to time *this* person, or *that* person, is described by himself or herself or others as a focal point for *all* light from the spirit world. It is a gross mis-description.

4   All individuals can be a focal point for a degree or portion of light, the degree or portion depending upon their capacity to *absorb and express* that light. But not even the *greatest* enlightened spiritual leaders of the ages were the channel for *all* light.

5   As a Blessed Soul says: "Not one individual or group is the focal point of *all* that is good, of *all* that is holy, of *all* that is beautiful."

6   Those who claim that distinction are *false*. Those who accept that claim are *blind*.

7   We in The Universal Spiritual Brother&Sisterhood are blessed in being part of the main stream of The Great Brotherhood, which is under the direction of truly great souls [101]. We are blessed in having received much of their teachings *directly* from them. And we are blessed in knowing that these teachings *are* the teachings of the new age. But we do *not* claim, and would *never* claim, the monopoly of light.

8   And we rejoice when we learn of *anyone*, or any *group*, *supporting* or *not* supporting the USB, *in* or *out* of the physical, that presents teachings true and undefiled, that *shares* our ideals, and that joins in the endeavor to make on earth a new heaven, where people might live in peace and love and tranquillity, and grow in stature and in strength spiritually [102:7].

14.6 THE PATH

1420 The Path to the Mountain Top

1   The climb to the mountain top is never an easy one [Sec. 7.8]. It cannot be. We are tried and tested time and again as we make our way to the heights.

2   The great prophets, the great teachers, the great seers of the ages—all had a difficult path to tread. All faced perils along the way. All were patient, content to take one step at a time, and to live one day at a time.

3   All had an inflexible purpose, a boundless faith, an unswerving determination, so that no disappointment or disillusionment could halt their upward journey.

4   We can learn much from them.

1421 Excerpts on Spiritual Progress

1   Only by consciously or unconsciously living in greater measure according to The Laws That Govern, can we raise ourselves one rung higher on the ladder of spiritual progression [503:5, 1139:4].

2   Those who strive, selflessly, to reach the heights or break down barriers or overcome obstacles, advance spiritually, regardless of the material outcome [773:4].

3   Everything that comes our way, so-called good and so-called bad alike, is a challenge to us—and an opportunity to use it as a spiritual stepping-stone [769:2].

4   We can grow in stature spiritually from the way we respond to challenges that problems present us [1408:13].

5   May we have grown *spiritually* for having overcome what *could* be overcome, and for learning to accept graciously, gratefully, and courageously, those adversities that have become a part of our life's pattern [A13:4].

6   *Every* tender thought directed to a soul in need, *every* kindly expression of brotherly and sisterly love—be it the spoken word, the silent prayer, the sincere handclasp, the friendly smile—every thought and expression is *recognized*. This recognition is manifested in the form of spiritual development, whether one is *aware* of that development or not; for by the very *effort* to help another, one reaches a *higher* state of consciousness [A12:2–3].

7   We benefit spiritually from giving only if the motive is selfless, without any expectation of reward [1405:3].

14.6 The Path

1422 Closeless to Spirit Inspirers

1 As an inspirer tells us:

2 There are many, many beautiful souls on earth who walk their path of life humbly and selflessly, seeking only to live a *spiritual* life. *They* are the souls who are commended. And while they may not be *conscious* of their closeness with spirit inspirers, they are nevertheless *walking* with them, and they are listening to the still small voice as they, in their *own* fashion, serve their fellow travellers.

1423 No One Can Walk the Spiritual Path for Another

1 A Blessed Soul says:

2 We cannot expand the horizon of *others*, but we can inspire them by the *example* we set. If *we* live according to our highest conceptions of what is noble, what is pure, what is beautiful, and what is true, many who cross our path will be touched, some to an astonishing degree.

3 The seeds we sow by the way we live, by the truths we share, and by our expression of what is good and godly, will find a fertile spot in some mentalities, there to take root and blossom and bloom, provided that the desire is there and the effort is made.

4 Where *others* are concerned, we can do no more than sow the seeds; the nurturing and the harvest rest with them and them alone. With all our love, with all our desire to help humanity, we can only point the way. *No one* can walk the spiritual path for another.

1424 Some Lessons That Can Be Learned Only on Earth

1 There are many lessons that can be learned on both sides [either side] of life, a far greater number that can be learned just in the spirit world, and some that can be learned on earth and only on earth.

2 The question, often put to us, "What are the lessons that can be learned only on earth?" sums up much that philosophers throughout the ages have asked (and attempted to answer) by other such questions as: "Why am I here?" — "Who am I?" — "Why am I living?" — and "Can this be all there is to existence?"

3   There are three points to bear in mind in considering the former question.

4   One is that the lessons that can be learned only on earth, and by that of course we mean in a physical [earthly] body, depend upon those particular experiences and opportunities for good or bad that are available here and nowhere else—at least as far as this planet and its spirit realms are concerned [1301]. The experiences may not always please us, but they are blessings if they provide us with opportunities to grow.

5   The second is that those lessons are not lessons that *all* need to learn, or to learn at the same time. The lessons we need to learn will vary, according to the state of our evolvement: It is a strictly personal, individual matter. We are the product of all that we have been, let us never forget; for that reason, few of us are the same in all respects, and none of us is the same at all times. So not all of us will need the very same battery of experiences and opportunities at the very same time.

6   The third point is that if we have learned our lessons well, we will prove it by refraining from wrongdoing *not* from fear of any possible retribution, but because the desire to do only what is right and good has become part of our *consciousness*—which is the sum total of what we have become.

7   If we review some of the experiences and opportunities that are present nowhere but on earth, we may discern some of the lessons that can be learned only on earth—lessons, alas, that scores upon scores of millions of people have yet to learn.

8   — Only on earth can one loot, vandalize, destroy, and kill.

9   — Only on earth can one achieve power or wealth by trampling over others.

10 — Only on earth is it ever possible to seize and *retain* something that does not belong to us, frequently by merely reaching out a hand.

11 — Only on earth can we suffer ills of the physical body and use them to grow spiritually—if we accept, graciously and courageously, what cannot be cured or alleviated, instead of indulging in lamentation and self-pity.

12 — Only on earth is it sometimes possible for us, by our outward appearance, to successfully deceive others, including some who are highly evolved spiritually. In the spirit world, we are open books to advanced souls.

14.6 The Path □ 1424

13. — Only on earth can we take the law into our own hands and sometimes seemingly get away with it. (In the long run, of course, we do *not*.)
14. — Only on earth do we have the opportunity to demonstrate that one who would serve must be prepared to sacrifice.
15. — Only on earth is there opportunity to deprive another of experiences necessary for growth. In the spirit world, one cannot live other people's lives for them.
16. — Only on earth do we have the opportunity to take up the defense for justice for others in the same realm of expression. In the spirit world, justice is automatic, though not always immediate.
17. — Only on earth can one gain in any way by sacrificing principle.
18. — Only on earth can one succeed in abusing or being cruel to animals.
19. — Only on earth is there the opportunity to develop a certain strength of character that comes from standing up for one's rights in a legitimate fashion, resisting domination, and refusing to be knowingly imposed upon.
20. — Only on earth can one profit by serving others for purely personal gain.
21. — Only on earth can one traffic in slavery or possess slaves.
22. — Only on earth can the unscrupulous ensnare or keep others in mental "bondage." Here there are lessons for both groups to learn: those who enslave, and those who permit themselves to be enslaved.

23. It is plain that life on earth usually serves at least two purposes. It gives us the opportunity to advance spiritually by resisting desires and impulses that we consciously or unconsciously know are unworthy. And it provides the means of determining the degree of our spirituality.

24. *Only if we are highly spiritual in a material world, do we demonstrate that there are no lessons, of those available only on earth, that we still need to learn.*

25. For only then will we in great measure live by The Laws That Govern, whether or not we are consciously aware of them.

26. Worthy of note in this connection, among lessons that can be learned on *both* sides of life, are the following two that can be far more easily learned on earth:

27. — Only on earth are there such *abundant* opportunities to demonstrate the courage of our convictions.

28 — And only on earth are there so *many* magnificent opportunities to exercise our reason. This is because of the vast array of truths and half-truths and lies, and teachings and misteachings, that on earth bombard us from all sides; and because it is easy, *here*, to mingle with people of many different levels of consciousness, including those of much higher levels. In the spirit realms, it is comparatively simple to descend and mingle with others of less rapid rates of vibration, but most difficult to ascend and mingle with others of much more rapid rates.

1425 Knowledge, as well as Spirituality, Is Essential for Progress

1 When we have learned all the lessons that can be learned only on earth, and live *spiritually* in a material world, we will then be prepared for further progress through the spheres. But spirituality, essential though it is, is not sufficient in itself to insure that progress. It must be accompanied by *knowledge*—a working knowledge—of The Laws That Govern.

2 One of the first and most basic lessons that many people learn in the spirit world—if they have not learned it on earth—is that they are always themselves, regardless of whether they are in a physical body or not. To countless millions, this facet of The Law of Life is most difficult to grasp, a facet that many take much time to understand.

3 We can see how important it is, while *still* on earth, to learn as much as possible about The Laws That Govern—or THE LAW—in preparation for our advance in spirit life to ever higher realms.

1426 On Fighting the Good Fight

1 While we are not expected or required to be perfect on earth [1409], we can, *on the whole*, live up to *our* highest conceptions of what is noble. We can show understanding and love and compassion for others, not least when we must discipline them. We can be true to ourselves and maintain our integrity, regardless of what others do. We can live by The Laws That Govern to the extent that we consciously or unconsciously understand them.

2 If we do that, we shall fight the good fight, which is all that can be expected or required of anyone. And we can then say, when it is time to leave the earth:

3   Weep not for me when I am gone,
          I shall have journeyed to the *known:*
        Old scenes; old friends to gaze upon,
          Greet and embrace—own of my own.
        The wells of memory shall be
          Unsealed, and all the glorious past,
        Half hidden now, revealed to me—
          A traveller home again at last.
        So I implore one thing of thee:
        Weep not; instead, *rejoice* for me.

14.7 THE USB VIEW

1427 *The Dawning*

1 Even if the night is black, and may become blacker, the light of a new age is here. Those on the mountaintop behold the rays of a glorious dawn that those in the valley cannot yet see.

1428 *The USB Path*

1 We who walk with The Universal Spiritual Brother&Sisterhood are truly blessed, for we are sisters and brothers on the most direct path. As an Illumined Soul says:

2   We realize there are many paths, and all these paths eventually lead back to God. But we know of *the* path, which is the *true* path; therefore naturally we are desirous that all shall tread that path, and find peace and tranquillity of spirit and harmony one with another in consequence.

1429 *For the Sower of Seeds*

1 Many of our Brother&Sisterhood's sowers of seeds journeyed along other paths before discovering the USB, before finding *in* the USB what they had long been seeking. Some of these sowers of seeds are beyond the first flush of youth; and if they become weary, it is understandable—

especially if they find that not all the seeds sown were planted in fertile soil.

2 But the sowing of seeds *must* go on; *it is vital*. And so we say this to those who would sow USB seeds:

3 Even though you tire, continue to shoulder the bag of seeds. Continue to plant a seed here, a seed there, as you make your way along the path of love and service.

4 Do not lose heart if some of our number fall by the wayside—or if some of the seeds were planted in what now seems to be barren soil.

5 If we sow the seeds; if from time to time we check on the growth of the seeds, to furnish any sustenance needed—this is as much as can be expected of any sower of seeds.

6 Let us remember, too, that the soil that appears barren may in some degree be fertile, so that it may *eventually* provide nourishment enough for the seeds to sprout. As an inspirer says:

7 There are some who question, who turn their back and walk away. But in the questioning, a seed may be sown. And one day, even though the back be still turned to us, the seed that was sown may take root and grow.

8 Many of our sisters and brothers are in close attunement with spirit people; and if they inquire, they will be assured of the usefulness of each sower of seeds of universal spiritual brother-and-sisterhood. And sowers who cheerfully and lovingly plant their seeds may look upon their efforts with rightful pride for contributing *their* share to the ultimate success of a great and momentous mission.

9 The sower of the seed of a rose is as indispensable to the beauty of the rose as the petals themselves. For the rose will not grow unless the seed is planted; just as it will not bloom to its fullest beauty without some attention, without some love, without some envisioning of the loveliness it will show to the world.

10 This suggests a thought we should hold in our mind: *What* this Brother-&Sisterhood is *becoming*. If the sowers of seeds will visualize the USB as it is *becoming*, they will realize that they are important to us, and valuable links in the movement.

14.7 The USB View

1430 Some USB Accomplishments

1 The USB has changed the *thinking* of a host of souls on both sides of life, as an Illumined Soul put it [in 1963], "of hundreds of people on earth, and many, many thousands in spirit life." Which is good. For all the worlds are *one*, and greater light in any *part*—greater light for anyone, anywhere—means greater light for the *whole*.

2 Thousands on the other side of life have been helped by visiting sisters and brothers on earth who, alone or gathered together, have humbleness of heart, sincerity of purpose, and the desire to be used to help others.

3 Much good comes from this. For many spirit people who walk in the shadows are invited or brought by enlightened souls to those on earth who open their doors in love and service.

4 The USB has made many realize that nothing is part of our universe unless we *live* it or live *by* it—that nothing is ours until we *apply* it—that knowledge without application is useless.

5 By the constructive thoughts and prayers of brothers and sisters on both sides of life, the USB has more than once helped to postpone or avert a world in flames—as of course have the prayers and thoughts of those who are *not* USB followers but share our ideals.

6 And the USB has given those who have weighed and accepted its teachings and philosophy not only a *new* life, in a sense, but a greater understanding of the *purpose* of life. In the USB teachings and philosophy, many have found something they had long been seeking—an oasis of truth and harmony in a vast desert of error and confusion.

1431 The Greatest Need

1 Awareness of the Laws that Govern is always needed. Knowledge of Survival and Communication is always needed. *Spiritual* mediumship is always needed.

2 But the greatest need today is *the realization that all people are sisters and brothers*, children of a living and loving God [601:2].

3 There is not one of us who cannot express that truth—by the way we live, by the words we say, by the things we do, by a smile or greeting or handclasp for those we meet, and by the love in our heart for all people everywhere.

4 The wounds people have inflicted on one another have been bitterest when some have looked down on others because of the color of their skin, or the slant of their eyes, or the way that they worship. We can help to bind the wounds by showing love to *all* who cross our path, and by both proclaiming and *living* by the principles of The Universal Spiritual Brother&Sisterhood.

1432 A Vision of Illumined Souls

1 Within two years of its founding on earth, the USB already had supporters in many countries, including the Americas, Australia, Britain, India, Malaysia, New Zealand, and South Africa.

2 Supporters form a band encircling the globe, a band that will widen with the years until it covers the entire world, to unite men and women everywhere in love and harmony and peace, in universal spiritual brother-and-sisterhood.

3 This heaven on earth—the love, peace, and harmony of a universal spiritual brother-and-sisterhood of all people everywhere—that brother-and-sisterhood which has been the vision of Illumined Souls for many, many centuries—will become a living reality within the lifetime of many of us. An Illumined Inspirer has emphasized this on a number of occasions.

1433 In The Brother&Sisterhood

1 The Brother&Sisterhood is a movement of hope and joy. Our step is firm. Our heart is light. And we rejoice. For we are ever conscious of the great and noble mission of the USB,[4] and therefore also of the Illumined Souls with whom we in The Brother&Sisterhood are linked.

---

[4] And you, dear reader, can be an important part of the USB mission. If you have read all or most of our chapters and appendices, you should have a good understanding of the purposes, methods, and goals of The Brother&Sisterhood, and of the significance and potential of our mission. So we now invite you to review *An Offer and a Call*, just before Chapter 1.

Appendices

APPENDIX CONTENTS

A	Addresses by Illumined Souls	495
B	Error and Misteachings	505
C	Reincarnation	533
D	Operation of the USB	537
E	The USB Leaflet	557
F	Glossary	565

A
Addresses by Illumined Souls

APPENDIX CONTENTS

A.1 Addresses[1]   **496**

- A01   An Illumined Soul, High Mountain, in 1956   496
  To those who wish to work with the USB
- A02   An Illumined Soul, High Mountain, in 1956   496
  The great need for the USB on earth; spirit support
- A03   An Illumined Soul, Alcoon, in 1957   498
  A call to join forces in service
- A04   An Illumined Soul, in 1958   498
  How to conduct ourselves and be good examples
- A05   An Illumined Soul, Alcoon, in 1958   499
  A call to service and to mediumship
- A06   An Illumined Soul, in 1959   499
  A greeting and benediction. Encouragement to help others, to share light
- A07   An Illumined Soul, in 1959   500
  A reminder of the USB way of life and its effects
- A08   An Illumined Soul, in 1960   500
  The linking and closeness to USB people in distant locations
- A09   An Illumined Soul, in early 1961   501
  To USB supporters—the great need for them to spread this truth
- A10   An Illumined Soul, in late 1961   502
  The responsibility that knowledge brings, to share, to do good
- A11   An Illumined Soul, in 1962   502
  Encouragement to spread joy, and to serve in one's own ways
- A12   An Illumined Soul, on New Year's Eve, 1963   503
  Every effort, thought, and intention is recognized
- A13   An Illumined Soul, in December 1965   503
  On learning from experiences, handling adversities, and growing spiritually

---

[1] These addresses are transcribed with permission from sittings and tape recordings made with the mediums mentioned in Michael Flagg's preface to this book. The first three addresses were given when Michael was discovering the USB mission and the part he was to play in it.

A.1 ADDRESSES

A01 An Illumined Soul, High Mountain, in 1956

1   In this great truth, in this movement, one must remember that each and everyone plays a part. Everyone has work to do. No one shall be greater than another. All shall work in love, and in harmony, and peace, and they shall rejoice that there is only one power that is a power, that is the power of love. It is the power of Goodness, the power of Justice, and the power of the Great Spirit. This power must permeate through all humanity.

2   And those whom we have chosen to be our representatives on earth, each and every one must be strong in themselves, of this power that flows through them, to serve humanity. And they must be humble in spirit. And they must not become one, as it were, with the ideals and the ideas of the earthly world. They must be people who are completely one in spirit and in truth, and who cast aside all material things, they must forget personal *desires* even, if called upon to do so. For the work of the spirit will supersede all the earthly things.

3   And the people that we need and use, must be those whose spiritual awareness is such that they desire only to serve the Great Spirit and to do the *work* of the Great Spirit, in *all* humility and humbleness of soul. For it is in that way that the work can be done, and only in that way. And they shall rise, and become indeed, spiritually great. Not materially so, but *spiritually* so.

4   For we come to develop the spirit, we come that we might inspire and give unto the earth world a great realization of the purpose of life, and what it can entail and what it can achieve when people approach all things from the spiritual aspect and desire only spiritual good for themselves and the world. For when people cast out all material condition, when they cast out fear, and put in its place that assurance within themselves that all is well because they are walking with the Great Spirit, then all these things shall come to pass, and each and every one shall be blessed.

A02 An Illumined Soul, High Mountain, in 1956

1   High Mountain very happy to have this opportunity once more to come and speak with brother [Michael]. High Mountain, with sister Alcoon, and other great souls here, look forward with great joy in our hearts to formation of organization for spiritual welfare of the children of earth. We

A.1 Addresses □ A02

know that from this can come great and glorious things. That the children of earth shall see and know and recognize the power of the Great Spirit, and of the love that He bears for His children of earth.

2   And so it is that you [Michael] come here to this new country [England], to receive further instruction from us, and confirmation of our desires and wishes. And when you return [to California], you commence this great work, in humble way. But it will grow, it will become big and strong and powerful, for *good* in the world. It will *only* be for good. And all who join with us, and are part of this great plan, must be humble in spirit, as instruments of the Most High, realizing that they have been called to serve humanity, to do the will of the Great Spirit; that His children may be blessed, that they may see and understand and know the laws of spirit; that they might find a peace and a joy while yet upon earth, in the things that are of spirit.

3   There is so much that we want to do. And it shall be achieved. For behind this great and momentous work are souls of *high* stature in spirit [life], some who you know, and many souls who you do not know. But all coming from the spheres of the highest [spiritual] attainment and achievement—realizing the need, as we do, that the earth shall have this knowledge, that it might save itself while there is yet time, from destruction.

4   In your world today there is chaos in people's hearts and minds throughout the world. In all nations, in all peoples, in all creeds, in all religions, there is doubt, there is fear, there is uncertainty. We come to bring assurance, we come to bring knowledge. And above all we come to bring love for the great Divine Creator of all, into the hearts, into the minds, that in time the peoples of earth shall see, and know, of that which is of God; and in themselves shall become changed, and shall become disciples of the Most High, that their one desire is to serve God, and to do God's work; to bring peace into your world, to bring love into the hearts of all God's children. And all the barriers that stand between people shall be broken down by the love and the power of the spirit.

5   You [Michael] are a humble instrument of our work. But we need many, many such as you. And they shall come, into the fold, and become one with us and for us. And our great and glorious truth shall set them free, and they shall know and realize the purposes of life. And they shall change the face of humanity upon earth. And joy and peace and love shall reign, where now chaos and hatred and intolerance reign. We see in your world the great need for our truths. If only there were more and

more disciples like unto yourself. But we shall find them.

6   And those who hear my voice now, I call upon them to come, to join with us, to organize this great spiritual work for humanity, that they might play a part now, that we can do together so much for the world, which is in such travail and torment of the soul. You have seen how human beings have brought into their lives such unhappiness, such bitterness. How, through wrong thinking and wrong living, they have created havoc, and indeed a hell upon earth. We come to sweep away many things of the old order. We come to break down many of the barriers that have stood between people. We come to break the chains that have bound them. We want to make them free and unfettered, in spirit and in truth. We need all the helpers.

[Michael established the USB on earth in December 1956]

A03 An Illumined Soul, Alcoon,[2] in 1957

1   To those who might yet listen to these recordings, I say: Be with us in heart and in spirit and in truth. Forget yourselves in love, and in true service.

2   Seek not the things of the earth, for they shall be taken from you. Seek the Kingdom of God, and all things shall be added unto you.

3   Remember the truths of the Great Ones of the past. Remember what they have sacrificed and done. Try therefore to be like unto them.

4   Be instruments of good in the truest sense, forgetting thyself in love and in service, and making thyself an altar, that those who would worship God can find through you a channel, that only what is pure and good shall come. For all who would serve must be pure in heart.

A04 An Illumined Soul, in 1958

1   You, who are the custodians of this great truth, must be an example in your world, and each of you must give forth that light which will illumine the path of others.

---

[2] A colleague of Alcoon's mentioned that she is known in the spirit world as "The Songbird of the Spheres."

A.1 Addresses

2   Cast from yourselves the weaknesses of the flesh—the envy, the bitterness, the pettiness, and the jealousies. Be of good faith and high moral courage, and know that the spirit of God floweth freely through to those whose minds and hearts are receiving stations in the true sense and.... meaning of that term.

A05   An Illumined Soul, Alcoon, in 1958

1   Come to us! Work with us! Give us the opportunity to serve through you! And the channels [mediums]—let them be found, let them be cleansed, let them be made whole. And we can serve through them, and work with them, and we can illumine the lives of all humanity.

2   Our task is God's task. And you who are God's servants, as we are also—let us strive together, in sincerity and in truth, and in complete oneness, in harmony, in brother-and-sisterhood.

A06   An Illumined Soul, in 1959

1   As these words are being directed to *all* of our sisters and brothers, I place my hands upon each of you, in benediction and love.

2   I greet you, and I look upon you, and I see my children, my brothers and sisters, each in your own fashion making your way unto the greater light of understanding, and each in your own way *living* your life in a fashion that you *alone* can live.

3   For each of you, in your *own* manner, serves your God. Each of you, in your *own* fashion, extends your hands and your heart to your fellow human beings. Each of you brings to your fellow traveller a bit of light as you *alone* can bring it, and as you *alone* can share it.

4   For each of you is personally making a way for not only yourself, but for those who travel with you. You are making the way a little lighter, and you are showing what *can* be done when one feels the glory of God within, and feels within that in order for that light to shine round and about, one must *share* some of that light with one's fellow travellers.

5   And to each of you I would say: Remember that we are *one* great band [or family or team], each individual contributing their just share to make a complete whole.

6   It is good. It is good. And I am well pleased.

7   With this greeting there comes a blessing as well, the blessedness of peace profound within you.

8   I shall come from time to time, and you shall *know* that I am with you.

9   It is so. I have spoken. It is so.

A07 An Illumined Soul, in 1959
(to those who join in the USB's way of life)

1   There will be many crossing our doorstep. There will be those brought to our door that would wish to enter in, and that would wish to join in our [the USB's] way of life. To all of these do we say:

2   Welcome, my sister, my brother, welcome! But please remember that our way of life is one that brings you closer to the All-High. And our way of life is one that would teach you not to overlook the trials and tribulations that pass your way, but to accept them cheerfully and to renew your strength spiritually, and to realize and understand their purpose.

3   Our way of life will *give* you strength of character. Our way of life will plant the seed of service more deeply within your being. And our way of life will encourage you to extend your hands—*both of them*—in brotherly and sisterly love across the seven seas to *all* the children of earth...

A08 An Illumined Soul, in 1960

1   We shall address ourselves at this time to those of our supporters in the far-distant places; and as we do, we shall bless each one with the great love of service to their fellow human beings.

2   Once again I address myself to *each* of you who are in the faraway places.

3   While we are indeed linked together as sisters and brothers in this great undertaking—those of you who are by yourselves or who are gathered together in small groups, attempting in your own fashion to spread the light, know that you have the blessings of The Most High.

4   Know that I at times draw nigh unto *each* of you, and feel the glow that permeates your being, and realize that *each* of you is indeed linked in a great and mighty chain, a chain that is forceful and dynamic, and a chain that will link one to the other, one to the other, until all who walk

A.1 Addresses   ☐ A09

the face of the earth *are* as brothers and sisters—are *indeed* as brothers and sisters in spirit.

5 While we make our way, we *are* being served. And as we serve one the other, know that the blessedness that comes from such service shall bring to each of you that which is your soul's desire.

6 Would that I could clasp *each* of you to me! Know that spiritually it is done.

7 And know that spiritually *each* of you is given the banner of Truth. Walk upright! And *let your voice be heard.*

A09 An Illumined Soul, in early 1961
(to those who support the USB)

1 As I greet you, children of earth, I do so with great joy—because of those of you who have gathered yourselves unto us, and brought with you your desires to serve and your desires to unfold your latent abilities.

2 As we have looked upon you, and have seen the sincerity of purpose that fills your being, we have been *very* grateful for the step you have taken. You have associated yourself with us. You have joined with us in our band [or family]. And we look ahead to the day, in the not too distant future, when more and more links shall be added to our chain, when there shall truly be upon the face of the earth The Brother&Sisterhood in its fullest expression.

3 For the need is *now*, and the need is *great*, for each of you in your *own* fashion to share your light with your fellow traveller; and to remember that as you do, so is added unto yourselves a still greater portion of what you are seeking, or what *is* the desire of your heart.

4 We are sisters and brothers, and we shall continue to seek for what shall bring to the children of earth the peace that they are searching for. We shall continue to bring to those hungry souls [spiritual] food to satisfy their craving [516:7].

5 And there shall be a glow within each child of earth that shall shine brightly, that shall bring to those who walk in the shadows a light that shall better enable them to make their way along the path that leads to greater understanding.

6 Let us take heart in the knowing that *each* of us plays an important role, *each* of us according to a plan, and *each* of us fulfilling that plan.

7   There are those among you who are not aware of the importance of this mission. And to those of you who come seeking for self alone, we say to you: "Bless you, my child; we do not share with you for self alone."

8   There are those among you who have a *great* realization of our mission —to free the children of earth from the shackles that bind them, and to bring to them the truth of the brother-and-sisterhood of humankind in its fullest expression, encircling the globe, and at last bringing peace to the children of earth.

9   I leave my blessings with each of you. And I pray that the God of your heart's understanding shall grant unto each of you *everything* that is the soul's desire.

A10 An Illumined Soul, in late 1961
(when asked whether he wished to greet our followers)

1   Of course do I greet them! Of course do I inspire them to realize the powers within themselves, and to remember that the knowledge within them brings—as knowledge *always* does—great and grave responsibility.

2   I know that *each* of them is reaching up for the light, and absorbing each grain, each kernel of truth, as best they can.

3   I know that they are *sharing* that light, and that truth, by a smile, by a handclasp, by a kindly word or thought or deed.

4   I continue to urge *each* of them, in their own fashion, in a manner that is their very own, and in the way that *they* understand it, to *go forth and do good!*

A11 An Illumined Soul, in 1962
(when asked to speak on anything dear to his heart)

1   What would I speak of? I would speak of *all* the hungry ones. I would speak for *all* of the weary ones, *all* who are heavily laden with burdens, and *all* who seek the light. I would speak *of* and *for* these children. And I would say that somewhere, somehow, there will be those leaders among leaders that shall be brought to an understanding with one another, so that their peoples may receive what is vital, and live each day free from the fear of annihilation...

2   *This* would I speak of, and much more. And *this* would I say to *all* people:

A.1 Addresses A13

3   Let your light so shine, that those who seek it shall absorb it! Let your heart so sing, that those who cross your path shall feel the joy that is yours.

4   The hands that serve, and the lips that pray, can combine their service for the good of humanity.

5   And when we say to our people to go forth and do good, let *each* be the sole judge as to *what* good they can do... Let each one, in their *own* way, in their *own* fashion, as it is *their* soul's desire, *go forth and do good.*

6   This would I say. *This* would I say!

A12 An Illumined Soul, on New Year's Eve, 1963
(when invited to address USB supporters)

1   What would I say to our people as they face another year? I would say *this*.

2   *Every* effort is recognized. *Every* tender thought directed to a soul in need, *every* kindly expression of brotherly and sisterly love—be it the spoken word, the silent prayer, the sincere handclasp, the friendly smile —every thought and expression are *recognized*, whether they are received, or whether they are repelled.

3   This recognition is manifested in the form of spiritual development, whether one is *aware* of that development or not; for by the very *effort* to help another, one reaches a *higher* state of consciousness. And so I would say to you: Let not *one* day go by without a kindly thought, expressed in your *own* fashion, for a fellow traveller.

4   Our lives are judged not by results alone, but by *intent* as well.

5   A life well lived is a life devoted not only to self-realization, but to *service* to one's fellow human beings.

6   And one cannot be of service to one's fellow human beings *without* being of service to one's God.

A13 An Illumined Soul, in December 1965

1   We have lived through another year. Many have been the experiences of each of us. *All* have been for good, whether or not we have been *conscious* of it.

2   As we approach the New Year, may we set in their *proper* niche our experiences of the past; and may they stand us in *good* stead during the experiences yet to come.

3   May we have learned much of *good* from what has been our lot. And may we look ahead to greater and more glorious adventures that shall be instrumental, *in time*, in bringing fulfillment of our desires.

4   May we have grown *spiritually* for having overcome what *could* be overcome, and for learning to accept graciously, gratefully, and courageously, those adversities that have become a part of our life's pattern.

5   May the next twelve months bring, within *each* of us, a greater *realization* that *we are sisters and brothers all!*

B
Error and Misteachings[1]

APPENDIX CONTENTS

B.1 Error — 506

   B01 On Teaching Untruth and Denying Truth to Others — 506
   B02 Of Some False "Leaders"—and the Gullibility of Some Humans — 506
   B03 Some Schools of Thought Hinder the Cause of Truth — 507
   B04 Of Orthodoxy and Mediumship — 508
   B05 Of Many Courses and Seminars — 510
   B06 Of a Certain "Seminar" — 510
   B07 Of Certain "Authorities"—the Blind Leading the Blind — 511
   B08 The Mine of Misinformation — 512
   B09 On Certain Psychic "Discoveries" — 513

B.2 Misteachings — 521

   B10 On Some Common Misteachings — 521
   B11 On Misteachings by Spirit "Teachers" — 524
   B12 On Misteachings by Mediums — 526
   B13 On Misteachings by Unorthodox Healers — 531

---

[1] We include these topics to enable the more serious investigator to exercise reason by studying and learning from the attitudes of USB inspirers to error and misteachings, and from examples of what the USB is convinced are error and misteachings, and also to help expose what we feel certain is false (325:1). We remind readers of the repeated declarations of Illumined Souls that they give us only truth as they see it (303:2), and that they advise us to accept or reject as we see fit (209:4). Also, we have pointed out more than once that those who enter the spirit world with profound misconceptions can experience many frustrations and heartaches (e.g., 1228:5–10, 324:n18, 324); so it is with the hope of *preventing* such distress of our sisters and brothers that we discuss significant misteachings that we have come to know of.

B.1 ERROR

B01 On Teaching Untruth and Denying Truth to Others

1 There are now more false teachers (and prophets and seers) than ever before, mostly capitalizing on the great hunger for spiritual Truth in this new age we are in. Some, who are opposed to certain truths, also hinder the spread of enlightenment wilfully.

2 Those who know the truth, but wilfully deny it to the humble seeker who is ready for it, commit an error that must be balanced.

3 To teach *any* untruth or to misrepresent a fact is to incur a debt that must be paid. To *wilfully* and *knowingly* do it, is to incur a greater debt. And for *each* seeker who is misled, a *separate* debt is incurred. That is The Law [407].

4 Some in positions of high responsibility on earth are incurring debts that will take them literally eons to pay. For when one is aware of the truths of Survival [of physical death] and Communication [with spirit people] (though perhaps not precisely as *we* understand them), and in fact has witnessed demonstrations of these truths, it is a grave error to deny them to the humble souls who inquire.

5 It is obviously far more grievous to wilfully, deliberately, determinedly, and sometimes even by the threat of extreme punishment, so terrify humble seekers that they seek no further, effectively barring them from the enlightenment and comfort and joy that these truths can bring.

6 Truth would free people from the crippling chains of dogmas and creeds and ignorance that bind them. It would mean the end of anyone having power over the people. False teachers know this. But regardless of motive, false teachers who assume authority for what people may or may not believe, what people may or may not think, what people may or may not investigate, or what people may or may not know—*such* teachers are incurring debts of a magnitude and duration that would astonish anyone who was not aware of The Law.

B02 Of Some False "Leaders"
—and the Gullibility of Some Humans

1 False claimants to Deity line the pages of history. This has persisted throughout the ages, and the past hundred years has been (and still is) no different.

B.1 Error ☐ B03

2 In the last few decades alone [before 1977], numerous people have either *claimed* to be God, or have tacitly approved of followers doing so on their behalf.

3 It is strange, and abundant testimony to the gullibility and lack of reason that are too common, that individuals have only to assert that they are God, or have others say that they are, to find hundreds and sometimes even thousands flocking to their banner, to worship them, to bow down before them, literally and metaphorically, to feel honored when given a mere glance by them, to delight in performing the most menial tasks in their service, tasks ordinarily performed only reluctantly or not at all, and to rejoice in living lives devoted to them—unless and until those followers come to their senses.

4 Others may not go so far as to claim to be God, but subtly or openly create and encourage the belief that they are of most exalted spiritual elevation—when the truth is far from it.

5 In both cases, the passion for unmerited acclaim and prestige overrides all other considerations.

6 We should pity those who "sell their soul" because of an excessive desire for admiration and adulation. For certainly no one would envy them their lot when the scales [of perfect justice] are balanced [409].

7 Of course truly Illumined Souls do *not* claim any special divinity other than the spark of the divine [601:2] that *every* child of God, on earth and in spirit life, possesses. They neither praise their own stature nor accept worship. As they teach:

8 We may love all, we may respect many, we may revere a few, but we should worship only God.

B03 Some Schools of Thought Hinder the Cause of Truth

1 While the cause of Truth presses forward slowly but surely, the advance has not been an unbroken one; for from time to time throughout the ages, the cause has been retarded here and there for a number of reasons, sometimes for a short span, sometimes for centuries. In comparatively recent times, the advance has been slowed by several schools of thought, and by two practices in particular.

2 In some schools of thought leaders have successfully used (or use) mediumship *not* as a channel to present truths that can set others free, but as a stepping stone towards the ignoble goal of personal glory or

aggrandizement or financial gain at the expense of Truth. Behind what to the undiscerning was (or is) an apparently humble exterior, they put themselves, or allow themselves to be placed by their admirers, on a pedestal to be worshipped, thus attracting and influencing people who do not think for themselves but look to *others* for a passport to "salvation."

3 In other schools of thought we find the after-death elevation, by their followers, of some who were truly humble and excellent mediums along certain lines, but who have since been credited with immensely greater personal wisdom and illumination than they actually possessed. The ranks of those followers have been swelled by others who are not very familiar with the mechanics and demonstration of certain phases of mediumship and psychic phenomena. And, sometimes in ignorance, sometimes deliberately, such followers in effect credit the *channel* with the message, instead of those who *used* the channel. It is rather like attributing a voice we hear on the telephone to the instrument itself, and not to the communicator at the other end of the line.

4 In almost all cases, unfortunately, the increasing denial or omission of *mediumship* and of psychic experiences *preceding* mediumship becomes more and more marked with the passage of time, even though in some instances that talent and those experiences were once acknowledged.

5 Some schools belittle mediums and mediumship, for one reason or another. Other schools shy away completely from those terms (even though many of their leaders *recognize* the truths of Survival and Communication), because of those few mediums who can be rightfully criticized for exploiting mediumship and twisting and distorting it for their own ends.

6 But one or several diseased trees are *not* the entire orchard. And while there are mediums who debase their talents—as occasionally happens, let us remember, in every profession—one should not condemn or disclaim *all* mediums because of the sins of some.

B04 Of Orthodoxy and Mediumship

1 An example of how some organizations newly discussing Survival and Communication may mislead searchers for spiritual truth was revealed in a psychic periodical some years ago. It reported on the program of a conference sponsored by a group whose declared purpose was to introduce psychic phenomena through *established orthodox organizations* [see also 322].

B.1 Error ☐ B04

2   The program included a lecture by an unnamed individual described—and the emphasis is ours—as having been "*for thirteen years a professional fake medium demonstrating all phases of physical and mental phenomena*," with the lecture hailed as "*a historic first in the annals of psychic research*... the only time a spiritually-based organization has presented a person completely qualified to address his audience on the *immensity* of the so-called 'spook business' as it now exists across the land."

3   While we would rather replace the phrase "annals of psychic research" by "annals of psychic confusion and error," more serious is the ignorance (and arrogance) revealed by that announcement.

4   The sponsors of the conference just mentioned obviously had little understanding of the process and mechanics of mediumship [1206]—*genuine* mediumship, that is—and seemingly thought that most seekers of the truth of spirit communication are incredibly gullible. What is hard to believe is that people claiming even remote acquaintance with psychic research would not know that:

5   — The *sham* in any field is not just an *imitation* of the real; it is also testimony to the *existence* of the real, because only the *real* can be counterfeited.

6   — Genuine mediums and seekers of spiritual truth have always *welcomed* the exposure of fake mediums. They know that virtually every field has its frauds, and that the sooner those frauds are exposed the better.

7   — For every fake demonstration of psychic phenomena, there are hundreds, even thousands of demonstrations of *genuine* phenomena.

8   — For each deplorable fraud who preys on the seeker or mourner, there are scores of genuine mediums who demonstrate that there is indeed *no* death to *the real self* and that *nothing* can separate those bound by ties of love.

9   Few can be lower on the scale spiritually than the individual who lies and cheats those seeking communication with people who have passed on to spirit life. To deliberately deceive others in such a sacred matter as communion with loved ones—for such communication *is* sacred—is to incur a debt that *must* be paid, with a *separate* debt created with *each* person victimized, each *time* they are victimized.

B05 Of Many Courses and Seminars

1. Springing up like mushrooms all over, in institutions of learning and out, to capitalize on the hunger of people for something that will give meaning and purpose to existence, have appeared a host of courses and seminars on the "occult" or "supernatural" or "paranormal."

2. Unfortunately they are often staffed by "educators" who not only reaffirm numerous errors of others, but who also compound them by ignorance and errors of their own.

3. In this connection it is well to remember a few things:

4. — A million quotations of an error cannot make it true. A ten-page bibliography cannot erase one fact. A thousand professors and their courses cannot cancel one truth.

5. — *No* theory or conjecture in these fields will lack support from "scientists" and "educators" as long as it does *not* confirm the truths of Survival and Communication. Some will support any hypothesis, however fantastic and implausible, rather than acknowledge that life continues, and that we can, under the right conditions, have sweet communion with those who have passed on to the spirit world.

6. — There are "educators" who, despite decades of "investigation" of psychic phenomena, remain apparently unaware that mediumship exists and that *the real self* does not die. United usually by a bond of academic degrees, and often a jargon intelligible only to themselves, they demonstrate again and again that scholastic "attainments" alone are little indication of wisdom or worth.

7. Let us not be impressed by individuals merely because they are writers or scientists or on the staff of educational institutions.

B06 Of a Certain "Seminar"

1. The flood of courses and seminars capitalizing on the hunger of people for something that will give meaning and purpose to existence continues. But whether the hunger is at all relieved is highly questionable.

2. One financially successful "seminar" followed a different tack from most of its fellows. Its "training course" was designed to convince troubled people that whatever their faults and errors may be, "they are perfect the way they are." No need to change, no need to strive for any improvement, no need to think of what they can *become*—they are perfect the way they are!

B.1 Error

3   They were *not* taught that the first step to curing a condition is to *recognize* it; or that it is one thing to *recognize* a condition, and another to *accept* it.

4   The spoken "instruction" was full of offensive comments, with the "students" addressed in most unpleasant terms; but many people were willing to pay the high "tuition fees," presumably because the course encouraged them to remove any "guilt feelings" and stifle the still small voice of conscience. Tens of thousands of people are "graduates" of the course.

5   That so many adults will accept treatment that shows such little respect for them, is puzzling.

6   What is more puzzling is that they seemingly did not realize that, however they may have felt they benefited from it, instruction presented in low language cannot possess much of upliftment or wisdom.

B07 Of Certain "Authorities"—the Blind Leading the Blind

1   As we have said, we should not be impressed by individuals merely because they are writers or scientists or on the staff of educational institutions.

2   The wisdom of that advice is confirmed over and over again by the views of many Doctors of Philosophy about almost anything relating to *parapsychology:* the branch of psychology that deals with the investigation of psychic phenomena. By and large, their attitude and lack of knowledge of the subject are pitiful [see also 323]. [This was written in 1976.]

3   *Inexcusable* is their frequent failure to study the immense and abundantly-documented evidence of psychic phenomena during the last hundred years and more. In no other field are the readily-available findings of the past so overwhelmingly and so unscientifically disregarded by "scientists" and "educators" who enter it.

4   Acting as if they were the pioneers in research into psychic phenomena —which they clearly are *not*—these "authorities" make unjustified comments, reach unjustified conclusions, learnedly quote one another's errors, complicate what is simple, and obscure what is clear.

5   An example is contained in the views on unorthodox healing expressed by the head of parapsychological research at a leading university. One statement was to the effect that no healer can cure anyone, and that healing depends on the patient's "awareness" of the "channels" opened up for them.

6   There are two major errors here.

7   For one thing, healers often *do* cure others, either directly or indirectly, as we point out elsewhere [Secs. 11.1–2].

8   For another thing—and any *thorough* researcher would know this—untold thousands of people have been relieved of afflictions without *any* knowledge that healing was directed to them. That number includes infants only a few days old; where would be the "awareness" in such cases?

9   Again we caution seekers of Truth to weigh well the words of *anyone*, regardless of outward indications of authority. We are by no means critical of all Doctors of Philosophy—that degree, by the way, seldom indicates excellence in the field of philosophy in general—but only of those who, by virtue of authority derived from their title, *add* to confusion in the minds of others.

10   Lack of knowledge about things of great importance is not uncommon, unfortunately. But it is particularly sad when displayed by those whose academic qualifications would suggest that they might know at least a little about what they express.

11   More and more courses in parapsychology are now flourishing in institutions of learning, with degrees awarded to those who successfully complete them. But as the courses are apparently in many cases conducted by individuals who are *not* aware of the truths of Survival and spirit communication, or of the *mechanics* of psychic phenomena, or of the part *spirit people* play in producing them, it is a classic example of *the blind leading the blind!*

12   The amount of misinformation presented and misteachings taught by people who presumably should know better is amazing.

B08 *The Mine of Misinformation*

1   There are more cults on earth today than in any other time in history, most of them teaching a mixture of fact and error, with error often predominating. The mine of misinformation becomes ever deeper, as people continue to preach of a soon-approaching day of judgement when a select few will be saved, while the rest of humankind is doomed either to annihilation or to start again on the lowest rung of the ladder of progression.

2   So seekers of Truth need to be more selective than ever, accepting and applying only what appeals to their reason and is unreservedly embraced

B.1 Error

by their inner being, and what they are convinced will better enable them to live in accordance with The Laws That Govern.

An example, reminding us of this need, is provided by a booklet describing a "master" and his teachings. Listing the things that it states individuals should or should not do to achieve spiritual elevation, it counsels them to avoid looking into the eyes of others, particularly those of the opposite sex.

How true are the words of a Blessed Soul:

> Many of the teachings of some so-called great ones are like the wind blowing through the trees!

B09 On Certain Psychic "Discoveries"

A popular book published some years ago [in the 1970s] dealt with psychic "discoveries" in certain countries in Eastern Europe. We place the word in quotes because most of those reported are *not* discoveries in the sense of bringing to light something that had existed but been previously unknown, but are in the sense of discoveries that someone makes that are well known to others. And most of the "discoveries" were made by scientists who *knew* that something happened, but did not know *how* or *why* it happened.

(We use the adjective *psychic* here with the meaning: "of, pertaining to, associated with, attributed to, or caused by some nonphysical force or agency.")

The book is most readable, fascinating in spots, and it does an excellent job of reporting on *reports*. But when the reports reported include many false assumptions, many incorrect conclusions, several extravagant and unsupported claims, some inexcusable misnomers, and some things that bear little relation to the psychic, can the book be more than just one of many that provoke much passing interest but little enlightenment?

There are those who claim that much that is expressed, however abounding in errors, still leads some people to seek further. That is probably true. But it also leads many people, and in our opinion a far greater number, to abandon the search altogether. We have pointed out that mediumship is often so poor as to drive away the searcher, who sometimes never returns. We can say the same about many books purporting to relate to the psychic or occult.

We cannot touch on more than just a very few of the "discoveries," and then only in the briefest fashion. It would take several hundred pages to discuss the many "breakthroughs" (reported in that and other volumes) that exist in name and imagination only, and the innumerable fancies and speculations that often overwhelm and camouflage the facts.

6   Our comments will contain some USB teachings; emphasize once again the wisdom of pondering well before completely accepting or rejecting statements made by anyone, anywhere; and hammer home the fact that *ignorance is the mother of misconceptions*, with one false premise capable of spawning a chain of many mistaken notions.

7   1. In any book devoted to scientific "discoveries," terms should be especially carefully defined and applied. Yet a whole chapter is titled and devoted to *"artificial reincarnation."* In our opinion, there is no justification for the use of this phrase, or for the noun as it is constantly used, or rather misused, by a psychiatrist. For while "artificial respiration," for instance, *is* respiration artificially induced, "artificial reincarnation" is not reincarnation in *any* sense of the word. What the psychiatrist quoted refers to repeatedly as reincarnation is nothing but acceptance of suggestions made to art students during hypnosis that they are great artists of the past.

8   It is undeniable that *suggestion*, whether made during hypnosis or not, is often powerful in bringing latent talents to the surface. It is equally undeniable that there is nothing scientific in calling any aspect of suggestion "reincarnation."

9   2. *Telekinesis* (TK) is confused with *psychokinesis* (PK) in the book, and the terms are used interchangeably. Those authors define PK as the ability to move matter with mind alone. But TK, according to the dictionary, and the emphasis is ours, is "the production of motion in a body, *apparently* without the application of material force." [And it states that PK is the *apparent* ability to influence physical objects *or events* by thought processes.]

10 Many of the misconceptions about PK or TK arise from the activities of a woman who some scientists claim had the ability to move objects merely by mind *alone*. The movement of objects, and the suspension of movement of objects, is well documented.

11 But the correct explanation is simple: the use of ectoplasmic rods, which we have already described [1122]; and with ectoplasmic rods being partly material and physical things [1121:1], the "mind over matter" theory of her activities has no basis in fact.

12 Under suitable and harmonious conditions, there is no doubt that the woman mentioned, who obviously has great psychic force and power, would be able to demonstrate her talents easily in a comparatively short time, and in a comfortable, relaxed state, instead of reportedly sometimes

B.1 Error

taking "two to four hours to rev up her supernormal powers," with an enormous increase in her pulse rate and other signs of tremendous bodily strain.

13 We would emphasize this: Mind works *with* mind, and *upon* mind, and *through* mind.

14 Of course mind can *indirectly* affect matter, and in many ways. The mind often affects the physical [earthly] body, for instance—and vice versa—a fact that has been known throughout the ages. And the mind, which includes one's emotions, can among other things affect the growth and well-being of plants and flowers, something that has been well demonstrated.

15 But as we have stated, the combined minds—and minds *alone*—of a billion people would not move a mountain or even a pin or a piece of paper one inch [a centimeter].[2]

16 3. One physicist states that the woman discussed can "cause third degree burns on her stomach by PK." How such a thing can happen we explain in "A Little About Stigmata" [1127]. There we point out that stigmata may occur as the result of a person's conscious or unconscious craving for their appearance; or as a result of the work of certain spirit chemists who when living on earth possessed, and now continue to possess, extraordinary religious fervor about certain convictions—a fervor they will do all they can to excite in others; or as a result of both circumstances, in which case it is much easier for them to appear.

17 If the third-degree-burns phenomenon was designed by her spirit associates to arouse wonder, it has been a success; if designed to stimulate thinking along spiritual lines, it has been a failure.

18 The case is a classic example of the widespread lack of knowledge of the great psychic power that some people possess. This lack of knowledge unfortunately seems to be [in 1971] more common among scientists generally than among humanity as a whole.

19 4. There is much confusion of the aura with the spirit [etheric] body (or "double") [1310:4]. As we have explained, the spirit body does *not* envelop the physical body [1310:3]. In any case, it is in no greater sense an "energy body" than any *other* body. For every single thing has energy, and every single thing *vibrates;* and vibration, which is energy in motion, is sensed as color, sound, and odor [414, 929].

---

[2] We here remind the reader of those less-evolved spirit people who for various reasons strive to mislead us (1124:8–10). They probably account for many strange results in investigations of the paranormal.

20   If these truths are remembered, the value of many premises and conclusions in some books will be apparent.

21   5. "Bio-energy," "biological plasma body," "fluctuating biological field," "force field," "energy body," "bioplasmic body," "psychotronic energy," and several other terms, to all of which much space is devoted, are new terms used to describe our old friend *the aura*—an aura apparently not understood by the scientists quoted. Like every other thing, the field of energy that is the aura is ceaselessly vibrating; but as the aura is a *representation* of all that we have been and are, the energy in a person's aura cannot be tapped and stored, despite "scientific" claims to the contrary.

22   What *is* sometimes tapped are the chemical essences in *the physical body*, as we noted in the mechanics of healing [1102:3, 1106:9]; but these chemical essences, if tapped, are tapped only by going *through* the aura.

23   We may momentarily impinge upon or go through the aura of hundreds or even thousands of people in a day: we do so every time we shake someone's hand, or touch or embrace someone or even just pass *close* to people; for auras, we repeat, vary in width from a few inches [centimeters] to many feet [meters; 1311:8].

24   Classic cases of tapping chemical essences from the physical body of someone is reported in scripture, where the Nazarene on occasion suddenly felt depleted when hemmed in and touched by the throng.

25   Of course when chemical essences are drawn from us, or supplied to us, the fact is instantly registered in our aura, which, like all auras, is never for a moment still.

26   Despite claims and theories to the contrary, the aura—no matter what terms are used to describe it—is not a separate unit of energy or "a whole unified organism in itself." It could not exist except for the thing, creature, or individual it emanates from and reflects.

27   6. Blindness, like many other physical handicaps, would not affect the "gift" of prophecy or any other facet of mediumship. This fact has been demonstrated by blind mediums of our own times who, guided by their spirit friends, were able to make their way safely through heavy pedestrian and vehicular traffic. And as we see all about us, many blind people make their way unaided except for their physical senses of hearing, touch, and smell, which are often heightened by the loss of sight.

28   Incidentally, in *true* blindfold billet reading [in which a blindfolded medium gives messages responding to people's writing on folded pieces of paper], which some find particularly impressive, the blindfold is often

B.1 Error

an *aid* to the demonstration, as it shuts out at least part of such distractions as light and undesirable sounds or movements.

29   7. It is of no surprise that measuring devices may find varying degrees of vibration in various areas of the aura. We have enumerated the seven psychic centers [1138:3]; and their *receptivity* will differ not only with different individuals, but at times even with the same individual.

30   8. In a report on acupuncture—the practice that attempts to cure illness by puncturing specified areas of the skin with needles—the Chinese are quoted as saying that the vital life force (or life force, vital energy, bio-energy, chi, or prana) can be tapped at seven hundred points in the skin.

31   Illumined Souls tell us that the vital energy can in fact be tapped anywhere on the body, with or without punctures. The psychic centers are receiving centers and storehouses of vital life force [1138:1]. And if there is a superabundance of that force in one center, and a deficiency in another—both of which would be displayed in the aura, which records everything—the imbalance needs to be corrected. If patients breathe in and out slowly and evenly during acupuncture, they can inhale the vital energy released from one area during the process; they can also aid in mentally directing it to the center or centers lacking a sufficient supply.

32   (Acupuncture is just one of many ways of relieving or releasing excessive pressure in certain areas of the body. Manipulative therapy is another. Both methods are often but not always successful. Still practiced in some countries is the practice of cupping; but virtually obsolete is the use of leeches, formerly much used in medicine for bloodletting.)

33   Spirit doctors and chemical engineers sometimes perform acupuncture to relieve patients in the physical, but of course without any actual material punctures made. Or they may inject needed vital energy into an area to which the passageway or vessels are partially or completely blocked.

34   9. What is described as *the* experiment in one country is the ability of some people to put others to sleep or to wake them up telepathically from a distance of a few yards [meters] to more than a thousand miles [thousand kilometers]. This of course is the result of suggestion, and is in effect distant hypnosis.

35   The principle is nothing new, and can be quite effective if the subjects are receptive, and especially if they are particularly susceptible to hypnosis. There are literally thousands or tens of thousands of people each year whose illnesses are cured or alleviated when "healers" (and their spirit helpers) project relief to them from immense distances, sometimes halfway around the globe, and sometimes without the afflicted even

being aware that distant healing is directed to them. If there is no wall of negation around them, people often can be helped regardless of distance; for with the speed of thought being as incredibly rapid as it is, distance is no barrier to such phenomena. Neither is any physical thing, regardless of its nature.

10. Telepathy between people and animals is nothing novel. Thousands of people have, for instance, taught their dog to fetch their slippers, or to retrieve a ball or stick or other objects. The dog, an intelligent animal, as most animals are, comes to understand the meaning of those words. And psychic as many animals are, more so than most humans, they can receive and often do carry out silent commands—which of course must be in language they *understand*.

There are many animals whose exploits in spelling and other demonstrations have proved astounding to those who do not know the mechanics of those demonstrations. A horse, to cite one example, may be trained to put a hoof successively on the letters M, A, R, and Y if the name Mary is mentioned. And the marvelous "tricks" of seals, porpoises, and even killer whales are a matter of record. They result from training, by word and gesture usually; and from that to performing on silent command or gesture is only a step, although perhaps a big step.

Another thing to remember is that some spirit people can impress animals to do what is desired. By the Law of Attraction, those on earth engaged in training animals to perform will usually have the help of spirit experts in that field.

11. Recounted is a previously published report of a hypnotist who, touring a clinic, was provided with a subject for demonstration of his technique. The subject, a nurse, fell quickly into hypnotic trance, and followed his instructions perfectly. Only later did he discover that she understood no English, the language he had spoken. The authors' explanation is that "she automatically used some sort of 'psychic transformer' to convert his English commands into action."

There are several possible and thoroughly legitimate explanations for the success of that particular experiment, but they do not include any "psychic transformer." A spirit interpreter could have translated the commands into the language the nurse knew. (This happens not infrequently at sittings where the medium and the sitter do not understand each other's tongue; here there are sometimes two interpreters—one on earth who accompanies the sitter to translate what the sitter says, the other on the spirit side to translate the response of the sitter's spirit friends into language the medium's controls will understand and relay to or through the medium.)

41 Or the nurse might have known English in some pre-existence, in which case, if she were in a deep enough hypnotic state, the knowledge buried in her consciousness could be brought to the surface. Or she might have been controlled while in the hypnotic state by a spirit guide who knew English and obeyed the commands. The first explanation—a spirit interpreter's translation of the instructions—is the most common in such cases.

42 As we have mentioned [1325:7], there are many skilled linguists in spirit life who serve as interpreters, and that there, as on earth, it is an honorable calling.

43 12. "Mental wizards" who can calculate faster than electronic machines are individuals, usually psychic, who are channels, whether they know it or not, for spirit mathematical geniuses.

44 And those individuals who have the seeming ability to instantly give the total of such things as dropped matches, coins in someone's pocket, or circles on a blackboard, are also channels.

45 13. That a person or object leaves impressions behind is nothing new. It is well known, for instance, that photographs of terrain taken by military planes in early daylight will often show the vibrations of vehicles that had passed during the night. Of course such vibrations will gradually disappear, sometimes within a few hours, sometimes within a few minutes.

46 The very basis of psychometry—which is the art or faculty of divining facts about an object itself or about its past or present owners [1012]—is the vibrations *left* by something or someone.

47 14. A psychologist states that the most important ingredient in "secret telepathic control" is *wishing*. That is just not so, regardless of the type of telepathy. Concentration, yes; visualization and holding the visualization, yes—all of which, by the way, the psychologist exercised, it is plain from the report. But wishing in itself, no.

48 15. Some incredible and in our opinion quite inexcusable observations are made about *time*.

49 "How does the thought you're thinking go instantly from you telepathically to somebody else, or from you to another part of the world?" ask the authors. They add that a certain astrophysicist believes he may have found this energy... and "He calls this energy 'Time' "!

50 Considering the two or three major meanings *time* has possessed for humanity throughout the ages, we find it highly unscientific and in fact

presumptuous for anyone, particularly a scientist, to use that word for something he *believes* he *may* have found. In the circumstances, would he not have been far wiser to coin some new term? In any case, what people have for scores of centuries termed "time" cannot be placed in the category of energy, and to interpret the word as he has done is beyond all understanding.

51   What the good scientist does not seem to realize is that the speed of thought is much more rapid than the speed of light [206:6]. Of course we refer to intense and directed thought—thought directed to others—and not to such casual thoughts as "It's a nice day."

52   The authors say that the astrophysicist's "time" has a number of properties which he says can be studied in the scientist's laboratory; and in a reference to telepathy, they quote him in part as follows: "Time would be thin near the sender of the thought and denser around the receiver." He obviously is unaware that this has *nothing* to do with time as people generally understand it—but may apply to the auras of sender and receiver. For while both sender and receiver may be psychic, it is usually the receiver who is the more psychic of the two. In fact, one dictionary definition of the adjective *psychic* is "specially sensitive to influences or forces of a nonphysical, apparently supernormal nature." The aura of receivers or psychics can be *expected* to show greater changes than the auras of others.

53   "Time appears immediately everywhere." What great observation is this?

54   16. No bibliography, however impressively long, is any indication, let alone guarantee, of worth, especially, unfortunately, with regard to psychic phenomena.

55   It is a great pity that many scientists who are entrusted with certain items of knowledge or who mistakenly think they "discover" them, misunderstand or misinterpret that knowledge, and use or coin terms that can only cause or compound confusion, instead of terms that are already clearly understood by literally millions of people. It is the same old story: with a few notable and most welcome exceptions, scientists as a whole not only have contributed little to the cause of Truth, as far as things of the spirit are concerned, but have in fact seriously hindered it [315, 323].

56   17. Many of the reported experiments and demonstrations touched on in the book are trifling and pale into insignificance beside the vast number of extraordinary and immensely more intricate and marvelous manifesta-

57 For as we have said, psychic phenomena, including communication with those in the spirit world, are determined by people in the *spirit* side of life [1215:3]. They are *not* at the command of those who head scientific laboratories on earth. And while truly highly evolved spirit beings may provide demonstrations and teachings and philosophy for those who are true and humble seekers, scientists or non-scientists, they will *not* appear or take part in experiments, elementary or advanced, by those whose aims are less than noble, or those who will propound any theory, however implausible or fantastic, rather than accept the demonstrable powers of the spirit.

58 An Illumined Soul says:

59 Many of your earth scientists are unwilling to accept what cannot be observed by the physical senses; and the truly important energies are not measurable by man-made instruments alone, certainly not as yet—and we don't know when or if they will be.

60 For example, scientists have not yet "discovered" the subtle and as yet unmeasured essence in oxygen that is vital to life [913:3].

B.2 MISTEACHINGS

B10 On Some Common Misteachings

1 We have emphasized that ignorance is the mother of misconceptions, with one false premise capable of spawning a chain of many mistaken notions.

2 And we have pointed out that thousands of people unthinkingly accept many misteachings.

3 Such misteachings come not only from people on earth, but also from some spirit people, not a few of whom are unduly revered by the uncritical.

4 But while some of those misteachings are harmless, others are not: They result in many errors of opinion, or are harmful, or cause great anguish, including to those who enter the spirit world with profound misconceptions.

5   In the world today there are, as always, numerous organizations that present what *they* understand as truth. Many of these organizations are genuinely moved by the desire to serve and enlighten humanity. But despite their sincerity, unfortunately some who serve Truth do not serve it well—a fact that applies to some students and teachers on *both* sides of life.

6   Due to misconceptions and ignorance, and an apparent readiness of some students to believe and share almost anything taught by others, *especially* by spirit teachers—and, in the case of students already in spirit life, taught by others who *preceded* them there—the flood of misconceptions and misinformation often increases, and there is already far too much.

7   One teacher has said: "Of course in spirit [life] there is no gender." The fact, however, is that *gender continues*, as knowledge of the spirit [etheric] body and of twin souls makes abundantly clear [1309, 1321]. Another asserts: "Jealousy does not exist in the spirit world." This statement is also quite incorrect.

8   It is true that jealousy does not exist in the *higher* spirit realms, whose occupants have long shed any unworthy traits they may have once possessed. But in the realms closer to earth, jealousy still exists, as do other unpleasant attributes; for the mere passing from this world to another expression of existence does not alter a person one bit—except for the change in their vehicle of expression.

9   We do *not* automatically advance to a plane *higher* than earth itself *unless* we have earned it. We can go a long way towards earning it if, while living on earth, we rid ourselves of any traits we may possess that we consider undesirable in others. Jealousy is one of them.

10   One spirit teacher states that God "has all the attributes of male and female" and "must contain within itself every expression of life for which it is responsible."

11   These are bold and sweeping and unjustified assertions, which seem to claim a far greater knowledge of The Creator than even Illumined Souls of the highest attainment possess.

12   Some teachers, on both sides of life, including some seemingly of above-average levels of consciousness, continue to declare that "good and evil are opposite sides of the same coin;" that "without darkness there could be no light;" and that "without hate there could be no love."

B.2 Misteachings

13 Let us reflect upon these three assertions.

14 The widest currency is given to the first: "Good and evil are opposite sides of the same coin." We have clearly stated elsewhere that *we completely reject this belief*, and we have explained why [829].

15 A corrected metaphor along the same lines would be: Good and evil are *separate* coins—one of *worth*, the other *worthless*.

16 As for the second assertion, one could as well say that without *light* there could be no darkness, and therefore *blame* light for the existence of darkness—literal or metaphorical.

17 The fact is that there *can* be, and very often *is* light without darkness. In the higher spirit realms there is no darkness of *any* sort; but residents there can, if they wish, create shade for themselves, either by the power of thought or by such things as blinds or curtains or draperies in their homes.

18 The third assertion—"without hate there could be no love"—is terribly wrong!

19 One of the signs of greater spirituality is greater love for others. And human beings, whichever side of life they live in, could as a whole *never* make much progress spiritually if every measure of love were counterbalanced by an equal measure of hate. All efforts to sweep the world with love and tenderness, as we and others with similar aims will in time succeed in doing, would be futile.

20 Some of the teachers we refer to go on to say that hate can be *transmuted* into love—not apparently realizing how that contradicts their declaration that there *must* be hate in order for love to exist! In any case, hate cannot be transmuted into love, as they are altogether different feelings, but it can be *displaced* or *supplanted* by it.

21 Hate, by the way, like all other emotions, exists or survives only in one's mind; dismissed from it, it ceases to be. (Unfortunately, of course, the *effects* of hate may linger long after the hate itself no longer exists—sometimes for years or even centuries.)

22 There are literally hundreds of other misteachings that are accepted without question by many people. Some of them are taught by men and women of the utmost integrity, but that does not make them less incorrect. Some are of such a nature that to accept them is to open the floodgates of error. We list a few of them here; we urge readers to doubly weigh *anything and everything* from anyone who proclaims or supports any of the following misteachings:

23. — that to ask a question is in itself evidence of inability to understand the answer.
24. — that mediums in general are vampires, that spirit communication is diabolic, and that we cannot commune with those no longer living on earth.
25. — that the world and things of the world are illusions [801:9].
26. — that anyone is a focal point for *all* light [1419:3-4].
27. — that belief in anyone, or allegiance to anyone, can absolve someone from personal responsibility or from The Law of Cause and Effect [705:1].
28. — that anyone can shoulder or erase the karma of another [705].
29. — that anyone can make a place in the sun for another, spiritually [705].
30. — that *all* illness springs from the mind [916].
31. — that illness starts in the *spirit [etheric]* body [1314].
32. — that there can be, and is, annihilation—in the sense of *ceasing to be*—of some individuals [1320].
33. — that gender may change from male to female, or from female to male, during one's existence [1321:13].
34. — that human beings have previously been animals [1308:10].
35. — that some human beings return to earth as animals [1406].
36. — that animals, in time, come to earth as human beings [1308:1-2,8].
37. — that human beings have evolved from the lowest form of life [808:12].
38. — that God is all, and that all that is, is God [502].
39. — that *denies* that God is The Creator [502:5].
40. — that *limits* God's creation to the lowest form of life [808].

B11 On Misteachings by Spirit "Teachers"

1. There have been many books containing spirit teachings. At best, unfortunately, many of them leave their readers little more informed, and vastly more confused. At worst, they bring darkness rather than light into the lives of those who read them without exercising reason.

2. These conclusions apply well to a series of volumes embodying the "teachings" of a certain spirit individual. In our opinion, they diverge far from truth, and they could greatly mislead the unthinking and uncritical. In these volumes:

B.2 Misteachings

1. The "teacher" constantly refers to his channel, a woman, as *he*. This should alert readers to the need to carefully weigh anything else he states [note 1321:13].

2. The "teacher" declares that nothing can help or harm people unless they *believe* it can.

The fact is, however, that thousands of sick people, infants included, have been cured by distant healing [1102:5–6, 1107] without knowing that it was directed to them, and often without having ever *heard* of that type of healing, so that belief (or disbelief) could not have entered into the picture.

Many in coma benefit from intravenous feeding, unaware that it is administered to them; so here, too, belief or disbelief can play no part.

People allergic to poison oak or poison ivy will be affected if they touch either, whether or not they believe these plants are harmful.

A person who drinks a fatal dose of a deadly poison will perish from it (unless an antidote is taken), even if they believe it is nectar they ingest.

3. The "teacher" maintains that no one dies at any time or under any circumstances unless and until they *decide* to die, and, by the power of their mind, they create the cause and manner of their death.

But if an infant is killed when a drunken driver's car mounts the sidewalk, who could believe that the infant actually *willed* its own death, and willed it to take place at *that* very moment and in *that* very way.

Some children are abused and some are killed. Does the "teacher" insist that such children *will* these things to happen to them?

4. The "teacher" states that vitamins only help those who *believe* that vitamins are beneficial.

The fact is that vitamins are absolutely necessary for health, whether contained in our daily food or provided as supplements when needed, and regardless of whether an individual knows about them or believes in them.

5. One thing more, a *crowning* misteaching. The "teacher" asserts the following about a being who has been loved and revered by hundreds of millions of people throughout the centuries for his love for humankind, the teachings he shared, and the example he set for humanity, and who was nailed to the cross for his pains: that he allowed an innocent man to be crucified in his place—first making sure that the victim was drugged.

We repeat what we so often urge: Weigh well the words of anyone, anywhere!

16   Especially the words of anyone in *spirit* life, we would add, for too many people assume that all speakers from the spirit world possess knowledge, wisdom, and integrity. Some do, of course; but *others do not*, as the "teacher" we have quoted clearly demonstrates.[3]

B12 On Misteachings by Mediums

1   It is not only some spirit individuals who provide a wealth of misinformation. Some on earth do so too, and thus also have much to account for.

2   We know of one medium whose *misteachings*, unthinkingly adopted by some in a third generation of "students" [in 1972], were still being further relayed by those who unquestioningly accepted them in the first place.

3   To help expose what we are convinced is false, and to help us all think more carefully about error, we present here (in boldface) a few of those many scores of misteachings—some senseless and incomprehensible but harmless, others so serious that to accept them would hinder an individual from living as fully as possible according to The Laws That Govern, or THE LAW. Our comments and responses follow them:

4   **— Having sittings with several different mediums is to risk putting our spirit guides in "spiritual captivity."** [See B12:60].

5   **— We can complete any unfinished work of our spirit guides and teachers, and thus furnish or "complete" their spiritual garb.**

6   This is not only incorrect; it is harmful. For if true, which it is *not*, it would nullify the principle of personal responsibility, from which no one can absolve another, and from which no one, anywhere, at any time, under any circumstances, is, if *normally* capable of reasoning, exempt.

7   We further point out, by the way, that actions committed under the "influence" of such things as alcohol or drugs do *not* set aside or lessen one's personal responsibility [404:2, 839:4].

8   We re-emphasize one of our cardinal teachings: If at all evolved, our guides come to inform and inspire us. They come to encourage and strengthen us spiritually. They come to remind us of the laws of God, a God that is all-love, all-wisdom, all-justice. They do not come to do our work for us, or to deprive us of the trials and tests which, well met, develop our character and enable us to progress spiritually [1221].

---

[3] Two other examples of misinformation given by spirit teachers are given in 1230:10–17.

B.2 Misteachings

9 — **One can open "a spiritual bank account"** [1405].

10 If the misteaching suggests that a good act will allow a person to commit a bad act with impunity, it is doubly wrong. Restoring a sum of money to the owner who drops it would not entitle anyone to rob another of an equal amount. And certainly saving *one* person's life would not entitle anyone to needlessly kill another!

11 — **In the spirit realms there is a specific limited number of "spheres" and planes within a sphere.**

12 As we have emphasized, there is *no* limit to the number of spirit planes or spheres, for those planes or spheres correspond to levels of consciousness [1301:7]. And as an Illumined Soul has pointed out: "The *people* make the plane, *not* the plane the people."

13 — **A speaker is best when he or she makes no preparation and talks under "inspiration" only.**

14 Many "inspired addresses" are rambling, disjointed, uninformative talks that confuse instead of enlighten their audiences. For unless one is a trance speaker controlled by highly advanced spirit guides—and this is rare—there is *no* substitute for preparation.

15 — ***Prana*** **[or vital life force, life force, vital energy, bioenergy, or chi] is "a point in time" and "a little yellow liquid that lives in the heart for distribution;" and** *oja*, **described as "a covering of prana" and "the material side of prana," when "transformed into spiritual force is stored in the brain."**

16 How a point in time can be a little yellow liquid we cannot understand. Likewise, how can something *material* cover "a point in time"? We wish more and more people would reflect, and reflect well, before incorporating *anything* into their universe.

17 — **Those developing psychic power should convert all their sexual energy into "ojas."** (This misteaching is mis-ascribed to "the illumined.")

18 Truly Illumined Souls recommend *the moderate path*. They do not preach continence, or asceticism, or abstinence, or fasting, but moderation in all things—except wrongdoing and evil, which of course should be avoided altogether.

19 — **We each have a definite, specified number of spirit guides, and the full complement includes guides representing such things as shame, laziness, jealousy, ignorance, duplicity, covetousness, indecision, regret, anxiety, conceit, arrogance, fear, and illusion.**

20 There is *no* limit to the number of spirit friends who may walk with us or work with us; the number depends on many things [1221:5–6].

21 **— Fairly advanced spirit "spheres" would include "planes" with such names as Ignorance, Superstition, Egotism, Hallucination, and Apprehension.**

22 **— An individual has a "mortal mind"** [in contrast to a mind that is not "mortal"].

23 Mind is mind; and one's mind or mentality, indissolubly fused with one's soul and spirit to make up *the real self*, does not automatically alter one iota when we pass on to spirit life [1319:15]. One's mind or mentality is no less and no more "mortal" there than here.

24 **— "All things manifest in the trinity," and all "faculties of being" do so too, with the constituents of each "faculty" being inseparable. One "faculty,"** according to this teacher, **consists of "spontaneity, realization, obedience." Another, "duty, tolerance, gratitude." Yet another, "simplicity, virtue, alertness." And so on.**

25 **— Mentality and spirituality are separate.**

26 The fact, however, is that our mentality *includes* our emotions, desires, thoughts, and spirituality if any—just as a house includes rooms that are a part of it.

27 **— We need have "no will apart from God"** (this may be considered to be a suggestion).

28 But the truth we teach is that one of our unsurrenderable possessions is the God-given gift of *free will* [701].

29 **— "Because the wise or illumined one does not strive, no man is his enemy."**

30 There are two errors here. For one thing, the illumined *do* strive; they strive to present enlightenment to humanity in general, and particularly to those who are ready to receive. They are fully conscious of the Law of Service: The greater our blessings, the greater our "gifts," the greater our awareness, the greater our opportunities, the greater is our responsibility to serve. For another thing, Illumined Souls *do* have enemies, and throughout the ages many of them were crucified, literally or metaphorically. The list is a long and distressing one.

31 Another book, written by a different, outstanding medium, provides further convincing evidence, if further evidence were needed, that mediumship in itself is no indication of either spirituality or wisdom.

B.2 Misteachings

32   The foreword, introduction, and conclusion describe the work as unique, invaluable, and transcendent, among other accolades. In our opinion it contains one of the sorriest collections of misteachings we know of, apparently drawn from many sources. It seems to attribute incredible knowledge to someone described as a "Master Teacher." We find much of it quite unintelligible. What concerns us the most, however, is that many of its misteachings can do little but hinder the spiritual progress of anyone who embraces them.

33   To help us all learn from thinking about errors, we quote (in boldface) just a few of those innumerable misteachings. And we quote them exactly as they are given, except we have omitted much emphasis that was indicated by boldface type, and we have not inserted sics[4] throughout. Our comments that follow them are based on our best understanding of Truth.

34   — **He who considers himself to be God, verily becomes God. As one thinks, so he becomes.**

35   The first thought is both absurd and irreverent. The second declaration is, as we have pointed out [817], a too-common belief that is unthinkingly accepted by too many.

36   — **There is no reality in the poverty of the poor.** This is beyond belief.

37   — **Honor and shame are the same as fear.**

38   — **Fortune and desires are the same as the person, so dignity and shame are inseparable on all occasions.**

39   — **The Spoken Word, if united with mind, may, after 24 hours have elapsed, take on the form of Nature Spirits.**

40   — **The first Sphere is about 3,000 miles [5,000 kilometers] above the earth plane.**

41   The spirit world or spirit realms are all around and about us, and consist of all the spheres or planes corresponding to levels of consciousness occupied by those who do not live in a physical [earthly] body, with each planet having its own spirit realms [1301].

42   — **I am part of God and He approves of all I do.**

43   *Part* of us, an important but infinitesimal part, *is* part of God, we repeat, but *we* are not part of God: The distinction should never be forgotten [503]. To assert that *we* are part of God is to reveal not only great

---

[4] Used in parentheses, (sic) shows that a quoted passage, especially one containing an error or something questionable, is reproduced precisely.

ignorance or imagination, or both, but a lack of the humility that marks those who are much, much farther along the road of progression, as we also observed. As for affirming that God approves of all one does, would this not imply that such affirmers consider themselves perfect?

44 Many of the affirmations recommended in the book do not make sense to us. In any case, we assert that *no* affirmation in itself will raise us one rung higher on the ladder of consciousness, or help us evolve in any way [768]. Only by living according to The Laws That Govern, by applying the knowledge we possess, and by *doing* rather than merely affirming or thinking, do we enlarge our consciousness or tend to become what we desire to be.

45 The "Master Teacher" repeatedly condemns the use of the word "I," but uses it in the above affirmation, and has little hesitation in saying: "Did I not say unto you..." — "Again I say..." — "Verily, I tell you..."

46 — **"Thou doest the work, oh Lord, but they say I do it."** ... **Mother, destroy in me all ideas that I am great, for who are they, but Thou in so many forms?**

47 — **In Creation everyone makes mistakes, but it is God's business to deliver us from evil.**

48 — **Acquire the conviction that everything is done by God's will.**

49 So we must believe that *God* is the cause of all the ills in the world, including people's inhumanity to others?

50 — **If one acquires the conviction... that one is only the tool in the hands of God, then is one free, even in this life.** So the Law of Personal Responsibility is not valid?

51 — **There is no such thing as cause and effect at all. There is... no reality in the law of cause and effect.** *Another* Law is repealed by the "Master Teacher"!

52 — **Students are urged to build a [spirit] home [while they are] here on this plane before passing out. If we don't, we will land there and have no place to go.**

53 What one prepares for oneself while on earth, as we explain more fully elsewhere [1307:24,27], is not an actual *dwelling* in the spirit world, but entry to an area, a plane or *level of consciousness*—the exact level of consciousness that one achieves on earth and that one will automatically gravitate to in the spirit realms, though not always at the very instant one passes. We also explain there why it usually would be pointless to build a spirit home while on earth, even if it were possible.

54 — **Our Spirit Guides become our mortal tools** [compare with 1223].

B.2 Misteachings   □ B13

55   **— Get truth for yourself. Don't try to get it for anyone else. Your brothers have the same opportunities that you have for getting it.**

56   What a contrast to the teachings of truly Illumined Souls!—to *share* truth with those we feel are ready to receive; and to post warnings of pitfalls on the path for those who may follow.

57   **— In case of premature death... the spirit [person has to] float around in space near the earth until the time of its natural passing out.**

58   This is a serious misteaching that could cause extreme grief to those whose loved ones do not die from natural causes. We have emphasized that there is no such thing as floating about in space for *anyone* who passes on, regardless of their errors of omission or commission or the manner of their passing [1319]. Does the "Master Teacher" hold the misteaching to apply to children killed, to people slain by robbers, to *all* victims of air crashes, and to *all* others who prematurely die?

59   **— You can throw your whole [spirit] band [of helpers] into captivity by becoming cranky, by criticizing something they have given you, some hope they have given you.**

60   This is absolutely incorrect, in our opinion. We reiterate that freedom is the heritage of every soul, on both sides of life, so that no one can put anyone else in "spiritual captivity," because *all souls have free will;* we also suggest that if a medium says that we can in any way place our spirit collaborators in "spiritual captivity," it is time to be finished with that medium once and for all.

61   **— The student asks: "Will I be able to obey to the fullest extent the commands that you give me?" Teacher's reply: "Verily, I tell you that your salvation is assured if you carry out even one-half of what I say unto you."** [Compare with 775:1, etc.]

62   We believe that this book provides overwhelming proof that a medium's reputation for excellence in demonstrating that life continues is *no* guarantee of anything approaching excellence in teachings and philosophy.

B13   On Misteachings by Unorthodox Healers

1   An article on healing [printed about 1980] contains the views of several [then] well-known unorthodox healers.

2   Their comments, on the whole, suggest that many healers then had little knowledge of the various forms of healing or of the *mechanics* of healing [1102, 1106].

3   One healer said that love and compassion, on the part of the healer, are the two vital ingredients in healing. Certainly they add much to the *power* of any healing flow, but they are not, strictly speaking, vital. Some healers, notably some who perform before immense audiences, are possessed not by compassion or love for their fellow human beings, but by the desire for the coin or currency of the realm; but they often do heal.

4   Another healer asserted that, in effect, it is always God who heals, a statement that cannot survive the light of reason.

5   God created Nature; and humans, by wisely using what *Nature* provides, can till and nourish the soil, plant the grain, and reap the harvest. But *God* does not do the tilling, the planting, and the reaping.

6   Any medication that may help to cure a condition is either a substance found in Nature or derived *from* Nature. It is *that* substance that may help to effect the cure, not God.

7   If a surgeon's skill averts a patient's death from, say, peritonitis, it is not God but the surgeon who saves a life.

8   Countless other examples could be furnished.

9   God has provided humanity with all that it needs, including curative substances necessary for healing. But it is *individuals* or groups of individuals—on earth or in spirit life, or both—who channel and direct those substances.

C
Reincarnation
by an editor

C01 On Reincarnation

1   Three times, between August 1990 and January 1992, Michael Flagg told me (John) that we *must* include a topic or brief chapter on reincarnation in this volume, to confirm its truth. We had discussed reincarnation a few times during the period when we were compiling the USB worldwide *Letters* into a manuscript for this volume [Intro:19]. But before we could finish the manuscript compilation, Michael developed a health condition that prevented him from working on it further. He was therefore also unable to prepare a topic on reincarnation for the volume, although until the end of his life here with us he always hoped to be able to work on the manuscript again.

2   Because I did not receive any formal material on reincarnation from Michael, and to try to comply with his wish to include something, I will here record whatever I can of related information that he *has* provided. I am treating this subject separately in this appendix because I am not able to pass it in the same way through the review by USB spirit leaders that the other material underwent. (However, see Intro:22.)

3   I gathered that, in the earlier years of the USB on earth, spirit leaders and Michael wanted to exclude mention of reincarnation, but later they came to see it differently. This is supported by the following. In the first (May 1958) version of the USB booklet, reincarnation is mentioned, together with vivisection and vegetarianism, as an example of controversial subjects to be avoided at USB public meetings. But, in later years, before distributing these booklets, Michael would mark a few corrections to them, and one of those corrections was to delete "reincarnation" from that list of subjects. He told me that now many more people believe in reincarnation and consider it important.

4   Other indications of the USB's position are given by the following.

APPENDIX C **Reincarnation**

In some of the early tape recordings made with the mediums mentioned in the preface of this book, when Michael was discovering the USB mission and the part he was to play in it, USB inspirers mentioned reincarnation a number of times. In the recording of a sitting in 1956, one can hear an Illumined Soul in spirit life discussing with Michael at least five incarnations that they had had together in the past. In at least eight other recordings, four different USB inspirers commented on or mentioned reincarnation. In all these cases they never questioned its truth.

In a 1958 newspaper article[1] about the then-new USB mission on earth and Michael's part in it, the editor who wrote it commented on the USB's lack of teachings on reincarnation. After introducing Michael and the USB, and discussing the USB's principles and values and what makes the USB different, the editor in his article (fully approved by Michael) wrote:

> I was somewhat surprised at the exclusion of the subject of reincarnation, for Flagg is as convinced of the truth of reincarnation —"without the trappings and nonsense so many invest it with!"— as he is of Survival [of physical death]. And he thinks that reincarnation, properly understood, is of even greater importance to us and our spiritual development.
>
> But he explains that there are many other avenues for discussion of controversial subjects that *divide* people; and that The Brotherhood's[2] aims are to *unite* people in peace and harmony— a peace and harmony based on love and service, knowledge of Survival, communication with those in other expressions of existence, enlightenment from Illumined Souls, and on the power of spirit [helpers] to heal.
>
> "When the world as a whole is ready for greater truths," he says, "they will be given, but even then only when the illumined inspirers of The Brotherhood so counsel."

From my discussions with Michael, I understand the "trappings and nonsense" that Michael referred to in the above quotation to include the following *incorrect* concepts: that people usually reincarnate immediately or soon after the death of their physical [earthly] body; that human beings can reincarnate as animals (1406:2); that people regularly change

---

[1] The reference and/or a copy are available upon request from USB headquarters.
[2] The original name of The Brother&Sisterhood (USB); see Intro:10.

C.1 Reincarnation

gender when they reincarnate (1321:13–14); and that there is a set time when the spirit enters the unborn physical body (1315).

11 My notes record that in 1990 and again in 1991 Michael told me, "Reincarnation is a great spiritual truth." In addition, reincarnation is indicated in Michael's preface (par. 16) and it seems to be strongly implied by Topic 1424.

12 Together, these particulars provide many instances of support for the truth of reincarnation, by both Michael and the USB spirit leaders. But in 1981 and again in 1991, Michael told me that we should only teach reincarnation to those who know about it and who are spiritually progressed. This, he said, is because we do not want people who lack sufficient understanding of spirituality and reincarnation to change their behavior due to a fear of punishment that reincarnation might represent to them. On other occasions he said that this book is for thinkers and those who seek spiritually something more.

D
Operation of the USB

APPENDIX CONTENTS

D.1 General Requirements — **539**

   D01 Some Requirements of the USB   539
   D02 No USB Affiliations   539
   D03 Simplicity and Humility   539
   D04 No Politics   540
   D05 Controversial Subjects   541
   D06 Financial Support   541
   D07 No Soliciting for Followers   542
   D08 On Linking Up with the USB   542
   D09 No Membership Fees   543
   D10 No Selling of Blessings   543
   D11 No "Fortune Telling"   543
   D12 "Laying On of Hands"   543
   D13 There Is Work for All   543
   D14 No Excessive Praise   544

D.2 Requirements and Recommendations for Meetings — **544**

   D15 Announcement of Meetings   544
   D16 Conduct of Meetings   544
   D17 Standing at Meetings Not Required   545
   D18 Reciting the USB Principles   545
   D19 Prayer in the USB   545
   D20 Collections at Meetings   545
   D21 Tobacco, Alcohol, and Drugs   546
   D22 Music   546
   D23 Platform Workers   546
   D24 Speakers and Writers   547
   D25 Mediums   548

continued...

D.3 Other Guidelines and Information — 549

D26	Qualities Needed	549
D27	What One Can Do	550
D28	Group Work Important—A Few Reminders	552
D29	What's in a Name? Sometimes, Much	553
D30	The USB Leaflet, Booklet, and Website	553
D31	USB Nonprofit Status	554
D32	A Little about Symbols—and Organizations	554
D33	The Inevitable Opposition	555
D34	Future USB Policies	556

D.1 GENERAL REQUIREMENTS

D01 Some Requirements of the USB

1 Truth has always suffered at the hands of some of its "disciples."

2 It suffers from those who twist and distort it for selfish ends—placing their own aggrandizement above the welfare of humanity, building nests of personal pride, and using spiritual movements for their own material gain and to enslave others.

3 That is why The Brother&Sisterhood has a few requirements, all of a *spiritual* nature, that people are expected to observe whenever they *officially* represent the USB in any capacity [see D27:13], [and that all are asked to observe at USB events]. What people do at other times is not for us to say.

4 These requirements are in harmony with noble teachings throughout the ages, and have had the blessing of USB spirit leaders and inspirers.

5 [The following topics in this section present and discuss the USB's more general requirements. Topic 107:1–2 regarding worship should also be considered a general requirement. Other requirements, relating to the conduct of USB meetings, are presented in Section D.2.]

D02 No USB Affiliations

1 The USB is *universal;* so while it therefore has room for all and everyone within its ranks, as an organization it is *not*, and *cannot* be, associated or linked with any other particular group or organization of *any* sort—religious, racial, national, political, or other. We *cannot* emphasize this too strongly.

2 (USB supporters are free to affiliate with whomever they wish [108], but they may not link activities of the USB or its representatives to activities of other organizations.)

D03 Simplicity and Humility

1 Simplicity and humility should mark the work of our movement in all its aspects—enlightenment, mediumship, and the "laying on of hands" [for healing, D12].

2   We do not glorify any individual. In our regular meeting places, if possible there should be no plaques or pictures of any individual, and no monuments of any sort to any individual.

3   No "day" may be set aside for any individual. Each day is a day for God only.

4   There may be no titles that separate our workers from the great flow of humanity. (This is one reason why we do not ordain ministers.) Titles of USB officers may be used only in their private meetings, and when legally required and expected; if really necessary, we may refer to them with others as "officers."

5   In our public meetings, group meetings, and publications, the only titles used in referring to our workers should be Sister, Brother, Mr., Mrs., Miss, and Ms. [or their equivalents in other languages].

6   While performing work for the USB, people should not wear unusual or outlandish clothing, or attire that represents or suggests any particular belief, following, or anything else that separates people spiritually.

7   Whenever possible, public meetings are to be held at places where there are no things that represent or suggest any particular person, group, belief, following, or anything else that separates people spiritually.

8   We do *not* condemn such things, which have value and meaning to many people. However, as an organization of spiritual truth for *all* people throughout the world, we cannot endorse, or appear to endorse, anything that tends to separate people spiritually.

9   What we also need to remember is that anything that separates people *spiritually* makes it even more difficult for highly evolved souls to draw near, because highly evolved souls all think in universal terms. It is a matter of attunement.

10 USB groups using premises that others place at their disposal should be grateful and appreciative, should not demand or expect changes to be made on their account, and should not comment on customs, views, and practices on those premises that differ from their own.

D04 *No Politics*

1   The USB is nonpolitical. It will never be political in any manner, shape, or form, and politics may not be discussed at any of its meetings. It will not in any way endorse or oppose the political ideas of any person or group of people. [This is also a legal requirement for the USB's nonprofit status.]

2   *Individuals* in the USB may engage in politics to their heart's content, but they must not attribute *their* political views or actions to the USB.

D.1 General Requirements □ *D06*

D05 Controversial Subjects

1 The Brother&Sisterhood takes no position on certain subjects which some consider controversial, such as vivisection, abortion, and vegetarianism, and such matters may not be discussed at its public meetings. (There are many other avenues for discussion of such subjects.)

2 Of course, there is *no* limitation to what USB supporters may discuss among themselves, or with others, provided they do not claim to voice *USB* views on subjects on which it takes no stand. So long as the discussions are friendly and harmonious, with each participant not only happy to share their own knowledge with others, but anxious to learn from one another, provided there is no wish to compel others to one's own way of thinking, and as long as we remember the great difference between discussion and debate, *any* exchange of opinion between people of good will is bound to be helpful.

3 (In *discussion*, we seek the facts; in *debate*, the triumph of a personal view or position.)

D06 Financial Support

1 All gifts to support the USB must be freely and voluntarily given. The USB does not solicit funds, contributions [D20], or donations.

2 On the other hand, it is quite proper to stress the aims of the USB and the need for funds to carry on its work.

3 As an Illumined Soul put it:

4 We realize in the material world that money must have its place, and to do this work—[the work of the USB]—there must be financial support. But it shall come . . . It shall come freely [voluntarily], and will come from people's hearts... That in itself will mean that the work can be done in the way we would wish it to be done. It will be done *with love.*

5 We know that those who support the USB's aims will of their own accord contribute what they can.[1]

---

[1] After study of our nonprofit organization (D31), the U. S. Treasury Department recognized The Brother&Sisterhood as a tax-exempt organization described in Section 501(c)(3) of the Internal Revenue Code. This means that contributions by U.S. taxpayers to the USB may generally be deducted when computing their taxable income.

6 [Except for those functions that are predominantly social events, the cost of attending all USB activities, as well as the cost of USB publications and recordings, shall be kept to a minimum, and shall be subsidized as far as possible by voluntarily-given financial support and by the services of volunteers. However, there shall be *no* admission charge for USB group meetings or services of worship. For all USB activities, including more formal ones like courses, workshops, lectures, and demonstrations of mediumship, financial arrangements and admission costs (if applicable) shall be agreed by a group or committee; except, for group meetings this is optional.]

7 [Organizers may explain to participants the expenses of USB group meetings (D28:2) and similar activities, and the financial circumstances under which they could be held or would have to be discontinued. But all financial support, including that for group meetings, must always be freely given (see also D20). And participation in USB activities must always be optional.]

D07 No Soliciting for Followers

1 We do *not* try to persuade others to follow or join the USB. We may suggest they consider it. But we prefer that others ask to join with us, rather than we persuading them.

D08 On Linking Up with the USB

1 [In accordance with Topic 111: anyone who feels the work of love of the great spirit beings who lead the USB is important to them; anyone who feels supportive of, committed to, and/or aligned with the illumined USB leaders, their philosophy, and their mission; anyone who wishes to be closely connected with those leaders or to "belong" to the USB—he or she can become a USB member. Membership is not "closed" or "special," it is free and open to everyone. The USB considers all humankind to be brothers and sisters; it recognizes no separation of people, rather it aims to unite them.]

2 Those who decide to become USB members need not give up other affiliations and/or beliefs they hold, in fact they need not give up anything; and they need not accept every one of the USB's purposes and principles.

D.1 General Requirements

D09 No Membership Fees

1   The USB will never have membership fees or dues of any kind.

D10 No Selling of Blessings

1   There may be nothing resembling the "selling of blessings." So there may be no statement or implication, from the platform or anywhere else, that any contribution to the USB will be returned many times over, or that contributors will in any way be rewarded for what they give.

D11 No "Fortune-Telling"

1   The USB does not permit anything resembling "fortune-telling."

2   Our guides come to inform and inspire us. They come to encourage and strengthen us spiritually. They come to remind us of the laws of God, a God that is all-love, all-wisdom, all-justice.

3   They do *not* come to do our work for us, or to deprive us of the trials and tests which, well met, develop our character and enable us to progress spiritually.

4   From time to time they may, from higher vantage points, see what appears on the horizon; but let us not forget that changes in our attitude and endeavors may, and often do, affect the picture. All is changeable except God and Truth, which includes God's laws [415:1].

D12 "Laying On of Hands"

1   We know that the power of spirit is unlimited, and that the more spiritual we are, the greater the channel we can be for healing if that is our avenue of service.

2   One form of healing is through the "laying on of hands" [1106:2].

3   Healers may lay on hands, with the hope that spirit power may flow through them, but they are *not* permitted to massage or manipulate the body when they represent the USB [and see 1110:20].

D13 There Is Work For All

1   "In this great truth, in this movement, one must remember that each and everyone plays a part. Everyone has work to do. No one shall be greater than another" [A01:1].

2   Indeed no worker shall be more important than another [and D03:4], even though some may have greater gifts or greater opportunities to serve. In the same way, no USB group is more important than another, regardless of its size, and no USB group has jurisdiction over any other.
3   We who work for the USB are one; and whatever any contribute, they contribute for all.
4   So we rejoice when others serve as well, or better. We rejoice when others hold the torch as high, or higher. We rejoice when others, in as great a measure or greater, help to fulfil the purposes of the USB.

D14 No Excessive Praise

1   The USB disapproves of excessive praise of any individual.
2   Kind reference to someone's work, if merited, is one thing; excessive or insincere praise is another.
3   Too often a speaker's talk is described as "words of wisdom" when it is little more than mediocre.

D.2 Requirements and Recommendations[2] for Meetings

D15 Announcement of Meetings

1   Whenever possible, advertisements or other announcements of USB meetings should include not only the name of the speaker, if any, but also the *topic* to be discussed.
2   This is only fair, to aid people in deciding whether to attend.
3   We should not fall into the error of smugness—of assuming that *anything* we offer will be of interest and value to everyone.

D16 Conduct of Meetings

1   For meetings of The Brother&Sisterhood there are no rituals, rites, or prescribed ceremonies.
2   Apart from an opening and closing prayer—which could well begin and end any aspect of our work—there are no rules for the content and order of such meetings.

---

[2] Recommendations (D18–D19) are clearly identified by the inclusion of that word; all others are requirements.

D.2 Requirements and Recommendations for Meetings   □ D20

3   Whenever possible, a public USB meeting should provide enlightenment, mediumship, and healing, not necessarily in that order.

D17 Standing at Meetings Not Required

1   Those attending USB meetings need not be required to stand at any time.

2   We should avoid frequent standing up at USB meetings, as this does not add to a service, and only inconveniences many people, the elderly in particular.

D18 Reciting the USB Principles

1   Whether or not the USB principles should be read or recited at its public meetings (preferably in unison by those who care to recite them) is up to those who preside.

2   We recommend one or the other at USB meetings that are open to the public, particularly when newcomers are present, because of the power of the spoken word when sincerely expressed; because the principles of this Brother&Sisterhood should be commonly known; and because they may touch the heart and mind of those who hear them. The manner of execution should be varied, to prevent it from developing into a ritual.

D19 Prayer in the USB

1   It is the right and privilege of members of any USB group to choose the prayers [if any] *they* would say aloud, the prayers *they* feel would make for greater harmony and greater attunement *within* the group—always provided that they reveal no worship of anyone but God [see 521:12–13].

2   Before reciting any particular prayer in unison, we recommend that the chair of a USB meeting should announce that the USB has *no* set prayers, and that those present should feel free to join or not join in the prayer to be offered.

3   We recommend a minute of silent prayer, with each person praying to the God of his or her own understanding.

D20 Collections at Meetings

1   Collection boxes may be left near the doors and at other suitable places at meetings, so that people may, if they wish, deposit contributions to help in the work of the USB. But the passing of collection boxes or plates is *not* permitted [D06].

D21 Tobacco, Alcohol, and Drugs

1. The use of tobacco, alcohol, and drugs, which are depressants and make it difficult if not impossible for advanced souls to come through, is of course not allowed at USB gatherings if evidence of Survival [of physical death] and communication with spirit people is desired or expected.

D22 Music

1. Any music at USB meetings should be joyous in nature and universal in appeal. We have much to be grateful for, much to rejoice in, and the music should reflect it.
2. Joyous and beautiful music also uplifts the atmosphere.
3. As this movement is universal, we should avoid any song or music that suggests any particular belief system.
4. We discourage any song or hymn that glorifies anyone but God.

D23 Platform Workers

1. Truth suffers severely from those who twist and distort it for selfish ends. It also suffers from those who, however well-meaning, are unprepared or ill-prepared to serve. These are some of the reasons why the USB has important requirements, that platform workers who identify themselves as USB mediums and/or USB speakers are expected to observe at all times, and that other visiting mediums and speakers are asked to observe at USB events.
2. The *wish* to serve is not enough. *Preparation and discipline are essential.*
3. Athletes train for weeks, or months, for one race. Pianists, however famous, practice to preserve or improve the dexterity of their fingers. [In the same way, mediums usually need years of development to become competent, and speakers (and writers) who are not controlled by highly advanced spirit co-workers need to have studied their subjects.]
4. But too many "disciples" of truth think that all that is necessary is to step upon a platform—and leave the rest to spirit helpers [1414].
5. To serve on the platform we need to prepare. We must realize that only when we ourselves do all we can, have we the right to seek the aid of spirit people.
6. We must realize that we owe it not only to our audience on earth, but to spirit co-workers as well, to *prepare* for any work we do.
7. The USB's policy on mediums and speakers is this:

D.2 Requirements and Recommendations for Meetings □ D24

8   Better no medium at all, than one whose work is so feeble and unconvincing as to create doubt in the newcomer of the truth of Survival and the reality of communion with spirit people [see also D25].

9   Better no speaker at all, than one who is poorly prepared, or who speaks fluently but says little [see also D24].

D24 Speakers and Writers

1   Unfortunately it is true that *speakers* often speak fluently but say very little.

2   To serve as speakers, we should never forget that no flood of words can atone for poverty of ideas.

3   We need to prepare notes, mental or written.

4   We need to stick to the subject, and avoid tiring our audiences with the same rambling generalities, as so often occurs.

5   If we do present an ounce [a few grams] of truth, we must be sure it is not so enveloped with a ton of fiction as to be unrecognizable.

6   We should be very cautious about speaking by "inspiration" only, as this usually leaves listeners confused instead of enlightened.

7   If we speak in trance, or semi-trance, we need to realize and remember that unless one is a trance speaker controlled by highly advanced spirit co-workers, there is *no* substitute for preparation.

8   Being controlled means nothing in itself—for not all spirit controls are enlightened or worth listening to. To be on the other side of life does not automatically give one wisdom, understanding, or the gift of instruction.

9   There are at least as many levels among spirit people as there are among "mortals." And The Law of Attraction is such that we do not attract more advanced spirit guides and controls than we merit. Their caliber depends at least in part on the degree in which we prepare.

10   When serving as USB speakers it is our duty to *prepare* what we are to say at our meetings, so that we can say it clearly, simply, and coherently.

11   We are not asked to say anything but the words that come from our hearts.

12   We are not asked to polish our phrases or to be flowery.

13   We are not asked to be out of character with ourselves.

14   But we *are* asked to prepare. We *are* asked to be sincere. We *are* asked to realize that a message is of little use if it isn't clear. We *are* asked to remember that truth, like all things beautiful, is simple. We *are* asked to remember that *the more we prepare, the better we can serve.* [See also D23.]

15 Sadly, we must add, too many **writers** also are wordy and say little.

16 Both groups forget—or perhaps assume that audiences haven't the intelligence to realize—that as we said, no flood of words can atone for poverty of ideas.

D25 Mediums

1 No one has a greater regard than The Brother&Sisterhood for truly *spiritual* mediums, and for the part they *can* play, and *are* playing, in helping to bring about a new heaven on earth [1207:6–7].

2 If we have strict requirements, as we *do* have, for mediums who represent the USB at *any* time, it is only because we know how a few mediums have used their mediumship for ignoble purposes, twisting and distorting truth when it suited them, or enslaving those they could enslave [1220].

3 Good mediumship, on and off the platform, is essential to provide convincing proof that life continues, that there is no death to the spirit, that love knows no barriers, and that there *is* communion with those who have passed on to the other side of life.

4 Unfortunately, however, mediumship is often so poor as to drive away the searcher, who sometimes never returns.

5 That is why it is USB policy to have no medium on the platform rather than a poor one.

6 There can be only one exception: a fully satisfactory medium *may* be preceded by a "beginner," provided that someone makes it clear that the beginner is *attempting* to serve, and that they ask the audience to be patient and understanding.

7 A medium, too, can prepare for service—by aspiring to be a completely open channel for the spirit world, and by being truly spiritual (and therefore humble and self-effacing). [See also D23.]

8 To serve on a high level, mediums need to be humble. They need to be completely open-minded. They need to place spiritual progress above personal desires. They need to put aside all personal opinions and prejudices. They need to not think of personal glory and power. They need to shun jealousy and envy and bitterness. They need to not cling to orthodox views, or imitate the orthodox churches, or desire form and ceremony at a meeting.

9 Only then may the vibrations be such as to permit a free and unfettered flow from a high spirit level.

10. Mediums need to always remember their responsibility to truth.
11. They need to always remember that they are the "telephone" over which the message comes, and not the message itself.
12. They must never attempt to give messages when they are not "moved by the spirit." In such cases, they should acknowledge the fact, frankly.
13. They must shun the worst sin of all—ascribing to the spirit world, or implying as coming from the spirit world, what does *not* come from the spirit world.

14. Any mediums who *consciously* permit their lips to give advice, from themselves or spirit people, that they know is unsound, unwise, misleading, or likely to cause acute distress, incur a great debt.

D.3 OTHER GUIDELINES AND INFORMATION

D26 Qualities Needed

1. Those who work for the USB should develop or foster many qualities within themselves.
2. Love, integrity, charity, understanding, compassion, gentleness, tolerance, patience, universality—all these are needed.
3. It may be hard to be patient with those who are consumed with envy and jealousy, or who lie and vilify and slander.
4. But if we are patient with the blind and the lame, and others who are physically afflicted, surely we should be patient with those who are *spiritually* afflicted—for spiritual ills are far longer lasting than any physical ills, and have far greater consequences.
5. What we need especially is to think *universally*—not in terms of one person or one people, but in terms of *all people*, in terms of *all humankind*.
6. We must remember that nothing is ours until we apply it. Love, charity, tolerance, the brother-and-sisterhood of humankind—these are idle words or phrases from our lips until we apply them in our daily lives. Only then do they become part of our universe.
7. Those who work for the USB owe it not only to themselves but to the USB to *live* by its principles. [See also Topic 309.]

D27 What One Can Do

1. [There are countless ways that we can help others, serve our society, and serve all humankind. Here we will discuss ways we can assist the work of the USB, which should always be another way of serving others.]

2. Much will depend on us who, as supporters and members of The Brother-&Sisterhood, are the nucleus of the work on this side of life. There are many ways we can contribute to the USB mission [see also 112]. [As much as possible of the USB's work will be done by volunteers.]

3. We need, each and all of us, to rid ourselves of our weaknesses, so that we can work one with another, with no thought of self, and with the common good of humanity uppermost in our thoughts.

4. Some of you have mentioned that your own individual efforts are insignificant. Don't underrate your work. Nothing is wasted. There is worth in even the humblest effort.

5. *Much of our work will be accomplished by small groups* in all parts of the world—groups that meet in love and harmony and aspiration to serve [D28], thus adding to the reservoir of spiritual power that will divert humanity from the road to destruction.

6. With all our supporters knowing exactly what the USB represents, and its position on every issue, each Sister and Brother becomes a guardian *of* truth; each assumes a responsibility *to* truth; and each can be vigilant in seeing that the USB light remains pure and undimmed. This includes guarding against anyone misrepresenting the USB in any way, wittingly or unwittingly, or anyone "adding" to the official USB teachings in this book [116:5,7]. [To help themselves be well informed for this, and for so many other purposes, supporters are encouraged to reread the teachings from time to time.]

7. [To help identify and prevent misteachings in the name of the USB, we require all subsequent authentic USB publications containing teachings and/or philosophy to display the following boxed statement in a prominent position:

> If any teaching and/or philosophy in this USB document is in conflict with or is not supported by *Spiritual Light* (ISBN 978-0-9912422-1-4 deluxe flex-cover, 978-0-9912422-2-1 paperback), which contains the only complete *official* teachings and philosophy of the USB, then *Spiritual Light* governs. The inclusion of this statement, in a box in a prominent position, and worded as in *Spiritual Light*, is required on every authentic USB publication containing its teachings and/or philosophy.

D.3 Other Guidelines and Information ☐ D27

This requirement also applies to all translations of this original English language version of the book into other languages. USB supporters can help assure that this requirement is followed, and can draw attention to any concerns about it.]

8   The USB is, by the way, registered—to guard against unauthorized use of the same or similar name by any individual or organization, and to prevent people from exploiting the USB for their own ends.

9   Each one of us, as a member or follower of the USB, has the right to give a word of light to others. However, we should never continue unless there is some response, some desire to hear more. We must *never* force our views on anyone.

10   In other words, we can say something about the USB—its accent on *spiritual* living; its emphasis on freedom and brother-and-sisterhood; its desire to reawaken humanity to the spark of God within each of us—and if others thirst for more particulars, *then* give them.

11   USB supporters can publicize the USB in the local press, in psychic papers, and in other places [see also par. 13]. This book is a storehouse of information not only for ready reference and guidance, but for *use*.

12   It has been good to see USB philosophy expressed in printed columns in various papers, often in the very words of the USB. Where possible, let us *mention* The Brother&Sisterhood; let us let others know *something* of our aims, principles, and policies.

13   [In the same spirit, group leaders, with the welcome assistance of others (per D28:4), can help the USB in the following ways. They can make the USB more widely known through various types of social networking and other communication methods, including broadcasting. Those with the necessary abilities are encouraged to make presentations and to foster and prepare publications that promote the principles and values of the USB (see 14–18), and that if possible mention the USB and this book. They can organize and lead other types of USB meetings besides USB groups (D28). Plans for all "larger" activities need to be discussed with headquarters.]

14   [*Anyone* is welcome to discuss with headquarters their proposed plans for ways of helping. And anyone, if they wish, can contribute financially (D06) and/or serve as a volunteer. *Everyone's* help is greatly appreciated; helpers are asked to follow the requirements of Appendix D and those with little experience of the USB are asked to seek the advice of a USB group leader. In all ways that they can take part, helpers will be aligning themselves with Illumined Souls and joining them as co-workers in their mission.]

15 This work [A05], in which each one of us associated with the USB is blessed and privileged to play a part, will flourish in the degree that we sink ourselves in service, and to the extent that we are prepared to sacrifice so that truth and enlightenment may go forth to the uttermost ends of the earth.

D28 Group Work Important—A Few Reminders

1 As we have said [D27:5], "much of our work will be accomplished by small groups in all parts of the world." We remind USB groups of the tremendous *importance* of harmony within the group [1311:40–41].

2 [Participation in a USB group will allow people to meet regularly with others having similar spiritual interests, for such purposes as discussion or study of USB teachings, communion (under the right conditions) with USB spirit friends, and/or personal development. It will provide searchers with better access to information. And it will help those who wish to participate in USB service (112, D27) to do so in cooperation with others. Each dedicated individual and group will be adding to the spiritual reservoir that Illumined Souls have said they need to enable them to bring about great changes for good (102:10–16).]

3 [People who feel a strong attraction to our philosophy and way of life, and who cannot find a suitable USB group in their area to join, should consider forming their own USB groups. If possible, group leaders should be very familiar with our teachings. We offer further guidance on forming and running groups.]

4 Anyone desiring to start and lead a USB group should write directly to headquarters [via the USB website, *www.theusb.org*]. (No individual outside headquarters has authority to give anyone permission to organize a group of the USB.) [To protect the integrity of the USB mission, all USB activities will be led either by headquarters or by USB-approved group leaders. Others are most welcome to offer their help.]

5 [Some groups may be formed to develop or use mediumship for purely spiritual purposes, in the hope that they may commune with Illumined Souls, or with other USB leaders and helpers from high levels in the spirit realms. For such communion, group members should remember that the most important requirement is their *spiritual* development (1407:2). Such groups should be either led or supervised by spiritual and experienced mediums (1242:7,23–27), who are also familiar with our teachings.]

6 We encourage USB groups to do all they can to spread truth and enlightenment [D27:9–14]. They are free to put out booklets, leaflets and such—

D.3 Other Guidelines and Information ☐ *D30*

always of course guided by the requirements and policies of the USB, and with their names and addresses on what they issue. (Material for nation-wide and world-wide distribution is the responsibility of national and international offices of the USB, with copies sent to its worldwide headquarters.)

7 Groups wishing to advertise are welcome to send proposed material to headquarters for comments and suggestions. In any case, they are expected to submit copies of printed advertisements [and references to or prints of digital advertisements] for headquarters' records.

8 Groups are also expected to send to headquarters a copy of any and all material reproduced for distribution, if that material is on the letterhead of a USB group or is represented as coming, directly or indirectly, from the USB. [Likewise, they are expected to inform headquarters of all USB-related websites or Web material they create.]

9 We do not ask those who direct USB groups to send a detailed account of each and every meeting. A brief quarterly summary is enough, unless they wish to write more often or in greater detail.

10 The important thing is that the USB is not misrepresented to others, and that nothing is misrepresented to headquarters.

D29 *What's in a Name? Sometimes, Much*

1 Any name for a Brother&Sisterhood group that meets from time to time could well include some such term as *group* or *center* or *branch* or *unit* or *meeting place*.

2 If we do not recommend terms like *church* or *mosque* or *synagogue*, it is only because to millions of people such words denote particular religions or denominations or sects. And the USB is a way of life, a way of life open to *all*, a way of life untrammelled by creeds and rituals and dogmas of any sort, a way of life that will in time embrace many other groups and organizations that exist today.

3 It is well, as we build, to avoid anything that limits or that would tend to limit the great and vital mission of this movement.

D30 *The USB Leaflet, Booklet, and Website*

1 Every USB member and supporter should have a copy of the USB leaflet or booklet and a copy of this book. Group leaders should keep on hand some extra copies of the leaflet and/or booklet.

2 The leaflet (Appendix E) has many purposes. Among other things, it will be a handy reference for helpers, who can do so much to further the

USB's work. Describing the USB, the leaflet mentions its aims and purposes, things it supports and things it opposes, and its guiding principle that "in all things we do, there is no cause greater than Truth" [304:1]. The leaflet will also answer many questions asked by people interested in learning more about the USB.

3   [The leaflet will be especially important to people who do not have access to the Internet. Printed on two sides of a single sheet (see Appendix E), it is easy to reproduce and distribute to people who are first learning of the USB.]

4   [While we hope that USB supporters will introduce the USB and its philosophy to people who appear to be seeking such information, please note that the USB does not actively seek members or promote membership (D07), so it does not push itself on anyone (D27:9). Instead, it prefers supporters and members to come from people who are searching for an organization and/or teachings like ours.]

5   [A more comprehensive introductory USB booklet may be prepared by headquarters if it is found to be needed by people who do not have access to our website.]

6   [The USB website, at *www.TheUSB.org*, provides much information about the USB.]

D31 USB Nonprofit Status

1   The Universal Spiritual Brother&Sisterhood on earth is a nonprofit organization, and "The property of this corporation is irrevocably dedicated to religious and charitable purposes and no part of the net income or assets of this corporation shall ever inure [accrue] to the benefit of any director, officer or member thereof or to the benefit of any private person..." (Articles of Incorporation, 1956, restated 2009.) [See also D06:n1.]

D32 A Little about Symbols—and Organizations

1   We have more than once been asked why the USB does not have a special symbol, one preferably that can be worn, so that members and supporters can recognize one another at a glance. There are several reasons.

2   To have a symbol of a material nature that could be displayed would be to follow the custom of organizations first founded on earth—which of course we are not.

3   Then, too, the average symbol sets aside one person from another—and that is not our purpose, not our mission.

D.3 Other Guidelines and Information ☐ D33

4 Our purpose, our mission—or rather, one *part* of our mission—is to bring people closer, to unite them, to form one great spiritual brother-and-sisterhood throughout the world.

5 The average symbol suggests that while *one* person is a sister or brother and walks the same path, another is *not*.

6 We do *not* separate one person from another. We recognize no separation, except separations that spring from people's ignorance and fear—and one of our purposes is to *remove* such barriers that separate peoples and nations and individuals.

7 We know that *all* people are brothers and sisters, whether or not they realize it, and whether or not they belong to the USB; and we hope that all links with the USB *live* by that knowledge and *spread* that knowledge.

8 Many organizations created by people are houses divided against themselves, despite their symbols. For while they follow certain paths and invite all to join, they separate their members according to the color of their skin or the faith they were born in.

9 There is no separation in the handclasp. The hands clasped in love and friendship cannot be misinterpreted by anyone who thinks about them. They symbolize the union of all people.

10 But we still do not claim the handclasp as our own special symbol.[3] For we have *no* secret signs, *no* secret symbols. What we have is open to all.

11 There is yet another reason why we do not have a symbol that can be worn. What is precious to us, what is holy to us, we do not outwardly display, but hold close to our heart.

D33 The Inevitable Opposition

1 Opposition to the USB grows as the USB grows. This is inevitable, especially from those who find their prestige and their power wane as more and more follow the USB and embrace its teachings and philosophy.

2 It is not only the betrayers of truth who oppose us. Some good and thoroughly well-meaning people have resented what they consider the intrusion of a "new" movement—unaware that it is the counterpart of the

---

[3] I interpret this topic to say that we may use the handclasp as a symbol of our welcome to all and of human togetherness and unity, as used on our 1958 booklet, but *not* as a symbol of the USB or its productions. –Ed.

original that has long existed in the higher spirit realms, unaware that Illumined Souls are its inspirers, and unaware that it is *the* movement planned in the spirit world for centuries *for* the earth for this very time and age.

3 We have been well prepared to expect opposition. We quote from two warnings received from inspirers at sittings in London as long ago as 1956 and 1957, the first given before the USB on earth was even officially launched.

4 > You're living in a material world; and although often people claim to be spiritually minded, often fundamentally they're very materialistic. And you're *bound* to have opposition—from sources which may even surprise you...

5 > There will be disappointments still, coming from individuals who perhaps you now hope will give you assistance. Remember that they have their *own* theories, their *own* ideas, cherished over long years.

6 > You might say to me: "How could they be in opposition to anything that we are trying to do?" I agree with you—there should be *no* opposition. But people often are strange creatures, with weaknesses within themselves which are not discernible within the face of things...

7 Opposition will come from those who see their strongholds weakening—threatened from without by Truth, threatened from within by the spirit of freedom.

8 They will learn, as others have learned before them, that all is built on quicksands that is not built on the rock of Truth, and that all ramparts must tumble unless bulwarked by freedom.

9 But whether it is the destructive or the well-meaning that oppose us, we do not condemn them [325:3–5].

D34 Future USB Policies

1 The Brother&Sisterhood on earth will remain under the inspiration, direction, and guidance of Illumined Souls. *No* changes in USB policies will ever be made unless *they* so direct, under conditions and circumstances similar to those at which *they* outlined the mission of the USB [in 1956], gave its full name, and confirmed its principles and policies [see e.g., Pref:5–7, Pref:26–36, A01:2–3, A02:2–3].

E
The USB Leaflet

E01 The USB Leaflet

1 This appendix describes the content and preparation of the USB leaflet. Its uses are discussed in Topic D30.

2 The leaflet is designed for easy duplication and distribution.

<u>Layout</u>

3 The text is arranged to fit into six panels or columns, three on each side of a single sheet of paper in landscape orientation. The panels are positioned as shown in the following two figures:

4 Inside:

United...	Purposes,	Mission
Universality	Principles	Humble
2	3	4

5 "Outside:"

Requirements	At a glance...	Front cover
Publications	(Back)	(handclasp)
5	6	(1)

Printing

6   There are two most common sizes of printer or copier paper in use in the world, and the leaflet has been designed separately for each of these. For either size, one may download the text from the website *www.TheUSB.org*.

7   Traditionally the leaflet has been printed on straw-colored paper, and preferably on paper a little heaver than common printer or copier paper.

8   Please check that the bottom column numbers on both sides are printed by the same edge.

Folding

9   The following information in Table E is provided to help anyone fold the leaflets they have downloaded from the USB website and printed, or to recreate the leaflets if they are unable to download them or obtain them from USB headquarters:

10
Table E

Dimension	ISO-A4 paper	American "letter" paper
Full sheet width	297 mm. ($11^{11}/_{16}$ inches)	11 inches (279.4 mm.)
Full sheet height	210 mm. ($8^{1}/_{4}$ inches)	$8^{1}/_{2}$ inches (215.9 mm.)
Text column width	82.5 mm. ($3^{1}/_{4}$ inches)	3 inches (76.2 mm.)
Text column height (including column #)	185 mm. ($7^{1}/_{4}$ inches)	$7^{1}/_{2}$ inches (190.5 mm.)
Outer margins width	10 mm. ($^{13}/_{32}$ inch)	$^{3}/_{8}$ inch (9.5 mm.)
Inner margins width	15 mm. ($^{19}/_{32}$ inch)	$^{5}/_{8}$ inch (15.9 mm.)
Right edge to 1st fold	98 mm. ($3^{7}/_{8}$ inches)	$3^{5}/_{8}$ inches (92.1 mm.)
Right edge to 2nd fold	197 mm. ($7^{3}/_{4}$ inches)	$7^{5}/_{16}$ inch (185.7 mm.)

11 When looking at the inside (columns 2–4), the two outer columns should be folded forward: first fold column 4 to cover column 3, and next fold column 2 to cover the other two. Columns 2–5 will then be hidden from view and columns 1 and 6 will be exposed.

Contents

12 If there is a need to recreate the text for the leaflet, the contents of its six panels, reduced in size to fit here, are given on the following six pages.

13 Before reprinting, please check if any information it gives has changed.

E.1 The USB Leaflet □ *E01*

Column (1):

The Universal Spiritual Brother&Sisterhood

USB

teaching

Spiritual Truth and Wisdom

and working towards

Universal Love and Harmony

Worldwide Headquarters
in CALIFORNIA, USA

www.TheUSB.org

E01 ☐   APPENDIX E *The USB Leaflet*

Column 2:

United in spirit, serving universally

By spreading spiritual teachings and truth received from exceptionally high and pure spirit sources, The Universal Spiritual Brother&Sisterhood* (USB) is striving to uplift, spiritualize, and unite humanity, to awaken us all to the many spiritual realities of life and to the God within. In this way it is working to bring peace and harmony to *all* people. (By "spiritual" we mean having high and noble qualities of spirit.)

Many of the greatest teachers and prophets who have lived on earth—who have since risen to even *greater* spiritual heights—are the originators and leaders of this movement. Surrounded by incredible auras and bright spiritual light, they have been described as "Beings of Light"; we usually call them Illumined Souls.

They offer to help all humanity. They see so much suffering on earth, and that from time to time all life on earth is in grave danger. They teach that humanity needs to live in accord with God's perfect spiritual laws. They call on all people, everywhere, to join in their enterprise.

They encourage us to form groups to study and discuss their philosophy, so that we may better understand and enjoy it, gain spiritual wisdom, and put it into practice and spread it in our daily lives.

The USB is **an organization of spiritual truth** (not a religion), working in concert with its parent organization that has long existed in the highest spirit realms. Supporters will always remember its guiding principle: "In all things we do, there is no cause greater than Truth."

These Illumined Souls humbly note that they offer us only Truth *as they see it*, from their (extraordinary) vantage point. They seek no unthinking acceptance. They ask us to accept only what our inner being tells us is true *and* our reason completely embraces.

---

*Founded in 1956 under its original name (The Universal Spiritual Brotherhood, the same name as its parent spirit organization), the USB is a 501c3 nonprofit organization, and none of its assets may inure (accrue) to any individual. Its property is irrevocably dedicated to charitable and religious purposes. (Articles of Incorporation.)

> If any teaching and/or philosophy in this USB document is in conflict with or is not supported by *Spiritual Light* (ISBN 978-0-9912422-1-4 deluxe flex-cover, 978-0-9912422-2-1 paperback), which contains the only complete and *official* teachings and philosophy of the USB, then *Spiritual Light* governs. The inclusion of this statement, in a box in a prominent position, and worded as in *Spiritual Light*, is required on every authentic USB publication containing its teachings and/or philosophy.

2

E.1 The USB Leaflet

Column 3:

USB PRINCIPLES

1. God is That Which is All-Good—a God of Love and Wisdom, of Law and Justice.
2. All humankind are God's children, and this means we are *all* spiritual brothers and sisters without exception.
3. Our lives are eternal and we shall retain our individualities after the change called death.
4. Under certain conditions we can commune with those in other expressions of life.
5. We are each personally responsible for all we say, think and do; and no belief in anyone, or allegiance to anyone, can absolve us from that responsibility.
6. The law of cause and effect, like all other spiritual laws, knows no exception; and as we sow we reap, here or hereafter.
7. The doors to spiritual progress are never closed to anyone—and loving ones will help us if we but reach out our hearts and minds to God.
8. Aspiration and effort are inseparable, so one cannot *truly* aspire without making the effort.
9. We should serve selflessly, as best we can, to bring love and peace and harmony to humanity, to bring the day ever nearer when all shall live in a universal spiritual brother-and-sisterhood.

USB PURPOSES

1. To unfold to humanity a way of life, and a new understanding of God's will and purpose.
2. To bring a universal awareness of the spark of God within each of us, and a realization that love is the greatest basis of spiritual life.
3. To bring to humanity peace and tranquillity of spirit, and happiness of heart and soul.
4. To break down the barriers that stand between one nation and another, between one people and another, and between one individual and another.
5. To break down the barriers of creeds and dogmas.
6. To cast aside ignorance and replace it with truth.
7. To form one great spiritual brother-and-sisterhood throughout the world.

3

Column 4:

THE USB MOVEMENT

The Illumined Souls in spirit life who lead the USB have presented a multitude of wise and beautiful teachings that are now compiled into books (see "USB Publications" in column 5). Their goals are to spread this knowledge, to encourage living by it, and to build a dedicated following.

Supporters working together in groups are very important to this mission. Each person who links up with this movement, and each group that meets from time to time in love and harmony for purely spiritual purposes, adds to the spiritual reservoir that will be used for great things in the years to come.

"There are great powers," says an Illumined Soul, *"greater than any that you or any soul upon earth know of..., whereby we can, through the right people, when the time comes, demonstrate the power of God that flows through us.*

"But we need thousands of souls"—*"souls afire with the desire to do the will of God."*

HUMBLE ALWAYS

This movement began in a humble way, but its power will grow with the years, and it will in time *"sweep the world with love and tenderness."*

But it will remain humble always, as must those who serve it. Illumined Souls themselves have said, *"We who come to you, ... though our development through the spheres has been great, ... we come in humbleness and in spiritual desire to work with you, and through you... We only ask that you accept us and treat us as brothers and sisters a little more enlightened."*

PERSONAL FREEDOM FOR ALL

You need not accept every USB purpose and principle to join with us. It is enough to realize that all humankind (on *both* sides of life) are God's children, and that this means we are all spiritual brothers and sisters.

Nor do you need to give up other beliefs and/or affiliations on joining with the USB.

Everyone must have *"above all things... personal freedom..."*

E.1 The USB Leaflet □ E01

Column 5:

SOME USB REQUIREMENTS

Supporters and workers are expected to observe certain requirements whenever they *officially* represent the USB (what they do at other times is not for us to say). Those requirements include:

Simplicity and humility must mark the USB's work in all its aspects—enlightenment, mediumship, and healing.

The USB discourages any worship of any one. We believe we should worship only God.

We do not glorify any individual.

There are no membership fees or dues of any kind. The USB does not solicit funds; there may be no passing of collection boxes or plates at its meetings. All contributions must come freely, from people's hearts, with love.

There are no rituals, rites, or prescribed ceremonies for USB meetings.

We do not permit anything resembling "fortune-telling."

The USB is non-political. Politics may not be discussed at any of its meetings.

MORE INFORMATION

This leaflet provides an introduction to the USB. If you wish to explore further, please do so at our extensive web site, in our publications, or by writing to us by e-mail.

USB PUBLICATIONS

The USB's principal volume of teachings, *Spiritual Light*, related documents, and study and organizational guides, are produced by our publishing division, USB Vision Press. More are planned. You may obtain a list (and see some) at our website, or from our headquarters.

THE GOAL WILL BE REACHED

Many hundreds of people in more than 20 countries have joined with the USB since its founding. They form a band encircling the globe, a band that will widen with the years until it covers the entire world, to unite people everywhere in love and peace and harmony, in universal spiritual brother-and-sisterhood.

Copyright © 2014 by The USB.   1 January 2014

Column 6:

At a glance, about the USB,

The Universal Spiritual Brother&Sisterhood

It is:

Universal because it recognizes great teachers among all ages and times, and acknowledges truth *wherever* it is found; because it regards *all* people as equally important, and so it makes no distinction between supporters by titles, attire, importance, etc.

Spiritual because this movement was planned and is led by teachers of the most advanced spirituality; because they teach spiritual truth, spirituality, simplicity, humility, and that love is the greatest basis of spiritual life; because it is dedicated to spreading teachings and philosophy from the highest spiritual realms; and because it only accepts financial support that is given *freely*, from the heart.

A brother-and-sisterhood because it is working to unite all people in peace, love, and harmony, in brother-and-sisterhood; and because the illumined leaders teach that we all have a spark of God and so are all linked as spiritual brothers and sisters.

Further, the USB emphasizes:
• spiritual truth • the use of reason • personal freedom for all (so no need to give up other beliefs or affiliations) • total personal responsibility • giving selfless service • an absence of commercialism and "glorification" • no rituals, debating, smugness, or politics in its activities • small local groups for study, service, development, and/or communion • the need to make a serious effort in support of our aspirations.

The USB is *a way of life*.

An organization of spiritual truth open to all, the USB is not linked in any way with any other organization on earth.
Wherever possible, it is operated by volunteers.

For more information see our website
or send e-mail to: staff@TheUSB.org

F
Glossary
containing only USB definitions

Apport: Any material thing that spirit people transport from one place to another (1129:1).

Astrology: The study that assumes and professes to interpret the influence of heavenly bodies upon people (1008:3).

Astronomy: The science of the material universe beyond the earth's atmosphere (313:5).

Aura: The magnetic field of energy that emanates from and envelops people, creatures, and all things. [Also known as the *odic field* and *electromagnetic field*.] (1311:1–2).

Bilocation: A [supposed and impossible] state of being, or ability to be, in two places at the same time (1313:1).

Bioplasm: The plasm used when a spirit person is both seen and heard (1121:8).

Blessed Soul: A very enlightened spirit individual, spiritually progressed and much revered, who may or may not be an Illumined Soul (*see below*). Blessed Souls referred to in this book are also leaders, inspirers, or supporters of the USB (102:n7).

Channel: *See* Medium.

Character: The sum total of traits that form one's individual nature (607:1).

Circle: *See* Home circle, Rescue circle.

Communication (with a capital C): Communication with spirit people (315:1).

Conscience: An inner knowledge or feeling of right and wrong, with a compulsion to do right (609:1).

Conscience with intuition: *See* Intuition with conscience.

Consciousness (of an individual): The sum total of what one is, what one has become (601:6).

565

Glossary

Control, spirit: A spirit guide who is in temporary control of a medium during trance (1232:1, 1126:5).

Cosmic pool, the: The thoughts of everyone, everywhere, on both sides of life. [Also known as the *cosmic sea* and *cosmic consciousness*.] (613:2).

Democracy: Government in which the supreme power is vested in the people and exercised by them or by those they elect under a free electoral system (861:1).

Direct voice: The term used when spirit communicators speak through either the vocal cords of the medium, or a "voice box" constructed in the atmosphere by skilled spirit chemists and scientists (1218:1).

Distant healing: The conscious directing of the flow of vital healing force to those at a distance. [Also known as *absent healing*.] (1102:5–6).

Divine: Only That which *always* manifests in order (1002:6).

Doorkeeper: A medium's spirit "protector" who screens spirits who would control the channel, who ensures that the medium is completely protected from all undesirable influences, and who engages in "dual control" (see below) when necessary (1242:24–26).

Dual control: A technique used by experienced spirit communicators to assist another spirit who wishes to speak through a channel but falters in the attempt (1242:24).

Duoplasm: The plasm used when a spirit person [or creature] is seen but not heard (1121:7).

Ectoplasm: An easily visible form of protoplasm; the outer layer of the protoplasmic cell (1121:3).

Ectoplasmic rods: Rigid rods, often with finger-like endings, formed from ectoplasm by skilled spirit chemists, to facilitate spirit phenomena (1122:2).

Enlightened Soul: The same as Illumined Soul (*see below*).

Enlightenment: Freedom from ignorance, prejudice, or superstition. It embraces both fact and truth (1417:1).

Exorcism: The use of ritual commands or religious or solemn ceremonies to expel an unwelcome and undesirable spirit person who is possessing the body of someone in the physical (1133:4).

Extra sensory perception (ESP): Perception or communication *outside of normal sensory activity* (1240:1).

Fact: A fact is often a reality for the moment only (compared with truth) (301:4).

Glossary

Faith: Confidence and trust based on experience (not automatic or unthinking acceptance) (208:7).

Glossolalia (speaking in tongues): Incomprehensible speech or jumbled syllables uttered by an individual or group of individuals in certain forms of worship, often during frenzy or "ecstasy" bordering on hysteria (1134:1–3).

God: That Which Is All-Good, The Supreme Power, The First Cause, The One Great Source, The Great Spirit, The Indescribable, All That Always Manifests in Order, That Which Creates and Expresses in and Controls the Universe (413:1, 501).

Group soul: A group of individuals united in a common purpose (1304:1).

Guide, spirit guide: Spirit people who touch our lives for varying lengths of time for various purposes (1221:1).

Home circle: A meeting in a home, in which a group of harmonious people sit in a circle for a common spiritual purpose, such as healing, distant healing, prayer, communion with spirit friends and loved ones, physical spirit phenomena, the development of mediumship, or "spirit rescue" (1242:1, 1110, 1322:3; *see* Rescue Circle).

Hypnosis: An artificially-induced state resembling sleep, characterized by heightened susceptibility to suggestion (1013:2).

Illumined Souls: Spirit people who live in, or are qualified to live in, the Kingdoms (1301:2). Illumined Souls specifically referred to in this book include the spirit founders, the spirit leaders, and some of the spirit inspirers and supporters of the USB, who are of the *highest* [spiritual] attainment (Intro:3, 1225, A02:3). Some of them have been revered here by hundreds of millions of people over the centuries [and some whose lives on earth are remembered are still so revered today] (Pref:5). (1225:n9 gives other terms used for them.)

Independent direct voice: The specific term used when spirit communicators speak through a "voice box" constructed in the atmosphere [near a medium] by skilled spirit chemists and scientists (1218:2).

Individuality: *The real self,* one's entire consciousness, one's triune of soul, spirit, and mind (mentality) (605:2).

Instinct: Either the tendency to behave in a way characteristic of a species, or a natural or acquired tendency, aptitude, or talent (609:6).

Instrument: See Medium (1216:18, 1220:7,14).

Integrity: Uprightness, honesty, and soundness of character that nothing can impair (711:1).

Glossary

Intellect: A person's capability to understand (601:7).

Intelligence: The degree of intellect in an individual (601:8).

Intuition: A receptive quality: the immediate knowing or learning of something without the conscious use of reasoning (609:3).

Intuition with conscience: The immediate (and usually unconscious) moral appraisal of a situation, sometimes accompanied by the knowledge of what to do and *doing* it (609:5).

Laying on of hands: A method of healing in which a healer (on either side of life) places his or her hands on [or near] a patient, to try to *help* bring about a cure (1106:2, 1107:7).

Love (in its noblest sense): Charity in thought, word, and deed; understanding, tenderness, and compassion; service to others without thought of reward; at times, sacrifice (510:4).

Magnetic healing: Healing accomplished by a magnetic curative essence that is manufactured within the physical [earthly] body of a gifted person and which, when the healer enters the auric emanation of a patient, exudes from the healer's body and gravitates to the part of the patient's body needing rehabilitation (1102:3).

Magnetize: To impregnate a physical object or person with an essence or essences to make it/him/her more conducive to phenomena (1109:3).

Mantra: A word, words, a sound, sounds, or formulas recited or sung (1139:3, 1140:11).

Materialization: In which spirit people, with the help of spirit specialists, mold ectoplasm (usually onto their spirit bodies) into a recognizable likeness of themselves, to make themselves visible to people on earth (1123:2–4).

Meditation: This may be: reflection; contemplation; extended thought; a reaching outward; a reaching inward; a receptivity that draws one closer to an attunement with what many call the still, small voice; a state of desiring nothing but to be used in some way for good; greater rapport with, and occasional manifestation by, loved ones and others in spirit life with whom we are linked (1140:4–6).

Medium: A person who is not only a psychic (see below) but, much more importantly, an instrument or channel used by spirit people to communicate with people on earth and to help in making some other psychic phenomena possible (1205:3).

Mental healing: The conscious directing of the flow of vital healing force either to one's own body or to those at a distance (1102:5).

Mentality: *A* mind, the portion of Universal Mind that an individual possesses (601:5).

Glossary

Microplasm: The plasm used either to transport the spirit body of a medium away from the scene, or to block out any interference (conscious or unconscious) from the medium's own mind, so that a full and free flow of communication is possible (1121:9).

Mind (not *a* mind): The same as Universal Mind (*see below*) (601:4).

Moxibustion: Health treatment by means of flammable substances placed on the skin at acupuncture points and burned to produce stimulation by heat (1104:5).

Obsession: When low or degrading spirit people are in control of someone's physical [earthly] body (1133:6).

Parapsychology: The branch of psychology that deals with the investigation of psychic phenomena (B07:2).

Personality: What one appears to be to others (605:3).

Possession: When people, usually mediums, invite or allow a spirit person to temporarily occupy their physical [earthly] bodies and use their vocal cords (1133:6).

Prayer: Intense or concentrated thought expressed silently or aloud (521:3).

Prophecy: The especial ability to see into the future (on earth, a form of mediumship) (1001:1).

Protoplasm: The living matter of all vegetable, animal, and human cells and tissues; the basic substance of all plasms that spirit chemists combine with certain spirit chemicals to help make possible various types of spirit manifestations (1121:1).

Psychic, a: A person on earth who is sensitive to forces or influences of a seemingly supernatural nature (1205:2).

Psychic centers (chakras): Seven especially sensitive regions in the physical [earthly] body that serve, among other things, as receiving centers and storehouses of vital life force (1138:1–3).

Psychokinesis (PK): The *apparent* ability to influence matter or events by mind alone (B09:9).

Psychometry: The process by which a medium, viewing or holding or touching an object, is able to obtain and relate information about it, or about some of those who are or have been associated with it (1012:2).

Real self: A person's individuality or entire consciousness, the eternal triune of soul, spirit, and mind (mentality) that each person is (602:2, 605:2, 1320:3).

Reason: The mental powers concerned with forming conclusions, judgements, or inferences (208:1).

Regression: The act of going back to a previous place or state (1013:3).

Glossary

Rescue circle: A meeting led by an experienced medium and assisted by spirit colleagues, in which sitters converse with "lost" spirit people, to help them realize that they are no longer in the physical, and/or to help them correct other misconceptions that are severely hampering their progress in the spirit realms (1228:n12, 1322:3).

Séance: The same as Sitting (*see below*).

Self, real: *See* Real self, *above*.

Shells: A term some use for astral bodies (1319:4) and for thought forms (1319:9).

Sitting: The same as a séance (1206:n5). A private sitting with a medium is usually for either communion with spirit friends and loved ones, or to experience physical spirit phenomena (1242:1, 1110). A group sitting is the same as a circle (*see* Home circle, Rescue circle).

Soul: The spark of the divine that is in each human being (601:2).

Spirit: The animating factor that is in each human being and all living things (601:3).

Spirit blindness: An inability of some spirit people to see certain things that they have previously been convinced they will be unable to see (1228:4–5).

Spirit body: The body comprised of all the various bodies we still retain at any time, other than the physical [earthly] body. [Also known as the *etheric, incorporeal, counterpart, subtle,* and *beta body,* and sometimes as the *etheric double.*] In ascending order of more rapid rates of vibration, it may include the astral body, the psychic body, the spiritual body, the celestial body, and others (1310:4–8).

Spirit chemists: Usually chemical engineers who confine their activities to preparing a medium's physical [earthly] body to absorb more of the vital chemicals needed in producing fuller and more complete and satisfactory manifestations of phenomena (1130:4).

Spirit guides: Spirit people who touch our lives for varying lengths of time for various purposes; not one of us is without them (1221:1).

Spirit healing: Healing given when a spirit guide enters the auric emanations of a medium and uses the physical [earthly] body of the medium to heal another person (1102:7).

Spirit realms: All the spheres or planes (levels of consciousness) occupied by those who do not live in an earthly body. In ascending order of more rapid rates of vibration, they consist of: the Astral Realms, the Spiritual Realms, the Celestial Realms, and the Kingdoms (1301:1–2).

Glossary

Spirit scientists: Those who undertake scientific research in the spirit world and/or help make certain spirit demonstrations possible (1130:3).

Spirit world (spirit realms): All around and about us, it consists of *all* the spheres or planes (corresponding to levels of consciousness) occupied by those who do not live in a physical [earthly] body (1301:1).

Spiritual healing: Healing that takes place when one or more spirit people heal the patient directly (1102:11).

Spirituality: Part of one's mentality, it is evidenced by the level of one's moral consciousness and the nobility of one's character, ideals, aspiration, and efforts; it is by far the most important of one's noble qualities (608:1–4).

Standby: A skilled spirit communicator who speaks for spirit people who have not mastered the techniques of voice communication [with people on earth] (1233:3).

Survival (with a capital S): Survival of death of the physical [earthly] body (315:1).

Survivalist: One who believes or knows that we all survive the change called death (1201:1).

Telekinesis (TK): The production of motion in a body, *apparently* without the application of material force (B09:9).

Teleplasm: The plasm used to reproduce audible sound (1121:6).

Thought forms: Resembling astral bodies, these are created and controlled usually by the minds of those who live on earth (1319:9–11,n9).

Trance: An altered state, in which spirit guides may have anywhere from slight to complete temporary control over the medium's speech and actions (1236:6–9, 1126:5).

Travelling clairvoyance: Describing what at the moment is taking place elsewhere, sometimes hundreds or thousands of miles [kilometers] away (1313:4). [Also known as *remote viewing.*]

Truth: That which is eternal (without end) (301:3).

Twin souls: The two halves of one soul (being), one male and one female, which will ultimately reunite (1321:2,13,18).

Universal Mind: The source of supply; power in essence; all that is known and unknown by humanity; an infinite reservoir of information (601:4).

USB: The Universal Spiritual Brother&Sisterhood on earth, The Universal Spiritual Brotherhood in the spirit world and formerly on earth (101:1,n1).

Glossary

Vital life force: A subtle and as-yet unmeasured essence contained in oxygen that is vital to life. [Also known as *life force, vital energy, bioenergy, chi*, and *prana*.] (913:3).

Voice box: An artificial larynx constructed by spirit chemists and scientists from various plasms contributed by the medium mostly, together with other chemicals they bring, for spirit communicators to use in speaking instead of using the medium's vocal cords (1122:2, 1218, 1233:7).

Will (of an individual): The part of one's consciousness that provides the power of choice and deliberate action or intention (701:1, 1231:4).

Wisdom: Knowledge of what is true or right coupled with just judgement as to action (861:5).

Index

Numbers cited in this index are those of topics, not pages; the numbers following colons indicate paragraph numbers within the topic, or footnote numbers if preceded by a letter n.

A

Abandoning the helm, 824:3
Abou Ben Adhem, 509
Absent healing (*see* Distant healing)
Accept:
    if cannot correct, 744:16, 756:6, 928:10, 1408:11, 1410:8, 1424:11
    a disagreeable condition, 742
    not blindly, 208:6, 309:5, 827:2, 1211:2, 1221:13, 1233:13, 1419:1
    not unthinkingly, Intro:43, 110:6, 316:5, 1234:5
    if think, 209:4, 848:3
    USB principles, 108:1, 111:5
    USB teachings, 110:6
Acceptance demanded, 107:7
Accidents:
    of birth, 1011:7
    happen?, 1410, 408:2
    and world confusion, 770:2
Accomplishments:
    by oneself, 731:3,9,11
    of USB, 1430
Achievement, 773:3
Achieving USB's goals, 1420–1432, 807:14–20
Acquisitions (fulfillment), instant, 747
Actions:
    consequences, 1410
    our own, 1410
    a philosophy, 736
    responsible for our, 1230:18

Acupuncture:
    and healing, 1104
    and prana, B09:30
    uses, B09:30–33
Addresses by Illumined Souls, A01–A13
Administration, need for change, 823:3
Admission charges, D06:7
Adulation, 107:5–7, 514:6, 723:4
Adulthood, those nearing, 907:8
Adults, and children, 907
Adversity, uses of, 1408, 1120:8
Affect one another, 1410:3–7
Affinity, the Law of, 412
    and attraction, 412
    for one only, 412
Affirmations (*see also* Mantras):
    effects and value, 768, 503:1,5
Afflicted, patience with the, 728:8
Affluence, test of, 846:3
Afterlife and misconceptions (*see* Misconceptions)
Age:
    best mediumship for this, 1236:2
    each is what we make it, 1007:10,12
    every, great souls visit, 1104:6
    new, 201, 101:5
    of responsibility, 839
Aggressors:
    appeasing, 860:7–9
    feeding, 860:7
Agnostics, 507
Agreements, repudiation, 716
Ailments and heredity, 1120:8

Index

Akashic records, 1312
Alcoholics, spirit protection of, 921:11
Alcoon, A03, A05, A02:1, A03:n2
   on God, 501:2
   on the path, 517:7
Allergies:
   a cause, 1311:24-28
   controlling, 1311:30–33
All, is not God, 502
Alone, we are never, 1222
Alternative healing, 1101:1
Anarchy or law, our choice, 838:4
Ancestor, common, 601:n1
Ancestors, 707
Ancient scrolls, *etc.*, 764
Ancient teachings, 314
Angel, guardian, 1221:8, 1224:4
"Angels of mercy," 1323:5
Animals:
   becoming human, 1308:8
   being awakened, 925:2
   the fate of, 1308
   and humans, 810, 811, 808:12
   humans never were, 1308:10, 1406:2
   kingdom, and humans, 810
   no divine spark, 601:2
   and phenomena, 1135, B09:36–38
   psychic ability, 812:3
   rejoining owners, 1135
   retain their identity, 1308:3–4
   saving humans, 812:2–3
   sense of smell, 929:5
   speech by, 811:2
   spirit direction of, B09:38
   telepathy with, B09:36
   vibration rates, 414:11
Annihilation, 308:3, 1316:2, 1413:10–13
Answers, to questions, 1307
Ant, and understanding, 506:2
Anyone can rise above, 770:5, 803:12, 1415:10
Apathy, of public, 715:28
Apparel, women's, 714
Appearance:
   in materializations, 1123:10–13
   presentable, 714
   of spirit people, 1309:7–8, 1315:4, 1310:17–19,21–23, 1330:12
Appeasement, folly of, 744:5, 754:3, 860:7–9
Appeasing aggressors, 860:7–9
Application, of knowledge, 1430:4
Apport, 1129
   and materialization, 1129:5
Armageddon, Pref:36
Art, 713:5–6, 836:4
Ask (pray), 756:4, 759:3, 1108:5
"As one thinks," 817:2
Aspiration, 411:1
   and effort, 103:8, 608:3, 717:5
Assisi, Francis of, 1405:4,n2
Astral:
   flights, 918:8, 1329:1
   projection, 918:8,n2
   realms, 1301:2
Astral body (shell), 1310:5–6, 1319, 1227:7
   and spirit controls, 1319:8
   and thought forms, 1319
Astrology, 1008–1009, 313:5
   interpretation in, 1008:4
   and planets, 1008:4,10–12
   predictions/prophesies, 1005, 1008:23
   of twins, 1009
Astronomy, 313:5
Atheists, 507
Atlantis, 805:3
Atom, power in, 507:10,n5, 727:17
Attitude(s), 719–733
   to avoid, 1203
   can block healing, 918:5
   closed-minded, 323:n17
   instilling in children, 907:12
   in prayer, 522:1
Attraction:
   and affinity, 411, 412
   laws of, 411–412
   and prophets, 1001:8
   and spirit guides, 1109:7
Attunement:
   to higher spirit realms, 413:12

Index

Aum, sound, 1139:1–2
Aura, 1311, 1312, 910:8
    colors, 1229
    cycles within, 1229:4
    detection instruments, 1311:n7, B09:29
    full record, our, 608:7
    incompatibilities, 1311:5,18–19,38
    misconceptions, 1311:42,46–47
    predominating color, 1229:3–4
    and prophecy, 1001:4
    of a psychic, B09:52
    rebuffs low thoughts, 207:2
    and spirit body, 1310:20, 1314:3, B09:19
    on tapping it, B09:21–26
    when about to die, 1237:3, 1311:46
Auric scientists, 1311:9,12-13
"Authorities", B07
Authors, 1209
Automatic writing, 1122:8
Average person, praised, 815, 323:12
Awareness:
    and responsibility, 405:1
    of spark of God, 104:2
    of time, 1328:1–4

B

Bad and good, 827–837
Banquet table of offerings, 316:3
Barriers:
    of creeds and dogmas, 104:5
    to enlightenment, 1221:18
    to knowledge, 1221:18
    to mediumship, 1216:9,17
    in spirit realms, 1327:2
    to truth, 309:6
Battle:
    spirit reenactments of, 1136, 841:3
    with forces of evil, 856
Beauty:
    of higher spirit realms, 521:4, 923:5, 1306:8–9
    and love, 730:1
    on sharing, 317
    thoughts on, 730
    and truth, 306
    in variety, 416:3

Becoming:
    no finality to our, 503:6
    more Godlike, 503:3
    we are always, 601:6, 764:6
Behavior, personal, 734–745
Beings:
    from other planets, 706
    spirit (*see* Spirit people)
    that guide nature, 809:7
Belief can absolve, misconception, B10:27
Beliefs and inhumanity, 817:3
Bend in the road, not death, 1316
Best, of old and new, 835
Beta body (*see* Spirit body)
Be true to one's *soul*, 729
Bibliographies, their worth, B09:54
Big lie, the, 848
Billet reading, blindfold, B09:28
Bilocation, 1313
Bioenergy (*see* Vital life force)
Bioplasm, 1121:8
Birth control, 821:9
Blessed, doubly, 317:7, 505:10, 516:7
Blessed Soul, 102:n8
Blessings, on counting ours, 737
Blindfold, billet reading, B09:28
Blindly following anyone, 208:6
Blindness:
    and mediumship, B09:27
    spirit, 1228:4–5,9, 1322:3
Body(ies):
    astral (*see* Astral body)
    beta (*see* Spirit body)
    celestial, 1310:1,8
    cherish them, 820:1
    counterpart (*see* Spirit body)
    etheric (*see* Spirit body)
    incorporeal (*see* Spirit body)
    and our appearance, 414:13
    out of, 1202:n2, 1313:3,8,10,n8
    physical (*see* Physical body)
    psychic, 1310:1,6
    replicas of physical, 1309
    spirit (*see* Spirit body)
    spiritual, 1310:1,7
    subtle (*see* Spirit body)
    we possess, 1310, 603:3

Index

Booklet, USB, D30:5
Books:
    and mediums and authors, 1209
    priceless, a parable, 726:1
    on "psychic discoveries," B09
Boxing, professional, 820
Brain:
    and mentality, 617:8
    surgery, 618
Brandeis, Louis, 852:3
Breathing exercises, 912
    and receptivity, 1138:4–6
Brother&Sisterhood (*see* USB)
Brotherly and Sisterly Love, the Law of, 410
Brothers and sisters:
    a chain of, A08:4
    realization needed, 1431:2
    their keeper, 1411
    we are all, A13:5
Browning, Robert, 307:n4
Burden, cannot bear other's, 704:5, 760:3
Burke, Edmund, 754:n10

C

Cancer:
    a grave misteaching, 915
    some causes, 915:4–5
Capital punishment, 841
Care of infants, 910
Cataclysm, 759:3
Catastrophes, 1004:10–16
Cause and Effect:
    the Law of, 407
    not all that happens to us, 1410
    for peoples, nations, humanity, 1007:11
Cause, no greater, 304
Cause of Truth, 102:5, 304:1
    and mediumship, B03
Celestial body, 1310:1,8
Celestial realms, 1301:2
Cells and healing, 1105:3
Center path, 734
Chain letters, 727:1–4
Chakras (*see* Psychic centers)

Challenges, 856–866, 1408–1410
    are necessary, 1113:2, 1408:13
    both good and bad, 769
    and opportunity, 769
Change, 835
    of administration, 823:3
    and/or correct, 756
    the Law of, 415
    mental, at physical death, 1319:15, B12:23
    the need for, 803, 415:4
    not merely for the sake of, 803:5
    produced by violence, 835:1
    and standards, 803:10–12
Channel (*see* Medium)
Channel for good, 1407:4
Channelling, 1218:n8
Chanting, 1139
    and spirituality, 1139:3
Character:
    disregard of weaknesses, 712:1
    inheriting, 1010:14, 1011:6
    and integrity, 711:2
    like a structure, 607:2
    and spirituality, 608:3
    strongest safeguard, 1242:6
    what it is, 607
Charges for admission, D06:7
Cheek, on turning, 744:2–11
Cheer, message of, 113
Cheerful countenance, 740
Cheerfulness in sittings and sick rooms, 1247
Chemicalization, 1216:9
Chemical raids during healing, 1106:10
    preventing, 1106:10
Chi (*see* Vital life force)
Childbirth, and death, 908:4–6
Children:
    and discipline, 704:1
    instilling attitudes, 907:12
    learning truth, 321, 911
    in spirit life, 1330, 1306:11
    too young to learn, 911
Chinese healing methods, 1104:5
    acupuncture, 1104

Index

Choice:
    between good and bad, 618:2,
        819:1, 832:2
    and freedom, 830:3–4
    gutter or the stars, 713:2
    of healers, 1117, 1118
    of nations, 854
Christmas 1976 prophecy (*see*
    Prophecy)
Cicero, Marcus Tullius, 811:n4
Circles:
    healing, suggestions for, 1110
    home (*see* Home circle)
    members spiritual, 1242:6
    rescue, 1322:3, 1228:6,n12
Clairaudience, 1001:n2
Clairvoyance, 1001:n2
    traveling (remote viewing), 918:n2,
        1313:4,9
    X-ray, 1102:9, 1311:17
Clones, 619, 802:n1
Clothing, spirit, 1306:11, 1329:9–12
Clouds, a face and figure in, 1003
Coin, opposite sides of, 829:1–2
Collections at USB meetings, D20
Collective unlimited source of supply,
    mythical, 1209:3
Collector of books, parable, 726:1
Color(s), 930
    in auras, 1229
    and healing, 1105:4
    for materialization, 1121:5
    and music, 931
    and prejudice, 813
    and sound, 929–931
    why people differ in color, 813:2
Coma, 617
    and mind, 617:7–8
    prolonged, reasons, 617:1–6
Command:
    by great souls, 1226
    one's spirit guides, 1223
Commercialism, 110:10
Common man (*see* Average person)
Communicating standbys, spirit, 1233
Communication:
    from other planets, 706:2

    particle, 206:n3
    spirit (*see* Spirit communication)
Compassion:
    developing, 905:2, 1408:4
    difficult, 515:2
    of Illumined Souls, 410:5, 1220:13
    leave the fallen with, 318:19
    part of consciousness, 604:5
    in USB workers, D26:2
    when disciplining, 1426:1
Compensation for mediums, 1214
Compensation, the Law of, 408, 1410
    and Law of Justice, 409
Complacency, the curse of, 823
Complicate what is simple, educators,
    323:13
Comprehend, ability to, 612:8
Compromise with wrong, and integrity,
    711:17
Computers, will never think, 806
Conceptions of God, 505:3
Concerts, spirit-realm, 1328:8
Condemn:
    no soul, 325:3, 1220:13, D33:9
    the sin, not the sinner, 325:3
Conditions:
    denying, 742
    on other planets, 816:10
    recognizing and correcting, 734:2
Confusion:
    aim of forces of evil, 706:4
    that some spirits bring, 1230:1
Conjecture, idle, 506
Connectedness, 206:n3
Conquest, the greatest, 1401:2
Conscience, 614, 609:1–2
    cowards resist, 614:1
    with intuition, 609:5
Consciousness, 601:6, 1111:3
    development variations, 604:4
    improving, 774:3, 836:2, 1230:3,
        1421:6, A12:2–3
    individual, 606
    levels of, 210:4, 601:6,1301:1–3,7,
        1307:24, 1331:2
    like a library, 606:4–8
    living (by) it, 208:10

Index

Consciousness—*Cont.*
  and mind, 801:6
  moral, 608:4, 609:1–2
  our individual, 606
  and our spirit guides, 1221:11
  planes of, 1301:1–7, 1307:24, B12:12,41,53
Conscious projection, 1310:15
Consequences of our actions, 1410
Consideration:
  and inhumanity, 819
  for others, 1404, 608:12, 849:4
Consumerism, and parents, 906:3
Contentment:
  meaning of, 733:2
  perfect peace, 758
  the secret of, 733, 709:5
Continuous life, one, 1301:13
Controls, spirit (*see* Spirit controls)
Controversial subjects, D05, 110:21
Convalescence, spirit-realm, 1307:26
Correct what can be corrected.., 744:16, 756:6, 1408:11
Cosmic pool, consciousness, sea, 613
  we contribute to, 613:5
Cosmic rays and healing, 1107:2
Countenance:
  cheerful, 740
  and food, 740:4
Counterpart body (*see* Spirit body)
Counting our blessings, 737
Courage, 309:2, 771:3
Courses and seminars, B05, B06
Courtesy, to spirit friends, 1224
Create life, 802
Create mind, humans will never, 806:7
Creation by spirit thought, 521:4, 1323:1–6
Creation of humans, 506:3–4
Cremation, 1317
Crime, 838–842
  causes of, 842
  deterrents to, 840
  influences on, 842:3–6
  and poverty, 842
  when silence is, 753
Crisis and opportunity, 822:3

Crookes, William, 315:3,n6
Crossing over, to spirit life, 1322
  everyone is met, 1322
Cruelty:
  around the world, 865:2
  in early religious texts, 1001:8
  low spirits craving, 1243:1
Cult of mediocrity, 836:2–3
Curse of envy, the, 723
Cycles, 928
  2000-year, Pref:32, 928:2
  humans not in, 928:7–9
  made by humans, 928:6
  of nature, 612:5, 928:3–5
  and time, 926–928
  within aura, 1229:4
Cynic, a, 814:8–9

D

Dam, breaking, 111:8
Dark matter, dark energy, 414:n6
Darkness, forces of (*see* Forces of evil)
Darkness, spirit-realm, B10:17
Dawning, the, 1427
Deaf and dumb, spirit people, 1324:3
Death (*see also* Passing on):
  and childbirth, 908:4–6
  fear of, 1207:2
  life's greatest experience, 908:n1
  penalty, 841
  the truth of survival, 909:1
"Death wish," 727:9
Debate, *vs.* discussion, D05:2–3
Debunkers, and heroes, 844
Decibel (db), 826:n7
Decisions, on making, 736
Deed, and the thought, 755
Deeding over possessions, 750:11
Deep-trance mediumship, 1242:23–27
Defense:
  from attack, 858
  for justice, 1424:16
Definition of:
  noble love, 510:4
  prayer, 521:3
  reason, 208:1
  truth, 301:3

Index

Degrees, academic, authority derived, B05:6, B07:9,11
Déjà dit, explanations, 1126
Déjà vu, explanations, 1126
Delphi, temple at, 611:1
Demanded acceptance, 107:7
Democracy, 861, 862
    decay of, 715:24–28
Demonstrations of healing, 1106:9–13
Demonstrators, silent, 845:4
Denying a condition, 742
Desires, 1311:44
    confused with needs, 718:3, 733:1,7
Destroy and expose error, duty to, 325
Destroyed, no soul ever, 1320, 308:3, 611:7, 1413:10–13
Destruction (*see* Life on earth)
Developing mediumship, 1216, 1210:7, 1219:1, 1236:4, 1242:1, 1245:3
Developing our being, facets of, 719:6, 1132:2
Developing the psychic centers, 1245:3
Development, spiritual, 1407, 774:7
    attunement with great souls, 608:23, 1407:3
    difference from psychic, 608:26
Devices to replace mediums, 1215
Dickson, James J., 1206:8
Dictatorship and government, 905:14
Diet and mediumship, 1219
Different, how the USB is, 110
Difficult path, 1420:2
Dignity, to express in, 851:3
Dimensions, multiple, 1301:n2
Directing our efforts, 759–764
Direct spirit communication, 1227:7, 1234:2, 1236:n15
Direct voice, 1218:1
    independent, 1218:2
Disagree, agreeing to, 719:12
Disagreement, 905:7
Disappointments and disillusionments, 728
Disaster:
    predictions of approaching, 1004
    widespread, 1004:2,4–5,18

Discipline children we love, 704:1
"Discoveries," psychic, B09
Discrimination, 813:6
    and inhumanity, 813:6
Discussion:
    vs. debate, D05:2–3
    at USB group meetings, D05:2–3
Disease, springs from mind, 916
Disorder, that manifests in, 502:8
Dissent, 855
    from dissenters, 855:1
Distant healing, 1102:6, 1107:1–2
    circle for, 1110
    mechanics of, 1107, 1102:5–6
    and thought, 1107:1
Distant hypnosis, B09:34–35
Distortion of teachings, 206:4
Diversions from truth, 1124:8–10,14–16, 1209:4–8, 1319:n10
Diversity, 721
Divine:
    always manifests in order, 502, 501:3, 1002:6
    to forgive is not, 1415:3
    prophesy and healing not, 1002
    spark, not in animals, 601:2
Divining arts, 1001–1013
Divining rod, 1128:1
Divinity:
    spark of (*see* Soul)
    transfer to animals, 1308:8
DNA "markers," 601:n1
Do, what we can, 765, 759, D27, 1426:1
Dogmas:
    bury truth, 201:5
    and youth, 907:10
Doorkeeper, duties, 1242:24
Doors:
    opened for us, 757:3, 1414:6
    to spiritual progress, 831, 103:7, 308:3, 607:3
Double, spirit or etheric, 1310:4
Doubly blessed, 317:7, 505:10, 516:7
Dowsing, 1128

Index

Doyle, Arthur Conan, 315:3,n6
   a profound student, 315:3
Dreams, 923, 924
   awakened from, 925:2–4
   and droes, 924
   interpretation of, 924:1–2
   REMs, 925:8–10
   and sleep, 925
   symbols, interpreted, 925:5–6
   two kinds of, 923:1–2
   what they are not, 925:5–6
   why mostly distorted, 925:7
   why not remember, 923:3–5
Droes and dreams, 924
Drugs, "psychedelic":
   and delusions, 1141:5–6
   God not reached by taking, 1141:28
   for psychic experiences, 1141
   and reality, 1141:3
   and spirit protection, 921:11
   and spirituality, 1141:11–13
Drummond, Sir William, 208:n4
Dual control, 1242:24
Duality, wave/particle, 414:n6
Duoplasm, 1121:7
Duplicates in spirit world, 1306
Duty to expose and destroy error, 325

E

Eagle, sparrow cannot become, 767
Earth:
   leaving, 1426:2–3
   lessons learned only on, 1424
   life on, 1408:6
   people here to be examples, 1120:8
   a proving ground, 711:4, 846:3, 1409:2
   weigh the words of those on, 853:7
Earthbound spirit people, 1331, 1332:9
Ectoplasm, 1122, 1121:3
   emanates in waves, 1122:2
   harmed by light, 1122:4
   and other plasms, 1121
   protectively sheathed, 1122:5–7, 1125:2,7
   used in materialization, 1121:5, 1123:2
   use in "marvels," 1125:2,7
   various colors, 1121:4
Ectoplasmic rods, 1122:2–3,7, 1124:3, 1137:6
Edifices, spirit, 1323:1
Educated, the, shun truths of survival, 323:3
Educators:
   complicate what is simple, 323:13
   psychic ignorance despite "investigations," B05:6
Effects of misconceptions, 309:16, 314:4, 1228:1,9, 1324:1,3
Effects of thought, 207
Effort:
   all recognized, 774:6, A12
   and aspiration, 103:8, 608:3, 717:5
   directing our, 759–764
   individual, 113:4
   and intent, 774
   need for, 757
   none is wasted, D27:4
   to walk through opened doorways, 757:3
Electronic voice phenomena (EVP), 1215:4,n6
Elements, 1246:4
"Elitists," ruthless, 862:5
Emotions:
   machines with, 806
   part of mentality, 604:7, 1311:44
   that defy speech, 1231:14
   unworthy, 207:3
Employees, responsibilities, 749
Employers, responsibilities, 749
Endeavor, 773
Energy poaching, 1244
   prevention, 1244
Enlightened:
   souls, work of, 759:3, 1414:4,6
   thinking directed, 774:2
   world receptivity, 757:1
Enlightened Soul (*see* Illumined Soul)
Enlightenment, 1417–1419
   barriers to, 1221:18
   greatest provider, 1417:2
   in sleep state, 1132:11

spreading, by the USB, D03:1,
  D27:9–14, D28:6
 at USB meetings, D16:3
Envy, the curse of, 723
Era, product of prior, 928:9
Err, those who, not destroy, 325:3
Error, B01–B09, 314:3–5
  cannot coexist with fact, 325:2
  duty to expose and destroy, 325
  in esoteric teachings, 314
  not destroy those who err, 325:3
  in publications, 310:2–3
  repeated quotes don't make truth,
    B05:4
  of self-satisfaction, smugness, 312
  of a spirit person, 1234:9–10
Esoteric teachings, 314
ESP (*see* Extrasensory perception)
Essences and impregnation, for healing,
  1107:6
Essence, vital in oxygen, 913:3
Eternal:
  the individual is, 601:2, 611:7
  values, 711:6
Etheric body (*see* Spirit body)
Etheric realms, etheria, 1301:2
Etheric (spirit) double, 1310:4
Etheric (spirit) flights, 1329, 918:8
Everlasting punishment, 308:3
Everyday life, 901–931
Evidence:
  of afterlife, 1202:2,n2
  of phenomena, 1202:n2, 1313:3–4,
    B07:3
Evil, 754, 829:3
  degrees of, 828:5
  forces of (*see* Forces of evil)
  good and evil, 828
  not absence of good, 828:2
  not opposite sides of coin, 829
  requirement for triumph of, 754:4
  on "resist not evil," 744:2–5
  and spirit realms, 829:3
  spirits, 1133:2,8,11
  take a stand against, 754:1–2
  why God allows, 830
Evolution:
  between species, 808:5
  evidence against, 808:5
  and involution, 1318:4
EVP, 1215:4,n6
Example, 843–848
  best, is way we live, 759:9
  and precept, 759:8
Excerpts from USB teachings (*see*
    Quotations)
Exercise reason, Intro:32,34, 208,
    210:5, 309:14, 314:1
Existence, laws governing, 403:3
Exorcism, 1133:1–4
Expecting too much, 513:12
Expediency, 711:5,17
Experience:
  can learn from others, 860
  a good teacher, 741:4
Expose and destroy error, duty to, 325
External mind, 617:n8
Extrasensory perception (ESP), 1240
  term often misapplied, 1240:1–2
Extremes, 834:2–5
Eye movements during sleep, 925:8,10

F

Facets:
  developing our, 1132:2
  of truth, 302
  of our personality, 605:3
Fact, 301:4
  cannot coexist with error, 325:2
Faculties, our:
  and genes, 1217:3–4
  not inherited, 1217:5,8
  objective, 1231:6
  and our mind, 1231
  their expression inherited, 1217:3,8
Faith, 208:7–8, 210:2
  and healing, 1106:13, 1113:5
  and material commitments, 743
  and reason, 210
Fake psychic phenomena, B04:2,7
False:
  claimants to be God, B02:2–3
  exposing what is, 325:1
  spirit information, 1003
  teachers, B01

Index

False leaders, *etc.*, 705, B02
  ill caused by, 705:10
  lives affected by, 1007:9
  prophets, 705:8–10, 1003:22, 1007:9
  some examples, 775:3–6
  a warning against, 1003
Family, 905–911
  of birth and heredity, 1120:8
  and government (state), 905:8–16
  importance of, 905:1–7
Fashion, 725
Fasting:
  the Buddha, 734:7
  no one becomes saintlier, 734:6–7
  woman who died from, 1230:12
Fate of animals, 1308
Faults, overlooking, 1416
Fear, 727
  healthy and unhealthy, 727:7–15
  preserves, destroys, 727:6
  sometimes helpful, 727:5
  of spirit people, spirits, 1133:n3
  in spirit world, 727:20
Feeding aggressors, 860:7
Fight or flight philosophy, 744:12–16
Finality, there is none, 503:6, 1325:12
Financial:
  integrity, 743:5
  support of USB, D06, D09, D20, 110:9
Finnemore, John, Contrib:3, Howto:n1, Intro:43
  his additions, Howto:n1
Fire-walking, 1125:1–6
First impressions, 203
FitzGerald, Edward, 741:n6
Flagg, Michael, Ackno:2,7,n1, Contrib:2, Howto:n1, Intro:3, Pref:36, 721:n2, C01:1,7
  early newspaper articles, 102:n7, C01:6
  poems, Ackno:7,n1, 301:n1
  position in the USB, Intro:9
  preparation for this work, Pref:16
Flexible, the need to be, 720
Flights, astral, spirit, 918:8, 1329:1

Fluorescein, 603:5
Follow anyone blindly, 208:6
Folly, 864
  of appeasement, 744:5, 754:3, 860:7–9
Food, destruction of, 819:8–10
Forces of evil/darkness:
  aims, 706:4–5, 1003:13, 1319:19
  battling with, 856
  do exist, 828:4
  existence, 828:4
  nature, methods, 856:1,5, 1003:17
Forces of nature, 1004:13
Forgive, 1415
  not divine, 1415:3
  not for us to, 744:4, 1415:8
  "until seventy times seven," 744:2
Forgiveness, 1415–1416
Forgotten, nothing ever is, 1415:9
Founders of the USB, Intro:10, 1225:2
Francis of Assisi, 1405:4,n2
Fraudulent mediums, 1220:10–12
Freedom, 849–855
  to accept or reject, 316:3
  to choose, 618:2, 819:1, 830:3–4
  enemies of, 861:3
  evolution of, 865:11
  and free will, 832, 830:3
  of interpretation, 850
  love it enough to die for it, 853:5
  must yield part, 853:8
  of nations, 854
  of peoples, 862:10–12
  personal, for all, 108, 849:2–5, 862:10
  of personal interpretation, 850
  of the press, 866
  the right to *not* do, 852:1
  to think and act, 114:8
  and tyrants, 853:5
  and the USB, 108, 849, 862:10
  and war, 857
Free speech, limitations, 849:4–5
Free will, 830:3
  misuse of, 502:8
Fulfillment (acquisitions), instant, 747
Full personal record, in aura, 608:7

Futility, 320
Future USB policies, D34

G

Gardener, responsibilities, 1412
Garden(s):
    spirit, 1323:1
    that is the USB, 1412:4
    thoughts are seeds in, 760:1
Gender:
    continues after passing, B10:7
    does not change, 1013:18, 1321:13–14
    issues for USB, 101:n2,n6
    neutral language, Intro:10, 101:n6
    of the soul, 1321:14
    of twin souls, 1321:13
Genes, and faculties, 1217:3,5
Genius, 1132
    and sleep, 1132:9
Gift(s):
    the greatest, 1119
    have to be earned, 1214:3
Gifts of the spirit:
    compensation for, 1214
    developing, unfolding, 1216
Gilbert, William Schwenck, 738:3,n5
Giving, 519
    in silence, 519:1–2
Glory, provided by God, 740:6
Glossolalia, 1134
Glow, spiritual, within, 505:7–11
God, 501–507
    according to USB leaders, Intro:4
    by Alcoon, 501:2
    always in order, 501:3
    children of, 103:2, 763:7–8
    claimants to be, B02:2–4
    differing understandings of, 1111:2
    does not inform prophets, 1001:8
    the existence of, 210:2
    glory provided by, 740:6
    intelligence of, 507, 502:7
    is not all, 502
    kingdom of, 505
    knowledge of, B10:11
    of Law, 501:6
    love and serve, 737:10
    of Love and Wisdom, *etc.*, 103:1, 705:3
    misconceptions, 502, 321:2, B12:48
    no disorder, 502:8
    not by a wand or drugs, 1141:28
    not of caprice, 501:6
    our conception of, 505:3
    power of, 612:8–9
    powers not ours, 503:4
    returning to, 1318:4
    and suffering, 830
    teaching excerpts on, 501
    think about, 506
    think and thank, 807
    understanding, 506:2
    we are not, only small part, 503
    why allows evil, *etc.*, 830
    works of, 502:7
Godlike, becoming more, 503:3
God's laws, 401
Golden rule, 901
Good:
    all that happens is not, 827
    and bad, 827–837
    and bad, choice between, 618:2, 819:1, 832:2
    channel for, 1407:4
    and evil, 828
    fight, fighting the, 1426
    and opposite sides of coin, 829:1–2
    to plant the seed, *etc.*, 320:2
    on sharing, 317
    and spiritual, 1402
Government:
    and dictatorship, 905:14
    one-world, 862
    (state) and family, 905:8–16
Grace, in theological sense, 1305:5
Grapes, parable of, 719:7–10
Grateful person, marks of, 737:10–14
Gratitude:
    and ingratitude, 738
    least of virtues, 737:4
    natural as breathing, 737:4
    not surrender our reason, 1211:3

Index

Gray, Thomas, 846:n9
Great Brotherhood of Light, 101:n1
Greatest:
    basis of spiritual life, 112:2, 508:3
    cause, 304
    conquest, 1401:2
    gift, 1119
    need, 1431
    provider, knowledge, 1417:2
    quest, 309:20–21
    responsibility of parents, 905:12
    service, 518:2
Great souls (*see also* Illumined Souls):
    a great teacher, and USB, 115
    impersonation of, 1234:6
    issuing commands, 1226
    mental attunement with, 1407:3
Great Spirit, 413:1, 501:n2, 1227:2
"Great unseen healing force," 1115
Great (White) Brotherhood, 101:1–7
    directed by, 101:1
    governing body of, 101:6
    representatives, 101:4
Greed, 748
    and inhumanity, 748:6
Grief, at loss, 1204
Group leaders, USB, D27:13–14
Group soul, 1304
Groups, USB (*see* USB groups)
Growth, don't force, 320:2
Guardian angels, 1221:8, 1224:4
    are more evolved, 1221:10
    do not leave us, 1224:4
Guides, spirit (*see* Spirit guides)

H

Habit, 607:4–5
Hamilton, Robert, 724:2, 724:n3
Handclasp, the, D32:9–10
Handling live coals, 1125:7–11
Hands, laying on of, 1106:2
Happenings, tragic, 865
Happens, not all for good, 827
Happiness and THE LAW, 740:7
Harm:
    bring none (in prayer), 521:10
    to nature, 809:2
    no "right" to cause, 853:9

    by psychical research societies, 315:1
    society protecting from, 719:5
Hate:
    long-lasting effects, B10:21
    only in the mind, B10:21
Healers, 1116–1120
    on choosing, 1117
    misteachings of, B13
    and patients, 1117
    their spirit helpers, 1106:3–9, 1112:4, 1118:4
    visiting several, 1118
Healing circle, suggestions for, 1110
Healing Touch, 1106:n1
Healing, unorthodox, 1101–1113, 1115
    absent (*see* distant)
    by acupuncture, *etc.*, 1104
    alternative, 1101:1
    blocking, by attitude, 918:5
    and chemical "raids," 1106:10
    choice of healers, 1117, 1118
    circle for, 1110
    and color, 1105:4
    and cosmic rays, 1107:2
    demonstrations, 1106:9–13
    different patient responses, 1113
    distant (absent), 1102:6, 1107:1–2
    essences and impregnation, 1107:6
    facilitating, 1231:16
    and faith, 1106:13, 1113:5
    four phases, 1102
    greatest gift, the, 1119
    "great unseen force," 1115
    helpers, spirit, 1106:3–9, 1112:4, 1118:4
    and Law of Life, 1105:3
    laying on of hands, 1106:2
    and love, 1105:1–2
    magnetic, 1102:3–4
    mechanics of, 1106
    mechanics of distant (absent), 1107, 1102:5–6
    mental, 1102:5–6
    a misconception, B13:4
    and music, 1245
    not divine, 1002

Index

prayers for, 1111
"precept," of, 1002:1–3
and receptivity, 1113:3,7, 1117:3
and rejoicing, 1110:15
spirit, 1102:7–10
spiritual, 1101:1, 1102:11–12
and spirituality, 1116
substances used, 1107:2,8–10
suggestions for circle, 1110
temperatures felt during, 1112
Therapeutic Touch, 1106:n1
and thought, 1107:1
and trees, 1103
unsuccessful, 1113
virus infections, 1114
and visualization, 1105:3–4, 1107:3
why some are not, 1113
Health, 912–917
and karma, 917:4–7
and spirituality, 917:1–3
"Heal thyself," 1120
why some healers cannot, 1120:7–8
Heaven, kingdom of, 505
Help:
by our thoughts, 204:10–12
from several healers, 1118
from spirit realms, 1207:9
them help themselves, 518:2, 704:3
the unable, *etc.*, 518:1
Herbs, and healing, 1104
Heredity:
and ailments, 1120:8
and family of birth, 1120:8
Hermes Trismegistus, 313:2–5, 314:5
distortion of teachings, 313:3
a founder of astronomy, 313:5
a USB Inspirer, 313:4
venerated by ancients, 313:2
Hermetic teachings, 313
resemble USB's, 313:4
Heroes, and debunkers, 844
Heroic deeds of pets, 812:3
Hierarchy, spiritual, planetary, 706:5, 1301:11
High Mountain, 517:5, A01, A02
History:
on changes by violence, *etc.*, 835:1

need not repeat itself, 860:6
teaches folly of appeasement, 860:7
Holmes, Oliver Wendell, 849:4
on free speech, limitations, 849:5
Holy, what makes a place, 837
Home and family, importance, 905
Home circles, 1242–1247
can do much good, 1216:15
for development, 1243:5–8
helpful measures, 1243
leader to be versed in psychic phenomena, 1242:7
members spiritual, 1242:6
one way of sitting, 1242
substances on hand at, 1246
Home, Daniel Dunglas, medium:
his levitation in daylight, 1122:6
a mistake, 1206:2
Home, our true, Intro:7, 1426:3
Honesty, Abraham Lincoln on, 715:14
Horoscope, 1008, 1009
Houses, spirit, 1323:6
How one can serve, 112
Human:
development, 719:6
laws, 838:2–8
nature, 818
origins, 506:3–4
purpose, 727:4
thinking, 770:3
Humans, 808–821
and animal kingdom, 810
and harm to nature, 809
and sense of rhythm, 931:13
and species evolution, 808
uniqueness, 811
Humility, humbleness, 309:6–7
false, 616
no banner, 616:5
and progress, 312:1
of spirit communicators, 1234:7
and understanding needed, 106:1
and the USB, 106, 102:18–19
and wisdom, 615
Humor, 1326:3–7
couplet, 1326:9
and the spirit realms, 1326

Index

Hunt, Leigh, 509:1,n7
Hypnosis:
    and change in gender, 1013:18
    distant, B09:34–35
    "regression" under, 1013

I

Icebergs, we are like, 1216:6
Identical twins, 619:8, 1008:16,
    1009:3–5
    dissimilarities, 619:8, 1009:4
Ignorance:
    in all races, nations, *etc.*, 615:1
    mother of misconceptions, B10:1
Illness:
    a grave cancer misteaching, 915
    misconception, 1314
    not from the mind, 916
    responses to treatment, 1113
    springs from mind, 916
    where it starts, 1314
Ills, caused by inhumanity, 830:2
Illumined Souls/Inspirers, 1225
    addresses by, A01–A13
    compassion of, 410:5, 1220:13
    greetings from, Greet:1–18
    impersonation of, 1234:6
    and mediums they use, 1207:8
    not perfect, 106:2, 520:6
    no praise or worship of, B02:7
    an offer and call, Call: 1–18
    prayers, 524
    question their offerings, 316:5
    on sharing, A09:7
    and spirit realms, 1225:1
    and truth, 316
    USB leaders, 1225:2
    vision of, 1432
    what we mean by, 1225
Illusion, 513:1–6
    and people, 513:3
Illusionists, 801
    children harmed by, 801:10
Impatience, a barrier, 1216:9
Impersonation:
    of Great Souls, 1234:6
    in materialization, 1123:9
Impregnate, 1107:6, 1109:3

Impressions, 613:3
Impulse:
    couplet, 728:7
    resist undesirable, 728:6
Inclination and will, 702
Incompatibilities with auras,
    1311:5,18–19,38
Incorporeal body (*see* Spirit body)
Independent direct voice, 1218
Indestructible real self, 301:6, 1320
Indissoluble triune, 602
Individuality:
    expands with progress, 1318:9
    and personality, 605
    and the real self, 605:2
    of spirit people, 1318:9
Individual, our:
    challenge, A04, A05, D27:3
    consciousness, 606
    interpretation, 114
Individual, the, 601–619
    can do many things, 765
    can rise above, triumph, 770
    characteristics, 601–609
    composed of, 601
    is eternal, 601:2, 611:7
    free to chose, 819:1, 832:2
    how one can serve, 112
    judgement of, 844:6
    knowledge of, 610–616
    medical aspects of, 617–619
    no one has all truth, 307
    opportunity to express, 865:3
    praise for the average, 815, 323:12
    product of our past, 734:5
    rights and non-rights, 851
    understanding of, 610–616
    what each can do, 759, D27
    what we can do, 1426:1
    when enters the physical, 1315
Infants, the care of, 910
Ingratitude, 738
Inherit, 1011:5
    not mental qualities, 619:8,
    1011:5–6
Inhibitions, 1140:29–30
Inhumanity, 819
    causes our ills, 830:2

Index

due to beliefs, 817:3
due to discrimination, 813:6
due to greed, 748:6
lack of consideration, 819:7–10
to Native North Americans, 1227:10
to others, 830:2
Injunctions, 744
  fight or flight, 744:12–16
  love thy neighbor, 510
  misascribed, 744:1
  resist not evil, 744:2,5
  turn the other cheek, 744:2,6–10
Injustice:
  no indignation over, 753:4
  none in the long run, 1410:6
Inner being senses, 310:4, 312:1
Inspiration, spirit, Contrib:1, 102:16, 924:4, 1231:12, 1418:1, D24:6
Instant fulfillment (acquisitions), 747
  lasting values cannot be, 747:9
Instinct, 609:6–7, 812
  for self-preservation, 727:9
Instrument (*see* Medium)
Instrumental transcommunication (ITC), 1215:4,n6
Integrity, 711–718
  anyone may possess, 711:3
  and character, 711:2
  characteristics of one with, 711:5
  financial, 743:5
  no compromise with wrong, 711:17
  root of a noble character, 711:2
  and some professions, 715
  tested, 711:4
  those who promote the false, 711:10–12
  various levels of, 711:13–15
Intellect, 601:7
"Intellectuals," ruthless, 862:5
Intelligence, 601:8
  of God, 507, 502:7
  and the Law of Life, 413:7
  and machines, 806
Intent, 774
Interpretation:
  in astrology, 1008:4
  of dreams, 924:1–2

freedom of personal, 850
individual, 114
of spirit communication, 1234:1–3
of spiritual Laws, 402:3
Interpreters, in spirit life, 1325:7
Intuition, 609:3–4
  with conscience, 609:5
Invasion, 859
Inventions, 1306:13
Involution and evolution, 1318:4
ITC, 1215:4,n6

J

Jealousy, spirit-realm, B10:8
Jerusalem, Pref:32
Jesus, 314:5, 1127:1
Joining the USB mission, 111
Judgement, of individual, 844:6
Judge others, is not for us, 325:4
Judges:
  and integrity, 715:17–23
  and justice, 715:23
  and laws, 715:19
Justice delayed, 840:3
Justice, the Law of, 409
  compensation, 1410:5–6
  laws of, 407–409

K

Kardec, Allan, 502:6,n3
Karma:
  debts, 1305:1–4
  erasing others', 1230:16–17
  and health, 917:4–7
  misteachings about, 917:4–7
Keats, John, 306
Keeper (of others), 1411
Kernels, USB presents, 1418
Khayyám, Omar, 741:2,n6
Kingdom of heaven, of God, 505
Kingdoms of nature, 809:8–9,n3
Kingdoms (of spirit realms), 1301:2
Know:
  about thyself, 611
  left hand, right hand, 519
  nothing, and a little, 612
  that we are, *etc.*, 506:4

Index

Knowledge, 210, 1425
    on acquiring, two ways, 610
    barriers to, 1221:18
    of the Creator, B10:11
    essential for progress, 1425
    and faith, 210
    greatest provider, 1417:2
    of Laws, and spirituality, 1425
    to live by, 611:15
    reason can bring, 210:4
    in sleep state, 1132:11
    spreading, by the USB, D03:1, D27:9–14, D28:6
    that sustains, 761
    at USB meetings, D16:3
    without application, 1430:4
    for youth, 907:9

L

Laborers and their hire, 710
Ladder, prayers climbing, 1111:4
Language, 1325
    low standards of, 713
    we think in, 1325:4–5
Lasting values not instantly acquired, 747:9
Law and order:
    evidence of, 612:4–5
    need for respect for, 838
Law(s), earthly, 838:2–8
    or anarchy, our choice, 838:4
    and judges, 715:19
    observance of, 401:4
    and order, needs respect, 838
    people's, 401
Law(s), natural, God's, 401–417
    about, 401–403
    of Affinity, 412
    of Attraction, 411
    of Attraction and organizations, 322:11
    of Attraction and privacy, 1222
    automatic, 830:8, 1413:7
    of Brotherly and Sisterly Love, 410
    of Cause and Effect, 407
    of Cause and Effect, and of Justice, 1410:6
    of Cause and Effect, and our disciplining, 830:8
    of Cause and Effect misunderstood, 1410:2
    of Change, 415
    of Compensation, 408
    of Compensation, and of Justice, 1410:6
    effects of thoughts, 207
    governing existence, 403:3
    and happiness, 740:7
    interpretation of, 402:3
    of Justice, 409, 1410:6
    know no exception, 103:6
    of Life, 413
    of Life, and healing, 1105:3
    of Life, and intelligence, 413:7
    love, about, 410
    and manifestations, 1131
    of Moderation, 734:16
    of Motion, 414
    of Multiplication, 417
    observance of, 401:4
    of Personal Responsibility, 404
    of Reciprocation, 406
    of Self-Preservation, 416:6, 812:1, 818:5
    of Service, 405
    of Service, a misteaching, B12:30
    when sharing truth, 317:2
    and suffering, 827:10
    for teaching untruth, B01:3
    That Govern, 401, 402, 403
    THE LAW, 402, 401:2
    translating, 403
    unkind actions recoil, 710:4
    of Variety, 416, 813:2
    of Variety and species, 808:8
    of Vibration, 414
Lawyers, 715:11–16
    and honesty, 715:14
    and integrity, 715:11–16
Laying on of hands, 1106:2
Leaders:
    can bring disaster, 861
    disastrous, 860:9
    false, 705, B02

Index

of nations, 718:5
need to do, 860:11
unworthy acts, 824:3
using the big lie, 848
who promise all things, 718:4
Leadership, 843–848
Leaflet, USB, printing, contents, E01
   copy to each, D30:1
   purposes, D30:2
Learn:
   from experience of others, 860, 323:9–10
   old dog, new tricks, 771
Leave it to spirit, 1414
Leaving earth, 1426:2–3
Lemuria, 805:3
Leopard, change its spots, 322
Lessons:
   of history, appeasement, 860:7
   to learn only on earth, 1424
   of politics before principle, 847:3
   of profits before people, 847:3
   use, and perish by, the sword, 847:2
Let us do our part, 759
Levels:
   among spirit guides, 1221:11
   of consciousness, 210:4, 601:6, 1301:1–3,7, 1307:24, 1331:2
   of integrity, 711:13–15
Levitation in daylight, 1122:6
Liberty (*see also* Freedom), 853:5–6, 857:3
   is not license, 823:6–7, 849:2
   and one-world government, 862:3
   the price of, 856:4
   ready to die for it, 853:5
   use and misuse, 865:6
   and vigilance, 863
   and war, 857:3–5
Library, and consciousness, 606:4–8
License, is not liberty, 823:6–7, 849:2
Lie, the big, 848
Life:
   consumes life, 810
   on earth, destruction of, 770:2, 1207:8, A02:3, D27:5
   everyday, 901–931

   laws of, 413–417
   one continuous, 1301:13
   records, in aura, 1312, 608:7
   reviews, misconception, 1311:13
   scientists will never create, 802
Life force (*see* Vital life force)
Life forms, other, 809:7
Light:
   all souls reach in time, 315:4
   of the new age is here, 1427
   no one a focal point for all, 1419
   reaching out for, 308:4
   of reason, a beacon, 208:9
Limitations, the wise recognize, 767
Lincoln, Abraham:
   on honesty, 715:14
   White House phenomena, 1122:6
Linguists, in spirit life, 1325:7
Living:
   right, 746–758
   ways of, 759
Location of the real self, 1310:2,4
Looking down on, 1203
Loss of loved ones, 1204
Love, 501–524
   and beauty, 730:1
   fulfilling a law, 514
   of God, 514:n8
   of God, and serving, 737:10
   and healing, 1105:1–2
   of humanity, 509:2, 510
   an injunction on, 510
   kinds of, 514:5–6
   labors of, 512:1
   a law about, 410
   noble: definition, 510:4
   personal, 904
   power of, 512:2
   principle of, 511:1
   and service, inseparable, 405:6–7
   in spirit realms, 1326:1
   unselfish, 511
   and the USB, 508
   if we cannot, 515
   and wisdom, 704:7, 865:1, 1321:16
   with eyes wide open, 513
Love and goodness, evidence, 612:4,6

Index

M

Machines with emotions, 806
Magnetic healing, 1102:3–4
Magnetize, 1109
Malevolent spirit people, 1013:17, 1236:n15, 1319:n10
Manifestations:
    according to natural Law, 1131
    require varied chemicals, 1216:9
    time to develop, 1242:22
Mantras (*see also* Affirmations), 1139, 1140:11
    and spirituality, 1139:3
"Marvels," "wonders," "miracles," 1125, 417:1–3, 1003:1,14, 1124:1,10,15–16, 1127:1, 1129:3, 1137:3,5–12, B09:17
    do not spiritualize, 1125:12–13
    of spirit communication, 1232:25
Massage, and healing, 1104
Mastery over self, 745:10
Materialization, 1123
    and apports, 1129:5
    control of appearance, 1123:10–13
    and impersonation, 1123:9
    mechanics of, 1123
    and plasms, 1121–1125
    source of colors for, 1121:5
Material possessions, 746
    and moderation, 746:15
Materials, spirit, 1307:13–16
Material world, 801–807
Meaning, the search for, 807:4
Mechanics of:
    distant healing, 1107, 1102:5–6
    healing, 1106
    materialization, 1123
    mediumship, 1206
    mediumship misunderstood, 1003:7
    prophesy, 1001:1–5,15–20
    reincarnation, C01:10
Mediocrity, cult of, 836:2–3
Meditation, 1140
    disadvantages of, 1140:27–32
    room, substances in 1246
    and thought forms, 1319:17
Mediums, 1205–1215, D25
    and books and authors, 1209
    if developed *and* spiritual, 1207:6
    devices to replace, 1215
    difference from psychics, 1205
    errors of, 1210
    exploring various, 1211
    a few bad ones, B03:6
    and former guides, 1213
    fraudulent, 1220:10–12
    highly-developed, 1216:n7
    and Illumined Souls, 1207:8
    and mechanics of mediumship, 1206
    misteachings of, B12
    overly acclaimed, B03:3
    psychic, 1205:n4
    and psychics, 1205
    remuneration of, 1214
    self-promotion, 1209:5
    spiritual, 1207:6–10, 1208:5
    time to develop, 1216:9,18
    training of, 1216:n7
    unscrupulous, 1210:5–9, 1220:5
    USB requirements for, D25
    USB's American, Intro:18, Pref:9, 908:n1, 1013:n8
    in various ways, 1216:21–22
    who divert people from Truth, 1209:4
    who prey on others, 1220:10
    who twisted truth, 1208:8
Mediumship, 1207, 1208, 1216–1220, D25:3
    belittled, denied, B03:4–5
    best for this age, 1236:2
    and blindness, B09:27
    and cause of Truth, slowed, B03
    deep-trance, 1242:23–27
    depends on, largely, 1219:9
    developing, 1216, 1210:7, 1219:1, 1236:4, 1242:1, 1245:3
    and diet, 1219
    direct voice, 1218:1
    errors of guides, 1210:1–4
    essential to communicate, 1215:11
    gift of, 1216
    good, is essential, 1208:1, D25:3

independent direct voice, 1218:2
limitations on, 1220:7
mechanics misunderstood, 1003:7
mechanics of, 1206
no royal road to, 1216:18
not inherited, 1217, 1217:9
and orthodoxy, B04
and phenomena, 1202:n2
and physical handicaps, B09:27
promise of, 1210:5–9
and psychic centers, 1217:3–6
revelations of, 1208:5, 1220:4
spirituality is unrelated, 1208:4
symbols in, 1237
tragedy, of some, 1001:13–14
trance (*see* Trance)
use and misuse, 1220
Meetings (*see* USB meetings)
Meet wronged in afterlife, 1333
Membership in USB, D08, 111:2,5
Mental:
asylums, a caution, 1142
attunement, 1407:3, 608:23
healing, 1102:5
includes spiritual, 1311:10,34
wizards, B09:43
Mentality (*see also* Mind), 604:7, 1311:44
and brain, 617:8
includes emotions, 604:7, 1311:44
needed to think with, 806:7
a portion of Universal Mind, 601:5
qualities not inherited, 619:8, 1011:5–6
a questioning, 209, 314:3
Mercy, not divine, 1415:6–7
Mescaline, and peyote, 1141:7
Message:
of cheer, USB's, 113
giver also important, 1235
relayed, 1233:6, 1234:2
Metal bending, 1124:1
Michael (Flagg), Ackno:2,7,n1, Contrib:2–3, Howto:n1, Intro:3,9–10,14–19,21,24, 26–29,31–33,41–43, Pref:36, Greet:0, 102:n7, 115:n10, 301:n1, 324:n18, 325:n19, 501:n1, 514:n8, 721:n2, 1119:n2, 1135:n4, 1225:n9,n10, 1307:n6,1319:n9, 1325:n11, A00:n1, A02:1–2,5,7, C01:1–3,5–6,10–12
Michael's misconceptions, 324:n18
Microplasm, 1121:9
Mind(s) (*see also* Mentality), 1311:44
affecting spirit communication, 1232:1
affects matter *indirectly*, B09:14–15
all we receive comes from, 613:3
and barriers to enlightenment, 1221:18
closed, 1221:18
and coma, 617:7–8
and consciousness, 801:6
credulous, 1221:18
humans will never create, 806:7
illness not spring from, 916
and indissoluble triune, 602
misconceptions, 1311:44, B09:10
move a pin or paper, 1124:6
objective, 1231:3–5,9–10
and our faculties, 1231
outside the brain, 617:n8
over matter, 1124, B09:11
people's shelters against, 739:2
subjective, 1231:7–9,12–15
and sunspots, 816
Universal, 601:4–5
works with mind, B09:13
Mine of misinformation, the, B08
Minorities, and tyrannizing, 845
"Miracles" (*see* "Marvels")
Mischievous spirits, 1003:6, 1013:17, 1133:30, 1236:n15, 1319:n10
Misconceptions affecting afterlife, (*see also* Misteachings)
belief can absolve one, B10:27
fate of animals, 1308:1
floating in space, B12:57
life reviews, 1311:13
no spirit gender, B10:7
no speech in spirit world, 1324:1,3
our saviors, 705:1

Index

Misconceptions and afterlife—*Cont.*
    reincarnation mechanics, C01:10
    retrogress below human, 1406:2
    spirit "blindness," 1228:1–9
    spirit planes, 1301:6–7
    spirit world duplicates, 1306:1
    three-day wait, 1317:1,3
Misconceptions, earth life (*see also* Misteachings), 324
    all healing is by God, B13:4
    all is God's will, B12:48
    the aura, mind, 1311:42,44,46–47
    building one's spirit home, 1307:23
    God not a creator, 502:5
    God of revenge and caprice, 321:2
    humans cause sunspots, 816:1
    illness from spirit body, 1314
    many, B10:25–40
    mind over matter, B09:9–11
    one is as one thinks, 817
    pits in the road, like, 324:1
    of racial superiority, 813:5
    sleep and dreams, 925
    soul-gender changes, 1321:13–14
    spirit body envelops the physical, 1310:12
    "spiritual bank account," 1405
    stigmata, 1127:1
    teach old dog new tricks, 771:2
    when soul enters physical, 1315
Misconceptions, effects of, 309:16, 314:4, B10:1
    floating in space, B12:57
    Michael's, 324:n18
    no speech in spirit world, 1324:1,3
    power of, 771:2, 1228:1,9,n12, 1317:3, 1324:1,3
    spirit "blindness," 1228:4–5,9, 1322:3
Misinformation:
    the mine of, B08
    from spirit people, 1230:10–17
Misinterpretation, 318:9
Misleading spirit people, 1124:8–10
Misteachings, B10–B13
    about all creatures peaceful, 810:1
    about cancer, cruel, 915

    consequences of, 911:1–6
    divinity to animals, 1308:8,10–11
    effects of, 208:2–3
    about God, 502, 503, B12:42
    harmed, die, vitamins, B11:4,9,12
    of healers, B13
    illness springs from mind, 916:1
    about illusion, 801
    judgement and destruction, 1320:1
    about karma, 917:4–7
    of mediums, B12
    no spirit gender or jealousy, B10:7
    about number of guides, B12:19
    on ojas, B12:17
    about prana, B12:15
    about selves, 604
    about speaker preparation, B12:13
    of spirit "teachers," B11
    about spirituality and mentality, B12:25
    about suicides, 1332:1–3
    about work of guides, B12:5
Misunderstood, the, 311
Moderation:
    the Law of, 734:16
    the path of, 734, B12:18
    path to lasting progress, 834
Modesty, 714:2–3,7
Molecular structure, alter, 1124:3,13, 1129:4–9
Moon, landings on, 804
Moral consciousness, 608:4, 609:1–2
Moses, 750:3, 1226:3
Mothers, parents, working, 906
Motion:
    each element has specific, 414:5
    the Law of, 414
Motive:
    alone is not enough, 722
    and spirituality, 1402
    and suicides, 1332:5–10
    weighs heavily, 722:1, 1332:5
Mountain, and resolutions, 717:9
Mountaintop, path to, 775, 1420, 318:5, 927:6, 1141:33, 1409:10
Move a pin or paper.., 1124:6
Moxibustion, and healing, 1104

Index

Multiplication, the Law of, 417
Music:
    and colors, 931
    dangers of, 826
    and healing, 1245
    how it affects us, 931:6
    lacking qualities, 836:16
    off-notes, 826:5
    of the spheres, 1302
Mythical source of supply, 1209:3

N

Nation, its needs, 844:2–4
Nations, society of, 854:1
Native North Americans, 1227
    injustices suffered, 1227:1–3
    and inhumanity, 1227:10
    noble of spirit, 1227:9
    purity of early, 1227:7
    spirit guides, 501:n2
Natural laws, 401
Nature:
    all vibrates in, 414:15
    bountiful, 821:13
    cycles of, 612:5, 928:3–5
    dominion over, 809:6
    forces of, 1004:13
    harm to, 809:2
    human, 818
    and humans, 809
    humans do not guide, 809:7
    is all in order, 816:6–9
    kingdoms of, 809:8–9,n3
    laws of, 401
    nothing wasted in, 809:5
    spirits, 809:7
    strikes a balance, 809:1
    of truth, 301–308
Nazarene, the, B09:24
Nearing adulthood, 907:8
Need(s):
    vs. desires, 718:3, 733:1,7
    the greatest, today, 1431
    is *now*, 824, A09:3
Neighbor, love thy, 510
New age, 201, 101:5
    every age is a, 201:1
    has already begun, 201:1
    its light is here, 1427
    the teachings of, 201:2, 1419:7
New, nothing under the sun, 805
New physics (*see* New science)
New science, Intro:26
    aura-detecting instruments, 1311:n7, B09:29
    dark matter, dark energy, 414:n6
    EVP voice recordings, 1215:4,n6
    mind outside the brain, 617:n8
    multiple dimensions, 1301:n2
    subatomic particles, 206:n3
    Therapeutic Touch, 1106:n1
    we're all related, per DNA, 601:n1
News disseminators, weigh well, 866
Noble:
    character, root of, 711:2
    love, definition, 510:4
    qualities, important, 608:1
No effort is wasted, D27:4
Noise, logarithmic scale, 826:n7
Non-human beings, 809:7
Nonprofit tax status, USB, D06:n1
North American Indians (*see* Native North Americans)
No's of the USB, positive, 110:11–22
Now, the, 927, 926:6–8
    to be thankful for, 927:4
    the joys of, 927, 927:4
    a time of trial and testing, 824

O

OBE, 1202:n2, 1228:n11, 1313:3,8,10,n8
Objective faculties, 1231:6
Objective mind, 1231:3–5,9–10
Obligation, a great, 319
Obsession, 1133:6–27
    and insanity, 1133:17
    protection against, 1133:18–27
    and puberty, 1133:28–29
Occupying, spirit beings, 1133:6–7,14
Occurrences, cause, 1410
Ocean, plowing, 320
Odor, 929:4–5
    each thing has own, 929:5

Index

Officeholders, and integrity, 715:25–28
Ojas, a misteaching, B12:17
Old and new, best of, 835
One continuous life, 1301:13
Oneself, can do much, 765
One-world government, 862
    potential disaster, 862:3
OOBE, 1313:3,8,10
Open mind, 309:12
Operation of the USB, D01–D34
Opportunity(ies):
    and challenge, 769
    how to use, 803:4,7–8
    not deprive others of, 851:3,5
Opposes, what the USB, 110:25
Opposite sides of a coin, 829
Opposition, to the USB, D33
Orchard, diseased trees in, B03:6
Order:
    all nature is in, 816:6–9
    and law, evidence of, 612:4–5
    and law, needs respect, 838
Organizations:
    and the Law of Attraction, 322:11
    persecution by, 309:2, 322:2
    and spiritual truths, 322
    and symbols, D32
    tenets rejected, 771:3
    that hinder truth, B03, B04, 322:5,8–9
    that repressed truth, 322:2,10
    unacceptable principles, 322:4
Origins:
    human, 506:3–4
    of the USB, 101–102
Others seek us, we prefer, D07
Other worlds, vibrations of, 919:3
Ouija board, 1236:11
Our own prophets, 611:14, 775:1
Our own saviors, 611:14, 705:1, 1007:4, 1008:31, 1413:6–8
Our part, let us do, 759
Our path of progress, 1318
Our world, 801–866
Out-of-body, 1202:n2, 1228:n11, 1313:3,8,10,n8
Overcome:
    cannot for others, 760:3
    a condition, 1410:8–9
Overlooking faults, wrongs, 1416
Overpopulation, 821
    rapid growth of, 821:1–7
Oxygen, vital essence in, 913:3

P

Paine, Thomas, 822:1–2,5–6
Palmistry, 1010
Parable:
    of the grapes, 719:7–10
    of the mountain road, 1001:16
Paragraph numbering, Howto:5
Paranormal demonstrations, 1122:6–7
Parapsychology, 315:1,n5, B07
Parents:
    on caring for infants, 910
    and consumerism, 906:3
    and discipline, 704:1
    greatest responsibility, 905:12
    importance of family, 905
    responsibilities, 907
    and teaching untruths, 911
    working, 906
    and youth, 907
Part, let us do our, 759, 807:20
Passing on, to spirit life (*see also* Death), 1322
    everyone is met, 1322
Past-life regression, 1202:n2
Path(s):
    center, 734
    difficult to tread, 113:5, 1420:2
    to God, 1428:2
    to lasting progress, 834
    of moderation, 734, B12:18
    most direct, the USB, 1428
    to the mountaintop, 775, 1420, 318:5, 927:6, 1141:33, 1409:10
    to a precipice, 1209:8
    of progress, our, 1318
    spiritual, the, 1420–1426, 612:4
    of truth, 102:13
    we cannot walk another's, 1423
    words of Alcoon, 517:7
Patience, 309:10, 807:16, 1420:2

Index

Patients:
    and healers, 1117
    varied responses of, 1113
Patriotism, 752
Peace:
    and constructive thoughts, 1004:20–21
    perfect, 758
Pearls, formation, 739:1
Pendulum, swing of, 834
People:
    barriers between, 1327:2
    make the plane, 1301:8, B12:12
    in praise of average, 815
    spirit (*see* Spirit people)
    variety among, 813:2
People's:
    inhumanity to others, 830:2
    laws, 401
    shelters against minds, 739:2
    similarities, remember, 763
Perfection:
    descending from, 1318:4–5
    on earth?, 1409
    and Illumined Souls, 106:2
    scheme of things, 501:8
Perfect peace, 758
Persecution, 309:2, 322:2
Persevering, 807:15
Persistence, 309:9
Personal interpretation (*see also* Interpretation), 114
    freedom of, 850
Personality, our:
    facets of, 605:3
    and individuality, 605
Personal love and affection, 904
Personal progress, 765–775
Personal relationships, 902
Personal responsibility (*see also* Responsibilities), 704–710
    age of, 839
    cannot absolve another from, 705
    Law of, 404
    not transferable, 707:6
    recognizing the importance of, 704
    on rewarding evaders, 708:3
    to serve, 520
    spiritual, 1411–1414
    and will, 701:6
Pets:
    heroic deeds of, 812:2–3
    psychic, 812:3, 1135:2–3
Peyote, and mescaline, 1141:7
Phenomena, 1101–1142
    and animals, 1135, B09:36–38
    apports, 1129
    déjà vu, déjà dit, 1126
    dowsing, 1128
    ectoplasm, 1121–1122
    evidence of, 1202:2, 1313:3–4, B07:3
    fake, B04:2,7
    glossolalia, 1134
    healing, unorthodox, 1101–1113, 1115
    incredible, 1012:10
    investigators of, 323, 1137:2, 1202:2, B05:6, B07:2–10
    and law, 1131
    materialization, 1123
    and mediumship, 1202:n2
    metal bending, 1124
    misunderstood, 1137
    obsession, 1133
    other, 1126–1137
    reenactments, 1136
    spirit determined, 1215:3
    and spirit scientists, 1130
    stigmata, 1127
    strange, B09:n2
Phrenology, 1011
Physical (earthly) body, 820, 414:13,16
    comfort in, 1120:9
    envelops spirit body, 1310:3,12
    its needs, 734:6–7
    our responsibility to, 820:2
    spirits occupying, 1133:6–7,14
    we retain a replica of, 1309
    when individual enters, 1315
Physical handicaps, and mediumship, B09:27
"Physician, heal thyself," 1120
    why some healers cannot, 1120:7–8

Index

Physicians, and integrity, 715:3–10
Physics, new (*see* New science)
Pipe, limited capacity, 734:15
Pitch, a component of sound, 929:3
PK (Psychokinesis), B09:9–15
Planes (of consciousness): 1301:1–9, 1307:24, B12:12,41,53
   of expression, 801:9
   made by people, 1301:8, B12:12
Planetary hierarchy, spiritual, 706:5, 1301:11
Planets:
   and astrology, 1008:4,10–12
   inhabitants, 1301:13
   their spiritual hierarchies, 706:5, 1301:11
   undiscovered, 1301:11,n4
   visiting, 919:2
   "visitors" from other, 706
Plasms, 1121
   and materialization, 1121–1125
Pleasure, 724:3
Plow the ocean, 320
Pluto, reclassified, 1008:n4
Poaching energy, 1244
   prevention, 1244
Poems:
   by Michael Flagg, 301, 721, 727, 728, 1326, 1426
   by Robert Hamilton, 724
   by Leigh Hunt, 509
   by John Keats, 306
   by Omar Khayyám, 741
   by Alexander Pope, 833
   by Grantland Rice, 745
   by William Shakespeare, 729
Poetry, 836:21–22
Politics, D04, 110:18
   before principle, 847:3
Poltergeist, 1122:7, 1133:30–31
Pope, Alexander, 833:8,n8
Population:
   rapid world growth of, 821:1–7
   spirit world, 821:3, 1301:9
   world, 821
Pornography, 836:27
Possession, 1133:6,11,13–14
   and rage, 735:2
Possessions, material, 746
Poverty and crime, 842
   a tribute, 842:8
Power:
   in atom, 507:10,n5, 727:17
   of God, 612:8–9
   of love, 512:2
   of misconceptions, 1228:1,9,n12, 1324:1,3
   at séances, 1232:17,22
   of thought, 206, 204:2–8, 1001:18, 1004:20,22, 1008:23, 1228:5
   of thought in spirit life, 1323, 1136:5, 1228:1,5,6,9,n11, 1306:11, 1307:4,6,14,16,n6, 1310:19,23, 1319:10, 1324:3
   use and abuse of, 846, 860:10
Praise:
   for average person, 815, 323:12
   not Illumined Souls, B02:7
Prana (*see* Vital life force)
Pray:
   how to, 521:8–10, 522:1, 1111:11
   starts up a Law, 522:3
Prayer(s), 521–524
   attitude in, 522:1
   bring no harm, 521:10
   climb a ladder, 1111:4
   definition, 521:3
   excerpts on, 522
   for healing, 1111, 1107:3
   of Illumined Souls, 524
   intensity is important, 521:3–5
   a noble, 703:3
   not answered, 522:4
   and rituals, 521:12
   for these times of trial, 825
   in USB groups, meetings, D19
   USB has no prescribed, 521:12
   of a USB Inspirer, 523
"Precepts," of prophesy and healing, 1002:1–3
Precognition of USB teachings, 1241:1,4
Predictions (*see* Prophesy), 1001–1007
Prejudice, and color, 813

Index

Presentable appearance, 714
Price, every person has a, 814
Priceless books, a parable, 726:1
Pride, 731
    double-edged sword, 731:5–7
    "sin" or virtue?, 731:1–4
Principle:
    of love, 511:1
    on surrendering, 824:3
Principles of the USB, 103
Privacy:
    considerate of others', 1222:6
    right to, 852
    spirit friends not "spies," 1222:7
Prizefighting (boxing), 820
Probers and seekers, 209:3
Problems:
    are necessary in our lives, 1408:13
    no one can escape all, 1408:10
    progress from responses to,
        1408:1–5, 1421:4
    tested by, 1408:6–9
Procrastination, 717:2–6
Professions and integrity, 715
    judges, 715:17–23
    lawyers, 715:11–16
    officeholders, 715:25–28
    physicians, 715:3–10
Profits before people, 847:3
Progress:
    from best of old and new, 835
    our path of, 1318
    personal, 765–775
    from raising the low, 836:39
Progress, spiritual, 774–5, 1421, 773:4
    doors to, 831, 103:7, 308:3, 607:3
    is earned, 1329:16
    essential knowledge for, 1425
    how to, 503:5
    is never closed to us, 103:7
    our path of, 1318
    from responses to problems,
        1408:1–5, 1421:4
Projection, conscious, 1310:15
Promise:
    all things, leaders who, 718:4

    of mediumship, 1210:5–9
Promises, keeping, 716
Prophecy, and predictions, 1001
    accuracy of, 1001:15–17
    of approaching disaster, 1004
    by astrology, 1005, 1008:23
    and the aura, 1001:4
    mechanics of, 1001:1–5,15–20
    most don't materialize, 1005
    mountain road parable, 1001:16
    not divine, 1002
    not infallible, 1001:17
    and power of thought, 1001:18
    "precept," of, 1002:1–3
    on "saviors," "fulfilling," 1007
    a warning for, 1006
Prophecy for Christmas 1967:
    face in clouds, 1003
    unmaterialized, 1003:10
Prophets:
    false, 705:8–10, 1007:9
    lives of great ones, 1420
    not informed by God, 1001:8
    we are our own, 611:14, 775:1
Protection by spirit friends, 206:8
Protective measure, energy, 1244
Protoplasm, 1121:1
Prototypes, spirit world, 1306:12–13
Provident, on being, 709
Proving ground, earth is a, 711:4,
    846:3, 1409:2
Psalm, twenty-third, 504
Psychiatrists, 909
    and aggravation, 909:2
Psychic:
    ability of animals, 812:3, 1135:2–3
    body, 1310:1,6
    centers (*see below*)
    development, 1407:2
    difference from medium, 1205
    "discoveries," books on, B09
    experiences, 1138–1142
    experiences and drugs, 1141
    experiences, relating, 1142
    ignorance of educators, B05:6
    medium, 1205:n4

Index

Psychic centers, 1138, 1205:7, 1217:3
   artificial stimulation of, 1141:10
   and breathing exercises, 1138:4–6
   chemicalize, 1216:9,20, 1236:3
   developing, and music, 1245:3
   locations, 1138:3
   and mediumship, 1217:3–6
   sensitivity inherited, 1217:3
   and vital life force, 1138:1
Psychic phenomena:
   circle leader to be versed in, 1242:7
   explanations of some, 1137
   fire-walking, 1125:1–6
   handling live coals, 1125:7–11
   mechanics misunderstood, 1003:7
   and puberty, 1133:30–31
   stigmata, 1127
   under spirit control, B09:57
Psychical research, 315
   societies done harm, 315:1
Psychics, and mediums, 1205
Psychokinesis (PK), B09:9–15
Psychometry, 1012, B09:46
   spirit guides impress, 1012:6
Puberty:
   and obsession, 1133:28–29
   and phenomena, 1133:30–31
Publications and error, 310:2–3
   seeker's safeguards, 310:4
Punishment:
   deterrent to crime, 840
   everlasting, 308:3
   of violence, 839:6, 840:5, 841:2
Purpose(s):
   human, 727:4
   of the USB, 104, Greet:4
Pushing others, not, 316:3, 318:14

Q

Qualities:
   desirable, 714:7
   noble, 833:10
   required during testing, 824:2
   of truth seekers, 309
Quantum mechanics, 414:n6
Quest:
   for freedom, 865:10
   greatest, 309:20–21, 1401:2
Questioning mentality, a, 209
Questions:
   about evil, tragedy, 830
   on "keeping" others, 1411
   on self-defense, 858
   on spirit life, 1307
   about water pollution, 914
Question, to help understand, 209:1–2
   all we are offered, 316:5
Quotations and excerpts from the
   USB, 739, 760
   on God, 501
   on love, 512
   on prayer, 522
   on service, 517
   on spirituality, 608, 1401
   on spiritual progress, 1421

R

Race, no superior, 813:7
   a misconception, 813:5
Rage, problems and effects of, 735
Raids, chemical, 1106:10
   preventing, 1106:10
Rate of vibration, determines, 414:7–13
Rays, 1229
Reaching out, for light, 308:4
Realization, sufficient, 506:5
Realms (*see* Spirit realms)
Real self, triune, 602
   composition, 729:4
   and gender, 1013:18
   indestructible, 301:6, 1320
   and individuality, 605, 607
   location, 1310:2,4
   and sleep, 918:7, 921:6, 1313:8
Reap what we sow, 745:11
Reason, 208–210, 309:14–16
   before accepting, 210:5
   can bring knowledge, 210:4
   chaos without, 1004:9
   definition, 208:1
   disaster learning without, 208:3
   embraces, 310:4, 312:1
   exercise it, Intro:32,34, 208:1–2,
      210:5, 309:14, 314:1, B00:n1

Index

in humans only, 811
its light a beacon, 208:9
opportunities on earth, 1424:24
and slavery, 208:12–13
Receptivity:
and breathing exercises, 1138:4–6
and communication, 1243:6
and music, 1245:2–3
regions of, 1138:3
Reciprocation, the Law of, 406
Recognition, for self, others, 731:10
Recognize, don't deny, 742
Recordings, Intro:33, Pref:8, C01:5
Records, our full, in aura, 1312, 608:7
Akashic, 1312
Reenactment of battle scenes, in spirit life, 1136
Reflection, 751
Regression, retrogression:
past-life, 1202:n2
spiritual, 1406
under hypnosis, 1013
Regrets, 741
Reincarnation, C01, Intro:27
"artificial," B09:7
a great spiritual truth, C01
mechanics, C01:10
Rejoicing:
for the departing, 1426:3
and healing, 1110:15
in prayer, 521:9
at sittings, 1247:3
Relationships, 901–904
freedom in, 903
personal, 902
Relayed communication, 1233:6
Relays:
in déjà vu, 1126:5
and distortion, 206:4
by the hypnotized, 1013:8
in the spirit world, 1215:9
by standbys, 1233:3,6
with an astral body, 1319:6
in work of mediums, 1209:3
Remember:
about our progress, 1408:5
the similarities, 763

to *think*, 848:2–3
a time to, 751
Remorseful, posters of the, 1333:5
Remote viewing, 918:n2, 1313:4,9
Remuneration of mediums, 1214
Replica of the physical body, 1309
Repudiation of agreements, 716:2
Research, psychical, 315
Rescue circles, 1228:6,n12, 1322:3
"Resist not evil," 744:2–5
Resist undesirable impulses, 728:6
Resolutions, 717
and mountain, 717:9
Respect, of friends, 719:12
Respond to things, how we, 1408
Responsibilities (*see also* Personal responsibility):
of employees, 749
of employers, 749
law of, 404
not for our ancestors, 707
for our actions, 1230:18
of parents, 907
to present truth simply, 318:9
of shepherd, 843
of teachers of truth, 202:4, 325:1
of USB followers, to truth, D27:6
Responsive chord (*see* Reason)
Responses to healing, varied, 1113
Retribution:
fear of, 1305:4, 1424:6
is according to Law, 1413:7
Retrogression (*see* regression)
Returning to God, 1318:4
Revelations of mediumship, 1208:5, 1220:4
Revenge, 857:6
Rhodamine, 603:5
Rice, Grantland, 745:n7
Ridicule, 323:6,n17
Right living, 746–758
Rights of the individual, 851
to be let alone, 852:3
to freedom, 865:6
must give up some, 853:9–10
to privacy, 852

Index

Rise above, anyone can, 770:5, 803:12, 1415:10
Rituals:
   buried truth, 201:5
   not in the USB, 110:13
   and prayer, 521:12
River, strength of, compared, 111:9
Rods, ectoplasmic, 1122:3,7, 1124:3, 1137:6

S

Safeguards at home circles, 1242:6
"Salvation:"
   to buy, 750:12
   through others, 706:1, 1209:8, 1413:1–2, B03:2
"Sapping" energy, 1244:3
Savior(s), 1413
   false, so-called, 1007
   "fulfilling" prophesies, 1007
   we are our own, 611:14, 705:1, 1007:4, 1008:31, 1413:6–8
   what false don't teach, 1007:4–6
   who adversely affect lives, 1007:9
Scenery, spirit, 1326:1
Sceptics, 1202, 1202:n3
Scheme of things, 501:8
Schools, that hinder truth, B03
Science, new (*see* New science)
Scientists:
   auric, 1311:9,12–13
   how they could share, 921:3
   ignore prior findings, 323:11
   support *any* other theory, B05:5
   and truth, 323
   unscientific, 323:4
   who complicate the simple, 323:13
   will never create life, 802
Scrolls, ancient, 764
Séance room, substances in, 1246
Séances (*see also* Circles, Sittings):
   cheerfulness at, 1247
   power at, 1232:17,22
   spirit people of the living at, 1239
Sea of Galilee, Pref:32
Search for meaning, the, 807:4
Searching for truth, 309–315
Seed, good to plant, but..., 320:2

Seeds, sowing, 1429, 112:3, 315:5, 317:5–7, 320:2, 760:1, 770:2, 865:4, 1320:4, 1423: 3–4
Seekers of truth:
   misleading them, B01:3
   not confined, 309:13
   opposition to, 311
   and probers, 209:3
   qualities needed, 309
   selectively, B08:2
   terrifying them, B01:5
   weigh well, 1230
Self (selves):
   be true to *soul*, 729
   consciousness not divided, 604
   to know *about*, 611
   no lower, higher, 604
   mastery over, 745:10
   real (*see* Real self)
Self-defense, questions about, 858
Self-determinism, 772
Selfishness, 821:17
Selfless (*see also* Service, selfless):
   and golden rule, 901:6
   and home circles, 1242:4,6
   and motive, 1405:3–4
   and spirit guides, 1221:19
   and spirituality, 608:20,24, 773:4
Self pity, the curse of, 732
Self-preservation:
   and "death wish," 727:9
   instinct for, 727:9
   Law of, 416:6, 812:1, 818:5
Self-satisfaction, error of, 312
Seminars, B05, B06
Sensing what is true, 312:1
Sensitivity:
   in sleep, 919
   usually inherited, 1217:3
Sensitize:
   for interplanetary travel, 919:3
   the psychic centers, 1216:20
   when magnetized, 1109:4
Serve:
   ever ready to, 737:11
   how one can, 112
   material/spiritual rewards, 519
   responsibility to, 520

Index

spirit friends, 1224:8
USB's desire, 111:6
Service, 516–520, D27:15
   the greatest, 518:2
   laws of, 405–406
   and love, inseparable, 405:6–7
   only unselfish, 516
   quotations on, 517
   selfless, 516, 103:9, 405:5
Shakespeare, William, 614:n7, 729:n4, 1008:n6
Sham, B04:5
Share, how much, 513:5
Shells (*see* Astral bodies *and* Thought forms)
Shepherd, responsibilities of, 843
Sick rooms, cheerfulness in 1247
Silence:
   giving in, 519:1–2
   sitting in the, 1231:12–14
Silent:
   demonstrators who remain, 845:4
   a time to be, 753
"Silver cord," 1310:16, 1311:21, 1313:12, 1317:1
Simplicity, 309:8, 1401:1
Sin:
   condemn, not the sinner, 325:3
   the great, 734:4
Singing at circles, no need, 1242:16
Sitters:
   and accompanying spirits, 1243:1
   should judge by content, 1233:24
Sittings (*also see* Circles):
   cheerfulness in 1247
   for development, factors, 1243:5–8
   each is an experiment, 1233:21
   spirit people of the living at, 1239
   at USB headquarters, 1241:3
   ways of holding, 1110, 1243
Skeptics, 1202, 1202:n3
Slates, on erasing our, 766, 1415:4
Slavery:
   acceptance of, 725:4
   to empty things, 725
   and snobbery, 725:3
Sleep, 918–925
   activities that fatigue, 920

   dreams and droes, 924
   and dreams, misconceptions, 925
   and geniuses, 1132:9
   knowledge in, 1132:11
   and the real self, 918:7, 921:6, 1228:n11, 1313:8
   sensitivity in, 919
   talking in, 922
   why we need, 918
Sleepwalking, 921
   and spirit controls, 921:6–9
Slogans, 853:3
Slow to decide, quick to act, 736
Small groups (*see* USB groups)
Smugness, the error of, 312
Snobbery, and voluntary slavery, 725:3
Society:
   to curb abusers, 849:2, 854:1
   to discipline wrongdoers, 840:2
   of nations, 854:1
   to protect itself, 719:5
Solar system:
   moons of, 1008:n5
   precise operation, 507:6
Solid objects, spirit-realm, 1323:8
Sorrow, 724
Soul(s), divine spark, 601:2
   be true to thy, 729
   fan spark into flame, 763:3
   gender, 1321:14
   great, never command, 1226
   human uniqueness, 811:3
   and Law of Life, 413:5
   location, 603
   none ever destroyed, 1320, 308:3, 611:7, 1413:10–13
   numbers of, 821:3
   spark of the divine, 601:2
   testing ground of, 1408:6
   when enters physical, 1315
Sound(s):
   aum, 1139:1–2
   chanting, uttering, 1139
   and color, 929–931
   has pitch and tone, 929:3
   most powerful, 1139:1
   a vibration, 929:1

Index

Source of supply:
   mythical collective, 1209:3
   universal mind, 601:4
Sow and reap, 745:11
Sowing seeds, 1429, 112:3, 315:5,
     317:5–7, 320:2, 760:1, 770:2,
     865:4, 1320:4, 1423: 3–4
Spark of God/the Divine (*see* Soul)
Sparrow cannot become an eagle, 767
Speak, a time to, 753
Speaking in tongues, 1134
Species:
   evolution, and humans, 808
   and Law of Variety, 416:1, 808:8
   and Law of Vibration, 414:14
   ranges of vibrations, 414:9
Speculation, pointless, 506
Speech:
   by animals, 811:2
   in spirit life, 1324, 1309:4
Speed of thought, 206:6–7
Speed, way of life, 747, 1216:n7
Spheres, spirit-world, 1301:1–7
   unlimited number, 1301:7
Spirit:
   animating factor, 601:3
   "blindness," 1228:1–9, 1322:3
   body(ies) (*see* Spirit body)
   clothing on flights, 1329:9–12
   communication (*see* Spirit
     communication)
   controls (*see* Spirit controls)
   developing gifts, 1216
   dormancy, 1413:13
   double (*see* Spirit double)
   edifices, 1323:1
   existence, 1315–1321
   false information, 1003
   flights, 1329
   gardens, 1323:1
   guides (*see* Spirit guides)
   healing, 1102:7–10
   home, misconception, 1307:23
   homes, 1307:21–27, 1323:6
   leave it to, 1414
   life, 1301–1333
   makeup, our, 1309–1314

   materials, 1307:13–16
   meanings of, 601:n2
   misinformation, 1230:10–17
   nature, 809:7
   people; spirits (*see* Spirit people)
   protection (*see* Spirit protection)
   realms (*see* Spirit realms)
   "rescue," 1228:6,n12, 1322:3
   "says," 1212
   scenery, 1326:1
   teachings, compared, Intro:8
   toys, 1306:11
   world (*see* Spirit world)
Spirit body(ies), 1310, 603:3–4, 775:4,
     919:3, 1303:5, 1307:5,9
   astral body, 1310:1,5
   and aura, 1310:20, 1314:3, 1311:42,
     B09:19
   "blindness," 1228:1–9, 1322:3
   cannot be harmed, 1307:5
   celestial body, 1310:1,8
   change appearance of, 1310:23
   and illness, 1314
   is within physical body, 1310:12
   of the living, at séances, 1239
   made up of, 1310:4–9
   psychic body, 1310:1,6
   replica of physical, 1310:17
   "silver cord," 1310:16
   and spirit travel, 918:7, 919:2
   spiritual body, 1310:1,7
   surgery on, 1314:5
Spirit communication, 1231–1241,
     1309:4
   determined by, 1208:3, 1215:3
   direct, 1227:7, 1234:2, 1236:n15
   factors affecting, 1232
   failure of, 1238
   and humility, 1234:7
   by inspiration, 102:16, 924:4,
     1231:12, 1418:1, D24:6
   interpretation of, 1234:1–3
   judge by content, 1233:24
   and language, 1325
   levels of, 1233:17
   minds affecting, 1232:1
   relayed, 1233:6, 1234:2

Index

restrictions on, 1232:13
same voices, reasons, 1233:1–7
scriptural condemnations of, 1133:n3
standbys, 1233
tardiness of, 1238
by thought, 1325:2,23
the truth of, 909:1
variety of forms, 1236
by voice, 1324, 1309:4
wonders of, 1232:25
weigh words well, 1230, 1234
Spirit controls, 1133:7, 1232:1, D24:8
and astral bodies, 1319:8
in déjà vu, 1126:5
in healing, 1116:3
meaning of, D24:8
in obsession, 1133:6–31
in sleep, 921:9, 922:2
in stupor, 921:10
understanding by, 1233:18
while sleepwalking, 921:6–9
Spirit double, 1310:4
Spirit guides (and friends), 1221–1230
children, 1247:1
closeness to, 1422
commanding them, 1223
and consciousness, 1221:11
courtesy owed, 1224
former, and mediums, 1213:8
helping healers, 1106:3–9, 1112:4, 1118:4
no "spiritual captivity," B12:60
not manifesting, 1232:20
not necessarily wise, *etc.*, 1221:15
not our servants, 1221:14, 1224:8
number, 1221:5–6
and privacy, 1222
standbys, communicating, 1233
"teachers," misteachings of, B11
that request or demand, 1230:7–8
their caliber, 1221:10–12
ways they can impress us, 1237
we are never alone, 1222
weigh words well, 1230
why they come, 1221:2,21, 1414:3–6

work problems through us, 1221:20
Spirit people (spirits; spirit beings):
aiding births, infants, 1315:3
appearance, 1309:7–8, 1315:4, 1310:17–19,21–23, 1330:12
barriers between, 1327:2
"blindness," 1228:1–9, 1322:3
chemists, 1107:3, 1130:4
chemists and ectoplasm, 1123:3
claiming supreme power, 1234:7
clothing, 1306:11, 1329:9–12
control psychic phenomena, B09:57
deaf and dumb, 1324:3
deceiving, 1236:11, 1319:18–19
direction of animals, B09:38
in dormancy, 1413:13
earthbound, 1331
fear of, 1133:n3
fervor of, religious, 1127:2, 1137:4, 1233:14, 1319:15, B09:16
floating in space, B12:57
Illumined Inspirers (*see*)
impersonations by, 1123:9, 1234:6
individuality, 1318:9
linguists, interpreters, 1325:7
malevolent, 1013:17, 1236:n15, 1319:n10
many levels of, 1013:17, 1221:15
meet those wronged on earth, 1333
mischievous, 1003:6, 1013:17, 1133:30, 1236:n15, 1319:n10
misleading, 1124:8–10
nature spirits, 809:7
numbers of, 821:3
occupying, 1133:6–7,14
projects for, 1210:2, 1230:7
protection of alcoholics, 921:11
"rescue," 1228:6,n12, 1322:3
scientists, 1130:3
sight, 1228
some bring confusion, 1230:1
specialists, 1111:8, 1115:3
speech among, 1324, 1309:4
surgeons, 1314:5
tardiness of, 1238
"teachers," misteachings of, B11
travel, 1329, 1310:14, 1313:n8

Index

Spirit people—*Cont.*
  trolls, 1319:n10
  undesirable, 735:2, 1013:10,
    1133:4,25, 1236:n15, 1243:1–2
  undeveloped, 1230:8, 1331:3
  ways they can impress us, 1237
  weigh their words well, 1230
Spirit protection, 206:8
  and drugs, 921:11
Spirit realms (Etheric realms, Etheria)
  (*see also* Spirit world), 1301
  astral realms, 1301:2
  attunement to higher, 413:12
  beauty of higher, 521:4, 923:5,
    1238:3, 1306:8–9, 1323:9
  celestial realms, 1301:2
  communication in (*see* Spirit
    communication)
  convalescence in, 1307:26
  creation of environment, 521:4
  darkness, B10:17
  and evil, 829:3
  help from, 1207:9
  higher, beauty of, 521:4, 923:5,
    1306:8–9
  and Illumined Souls, 1225:1
  kingdoms, 1301:2
  made by people, B12:12
  music of the spheres, 1302:2
  planes, misconceptions, 1301:6–7
  spiritual, 1301:2
  warmth and happiness, 1326:8
Spirits (*see* Spirit people)
Spirit world (*see also* Spirit realms),
  1301–1308
  activities, 1325:27
  children, 1330
  communication in (*see* Spirit
    communication)
  concerts, 1328:8
  counterparts, 1306:1
  duplicates, 1306
  duplicates don't exist, 1306:7
  and earth emanations, 1303
  fear in, 727:20
  humor in, 1326

  jealousy, B10:8
  leaders of, 1004:15
  living in, 1322–1333, 1307
  love and affection, 1326:1
  mediums in, 1215:9
  new arrivals, 1307:21–22
  population, 821:3, 1301:9
  prototypes, 1306:12–13
  solid objects, 1323:8
  speech in, 1324, 1309:4
  spheres, 1301:1–7
  spirit realms (*see above*)
  thought in, power (*see* Power, of
    thought in spirit life)
  time in, 1328, 1136:5, 1238:4
  titles, 1327
  travel, 1329, 1310:14, 1313:n8
  weigh their words well, 1230
  when passing on to, 1322, 771:2,
    1228:10, 1317:3
Spiritual:
  acts are recognized, 1421:6
  "bank account," 1405
  body, 1310:1,7
  "captivity," B12:59–60
  circle members should be, 1242:6
  development, 1407, 506:6, 774:7
  glow, within, 505:7–10
  and good, 1402
  healing, 1101:1, 1102:11–12
  hierarchy, planetary, 706:5, 1301:11
  ills, 728:8
  lives simply, 1401:1
  and moral consciousness, 609:1
  path, 1423, 612:4
  progress (*see* Spiritual progress)
  realms, 1301:2
  regression, 1406
  strength, 1408:12
  truths, and organizations, 322
Spiritual Light (this book):
  assembly, Intro:19–29
  contributors to, Contrib, Intro:3,37
  how to use it, Howto:1–9
  spirit review of, Intro:18
  writing for, Intro:14–18

Index

Spiritual progress, 775, 1401–1433, A13:4
  doors to, 831, 103:7, 308:3, 607:3
  essential knowledge for, 1425
  excerpts on, 1421
  how to make, 503:5, 520:6
  is earned, 1329:16
  is never closed to us, 103:7, 831
  the path of, 1420–1426, 1318, 612:4
  from responses to problems, 1408:1–5, 1421:4
  and responsibility, 705:1
  stepping stones, 769:2, 803:4
  tests of, 769:3
  and The Law, 1425, 1139:4
  the USB view, 1427–1433
Spirituality, 608, 1401–1407
  and chanting, 1139:3
  evidenced by deeds, 1403:2
  expression of, 1403:3
  growth of, 503:3, 1408:13
  and healing, 1116
  and health, 917:1–3
  and knowledge of Laws, 1425
  in a material world, 1424:24
  mediumship is unrelated, 1208:4
  and mental outlook, 1408:12
  part of our minds, 1311:10,44
  and technical progress, 804:5–6
  unrelated to mediumship, 1208:4
Spiritually afflicted, the, 728:8
Spoon bending, 1124:1
Sports and sporting behavior, 745
Spreading enlightenment, by the USB, D03:1, D27:9–14, D28:6
Spreading truth, 316–325
Stand, take against evil, 754:1–2
Standards, 711–718
  the decline in, 836
  of education, 836:5–11
  of language, 713
  of morality, 836:24–28
  of music, 836:15–16
  in news media, 836:17–19
  personal, 712
  of poetry, 836:21–22
  reversing decline in, 836:29–39
  of sculpture, painting, 836:23
  self-discipline, 803:11–12
  set high, 712:4
  of writing, literature, 836:20
Standbys, communicating, 1233
Stars (*see* Astrology)
Stepping stones, spiritual, 769:2, 803:4
Stigmata, 1127
Strength of a river, compared, 111:9
Strength, use and misuse of, 860:10
Stupidity, 615:1
  disastrous to a nation, 860:9
Sub-atomic levels, 206:n3, 1301:n2
Subjective mind, faculties, 1231:3,5,7–9,12–15
Substances, in séance/meditation room, 1246
Subtle body (*see* Spirit body)
Success, attribution of, 737:9
Suffering:
  and God, 830
  on seeing loved ones, 908
  and THE LAW, 827:10
Suggestion, and latent talents, B09:8
Suicides, 1332, 1331:2–3
  a grave misteaching, 1332:1–3
  and motive, 1332:5–10
  not all earthbound, 1332:9
"Summerland," 1408:7
Sun, nothing new under, 805
Sunspots and mind, 816
Superiority:
  racial, 813:7, 1004:15
  self-assumed, 813:6
Superstition, 727:4
Supporters of truth, 323:2
Surgery:
  brain, 618
  on spirit body, 1314:5
Survival beyond physical death, 1201–1204
  proof is only a first step, 1220:4
  revelations beyond, 1201:4
  the truth of, 909:1
Survival instinct, 812
Survivalists, 1201
Sword, 325:5, 847:2

Index

Symbols:
    in dreams, 925:5–6
    in mediumship, 1237
    and organizations, D32

T

Table turning/tipping, 1122:7
Talents, are earned, 1214:3
Talking in sleep, 922
Tape recording, Intro:33, Pref:8, C01:5
Tapestry of our efforts, 405:9–11
Tapping the aura, B09:21–26
Tax-exempt, USB, D06:n1
Teach:
    any untruth, B01
    old dog new tricks, 771
Teacher:
    false, B01
    a "master," B12:32–61
    self-promotion, 513:7
    spirit, B11
    true, of truth, 318
    truth more important, 726:3–4
Teachings, 201–203
    esoteric and ancient, 314
    like wind through trees, B08:5
    of the New Age, 201
    pondering over these, 1418
    of the USB (*see* USB teachings)
Teaching untruths, B01
    to children, 911:1–6
Tears, and relief, 1204:4
Technological progress and spirituality, 804:5–6
Telekinesis (TK), B09:9
    confusion with PK, B09:9
Telepathy with animals, B09:36
Teleplasm, 1121:6
Television:
    dangers of, 833
    and violence, 833:4–10, 836:18
Temperatures felt during healing, 1112
Terms, defining, 202
Testing ground, soul's, 1408:6
Testing integrity, 711:4
Testing, present, 824:2
Thanksgiving, 737:1

The Laws That Govern, 402, 403
Therapeutic Touch, 1106:n1
Think (*see also* Thought), 209:1–2,4
    and accept, *etc.*, 209:4, 848:3
    as one thinks...?, 817
    constructively, positively, 204
    about God, 506
    and know, be, express, 204:1
    in language, 1325:4–5
    and probe, 209:3
    and spirit-create, 1323, 521:4
    and thank God, 807
    universally, 205, D26:5
Thinking of humanity, the, 770:3
Thought(s) (*see also* Think), 204–207
    are seeds, 760:1
    creation by, spirit, 521:4, 1323:1–6
    and the deed, 755
    and distant healing, 1107:1
    distortion of directed, 206:4
    effects of, 207
    forms (*see below*)
    how to help, by our, 204:10–12
    is vibration, 206:3
    no original, new, 805:6
    power in spirit life (*see* Power, of thought in spirit life)
    power of (*see* Power, of thought)
    projection, 1231:10, 1319:11
    speed of, 206:6–7
    spirit communication by, 1324
    and spirit house, 1323:6
    unworthy, 1409:7
    uses in spirit life, 1323, 1329, 1309:4, 1310:23, 1325:23, 1328:5, 1329:12
Thought forms (shells), 1319, 322:12, 1136:4, 1319:n9,n10
    and astral bodies, 1319
    and meditation, 1319:17
Three-day waiting period, 1317
Thyself, know *about*, 611
Time (*see also* Times):
    and cycles, 926–928
    to develop manifestations, 1242:22
    exists; how it affects us, 926:5
    misuse of term, B09:48–53

Index

the Now, 926:6–8
often misunderstood, 926:1
our use of, 747:6
past, present, future not one, 926:2
refer to spirit events, 1328:1
to speak, and to be silent, 753
in spirit life, 1328, 1136:5, 1238:4
in spirit life and on earth, 1328
Times (*see also* Time):
   of crisis and change, a trial, 822
   a prayer for these, 825
   these, 822–826
   of trial and testing, now, 824
Timidity of leaders, 860:9
Tithing, 750
Titles, in spirit life, 1327
TK (*see* Telekinesis)
Tolerance, 719, 311:5
   of the intolerant, 719:5
Tone, component of sound, 929:3
Tongues, speaking in, 1134
Torch of Truth, Pref:36, 112:12
Toys, spirit, 1306:11
Tradition, need for, 844:3
Tragic happenings, 859, 865
Trance (*see also* Mediumship):
   advice to sitters, 1242: 6–21
   deep, 1242:23–27
   deep, advantages, 1236:7–9
   light, deep, compared, 1236:5–9
   and sneezing, coughing, 1133:15
   a warning, 1242: 23–27
Tranquillity, 758:4
Translating the Laws, 403
Translators, 403:1
Travel, spirit, 1329, 1310:14, 1313:n8
Travelling clairvoyance (remote
     viewing), 918:n2, 1313:4,9
Treason, 860:9
Trees and healing, 1103
Trials (*see also* Testing):
   in crisis, 824:1–2
   trying times, 822
Tricks, teach an old dog, 771
Triumph of evil, requires, 754:4
Triune, individual is, 602 (*see* Real
     self)

Trolls, 1319:n10
True:
   inner self senses is, 312:1
Truth(s), 301–325
   bearer's responsibilities, 734:13,15
   and beauty, 306
   buried by rituals, 201:5
   the cause of, 102:5, 304:1
   children learning, 321, 911
   dangers from organizations, 322
   definition of, 301:3
   diversions from, 1124:8–12,
     1319:n10
   the enemy of, 742:1
   examples of, 301:6–8
   facets of, 302
   and fact compared, 301:4
   the greatest quest, 309:20–21
   harmed by additions, 305:4
   and Illumined Souls, 316
   and the individual, 308
   Inspirers view of, 303
   is no beggar, 304:4
   the jewel that is, 201:3
   the lot of many seekers, 311
   misconceptions, 324
   monopoly of, 316:1
   nature of, 301–308
   needs to be simple, clear, 201:6
   never conflict, 302:2
   no greater cause, 304
   no one possesses all, 307
   not made by repeated quotations,
     B05:4
   our responsibility to, D27:6
   outweigh their presenter, 726:4
   the path of, 102:13
   perception of, 303:1
   presented simply, 305
   the quest for, 309:1
   and reason, 208
   renouncing past errors, 319
   repressed, 322:2
   responses to, 308
   restatement of, 201:6
   reveal to seekers, 317
   sacrificed, jeopardized, 304:2

Index

Truth(s)—*Cont.*
  safeguards for searchers, 310
  schools that hinder, B03
  and scientists, 323
  searching for, 309–315, B08:2
  seeker qualities, 309
  sharing of, 317
  some do not serve it well, B10:5
  source of, 307:7
  spiritual, Intro:6, 111:1
  spreading, 316–325
  supporters of, 323:2
  of survival, shunned, 323:3
  torch of, Pref:36, 112:12
  true teacher of, 318
  truths collectively, 301:7
  what it is, poem, 301:1
  who consider single source, 309:5
  why some discredit, 315:2
Trying times, 822
"Turn the other cheek," 744:2–11
Twenty-third psalm, 504
Twins, 1009, 1008:16
  and astrology, 1009
  identical, 619:8, 1008:16, 1009:3–5
Twin souls, 1321
  and gender change, 1321:13
Tyranny, 845, 309:2
Tyrants and freedom, 322:5, 853:5

U

Understanding, 106:1, 807:19
  and an ant, 506:2
  God's, 830:6
Understandings of God differ, 1111:2
Undesirable spirits, 735:2, 1013:10, 1133:4,25, 1236:n15, 1243:1–2
Undiscovered planets, 1301:n4
Undoing by overdoing, 762:3
Unfoldment/development:
  of mediumship, 1216
  spiritual, 1407
Unity of expression, 416:1–4
Universal Mind, 601:4–5
  source of supply, 601:4
Universal Spiritual Brother&Sisterhood (*see* USB, *below*)

Universality, USB, 105
Universally, think, 205, D26:5
Unorthodox healing (*see* Healing)
Unscientific scientists, 323:4
"Unseen healing force," great, 1115
Unselfish love, 511
Unselfish service, 509, 516
Unspoken word, the, 1231:14
Unthinking acceptance, Intro:43, 110:6, 316:5, 1234:5
Unthinking people, disillusioning, 1003:17, 1319:19
Untruths, teaching, B01
  to children, 911:1–6
Unworthy emotions, 207:3
Us:
  the ever-changing, 607
  the real self, individuality, 605, 602
USB, 101–116, 1433
  acceptance of truth, 105:1
  accomplishments, 1430
  achieving its goals, 1420–1432, 807:14–20
  acronym, 101:n6
  affiliations, D02
  blessing and benediction, A06
  book, this (*see Spiritual Light*)
  call for helpers, Call:13–18
  and controversial subjects, D05
  and current issues, 114
  different, how, 110
  directed by, 101:1
  doctrines, no, 734:1
  encouragement from, 102:9–18
  especial desire, 111:6
  excessive praise, no, D14
  financial support of, D06, D09, D20, 110:9
  followers, encouragement to, A04
  following, 111
  "fortune-telling," no, D11
  founders, Intro:10, 1225:2
  and freedom, 108, 849, 862:10
  future policies, D34
  garden, 1412:4
  gender issues, Intro:10, 101:n2,n6
  goal, 102:8

Index

groups, (*see below*)
helpers, workers, search for, A02:5–6, A03, A05
and humility, 102:18–19, D03
Illumined Souls/Inspirers, 1225
Inspirers, Intro:30–42
Inspirer's prayer, 523
joining with its mission, 111
and "laying on of hands," D12
leaflet, D30, E01
linking of supporters, A08, D08
and love, 508
the main stream of The (Great) White Brotherhood, 101:5
mediums, D25
meetings (*see below*)
membership, D08, 111:2,5
membership fees, no, D09
message of cheer, 113
Michael's position in, Intro:9
mission, 101:10–11, 102:5–9, 108:1, 114:5, 508:1
more requirements for, D26–D34
movement, the, 102
name, original, 101:n2
newsletters, Inrto:18
no doctrine of fear, 113:1, 734:1
no misrepresentation to, D28:10
nonprofit tax status, D06:n1
no requirements to join, 108:4
no set prayers, 521:12
not linked, 110:8
not misrepresented, D28:10
not political, 101:10
offer of help, Call:3–12
official representatives, 101:1,5
operation of, D01–D34
opposition to, D33
organization, the, 101
originators, 102:3–4
origins, 101–102
outlook, 111–116
path, the most direct, 1428
platform workers, D23
and politics, D04
positive no's, 110:11–22
prayer in, D19

presents kernels, 1418
principles, 103
project, the, Intro:3–13,41–42
publicizing, D27:12
purposes, 104, Greet:4, A01:4
representatives, A01:2–3
requirements, D01–D25
responsibility to truth, D27:6
selling of blessings, no, D10
serve, how one can, D27
similar organizations, 1419:8
and simplicity, D03
sittings, Intro:31–32
sittings at headquarters, 1241:3
and soliciting for followers, D07
spirit leaders, Intro:3, 1225:2
spirit supporters, Pref:13,20,34, A02:3
and spiritual progress, 1427–1433
spreading knowledge, D27:9–14, D28:6, D37:2
sword, it wields, 325:5
on a symbol, D32
task, 101:11
tax-exempt status, D06:n1
teachings (*see below*)
torch held high, 807:14
values, 103–110
vision, 1432
way of life, 111:3, A07
what it is becoming, 1429:10
what it opposes, 110:25
workers, efforts of, A09–A11
work for all, there is, D13
USB (local) groups, D28
adding to spiritual reservoir, 102:10
discussion at, D05:2
forming, D28:3
harmony in, 1311:39–41, D28:1
importance of, D27:5
jurisdiction over other, D13:2
leaders, D27:13–14
leading, D28:4
meetings, D05:2–3
prayers of, D19
what they can do, D28

Index

USB meetings:
    collections at, D20
    enlightenment at, D16:3
    knowledge at, D16:3
    no rituals, 110:13
    prayers at, D19
    requirements for, D15–D25
USB teachings:
    book, this (*see* Spiritual Light)
    combined with others, 116:7
    excerpts on God, 501
    excerpts on prayer, 522
    excerpts on spirituality, 608
    excerpts on spiritual progress, 1421
    on God, by leaders, Intro:4
    of the New Age, 201:2, 1419:7
    the only official, 116:5
    pondering over these, 1418
    positive no's, 110:11–22
    precognition of, 1241:1,4
    purity, 101:7
    purpose of, 201:2
    received *directly*, 1419:7
    resemble Hermetic, 313:4
    their delivery, 1241:3–5

V

Values:
    of anything, 853:4
    eternal, 711:6
    need return to worthy, 718
    of the USB, 103–110
Variety:
    among people, 813:2
    beauty in, 416:3
    the Law of, 416
    of manifestation/appearance, 416:1–6
    operates everywhere, 908:6
Vibration(s):
    cleansed by water, 837:6, 913:5
    the Law of, 414
    of other worlds, 919:3
    rate determines, 414:7–13
    rates of animals, 414:11
    of rejoicing, 521:9
    as sound, color, and odor, 929
    within, 414:15–23

Vice, 833:9
Vigilance, and liberty, 863
Vineyard, grapes in the, 719:8–10
Violence:
    controlling, 823:3
    of prizefighting (boxing), 820:4
    producing change, 835:1
    punishment of, 839:6, 840:5, 841:2
    and television, 833:4–10, 836:18
    and youth, 907:27
Virtues, 718:2
Virus infections, healing, 1114
"Visitors" from other planets, 706
Visualization and healing, 1105:3–4, 1107:3
Visualize:
    good, 204:7, 1004:24
    leaders in harmony, 759:5
    peace and understanding, 822:3
Vital energy (*see* Vital life force *below*)
Vital life force, 913:3
    and acupuncture, B09:30
    other names, 913:3, 1103:3
    in oxygen, 913:3, 1103:3
    at psychic centers, 1138:1
    storehouses of, B09:31
    and water, 913:3, 1103:3
    and water pollution, 914
Vocabulary, 1325
Voice:
    electronic phenomena (EVP), 1215:4,n6
    recognition, 1215:4,n6
Voice box, 1122:2, 1233:7

W

Wait, three-day, 1317:1,3
Walking on fire, 1125:1–6
Wallace, Alfred Russel, 315:3,n6, 323:5,n9
War:
    and freedom, 857
    one can rise above, 770:5
    a prayer, 524:1
    will continue until, 770:4
    worse things than, 857:3
    WWII, 907:19

Index

Warmth, spirit-realm, 1326:8
Warning:
   mental asylums, 1142
   misteachings, 116
   about predicting, 1006
   to weigh words well, 1013:23
Waste, 315:5
Wasted:
   no effort is, D27:4
   not one day is, 774:2–4
Water, 913
   by bedside, 913:4
   as cleanser, 837:6, 913:5, 1106:8
   cleanser of vibrations, 837:6, 913:5
   pollution, effects of, 914
   vital life essence in, 913:3
Way of life:
   a Great Teacher taught, 115:5
   speed, 747
   the USB's, Greet:5–6, 111:3, A07
Wayshowers, 771:4
Weeping, and relief, 1204:4
Weigh words, 853:7, 1013:23, 1230
What *we* do, that matters, 712:3
White Brotherhood, 101:n1
   white represents, 101:n1
White House, psychic phenomena in, 1122:6
Will, 701–703, 1231:4
   free, 308:3, 830:3
   and inclination, 702
   and personal responsibility, 701:6
   Thy will be done, 703
   unsurrenderable, 701
"Wind through the trees," B08:5
Wisdom, 861:5
   concern for, 703:3
   evidence of, 612:4,7
   and humility, 615
   learning, 860:3
   and love, 704, 865:1, 1321:16
   not monopolized, 615:1
Wise counsel, 762
Women's apparel, 714
"Wonders" (*see* "Marvels")
Word, keeping one's, 716
Work, of our guides, 1221:20–22
Working mothers, parents, 906
World, our, 801–866
   advances made, 807:11–12
   chaos and confusion, 770:2
   generally good, 734:4
   government, 862
   material, 801–807
   population, 821
   real, not illusion, 801
Worship:
   best way, 110:5
   not Illumined Souls, B02:7
   only God, 107, B02:8
Worth, not accomplish alone, 731:9
Worthy values, need return to, 718
Writing, automatic, 1122:8
Wrong, no compromise with, 711:17
Wrongdoing, refraining from, 1424:6
Wrongs, overlooking, 1416

X

Xenoglossy, 1134:2
X-ray vision, 1102:9, 1311:17

Y

Young children and truth, 321
Youth:
   knowledge for, 907:9
   and parents, 907
   and their entertainment, 826
   and violence, 907:27
   and working parents, 906

To order additional copies of *Spiritual Light*
please visit the Bookstore page of the USB website

www.TheUSB.org

for information on the deluxe and paperback versions,
international availability,
and US domestic and international shipping.

www.ingramcontent.com/pod-product-compliance
Lightning Source LLC
Chambersburg PA
CBHW050117170426
43197CB00011B/1611